PROVOCATIONS

PROVOCATIONS

COLLECTED ESSAYS

CAMILLE PAGLIA

PANTHEON BOOKS, NEW YORK

Pantheon Books and colophon are registered trademarks of
Penguin Random House LLC.

Information on previous publication, permissions acknowledgments,
and illustration credits appears on pages 703–713.

Library of Congress Cataloging-in-Publication Data
Name: Paglia, Camille, [date] author.
Title: Provocations : collected essays / Camille Paglia.
Description: New York : Pantheon, 2018. Includes index.
Identifiers: LCCN 2018005846. ISBN 9781524746896 (hardcover).
ISBN 9781524747619 (ebook).
Subjects: LCSH: Popular culture—United States—History—
20th century. United States—Intellectual life—21st century.
Arts, American—21st century. BISAC: SOCIAL SCIENCE /
Women's Studies. SOCIAL SCIENCE / Feminism & Feminist Theory.
SOCIAL SCIENCE / Essays.
Classification: LCC E169.12 .P325 2018 | DDC 306.0973/0904—dc23 |
LC record available at lccn.loc.gov/2018005846

www.pantheonbooks.com

Jacket design by Janet Hansen

Printed in the United States of America

First Edition

2   4   6   8   9   7   5   3   1

CONTENTS

SEX, GENDER, WOMEN

LITERATURE

ART

EDUCATION

INTRODUCTION

This book is not for everyone.

It is not for those who believe that they and their friends, allies, political parties, or churches have found the absolute truth about mankind, present or future.

It is not for those who believe that language must be policed to serve what they view as a higher social good, nor is it for those who grant to government and its proxies on college campuses the right to require and enforce "correct" thinking.

It is not for those who believe that art is a servant of political agendas or philanthropic goals or that it contains hidden coercive messages that must be exposed and destroyed.

It is not for those who see women as victims and men as the enemy or who think that women are incapable of asserting their rights and human dignity everywhere, including the workplace, without the intervention and protection of authority figures deputized by the power of the state.

It is not for those who see human behavior as wholly formed by oppressive social forces and who deny the shadowy influence of evolution and biology on desire, fantasy, and anarchic impulse, from love to crime.

This book is instead for those who elevate free thought and free speech over all other values, including material considerations of wealth, status, or physical well-being.

It is for those who see art and the contemplation of art as a medium of intuition and revelation, a web work of meaning that should be enhanced and celebrated and not demeaned by teachers who cynically deny the possibility of meaning.

It is for those who see women as men's equals who, in their just and necessary demand for equality before the law, do not plead for special protections for women as a weaker sex.

It is for those who see nature as a vast and sublime force which mankind is too puny to control or alter and which fatefully shapes us as individuals and as a species.

It is for those who see life in spiritual terms as a quest for enlight-enment, a dynamic process of ceaseless observation, reflection, and self-education.

A premise of this book, following the great cultural revolution of the 1960s, which was thwarted by the reactionary and elitist forces of academic postmodernism, is that higher consciousness transcends all distinctions of race, class, and gender. Sixties multiculturalism was energized by a convergence of influences from world religions—both Buddhism (a legacy of the Beat writers) and Hinduism, which suf-fused popular music. Standard interpretation of the radical 1960s in exclusively political terms is a common but major error that I address in detail in an essay collected here, "Cults and Cosmic Consciousness: Religious Vision in the American 1960s."

Although I am an atheist, I have immense admiration and respect for religion as a comprehensive symbol-system, far more profound in its poetry, insight, and metaphysical sweep than anything currently offered by secular humanism. In my Cornerstone Arts Lecture at Colorado College, "Religion and the Arts in America" (also collected here), I demonstrate how central religion has been to American cul-ture and how its emotionally expressive and multiracial gospel tra-dition remains the principal reason for America's continued world dominance in commercial popular music.

I have argued for decades that true multiculturalism would be achieved in education not by splintering the curriculum into politi-cized fiefdoms but by making comparative religion the core curricu-lum of world education. An early piece on this subject (published in my first essay collection, *Sex, Art, and American Culture* in 1992) was "East and West: An Experiment in Multiculturalism," a chronicle of an interdisciplinary humanities course that I co-taught with artist and social activist Lily Yeh at the University of the Arts. In the present volume, the same theme is addressed in my opening statement for a 2017 debate at the Yale Political Union, "Resolved: Religion Belongs in the Curriculum."

Provocations covers the two and a half decades since my last general essay collection, *Vamps & Tramps*, in 1994. Some of my articles and lectures on sex, gender, and feminism were published separately a year ago in *Free Women, Free Men*. The latter volume contains my 1991 New York *Newsday* op-ed on date-rape that caused prolonged controversy as the first public protest against an escalating hysteria around that issue on college campuses and in the media. I continue to espouse my code of "street-smart feminism," which frankly acknowledges the risks and dangers of life and encourages women to remain eternally vigilant and alert and to accept responsibility for their choices and adventures.

However, as the generations pass since the sexual revolution launched in 1960 by the release of the first birth-control pill, discourse about sex has become progressively more ideological, rigid, and banal. The feminist rejection of Freud as sexist has eliminated basic tools of psychological analysis once standard in cultural criticism. Few young adults with elite school degrees today appear to realize how romantic attractions and interactions often repeat patterns rooted in early family life. Nor do they seem to have heard of the complex principle of ambivalence, which produces mixed messages that can disastrously complicate social encounters.

In my first book, *Sexual Personae* (1990), I wrote extensively about the tormented fragility of male sexual identity—which most feminist theory, with its bitterly anti-male premises, seems incapable of recognizing. Too often, women fail to realize how much power they have over men, whose ambition and achievement in the public realm are often wedded to remorseless anxiety and insecurity. Canonical feminist theory has also missed the emotional and conceptual symbolism in sexual behavior—as in the infantile penile displays of entertainment industry moguls who appear to have routinely chosen as targets women who would show embarrassment, confusion, or fear and not those who would laugh, scold, or whack that tender member with the nearest shoe, purse, hairbrush, or lamp. Interpreting such pathetically squalid scenes in exclusively political rather than psychological terms does not help women to make their way through the minefield of a professional world that will always be stressful, competitive, and uncertain for aspirants of both sexes.

The masculine dream of sexual freedom is writ large in the drawings of Tom of Finland, who heavily influenced gay male iconography after World War Two and directly inspired photographer Robert Mapplethorpe (whom I defended in *Sex, Art, and American Culture*). My essay, "Sex Quest in Tom of Finland," which was written for the massive Taschen edition of Tom's collected works, stresses the pagan energy, vitality, and humor of Tom's pornographic all-male world, with its panoply of archetypes borrowed from Hollywood and Nazi-era Finland.

The initial theme of my work, however, was not masculinity but androgyny, the subject of my doctoral dissertation at Yale. (Its title was *Sexual Personae: The Androgyne in Literature and Art*.) When the prospectus for my thesis was accepted in 1971, it was the only dissertation on sex at the Yale Graduate School. While completing its writing at my first teaching job at Bennington College, I was electrified by David Bowie in his Ziggy Stardust phase, which seemed to encapsulate everything that I had been thinking about gender. Forty years later, Bowie would put *Sexual Personae* on a list of his 100 favorite books. It did not surprise me: that great artist was sensing himself mirrored back from my pages. It was a tremendous honor to be invited by London's Victoria & Albert Museum to write the article on gender for the catalog of its mammoth 2013 exhibition of Bowie costumes, which then toured the world. That essay, "Theater of Gender: David Bowie at the Climax of the Sexual Revolution," is reprinted here.

As I have often said, my own protest against gender norms began in childhood with my flagrantly dissident Halloween costumes: Robin Hood at age five; a toreador at six; a Roman soldier at seven; Napoleon at eight; Hamlet at nine. (A photo of me as Napoleon appears elsewhere in this book.) From college on, I adopted the gender-bending styles of Mod London, which were effectively transvestite. However, despite my lifelong transgender identification, I do not accept most of the current transgender agenda, which denies biological sex differences, dictates pronouns, and recklessly promotes medical and surgical interventions. An excerpt from an interview with *The Weekly Standard*, where I condemn the use of puberty blockers on children as a violation of human rights, is collected here. When *Sexual Personae* was released, I called it "the biggest sex change in history." Gore Vidal rightly said that the voice of *Sexual Personae* was the voice of his transsexual heroine, Myra Breckinridge. Aggressive, implacable, and scathingly satirical, that voice is a transgender construction, using the materials of language and mind. To questioning young people drawn to the siren song of hormones and surgery, I say: Stay fluid! Stay free!

It is surely my sexually dual perspective that has allowed me to understand and sympathize with Alfred Hitchcock's awed and quasi-mystical view of women, which so many other feminists have reductively condemned as "misogynous." I defended Hitchcock in my British Film Institute book on *The Birds* (1998), as well as in essays such as "Women and Magic in Alfred Hitchcock," written for the BFI's 2012 Hitchcock retrospective and collected here. Other pieces on film in this book celebrate movie music and lament the waning of European art film as well as the decline of film criticism.

One of my principal ambitions since my student days has been to develop an interpretative style that could integrate high and popular culture, which had exploded during the 1960s. I call myself a Warholite: Andy Warhol's improvisational, avant-garde short films (starring gay hustlers and drag queens) and his conversion of publicity photos of Hollywood stars into radiant Byzantine icons provided an inspiring template for my work. In contrast, I detest and oppose academic media studies that monotonously recycle judgmental, politicized terminology from the passé Frankfurt School, which has no feeling whatever for popular culture.

Provocations, I submit, demonstrates the range and flexibility of my system of interpretation, which fiercely attacks when necessary but which respectfully illuminates both the artist and the artwork, from Old Masters like Shakespeare and Leonardo to modern music stars like Prince and Rihanna. In college, I was impatient with the

New Criticism, which I felt was too narrow and genteel and had to be urgently expanded with history and psychology. But I have continued to apply the New Critical technique of close textual analysis to everything I write about, as in my pieces here on Picasso's *Girl Before a Mirror* or on what I call the "psychotic mysticism" of poet Theodore Roethke. One of my long-range goals in college was to break down the barriers between genres, and I believe that my interdisciplinary method has in fact done that—extending the same minute focus and dramatic commentary to all of the arts but also to contemporary politics.

My columns and op-eds on politics over the past quarter century are too numerous to reprint or even catalog. I think I showed special facility for analyzing the horse race of presidential primaries, when my reviews of televised debates, for example, were usually far more attuned than those of the major media to how the candidates were actually being perceived by mainstream voters. I consider the cover-story Salon.com interview (collected here) that I did with editor-in-chief David Talbot in February 2003 to be a supreme highlight of my career: I was virtually alone among political commentators in condemning the imminent invasion of Iraq. Other leading media, including *The New York Times* and *The New Yorker*, had shockingly surrendered to tissue-thin government propaganda.

Full columns have been reproduced here on three political figures: Bill Clinton, Sarah Palin, and Donald Trump. I have written so voluminously and variously about Hillary Clinton since the Clintons' arrival on the national scene in 1992 that there was no one piece that could be considered representative. Hence I have interwoven excerpts about her from numerous articles in the "Media Chronicle" at the back of the book. (It lists articles in English only. My extensive articles and interviews on politics, art, and other subjects in the foreign press, particularly in Italy and Brazil, have been omitted.) The reader should be forewarned that I began as a Hillary fan but became steadily disillusioned over the years.

I was speaking, writing, and crusading about the first woman president throughout the 1990s, when most other feminists were absorbed with policy issues. Reproduced in this book is a poster advertising my appearance at a 1996 debate at the Yale Political Union ("Resolved: America Needs a Female President"), which was recorded for national TV broadcast by C-SPAN. The "Media Chronicle" also contains excerpts of then-controversial columns or articles where I was notably prescient, as a registered Democrat, about developing problems and evasions in my own party that would eventually lead, many years later, to its stunning surprise defeat in the 2016 presidential election.

Education is a major theme in this book. As a career teacher of nearly half a century, I have watched American universities miss their epochal opportunity for radical curricular reform in the 1970s and descend decade by decade into the balkanized, bureaucratic, therapeutic customer-service operations that they are today. High scholarly standards and deep erudition (as admirably exemplified by the stiff, stuffy, old-guard professors at Yale when I arrived as a graduate student) have so vanished that their value and indeed their very existence are denied by today's bright, shiny, and shallow academic theorists. The real revolution would have been to smash the departmental structure of the humanities, reunite the fragmented fields of literature and art, and create an authentically multicultural global curriculum.

A principal piece in this volume is "The North American Intellectual Tradition," which was given as the Second Annual Marshall McLuhan Lecture at Fordham University. There as in my long exposé, "Junk Bonds and Corporate Raiders" (published by Arion in 1991 and reprinted in Sex, Art, and American Culture), I reject European post-structuralism and call for a reorientation toward North American pragmatism, grounded in nature. The academic stampede toward pretentious, abstruse French theorists in the 1970s was a grotesque betrayal of the American 1960s, which was animated by a Romantic return to nature and a reconnection of art with the sensory—the dynamic life of the body. Michel Foucault's primary influence, by his own admission, was playwright Samuel Beckett—whose depressive postwar nihilism was swept away by the communal music and dance of the 1960s. Today's jargon-spouting academic postmodernists with their snidely debunking style are not the heirs of '60s leftism but retrograde bourgeois elitists, still picking through the shards of T. S. Eliot's Waste Land.

This book contains multiple examples of my early involvement with the Web. "Dispatches from the New Frontier: Writing for the Internet" documents the process by which I developed the unique format of my long-running Salon.com column, which debuted on January 13, 1997. Because articles written for the Web are viewed on a screen rather than a page, adjustments must be made in syntax, diction, and visual design. A continuing failure to recognize this has produced the reams of slack, verbose, meandering prose that currently clogs the Web on both news sites and blogs. Historically, it will eventually be recognized that my lengthy, multi-part Salon column, with its variety of tone and topics and its gradual incorporation of reader letters, was the first blog, a new literary genre of the digital age. During the first few years of my column, only Mickey Kaus (whose online profile began after mine) was doing anything comparable, but his Slate .com column and later Web site were wholly focused on politics. My narrative and autobiographical diary approach was so new that Salon's editor-in-chief relayed complaints from other staffers that there was too much of me in my columns. In retrospect, it is clear that my work for Salon prefigured today's universal social media.

"Dispatches from the New Frontier" also describes how the geographically scattered, maverick founders of the Web instantly understood and supported my libertarian and multi-media ideas. In the early 1990s, while my work was being ostracized by the academic establishment, the dissidents on The Well were discussing it from coast to coast. Stewart Brand, a co-founder of The Well, interviewed me in 1993 for the premiere issue of *Wired*, which called me "possibly the next Marshall McLuhan." I co-hosted early online chats, an innovative interactive genre whose format was, by today's standards, strikingly primitive.

Included in this book is the transcript of a collaboration I did on "Oscar Style" with Glenn Belverio (in his drag persona as Glennda Orgasm) for an America Online "CyberPlex Auditorium" in 1996. The low-tech print-out format of our dialogue with real-time questioners, on the day after the Academy Awards ceremony, has been reproduced as exactly as possible. Before the Web, people had to wait more than a full day before there could be newspaper coverage of the Oscars, with their climactic late-night finale. Hence I lobbied David Talbot about the Web's potential for rapid response to the Oscars broadcast, and the result was a yearly feature on Salon, "Camille Does the Oscars." I also campaigned in Salon and *Interview* magazine for comprehensive reporting on Oscars fashions—another of my prophetic themes: the red carpet would eventually win epic coverage by Joan Rivers and become a media staple, currently on the verge of excess.

Finally, two interviews here focus on my philosophy and practice as a writer. My writing has always been motivated by the search for a voice—or rather for many voices, keyed to the moment. There is nothing more important to me than the power of words to describe, re-create, entrance, and provoke.

POPULAR CULTURE

1

THE GRANDEUR OF OLD HOLLYWOOD

As a child, I had two pagan high holy days every year. The first was Halloween, where I advertised my transgender soul by masquerading as a matador, a Roman soldier, Napoleon, or Hamlet. The second was Oscars night, when Hollywood put its dazzling glamour on heady display for the whole world.

As I was growing up in the drearily conformist 1950s and early '60s, it was hard to find information about popular culture, which wasn't taken seriously. Deep-think European art films were drawing tiny coteries of intellectuals to small, seedy theaters, but flamboyant mainstream Hollywood was still dismissed as crass, commercial trash.

Confidential magazine, a splashy rag specializing in steamy innuendo, was my main news source about all things Hollywood. I avidly followed the lurid adventures of my favorite movie star, Elizabeth Taylor, as she breezily acquired and shed husbands at the drop of a hat. Eventually, my collection of Taylor clippings and photos reached 599.

As a brash Italian-American oppressed by the postwar cult of cheerful, girly blondeness, I celebrated when the voluptuous, brunette Taylor stole singer Eddie Fisher from that petite juggernaut of peppy blonde niceness, Debbie Reynolds. Much later, I learned to deeply respect the indomitable spunk, professionalism, and craft of both Doris Day and Debbie Reynolds, but at the time, I darkly viewed them as ruthless tyrants of an ossified WASP establishment.

["Camille Paglia on Oscar Glamour Then and Now: 'The Mythic Grandeur of Old Hollywood Is Gone,' " *The Hollywood Reporter,* February 23, 2017.]

Most of the country automatically took Debbie's side in the 1958 Fisher scandal, a sympathy stoked by her shrewd posing for an endless series of upbeat, homey photos with her two small children, Carrie and Todd. Her adulterous rival was publicly excoriated as a vixen and tramp, a heartless home-wrecker.

This was the backstory to the supreme Oscar moment of my lifetime—when Elizabeth Taylor, having just survived a near-death tracheotomy during an episode of pneumonia in London, won the award for Best Actress for her spectacular performance as a sleek Manhattan call girl in *Butterfield 8* (1960). Three years after her treacherous adultery, Hollywood was formally forgiving her and welcoming her back to the fold.

Watching the Oscars on TV in upstate New York, I was in near-delirium at Taylor's unexpected win. My breathless state of ecstasy lasted for the entire next school day, where I felt like I was floating on a cloud. In retrospect, I realize that Taylor's triumph was indeed a huge cultural watershed, a prefiguration of the coming sexual revolution.

But a surprise waited. The 1961 Oscars were still being broadcast in black and white. A week later, a gorgeous full-color photo of Taylor regally seated at the Oscars party appeared on the cover of *Life* magazine. Her white cigarette holder was elegantly raised above a full champagne glass near a bottle of Dom Perignon resting on ice.

The billowing white skirt of her floral-embellished Christian Dior dress was barely glimpsed. We saw only her starkly simple, pale yellow bodice that seemed to be channeling the golden glow of the Oscar statuette, which was offering her its adoration from amid a burst of red tulips, matching her full, crimson lips.

That night, with her magnetic composure and luminous charisma, Taylor exuded all the pomp and power of old Hollywood, from which she had emerged as a child star just before the decline of the studio system. Even her glossy raven bouffant was a work of art, because surely those intricate petals had been sculpted by her close friend, hair stylist Sydney Guilaroff, one of the creative geniuses of MGM production at its height.

The *Life* cover also revealed a strange perversity: austerely presenting herself without necklace or brooch, Taylor seemed to be wearing the vertical, white tracheotomy scar on her throat as a fashion accessory. It was a tour de force of ambiguous eroticism, like a Catholic saint's statue of a martyr flaunting her wounds.

Taylor enthroned with her *Butterfield 8* trophy is probably the greatest post-Oscars photo ever taken. Next would be Terry O'Neill's picture of Faye Dunaway breakfasting at the Beverly Hills Hotel the morning after she won the Best Actress award for *Network* (1976). Lounging at poolside in her creamy silk dressing gown, newspapers scattered at her feet, Dunaway contemplates her Oscar with a tinge of ironic detachment and fatigue.

This bleak, brilliant photo marks the arrival of a new generation in Hollywood, hip, smart, and cynical. The mythic grandeur of old Hollywood and its pantheon of celestial stars is already gone.

2

ART OF SONG LYRIC

Thirty years ago, during my second year of teaching humanities at the Philadelphia College of Performing Arts (1985–86), I created an elective two-semester course called "Lyric" that began with ancient Greek poetry and ended with modern song lyrics, from Broadway musicals to folk-rock. In the course catalog, I described it as "a study of how contemporary song lyrics developed from the tradition of lyric poetry and folk ballads." My aim was to demonstrate how poetry had begun as ritual performance, accompanied on the lyre, and how after a half millennium of the Gutenberg print era, poetry had returned to its performance roots and its spiritual bonding with music.

My immediate target was our music majors in both the classical and jazz programs. Many young guitarists and drummers were playing in bar bands and trying to develop their own material, in hopes of landing a record contract. The writing requirement for the course was "critical or creative," with the option to compose original song lyrics. The second semester, which covered Romanticism to modernism, had a natural organic shape, because *Lyrical Ballads,* the revolutionary 1798 volume of poems by William Wordsworth and Samuel Taylor Coleridge, was partly inspired by the new interest in folk culture typified by Robert Burns' collecting of rural Scottish ballads.

I was concerned about the declining quality and prestige of popular song lyrics in the 1980s, when visual flash, tailored to the exciting new genre of music videos, was increasingly dominating music-industry

[Salon.com, March 31, 2016.]

priorities. In hard rock, flamboyant virtuoso guitar solos were replacing the marriage of vivid lyrics with expressive vocals. Working with aspiring songwriters, I found that exposure to major poetry sharpened their awareness of the power and possibilities of language. Simple strategies—such as typing up their own lyrics-in-process to peruse visually—helped them clarify basic issues of theme and form and detect any inconsistencies in point of view.

After a merger in 1987 with our next-door neighbor, the Philadelphia College of Art, to form the University of the Arts, "Lyric" evolved into its present one-semester incarnation, "Art of Song Lyric," a course of general cultural appreciation for students from all majors. As my coverage of music history expanded, poetry per se was dropped for reasons of time, and the creative writing component was also discontinued. Term papers now focused on popular, jazz, or art song in any time period or world region. Frequent topics remain leading lyricists and vocalists, past or present, as well as musical groups, famous or not. For example, I have periodically gotten intriguing papers about struggling club bands in metropolitan Philadelphia and New Jersey.

My classroom procedure remains the same: I distribute lyric sheets of selected songs, and we methodically analyze them like poems, with close attention paid to voice, tone, imagery, and narrative (if relevant), with its ancillary premises of character, scene, and time. It is crucial to do my own lyric sheets, because published versions of even classic hit songs are often startlingly inaccurate, with misheard words, jumbled-together lines, or missing stanza divisions that obscure a shapely song structure. I play the song twice, before and after our discussion. Ideally, the students on second hearing will experience a sense of pleasurable surprise and revelation, as the song seems to have strangely altered and expanded on its own.

My song choices have steadily changed, but one favorite remains fixed because of its resounding success over the decades: I always begin the semester with "Silver Dagger," the traditional ballad from the Southern Appalachian Mountains with which Joan Baez opened her blockbuster first album in 1960. The economy and compression of this haunting song, streamlined by generations of oral transmission, should stand as an inspiration to any writer.

Don't sing love songs, you'll wake my mother,
She's sleeping here right by my side,
And in her right hand a silver dagger,
She says that I can't be your bride.

All men are false, says my mother,
They'll tell you wicked, lovin' lies,
And the very next evening, they'll court another,
Leave you alone to pine and sigh.

My daddy is a handsome devil,
He's got a chain five miles long,
And on every link a heart does dangle
Of another maid he's loved and wronged.

Go court another tender maiden
And hope that she will be your wife,
For I have been warned, and I've decided
To sleep alone all of my life.

In this brilliant theater of the here and now, a young woman conducts a tense exchange with her serenading suitor through the open window of what may well be a one-room shack. She urgently hushes him; his song is stifled so that hers can begin—a searing elegy for lost hopes. Poverty cancels out impropriety: she is sitting up in bed, next to her sleeping mother, whose steel dagger gleams silver, as if in moonlight. The mother's tight grip represents her world of fear, her thirst for vengeance, and ultimately her choking of her daughter's life.

In the British and Scots-Irish ballad tradition, from which today's country music developed, men are mobile, roaming free while women endlessly wait, abandoned or pinned down by duty. The brooding mother is poisoned with cynicism: "All men are false"; all men lie, seduce, humiliate. The daughter, however, sees her absent, derelict father from an appreciative distance: he's a "handsome devil," predatory and amoral but charismatic and irresistible. He collects hearts like scalps. His scattered conquests, still infatuated, are like dazed prisoners in a chain gang. His emblem is the coldly metallic—the chain's iron links as well as the mother's fetishistic dagger, portraying the penis as impersonally wounding to women, defined as the "tender" and vulnerable. Gender is inescapably polarized.

The song, just four stanzas long, has a wonderfully lucid design, beginning in the present, jumping backward to sketch in the past, then returning to the present. There is no future—or rather the future is murdered by the mother's bitterness and her daughter's renunciation. Torn by pity and loyalty, the daughter chooses her mother's paralyzed state of endless war, a stubborn mountain feud. The two are self-entombed with suffocating bad memories. There will be no more risky love and thus no children or posterity. Time stops.

Although only 19 when she recorded this debut album, where she accompanies herself on acoustic guitar, Baez already had exquisite vocal phrasing as well as a mastery of poignantly modulated dynamics. Other ballads on the album also work well in the classroom, such as "John Riley," the homecoming tale of a seafarer so changed by seven harsh years away that he is unrecognized by his faithful betrothed, or "Mary Hamilton," a complex saga of seduction, infanticide, and execution on the gallows that may descend from a seventeenth-century scandal at a royal court.

While Joan Baez has unfailingly impressed, her colleague and sometime flame Bob Dylan has not. To my dismay, Dylan was a very hard sell in my classes throughout the 1980s. His voice struck many students as thin and grating, while the relentless hyper-verbalism and attack style of his protest songs seemed out of sync with the times. That thankfully changed in the 1990s, probably because of the impact of aggressively political rap, which had become hugely popular among white male teenagers trapped in the blandness and materialism of suburban shopping-mall culture. Dylan's message-heavy intensity seemed relevant again, a recovered stature happily sustained in the new century.

"Subterranean Homesick Blues," Dylan's 1965 breakthrough radio hit, is actually a proto-rap song in the rural "talking blues" tradition. Its delirious barrage of satiric blows at a surveillance society of corrupt authority figures, economic exploitation, and assembly-line institutions speaks directly to our time. I have repeatedly used the song to demonstrate how much can be packed into a very short space (two minutes, twenty seconds).

But Dylan's true masterpiece, in my view, is "Desolation Row," the more than eleven-minute song that closes *Highway 61 Revisited* (1965). I submit that this lyric is the most important poem in English since Allen Ginsberg's *Howl* (which influenced it) and that it is far greater than anything produced since then by the official poets canonized by the American or British critical establishment. The epic ambition, daring scenarios, and emotionally compelling detail of "Desolation Row" make John Ashbery's multiple-prize-winning *Self-Portrait in a Convex Mirror* (1975) look like the verbose, affected academic exercise that it is. I have written elsewhere (in regard to the selection process for my book on poetry, *Break, Blow, Burn*) of my rejection of the pretentious pseudo-philosophizing of overpraised contemporary poets like Harvard's Jorie Graham, none of whom come anywhere near the high artistic rank of Bob Dylan.

"Desolation Row" is so long—four printed pages, taking three class days to discuss—that I rarely do it now. But it is a stunning achievement, with all the passion and vision missing from today's writers in virtually every genre. When I first transcribed the song for classroom use, its elegantly symmetrical structure leapt into view: ten triads (sets of three stanzas), each ending in the rhythmic refrain, "Desolation Row." As recorded, the song is accompanied by acoustic guitars that begin quietly and become lashingly emphatic.

Modeling himself on his mentor, the working-class bard Woody Guthrie, Dylan has chronically concealed and denied his wide reading. "Desolation Row" uses Rimbaud's hallucinatory surrealism to fuse T. S. Eliot's *Waste Land* vision of Western civilization to the comic archetypal mythologies of James Joyce's *Ulysses*. The Bible, Roman history, fairy tales, Shakespeare, and Hollywood movies fly by. Dylan's muse here is, I believe, Billie Holiday: "As Lady and I look out tonight / From Desolation Row." He is listening to a record by Lady Day (as she was reverently called by jazz musicians) and has assumed her melancholy insight and personal trauma as his own.

Each triad of "Desolation Row" exposes the lies, limitations, cruelties, or collateral damage in different sectors of society: politics, law enforcement, and racial injustice; heterosexuality (set in a hostile gay bar); religion; science; psychiatry; the legitimate theater; corporate careerism; universities and English departments. Desolation Row is a state of mind, a self-positioning at the margins, where the artist identifies himself, like the Romantics, with the dispossessed, the outcasts and losers.

In the final triad, after a mournfully piercing harmonica solo, Dylan himself appears, addressing someone whom I suspect is his mother. She has probably sent him a chatty letter about his Zimmerman relatives, whose name he had long cast off. Dylan the artist, taking Lady Day as his foster mother, bids goodbye to his old identity and to books and letters and everything processed by social norms. He will seek truth, if it is ever to be had, in direct experience and spiritual intuition.

After many experiments and permutations, "Art of Song Lyric" now has a dual trajectory. I begin with the Appalachian ballad tradition from its politicization during the violent unionization of Kentucky coal-miners in the 1930s through the protest-oriented folk movement shepherded by Pete Seeger to Bob Dylan's controversial turn to the electric guitar, then a symbol of commercialized rock 'n' roll. Folk-rock, Dylan's creation, lasts barely five years but produces innumerable lyrics of high poetic quality, from Donovan's "Season of the Witch" to Crosby, Stills, and Nash's dreamily jazz-inflected yet ominously apocalyptic "Wooden Ships" (co-written by Paul Kantner).

Next we follow the African-American tradition from its roots in West Africa to the emergence of the blues in the rural South. YouTube has become a tremendous resource for video clips of West African "speaking drums," call-and-response group singing, and melismatic vocal technique (probably Islamic in origin) that survived in American blues. The powerful religious current in African-American culture surfaced in the Negro spirituals (a fusion of blues tonalities with Protestant hymn measure) that white audiences first heard from the Fisk Jubilee Singers on international tour after the Civil War.

The blues spread into jazz and torch singing and then Chicago electric blues, the crucible of rock 'n' roll. The British blues revival of the 1950s and '60s produced great bands like the Yardbirds, the Rolling Stones, and Led Zeppelin. Simultaneously, African-American soul music merged gospel singing with secular, romantic themes and, in Marvin Gaye's landmark *What's Going On*, a topical social consciousness.

James Brown, "the godfather of soul," shattered European song format by returning popular music to West African style, an endless stream of exclamatory riffs over heavy, "funky" bass and percussion that gave birth to disco. In the 1970s, lyrics lost importance in hedonistic, producer-driven disco; with a few exceptions, political content vanished. But the invisible mastermind d.j.'s of disco clubs took their dual-turntable technology to the streets and by the late 1970s had created rap (influenced by Jamaican "toasting") in the Bronx. Elements of rap had long existed in African-American culture, where rhythmic speech as performance was already recorded in the 1920s and probably had antecedents in the recitations of African griots (tribal bards).

Rap spread globally in the late twentieth century and, under the general rubric of hip-hop, now dominates music industry sales. It helped inspire the poetry slam movement, which began in Chicago in the mid-1980s and went national in the '90s. Rap as an incantatory, improvisational form descends from the "dozens" or "snaps," a competitive African-American game of escalating put-downs, cheered on by the group. Its fast pace and bouncing internal rhymes have enormous propulsive vitality. As an artistic style, rap is energizing and confrontational rather than contemplative or self-analytic. The voice is so weaponized that admission of fears, doubts, or ambiguities can be difficult. Themes are sometimes scattershot or undeveloped. Nevertheless, rap's extemporaneous channeling of colloquial speech is so robust and dynamic that it makes most contemporary American and British poetry seem stilted, stale, and cloistered.

To complete the spectrum in "Art of Song Lyric," I do a brief survey of the major genres of hymn, aria, lieder, cabaret, and musical theater. But my primary goal is to give historical shape and context to the enormous body of modern popular music that young people now hear in random digital isolation, without the framing commentary by d.j.'s in the old era of radio airplay. High-level song production is becoming depersonalized, with beats invented by digital whiz kids being handed off for slapped-on lyrics—an assembly-line contrivance then dropped in the lap of a star vocalist. The integral artistic bonding of music and lyrics is weakening. There is one solution, perhaps the only one: immersion in the lost poetry of music.

3

ON RIHANNA

The songs I most admire on Rihanna's latest album, *Anti*, are "Desperado," "Never Ending" (with its lilting old Caribbean sea chanty refrain), and "Love on the Brain," a piercing aria of retro-soul grand opera. Only the husky, soul-baring Adele right now is matching Rihanna's emotional intensity and authenticity.

My favorite Rihanna song is probably the hypnotic "Pour It Up," from *Unapologetic*. I think it is a true work of art, with a chilly avant-garde edge. The stunningly sensual strip-club setting of the official video has unfortunately distracted people from the eerie power of the song itself, which is about a state of mind rather than a banquet of vibrating flesh.

Certainly, I applaud the steely exhibitionism of the regally enthroned Rihanna and her phalanx of twerking pole-dancers: the video correctly represents strip clubs as citadels of female power, not as pigstys for rutting male buffoons, as they were once routinely portrayed by feminist puritans. For an article called "Woman as Goddess" in the October 1994 issue of *Penthouse* magazine, I took a woman journalist on a tour of New York strip clubs to demonstrate how admiring and visibly cowed the men were in the pagan presence of a dynamic woman dancer. Men's money in that ritual environment does not control women but rather the opposite: money is the poor tribute by which desperate men win a dominant woman's momentary attention.

["Uncensored: Camille Paglia on Rihanna, Identity Politics, and Sexuality," interview with Alex Kazemi, *V* magazine, March 27, 2017.]

When one listens to "Pour It Up" without the video's luscious visual stimulations, its infernal soundscape (almost like the jittery electronic soundtrack of Alfred Hitchcock's *The Birds*) is overwhelming. We are in *The Twilight Zone*, where a leading woman artist who grew up married to idyllic nature on a sun-drenched island is wandering in a murky, directionless urban world of overwhelming wealth and material display. No recent song to my knowledge has so directly confronted the contemporary search for meaning—which too many people have deflected into the toxic flux of an insanely polarized politics.

Rihanna is virtually the only performer today who consistently intrigues and fascinates me. My exacting high standards were formed by the golden age of the entertainment industry, which began in the 1920s (with jazz, radio, and sound movies) and which precipitously declined by the late 1990s, as the Web achieved hegemony. It's as if the Muses have abandoned us: look at how painfully clumsy a proven genius like Madonna seems as she struggles to regain the creative brilliance and global impact of her early years, when every taboo-breaking video she released was electrifying.

At a time when too many Hollywood actors are hopelessly depthless and try to compensate for their mediocrity by hijacking arts-celebrating ceremonies for clichéd political rants, Rihanna exudes the complexity, mystery, and magic of classic stars like Ava Gardner, a country-girl renegade who lived and loved spontaneously, her stormy melodramas periodically erupting into the news. I love to monitor Rihanna's transnational doings via the *Daily Mail*, with its pap shots of her enigmatic predawn exits from nightclubs or her grand arrivals in full drag at glittering events. What maverick fashion smarts she has—that startling profusion of sculptural looks and the ingenious array of accessories and makeup in dazzling rainbow colors. Rihanna is an instinctive performance artist born for the camera.

I wrote two cover stories on Rihanna four years ago, one in *The Sunday Times Magazine* in London and the other in the magazine supplement of *La Repubblica* in Rome. There is a piquant saga attached to the London piece, in which I warned that by increasingly Instagramming fabulously sexy photos of herself to taunt her bad-boy ex,

Chris Brown, Rihanna was ominously headed down the same path as Diana, Princess of Wales. The charismatic Diana seduced the media and skillfully used them as a propaganda tool against her errant husband, the callously adulterous Charles. But then Diana was stalked nonstop for years by the ravenous media wolf pack—leading directly to her fatal 1997 car crash in the Alma tunnel in Paris. In its resumé of my article, the *Daily Mail* published the most sensational of Rihanna's Instagrams (from the superbly atmospheric fireplace series taken by her longtime close friend, the gifted Melissa Forde).

By some strange alchemy, my *Sunday Times Magazine* cover story was published by chance on the very weekend that Rihanna arrived in London to debut her fashion line. Returning to her hotel early Sunday morning after a heavy night of pub-crawling, she found the newspaper waiting outside her room and was amazed to see herself linked on the front page to the legendary Diana, whom she loved. She tweeted two images to her millions of followers—the magazine section lying on her bed and the front page where she was flagged above the headline—the big surprise that greeted her when (as she tweeted) she "came home drunk" to her hotel.

There is a melancholy coda to this story. Rihanna's conservative, church-going mother in Barbados eventually saw the sexy fireplace photos and came down hard on her. Rihanna told *Elle* magazine, "I'm not afraid of any person in this world but my mother—I'm terrified of her. . . . She went crazy on me. . . . I felt like I got my ass whipped in front of the class in school." So Rihanna's blazing career in ultra-sophisticated soft-core online porn seems, alas, to be over. If I played any role, however small, in that major cultural loss, I do publicly repent here and now!

4

THE DEATH OF PRINCE

I would certainly classify Prince as a major artist of the late twentieth century, but I must admit some disappointment with how his brilliant career developed or failed to develop over time. His great period was his early one, from the late 1970s to the mid-1980s, when he created a brand-new sonic landscape and used the emergent genre of music videos as a flamboyant medium of performance art. Musically, he downscaled Rick James' massive macho funk chords into a bewitching web work of intricate rhythms, intimate and sensual. As a sexual persona, he borrowed transgender motifs from Little Richard and Jimi Hendrix and refashioned himself first as a half-naked s&m rent boy and then as an aristocratic dandy, dripping silk and lace.

There is both a Mardi Gras and voodoo element in Prince: all four of his grandparents were born in Louisiana (and photos of his parents suggest they were at least partly Creole). He was one of the most photogenic people on the planet: his personal magnetism and artistic intensity verged on the eerie and mystical. But it's clear that, like Michael Jackson, Prince became a prisoner of his own fame. I was horrified by the aerial views of Paisley Park published after his death: I had no idea Prince was living like that—in a lavish windowless bunker as characterless as an office park. Paisley Park is of course mainly a recording studio, but as a residence, it looks like a set for Edgar Allan Poe's "Masque of the Red Death."

No music fan who lived through Prince's sensational *Purple Rain*

[Response to a reader question about Prince, Salon.com column, May 5, 2016.]

period in 1984 will ever forget it. We were all drenched in the florid extravagance of his swashbuckling self-presentation and the searing confession of his half-crippling melancholy. The long, climactic title song of that movie still has a tremendous, near-religious charge. But then what? By the late 1980s, Prince remained highly productive, but there was a lapse in originality, and very few of his songs ever reached the top of the charts again. Changing his name to a love symbol seemed like a silly stunt to me, and I wasn't impressed by a multimillionaire writing "slave" on his face as a gesture against his record company.

The news about Prince's death two weeks ago was announced while my "Art of Song Lyric" course was meeting. We were in fact doing the period from James Brown through soul, disco, and funk. I was incredulous when I got back to my office and saw the shocking headline on the Drudge Report. At our next class, I immediately showed Prince's "Kiss" video (1986) to demonstrate what pure talent looks like. What a low-budget masterpiece that beautifully edited video is—nothing but dance, gesture, seductive rhythm, and witty warmth.

And then I showed a new discovery, a Patti Labelle song from 1989 that I hadn't heard in decades and had completely forgotten—"Yo Mister." I had no idea that Prince had written, produced, and played on that powerful song about a young girl dying of a drug overdose until I read it in the *Daily Mail* after his death. In the video, Patti is shown (like a *deus ex machina* on a Philadelphia balcony) condemning the girl's hard-hearted father as he stonily walks away from her grave in the Louisiana countryside, where a New Orleans funeral march is being performed. This song, with its complex church bell reverberation, suggests the serious, avant-garde direction that Prince's later career could have taken but unfortunately did not.

As for Prince remaining in Minnesota instead of moving to New York or Los Angeles, I think that was a terrific decision on his part. His creative imagination was rich enough—and he had the resources to explore every aspect of the arts on his own. Because of stratospherically rising property costs, New York was no longer the mecca for daring and impoverished young artists that it had been up to the early 1970s. And as for Los Angeles, it has always been about show and status, a cosmos of perpetual anxiety. It was hardly the place for a sensitive soul like the reticent Prince, who preferred enigmatic silence to conversation with strangers. If Prince's idea stream began to run thin toward the end, it was not due to Minnesota, with its exhilaratingly clear Canadian air, but to a waning in his own confidence and ambition.

5

THEATER OF GENDER:
DAVID BOWIE AT THE CLIMAX
OF THE SEXUAL REVOLUTION

David Bowie burst onto the international scene at a pivotal point in modern sexual history. The heady utopian dreams of the 1960s, which saw free love as an agent of radical political change, were evaporating. Generational solidarity was proving illusory, while experimentation with psychedelic drugs had expanded identity but sometimes at a cost of disorientation and paranoia. By the early 1970s, hints of decadence and apocalypse were trailing into popular culture. Bowie's prophetic attunement to this major shift was registered in his breakthrough song, "Space Oddity" (1969), whose wistful astronaut Major Tom secedes from Earth itself. Recorded several months before the Woodstock Music Festival, "Space Oddity," with its haunting isolation and asexual purity and passivity, forecast the end of the carnival of the Dionysian 1960s.

In its rebellious liberalism, nature worship, and celebration of sex and emotion, the 1960s can be seen as a Romantic revival. Folk and rock music, emerging from both black and white working-class traditions, were the vernacular analogue to William Wordsworth and Samuel Taylor Coleridge's epochal *Lyrical Ballads* (1798), which used rural

[Catalog essay for "David Bowie Is," retrospective exhibit of Bowie costumes, The Victoria & Albert Museum, London, March 23–August 11, 2013.]

popular forms against an ossified literary establishment. But events, mirrored and magnified by mass media, had such force and velocity in the '60s that Romanticism soon flipped over into its decadent late phase. Bowie was the herald and leading symbol of that rapid transformation—as if Oscar Wilde had appeared less than a decade after Wordsworth. Bowie has in fact described himself as an artist "who tries to capture the rate of change"—the theme of one of his signature songs, "Changes."[1]

Bowie assumed the persona of a Romantic precursor, Lord Byron, in the video for "Blue Jean" (1984), excerpted from a 20-minute narrative, "Jazzin' for Blue Jean," directed by Julien Temple. Like Bowie, Byron was a charismatic, bisexual exile of enormous and at that time unprecedented scandalous fame. Now reduced to a footloose, effeminate nightclub entertainer, Screaming Lord Byron, he is mounting his over-the-top act at the Bosphorus Rooms ("only London appearance," blares a poster), attended by enthusiastic but depthless dating couples. His fancy Aladdin outfit of turban, Turkish trousers, and gold slippers with turned-up toes recalls the 1813 portrait of Byron in the opulent crimson and gold Albanian dress of a Greek patriot. Bowie's ingeniously shadowed trompe l'oeil makeup also evokes two other of his sexually ambiguous antecedents, the dancer Vaslav Nijinsky in Ballets Russes productions of *Scheherazade* and *Afternoon of a Faun,* and Rudolph Valentino, silent-film star of *The Sheik,* who was excoriated by the press for his face powder, mascara, "floppy pants," and platinum slave bracelet.

But Bowie is closer in spirit to the late Romantic Wilde, a provocative man of the theater and a lover of masks. Like Wilde, who satirized Wordsworth's cult of nature, Bowie has always been urban in sensibility: the city is his wilderness and his stage. Artifice is his watchword; indeed, except for cartoonish predators like interplanetary spiders or hybrid dog-men, nature appears in Bowie mainly as the blank void of outer space. Like Wilde, who free-lanced as a fashion journalist, Bowie is a dandy for whom costume is an art form. But his lineage descends not direct from Beau Brummell but refracted through the English dandyism imported by French decadents such as the poet Charles Baudelaire, who portrayed the dandy as an arbiter of distinc tion, elegance, and cold apartness—exactly like the Thin White Duke persona of Bowie's 1975–76 tours. Barbey D'Aurevilly, Baudelaire's friend and ally, called dandies "the Androgynes of History."

Music was not the only or even the primary mode through which Bowie first conveyed his vision to the world: he was an iconoclast who was also an image-maker. Bowie's command of the visual was displayed in his acute instinct for the still camera, honed by his attentiveness to classic Hollywood publicity photographs, contemporary fashion magazines, and European art films. His flair for choreography and body language had been developed by his study of pantomime and stagecraft with the innovative Lindsay Kemp troupe in London in the late 1960s. Bowie's earliest ambition was to be a painter, and he has continued to paint throughout his life—especially, he has said, when he is having trouble writing songs.[2] The multimedia approaches that were gaining ascendance over the traditional fine arts during the 1960s also helped foster his desire to fuse music with visuals onstage. While working at an advertising agency when he was 16, he learned story-boarding techniques that he later employed for his videos.

As he was searching for a voice and place in the music industry, Bowie's look steadily changed. Beatifically singing "Let Me Sleep Beside You" for a 1969 promotional film, he appeared in standard Mod dress of open-necked floral shirt and hip-huggers and projected the harmless, wiggly charm of the bashful boy next door. By his third album the following year, however, he had embarked on a challenging new course, putting his commercial acceptance at risk through unsettling cross-dressing scenarios. The cover of *The Man Who Sold the World* shows him sporting heavy, winsome, shoulder-length locks and wearing a luxuriously patterned pink-and-blue velvet maxi-dress over tight knee-high boots normally associated with stylish young women. (This "man-dress" was designed by Michael Fish, who also did Mick Jagger's short white dress for the Rolling Stones' free Hyde Park concert in 1969.) Bowie's languidly seductive, serpentine reclining posture is equally cheeky—a parody of Canova's nude statue of Pauline Borghese (Napoleon's sister) as Venus. This cover was so sexually radical at the time that it was vetoed by his record company for distribution in the U.S. A cartoon by Michael J. Weller showing the mental hospital to which Bowie's half brother Terry had been committed was hastily substituted instead. It was replaced in 1972 by a mediocre black-and-white shot of a blurry Bowie kicking up his heels onstage.

In the close-up portrait on the cover for *Hunky Dory* (1971), his next album, Bowie adopted a dreamy expression of sentimental, heavenward yearning drawn from the lexicon of studio-era Hollywood for women stars. Also startlingly feminine is his gesture of frank self-touching, as he smooths his long blonde hair back with both hands. The picture cleverly combines two images from Edward Steichen's great 1928 photo series of Greta Garbo draped in black (republished by *LIFE* magazine in 1955). The *Hunky Dory* cover was stunning at release not only for its daring gender play but for its evocation of Hollywood glamour, which was not yet taken seriously in nascent film studies. Its unnatural, metallic-yellow tinting of Bowie's hair had a Pop Art edge but also recalled airbrushing conventions of 1920s fan magazines, while its soft focus replicated the flattering aura of ageless mystery produced in Hollywood by applying Vaseline to the camera lens.

On the back of *Hunky Dory*, a long-haired Bowie somberly stands in blousy, flowing trousers, tailored in what was then a highly unusual retro 1930s cut (preceding Halston's contemporary variation on it). The picture resembles a canonical 1939 photo of Katharine Hepburn fiercely standing with shoulder-length hair and in similar tan slacks before a fireplace on the New York stage set of *The Philadelphia Story* (a year before it was filmed). Although Bowie cited Pre-Raphaelite precedents, the oblique inwardness and intriguingly half-concealing Veronica Lake hair were partly influenced, as was his beret photo on the back of *The Man Who Sold the World,* by Rachel Harlow (born Richard Finocchio), a Philadelphia drag queen.[3] Harlow had gained passing attention as the star of *The Queen,* a 1968 documentary chronicling a New York drag beauty pageant the prior year where the panel of judges (Andy Warhol, Edie Sedgwick, and journalist George Plimpton) awarded her the crown. The film, which Bowie saw and which created a press stir at the Cannes Film Festival, showed the furious backlash by disappointed fellow contestants: Harlow's soft, feminine look was a marked departure from drag queens' traditional "hard glamour," modeled on Hollywood stars like Marlene Dietrich. Harlow, who became a transsexual in 1972, was later linked to a rumored scandal involving Grace Kelly's brother Jack, who dropped out of the Philadelphia mayoral race because of it.

The cover art for Bowie's fifth album, *The Rise and Fall of Ziggy Stardust and the Spiders from Mars* (1972), enacted a brisk gender reversal from the prior two albums: a now short-haired, Nordically blonde Bowie is posted in macho mode, leg up on a rubbish bin on a London night street, his guitar slung like a rifle at his side while he warily scans the distance like a soldier on patrol. But the garish colors (superimposed afterward) of his turquoise jumpsuit and purple wrestler's boots, inspired by the army boots of the marauding "droogs" of Stanley Kubrick's film *A Clockwork Orange* (1971), betray another subtext. That sexual contrary is revealed by the sensational photograph on the back of the album: Bowie piercingly meeting the viewer's eyes from within a lighted telephone box, where he loiters with the graceful hands and hip-shot stance of a woman but the bare chest and bulging crotch of a male hustler (recalling Renaissance codpieces as well as the oversized jockstraps of *A Clockwork Orange*). Bowie's eccentric posture here was his first public use of drag queen mannerisms, which have been highly stylized since the Victorian era and probably long before. The exhibitionistic brazenness of the scenario—a rent boy waiting at a telephone—markedly departed from the relaxed domestic transvestism of the cover of *The Man Who Sold the World*, where Bowie could be mistaken for a rumpled eighteenth-century lord at his glossy leisure, like Thomas Gainsborough's *Blue Boy*. There was also a disconnect in the gay persona of the telephone box: in that period, male hustlers ("rough trade") would normally affect a stereotypical masculine look, such as that of a sailor, laborer, motorcyclist, or cowboy. Bowie created something entirely new in this taunting yet fey street tough, based on his own observation of the rent boys who lingered around London's hot spots and who paralleled the hunky male hustlers whom Andy Warhol filmed gamboling with the gamine Edie Sedgwick in his grainy early short films in New York.

Ziggy Stardust, Bowie's most famous invented character, did not appear on the cover of the album that bears his name but was theatrically developed on the unusually long world tour (January 1972–July 1973). Ziggy became so potent an entity that he virtually annihilated his creator and spun Bowie, by his own admission, into a fragile psychological state, exacerbated by cocaine, that was near "schizophrenia."[4] Ziggy's flamboyant makeup, rooster comb of spiky, razor-cut red hair, and futuristic costumes designed by Kansai Yamamoto turned him into an alien rock "messiah" (Bowie's term), leader of a band of space invaders come to redeem errant earthlings.[5] Bowie said Ziggy was modeled on Vince Taylor, a British-born pop singer who had lived in the U.S. and achieved second-tier prominence in England and France until he began to suffer drug-related religious hallucinations on stage. However, there was little sexual ambiguity in Taylor's self-presentation, which surviving TV clips show to have been a straight rockabilly knockoff of Gene Vincent, a hyperactive, black-leather-clad peer of the hip-swiveling Elvis Presley.

Bowie pushed Ziggy's gender into another dimension of space-time, where sexual personae of both East and West met and melded. Then very intrigued by Asian culture, he made Ziggy a strange amalgam of samurai warrior and kabuki *onnagata*—the male actor who played female roles in traditional Japanese theater. (On tour in Japan in April 1973, Bowie received instruction in kabuki makeup from Tamasaburo Bando, Japan's foremost living *onnagata*.) But Bowie's cynically suggestive stage manner (most overt in "Time," with its sinister honky-tonk piano) was drawn from German cabaret. The Broadway musical *Cabaret* had had a successful London run, with Judi Dench as Sally Bowles, in 1968; a revival of Bertolt Brecht and Kurt Weill's *Threepenny Opera*, starring Hermione Baddeley and Vanessa Redgrave, opened in the West End in early 1972. Bob Fosse's movie of *Cabaret* was released the same year: Joel Gray would win one of the film's eight Academy Awards for his insinuating, repellently flirtatious performance as an epicene master of ceremonies. Bowie's very title, *The Rise and Fall of Ziggy Stardust*, alluded to Brecht and Weill's *The Rise and Fall of the City of Mahagonny*, a satire of America from which came "Alabama Song," later performed by Bowie on his 1978 world tour.

Ziggy flashes with Weimar decadence, from the insomniac black-

ened hollows of his eyes to his impudent feather boa, a femme accessory that once belonged to Lindsay Kemp and that descended from
Marlene Dietrich's early film roles as a cabaret singer. The love god
Jimi Hendrix had often affected a pink boa, solarized to a psychedelic orange on the cover of his 1967 debut album, but it generally
receded in the rainbow riot of his Portobello Road retro wear. Marc
Bolan, with whom Bowie co-invented glam rock, had become known
for an arch combination of lavish boa and shiny top hat that almost
certainly came from Helmut Berger's drag routine as Dietrich in *The
Damned,* Luchino Visconti's 1969 film about the Third Reich's war on
Weimar excess. Ziggy's shoulder shimmies or bouts of hand-on-hip
swish frankly signaled Weimar sleaze and *nostalgie de la boue,* which
were most notoriously captured by Mick Rock's classic photo of Bowie
fallen to his knees and avidly mouthing Mick Ronson's vamping guitar. Gay fellatio was shocking enough at the time, yet even more notable in that perverse ritual was that a major male star was unashamedly
exhibiting himself in a sexually subordinate role. The *Ziggy* album
abounds with overtly gay references, from the title song's boast about
"God-given ass" to the provocative "Put your ray gun to my head" and
"The church of man love is such a holy place to be" ("Moonage Daydream").

But beyond his besmirched decadence, Ziggy Stardust also had
a dazzling visionary beauty, above all when Bowie was wearing his
short-skirted white silk kimono and high buskins, which made him
resemble an Amazonian huntress like Belphoebe in Edmund Spenser's *Faerie Queene.* With his silver lipstick and forehead astral sphere,
he evoked the radiant allegorical figures of courtly masque. At key
moments in the Ziggy gender mirage, Bowie would plant his feet
wide and show off his rippling, muscled thighs, a blazon of his underlying masculine athleticism. Indeed, in Ziggy Stardust's supernormal
militant energy and shuffled masks, we may have come closer than we
ever will again to glimpsing how Shakespeare's virtuoso boy actors performed the roles of Rosalind, Cleopatra, and Lady Macbeth. With his
haughty architectonic cheekbones and implacable will, Ziggy at times
resembled the young Katharine Hepburn, another sexually heterodox
personality who chopped off her hair and called herself "Jimmy" in

childhood and who made a spectacular Broadway entrance in 1932 as an Amazon warrior leaping down a flight of steps with a dead stag over her shoulders. Ziggy at his most lashing and relentless also re called Mary Woronov's brilliant improvisation as Hanoi Hannah in Warhol's epic *Chelsea Girls* (1966), a flight of ferocity so breathtaking that some viewers mistook her for a rampaging drag queen. Woronov played a dominatrix doing a whip dance with the poet Gerard Malanga in a multimedia show, the *Exploding Plastic Inevitable*, staged by the Velvet Underground, a group which had a heavy influence on Bowie. Indeed, Bowie prefaced the encore to his final concert performance as Ziggy, as can be seen in D. A. Pennebaker's documentary, with a heartfelt tribute to the Velvet's Lou Reed, who was then recording in a London studio. Bowie elsewhere called Reed "the most important writer in modern rock" and lauded "the street-gut level" of his work.[6] The title of Bowie's song, "Velvet Goldmine" (later borrowed by Todd Haynes for a 1998 movie), clearly riffs on Reed's band.

By the time we saw him on the front of an album, *Aladdin Sane* (1973), Ziggy Stardust was already in eclipse. The cover photograph by Brian Duffy with its red-and-blue lightning bolt crossing Bowie's face has become one of the most emblematic and influential art images of the past half-century, reproduced or parodied in advertising, media, and entertainment worldwide. It contains all of Romanticism, focused on the artist as mutilated victim of his own febrile imagination. Like Herman Melville's Captain Ahab, whose body was scarred by lightning in his quest for the white whale, Bowie as Ziggy is a voyager who has defied ordinary human limits and paid the price. Aladdin sane in the realm of art is a lad insane everywhere else. A jolt of artistic inspiration has stunned him into trance or catatonia. He is blind to the outer world and its "social contacts"—Bowie's recurrent term for an area of experience that had proved troublesome for Major Tom as well as himself.[7]

Pierre La Roche's ingenious zigzag makeup looks at first glance like a bloody wound—an ax blow through the skull of a Viking warrior laid out on his bier. Ziggy appears to be in hibernation or suspended animation, like the doomed astronauts in their mummiform chambers in Stanley Kubrick's *2001: A Space Odyssey* (1968), which had inspired Bowie's "Space Oddity." The background blankness is encroaching like a freezing cryogenic wave upon the figure. It's as clinical as an autopsy, with a glob of extracted flesh lodged on the collarbone. This teardrop of phalliform jelly resembles the unidentifiable bits of protoplasm and biomorphic conglomerations that stud the sexualized landscapes of Salvador Dalí. Also Surrealist are the inflamed creases of Ziggy's armpits, which look like fresh surgical scars as well as raw female genitalia. Like Prometheus, a rebel hero to the Romantics, he has lost his liver for stealing the fire of the gods. Like the solitary space traveler in 2001, he may be regressing to the embryonic stage to give birth to himself.

With his smooth, lithe, hairless body, *Aladdin Sane*'s rouged androgyne has evolved past gender, as blatantly dramatized by the full-length picture in the inside gatefold, where Ziggy's long legs and sleek, sexless torso are turning silver robotic. His proudly aristocratic stance with its streamlined waist grip is another quotation from Katharine Hepburn's unique publicity pose for *The Philadelphia Story*, combined with a salute to Veruschka von Lehndorff, the great supermodel (seen in Michelangelo Antonioni's *Blow-Up*) who had posed nude in spectacular body paint in a 1966 photo shoot in Kenya with Peter Beard and Salvador Dalí. In a 1977 interview on American TV, Bowie compared his friend Iggy Pop's method of working to his own: Iggy's ideas, said Bowie, blocking off space with both hands, came from the viscera and crotch, while his own ideas came from the chest and head: "I'm a cyborg," he declared.[8] The bust-like cover of *Aladdin Sane* shows the artist in creative process, having jettisoned the mundane appetites of belly and genitals. This dreaming head is lifting off into a shamanistic zone of vision purged of people and matter itself.

For the cover of his next album, *Pinups* (1973), a vigorous collection of cover versions of hard-rock classics, Bowie used a photograph of himself with Twiggy taken in Paris by Justin de Villeneuve for *Vogue*. The two look lost and stricken, like Adam and Eve after the Fall. Who are these waifs? They appear to be wearing masks—actually cleverly drawn on with makeup. The striking color contrast on Twiggy (she was tanned from a Bermuda holiday) sparks a frisson of uncertainty about both race and gender: it might very well be a black man in a female mask leaning his head so confidingly on the tensely alert Bowie. As a pop idol now bruised by fame, Bowie had arrived in the purgatorial territory of Twiggy's declining star—she who as a coltish girl-boy had been a supreme symbol of the 1960s youthquake.

Bowie returned to Weimar sensibility for the cover of *Diamond Dogs* (1974), a lurid drawing by Guy Peellaert in a German Expressionist style complementing the album's dystopian narrative, which had been inspired by Fritz Lang's 1925 film, *Metropolis*. The opening howl, recitation about "rotting corpses," and graphic bestiality—Bowie and two crouching, ghoulish women are depicted in half-dog form—was the closest he ever came to the Grand Guignol horror-movie gambits of Alice Cooper, whose 1971 European tour had been attended by both Bowie and Elton John. The setting of the *Diamond Dogs* cover is a sideshow ("The Strangest Living Curiosities") drawn from Tod Browning's disturbing 1932 film, *Freaks*, which is glossed in the title song. Bowie's canine loins (presumably alluding to Iggy Pop's breakthrough song, "I Wanna Be Your Dog") may have been glaringly male—the genitalia were soon airbrushed away to head off rising controversy— but the rest of him is a bitch. He wears a large loop earring, a lushly enhanced silhouette of red lipstick, and a lavishly teased bouffant variation of his Ziggy haircut. Despite his sinewy arms, the effect is sensuously female—an alluring prone pose propped up on elbows that was commonly used for publicity shots of bosomy studio-era stars like Lana Turner and even the mature Gloria Swanson. Peellaert worked from two sketches drawn by Bowie of his variation on an Egyptian sphinx. Precedents for the picture can be found in Symbolist paintings of femmes fatales, specifically Fernand Khnopff's *Sphinx* (1896), where a reclining leopard with a woman's face smugly caresses a girlish Oedipus. The songs on *Diamond Dogs* portray a decadent world of fast sex in city doorways ("Sweet Thing") and trampy boys in torn dresses and smudged makeup ("Rebel Rebel").

Young Americans (1975) was the last album cover that Bowie used as a gender canvas. Once again he meets the viewer's eyes but no longer with the hard edge of urban prostitution seen on *Diamond Dogs*. It is another Hollywood glamour portrait, his short but flowing hair softly backlit to form a halo. The startlingly feminine silver bangle bracelets, jarringly juxtaposed with a subtly Art Deco man's plaid shirt, gleam like a starburst. The impression of wavering gender is accentuated by his discreet pink lipstick and longish manicured fingernails. (Russet nail polish, missing from the U.S. album, was restored to the picture for the 1999 remastered CD release.) A ghostly spiral of cigarette smoke, airbrushed in, is another vintage Hollywood touch. This wistful, cloistered figure might be a kept boy or a neurasthenic aesthete, like the artist Aubrey Beardsley or the poet Lord Alfred Douglas, who brought down Oscar Wilde. A similar pensive brand of guarded androgynous male beauty was captured by Peter O'Toole in his multifaceted portrayal of the cultivated, tormented Lawrence of Arabia in David Lean's 1962 film.

What must be observed about Bowie's gender fantasia is how rarely he ever did straight drag. The significant exception was a video directed by David Mallet for "Boys Keep Swinging," a song on *Lodger* (1979), the final album in Bowie and Brian Eno's "Berlin Trilogy." The song was not released in the U.S. because of record company fears about the video's unpalatable transvestism. It begins with Bowie as a Cliff Richard–style early 1960's rock 'n' roll singer clad in a generic dark suit and rollicking away with standard kinetic moves at a standing microphone. Attention then shifts to his trio of hilariously bored female back-up singers, each one played by Bowie in drag. There is a blowsy, blasé, gum-cracking Elizabeth Taylor in a tendrilous bun wig and a big crinoline skirt topped with a violet cinch belt—Taylor's signature color. Bowie had met John Lennon five years earlier at a party at Taylor's Los Angeles house. Photos of the zaftig Taylor bearhugging the alarmingly frail Bowie—she was wearing his fedora—made it seem as if she could crush him like an eggshell.

Next in the video is an icy Valkyrie in a svelte metallic-gold sheath dress with fetishistically deformed sleeves—boxy Joan Crawford shoulder pads sprouting lateral wings like shark fins. Her full, dark hair resembles that of the enigmatic Lauren Bacall in *To Have and Have Not* as well as the stormy Bette Davis in *All About Eve*. The dress itself recalls the clinging metallic moth costume worn by Katharine Hepburn (playing an aviatrix modeled on Amelia Earhart) in *Christopher Strong* and also the spectacular, skin-tight "nude dress" of beaded

silk soufflé designed in 1953 by Jean Louis for Marlene Dietrich's cabaret concerts. (For the second half of those shows, which toured the
world, Dietrich changed into the top hat and tails of her 1930 film,
Morocco.) There is also a suggestion of the fashion model Jerry Hall's
disruptive, sashaying entrance in a black-slashed gold tiger gown in
Bryan Ferry's 1976 video for "Let's Stick Together." At the end of the
sequence, Bowie breaks role by aggressively whipping off his wig
and smearing his lipstick with the back of his hand, staring down the
viewer with a frightening sneer of rage—a reversal of the usual hilar-
ity and applause-inviting bonhomie accompanying the gender revelation at the end of drag acts. This golden androgyne is truly Bowie's
"Queen Bitch" (the tenth song on *Hunky Dory*).

The third drag impersonation is of Dietrich herself, with whom
Bowie had recently starred in *Just a Gigolo* (1978), directed by David
Hemmings. Bizarrely, they never met: Bowie's dialogue with Dietrich
was spliced together in post-production. In "Boys Keep Swinging,"
he got his revenge: the aged Dietrich, dressed in an understated knit
Chanel suit, walks haltingly with a cane down the fashion catwalk,
from which old women are normally banned. Pausing at the edge,
she feebly yet contemptuously blows a kiss at the viewer with her cigarette, the fading superstar still hungry for dominance. In this video,
Bowie penetrated to the cold masculine soul and monstrous lust for
power of the great female stars, which drag queens had always sensed
and turned into rambunctious comedy.

The video for "Boys Keep Swinging" had camp wit but shabby production values. That all changed the following year with "Ashes to
Ashes," from the *Scary Monsters (and Super Creeps)* album. Directed
by Bowie and David Mallett (working from Bowie's own storyboards),
it was at the time the most expensive music video ever made. This
mini-movie, with its dreamlike collage, profoundly influenced the
direction of music videos, which exploded with the spread of cable
TV and the introduction of a round-the-clock music channel, MTV, in
1981. Bowie called the song "Ashes to Ashes" "an ode to childhood,"
but its video became a portrait of the isolated, suffering artist, with
motifs and techniques drawn from the entire history of European art
films—from Carl Dreyer's *The Passion of Joan of Arc* and Luis Buñuel

and Salvador Dalí's *Un Chien Andalou* to Jean Cocteau's *Orphée* and Ingmar Bergman's *The Seventh Seal*. The song's self-referential nature was signaled by the return of Bowie's debut character, Major Tom, now a notorious "junkie" in a crisis of addiction.

In "Ashes to Ashes" (a phrase from the Anglican funeral service), Bowie assumes the role of Pierrot, a figure of seventeenth-century Commedia dell'arte who became prominent in French pantomime. Many painters, such as Watteau, saw themselves in the melancholy Pierrot, with his tenderness and naïveté and his humbling enforced straddling of the line between art and entertainment. Bowie's Pierrot, wearing a tufted white clown costume and dunce cap, has a gangly awkwardness and a timid, pre-sexual innocence. In other scenes, however, an elegantly handsome Major Tom sits caged in a padded cell and an exploding kitchen or, haggard and stony, hangs moribund in a watery grotto that is half wrecked spaceship and half nightmare womb.

Bowie has rarely spoken publicly of his mother and, in the 1970s, curtly rebuffed prominent British and American TV interviewers when they presumptuously prodded him about it.[9] The finale of "Ashes to Ashes" addresses the matter in dramatic symbolism, like the depressed film director Guido's dream encounter with his parents in a cemetery in Federico Fellini's *8½*. Hectored by a small, gesticulating older woman, who Bowie said (when introducing this video for a 1993 MTV retrospective) resembled his mother, Pierrot strolls with abashed attentiveness and dutiful resignation along the edge of an infernal underground sea.[10] A moment before, he stands flinching and paralyzed from the camera flash of a merciless paparazzo: the shooting of a picture (the video's third photo portrait) becomes a real bullet shot. Is Pierrot now dead and his mother come to reclaim his body—like Mary for a pietà? Bowie's ending evokes that of *The Tramp*, where another childlike, genderless clown, Charlie Chaplin in a fake mustache, rambles away down a dirt road. There are also striking visual parallels to a mordant moment in Fellini's *La Dolce Vita* where a fierce matriarch of the old Italian nobility materializes at dawn with a priest and imperiously summons her carousing adult children to Mass. The other decadent partygoers stand stupefied as they watch their recently priapic but now cowed playfellows fall in line and obediently troop away.

In the finale of "Ashes to Ashes," Bowie was questioning his identity as an artist and a man. Despite his wandering, he evidently still felt the stubborn tug of his origins, a regulated suburban conformity from which he had escaped to a vivid universe of omnisexual fantasy that had bewitched an entire generation. In the video, his mother is both peripheral and central, a voice he can't get out of his head. The poignant refrain, echoing a traditional British children's song, identifies the mother with pressing practical reality: "My mother said to get things done / You'd better not mess with Major Tom." Tom is Bowie the daydreamer who spaces out. His mother is like the poet Wallace Stevens' contrary Mrs. Alfred Uruguay, who boasts, "I have wiped away moonlight like mud."

The video's bleak, solarized color suggests that, at this moment, the mother is winning. Pierrot sinks slowly in the sea, while the landscape seems to be losing its fictive energy, like the anemic, fading characters in Jacques Rivette's 1974 film, *Céline and Julie Go Boating*. Bowie's scathingly self-critical dual perspective would soon take comic form in "Jazzin' for Blue Jean," where Screaming Lord Byron's excess and vanity are satirized by Bowie himself playing a dual role as a maladroit nerd who shouts at Byron, "You conniving, randy, bogus Oriental old queen! Your record sleeves are better than your songs!" In "Ashes to Ashes," the limited personal mother is only an instrument of or proxy for larger processes of fate. The mammoth bulldozer, for example, which menacingly follows Pierrot and his troupe of female priests is a modernization of "Time's winged chariot hurrying near" (from Andrew Marvell's "To His Coy Mistress")—a fascist force pushing all of humanity into a mass grave.

The subterranean disturbances in Bowie's oeuvre around the issue of women and their ungovernable power can be detected in "Suffragette City" (from *The Rise and Fall of Ziggy Stardust*), with its heady refrain, "Don't lean on me, man, because you can't afford the ticket back from Suffragette City!" Gender relations were changing fast after the rebirth of feminism in the late 1960s. This line shows men unprepared for the shift and running around in circles like antic squirrels.

It says in effect, "Don't ask *me* for advice, because I sure can't help!" It implies that castration, metaphorical or otherwise, is the toll exacted by women whose quest for equality may sometimes conceal a drive for dominance. The song's other blazing refrain, "Wham, bam, thank you, ma'am!"—a common old American catchphrase probably about prostitution—tauntingly suggests that loveless hit-and-run sex is one foolproof way to avoid swampy entrapment by women.

Few if any songs in Bowie's great period contain a fully developed portrait of a woman, positive or negative, comparable to Bob Dylan's sympathetic "Sad-Eyed Lady of the Lowlands" or the toweringly furious "Like a Rolling Stone." Bowie's exhilarating "China Girl" (1983), with its wonderfully expansive video directed by David Mallet, substitutes political for psychological issues and was in any case co-written by Iggy Pop about an Asian woman he was courting in Switzerland. Bowie's most concentrated meditation on sexual identity and gender relations is contained in the staggered finale of *Aladdin Sane*—a matched set of songs, one inspired by an American man and the other by an American woman. They are pointedly introduced by a cover version of the Rolling Stones' "Let's Spend the Night Together," which in this context posits not just sexual intercourse but dialogue and détente—which may prove impossible between the entrenched positions of the new gender wars.

The first song, "The Jean Genie," is an anthem to boy power partly inspired by Iggy Pop, one of Bowie's closest friends in the 1970s and his flatmate during his low-profile exile in Berlin after the burn-out of Ziggy Stardust. Bowie said that in this song he wanted "to locate Ziggy as a kind of Hollywood street rat"—in other words, one of the homeless, rootless kids who flocked to the Sunset Strip in the late 1960s and '70s, a colorful scene rife with drugs and prostitution that was also a matrix of new music and style.[11] (A male "trick" from Sunset and Vine forces a closeted star to his knees earlier on the album in "Cracked Actor.") The jean genie is a "reptile," a "rattlesnake," a scrappy sprite and male hustler slithering outside the system who, like Peter Pan, retains his freedom by never growing up. If there is a reference to Jean Genet in his name (as Bowie later admitted was possible), then he is Genet's ideal of the thief and outcast, representing the association of homosexuality with heroic Romantic criminality that Genet got from André Gide and that Gide got from Wilde.[12] Denim (preceding the designer jeans trend of the late '70s) still had an outlaw connotation, as shown in Warhol's snapshot of the crotch of a jeans-clad male hustler for the zippered cover of the Rolling Stones' 1971 album, *Sticky Fingers*.

Bowie's jean genie is a vagabond and derelict who savors squalor and filth as a defiance of female order and control and who even asserts the right to slash, maim, and violate his own mother-made flesh. ("Ate all your razors" is a splendid Beat-style line vividly referencing the stage-diving Iggy's notorious self-cutting on broken glass.) The genie's delirious manic motion is caught by the buzz and fuzz of the aggressive guitars, which evoke the unleashed boy energy of the rave-up Yardbirds in their covers of Bo Diddley's braggart "I'm a Man" and Howlin' Wolf's "Smokestack Lightning," which pictures sex and its betrayals as a constantly hurtling train. (The genie "loves chimney stacks"—belching, sparking phallic totems as well as soft entry points for home burglary.) Bowie, who daringly talks rather than sings this song, can be heard doing the legendary bluesman's eerie "whoo-hoo" (the train's receding siren) as a chorus.

But woman gets the last word on *Aladdin Sane*. "Lady Grinning Soul" was reportedly inspired by Claudia Lennear, an African-American soul singer who had been one of Ike and Tina Turner's back-up Ikettes. (Despite widespread claims, it remains unclear whether it was Lennear or another American, Marsha Hunt, mother of Mick Jagger's first child, who was the model for the Rolling Stones' "Brown Sugar.") "Lady Grinning Soul" becomes a great archetypal sexual vision that transcends its origins—much as Percy Bysshe Shelley's "Epipsychidion" left Emilia Viviani behind. From the first entrance of Bowie's voice, apprehensively a capella and distorted by echoes, we know we are in perilous territory.

The title alludes to Aretha Franklin's 1968 album, *Lady Soul*, but that phrase is now split by a death's head.[13] "Grinning" almost certainly comes from "Pirate Jenny" in *The Threepenny Opera*, a song premiered by Lotte Lenya in Berlin in 1928 and volcanically performed at New York's Carnegie Hall in 1964 by Nina Simone, who fused it with black radical politics. (Bowie deeply admired Simone and met her in Los Angeles in 1975; he recorded "Wild Is the Wind," from her 1966 album of that name, as the finale of *Station to Station*.)[14] Jenny is a hotel chambermaid who harbors secret thoughts of class revenge and pitiless massacre: "I'm kind of grinning while I'm scrubbing. And you say, 'What's she got to grin?'" Her chilling refrain forecasts the arrival of a black freighter with a skull on its masthead as well as the privileged choice now handed to her: "Kill them now or later?"

Bowie's chambermaid is more chatelaine or cool adventuress than brooding, vengeful servant, but "the clothes are strewn" here too—a messy trail of sexual haste. "Don't be afraid of the room," he confidently sings, but this is whistling in the dark (shown by his rise to vulnerable falsetto), for she rules the womb-tomb of the female body. After the brisk fresh air of the peripatetic genie, we are in a dark sensory zone of intoxicating hormonal scents—cologne and "musky oil" from African civets. With her full breasts and impenetrable psyche, Lady Grinning Soul represents absolute sexual difference, not the misty, blurred ground of gender experiment that Bowie normally traverses. It is as if he has come face to face with Homer's Circe or Calypso, in whose realms men shrink to swine or slaves. But she is also a series of other seductive femmes fatales—Carmen (suggested by the Spanish guitar), Gustav Klimt's Judith (whose supercilious lolling head is mimicked by Bowie in his 1973 video of "Life on Mars"), and Alban Berg's heartless Lulu. The female principle is shown as mysterious, elusive, ungraspable. "She will be your living end," croons Bowie in the hypnotic, achingly elegiac refrain: pleasure and pain, love and death (as in Wagner's *Liebestod*) are intertwined. Any man's victory in sex with a woman is transient and illusory.

The genesis of "Lady Grinning Soul" may have been in the lyrics of a Jacques Brel song, "My Death," a flawed translation of which Bowie had been singing on the Ziggy Stardust tour: "Angel or devil, I don't care. . . . My death waits there between your thighs." Bowie turned it into a stark encounter with elemental realities, a descent to the underworld. "Lady Grinning Soul" has hauntingly immersive atmospherics and an incisive power that standard poetry written in English was losing in the 1970s. Indeed, in its hair-raising candor yet sardonic banter, the song bears comparison to Sylvia Plath's savage Oedipal nursery rhyme, "Daddy" (written in England in 1962). "She comes, she goes": Bowie's restless, piratical traveler who trifles with men and has a way with cards sounds like a capricious, fortune-telling Muse, flooding the artist with ideas and then leaving him high and dry.

Art-rock, a genre that showed enormous promise but failed to develop and deliver over time, produced only two enduring master-pieces: the Doors' 1967 Freudian-Jungian psychodrama, "The End," and Bowie's "Lady Grinning Soul" (which ends with virtually the same words as begin the Doors song). Crucially contributing to the late Romantic lyricism of "Lady Grinning Soul" is Mike Garson's amaz-ing piano work, a sumptuously florid improvisation that exposes the rifts, fractures, illusions, and turmoil of sexual desire. Beginning in an ominous mood of decadent Vienna and Berlin, Garson creates a compelling emotional world of anxiety and entrancement, tinged with panic and despair. With fistfuls of virtuoso runs and trills, he invokes the most flamboyant Romantic music-making from Liszt and Rach-maninoff to Liberace and Ferrante and Teicher—a style often used in classic movies such as the 1941 British film, *Dangerous Moonlight,* where Richard Addinsell's *Warsaw Concerto* is played amid the rubble of the Nazi invasion of Poland. Nina Simone used the same rapid, rippling piano style to accompany herself on the 1966 album version of "Wild Is the Wind." Bowie has reportedly never performed "Lady Grinning Soul" live—a testament perhaps to its excruciatingly sen-sitive material. After the infectious gaiety of "The Jean Genie," this harrowing sojourn into the female boudoir, which is both burrow and palace, yields a Wildean revelation: men are simple, women complex.

Bowie's theater of gender resembles the magic lantern shows or phantasmagoria that preceded the development of motion-picture projection. The multiplicity of his gender images was partly inspired by the rapid changes in modern art, which had begun with neoclassi-cism sweeping away rococo in the late eighteenth century and which reached a fever pitch before, during, and after World War One. Bowie told a TV interviewer in 1976, "I was always totally bedazzled by all the art forms of the twentieth century, and my interpretation comes out *my way* of these art forms from Expressionism to Dadaism." "Even if the definition isn't understood," he tried to "break it down" to convey his own "feeling" to the audience."[15] One of Bowie's leading achievements is his linkage of gender to the restless perpetual motion machine of modern culture. "I have no style loyalty," he has declared.[16] His signature style is syncretism—a fusion or "synthesising" (his word) of many styles that is characteristic of late phases such as the hybrid, polyglot Hellenistic era, when religions too seeped into one another.[17] Bowie has in fact used the word "hybrid" to describe his approach.[18] His stylistic eclecticism in performance genres—combining music hall, vaudeville, pantomime, movies, musical comedy, cabaret, theater of cruelty, modern dance, French chanson, and American blues, folk, rock, and soul—created countless new angles of perception and startling juxtapositions.

A superb example of the way Bowie brings art and gender into single focus was his adaptation of the mannequin style, a prototypical twentieth-century motif. As women were liberated in the Jazz Age, fashion sped up, promulgated by new media like high-budget movies and glossy magazines with vastly improved techniques of photographic printing. Mannequins as living models as well as department-store dummies became vivid cultural presences, as shown by the frequency of elaborate fashion-show sequences in prestige Hollywood films like *The Women* (1939). The way that the self-conscious mannequin style had been instantly absorbed by the new woman can be seen in Man Ray's 1926 photograph of heiress Nancy Cunard with her arms robotically stacked with big African bangle bracelets and in August Sander's 1931 photographs of a slender secretary with boyishly cropped hair at a West German radio station in Cologne. These two women with their penetrating eyes and steely emancipation capture the intersexual look of avant-garde modernism and eerily anticipate the classic androgyny of David Bowie himself. The mannequin theme is overt when Bowie calls his diamond dogs, on the title song of that album, "mannequins with kill appeal." In the same lyric, the chillingly faceless "little hussy" of his alter ego Halloween Jack wears "a Dalí brooch," recalling the jellied teardrop fixed to the collarbone of Aladdin Sane. Mannequins became automaton-like agents of what Bowie elsewhere called a "ritualizing of the body" in art that interested him.[19]

The Surrealists, who emerged from Dada, seized on the fashion mannequin as a symbol of modern personality—assertive and hard-contoured yet empty and paralyzed. They were partly following the precedent of the Metaphysical painter, Giorgio de Chirico, who showed genderless tailors' dummies marooned in twilit deserted plazas. (Bowie explicitly voiced his admiration for de Chirico and later replicated his work, as well as that of the Surrealist René Magritte, in the hallucinatory sets for the 1985 video of "Loving the Alien.")[20] Mannequins were major players in the 1938 International Surrealist Exhibition in Paris, where the entry courtyard was dominated by Dalí's installation, "Rainy Taxi," with its nude mannequin seated amid 200 live snails on a bed of lettuce. Inside the building was an avenue of mannequins stationed like streetwalkers and festooned with symbolic regalia and outright junk. In 1945, the Dadaist Marcel Duchamp, who had posed in drag as his alter ego Rrose Sélavy for Man Ray two decades before, inserted a headless, book-reading mannequin in a skimpy negligee into the window of New York's Gotham Book Mart to advertise the latest release by André Breton, the father of Surrealism. In the age of abstraction, the plaster mannequin, so easily chipped and seedy, was the derelict heir of canonical life-size Western sculpture in marble or bronze. The mannequin was so artificial that it eventually became gender-neutral. Its spectral aura was well captured in "The After Hours" (1960) from the first season of *The Twilight Zone,* a TV series launched by America's greatest native Surrealist, Rod Serling: here department-store mannequins are tracked as they roam, freeze, and frighteningly come alive again.

Bowie's stunning variation on the Surrealist mannequin was that he became it: never before had a major male artist so completely submerged himself in a female *objet de culte.* Bowie's genius for using the camera as others use a paint brush or chisel—not from behind the camera but before it—was dramatized in *The 1980 Floor Show,* his last appearance as Ziggy Stardust. This cabaret-structured program was recorded over three nights in October 1973 at the Marquee Club in London and was broadcast on American TV the following month. (It was never aired in Britain, and the film footage was thought lost for many decades.) In one routine, Bowie wore a see-through black fishnet body suit (designed by him and Freddie Burretti) adorned with two gold-painted mannequin's hands attached to his chest. A third hand affixed to the crotch had been scuttled after a battle royal with the NBC film crew, who also insisted that Bowie cover up his black jockstrap with gold semi-leggings. The two cupped hands formed a bizarre brassiere that made it seem as if Bowie had sprouted breasts. Yet given women's swerve away from nail lacquer since the mid-1960s, the hands' black varnished nails (a nihilist color not yet in the female arsenal) also suggested a man in drag: it was as if Bowie were being

David Bowie in his gold and black fishnet body suit, topped with a Surrealist brassiere of mannequin's hands. *The 1980 Floor Show,* London, October 1973. Bowie's last appearance as Ziggy Stardust.

sexually pawed and clawed from behind by a raging queen in heat. Or was he split in gender and acrobatically embracing himself?—a trick (imitated by Bowie on tour) often employed in burlesque by strippers turning their backs to the audience. Furthermore, it seemed as if his body were being played like a piano—not unlike the way Man Ray turned the body of Kiki de Montparnasse into a sensuous violin. The eye was titillated and confounded by an optical illusion: Which of the multiple hands, including that on Bowie's glitter-sheathed right arm, were the real ones?

Bowie's mannequin masque was a tremendous tour de force, Dadaist in impulse and Surrealist in conception and execution. It fulfilled Baudelaire's dictum in *The Painter of Modern Life* that fashion should be "a sublime deformation of nature." In that one event, seen only by Americans, Bowie inserted himself permanently into the story of modern art. He instantly revived and renewed the Warhol legacy, which had been flagging since Warhol was shot and nearly killed in 1968, leaving him physically depleted and unable to advance beyond his set formulas. The Bowie broadcast on NBC's late-night variety show, *The Midnight Special*, was electrifying in its direct address to Americans who had been following the sexual radicalism of Warhol and his circle since his pioneering short films of the 1960s—notably *Harlot* (1965), Warhol's first sound film, starring Mario Montez as a charismatic blonde drag diva photographed with slow, ritualistic solemnity.

Bowie said that America had always been "a myth land" for him.[21] The "idol" of his youth had been Little Richard, the gender-bending, high-wattage rock 'n' roller whom he had seen in person at the Brixton Odeon.[22] Andy Warhol and his coterie represented the next stage in Bowie's Anglo-American artistic journey. His contacts with Warhol figures are well-documented. In August 1971, Bowie saw the London production of *Pork*, a self-satirizing farce by the Warhol coterie of Andy's obsession with gossipy telephone calls. (The stage was adorned with two nude, fetchingly long-haired boys.) A slew of *Pork* personnel were immediately hired by Bowie, including Cherry Vanilla, Tony Zanetta, and Leee Black Childers. Bowie and Warhol met just once the following month in New York, an awkward and mutually diffident encounter from which survives a video of the long-haired Bowie in a raffish black hat doing a strangely self-disemboweling mime. In his song, "Andy Warhol" on *Hunky Dory* (released December 1971), Bowie hailed Warhol's perverse, voyeuristic theatricality by envisioning him as an art gallery and "silver screen," a "cinema" of the mind that he longed to emulate. However, the refrain "Andy Warhol looks a scream" upset and offended Warhol. Bowie would later use the dead Warhol's own wig and eyeglasses to play him in Julian Schnabel's 1996 film, *Basquiat.* In 1975, Bowie co-produced Lou Reed's only hit song, "Walk on the Wild Side," with its litany of drag queens and hustlers from the Warhol Factory. Bowie gave one of them, Joe Dallesandro, a cameo role in his 1987 video, "Never Let Me Down," directed by Jean-Baptiste Mondino.

In its brash humor and dreamlike fantasy, Pop Art, as is widely accepted, was the heir of Dada and Surrealism. But by embracing commercial popular culture, Pop ended the oppositional avant-garde tradition that had been born with Romanticism. The momentum of new art styles immediately slowed after Pop and soon stopped altogether. No one style has dominated any period since. Thus Bowie, with his protean multiplicity of styles, must be acknowledged as having taken the next important step in the fine arts after Warhol. He remains Warhol's true successor. It is indisputable that Bowie, through his prolific work in the 1970s, was one of the principal creators of performance art, which would flood the cultural scene in the 1980s and '90s. Another seminal figure in that movement, Eleanor Antin, who emerged from American radical theater and Conceptual Art after Fluxus, boldly declared Bowie "one of my favorite artists" in 1973, when he was still being dismissed by many critics as a flashy fad. She explicitly paralleled his creation of volatile, autonomous cross-dressing characters to her own (such as a bearded ballerina or a melancholy vagrant king modeled on Charles I). "Something is in the air," Antin said. "Maybe it's in the stars."[23]

What Bowie and Antin were separately formulating was a theory of gender as representation or performance, antecedents for which can be found in Shakespeare's plays, where theater becomes a master metaphor for life. Role-playing as constitutive of identity had been a basic premise of social psychology since the 1920s and had been most fully analyzed in the Canadian-American sociologist Erving Goffman's highly influential 1959 book, *The Presentation of Self in Everyday Life*, which applied theater metaphors of acting, costume, props, script, setting, and stage to social behavior. (Goffman's theory of the performative self was a primary source for Michel Foucault, to whom these ideas are often incorrectly attributed.) Gender roles were in flux from the mid-1960s well into the '70s due to a convergence of dissident energies from the reawakened women's movement in the U.S. and from a pop culture revolution that had started even earlier in England. The unisex crusade of the 1960s was born in Mod London and spread to the world—cropped haircuts, pinstriped trousers, and sailors' pea coats for urchin girls; crimson satin, purple velvet, and flouncy Tom Jones shirts for peacock boys.

But transsexual impersonation of the kind undertaken by David Bowie and Eleanor Antin was something new and different—or rather something as old as Teiresias, the shaman and prophet who crossed into forbidden sexual terrain. Drag was a familiar quantity in British music hall, with its rambunctiously outspoken "pantomime dame," whose roots were in the rigidly conformist Victorian era and who begot the immensely popular entertainer Danny La Rue. From the 1920s on in Britain, Germany, and the U.S., gay nightclubs featured drag queens doing campy parodies of glamorous Hollywood stars or lip-syncing to rousing cult classic songs. (By Bowie's formative years, the international drag anthem was Shirley Bassey's incendiary "Goldfinger," perhaps the most terrifying manifestation of ruthless star power ever recorded.) Bowie never had a triumphalist view of sexual liberation or gender games. He told an American magazine in 2000 (in response to a question about the song "Boys Keep Swinging"), "I do not feel that there is anything remotely glorious about being either male or female."[24] On the contrary, he had always systematically experimented with disorienting suspensions of gender, as in his ode to the "Homo Superior," "Oh! You Pretty Things" (on *Hunky Dory*), where sexually ambiguous boys and girls have shifted into an indeterminate "thing" state, like works of art.

Bowie's shocking proclamation of his gayness to *Melody Maker* in

1972 was unprecedented for a major star at the height of his fame. It was a bold and even reckless career gamble. But the overall pattern of Bowie's life has been bisexual, something paradoxically far more difficult for many gay activists to accept, then and now. His open marriage to the equally bisexual Angie Barnett (another of his American alliances) went further toward bohemianism than did the communal '60s hippie ménage typified by the Mamas & the Papas in Charlotte Amalie and Laurel Canyon. His loquacious wife, with her brazen verve, encouraged his androgyny and helped costume it, notably a propos his "man-dresses."

Yet despite his pioneering stand, Bowie was on a trajectory diverging from that of both feminism and the gay liberation movement which sprang up after the 1969 riots at New York's Stonewall Inn. Although black and Latino drag queens had been central in that first resistance to a routine police raid, the drag queen soon became persona non grata to gay men who wanted to distance themselves from the age-old imputation of effeminacy. Similarly, the women's movement was hostile to drag queens for their supposed "mockery" of women. The flaming lipstick and rouge of glam rock flouted feminists' mass flight from makeup: cosmetics were among the accoutrements of female oppression flung into a "Freedom Trash Can" on the boardwalk at the famous feminist protest at the Miss America pageant in Atlantic City in 1968. Bowie's orientation toward fashion, glamour, and Hollywood went completely against the feminist grain in the 1970s, when identity politics made a highly ideological landfall in academe. Although "lipstick lesbians" emerged in San Francisco in the late 1980s, the cult of beauty would not be restored to feminism until Madonna led the way in 1990 with her "Vogue" video glamorizing high fashion and Hollywood love goddesses.

Just as Bowie was debuting Ziggy Stardust, furthermore, gay men were heading in a macho direction—first with San Francisco's Castro Street "hippie clone" look of beards, t-shirts, and tight hip-hugger jeans and later with New York's "Christopher Street clone" uniform of thick mustaches, flannel lumberjack shirts, riveted farm jeans, and work boots. The gay stereotypes were already fixed by the 1977 debut of the Village People, a comedic novelty band that won surprising mainstream acceptance. The icon-maker of that period was Tom of Finland, whose ebullient beefcake drawings of gigantically endowed, black-leather-clad orgiasts shaped the sadomasochistic urban underground documented by Robert Mapplethorpe's photographs. Bowie's first concession to this trend was the cover of *Heroes* (1977), where he wears a soft, chicly continental black-leather jacket, offset by the angular hand gestures of an avant-garde dancer. The pose combines Nijinsky's stylized imitation of Greek vase-painting with the stigmata scene in *Un Chien Andalou*.

After his half-dozen years of uneven success on the London music scene, Bowie's artistic persona suddenly coalesced in the early 1970s at the climax of the sexual revolution. The idealism of the '60s, stoked by peaceable, communal, giddy-making marijuana, had drifted and stalled. Now dawned the cynical disillusion of the '70s, symbolized by nervous, ego-inflating, jealously secreted cocaine. Spontaneous romantic romps in the sunny or soggy meadows at Woodstock would yield to predatory stalking and anonymous pickups in murky, mobbed, deafening disco clubs or barricaded elite venues like Studio 54. Bowie's archly knowing and seductively manipulative Ziggy Stardust sprang into being at the invisible transition into this exciting but mechanically hedonistic sexual landscape.

Although himself a hyperactive athlete of the new libertinism, Bowie never viewed sex as salvation. In his classic work, identity is a series of gestures or poses. Sex is represented as a theatrical entry into another dimension, parallel to but not coexistent with social reality. Like Wilde, Bowie made sex a medium for a sharpening of self-consciousness rather than its Dionysian obliteration. The megalomania and delusionalism of Ziggy Stardust marked the start of the long and confused period of gender relations that we still inhabit. The fall of the old taboos has not enhanced eroticism but perhaps done the opposite. Women have gained widespread career status, and homophobia has receded, but divorce has soared, and the sexes still collide in bitter public recriminations. The evident progress in sexual freedom and tolerance in the secular West—given that it is hemmed in by populous conservative cultures that consider it decadent—might be just as evanescent as it was during the Roman Empire.

Bowie's darker intimations about the sexual and cultural revolution were signaled in his background vocal for Mott the Hoople's "All the Young Dudes" (1972), which he wrote for the group when they seemed to be disbanding. The song, with its spunky androgynous misfits ("he dresses like a queen but he can kick like a mule"), was widely interpreted as a celebration of the glam rock insurgency, but Bowie warned that it was "no hymn to the youth" but "completely the opposite," a prelude to "the end of the earth."[25] That storm clouds were already gathering over the defiant new dandies can be sensed in the song's dirge-like foreboding, nowhere clearer than in the unforgettable refrain, "All the young dudes carry the news": the smoothly harmonizing Bowie breaks "news" into two syllables, a rupture that sounds like a sob (boo-hoo). It was oracular prescience: the apocalypse came a decade later as the plague of AIDS, which decimated an entire generation of gifted young writers, artists, musicians, and fashion stylists.

The Aeolian lyre, a harp hanging in the wind, was a cardinal metaphor for the Romantic poet, passively played upon by the forces of nature. During his supreme decade of the 1970s, David Bowie too was an Aeolian lyre, with the totality of the fine and popular arts of the time playing through him. Even when Bowie at his most alienated sings in a dissonant, jagged, splintered, or wandering way (partly drawing from his early history as a saxophone player), there is always a high emotional charge to his work. Here is his salient distinction from the postmodernist artists and theorists of the 1980s with their ironic "appropriations" and derivative pastiches. Bowie's emotional expressiveness, heard at its height in songs like "Look Back in Anger" (whose artist's garret video adapts Wilde's *The Picture of Dorian Gray*), would help trigger the foppish New Romantic movement in British music of the late 1970s and '80s that produced Duran Duran, Boy George of Culture Club, and eventually Depeche Mode.

Bowie's empathic virtuosity is on magnificent display in the gospel-inflected "Fascination," which he wrote with Luther Vandross in Philadelphia for *Young Americans*. It is a song so passionate, powerful, and grand that it can be understood as Bowie's artistic manifesto, addressed to no one but himself. "I've got to use her": if she is a drug, then it is merely a coin of passage to his inner realm. The song describes his violent seizure by and enamored fascination with his own aspiring, gender-conflating mind. He is his own Muse. "Can a heartbeat / Live in the fever / Raging inside of me?" Is there room for personal love or even life itself for the artist driven by uncontrollable flashes of inspiration? Bowie's mesmerizing theater of costume, music, and dance is animated by mercurial yet profound emotion— the universal language that transcends gender.

1. *TopPop* TV program, The Netherlands, October 1977.

2. Interview with Jools Holland on *The Tube*, Channel 4, March 1987. Bowie: "If I'm writing and recording, I find I don't need to paint. But if I'm not doing very well, and I can't write, and there's a kind of block or a blank there, then I revert to painting, and it opens up like a watershed of ideas and associations and things." In an interview recorded on May 16, 1978, in Cologne, Germany, for the BBC2 documentary series *Arena*, Bowie told Alan Yentob that when he returned to Europe after living in Los Angeles, painting helped him "get back into music." He described his painting style as "a form of Expressionistic Realism."

3. Bowie said he had "a Pre-Raphaelite kind of look" on *Hunky Dory*. Interview with Ian "Molly" Meldrum for *Countdown*, a weekly Australian music television program, taped in October 1980 in a Japanese restaurant in New York during Bowie's run in *The Elephant Man* on Broadway.

4. "I was so lost in Ziggy, it was all a schizophrenia." *Cracked Actor*, BBC documentary filmed in 1974 and first aired on January 26, 1975.

5. Bowie about Ziggy Stardust: "I wanted to define the archetype 'messiah/ rock star'—that's all I wanted to do." Interviewed by musicians Flo and Eddie of the Turtles and Mothers of Invention for *90 Minutes Live*, CBC, November 25, 1977. In the 1978 Yentob interview for BBC2, Bowie said about his stage characters, "They're all messiah figures." Bowie about Yamamoto in an interview for NBC's *The Today Show*, April 1987: "I wanted the best of the contemporary fields working with me, kind of like Diaghilev did when he was doing ballets."

6. Craig Copetas, "Beat Godfather Meets Glitter Mainman," *Rolling Stone*, February 28, 1974. Conversation between Bowie and author William S. Burroughs the prior November at Bowie's London home. Bowie reveals he had taken the name of American frontiersman Jim Bowie, inventor

of the massive Bowie knife, because "I wanted a truism about cutting through the lies." In a 1996 interview with Avi Lewis for the Canadian television program *The New Music*, Bowie said that "however many critics were saying how important the Beatles were" at the time, "the artists" were talking instead about the Velvet Underground: "Tomorrow's culture is always dictated by the artists. . . . The artists make culture, not the critics."

7. Bowie about Major Tom: "He was my own ideal of what I wanted to do, somebody totally in his own world. . . . He was a hero to me but an anti-hero—he didn't have any social contacts [*laughs*]." (Interview in 1980 with Ian "Molly" Meldrum for *Countdown*.) In a 1979 interview with Mavis Nicholson, Bowie recalled putting himself in "dangerous situations," specifically "areas where I have to be in social contact with people, which I'm not very good at doing." (*Afternoon Plus*, Thames Television, recorded February 12, 1979.)

8. *Dinah!*, CBS TV talk show, April 15, 1977. Iggy Pop sat on the couch between Bowie and Dinah Shore, the motherly blonde host. Bowie's pelvic thrust punctuating his analysis of Iggy's method drew a faux-naïf response of "I wonder what he means by that! Gee whiz!" (producing audience laughter) from the other guest, Rosemary Clooney, a veteran big-band singer like Shore. Despite his gentlemanly British manner, Bowie had managed to break the code of American television, then very strict on daytime programs directed to homemakers.

9. *The Dick Cavett Show*, ABC, recorded in New York, December 2, 1974; aired December 5. Cavett asked Bowie about his mother, "Does she have any trouble explaining you to the neighbors?" Bowie replies, "I think she pretends I'm not hers [*laughs*]. . . . We were never that close particularly. We have an understanding." In a remote-camera interview from London, Russell Harty condescendingly probed Bowie (in Burbank, California) about his mother. Bowie coldly replied, "That's really my own business." (*The Russell Harty Show*, BBC, recorded November 28, 1975.) Cavett asked Bowie what he was reading: "What would we find on your coffee table in your apartment?" Bowie responded, "At the moment, mainly pictures. I bought Diane Arbus's book of photographs, a photographer I like very much."

10. Bowie on the making of the "Ashes to Ashes" video: "We went down to the beach, and I took a woman there who looked like my mother. That's the surrealistic part of making movies." (*David Bowie Weekend* on MTV, April 4 and 5, 1993.) The actress was Wyn Mac, wife of comedian Jimmy Mac, who played Warwick on the BBC sitcom *Are You Being Served?*

11. David Bowie and Mick Rock, *Moonage Daydream: The Life and Times of Ziggy Stardust* (New York, 2005), p. 140.

12. Charles Shaar Murray, "David Bowie: Gay Guerrillas & Private Movies," *New Musical Express*, February 24, 1973.

13. Aretha Franklin can be heard singing a smash hit from *Lady Soul*, "(You Make Me Feel Like) A Natural Woman," in the limousine crossing the desert in the 1975 BBC documentary *Cracked Actor*, where Bowie drinks milk from a large carton and is questioned by Alan Yentob. (Aired January 26, 1975.) It was this sequence which convinced director Nicolas Roeg to cast Bowie as the alien star of *The Man Who Fell to Earth* (1976).

14. Introducing his version of "Wild Is the Wind," Bowie said, "During the mid-1970s, I got to know Nina Simone, whom I've got incredible respect for as an artist and a composer and a singer." Even though she had not written this song, her "tremendous" performance of it had "affected" him greatly: "I recorded it as an *hommage* to Nina" (*David Bowie Weekend* on MTV, April 4 and 5, 1993).

15. *Dinah!*, CBS TV talk show recorded in Los Angeles, February 24, 1976. Dinah Shore's other guests were Nancy Walker and Henry Winkler. Earlier Bowie says about his continual openness to and influence by other performers and styles, "I'm usually saturated."

16. Interview with Alan Yentob, recorded May 16, 1978, in Cologne for the BBC2 documentary series *Arena*.

17. Ibid.

18. *Parkinson*, BBC1 talk show, recorded November 27, 2003. Parkinson asks, "What was Ziggy about?" Bowie replies, "It was about pushing together all the pieces and all the things that fascinated me culturally—everything from kabuki theater to Jacques Brel to Little Richard to drag acts. Everything about it was sort of a hybrid of everything I liked."

19. Interview at Stadthalle, Vienna, 1996. Bowie says, "I was trying to pinpoint a tradition of ritualizing of the body." He cites as a "semi-nihilistic equation" André Breton's definition of the ultimate Surrealist act as shooting a pistol randomly into a crowd (from the *Second Surrealist Manifesto* of 1930). Bowie calls it "as potent an image" as Duchamp's urinal in presenting the body as "a ritualistic way of articulating twentieth-century experience." (In the first *Surrealist Manifesto* of 1924, Breton compared "the modern mannequin" to "romantic ruins" in exemplifying the "marvelous," a central Surrealist principle.) Bowie mentions as an antecedent the Romantic writer Thomas De Quincey's 1827 essay, "On Murder

Considered as One of the Fine Arts." In the same interview, he says that he liked Expressionism since he was "a kid" and that he had especially admired Gustav Klimt, Egon Schiele, and the Blaue Reiter group.

20. In a 1987 interview, Bowie said, "I was always very seriously affected by my dreams. . . . I found the dream state magnetic. It just captured everything for me." When he saw the films of Dalí and Buñuel and the paintings of de Chirico, he thought, "Yes, that's exactly how I want to write. How do you work like that?" (*Day In, Day Out*, MTV special during Bowie's Glass Spider tour.)

21. *Cracked Actor.*

22. In an Australian interview, Bowie said of Little Richard, "He was my idol" (November 28, 1978). Elsewhere Bowie said, "I wanted to be a white Little Richard at eight—or at least his sax player" (*David Bowie: Sound and Vision*, A&E network's *Biography* series, October 6, 2002). In 1980, Bowie told ABC's *20/20*, "I fell in love with the Little Richard band. I had never heard anything that lived in such bright colors in the air. It really just painted the whole room for me" (November 13, 1980).

23. *Art Talk: Conversations with 15 Women Artists*, ed. Cindy Nemser (1975; rev. ed. 1995), p. 252.

24. "Watch That Man," *BUST* magazine, Fall 2000.

25. Copetas, "Beat Godfather Meets Glitter Mainman." Bowie tells Burroughs that "All the Young Dudes" refers to the "terrible news" collected by Ziggy Stardust, who is torn to pieces on stage by the "black hole" of the "infinites." This news, Bowie says, appears in "Five Years," his first song on the *Ziggy Stardust* album: "News had just come over, we had five years left to cry in. . . . Five years, that's all we've got."

6

PUNK ROCK

The Sex Pistols, the British band that is often given credit for starting the punk movement, burst on the rock scene with "Anarchy in the UK" (1976) and "God Save the Queen" (1977). They were never able to reproduce their success in the United States, since their ferocious anti-establishment stance was so geared to the ossified class system that has weakened but that remains an overt feature of British life.

The Sex Pistols' 1977–78 tour fell flat partly because they were out of sync with the inner dynamic of American music. London may have needed a retro kick in the ass to restore primal, masculine rock energy after the dissolving androgyny of the glam and glitter period, but we Americans had already been ravished by the punk artistry of Patti Smith, whose 1975 album, *Horses,* remains one of the greatest products of the rock genre. Television, whom I saw in 1977 at CBGB's in downtown New York, and early Talking Heads (though not the Ramones) were the punk avatars for me and my circle.

The Sex Pistols undoubtedly struck many young listeners as highly original, but in the late 1970s, I was already 30 and had gotten my punk zap from the Velvet Underground, whose mesmerizing first album was released in 1967, when I was in college. In their first phase (the early- to mid-1960s), the Rolling Stones and the Who had also been aggressively punk in assumptions and attitude. Furthermore, by the time the Sex Pistols arrived in the U.S., disco was in full swing—a

[Response to a reader question about the failure of the Sex Pistols in the U.S., Salon.com column, January 20, 1999.]

much-derided style that I took seriously and had been closely following since James Brown begat funk.

Although their manic influence can be traced in rhythmic terms to thrash rock and in performance terms to brash boy personae as far afield as Billy Idol and Anthony Kiedis of the Red Hot Chili Peppers, the Sex Pistols self-destructed too soon to leave much of a musical legacy. Nothing they composed remotely approaches the enduring brilliance of David Bowie albums like *Aladdin Sane* (1973) and *Diamond Dogs* (1974). (Bowie's baroque art-rock was a primary punk target, and he briefly took refuge in Berlin, where he revamped his style.)

Punk anarchism may be an adolescent phase of simplistic rebellion against authority. The Rolling Stones' canonical late-1960s songs, "Sympathy for the Devil," "Jumpin' Jack Flash," "Street Fighting Man," and "Gimme Shelter," are far more comprehensive statements about life and its inevitable conflicts between individualism and order. The Sex Pistols' Sid Vicious, who died of a drug overdose in 1979 several months after he was charged with murdering his girlfriend, didn't live long enough to work through his early punk positions.

I would cite the Who's magnificent, rumbling "Eminence Front" (from the 1982 *It's Hard* album), with its penetrating insights into psychology and politics, as an example of what an evolved punk can and should achieve. Anarchism is glorified thumb-sucking. Off with the diapers, and on to business! Construction, not destruction, is the name of the human game.

7

LIVING WITH MUSIC:
A PLAYLIST

1) **Train Kept A-Rollin'**, The Yardbirds (1965). An addictive London Mod rave-up epitomizing the accelerating mania of the 1960s, which finally self-destructed. Based on a 1951 song by an African-American musician, Tiny Bradshaw.

2) **Ballad of a Thin Man**, Bob Dylan (1965). Sinister atmospherics of the garish sexual underground in the repressive pre-Stonewall world. A naïve voyeur reporter steps through the looking-glass and may or may not escape.

3) **Season of the Witch**, Donovan (1966). Nature and society in turmoil, as identity dissolves in the psychedelic '60s. The witch marks the return of the occult, a pagan subversion of organized religion.

4) **8 Miles High**, The Byrds (1966). Shimmering Hindu sitar riffs with jet flight as a metaphor for mental expansion. The song's ultimate theme isn't drugs but cosmic consciousness, a now forgotten '60s goal.

5) **Foxy Lady**, Jimi Hendrix (1967). Oh, those crazed, strutting, supersonic, wham-bam chords! Their shock on the nerves still excites, more than 40 years later.

6) **Lickin' Stick**, James Brown (1968). A deliciously sly exercise in

["Living with Music" series, Dwight Garner, ed.,
The New York Times, July 16, 2008.]

sexual suggestiveness underpinned by Brown's hypnotic, trademark, heavy-bass rhythms. Is the lickin' stick an antebellum whip or melting phallic candy?

7) **Wooden Ships**, Jefferson Airplane (1969). An apocalyptic spectacle of wandering survivors of nuclear war. Male and female voices meet and bond as humanity renounces aggressive nationalism.

8) **Bitch**, The Rolling Stones (1971). Powerful, jagged, stabbing chords that seize the mind. Is the Stones' bitch goddess a capricious woman or enslaving heroin?

9) **Hotel California,** The Eagles (1976). West Coast hippie hedonism meets the new satanism. Staggeringly brilliant double guitar solos ecstatically entwining—men in love!

10) **On Broadway**, George Benson (1977). The Drifters' aspirational 1963 hit song tooling along on a seductive Latin jazz beat. Benson explicitly flaunts his guitar as his artistic alter ego.

11) **Straight on for You**, Heart (1978). The Wilson sisters give a throbbing, sonorous tour of erotic neurology. Phenomenal display of basic, stripped rock rhythms.

12) **Edge of Seventeen**, Stevie Nicks (1981). The only woman rocker with a majestic orchestral flair. Stevie as Druid seer showering her maternal compassion on youthful romantic trauma.

13) **Coming Out of Hiding**, Pamala Stanley (1983). Now a gay anthem, this song is actually a soaring assertion of female power. It's an exuberant war whoop, flawlessly executed by Stanley's witty, knockout voice.

14) **Ain't Nobody,** Chaka Khan with Rufus (1983). A masterpiece of modern popular culture. The passionate lead voice stays cool and low amid the pulsing, swooping neo-African rhythms. This song is a living, breathing organism.

15) **Middle of the Road**, The Pretenders (1983). Chrissie Hynde at Dante's midlife crisis. She ingeniously fuses explosive, in-your-face street attitude with rueful reflections on her new role as mother.

16) **On the Turning Away**, Pink Floyd (1987). Celtic mysticism rising to a grand, Wagnerian finale. David Gilmour's luminous lead guitar is ravishing beyond words.

17) **Hazy Shade of Winter,** The Bangles (1987). The best rocking the Bangles ever did. Simon and Garfunkel's classic aria of angst given a crisp, slamming treatment. The drums are like artillery fire.

18) **Black,** Pearl Jam (1991). Deep-sea diving in the inky depths of male emotion, explored by Eddie Vedder's rich, keening, achingly honest baritone. Wonderful interplay with the band's virtuoso instrumentalists.

19) **Un-break My Heart,** Toni Braxton (1996). Two centuries of African-American church singing produced the expert dynamics and peaking structure of this elegant display of musical theater. Poignant and devastating.

20) **Easy,** Groove Armada (2002). An ultra-sophisticated Euro-tech descendant of Giorgio Moroder's seminal disco collaboration with Donna Summer. Sunshine Anderson (a North Carolinian in a British band) brings introspective intensity to the moody, multi-layered soundscape.

8

OSCAR STYLE

STYLE Q

Style Q: Exercise Your Brain

To the Photo Gallery

Paglia Wired for the Oscars

Camille Paglia Does Oscar, Live!

America's most provocative, and, if we may add, attractive public thinker will lead a live tour of the high, low, and finer points of Oscar fashion 96, on Tuesday, March 26, at 10 p.m. in the ABC Cyberplex. How do today's stars stack up against the glamour-pusses of yesteryear? Well, it just so happens that Camille, author of Vamps and Tramps and Sexual Personae, has a rather strong opinion on that topic. Join her - and special guest Glennda Orgasm (aka Glenn Belverio) - Tuesday the 26th, and hash out the meaning of Oscar style once and for all.

Screen shot made by America Online (later AOL Inc.) of March 1996 advertisement for online dialogue by Camille Paglia and Glenn Belverio. Paglia did everything she could to support the development of the Web at a time when it was still not taken seriously by established writers, journalists, and academics.

[Transcript of Camille Paglia and Glenn Belverio (in his drag persona as Glennda Orgasm) on "Oscar Style," Style Channel Live, America Online/ABC CyberPlex Auditorium, an interactive online event, March 26, 1996. The text has been slightly shortened but has been reproduced exactly as it appeared in process on the computer screen. Belverio was at home in New York, while Paglia was in Philadelphia.]

StyleABC: Hello and welcome to Style Channel's CyberPlex!
              Coming up next—Camille Paglia and Glennda
              Orgasm to discuss Oscar fashion.
              Send in your questions and comments for Camille and
              Glennda. Click on INTERACT.
              Go to keyword PICS to see the Oscar picture show!
              Welcome Camille and Glennda!

CamillePag: It's great to be here!

OnlineHost: Welcome to Style Channel Live in the CyberPlex.
              We are thrilled to present America's hottest
              intellectual, Camille Paglia, and her special guest,
              Glennda O (aka Glenn Belverio).
              The two recently starred in the frock-u-drama, *Glennda
              and Camille Do Fashion Avenue.* Our topic this evening
              is Oscar Style, last night
              and every Oscar night.

GlenndaO: Here we are together again, Glennda and Camille.

StyleABC: Here's our first question . . .

Question: Didn't Whoopie look REALLY bad last night? What
              was with that dress?

CamillePag: I thought it looked like a gospel choir robe!

GlenndaO: Whoopie looked like Darth Vader.

CamillePag: It could have been a fabulous opera diva look, but she
              didn't practice whipping it around!

GlenndaO: Where are her eyebrows?

CamillePag: Her makeup was disastrous—her face and neck didn't
              match her bosom.

GlenndaO: It needs to be blended. BLEND!!!

CamillePag: Where were the makeup artists throughout the show?

GlenndaO: The podium was really distracting—it had glitter on it!

GlenndaO: I thought everyone had sequins on the lower half of their outfits.

CamillePag: The main problem for me is that hardly any of the women knew how
to wear a period dress.

StyleABC: Darracq wants to know about Sharon Stone . . .

Question: A question for Glennda: Does Sharon Stone's sensuality seem "armored" and unreal to you, or is she really a sensual person?

GlenndaO: How can one be armored in a GAP t-shirt?

CamillePag: I love the idea of armored and unreal!

GlenndaO: She looked like she was going to a tennis match.

CamillePag: It's very Amazon like! I adore Sharon Stone!
I thought she looked fabulous—
because everyone at the show was doing her in
Casino, that 70's
Sharon Tate look, and she
surprised everyone and in fact upstaged everyone by coming out
in a very minimalist costume that accentuated her blonde beauty!

GlenndaO: It was really inappropriate for the Oscars—even though it was iconoclastic.
She was single handedly trying to revive grunge!
GAP sales will go through the roof.

StyleABC: Next question . . .

Question: What did you people think of Mira Sorvino?

CamillePag: I thought she was one of the few actresses at the Oscars

who showed real old-style movie star class.
She had a wonderful early 50's look to her.

GlenndaO: She defined the whole jewelry motif of the night!
She was great!

CamillePag: And she was one of the few women last night who had
appropriately sized jewelry.
Half the women looked like they were in dog collars
or suffocating
in King Tut's mummy pectorals totally out of
proportion to their anatomy!
Her hair was quite beautifully styled in that complex
way—very
eighteenth-century French, I thought.

GlenndaO: Sandra Bullock had on an antique choker.

CamillePag: I liked Sandra's lush, flowing hair, which was a nice
change from her usual sorority girl look
but I thought the choke collar was quite wrong
and looked as if the Marquis de Sade had designed
it. And
I also thought that very beautifully styled dress was
too flat a brown
for her—she needed more highlights in the color.

GlenndaO: The choker was from 1910 when women were smaller.
She had a perfect *Valley of the Dolls* look.

CamillePag: And we do adore *Valley of the Dolls*—it's one
of my favorite movies of all time!

GlenndaO: She was playing against her "plain-jane" type.

Online Host: For those of you who are just joining us,
Style Channel's guests are intellectual extraordinaire
Camille Paglia and drag queen
extraordinaire, Glennda O (Glenn Belverio).
Our topic: Oscar style—who had it, who didn't,

and who ought to just give up and slink
out of the limelight. Click INTERACT to
send Camille and Glennda a question.

StyleABC: Go to keyword PICS to see the Oscar Photo Show!
Our next question is from Kyle Mile . . .

Question: What did you think of Emma Thompson?

CamillePag: I thought she had a Queen Mum look

GlenndaO: The Queen Mum approved her outfit.

CamillePag: and although it was a gorgeous glittering fabric
it was far too conservatively cut at the neck area.
And she looked like she was on her way to a secretarial
job!

GlenndaO: She took her pumps off after the show, no self-
respecting woman would do that.
But she was very prim and proper in the British
tradition, I approve of that.

CamillePag: But I did love her hair—very lavishly styled, like
Hillary on the way to her Whitewater testimony—
and the color was a very vibrant blonde.

GlenndaO: Did Emma Thompson find any document outside her
bedroom?

StyleABC: Dykedr wants to know about sweet Winona . . .

Question: What about Winona Ryder's look? Old-style too?

CamillePag: Someone should slap Winona and give her some
color!

GlenndaO: She had nice finger waves, but a flesh tone dress . . .
NO!!!!!!
I don't approve of dresses that match skin tones.

CamillePag: She was totally drab and washed out, and

it didn't help that she introduced Bruce Springsteen in a whiney, wimpy manner. She
needs some spunk, some spine—even
though her hair was nicely styled in a late 20's way.

GlenndaO: But she had great cleavage, and we love that!

StyleABC: Let's get down to basics . . .

Question: What do you think of the Wonderbra. It seemed to be all over the
Oscars (except of course, on Sharon Stone). Is it revolutionary for women?

CamillePag: I believe that if the dress is correctly cut, the more bosom the better!

StyleABC: RedTiger1 wants to know about . . .

Question: How could Nicole Kidman look so great in everything she wore in *To*
Die For . . . and then
wear that THING to the Oscars?

CamillePag: She was in tatters!

GlenndaO: She was wearing lingerie that looked like she sewed it on a toy sewing machine that morning.
It must've been her revenge outfit for not being nominated.

CamillePag: Her silhouette was too faint.

GlenndaO: Tom looked embarrassed.

CamillePag: She is a large, handsome woman who could have made a truly spectacular effect.

StyleABC: Check out our photo show—keyword PICS. Next question . . .

Question: Why does Brad Pitt always look so homeless?

GlenndaO: He lost his bowtie in the limo.
It was casual. I approve of that.

CamillePag: He looked like a 70's gigolo.

GlenndaO: We knew he wasn't gonna win anyway.

Question: There seemed to be an Audrey Hepburn revival
going on at the Oscars. You both admittedly
adore her. Why are we suddenly so fascinated by her
again?

CamillePag: We are certainly part of that!
We worship Audrey and regard her as a paragon of
modern chic.

GlenndaO: NO—Audrey had more taste. I was disappointed to
not see any
Givenchy. But there were some nice Galliano's.
Her dress in *Breakfast* was a flashpoint between the
50's and 60's.

CamillePag: Most of the young women in Hollywood have no taste
whatever—
it all began with Daryl Hannah, whom I publicly
prodded to get
some taste. My efforts do appear to have partially
succeeded.

CamillePag: On a more serious note, I think the massive deaths
from AIDS
of so many gay men took out of the New York and
Los Angeles
scenes the principal tastemakers who helped these
young girls along.

GlenndaO: Jessica Lange was GORGEOUS!
I've loved her ever since *King Kong*.

CamillePag: I think she looked like a bag of beans!
And you talk about droopy boobs?

StyleABC: A question from Hottieboy . . .

Question: Whoopi made a slick comment about breast implants last night.
What's the consensus, guys:
enhancer of sexuality (e.g. Demi) or silly, unnatural body ornamentation?

GlenndaO: Some women feel self-conscious about their breasts. I'm sensitive to that.

CamillePag: If any person, male or female, wants to use the body as a living sculpture,
I approve of it!
But we must be prepared to face the toxic or mutilating consequences!

GlenndaO: Silicon breast implants are dangerous.
I saw a documentary on PBS about it and I'm very concerned.

StyleABC: Getting personal . . .

Question: Camille, do you own any designer clothing? Why? Why not?

CamillePag: I do own a few remnants from Syms!
But I really don't have the finances to afford anything major.
However, my lecture tour look for 1994 made a huge effect
with my Donna Karan tuxedo outfit!

GlenndaO: I wear Halston. He and I were close in the 70's.

StyleABC: BO DOME wants to know . . .
What do you think of all of the vests worn by the men?

CamillePag: I liked them very much,
because I love the dandy look of the nineteenth century.

GlenndaO: Contrast vests were the look for men this year. It was a great
                departure from the monochromatic look.
                Steven Spielberg lost out with his tired monochromatic look.
                Will Smith was wearing an ascot.

CamillePag: Spielberg is too small
                to wear jackets with huge lapels. He looked like he was wearing a bathrobe!

StyleABC: Finally, a question about Joanie . . .

Question: What do you think of the way Joan Rivers looked?

CamillePag: I hope to catch re-runs later, but I adore Joan Rivers— she is
                my patron goddess. I am called the academic Joan Rivers.

Question: Who do you think was the hottest couple at the Oscars? Claudia and David or Nicole and Tom?

GlenndaO: Goldie Hawn and Kurt Russell were my faves.

CamillePag: Me too.

GlenndaO: I loved Goldie's pistachio CK gown.

CamillePag: Goldie knows how to wear a dress
                and walk across a stage—
                she has that superb dancer's carriage.
                However, that stringy hairdo does not go with elaborate diamond pectorals.

GlenndaO: She had a great flower power look during the *Laugh-In* era.

StyleABC: Good question . . .

Question: Is there any difference between the Oscars and a drag ball?

CamillePag: A drag ball is more vicious.
People will use their stiletto heels and
pierce your instep.

GlenndaO: There's more real designer gowns at a drag ball. And
everyone has eyebrows.

GlenndaO: You would never see GAP at a drag ball.

StyleABC: Racybird asks about lovely Alicia . . .

Question: What about Alicia Silverstone's 'look'? A far cry from
Clueless.

GlenndaO: AWFUL—
especially for an actress in a movie about fashion and
style.
And she forgot to brush her hair before she left the
house.

CamillePag: I love Alicia, but
she looked like a bag lady.
No one was there to help her learn how to walk in
a dress of that consequence—much less how to
handle that fiendish chiffon wrap.

GlenndaO: I thought it looked tulle.

StyleABC: Onlysis wants to know about the SUPERMODELS:

Question: Do you think supermodels are out of place at the
Oscars?

CamillePag: Supermodels are the heirs of the great Hollywood
studio system
past and therefore do belong at the Oscars.
But they were horrendously misused and looked like
jerks for the most part—
They were awkward, sheepish, off-balance.
That production number should have been brilliant,
but it was a huge waste of everyone's time and money.

GlenndaO: That fashion production will come to define the 90's much the way Debbie Allen defined the 80's.

CamillePag: For heaven's sake, if you wear Jane Austen clothes, you'd better learn how to walk in them and how to move your arms in a graceful manner.

GlenndaO: It was gratuitous to name all the models—it was an unholy marriage
between Hollywood Blvd. and 7th Ave.

StyleABC: Writer595 writes . . .

Question: Camille—Been a fan for some time. :). I'm curious . . . what do you
think of the choices for
best actor/actress and what they say about Hollywood and ourselves?

CamillePag: I love Susan Sarandon,
and it's about time she was honored by the industry. She is one
of the most intelligent of all contemporary performing artists.
However, I am underwhelmed by Nick Cage
and do not find him interesting at all.

StyleABC: It all comes back to Streisand:

Question: Remember Streisand in her *Funny Girl* Oscar outfit?
Does anyone
have individual style anymore?

GlenndaO: Where was Barbra?
We needed her there.

CamillePag: People in general have lost the individuality of the Sixties/early Seventies.

GlenndaO: Her Scaasi outfit was the best ever in history.

Question: Do you think men wore too much jewelry at this year's awards?

CamillePag: Well, there were so many diamonds on the women that surely the men must compete somehow.

GlenndaO: I hated Mel Gibson's tacky sword in the lapel. Nothing should go
into men's lapels at the Oscars.

CamillePag: Of course, I adore martial symbolism of all kinds—since I am a natural born pugilist.

GlenndaO: Women can wear flowers and jewelry, but I would discourage men from doing it.

Online host: For those of you who are just joining us,
Style Channel's guests are intellectual
extraordinaire Camille Paglia and drag queen
extraordinaire, Glennda O (Glenn Belverio).
Our topic: Oscar style—who had it, who didn't,
and who ought to just give up and slink
out of the limelight. Click INTERACT
to send Camille and Glennda a question.

Question: What do you think was this year's worst fashion mistake? Be brutal.

GlenndaO: There were so many.
I'm tempted to say Sharon Stone, but I'm gonna have to go with Nicole Kidman.

CamillePag: I think we both agree it was Nicole in rags.

GlenndaO: Poor Nicole!!

CamillePag: Claudia Schiffer's gown made her look trivial, I thought.

GlenndaO: Pity what happened to Anjelica Huston. Her off the
shoulder number
looked great on her huge shoulders.

CamillePag: I thought Anjelica made an enormous, regal
impression in that strikingly simple dress.

GlenndaO: The winner of the night was Susan Sarandon. Her
hair matched her
dress. GENIUS!

CamillePag: I loved Susan's spiky copper hair—almost punk.

GlenndaO: I liked how she managed to sneak in a social message.
I'm with her on her non-violence stance.

CamillePag: Vanessa Williams was amazing in that gold metallic
gown with her
tawny lioness hair and luminous skin.

GlenndaO: We like her because she appeared in *Penthouse*.

CamillePag: I've been a fan of Vanessa's since that huge
controversy.
Another person who looked great was Lawrence
Fishburne—
I thought he was the handsomest and best-dressed of
the men, with
that beautiful grey tie.

GlenndaO: Angela Bassett had 60's Joan Crawford hair.
GORGEOUS!!

StyleABC: LilyZ asks . . .

Question: Camille—what would you have worn if you were
presenting??

CamillePag: I would have found some elegant sportive pant suit.

GlenndaO: That old Givenchy that I have in the closet. I can't
possibly wear another Halston in public.

CamillePag: There appears to have been only one Dutch dyke
wearing pants—it was a dress fest!

StyleABC: Astorian wants to know about Bruce . . .

Question: What happened to Bruce Springsteen? He used to be
so cool, and now
he's a pompous, mumbling, preachy bore!

CamillePag: Well, he began as a preachy bore, in my view,
when he ripped off Bob Dylan without
understanding all the
learning that goes into brilliant surreal lyric writing of
that kind.
Bruce had a nice middle period that I appreciated,
but he seems to be knee deep in the compassion
sweepstakes these days,
writing heavy penance songs.

GlenndaO: I went to the bathroom while he was on to fix my
makeup.
One word for the Boss . . . ROGAINE.

StyleABC: Mar f g asks . . .

Question: Didn't the evening seem incomplete without Jodie in
her Armani?

CamillePag: I'm a bit tired of Jodie and her supercilious Yale
know-it-all manner.
And I think she needs to do some deep meditation
about womanliness and take some lessons from
Vanessa Williams!

GlenndaO: She gave Mel Gibson some tacky war beads. She
hasn't had a good role since *Foxes*.

Question: Are designers doing a better (or worse) job dressing
stars than studio wardrobers in the fifties?

CamillePag: Emphatically not—the great studio designers

had much more distinction in their conceptions, since they were drawing on the classical past in art history and theater design.

And furthermore, women were coached more seriously at that time in dignity of bearing and placement of arms and hands— a real lady should know how to use her hands!

GlenndaO: Edith Head ruled the Oscars from 1953 to 1969—no one got on that stage without her approval.

CamillePag: Edith Head was one of the great artistic tyrants of all time—she was a creative genius!

CamillePag: The Oscar shows have got to expand that introductory section more.

CamillePag: The entire world audience is tuning in to see the stars get out of their limousines.
It infuriates me how the theatricality of that moment is underplayed year after year by the television network. We must demand a return to the old Hollywood idea of the Oscars as a panorama of style!

StyleABC: Another good question . . .

Question: Why do we care so much what the stars wear?

CamillePag: For me, glamour is ART!
It is not superficial—it is the essence of human beauty. It is godlike, in the pagan way.

Question: The late great Gloria Swanson said in *Sunset Boulevard* that "we had faces!" Where are today's Hollywood faces—surely not in the likes of Meg Ryan/Daryl Hannah/Geena Davis. Who in your opinion has THE FACES today?

CamillePag: Sharon Stone is magnificent for me.
The way she showed herself last night to dramatize her facial contours—that black outfit combined with her gold complexion—proves my point.

GlenndaO: Joel West, the model, has a great face. He looks like an extra from
the finale of *Close Encounters of the Third Kind.*

StyleABC: IGP89 asks . . .

Question: I wonder if Prof. Paglia noticed the resurgence of the strapless
gown, and if she sees
any import in this new trend. I am a gay designer and appreciate her respect for our art, btw.

CamillePag: Yes, I think that it shows the influence of Rita Hayworth in *Gilda*—
that amazing cantilevered gown constructed with all the care of a
Gothic cathedral!
I love the return of the strapless, because it echoes our new interest in traditional sex roles—
it's very difficult for men in drag to replicate the soft plushiness of a woman's natural bosom.

GlenndaO: It goes back to the 50's motif. It calls for creative bra-wearing. I have a problem wearing that look!

StyleABC: Our last question is . . . What are you wearing right now?

GlenndaO: My silk pajamas that Doris Day gave me with my fluffy slingback slippers. It's very comfortable.

CamillePag: I am in my characteristic at-home writing garb—sweatpants and t-shirt and sneakers. Yes, I am quite dowdy in real life! Glennda is the
one with the glamour in this collaboration!

CamillePag: My advice for next year's Oscars attendees
                is to practice, practice, practice with those gowns in
                front of a mirror and then have a very
                waspish gay man critique you!

GlenndaO: Maybe everyone should wear GAP—to hell with the
                designers!!!! And
                more tans and blond hair, i.e.
                Donatella Versace!

Online Host: Thank you, Camille and Glennda,
                for sharing your expertise with us tonight.
                And thanks to all of you in the audience.
                Remember, though Oscar night comes but once
                a year, you can always keep an eye on what the
                stars are wearing by visiting the Style Channel.
                And you can learn more about glamour and
                gender at the Gay and Lesbian Community Forum.

CamillePag: Good night, everyone!

GlenndaO: Good night, everyone.

StyleABC: Good night, everyone. Thanks for joining us! Sweet
                Oscar dreams.

9

A LOVE LETTER TO JOAN RIVERS

Joan Rivers is a force of nature. Her caustic voice, relentless energy, and driving ambition are formidable, while her flinty toughness and grit have carried her through bruising career reverses and shocking personal tragedies. Joan is the queen of comebacks and a master of all media, having invaded every genre and format from stand-up comedy, theater, movies, and books to talk shows, shopping channels, reality TV, radio, and the Web.

When I arrived on the public scene after the release of my first book in 1990, I was called "the academic Joan Rivers"—a title I loved. Yes, Joan influenced me profoundly. Watching her for decades on TV, I learned so much about how to work a crowd or even how to wake up groggy students in my morning classes. With her combative, rapid-fire style, Joan has shown several generations of women how to command a stage and make it your own.

In her most recent book, *I Hate Everyone . . . Starting with Me,* Joan demonstrates her scathing rejection of humanitarian pieties and political platitudes. Unlike virtually all American comedians these days, she never preaches to the liberal choir for easy laughs. On the contrary, she goes against the grain and overtly offends and repels. She has endeared herself to free-thinking gay men by her pitiless attacks on political correctness. She cracks jokes about Nazis, mass murder-

["Camille Paglia Pens Love Letter to Joan Rivers, Iconic Feminist Role Model," in "Joan Rivers Turns 80," a roundtable package of tributes for *The Hollywood Reporter,* June 12, 2013.]

ers, the handicapped, the homeless, the elderly, starving children, racial minorities, stroke victims, and even suicides (despite the suicide of her second husband, Edgar Rosenberg).

Joan's relationship with the entertainment industry remains uneasy: in an era of soft celebrity journalism, she treats stars with an impish mockery that borders on cruelty, as when she dogged Elizabeth Taylor and Kirstie Alley about their weight. Her feuds (as with her former benefactor, Johnny Carson) are infamous. But ever since Greco-Roman times, true satire stings and bites. Joan is just as mean about herself, frankly admitting her countless plastic surgeries ("I've undergone more reconstruction than Baghdad") and the foibles of her sex life.

Born in Brooklyn but raised in affluent Westchester County, Joan Alexandra Molinsky graduated from Barnard College in 1954. She bounced around in minor advertising and fashion jobs until she discovered her vocation as a comic in Greenwich Village coffeehouses during the early 1960s.

After World War Two, it was Jewish comedians—Lenny Bruce and Mort Sahl—who transformed stand-up comedy into social commentary, a legacy of Jewish political activism in the unionization and civil rights movements. Before that, stand-up on the vaudeville circuit was just a string of harmless gags. Bruce in particular had a beatnik edginess, which he uncomfortably turned against the audience, as in avant-garde theater.

In the 1950s, virtually the only woman daring to do stand-up comedy was Phyllis Diller, who dressed like a clown in a fright wig to erase any hint of sex appeal but whose body language was as coolly contained as her mentor Bob Hope's. Joan Rivers, in contrast, took Lenny Bruce's slouching, surly menace and converted it into a hyperkinetic prowling of the stage, from which she launched abrasive provocations. She lambasted the audience for its sentimentality or hypocrisy and insisted on comedy's mission as a vehicle of harsh truths: "*Please. Can we talk?*"

What Joan brilliantly represents is power of voice, which she was developing for years before Betty Friedan co-founded the National Organization for Women. Jewish-American women (including Friedan herself) already had a startling candor and audacity, producing the shrill ethnic stereotype of the "Jewish seagull." Joan Rivers turned the seagull into a lioness. Although her self-deprecating acceptance of the iron law of female beauty initially put her at odds with the women's movement, Joan must be recognized as an iconic feminist role model. Everything she says or does, even when following her killer instinct for marketing and publicity, is about personal empowerment and ferocious independence. Her work ethic alone is a constant inspiration.

That Joan Rivers is a comic genius is incontrovertible—even in her George Burns and Gracie Allen exchanges with her daughter Melissa, who deftly plays the straight man. Joan has a better ear than most living poets for the spare, sinewy rhythms of modern English. Profane, irreverent, and fearless, Joan Rivers is a legend in her own time.

10

ROCK AROUND THE CLOCK

Nature's clock ticks behind technology's facade. Try as we will to perfect society's gleaming latticework of metal and microfiber, we are hostage to our stubborn bodies, which still pulse to primeval rhythms.

We were once wedded to the sun. In the agrarian past, the calendar was fixed by seasons, and days began and ended with the light. On farms, there was steady, perpetual movement. Work never ended, and energy had to be conserved.

I felt that stately, archaic sense of time in my Italian grandmothers' kitchens when I was a small child in upstate New York. My grandmothers never rushed. Yet they were always on their feet, and they never seemed to sit, even at meals. They tended the stove all day and hovered at the table.

Time seemed hypnotically dense at my grandmothers'; it was something one could almost swim in. That this was no childhood illusion was dramatically proven to me 35 years later, just after I began teaching in Philadelphia. After an exhausting day at my university in Center City, I decided to try to track down a barbecued-rib restaurant I had heard was located in the vast black community of West Philadelphia.

Zigzagging my car in and out of rush-hour traffic, I finally found what I was looking for and, in my usual manic, blitzkrieg style, parked, jumped out, ran down the block, dashed through the door—and nearly fell on my face. I hit agrarian time, or rather it hit me. My

[Special issue on time, *Forbes ASAP* magazine, November 30, 1998.]

mind could not process rapidly enough what I felt literally on my skin. The only comparable sensation I have ever had was when, as an adolescent traveling with my parents, I jumped into the Manatee River at a Florida campground and felt the reddish, brackish, mineral-laden water heavily swirling, thick as syrup.

At the restaurant, it was as if I had glided through a wall and stepped into another dimension in Rod Serling's *The Twilight Zone*. There were no tables, just a large, dimly lit room packed with chatting customers, patiently waiting for their take-out orders. Several generations of the black family who owned the restaurant methodically circulated behind the long wooden counter, hefting and chopping hunks of succulent grilled meat, spooning out salads, and wrapping up bags.

Everything seemed in dreamlike slow motion.

As if struck by a thunderbolt, I was ecstatically transported back to my grandmothers' kitchens. Here once again was that majestic rhythm, unanxious and unhurried, startlingly removed in this case from the hectic urban clatter outside. I immediately sensed the nearness of the Southern rural roots of the restaurant owners as well as many of its patrons.

In hot regions, like the Mediterranean or the American South, people must pace themselves or suffer sunstroke. Hence contemporary Italians from Rome southward still close their shutters and take a midday siesta, after which shops casually reopen at staggered times in the late afternoon. It is a practice that baffles and infuriates Anglo-American tourists, who are used to the stricter business clock invented some 200 years ago by the Northern European industrial revolution.

In *A Passage to India*, E. M. Forster describes the comic clash between British and Hindu cultures, with their quite different expectations about organization and efficiency. In college in the 1960s, during my generation's tilt toward the Far East, Hindu and Buddhist ideas about time were everywhere. Even in a class on seventeenth-century poetry I heard about the "Eternal Now," the suspension of linear clock time in religious meditation, experienced as well by Christian mystics.

The massive drug-taking of my peers (from which, thanks to my Mediterranean preference for Dionysian liquors, I miraculously escaped) was an artificial way to interrupt the Western clock. Its aim

was to stop cold the careerist pressure from parents and authority figures on the young to enter the materialistic "system." Marijuana in
particular, which squeezes or stretches the ordinary sense of time, was
used to blot out external pressures.

So much great 1960s pop music still communicates that hazy
reshaping of time, from the Beatles' "Strawberry Fields Forever" to
Vanilla Fudge's operatic version of "You Keep Me Hangin' On." The
psychedelic style, fueled by LSD, was ideologically hallucinatory,
transforming concrete space and time into a higher realm of imagination and art.

However, this was a journey from which many of my generation
never returned, their brains so chemically altered that they could no
longer focus their energies enough to contribute meaningfully to
society.

Salvador Dalí's famous melting watches symbolize the relativity
of Western notions of time, which Freud saw subverted every night in
our unconscious dream life. This Freudian and Surrealist vision was
prefigured in Lewis Carroll's influential Alice books, which open with
the frantic White Rabbit, a parody of a British businessman constantly
checking his watch ("I'm late! I'm late! For a very important date!" the
sputtering rabbit sings in Walt Disney's cartoon film).

The Jefferson Airplane's great song, "White Rabbit," from *Surrealistic Pillow* (1967), became a generational anthem because it describes
young people's experience of falling down the rabbit hole of drugs, by
which they were trying (as the Doors put it) to "break on through to
the other side" of reality.

Back then, I had my own interpretation of time resculpting. In
one of my elaborate college pranks (40 in all, which got me put on
probation for a semester), I created a Surrealist homage to Dalí. Pok-
ing around my dormitory, I had figured out that the big, white campus
clocks, sunk into the walls of hallways and classrooms, were easily
pried out and unplugged.

So late one weekend night, while everyone was off at a beer blast,
I lifted two of these clocks (each the size of a large pizza) and tucked
them into the twin beds of my dorm's senior student resident advi-

sors. Each clock seemed to be sleeping peacefully on a pillow, with the sheet and blanket neatly pulled up under its chin.

I thought the effect was quite striking and humorous—an anthropomorphic allegory of suspended time. However, the advisors did not find it so wonderful, staggering drunk into their room at 3 AM and screaming in surprise and terror. I don't think they ever spoke to me again.

Modern culture has been obsessed with speed since the invention of the steam-powered locomotive in the early nineteenth century. Our sense of space has progressively contracted and collapsed because of our ability to cross huge distances with magical effortlessness. Many chronic, stress-related medical complaints are certainly aggravated by this headlong pace, which has disrupted our physical perception of time.

My theory is that the massive rise of rhythmically intense pop music over the past 70 years is partly due to our urgent need to reset our inner clocks to match this new world. Similarly, the modern pornography industry serves an important function in reorienting our high-tech consciousness toward our baseline identity in the fleshly and the organic. Love poets in the lascivious *carpe diem* tradition have always known time is transient, as written in the human body, which blooms only to decay.

11

THE *GUARDIAN* QUESTIONNAIRE

When were you happiest?

Snorkeling for an hour with a comically disciplined and curiously attentive squadron of six, fat Caribbean reef squid off Akumal beach in Mexico.

What is your greatest fear?

Imprisonment. I must be free!

What is your earliest memory?

Green olives bobbing in dark water in a wooden barrel at Tedeschi's grocery in Endicott, New York, the factory town where I was born.

Which living person do you most admire and why?

Germaine Greer. She is a feminist colossus—bold, learned, and devastatingly witty.

What is the trait you most deplore in yourself?

Furious impatience with bureaucratic inefficiency and torpor, the stubborn realities of modern life.

What is the trait you most deplore in others?

Ruthless, soulless careerism, a leading attribute of elite academics in the U.S.

[Rosanna Greenstreet, interviewer, *The Guardian* (U.K.), April 4, 2008.]

What was your most embarrassing moment?

When I caused a violent methane explosion by dumping too much lime into the latrine at the Spruce Ridge Girl Scout Camp in the Adirondack Mountains. Toxic brown clouds churned up into the trees for half an hour. I was utterly mortified.

What is your most treasured possession?

A massive brass 105 MM Howitzer artillery shell given to my family 50 years ago by an uncle in the National Guard.

What do you most dislike about your appearance?

I am small, plain, and worn. However, this mediocrity has proved advantageous to me as a social observer. I can lurk at the margins and fade into the woodwork.

Who would play you in the film of your life?

Brenda Vaccaro crossed with Judy Davis.

What is your favourite smell?

Freshly laundered white cotton sheets sun-dried on a line—now only a poignant memory with today's sterile launderettes.

What is your favourite book?

Lewis Carroll's *Through the Looking-Glass.*

What would you most like to wear to a costume party?

David Hemmings' gold-braided hussars uniform with rakish double jacket in *The Charge of the Light Brigade.*

Cat or dog?

I adore the Egyptian elegance and proud independence of cats. (I have two.) Dogs are good-hearted but too pantingly sycophantish.

What do you owe your parents?

Social critique. From my infancy, I listened to them sharply analyze American culture from the immigrant outsider's point of view.

What or who is the greatest love of your life?

Writing—a strange process of anxiety crowned by pleasure.

Which living person do you most despise and why?

Vice President Dick Cheney, who sat on George W. Bush like a mattress and stampeded the U.S. into the folly of invading Iraq.

Which words or phrases do you most overuse?

"Okay?" It's my annoyingly default cattle prod to ensure that weary listeners are surviving the rapid-fire barrage.

What is the worst job you've ever done?

I earned just one badge in Girl Scouts and was sternly informed by the troop leader that I was the "least-qualified camper." Camping, with its grubby dampness, remains my *bête noire*.

What has been your biggest disappointment?

The shocking decline of artistic quality in Hollywood movies over the past 15 years.

If you could edit your past, what would you change?

The arrogantly militant Amazon feminism which I foolishly tried to impose on an entire campus during my first teaching job at Bennington College in the 1970s.

If you could go back in time, where would you go?

The 1920s, when jazz, theater, movies, Art Deco, and smart-mouthed flappers were on the boil.

What do you consider your greatest achievement?

Persisting with the insanely gargantuan project of *Sexual Personae*, which took twenty years to write and was rejected by seven publishers. It was finally released, to a storm of controversy, as a 700-page book by Yale University Press in 1990.

How would you like to be remembered?

As a dissident writer who defended free thought and free speech.

What is the most important lesson life has taught you?

Deep social change takes time.

12

THE DEATH OF GIANNI VERSACE

DEAR CAMILLE:

Do you share the gushing press appraisals of fashion mogul Versace that have appeared since his murder?

READY TO WEAR

DEAR READY TO WEAR:

Yes, indeed, I am a Versace fan and in fact defended him to *The New York Times* in 1992 when he was under heavy feminist attack for his s&m designs (see index of *Vamps & Tramps*). Gianni Versace was a true decadent artist—that is, a visionary of a "late" phase in culture, with its cosmopolitan breadth, sexual pluralism, and stylistic "too muchness."

With his deep knowledge of art history, theater, opera, ballet, and film, Versace synthesized Western sexual personae and re-projected them not just on the fashion-show runway but in his brilliant magazine layouts, where the models seemed like towering, brazen, pagan idols. I loved his deft allusions to classical antiquity, the Renaissance, Weimar Berlin, and so on. His gaudy, glittering, iridescent patterns always reminded me of that master genius of the Baroque, Bernini (one of my idols), who used twenty different colored marbles for the Cornaro Chapel in Rome. Artistically, Versace understood both surface and structure—a rare combination.

["Ask Camille," Salon.com column, July 22, 1997.]

Versace had a wonderful instinct for how to present public women on key occasions. His eye-popping, see-through, premiere-night dress for Elizabeth Hurley—a couture version of a feverish Frederick's of Hollywood fantasy that twenty years ago only s&m call girls would have worn—instantly propelled her onto the world stage. Versace's simple, elegant white dress for Courtney Love at this year's Academy Awards not only exquisitely redefined her in the public eye (after her grungy past as rock-waif/widow and strung-out porn-concubine in Milos Forman's film) but seemed to magically reshape her own world-view, so that as an onstage presenter, she floated above and out-classed the formidable Madonna herself, who was huffing and puffing through a flat *Evita* tune.

Versace clearly had a symbiotic relationship with his tough-as-nails sister Donatella, who was not only his creative Muse but in some way his transsexual alter ego. She's like a School of Monica Vitti tigress/drag queen. It's very interesting that Versace's omnipresent logo is the head of Medusa. He constantly acknowledged how much he owed to his seamstress mother, who ran a factory-like dress shop with a corps of toiling females. Versace was a classic example of the kind of mother-dependent, mother-adoring, but mother-fearing gay man who ruled the pre-Stonewall fashion and performing arts world. Snaky Medusa is, of course, the ultimate earth-cult symbol of woman as barbaric dominatrix of the universe. Freud interpreted her writhing hair as a pubic motif, representing boys' castration anxiety at their horrifying first sight of female genitals.

The Versace shocker is reminiscent of one of my favorite films, *The Eyes of Laura Mars* (1978), where Faye Dunaway at her most fabulous is a take-it-to-the-limits fashion photographer trifling with Helmut Newton/Deborah Turbeville s&m scenarios. It degenerates after 45 minutes, but that mix of fashion, decadence, and murder was amazing and amusing. I also recall a made-for-TV movie—possibly *She's Dressed to Kill*—from the late 1970s or early 1980s where Jessica Walter (I've loved her since *The Group* and *Play Misty for Me*) imperiously presided over a resort fashion show inconveniently strewn with corpses.

13

THE ITALIAN WAY OF DEATH

Italians are masters of the concrete, from the vast engineering projects of the Roman Empire to the gritty manual labor of Renaissance painting and sculpture to our domination of the trade in paving, masonry, ironwork, garden ornaments, and gravestones in modern America. We specialize in the markers and monuments of the messy human transit of birth and death.

Italians view death in simple, pragmatic terms, as a physical process to be efficiently planned and managed. Our culture is strongly ritualistic, with the public theatricality of early tribalism. Italian funerals are major events where, despite our reputation for histrionics, extreme emotion is strictly limited. The gravity and dignity of Italian funerals predate Catholic ceremonialism and probably originate in the Etruscan death cult, whose inspiration may have been Egyptian.

As an Italian-American, I was raised with respect for but not fear of death. Italians dread incapacity and dependency, not extinction. Since the dead are always remembered, they are never really gone. In rural Italy, cemeteries are like parks where the survivors picnic and tend the graves. In America, family plots are purchased like vacation condos; one knows one's future address decades in advance.

An education in death is part of the Italian facts of life. From childhood, I was accustomed not only to seeing the dead laid out in open caskets but also to kissing the corpse's chilly forehead on the morn-

[Salon.com (www.salon1999.com), April 18, 1996.
Reprinted in *The Italian-American Reader*, ed. Bill Tonelli (2003).]

ing of burial. At home, elderly relatives burned votive candles before framed photographs of the deceased. Anniversaries of the date of death, recorded on plasticized saints' cards, are still marked by special Masses and devotions.

The Italian realism about death was formed by the primitive harshness of agricultural life, where food, water, shelter, and sex were crucial to survival. Country people are notoriously blunt and unsentimental about accidents and disasters, which tend to traumatize today's pampered, squeamish middle-class professionals. Bobbie Gentry's 1967 hit song, "Ode to Billie Joe," preserves something of that pre-modern flavor when a crusty Mississippi farmer, indifferent to his daughter's feelings, reacts to the news of a young man's fatal plunge off a bridge by remarking, "Well, Billie Joe never had a lick of sense. Pass the biscuits, please."

The steely Italian stoicism and even irreverence about death have often gotten me into trouble in American academe, where bourgeois pieties reign supreme. Hamlet's black humor about Polonius' corpse—"I'll lug the guts into the neighbor room"—is very Italian. Informed of a death, we shun the usual polite, unctuous hush and take great interest instead in the technicalities: "How did it happen?" Italians recognize both the inevitability of death and its unique grisly signature, which seems fascinating to us in a way that strikes other people as morbid or insensitive. And as in TV soap operas, we like prolonged debate about how a death will affect others—pathos and voyeurism as mass entertainment.

Movies about Italian-Americans have rarely caught our essence. We are, after blacks, the most defamed and stereotyped minority group. The over-praised *Prizzi's Honor* (1985) and *Moonstruck* (1987), for example, are grotesquely bad, with all the ethnic verisimilitude of a minstrel show. Woody Allen's films, in contrast, convey a keen sense of America's social codes as perceived by an anxious, alienated Jew. Allen's *Broadway Danny Rose* (1984) deserves more attention for its comparison study of Italian and Jewish style and thought, notably in regard to death.

Allen's preoccupation with death is well-known, a haunted pessimism partly produced by the persecutions of Jewish history. But Allen turns his terrors into candidly self-revealing comedy, which is why I prefer his work to that of overly ironic literary modernists like T. S. Eliot and Samuel Beckett. In *Annie Hall* (1977), his alter ego, Alvy Singer (played by himself), announces, "I'm obsessed with death," as he presents two books as love gifts to the perky, ultra-WASPy Annie (Diane Keaton) after their first sexual encounter—*The Denial of Death* and *Death and Western Thought*. The film's amusing refrain is Alvy's attempt to reeducate Annie by repeatedly taking her to Marcel Ophuls' dour, four-hour epic on Nazism, *The Sorrow and the Pity*. Busily packing boxes after their breakup, she reminds him, "All the books on death and dying are yours."

In *Broadway Danny Rose*, Allen plays a compassionate, ethical Jew for whom suffering and death define the human condition. He belongs to an exquisitely internalized guilt culture: "I'm guilty all the time, and I never did anything," he sighs. Danny has a madcap adventure with a tough New Jersey broad, Tina (brilliantly played by Mia Farrow), whose honor-based, vendetta-filled shame culture is completely Italian: "I never feel guilty. You gotta do what you gotta do," she proclaims. Her slangy speech has an aggressive Mediterranean flamboyance: "You're lucky I don't stick an ice pick in your goddamned chest!" she yells at her lover as she trashes the apartment. "Drop dead!"

Allen wonderfully catches the brusquely routine Italian attitude toward death when Danny drives Tina away from a (somewhat caricatured) Mafia lawn party. He asks if she and her husband are divorced. "Some guy shot him in the eyes," she says casually. "Really," says Danny, horrified. "He's blind?" "Dead," she flatly replies. Danny cringes with pained, nauseated empathy: "Dead? Of course—because the bullets go right through—[gestures behind his glasses]. Oh, my God! You must have been in shock!" "Nah," she replies, "he had it coming." Ethnicity has reversed the sex roles here, with a man about to faint from a woman's bloodthirsty bluster.

That the Italian directness about death is part of a more general world-view is clear in the first two parts of Francis Ford Coppola's *The Godfather* (1972, 1974), based on Mario Puzo's bestselling novel. True masterpieces of our time, they dramatically demonstrate the residual paganism of Italian culture, with its energy, passion, clannishness, and implacable willfulness. The stunning, choreographic violence of these films is like a sacrificial slaughter where blood flows as freely as the waters of life. Coppola constantly juxtaposes and intercuts images of food and death to suggest the archaic Italian, or rather pre-Christian, cycle of fertility, destruction, and rebirth.

Don Corleone's right-hand man, Peter Clemenza (Richard Castellano), is the primary vehicle of this theme. "Don't forget the cannolis!" his wife calls out to him from the front porch. On an airy highway in the New Jersey marshlands, he says, "Hey, pull over, will ya—I gotta take a leak." While his back is turned, three shots blast into the driver's skull from the shadowy backseat. Ambling back to the car, Clemenza curtly tells his henchman, "Leave the gun. Take the cannolis." The white pastry box is tenderly lifted from its place next to the corpse bloodily jammed against the steering wheel, and burly Clemenza primly carries the pastries away. Now, that's Italian!

In another scene, the don's inner circle hangs out, tensely waiting for news of his condition after an assassination attempt. Clemenza is happily making tomato sauce. "Hey, come over here, kid," he calls to the don's youngest son, Michael (Al Pacino). "Learn sumpin'. You never know, you might have to cook for twenty guys someday!" Instructions follow about olive oil, garlic, tomato paste. "You shove in all your sausage and your meatballs": as Clemenza's big, hammy hand slides the grey meats into the pot, we can't help thinking of the corpses piling up in the plot. And indeed his next remark is a cheerful aside about the roadside execution: "Oh, Paulie—you won't see him no more!" Cooking and killing are as intimately related as in the Stone Age, with past guests easily ending up on the menu.

One of *The Godfather*'s most gruesome rub-outs occurs at Louis's Restaurant, "a small family place" in the Bronx where a drug kingpin advises his crony, a corrupt police captain, "Try the veal—it's the best in the city." Moments later, their dinner companion, Michael Corleone, shoots them both in the face with a pistol. The astonished captain, laden fork raised over his bib, gurgles and chokes as if still chewing, then slams headfirst on the table, bringing everything to the floor with a crash. As Michael flees, we can see the overturned table stained with red splotches that could be wine, tomato sauce, or blood—or perhaps, in the Italian way, all three. Coppola then inserts a montage of headlines with real police photos of gory gangland hits, followed by a staged shot of a big bowl of leftover spaghetti being dumped into a garbage can. *Sic transit gloria mundi.*

The Godfather is full of these vivid visual effects that show death as a barbarically sensual experience, integrated with the body's normal and abnormal functions and spasms. For example, in his famous final scene as Don Corleone, Marlon Brando, cutting monster teeth out of an orange peel, frolics with his grandson among his tomato plants in his arbor, a re-created patch of Italy. Death comes quickly but subtly: the don's steps turn to a stagger and his laughter to gasps for breath, until his heavy form topples and sprawls on the ground. Or death can be a terrible explosion of the nerves, as when the don's disloyal, pretty boy son-in-law, Carlo, is garroted from behind by Clemenza and convulsively kicks out the windshield of a moving car.

My favorite scene in *The Godfather* (sometimes censored for TV broadcast) shows the Italian cultivation of death as an artistic strategy, an operatic spectacle of hands-on activism. Vito Corleone (played as a young adult by Robert De Niro) revisits Sicily to settle an old score— the murder of his parents decades before by the ruthless Don Ciccio. Vito and his local business partner, bearing a gallon of olive oil, respectfully approach the feeble and nearly deaf don, who genially asks, "What was your father's name?" Leaning in close on the sunny veranda, Vito softly replies, "His name was Antonio Andolini, and this is for you"—as he jams the don with a knife, ripping his gut crosswise to the top of his chest. Magnificent and inspiring, in my Homeric view. "Turn the other cheek" has never made much of a dent in Italian consciousness. Death Italian style is a luscious banquet, a bruising game of chance, or crime and punishment as pagan survival of the fittest.

FILM

14

WOMEN AND MAGIC IN ALFRED HITCHCOCK

Kim Novak and director Alfred Hitchcock on the set of *Vertigo*

With a spate of new movies being made about Alfred Hitchcock, charges about his reputed misogyny will soon be back in the air. There is abundant evidence of Hitchcock's insistence on total and sometimes autocratic control of his productions as well as of his leading ladies. But misogyny is a hopelessly simplistic and reductive term

[From *39 Steps to the Genius of Alfred Hitchcock*, ed. James Bell,
a book of essays accompanying the British Film Institute's retrospective,
"The Genius of Hitchcock," at BFI Southbank, London (August–October 2012).]

Kim Novak as the enigmatic
Madeleine in *Vertigo*

for the passionately conflicted attitude of major male artists toward women. Art-making is not just a formal exercise but a quest for identity, a strategy of defense against turbulent reality.

Hitchcock's view of women is not politically correct. But his haunting films continue to gain power over time because of the profound depth and searing truth of his emotional world. What he records is the agonized complexity of men's relationship to women—a roiling mass of admiration, longing, neediness, and desperation. Heterosexual men instinctively know that women have magic. Gay men know it and, through high fashion, ingeniously enhance it. Drag queens heartily mimic it. Most heterosexual women keenly observe, appreciate, and competitively monitor the magic of other women. Only feminist theorists, evidently, fail to see that magic—or they contemptuously dismiss it as a product of social conditioning and commercial manipulation.

Hitchcock's great films of the 1950s and early '60s show the tension between men's fear of emotional dependency and their worship of women's beauty, which floods the eye and enforces an erotic response over which a man has ethical but not conceptual control. Beautiful women are a fascinating conflation of nature and art. They often have an elusive, dreamy apartness, suggesting a remote inner realm to which a man can claim only momentary access. It is a theme in Botticelli's *Birth of Venus,* Raphael's Madonnas, and Leonardo's *Mona Lisa.* It can be seen in more sexually perverse form in Rossetti's florid somnambules and the drugged odalisques of Ingres and Renoir. Beautiful young men too may have that reserve and distance, as captured from Greek art to Wilde's *The Picture of Dorian Gray.* Jean Cocteau saluted Wilde in declaring, "The privileges of beauty are enormous." Similarly, Tennessee Williams' Mrs. Stone says, "People who are very beautiful make their own laws."

The two poles of Hitchcock's erotic vision are woman as objet d'art and woman as devouring mother. One pleasures the eye, and the other assaults it. Hitchcock warned Janet Leigh before *Psycho,* "My camera is absolute." His camera habitually frames woman as a gorgeous cult object whom he loves to dress and drape. We know from Edith Head that Hitchcock designed Grace Kelly's clothes for *Rear Window;* everything was already specified, from color to fabric, in the script. He chose Kim Novak's magnificently varied clothing for *Vertigo,* forcing a now-classic grey suit on her that she hated. He took Eva Marie Saint to Bergdorf Goodman's, sat with her as mannequins paraded, and turned her into a fashion plate for *North by Northwest.* He shaped every detail of Tippi Hedren's look in *The Birds,* including her makeup, jewelry, and mink coat.

Simultaneously in Hitchcock, there is a dread of the imperialistic power of mothers, who are often belittling, hectoring, or suffocating. The ultimate symbol of this is the mummified mother's laughing skull in *Psycho:* horrific Mrs. Bates, with her flapping jaw, is the flip side of *Rear Window*'s chic Lisa Fremont, "who never wears the same dress twice." Life's eternal paradox is that all beauty vanishes, a victim of ruthless time. This process is particularly cruel to women, with their thinner skin. Feminism has decreed that rejection or marginalization of the aging woman is sexist. But the witch-crone is a universal archetype, registering an atavistic dread of loss of fertility, the life force itself. The Western career woman, peaking in competence and rank at menopause, is understandably indignant at being supplanted by the young and beautiful, but it is a hard law of nature.

Themes of sexual allure or fetishism are found in Hitchcock's early films, such as *The Lodger*, where a serial murderer ("the Avenger") is stalking blondes. Overt magic, however, begins with *Rebecca*, a Gothic romance where a beautiful dead woman's spectral presence suffuses a gloomy house. Her obsessive guardian, Mrs. Danvers, keeps shockingly materializing, stock-still, near the nameless heroine, a timorous second wife. Mrs. Danvers is like an evil stepmother blighting a hapless fairy-tale princess. Even the mansion's location is ambiguous: it is a state of mind, a climate of fear.

Magic is first acquired by a signature Hitchcock blonde in *Rear Window*, where Lisa (Grace Kelly) advances on her sleeping, crippled target Jeff (James Stewart) like a floating, dazzling apparition. As she looms like a goddess and leans down to kiss him, Hitchcock shook the camera, and he later double-printed several frames to make the moment more shimmering and dreamlike. As if in a masque from *The Tempest*, she summons up rich food by a snap of her fingers: a waiter from the 21 Club appears at the door with lobster and wine. Introducing herself with her three names ("reading from top to bottom," as if on a triumphal column), she switches three lamps on—a ritualistic triplicate reminiscent of the witches of *Macbeth*. The deep structure is imprisonment: Jeff is her captive audience as she tries to mold him into a pliable consort and social ornament in "a dark blue flannel suit." That there is something subliminally aggressive about her was confirmed by Hitchcock, who told an interviewer that Lisa is a "typical active New Yorker," a class of women "more like men." Meanwhile, Stella (Thelma Ritter), anticipating Midge (Barbara Bel Geddes) in *Vertigo*, is the wisecracking, pragmatic, and resolutely unmagical foster mother, satirizing Jeff, bossing him around, and slapping his flaccid muscles like a testy cook kneading dough.

In *To Catch a Thief*, Grace Kelly plays another ultra-fashionable young woman whose fabulous outfits set her apart from her environment even at Cannes. Francie Stevens seems to be coolly contained within her own mental zone. When she invites reformed cat burglar John Robie (Cary Grant) to touch her diamonds, the erotic charge is so intense that it seems as if her mana or divine energy is flowing through them. Hitchcock's mischievous evasion of the studio production code is blatant (he called the background fireworks "pure orgasm"), but Robie does seem zapped and chained by some uncanny force. When Francie whizzes him along the Grande Corniche in her open sports car, his nerves and her confidence make her seem like a heedlessly impervious winged goddess kidnapping a boy toy. She is a tremendous prize, but as soon as he wins her, the film ends, as Hitchcock sardonically said, on a "grim" note: Francie exclaims about Robie's airy country house, "Mother will love it here!" So dies the male dream of freedom.

Hitchcock's magic is most overt in *Vertigo,* where the sexual woman is in league with the forces of nature and the death principle. Midge, the busy, capable professional, is a pleasant if teasing companion, but she completely lacks erotic mystique; worse, she even calls herself "Mother." Vampirism by the dead is illustrated in Madeleine's possession by her great-grandmother, Carlotta Valdes, a false tale in fact realized through the murdered Madeleine possessing the soul of working-class Judy (Kim Novak). Madeleine drifts through the labyrinth of San Francisco in a hypnotic bubble of seductive abstraction. That she belongs to the nonhuman world or has some special communication with it is suggested by her fleet passage in a green Jaguar (half vegetable, half animal) and her melancholy, tender address to a giant sequoia tree as "you." The primal, elemental drama in sex is wonderfully portrayed by the ecstatic embrace of Madeleine and Scottie (James Stewart) against a rocky seascape at Cypress Point.

The central occult moments in *Vertigo* are Madeleine's entrancement by Carlotta's gravestone and portrait; Madeleine's inexplicable disappearance at the Victorian-era Hotel McKittrick; her momentary vanishing in the sequoia woods; and the cosmetically transformed Judy emerging as Madeleine's ghost from a green fog at the Empire Hotel. Madeleine's first appearance in the film is a spectacular tableau vivant: slow and stately in her black evening gown and green cape, she pauses in voluptuous, Olympian profile like a monumental objet d'art.

Kim Novak's sensational success with *Vertigo*'s supernatural subtext would carry over into *Bell, Book, and Candle,* where she rejoined James Stewart to play a Manhattan witch, and Robert Aldrich's *The Legend of Lylah Clare,* where she is a naïve young woman possessed by the caustic spirit of a bisexual movie queen modeled on Marlene Dietrich.

In *North by Northwest,* Eve Kendall (Eva Marie Saint) has a suavely impenetrable composure that recalls Madeleine's deceptive magnetism. Eve's languid charm is almost armored, as when she fends off the suspicious police in her train compartment—a virtuoso face-off that surely inspired the brilliant police station interrogation scene in *Basic Instinct.* Throughout this exchange, Roger Thornhill (Cary Grant), with his cryptically sexual name (phallus plus Venusberg), is trapped in a folding bed, to which Eve holds the stolen key. He has become a homunculus, smothered and smashed (breaking his sunglasses). This movie too has a deflating mother, who chides and ridicules the elegant hero in public.

Psycho revives *Rebecca*'s haunted house, now inhabited by another dead woman, a tattered fetish preserved in a fruit cellar—like the shrunken heads of Hitchcock's *Under Capricorn.* Norman Bates (Anthony Perkins) is like a devotee of the pitiless goddess Cybele, whose priests castrated themselves and dressed in her robes. There is a ritualistic formality in the way Marion Crane (Janet Leigh) dresses herself, pirouetting in her formidably structured brassieres, now white, now black. The frightful shower murder is like a ceremonial purification and slaughter, a blood sacrifice to a jealous local goddess who will brook no rivals. Mrs. Bates vampirically lives through her psychotic son, her skeletal face being briefly superimposed over his at the end, as we hear her crotchety voice usurping his inner thoughts.

In *The Birds,* mothers are either coldly absent, coldly present, or chokingly intrusive, as when an itinerant mother, in the name of protection, oppressively injects her own hysteria into her children at the diner. Its capricious heroine, Melanie Daniels (Tippi Hedren), moves with exhilarating speed through the landscape in her spring-green suit and sky-blue sports car. Is she in mystic synchronicity with nature? Does she carry a curse that triggers the bird attacks? Birds do seem drawn to her, as when they ominously gather behind her on the schoolyard jungle gym. Something occult seems implied by a gull killing itself against a front door under a full moon, beneath which Melanie and Annic Hayworth (Suzanne Pleshette) stand frozen.

But Hitchcock renounced his magic after the ordeal of *Marnie*, where he reportedly made crude overtures to Tippi Hedren and then maliciously sabotaged her career. This clumsy literalization of his artistic ideals, which were primarily voyeuristic, broke the spell. Hedren was the last of his glamorous blondes. But Hitchcock's sexual magic lived on in film after film which he influenced. We see it in Anita Ekberg strolling through night-time Rome in *La Dolce Vita;* in Delphine Seyrig as the chic mystery woman of *Last Year at Marienbad, Accident,* and *Daughters of Darkness*; in Stéphane Audran as a predatory sophisticate in *Les Biches*; in Catherine Deneuve as a dangerous day-dreamer in *Repulsion, Belle de Jour,* and *The Hunger;* in Sharon Stone as a tauntingly mysterious adventuress first seen on a high patio over rocks and water in *Basic Instinct*. It is even in Visconti's *Death in Venice,* where Aschenbach (Dirk Bogarde) trails a beautiful boy through pestilent streets as the soundtrack surges with Mahler.

Hitchcock's acute sense of women's magic paralleled that of the Surrealists, who intrigued and influenced him. Like Salvador Dalí, whom he commissioned to design the dreams for *Spellbound,* Hitchcock was prankish, uxorious, and ruled by an outspoken wife. Like René Magritte, Hitchcock dressed in a bourgeois suit and presented an impassive face to society. A critic said Magritte painted "transparent enigmas"—a perfect description of Hitchcock's films, with their sparklingly lucid surface and disturbing secret sorcery.

15

THE WANING OF EUROPEAN ART FILM

On the culture front, fabled film directors Ingmar Bergman and Michelangelo Antonioni dying on the same day was certainly a cold douche for my narcissistic generation of the 1960s. We who revered those great artists, we who sat stunned and spellbound before their masterpieces—what have we achieved? Aside from Francis Ford Coppola's *Godfather* series, with its deft flashbacks and gritty social realism, is there a single film produced over the past 35 years that is arguably of equal philosophical weight or virtuosity of execution to Bergman's *The Seventh Seal* or *Persona*? Perhaps only George Lucas' multi-layered, six-film *Star Wars* epic can genuinely claim classic status, and it descends not from Bergman or Antonioni but from Stanley Kubrick and his pop antecedents in Hollywood science-fiction.

Tragically, very few young people today, teethed on dazzling special effects and a hyperactive visual style, seem to have patience for the long, slow take that deep-think European directors once specialized in. It's a technique already painfully time-bound—that luxurious scrutiny of the tiniest facial expressions or the chilly sweep of a sterile room or bleak landscape. What my generation was passionately responding to in European films was their sexual candor and their low-budget protest against the peachy Technicolor artifice and forced jollity of mainstream Hollywood film-making in the Marilyn Monroe/ Rock Hudson/Doris Day era, with its postwar myths of ever-imperiled virginity and ideal marriage.

[Salon.com column, August 8, 2007.]

I'm not sure who, if anyone, still views movie-going as a quasi-mystical experience. As a college student in the mid-'60s, I saw the movie screen as a door into another world. When Roman Polanski's hypnotic *Knife in the Water* was shown in my very first semester at Harpur College (the State University of New York at Binghamton), life seemed to change overnight. Jean Cocteau's *Orphée,* a surreal modernization of the Orpheus legend in existential Paris, sent me staggering out speechless under the twinkling upstate stars.

Other indelible memories: the grinding of the collapsing stone balustrade in the baroque gardens of Alain Resnais' *Last Year at Marienbad.* The night wind eerily stirring the spray-painted green trees in the London park of Antonioni's *Blow-Up.* The column of army tanks ominously rumbling through the city street in the unknown land of Bergman's *The Silence.* The life-giving waters of the Fountain of Trevi suddenly stopping in Federico Fellini's *La Dolce Vita,* stranding Marcello Mastroianni and Anita Ekberg mid-kiss.

When Antonioni's plotless *L'Avventura* was shown at Harpur, the entire theater emptied within a half hour—except for the front row of me and my friends, transfixed by the aquiline profile of a very anxious Monica Vitti, her blonde locks tossed this way and that, as she searched a desolate Italian island for her capriciously absent friend. When I saw Bergman's *Persona* at its first release in New York in 1967, I felt that it was the electrifying summation of everything I had ever pondered about Western gender and identity. The title of my doctoral dissertation and first book, *Sexual Personae,* was an explicit homage to Bergman. On a British lecture tour for the National Film Theatre in 1999, I asked to sleep with *Persona*—whose five reels, like holy icons, rested in two silver cans next to my bed.

But art movies are gone, gone with the wind. In some cases, what once seemed suggestive and profound now feels tortured and pretentious. For example, why should the rivetingly super-sophisticated Jeanne Moreau have to drive her car off that damned bridge at the end of François Truffaut's *Jules and Jim?* It's factitious and absurd. All of the major European directors hit the skids in the '70s. I for one had little interest in late Bergman, Antonioni, or Fellini, who seemed to decline into pastiche and self-parody. With Bergman in particular, the austere turned sentimental. But why should any artist have to compete with his or her peak period? We should be satisfied with the priceless legacy of genius.

Art film as a genre has waned with the high modernism that produced it. The premiere modernists—from James Joyce, Marcel Proust, and Virginia Woolf to Igor Stravinsky, Pablo Picasso, and Martha Graham—were rebelling against a hierarchical, authoritarian tradition which suffocated their youth but whose very power energized their work. They became larger from what they opposed and overcame. Today, anything goes, and nothing lasts.

Ingmar Bergman's creativity was certainly stimulated by the overly cerebral, puritanical Protestantism in which he was raised. In film after film, he militantly made space for emotion and intuition, usually embodied in elusive, charismatic women, whose faces his inquiring camera obsessively searched. Bergman's artistic drive was inextricable from the religious impulse.

Now, in contrast, aspiring young filmmakers are stampeded toward simplistic rejection of religion based on liberal bromides (sexism, homophobia, etc.). Religion as metaphysics or cosmic vision is no longer valued except in the New Age movement, to which I still strongly subscribe, despite its sometimes outlandish excesses. As a professed atheist, I detest the current crop of snide manifestos against religion written by professional cynics, flaneurs, and imaginatively crimped and culturally challenged scientists. The narrow mental world they project is very grim indeed—and fatal to future art.

My pagan brand of atheism is predicated on worship of both nature and art. I want the great world religions taught in every school. Secular humanism has reached a dead end—and any liberals who don't recognize that are simply enabling the worldwide conservative reaction of fundamentalism in both Christianity and Islam. The human quest for meaning is innate and ineradicable. When the gods are toppled, new ones will soon be invented. "Better Jehovah than Foucault," I once warned.

16

THE DECLINE OF FILM CRITICISM

Film criticism, at its height from the late 1950s to the early '70s, has obviously totally lost its cultural centrality, with the overall decline in the quality of films and with the massive growth of pre-release publicity campaigns geared to television. By the time a movie actually opens, we've been inundated in so many advance clips that we hardly need a reviewer to tell us whether the movie is worth seeing or not. How stupid the studios are to destroy their films' best surprises, particularly the funny one-liners that lose their impact in theaters because we've heard them dozens of times already in ads.

Parker Tyler, an audacious gay aesthete, was my favorite film critic and the one most influential on my practice. Second was the unfailingly perceptive Pauline Kael, whose tart, lively, colloquial style I thought exactly right for a mass form like the movies. However, I became somewhat disillusioned with Kael because of her dismissive attitude toward the decadent European films I loved (*La Dolce Vita, Last Year at Marienbad,* etc.). Third was Andrew Sarris, whose acute columns during the high period of *The Village Voice* celebrated the attention to physical beauty and staging of cinematic stylists like Claude Chabrol.

[In response to a reader question about film criticism, "Ask Camille," Salon.com (www.salon1999.com), December 9, 1997. "Ask Camille" revived the "agony aunt" format of Paglia's advice column in *Spy* magazine, which announced her debut on the February 1993 cover depicting Hillary Clinton as a busty, beaming dominatrix enthroned in the Oval Office.]

Like Parker Tyler, I am primarily a myth-critic and pagan cultist—something which cannot be said of the sensible, pragmatic Kael, who never indulges in feverish Tyler-Paglia gay mysticism. Kael and I do resemble each other in our snappy humor and very modern, very *American* voices. That punchy, scrappy, take-no-prisoners tone of mine long predates my introduction to Kael (which came in graduate school via her published collections of reviews; *The New Yorker* wasn't part of my world) and descends first from Dorothy Parker, whose famous put-downs I adored as an adolescent, and second from Ann Landers ("Wake up and smell the coffee!"), whose advice column was a fixture of my family newspaper in Syracuse.

Ann Landers has never gotten the credit she deserves for creating a radically outspoken female persona during the drowsily domestic and ethnically repressive postwar period. Landers is, of course, the patron saint and august foremother of "Ask Camille."

17

MOVIE MUSIC

Movie soundtracks are my hymns and oratorios, which I listen to in a state of religious ecstasy. They have been a primary inspiration to me throughout my career as a writer, and I have often played them as I was writing my books. I long to reproduce in my prose their evocativeness, sweep, and sensory impact.

I grew up in the 1950s when Hollywood was turning out widescreen Technicolor epics to compete with the threat of television. Hard to imagine now, movies were still not taken seriously. European art films would gradually win critical stature, but it took decades for Hollywood productions to be accepted as their equals.

While I always appreciated a score's telepathic portrayal of the characters' inner state—their gusts of joy or impulses of desire and fear—it was the grandiose and operatic scores that most enraptured me. The first soundtrack I ever owned was a vinyl recording of Max Steiner's *Gone with the Wind,* which I listened to endlessly as a teenager. What I heard in its variation on nineteenth-century orchestral music was the very sound of history itself, whose radical changes Steiner, born to a wealthy Jewish family in Vienna during the decline of the Austro-Hungarian Empire, had witnessed and experienced in his own time. For me, *Gone with the Wind* extended the dark vision of

["The Essay: Sound of Cinema," broadcast on BBC Radio 3 on October 2, 2013. Recorded at WHYY public broadcasting studios on Independence Mall in Philadelphia. This is the original script, as approved by the BBC. At the recording session, several of the final tracks had to be dropped for reasons of time.]

the competing forces in Western culture that I also heard in Brahms' four symphonies, which would be crucial in forming the system of thought in my books.

Among movies released during my teenage years, I adored Miklos Rosza's score for *Ben-Hur*, which conveys the arrogance and majesty of imperial Rome, implacable in its assertions yet vulnerable to the soft invasion of Christianity. Rosza presents compassion and caritas as spiritually feminizing, canceling out Rome's rigid claims to worldly power. And he subtly interweaves European with Near Eastern tonalities, projecting a clash of cultures that lingers in our headlines today.

A similar symbolic use of gender can be detected in the ravishingly beautiful score for *The Egyptian*, composed by Alfred Newman and Bernard Herrmann. This obscure 1954 film, which I discovered on late-night TV, follows the wanderings and travails of an Egyptian doctor. He is caught up in an extraordinary moment in history, when the pharaoh Akhenaten and Queen Nefertiti are establishing monotheism in the face of a stubbornly conservative priesthood and military. The tragedy of the naïvely innocent Akhenaten, whose new city would be destroyed and his name blotted out for 3,000 years, is caught by the music, which suggests mystical aspiration shadowed by doom. The exalted "Hymn to Aton" is particularly eloquent in expressing an idea—that of one god—whose time had not yet come.

Another score phenomenally capturing the sound of history itself was Maurice Jarre's soundtrack for David Lean's *Lawrence of Arabia*. This 1962 film had a stunning effect on my generation, who had been raised in a political vacuum in the U.S. It opened up a vast geography of complex, roiling ethnicities as the Ottoman Empire was being carved up by imperialistic powers after World War One. The movie was a primer in cold Realpolitik, the chess-like manipulations and ethical ambiguities in political decision-making.

The thrilling overture of *Lawrence of Arabia* still makes my hair stand on end. Those thunderous Bedouin drums, played on timpani, are pure, masculine, and harshly ascetic, representing Arabia's entrenched ancient tribalism. The drums are followed by a Steiner-like romanticism, as we hear T. E. Lawrence's attraction to the expansiveness and isolation of the desert. Prince Feisal, played by Alec Guinness, dryly remarks to Peter O'Toole's Lawrence that he is another of these "desert-loving" Englishmen. What we hear in that famous gorgeous theme, therefore, is Lawrence's own quest for identity, his self-purgation and self-punishment, along with his well-intentioned misunderstanding of the very peoples he tried to help.

A sense of exhilarating open space as well as the hurtling movement of history is also conveyed by Bronislau Kaper in his score for the 1962 version of *Mutiny on the Bounty,* starring Marlon Brando as Fletcher Christian. Here is the exhilarating sound of the *Bounty* sailing toward Tahiti, where one practically sees the three-masted ship gloriously skimming across the sea under an open sky. And then there is Kaper's Tahitian love song, which is hauntingly beautiful—despite the confused Hollywood exoticism betrayed by a touch of Brazilian samba.

The film scores of Bronislau Kaper, born in 1902 in Warsaw, are currently unheralded and warrant revival. For example, Kaper's soundtrack for *Butterfield 8* created the entire sophisticated urban milieu through which Elizabeth Taylor as a high-priced Manhattan call girl moved. Released during a suffocatingly puritanical period in the U.S., *Butterfield 8* had a tremendous impact on me and helped form my later libertarian theories about sex. Kaper's elegant piano bar music deftly captures the glittering yet empty world so supplely traversed by the film's jaded heroine.

A similar atmosphere of feline sexual sophistication was created by John Dankworth in his marvelously atmospheric scores for a series of films that imprinted the fabulous image of Mod London on the minds of my sheltered generation in the U.S.—notably *The Servant, Darling,* and *Accident.* Dankworth's score for Joseph Losey's *Accident* mirrors the film's mercurial conflation of moral ambiguities, so oblique and ironic, so delicate and sensuous.

The reputation of film composer Bernard Herrmann has steadily risen with that of Alfred Hitchcock, who was once dismissed as a purveyor of potboiler murder mysteries but who was hailed as an auteur by the cheeky young directors of the French New Wave. Herrmann's unstable world of existential angst is now universally admired. His overture for Hitchcock's *North by Northwest,* as conflated with Saul

Bass' dynamic title design, can in my view stand alone as a major work of modern art—a minimalist scrum of horizontals and verticals as the angled wall of a glass-skinned office tower comes into focus. Herrmann wrote an impudent and slightly deranged fandango, combined with great bolts of embattled chords in the avant-garde style of Stravinsky and Bartók. It captures the turmoil of urban life, as the mirrored wall dissolves into real people, work slaves scurrying to survive in a grid imposed by faceless powers.

Sexual passion drives Jules Dassin's *Phaedra,* a neglected 1962 film that is one of the most compelling modernizations of a classical myth ever made. The proud Greek kings have become modern Greek shipping magnates, ruthlessly ruling the world. Melina Mercouri plays Euripides' Phaedra, obsessed with her adoptive son Hippolytus, played by Anthony Perkins fresh from his matricidal role in *Psycho.* Mikis Theodorakis' cascading score conveys the madness and propulsiveness of Fate or Necessity, from which Phaedra cannot escape. The music erupts like an inner storm whipped by Furies. Later, the main theme is quietly restated with traditional Greek folk instruments, to heartbreakingly elegiac effect.

Movie music descends from often underrated nineteenth-century program music like Rimsky-Korsakov's enchanting *Scheherazade.* But I would argue that film music is a visionary mode, like Pindar's odes to the radiant divinity of victorious Greek athletes. I believe that soundtracks, heard apart from the films themselves, trigger an area of the mind that is otherwise inaccessible except in dreaming—a place where sound and image fuse in a primitive form of communication that preceded the development of language. Movie music has the power to seize and transport us to another dimension, where pictures flash and the movie never ends.

18

HOMER ON FILM:
A VOYAGE THROUGH *THE ODYSSEY, ULYSSES,*
HELEN OF TROY, AND *CONTEMPT*

The May 1997 NBC television miniseries of *The Odyssey*, a production of Francis Ford Coppola's American Zoetrope in association with Hallmark Entertainment, should give courage to the faint of heart in the culture wars. The canon lives!

The Odyssey's executive producer, Robert Halmi, Sr., 73, who worked in the Hungarian Resistance during World War Two, is an author and photographer as well as producer of nearly 200 feature films and television dramas, such as *Svengali* (1983), *The Josephine Baker Story* (1991), *Lonesome Dove* (1987), and *Gulliver's Travels* (1996). The popular and critical success of *Gulliver's Travels*—the miniseries drew over thirty million viewers nightly and won five Emmys— led to NBC's quick approval of Halmi's proposal to do *The Odyssey* as a two-part, four-hour telecast. With evangelical fervor, Halmi has now devoted himself to bringing the classics to a mass audience: his productions of Dickens' *David Copperfield*, Melville's *Moby-Dick*, Dostoyevsky's *Crime and Punishment,* and Dante's *Inferno* are either nearing completion or in planning.

[*The Odyssey*, directed by Andrei Konchalovsky. Miniseries produced by American Zoetrope and Hallmark Entertainment for NBC (May 18 and 19, 1997). Review commissioned by editor-in-chief Herbert Golder for *Arion*, Fall 1997.]

Andrei Konchalovsky, the director of *The Odyssey*, was born in Russia and was trained as a classical pianist and then as a filmmaker. Lured to Hollywood after his epic, *Siberiade*, won the Special Jury Prize at the 1979 Cannes Film Festival, he has directed a variety of middling films, of which the best known is *Runaway Train* (1985). Konchalovsky has a reputation for Russian emotional intensity and benevolent despotism on the set. For this project, however, his control may not have extended to casting, since producer Halmi, a whirlwind impresario in the old-fashioned studio-mogul style, likes to handpick his principal actors.

Though reliable figures are hazy, NBC's *Odyssey* apparently cost $32 million, more than any miniseries in television history. Much of the budget was consumed by logistics: the four-month shooting schedule required equipment and basic supplies to be flown and trucked into remote areas of Turkey without roads. There were 2,000 local extras and the massive props normally commissioned only for epic movies: a sixty-foot wooden Trojan Horse on wheels; two full-scale, twenty-oar Greek ships costing nearly a quarter of a million dollars; and a water tank longer than a football field erected on a Maltese beach for Odysseus' scenes at sea. Special effects were also costly. London's Framestore designed the computerized graphics, which created storms, caverns, gods, and the Greek army and war fleet, consisting of mechanically multiplied images of soldiers and ships. The Creature Shop (the Muppet factory now run by the late Jim Henson's son, Brian) built the monstrous Scylla; Laocoön's deadly sea serpent; and the one-eyed Cyclops' giant head, worn by a real-life sumo wrestler, Reid Asato.

How did *The Odyssey* fare? Media reviews ranged from lukewarm to enthusiastic. Part one (Sunday, May 18) drew 28,770,000 viewers and part two, aired the next night, 26,320,000 (these are technically "homes" tuned in, estimated by an A. C. Nielsen media rating); both ranked among the top three programs of their weeks. Many literary scholars and classicists will certainly raise serious objections to the production's historical accuracy, not to mention the fidelity of the teleplay, written by Konchalovsky and Christopher Solimine, to the original poem. However, in a technological age of declining literacy, popular

culture is crucial to sustaining the vitality of great literature and art
(which have been systematically undermined by post-structuralists,
postmodernists, New Historicists, Stalinist feminists, and the rest of
that crew). Market saturation by the NBC publicity machine in the
month before the broadcast did enormous good for the imperilled
field of classical studies. Tie-in paperback special editions of *The Odyssey* were stacked among mass-market bestsellers near cash registers,
and eye-catching posters of a fierce, sword-wielding Armand Assante
as Odysseus rolled by on the side of city buses.

Film versions of novels, plays, and narrative poems often disap-
point because the director and screenwriter have failed to translate
word-bound ideas into simple visual form. Plot must be condensed
and scenes economically structured: good screenplays look rather
skeletal on the page. Character and conflict are more quickly revealed
by film because of its basic tools of close-up and soundtrack, which
register subtle emotion and create mood. Movies that remain too tied
to their literary originals, or that slight the camera's gift for showing
space, end up seeming preachy, tedious, and claustrophobic.

Successful movies of great books are rare. *Anna Karenina* (1948),
starring a beautifully controlled Vivien Leigh, shows what is possible in the respectful re-creation of a vanished, hierarchical society.
Wuthering Heights (1939), on the other hand, the Laurence Olivier–
Merle Oberon vehicle often cited as a peak of Hollywood film-making,
sentimentalizes and sanitizes Emily Brontë's unsettling novel. The
recent feature films of Jane Austen's novels, including a slack, coy
Sense and Sensibility (1995) starring Emma Thompson, have similarly
been vastly overpraised. In contrast, the six-part British television
series of Austen's *Pride and Prejudice* (1995), produced by the A&E
network in conjunction with the BBC, is extraordinary work of the
highest quality, in terms of both history and psychology. Generally, the
best films-from-novels, like *Gone with the Wind* (1939) and *The Godfather* (1972, 1974), have been based on popular blockbuster bestsellers
rather than revered canonical texts.

Already designed for performance, plays make the transition to
film much more easily than novels. Shakespeare's brash, volatile, rule-
breaking style, which led to his disrepute among neoclassical critics,

is exactly what makes his plays good movie material, first persuasively demonstrated by the Laurence Olivier *Hamlet* (1948). Classic films, directed by Elia Kazan and Mike Nichols respectively, have been made of Tennessee Williams' *A Streetcar Named Desire* (1951) and Edward Albee's *Who's Afraid of Virginia Woolf?* (1966). Four favorite films of mine, which illustrate the importance of good casting, direction, and editing, were based on hit stage comedies: *The Women* (1939), *The Philadelphia Story* (1940), *His Girl Friday* (1940), and *Auntie Mame* (1956).

Pagan antiquity is an ideal subject for Hollywood spectacle, at its zenith during the widescreen CinemaScope years of the 1950s, when the retrenching film industry was trying to compete with the new medium of television. My great faith in Hollywood comes from the fact that I grew up with masterpieces like *The Ten Commandments* (1956), *Ben-Hur* (1959), *Spartacus* (1960), and even *Cleopatra* (1963), whose outstanding military and political content has been overshadowed by the production's financial crises and personnel scandals, not to mention the screenplay's heavy-breathing, one-dimensional treatment of the lead role, played by a sumptuous Elizabeth Taylor.

Attempts to film Homer have been surprisingly few, considering the number of movies based on the Bible, such as *Samson and Delilah* (1949) and *Salome* (1953), or on Greek mythology, notably the series of fancifully embroidered Hercules movies starring Steve Reeves and his beefcake imitators that were made in Italy from the late 1950s through the 1960s. Again, plays have proved more manageable. In the 1970s, an exhilarating new age of film adaptations of ancient drama seemed to be dawning: Pier Paolo Pasolini cast Maria Callas in his dust-choked but electrifying *Medea* (1970), and Michael Cacoyannis, who had already directed *Electra* (1961), released a searing, all-star production of *The Trojan Women* (1971), followed by *Iphigenia* (1977). But with the overall waning of European art film in the 1980s, such experiments have gradually ceased.

The best films based on ancient texts, in my opinion, are influenced by or resemble grand opera, which has a rich history of classical adaptation, from Monteverdi's *Orfeo* (1607) and *The Return of Ulysses to His Homeland* (1641) to Richard Strauss' insomniac *Elektra* (1909),

Ariadne auf Naxos (1912), and *Helen in Egypt* (1928). The operatic emotionalism of Jules Dassin's *Phaedra* (1962), an ingenious modernization starring Melina Mercouri (Dassin's wife), Raf Vallone, and Anthony Perkins, with a haunting soundtrack by Mikis Theodorakis, seemed grotesquely overblown to critics and audiences alike, but this excellent film may simply have been ahead of its time. The most dazzlingly artistic film modernization of a classical story is probably Jean Cocteau's surrealist *Orphée* (1949), which shows how a low budget can sometimes stimulate imagination.

Finally, dramatizations of classical stories must take into account the European high art tradition since the Renaissance, which has produced an overwhelming number of iconic Greco-Roman images in painting and sculpture that have entered the world canon. French neoclassicism in particular treated gods, heroes, and warriors in a forceful, luminous way that filmmakers should closely study. Good examples are Jacques-Louis David's seminal *Oath of the Horatii* (1784), with its gleaming weapons and straining muscles, as well as Jean-Auguste-Dominique Ingres' glowering *Jupiter and Thetis* (1811) and his daunting *Oedipus and the Sphinx* (1827). Conventional Salon art soon reduced the spare, severe neoclassical style to mere illustration, but we must still admire the sheer craftsmanship of academic painters like Adolphe Bouguereau and Lawrence Alma-Tadema, with their ancient fantasies of nymphs, satyrs, ephebes, patricians, and emperors. By the fin de siècle, mummification set in: John William Waterhouse's *Ulysses and the Sirens* (1891), for example, with its flying squadron of female-headed vultures, makes the bearded hero lashed to his mast seem like a spoon stuck in a jam pot being eyed by some rather large moths.

NBC's *Odyssey* must be measured against all these precedents in the depiction of ancient culture. Each viewer will of course bring his or her premises to such a project. My own, as set forth in my book *Sexual Personae* (1990), are that Homer is an instinctively "cinematic" artist and that he bequeathed his long sight lines and striving, densely visualized personalities to the rest of Western literature and art. While convinced that superlative films of the *Iliad* and the *Odyssey* can and should be made, I also think, as a fan of sensationalistic Hollywood "B" pictures and television soap opera, that I have realistic expectations about what network television can provide its mass audience.

Homer's poem opens with an assembly of the gods, from which Athena descends to Ithaca to help Odysseus' beleaguered son, Telemachus, step over the borderline into manhood. The warrior goddess disguises herself as a traveling prince for her visit, where she sees first-hand the disorder in the palace caused by queen Penelope's callow, carousing suitors. Odysseus' twenty-year absence has left a power vacuum in his realm. Telemachus receives the stranger with great hospitality, which in the ancient world had a moral meaning. The guest is seated comfortably, his hands are washed, and he is liberally provided with food and drink.

To discard these two matched, smoothly formulaic scenes, with their backdrop of human chaos, a modern screenwriter has got to come up with something better. Homer's practical experience as a bard, reshaping and refining a huge, contradictory mass of inherited oral material, shows everywhere in the decisions he made about exposition, development, and climax. The NBC *Odyssey* begins in disorder, but for a newfangled reason: we see Odysseus himself running madly through the woods. Penelope (Greta Scacchi) has gone into labor, and all the men are hysterical. The servants are shrieking for Odysseus' mother, Anticleia (Irene Papas), who drags her feet and never does get there in time. Instead, the infant Telemachus is born (suspiciously clean and dry) virtually in the open in Eumaeus' hut, supervised by the handy Odysseus himself.

This arbitrary alteration of Homer's plot is as ridiculous an example of political correctness as we have seen in years. Lest anyone think the production is glorifying machismo, evidently, we must have the great Greek warrior introduced as Mr. Mom, Lamaze graduate. Nowhere in world history until the advent of the obstetrician, with the proliferation of modern medical specialties, did men have any role in the birthing process. On the contrary, until this century, the latter was the primary occasion for women as a group to assert their special knowledge, power, and solidarity. Not only is it absurd to imagine that the king of Ithaca would make a spectacle of himself by running toward the scene (hightailing in another direction would be more the male style), but a man of any rank who tried to force himself into a childbirth would likely get swatted in the chops. In this case, Odysseus' own nurse, Eurykleia (a wan Geraldine Chaplin), is already on the scene and would have automatically taken charge.

Director Konchalovsky made a big point of convincing the cast that they were depicting, in his words, "a tribal lifestyle"—something he appears to know little about. Modern touchy-feely liberalism is clueless about the formality and strictness of tribal life, which was a web of sacrosanct conventions. Konchalovsky misses every important theme in Homer's opening: in this production, the gods are either omitted or feminized; no attention is paid to good government or household economy; and there is not a shred of feeling for the rituals of hospitality, food preparation and consumption, or gift-giving—all major themes in Homer.

Armand Assante was a credible choice to play Odysseus, but he obviously didn't get much help from the director in understanding his role. Like Richard Burton as Mark Antony in *Cleopatra*, he seems to lack brawn and certainly wasn't helped by the costume designers, whose prime inspiration seems to have been the daily garb of medieval serfs. Wobbling in approach from mumbling Marlon Brando to taciturn Sylvester Stallone, Assante changes very little in age or expression over the twenty-year span of the story; much of the time, he resembles a blowsy, unshaven, and very haggard Paul McCartney. Apparently, the cast and crew were constantly sick with flu: Assante had it four times and was later hospitalized with pneumonia.

The kick-off plot conceit of the NBC *Odyssey* is that the hero is abruptly called away to Troy on the day of his son's birth—as if preparations of supplies for voyages, much less war, were not elaborate operations. Papas, a perennial in Greek movies, is excellent as Odysseus' fierce mother, who bids him farewell ("Turn Troy to dust!") by daubing his forehead with blood. However, Odysseus' divine patron, Athena, despite her chillingly archaic statue in his household shrine, is treated abysmally. Her "advice" consists mainly of whimsical smirks and giggles, and except for one effective shot of her cold, blue eye, through which we pass to the next scene, there's never any sense of what proficiencies of technical skill or mental agility the goddess represents. The casting is ludicrous: Isabella Rossellini might play Aphrodite, but never Athena. Here she looks like she stepped straight out of her usual Lancôme cosmetics ads. She's dressed not in armor or a simple robe but in a poorly cut, pleated, dull khaki silk dress that I suspect is supposed to be olive-green, alluding to Athena's connection with the olive tree. Her aegis is a gloppy pectoral that's basically a brassy bib. Odysseus recognizes her by her glitzy golden sandals, which look like something Leona Helmsley might bag on Rodeo Drive.

The ramparts of Troy are impressively done by computer simulation, even if the beige stone is too clean and evenly planed: one would expect a more intimidating and roughhewn surface, as on the megalithic walls at Mycenae. The battle scenes on the plain are cursory and badly shot, mere skirmishes that look like a schoolyard shoving match. Assante looks good in Odysseus' leather armor, but why is he fighting without a helmet? And why is Achilles, a Fabio lookalike with long blonde surfer tresses, fighting bare-chested? This production has completely missed the symbolism of armor as artifact in Homer: in the *Iliad,* the forging of Achilles' armor and shield, with its multiple narrative scenes, is a metaphor for the poem and ultimately for civilization itself. The production also ignores an important class distinction between the foot-soldiers and the chariot-riding kings and princes, whose plumed helmets were invitations to single combat. Konchalovsky is a lousy anthropologist: like the Marija Gimbutas school of goddess feminism, he thinks preliterate tribes were egalitarian.

The pivotal fight between Achilles and Hector is given short shrift (and Patroclus is conspicuously missing), but we get a dramatic helicopter shot of Achilles' chariot dragging Hector's body at full speed along a cliff road—a scene lifted from *Phaedra,* where Anthony Perkins as hysterical Hippolytus is killed in a crash while zooming his sports car along just such a road. What is Achilles doing with Hector's body out there anyhow? The whole point is to drag it around the city walls to torment and humiliate the Trojans by abusing a princely corpse. And where exactly is that cliff? Troy was a promontory overlooking a now-receded harbor. Has Achilles' Californian hair transported him to Big Sur? Bizarrely, we never see him get killed in turn—one of the

most famous lucky hits in history, when Paris' arrow strikes the vulnerable tendon that still bears Achilles' name. We do get to see Achilles' body (a large wax doll) burning up on its bier. Odysseus looks like
he's exhorting the troops with a showy funeral oration (à la Brando as
Mark Antony in *Julius Caesar* [1953]), but wouldn't that privilege have
belonged to a commander like Agamemnon or Menelaus?

Meanwhile, back on Ithaca, there's trouble brewing between
Penelope and her mother-in-law, whom Papas plays like Helen Hayes
as the weary, haughty empress in *Anastasia* (1956). Anticleia is picky,
picky about Penelope's leniency with Telemachus. Penelope oversees
the making of olive oil, which is credible, but surely servants rather
than the queen would be doing the actual muscle work of toting bas-
kets of olives and pulling the press pole (though even today Mediterranean dowagers typically horn in to demonstrate to the useless young
precisely how things should be done). At night, pining Penelope cools
her libido off with indecorous and very un-Homeric sitz baths in the
harbor, a scene that smacks of skinny-dipping Hedy Lamarr or lonely,
pill-dazed Barbara Parkins staggering onto the dark beach in *Valley of
the Dolls* (1967).

At Troy, the Greeks have left their trick gift of the wooden horse,
which is convincingly done in rough, dun wood. Laocoön's warning
lacks punch, and when he is attacked by the sea serpent, guffaws surely
shook the nation. We know this grisly scene too well from the restored
Hellenistic statue group of a giant serpent strangling the heroically
muscular priest and his two sons. NBC's wormy monster, certainly
at some pain to the budget, looks like a pretzel combined with a hair
dryer, and it awkwardly whips Laocoön into the harbor like an errant
Jet Ski at Disney World. The horse's stately passage through the gates
is done extremely well. The city falls, of course, but not apocalyptically.
The writers failed to glean a few hints from Vergil's *Aeneid*, so the
burning takes very little time, and the slaughter is minimized. Some
random profanation of altars would have been nice, but we do get
a potent flight of hubris when Odysseus, seen against a picturesque
natural rock arch pounded by heavy surf, insults Poseidon by boast-
fully taking full credit for Troy's destruction.

Now begin Odysseus' attempts to get home. The scenes on ship are too farcical at times, as if Joseph Papp had imported one of his go-for-the-lowest-common-denominator Shakespearean comedy casts, with their oafish, gratingly jolly "types." I kept wondering where all the Trojan booty was on board; they're traveling awfully light. The episode in Cyclops' cave is fairly well-done, especially the giant's zestful, crunching bisection of one of Odysseus' men. But the stone blocking the cave entrance should be a boulder rather than a wheel, which looks too much like a rolling tomb door of old Jerusalem. In the escape from the cave, the screenplay inexplicably omits Homer's memorable detail of Odysseus hanging from the belly of a ram.

The approach to Aeolus' rocky island captures the constant anxiety of ancient seafaring in unknown waters. But then we hear Aeolus' lispy voice emerging from an interestingly ghoulish apparition in a waterfall, and it's Papp time again: in an irritating piece of stunt casting, Aeolus is played by a tittering, roly-poly Michael J. Pollard, who looks the part but whose braying New Jersey accent and smarmy Whoopi Goldberg shtik are foolishly disruptive. Nevertheless, the special effects wizards make this episode a spectacular success: summoned by Aeolus on his parapet, the winds come whistling down in a black tornado (inspired by the parting of the Red Sea in *The Ten Commandments*) and disappear into a leather bag. The sound effects are superb here—first the whooshing winds and then, onboard, the creaking of ropes and timbers. When the men see Ithaca—and get blown sky-high by the surreptitiously opened bag of winds—I was vexed by another matter: these sailors look way too pale for men who have spent their lives outdoors under a Mediterranean sun. For heaven's sake, how much could body makeup cost these days, when self-tanning creams are a staple in every drug store?

The Circe episode begins inauspiciously when the entire story of the men's disastrous metamorphosis into swine is told in advance, with excessive verbosity—a rare case where a film might improve on Homer by just showing the scene unmediated. Odysseus' search for his men, however, is quite captivating. He explores a rocky gorge filled with a menagerie of exotic animals from all over the world and then sweats and strains up the sheer face of a cliff, with a magnificent panorama behind him of forests and sea. Suddenly, floating next to him in midair, with taunting supernatural ease, is the god Hermes (Freddie Douglas), a dimpled pretty boy with frosted curls, bare chest and feet, and winged, gold greaves who looks like a cross between David Bowie as Ziggy Stardust and John Phillip Law as the effete blind angel in *Barbarella* (1968). The contrast between human frailty and divine perfection is brilliant. After archly delivering his instructions (and force-feeding Odysseus some tufts of grass, allegedly protective moly), the Ariel-like Hermes flits and dives away into the distance, with the exhilarating freedom of a bird.

When, with scraped hands and bloody fingers, he finally hefts himself to the top of the cliff, Odysseus oddly finds a complete Edfu-type Egyptian temple with a lion pacing the peristyle courtyard—not the most domestic of arrangements, even for a demigoddess. The music is appropriately eerie. But then all this tremendous, evocative build-up is wasted when we get a gander at the NBC Circe: Bernadette Peters, an over-the-hill musical comedy star who's never done anything deeper than *Dames at Sea* and *Pennies from Heaven*. Why would anyone think that diminutive, cutesy-pie Peters, with her button mouth and squeaky, little-girl voice, has a prayer of playing one of the most seductive, sinister femmes fatales in world mythology? Words like "asinine" and "moronic" spring to mind. Perhaps chits from murky past show biz alliances were cashed in here, since it's sure hard to believe that Peters won this choice role on talent alone.

Back on Ithaca, Penelope is bickering with Telemachus and trying to stop Anticleia, the ultimate guilt-tripping Jewish mother, from killing herself. After a lot of screeching on all sides, Anticleia, who misses her son a bit too much, marches off to drown herself in broad daylight in the very tranquil harbor—where one expects a bevy of *Baywatch* beauties to come bounding earnestly to her rescue. The scene is so misconceived and clumsily directed that it seems like a parody on the old *Carol Burnett Show*. Circe, meanwhile, is jealous that, despite all the amnesiac, edible lotus flowers that she and her Egyptian maidens have been pressing on the Greeks, her lover Odysseus still can't forget Penelope, so she realizes she must let him go. But first there's Hades:

poor Bernadette Peters, having to deliver lines like "You must cross the river of fire and sacrifice a ram," is as inept as Madonna in *Shanghai Surprise* (1986).

The voyage to Hades is highly effective. In fact, the sea always looks great in this production—its choppy waves, its changes of color from grey-black to turquoise-green. As Odysseus' ship approaches Hades, with its burning water, smoke, and meteor showers of fiery rocks, there are some spectacular shots that resemble Turner paintings. Assante looks his best in this episode, as he disembarks and, hefting an unwieldy and sometimes impatient ram, strides up a corridor of huge pillars—a conception of hell far too architectural, incidentally, for this period in ancient mythology. Part one ends as the ghosts appear, materializing ominously from the air. When part two resumes at the same point, the follies begin. We meet a phlegmatic, then madly cackling but disappointingly non-androgynous Teiresias sitting by a steaming lava bath—a detail stolen from Fellini's prelates-at-the-spa scene in *8½* (1963). Homer correctly, *tribally* had Odysseus dig a trench in the earth and cut the sheep's throats over it, so the ghosts would drink the blood and speak. Here he cavalierly tosses the ram into the magma—which takes the Society of Sophists' Dopey Writing Award. After two decades of slasher films, beloved by American adolescents, did the producers think incineration more decorous for the bourgeois home? Through all of this, we are inundated with spooky synthesizer music in the now clichéd Eurotech style.

The looming rocks of the straits of Scylla (forecast by Teiresias rather than Homer's Circe) are impressive, but when Odysseus' ship gets closer, things degenerate. It seems like we're in another generic, dusky cavern instead of between towering, open-air rocks, and Scylla is photographed so poorly that the enormous expense of her construction is wasted. There's a blindingly fast in-and-out of something that looks vaguely like an aluminum can-opener capped with plastic dandelions, accompanied by the whizzing, slicing sound of a scythe and a pulpy shower of blood and sawdust, and that's it. With her spindly arms, lunging claws, serpent necks, and bared teeth, Scylla just seems like a rip-off of the *Alien* monster whom Sigourney Weaver started grappling with eighteen years ago, leading to inevitable sequels. Scylla would be much more frightening, in my opinion, if she were recognizably female and therefore part of Homer's ongoing sex theme.

Charybdis—the whirlpool formed by seawater rushing through the Straits of Messina between Sicily and the Italian peninsula—is very well done by the special effects unit. Again, this scene is too short, but what's here is extraordinary. As the men grunt at their oars, trying to get past rapacious Scylla, the ship topples over the edge of the maelstrom and, sailors flying, falls a dizzying distance. The column of thundering water blooms like a carnivorous flower and turns into huge, living claws closing over the ship, which vanishes in a churning swirl of white water. *Bravissimo!* In Homer, of course, the ship is lost not in the whirlpool but in a divine storm sent to avenge the Greeks' killing of the cattle of the sun god.

As Odysseus undergoes these travails, we keep cutting back to Ithaca, where Penelope is trying to stall the suitors. Greta Scacchi has a regal bearing and a melancholy, Mona Lisa quality that suits the role, and she looks particularly beautiful in her public address, where she steps forth in a deep-blue robe with her face half covered. The design of the shroud she weaves—Odysseus' ship, its red sail adorned with Athena's apotropaic Gorgon face—is no great shakes. Eurycleia is in a constant snit, rocketing around the house and doing a lot of spitting at suitors, which Geraldine Chaplin is too ladylike to really carry off. Also, Chaplin looks way too young and frail for the role of Odysseus' nurse, who needs a bossy robustness like that of Hattie McDaniel's Oscar-winning Mammy in *Gone with the Wind.*

Now comes one of the production's most successful episodes, Odysseus' long sojourn with Calypso, beautifully played by singer Vanessa Williams, who had lobbied for the part of Circe and, because of her acclaimed Broadway performance as the lead in *Kiss of the Spider Woman,* deserved to get it. Ironically, Assante has much more chemistry with Williams than he does with Scacchi (or Peters!), proved by the fact that NBC's official publicity photos present him and the latter two ladies in separate, solitary poses: the sole joint photo, which was widely reproduced (and interracial to boot), is of sensuous, strong-willed Calypso tenderly shielding an exhausted Odysseus. This episode shows the hero weeping for his lost men—a rare example of a screenplay admirably capturing the charming Mediterranean tearfulness of Homer's warriors.

Calypso is attended by a troop of sexy ladies in black, who do lots of Calvin Klein–like lounging amid pretty green pools on salt cliffs hung with Persian rugs. (It would be oh, so wrong of us to be reminded of Vanessa Williams surrendering her Miss America crown in 1984 because of old lesbian photos resurfacing in *Penthouse*.) The scene where the castaway Odysseus is spotted by these giggling girls with their stand-tall mistress is a direct copy of the scene in *The Ten Commandments* where the exile Moses comes to the aid of the shepherdess daughters of the sheik of Midian. There is a superb moment when effeminate Hermes arrives to nag Calypso about letting Odysseus return home; the two spar and quibble, and then Hermes sternly darts off, disappearing again over the blue sea. If only the entire production had been executed at this level of excellence!—though there are several awkward shots where Hermes appears to be sporting a Cupid-like diaper and where Odysseus, who has gone native, is soulfully beating a drum. Williams is so good as Calypso that she has become my leading candidate to play the unplayable—Shakespeare's fierce, "tawny," mercurial Cleopatra, whom no actress has yet been able to do. The shore scene where a desolate Calypso watches Odysseus grittily building his raft with makeshift tools is truly affecting.

Telemachus, meanwhile, is having tantrums—trying to string his father's bow and throwing things around when he can't—and finally calls an assembly of Ithacans. Here wise venerable Mentor, whom Odysseus left in charge of his household and whose name has entered our language, is shockingly shown as a fat buffoon resembling a gouty W. C. Fields. Traveling to Sparta to find news of his father, Telemachus passes a startlingly out-of-place camel and arrives at the surely too brightly painted palace of dark-haired Menelaus (whose Homeric epithet is "red-haired" but whose long kinky locks are well cut here in a kouros-like triangle). Some nifty, bronze-wheeled chariots go by that are right off Geometric vases of the period. Bizarrely, Telemachus is not honorably received and lavishly entertained by Menelaus, as in Homer. Instead, after a brief chat, Telemachus is sent off without even a bite for the road. I especially missed Helen's presence—not only her drugging everyone's wine for forgetfulness but her "Silly me!" account of how she caused the whole war by running off with Paris.

Odysseus is cast ashore on his last stop, Phaeacia, by the wrath of Poseidon, whose big, blue, cartoonlike face and speaking mouth appear in a giant wave of *Hawaii Five-O* dimensions—not incredible considering the tsunami after the cataclysmic eruption of Thera that may have destroyed the Cretan ports and even reached Egypt (influencing, some speculate, the account of God's vengeance against Pharaoh in Exodus). The clever re-creation of Poseidon, with his deep, rumbling voice (like God's on Mount Sinai in *The Ten Commandments*), makes one lament all the more the failure to exploit cutting-edge morphing technology for Athena's transsexual disguises, an au courant theme of psychic androgyny which the production for some reason completely ignores: Isabella Rossellini is the same boring, orchid-heavy flirt from start to finish. Discovered unconscious by the Phaeacian princess, Nausikaä, who is very authentically beating laundry on the rocks with her maids, Odysseus is certainly not as battered or "salt-begrimed" (in Homer's phrase) as one might expect after punishing near-death at sea. Nausikaä, one of my favorite characters from ancient literature, is left undeveloped. She's a mere girl here; Odysseus makes no fine speech-in-the-nude to prove his rank, and no premarital sparks fly between them. At court, her father the king wears a surprising amount of makeup, and her ripe, fleshy mother looks like Rahotep's wife Nofret, in a splendid dual tomb sculpture from Old Kingdom Egypt.

Carried back to Ithaca on a Phaeacian ship, Odysseus now undertakes his complex homecoming, which Homer draws out into so many fascinating stages. Naturally, this production is too obtuse to catch the ritual symmetries of it all. The swineherd Eumaeus immediately recognizes his long-gone master, so there's no suspense there, and we're left to wonder why Eumaeus is living in what looks like a see-through, faux-palm Daytona Beach Coke-and-fries stand. At the first encounter of father and son, far from Telemachus courteously giving the stranger the best seat, the young man hammily draws his menacing sword instead. As for Argus, the old, neglected hound who has waited faithfully for his master for twenty years—well, no Argus, doggone it!

When Telemachus returns to the palace, the suitors twit him about his wispy, newly sprouted whiskers ("Does he have a hormone imbalance?" I asked myself. "The guy's twenty!"). In a very badly photographed scene, Eurycleia washing the beggar's feet recognizes Odysseus' identifying scar more by sight than by shadowy touch; worse, the scar is shown as a simple, shiny shin scrape, contradicting Williams/Calypso's earlier flirtatious palpation of the boar wound correctly placed above Odysseus' knee. Alas, there's no resounding clang—that wonderful Homeric detail—as the joyful Eurycleia drops Odysseus' foot into the basin, nor does he grip her by the throat to silence her (there's real tribalism for you). As we see and clearly hear when it is being swept, the floor of the banquet hall where the suitors will meet their deaths is paved with stone—a flagrant error, since Homer specifically describes how the primitive dirt floor must be scraped afterward to remove the buckets of blood.

There's an exquisite shot (like an Alma-Tadema painting) of Telemachus brooding near a window in his airy bedroom, with weapons hung behind him on the wall, attractively painted in Minoan hues—orange-red and green with bands of blue. Odysseus' great bow has been sharing a storeroom with wonderful, giant terra-cotta amphoras, which are glimpsed far too briefly and could have given a better sense of ancient household operations. The stringing of the bow scene—surely one of the most thrilling episodes in the history of literature—is poorly directed. When the beggar Odysseus picks up the bow, the suitors shouldn't stop dead in their tracks and gawk; they should be laughing, careless, inattentive, dismissive. When the beggar not only easily strings the bow but sends the arrow through the ax-heads, *then* the suitors should pause, puzzled but still uncomprehending. When Odysseus throws off his rags and leaps onto the threshold, their bafflement must turn to horror. This production jumbles the brutal, escalating, unstoppable rhythm of Homer's scene, reducing its power. Interestingly added, however, is the slamming of the doors (already secretly locked in Homer) as Odysseus strings the bow, followed by the magical transformation into a red robe after he lets the first arrow fly. But things get incredible as Odysseus lackadaisically seats himself on his throne and jaws at the curiously slow-moving and witless suitors, who are felled far too easily.

An unlikely piece of casting that does work is Eric Roberts (Julia's alienated brother) as Eurymachus, the vilest of the suitors. Roberts, who worked with Konchalovsky more than a decade ago on *Runaway Train,* is surprisingly effective, not only looking like a Greek warrior but projecting exactly the right degree of decadent insolence. A single arrow ingeniously pierces both Eurymachus and his lover, the treacherous maid, Melanthe, when she tries to save him by opening the door (in the poem, she's hanged later with her sister quislings). Penelope, meanwhile, has un-Homerically fainted at all the slaughter. There is no final testing scene between Odysseus and his wife, but the marriage bed carved out of the living olive tree is indeed gratifyingly shown. However, the teleplay, unhelped by sluggish editing, misgauges the timing of the finale, which is too drawn out. Odysseus and Penelope mind-meld to awful, synthesized *Little House on the Prairie* music. As William Blake said, "Enough! or Too much."

With the video of the NBC miniseries released to stores in August 1997, classical studies will be stuck, for better or worse, with this version of *The Odyssey* for the foreseeable future. Whatever its deficiencies, it will prove a useful pedagogical tool for courses on both the high school and college levels. I have had good luck with comparative projects: students enjoy and find profitable term papers that analyze a literary text and its adaptations by opera and film. Despite the fact that I have taught *The Odyssey* many times (using E. V. Rieu's Penguin prose translation), the miniseries gave me renewed appreciation of Homer's masterful shaping and structuring of plot. Nine out of ten times, the teleplay went wrong when it tried to improve on Homer, who after nearly three millennia has never lost his relevance and broad appeal.

My view of the miniseries is probably biased by my long devotion to the Italian-made movie version of Homer's poem, *Ulysses* (1954), starring Kirk Douglas, which I first saw on late-night television in the early 1970s. It is available on Warner Home Video but difficult to find. The miniseries will probably spark the video's re-release and wider distribution, but a new copy ought to be made from a fresh or restored print of the film, since the colors have dulled. *Ulysses* was a risky venture produced by the then-unknown Dino De Laurentiis and Carlo Ponti. The director was Mario Camerini, and seven people, including Ben Hecht and Irwin Shaw, worked on the screenplay. The dialogue often sounds stilted to contemporary ears, since everyone in the international cast spoke the lines in his or her own language, with dubbing done afterward for each country where the film was shown.

The imaginative quality of *Ulysses* is shown even in the credits, which contain a story in themselves, sweepingly scored: a tranquil sea gradually darkens until a storm batters and overwhelms a Greek sailing ship; then the sea quiets, and the sun returns. (The credits claim the production's "exteriors" were shot on "the Mediterranean coasts and islands described in Homer's *Odyssey*.") Perhaps the film's most daring innovation is to have Penelope and Circe played by the same actress, Silvana Mangano, De Laurentiis' wife. Ulysses as Everyman therefore encounters the two faces of Eve, the ambiguous duality of woman that Western culture polarizes as Madonna and whore.

The story begins as it should with Ulysses' house invaded by suitors, over whom his wife struggles to maintain authority. Mangano makes a very grand and statuesque Penelope, whose inner suffering we feel. The nurse Eurycleia, I am happy to say, is as old as she should be, but the suitors are too fat, middle-aged, and epicene. We quickly get a performance by the Ithacan bard, Phemius, playing his lyre with a gorgeously ornamented mother-of-pearl pick, seen in close-up; his tale is the fall of Troy, which takes us into flashback.

Bearded Kirk Douglas as Ulysses is crouching inside the belly of the wooden horse. When the Greeks emerge to take the city, the chaos in the streets is done far more completely than in the NBC miniseries. Fire, massacre, and rape are shown, as well as the insult to Neptune's shrine by a gloating, wild-eyed Ulysses, who topples the god's statue and gets a curse laid on him by the ranting princess, Cassandra. Even though the gods are never actually seen in this film, Italian Catholic culture, with its residual pagan superstition, seems to have given the makers of *Ulysses* an instinct for the crucial religious elements of Homer's story.

Now we jump back to Ithaca in the present: Penelope boldly chides the suitors, who are carousing with the slutty maids. We clearly catch the Homeric dirt floor of the great hall, with its central open pit where meat turns on spits. The dark stone walls, however, with their flat, squared blocks, look too medieval. As Penelope mourns her absent husband, there is a spectacular dissolve from her pensive face to the open sea; the camera pans down to find Ulysses lying face down in the sand, his body entwined with seaweed; a broken mast and shredded sail bob further out on the rocks.

Nausikaä (Rossana Podestà), who gets a satisfyingly full-scale treatment in this film, is playing ball with her maids. Unfortunately, the girls are decked out in glaringly anachronistic, off-the-shoulder, rainbow-pastel prom dresses with frilly bodice ruffs. Still, the scene captures Homer's moving contrast between the bruised, traumatized castaway and the merry young people of peacetime affluence, who think they've stumbled on a corpse. The screenplay's sustained plot device is for the shaky, near-drowned Ulysses not to remember who he is or where he's from. Nausikaä is instantly smitten but comports herself with a princess's proper dignity.

At her father's court, the jewelry-laden king and his men are peculiarly wearing glittery, decolleté dresses with puffed sleeves and have their hair styled in dangly, oiled, Louisa May Alcott ringlets. Ulysses naturally comes across as very masculine in this near-drag environment. At the poem's festive Phaeacian games (omitted by the miniseries but included here), the baited Odysseus reluctantly proves his mettle by hurling a heavy discus and challenging the vain young bucks to a test in any sport. In *Ulysses*, Douglas, who was a wrestling champion in college, does a great job of Greco-Roman wrestling with Umberto Silvestri, a renowned Italian athlete. Regrettably, Homer's intergenerational theme—the seasoned veteran vanquishing novices who are the suitors' age—is overlooked.

Meanwhile, back on Ithaca, Eurycleia, with true tribal vigor, is furiously whipping the servant maid who betrayed the secret of Penelope's nightly undone shroud to the suitors. The latter are busy outside with competitive games; the Homeric prominence of athletics in this film again exposes the conceptual weakness of the NBC miniseries. Antinous, the obnoxious head suitor, is well played by a swaggering Anthony Quinn in elegant, Darth Vader black. The Ithacan marriage theme is paralleled on Phaeacia, where the wedding day of Ulysses and Nausikaä has dawned. The princess's bridal dress is an exact copy of the full-skirted, cinch-waisted costume of Cretan snake-priestess statuettes—minus the bare breasts: a modest cloth panel censors that glorious pagan display for modern consumption. But where's the groom? The troubled Ulysses has wandered off to brood on the beach: "My name, my deeds—who am I?"

Now we again move gracefully into flashback, as Ulysses slowly begins to remember the disasters that led to his marooning on Phaeacia, most of all his boastful self-confidence and sacrilegious denial of the gods. The screenplay treats the Cyclops episode with great respect. For example, when the trapped Ulysses begs for mercy by appealing to Zeus' sacred "laws of hospitality," Polyphemus scornfully laughs: "What have I to do with *Zeus*? I am Neptune's son!"—at which Ulysses' men groan in despair. As the leader who must sustain morale and find some stratagem for escape, Douglas is charismatically convincing. I've always loved the lusty way, on arrival in Cyclops' cave, he is shown grabbing a fistful of soft cheese and cramming it greedily in his mouth. In his autobiography, Douglas reveals that filming this detail was no easy matter: "We did seven takes of a scene where I had to taste giant white cheeses. They used the real thing, strong Italian goat cheese. I was so nauseated, for the eighth take, I had them slip in little pieces of banana."[1]

Later, as the Greeks barely escape on their ship, Ulysses cannot resist tempting fate. "Who's master now—Neptune or Ulysses?" he exults. Roughly shoving past his own men on deck, who try to restrain him, he shouts back at the Cyclops howling on his cliff: "When your father asks who took your eye, tell him it was *Ulysses*! Ulysses—destroyer of cities, sacker of Troy, son of Laertes, and *king of Ithaca*!" Douglas delivers these soaring, trumpet-like lines to perfection, grinning, laughing, and roaring like a rampaging lion. Nowhere in film have I ever seen a better depiction of the terrifying vitality and half-mad hubris of ancient warriors.

With a powerful sense of dynamics, the film cuts momentarily back to Ulysses in the glum present, as he stands mute and uncertain on the Phaeacian shore; then we return to him on his ship, where he is relaxed, leaning on the rail and staring out at the twilit sea. Chuckling, he says wistfully to his companion: "There's a part of me that loves the familiar, the end of the journey, the cooking fires at home. There's always the *other* part—that part loves the voyage, the open sea, storms, strange shapes of uncharted islands, demons, giants. Yes, Eurylochus, there's part of me that's always homesick for the unknown." As an example of deftly condensed screenwriting, this passage is as fine an adaptation of a major work as any scholar can ask for. And Douglas again shows his virtuosity: he is as eloquent with these quiet, rueful, poetic lines as he is in his paroxysmic, full-volume gibes at the Cyclops.

In another smooth segue, the two men conversing at the rail become aware of an eerie calm on the water and then an odor of dead flowers: they are approaching the fearsome island of the Sirens. We see a broken ship, then dismembered skeletons strewn on rocks. The latter might well be impressive on a theater screen, but in miniature video format, the bones just look like random paper litter under a boardwalk. Homer visualized it much more horrifically—the Sirens sitting in a meadow heaped with rotting male skeletons, from which the withered skin still hangs. Having ordered himself tied to the mast, Ulysses is tormented by the Sirens' song, which, in a nice touch by the screenplay, takes the alluring form of the voices of his wife and son, urging him to come ashore, for this is "Ithaca." Deceived, he screams in agony and grief, his neck muscles bulging as he struggles to get free.

Altering the poem's sequence of events, the film next brings Ulysses to landfall on Circe's island: she herself has pulled the ship off course. When she first appears, Circe is standing eerily in the dusk in an archetypal rocky cleft on a hill. She wears magical sea-green veils over a svelte beaded gown; even her hair is sea-mist green. Silvana Mangano gives Circe all the serene, evil magnetism that Bernadette Peters utterly lacks. Circe lives not in a stone house, as in Homer, but in a cavern dripping with underground water, like a mineral-encrusted Gustave Moreau painting. Once he falls under her spell, Ulysses loses track of time. When his men come to berate him, six months have passed in the blink of an eye, and he is paddling in Circe's indoor pond, with its floating, forgetfulness-inducing lotus blossoms (as in the miniseries, borrowed from the omitted episode of the Lotus-eaters). Emerging, he narcissistically primps in a mirror and dons a metallic-green robe—signifying his enslavement by Circe. This hedonistic transformation and loss of manhood are made completely believable by Douglas' nonchalant charm.

The screenplay sinks Ulysses' ship and drowns his men when the latter try to leave Circe's island. When he finally steels himself and starts to build an escape raft, Ulysses (like Jesus in the wilderness) is subjected to the wiles of the Tempter: Circe offers him immortality—a detail, like the raft, transferred from Homer's Calypso idyll. The screenwriting here is splendid. Circe declares, "This very night, Olympus shall welcome a new god—Ulysses." He pauses with tool in hand, a look of wonder on his face. But then comes his firm answer: "No. There are greater gifts: to be born and to die—and in between to live like a man." Kirk Douglas and Charlton Heston are among the very few, genuinely masculine American actors who can give such stirring lines their proper sturdy sound.

To try to convince him, Circe now summons the dead, so that Homer's voyage-preceded descent to the underworld is collapsed into this single scene by the raft. Agamemnon, Ajax, and Achilles, in full armor, step out of the fog to urge Ulysses to stay with Circe and accept her offer. But just as he starts to yield, his mother—ever the wet blanket!—arrives to put the kibosh on the idea. Circe furiously yells at Anticleia but (as in modern Italy, where mothers still rule) must concede her greater power over her son, whom Circe bitterly releases to return home.

The screenplay immediately takes us back to Phaeacia, where Ulysses' memory is now fully restored, just as the frantic wedding party discovers him on the shore. To young Nausikaä's poignant disappointment, he cannot take a new bride, when another wife waits for him in Ithaca. Ulysses' dramatic homecoming is done with enormous energy, but Homer's details have been trimmed. There is neither swineherd nor scar, and while Argus does appear, he seems to be resting comfortably indoors instead of abandoned on a dung heap. If this recognition scene seems muted, it's because it had to be shot fifteen times: the blasé Italian dog kept exiting as Douglas entered and finally had to be drugged. Argus' undetectable acknowledgment of his master (Douglas has to grip and fondle its snout) unconvincingly produces the passing Telemachus' recognition of his father—perhaps the film's weakest moment, though the men's bonding is touchingly quickened and sealed by the sound of Penelope weeping upstairs.

The contest in the great hall is presented with due formality. Penelope descends, elegant in white, and the film conveys what the miniseries, despite lovely Greta Scacchi, does not: the blindingly charismatic desirability of this ultimate trophy wife, whose classiness makes the relatively well-born suitors look like clods and ruffians, much like early medieval warriors before the spread of chivalry and the courts of love from southern France. The beggar Ulysses is mocked, scorned, and spattered with wine; Quinn as Antinous is properly loathsome, kicking the beggar's alms dish out of his hands. The bending-of-the-bow scene is long and riveting; Antinous comes closest to succeeding—and is later, as in Homer, the first to die, with an arrow gorily piercing his throat. Vengeful Ulysses goes into full furor, even yanking out an ax-head to chop a cringing suitor savagely in the face.

Running to her quarters, while the battle still rages, to thank Athena for Ulysses' return, Penelope flings herself down on an enormous, thick, white sheepskin blanketing the steps beneath the goddess's image. This seems to be a substitute for the marriage-bed motif, which is otherwise missing. Below, the hall is in total shambles—with corpses, cushions, robes, vessels, and utensils heaped and thrown about. The film understands the importance in Homer's poem of the house, another symbol for civilization. Surveying the mess, Douglas magnificently delivers, with raw, throbbing voice and simple, expressive gestures, these superb lines: "Many terrible things have happened to me, Telemachus, but none more terrible than to bring death into my house on the day of my homecoming. Tell the servants to purify the room with fire, and may the revenge of the dead never overtake us." After washing his bloody hands and arms, Ulysses goes upstairs to embrace his wife, and the story crisply ends.

Despite its strident dubbing and plot omissions—I particularly lament the absence of Calypso, as well as the gods—*Ulysses* is a model of well-paced, emotionally rich, and intelligent moviemaking about ancient culture. Even the film's final image is arresting. A script unrolls: "For the immortality that Ulysses refused of a Goddess was later given to him by a poet. . . . And the epic poem that Homer sang of the hero's wanderings and of his yearning for home will live for all time." Then "THE END" is superimposed on Penelope's shroud: it is woven with authentically period figures of a man in a long Greek robe driving a bull pulling a plow, watched by a quizzical dog and a woman with a babe in arms while a vine of grape leaves swirls overhead. The scene seems to allude to the post-Homeric legend of Odysseus, who feigned madness to avoid going to Troy and was exposed by the warrior Palamedes' trick of tossing infant Telemachus before his father's plow. But in historical context of the film's production in ravaged postwar Italy, the image seems to celebrate the return to love, family, fertility, and prosperity, made possible by peace.

If *Ulysses*, with its lean narrative and psychological astuteness, makes NBC's *Odyssey* seem fragmented and superficial, what can we say about *Helen of Troy?*—a pretentious, American-Italian extravaganza based on the *Iliad* that, at its superheated release in 1956, aimed for greatness and fell flat on its face.

Starring as Helen is Rossana Podestà, whom we last saw as Nausikaä in *Ulysses*. Others in the cast include Stanley Baker, Cedric Hardwicke, Harry Andrews, and a very young, brown-haired Brigitte Bardot in a bit part as Helen's slave, Andraste. It's hard to say which is more awful, the screenplay or the direction. Remarkably, Robert Wise, the director of *Helen of Troy*, is one of the most accomplished figures in Hollywood history: he edited *Citizen Kane* (1941) and directed *The Curse of the Cat People* (1944), *The Day the Earth Stood Still* (1951),

Run Silent, Run Deep (1958), *West Side Story* (1961), *The Sound of Music* (1965), *The Andromeda Strain* (1971), and *Star Trek* (1979). But whatever special combination of skills is needed to direct a successful ancient epic is woefully beyond Wise's repertoire.

On the same tape as its color video of *Helen of Troy*, Warner Home Video has released four black-and-white publicity segments produced for television and introduced by a very dapper Gig Young as host of *Warner Brothers Presents,* a short-lived ABC drama series that ran from 1955 to 1956. In the first, Young touts the spectacular wide-screen CinemaScope of *Helen of Troy,* which was to be presented in a first-time-ever worldwide premiere, opening simultaneously in (a presumably numerological) 56 cities. Young steps over to a placard propped on an easel: it's a cutaway section map, "Walls of Homeric Troy—Built 1500 B.C.," showing the city's pancaked levels from the Stone Age through the Roman period.

In the second segment, Young in his sleek business suit jauntily visits a makeshift Trojan battlement, where he is accosted by a soldier in full armor who barks, "Whence came you?"—the standard corkscrew Hollywoodese that passes for archaic diction. Unfazed, Young ambles over to chat with Helen, the glowingly fleshy, petite, white-blonde Podestà, who was being groomed as a Marilyn Monroe lookalike but whose career never took off. (She more resembles the winsome Arielle Dombasle of Eric Rohmer's *Pauline at the Beach* [1983].) In the next segment, Young appears posing with a Greek bow, then takes us to visit the sound engineers who must reproduce the twang of an arrow leaving its string or the thud of it striking flesh, illustrated by a clip of Achilles felled by Paris. The technicians are also shown simulating iron doors echoing, siege platforms dropping, chariots charging, and the footsteps of kings on marble floors—as Young grandiloquently puts it, "the sounds that haven't been heard for 3,000 years."

In the final segment, we're treated to the in-theater trailers or "coming attractions" announcing the film's release: "Her name was burned into the pages of history in letters of fire." We then see the yellow script of the title, *Helen of Troy,* literally catching on fire! We're promised "All the Storied Wonders of Homer's Immortal 'Iliad,'" which include "the sweeping saga of the mortal struggle between the legions of imperial Greece and the forces of impregnable Troy," not to mention "Bacchanalian revels of unbridled abandon." However, even as our hopes are raised, there's something dispiriting about the brief glimpses we get of the Kewpie doll Podestà (shades of Bernadette Peters) and her equally artificially blonde co-star, Jacques Sernas, who seems a bit too Troy Donahue to be a credible Paris.

Helen of Troy is prefaced with a five-minute "Overture," designed to increase suspense as theatergoers were taking their seats and fiddling with popcorn. A grand columned ancient hallway occupies the screen, with a weird statue at the far end that looks inappropriately Hindu. Meanwhile, generic movie music is pouring at us—probably the most mediocre score in Max Steiner's illustrious career. The story begins with a booming voiceover, as we are shown a map of the Hellespont and informed of its commercial importance. The first person we see is the Trojan prince Aeneas pulling up in a chariot—and we might as well bolt into the aisles and go home. For such a high-budget film (it was shot at Cinecittà near Rome), the flimsy costumes, wiry wigs, and cotton-candy beards are dreadful beyond belief.

The opening scene takes place in the council room of King Priam, whose wavy-backed throne (like Odysseus' in the miniseries) is a copy of the Minoan one found at Knossos. Hector seems awfully long in the tooth, and Paris has great biceps and pecs but looks like he's wandered in from an Alan Ladd movie. Like Hippolytus, Paris is chided for worshipping Aphrodite too much. Lining the chamber is a row of what look like white papier-mâché statues of gods: a hideously ugly Athena grimaces, and Aphrodite seems to be vaguely waving. Right from the start, the movie takes the Trojan side: the Greeks are coarse, greedy, quarrelsome Nazi fools without German organizational sense, and the Trojans are mellow, cultured, peace-loving innocents (though their taste in sculpture needs improvement).

The initial plot device is that Paris, who sets sail on a diplomatic mission to Greece in a wonderful ship awesomely outfitted with two tiers of oars, gets marooned after he bravely climbs a mast in a lightning storm and is knocked into the sea. Shamelessly pirating the Nausikaä episode of the *Odyssey*, the movie has the Spartan queen Helen discover the unconscious Paris washed up on shore: ex-Nausikaä Rossana Podestà must have felt she was stuck in a casting rut. Paris thinks she's Aphrodite and then, when mutual attraction kindles, accepts her story that she's a slave. This is probably a cautious 1950s device to whitewash the blatant adultery of the famed romance. Paris determines to buy the comely slave from her owners so that he can make her "princess of Troy" ("Oh, sure," I said to myself. "That's just how Trojan princesses were made!").

Paris' political timing could not be better, since at that very moment a council of Greek kings is meeting up at Menelaus' palace. They all look pasty, paunchy, fuzzy, and ill-dressed, but they love to josh each other with macho brio. Odysseus, a cross between Abe Lincoln and a leprechaun, is teased for the babe-in-the-furrow tale, and Achilles, a repulsive braggart, takes his licks for dressing like a woman on Scyros until Odysseus collars him. When the shipwrecked Paris is dragged in, he must prove his identity by an ad hoc cestus match, where he fights Ajax and wins. On the sidelines, however, the overconcerned Helen—prettily dressed in a pink and blue costume based on the Archaic korai of the Athenian Acropolis—blunderingly betrays her love to the much older (and predictably dark-haired) Menelaus, who glares and plots.

There's a pleasant scene where Bardot as Andraste (who's never without her pet whippet) is combing Helen's hair, but one starts to feel that this movie that's supposedly about Troy is taking *forever* to get out of Sparta. The best thing in this sequence is the queen's big heavy bronze doors, ornamented with Medusa's face; they get clangorously pounded on, to the credit of the sound engineers kvelled over by Gig Young. Running away together, Paris and Helen leap off a cliff into the sea, while an orgy rages back at the palace, which is presented like Elsinore disarrayed by morose king Claudius' beer parties in *Hamlet*.

When the lovers arrive at Troy, thanks to a Phoenician rental bark, not everyone is thrilled with Helen. "Her name is *Death!*" snaps Cassandra, an unexpectedly pert, freckled, button-nosed teen in the Anglo-American style of Kathleen Widdoes. The fickle people quickly turn against Paris (who does look spiffy in leopardskin), and the city prepares itself for war. Now there is a rushed montage of armaments manufacturing that could have been truly brilliant. Hephaestus knows the production expense of these scenes!—smiths hammering iron and forging gleaming rows of sword blades; forests of spears being sorted and propped on racks; wood being cut for bows, then plunged in treatment baths and gathered up after air drying. This fascinating material about artisanship represents the very substance of premodern life. But the makers of *Helen of Troy*—we don't know exactly who; directors sometimes lose control during editing—gave these technical scenes brusquely short shrift, in the general haste to return to Helen and Paris' soggy, tedious affair.

When the Greek ships arrive, it's night, and there is a wonderful scene of Priam and the other elders, summoned by signal gong, as they stare out from the battlements at the sight of hundreds of lights ominously glowing in the harbor. An unnecessary expenditure was surely the laborious footage of the Greeks assembling their wooden siege engines, which are unremarkable objects that don't photograph well. The Greeks on the march definitely make a good impression, with their sharp assortment of round shield designs—geometric emblems of bird, snake, horse, and so on. But don't look too closely at the battalions, since the budget clearly didn't stretch to arming the rear rows of extras, who trudge along in plain burlap tunics.

Considering the size of the opposing forces, it's quite coincidental that rivals Menelaus and Paris, as well as Achilles and Hector, manage to come face to face for some tense swordplay in a stairwell after the Greeks first pour over the wall—an engagement from which the latter abruptly flee, though suffering no discernible reverse. Just to make sure the audience stays on the right side, a voiceover informs us that the Greeks later "looted and raped the small surrounding villages": we get a few shots of girls doing excessively enthusiastic, midair butterfly kicks as they are hauled away by their raptors.

An indeterminate amount of time must have passed, since we next see Helen at home complaining about air pollution: "Must the Trojans always put their funeral pyres so near this house? How long will they accuse me?" No wonder she's aggravated: her view out her patio-balcony is spoiled by rising smoke columns. I loved this scene, since it seems inspired by Gustave Moreau's *Helen at the Scaean Gate* (1880; reproduced in *Sexual Personae*), where like a promenading mannequin, Helen turns her back on the heaps of bloody corpses and smoldering pyres. The very dignified Queen Hecuba, meanwhile, is quite warm and welcoming to beleaguered Helen—unlike the way Elizabeth II, I groused, treated the Princess of Wales. We begin to warm up to Paris, since the clean-shaven, neatly tressed Sernas (a mildly homoerotic, gracefully athletic Jean Marais type) doesn't force us to look at bad wigs and mossy face fur.

The occasional excellent scene makes us more impatient with the rest of the film. For example, the aborted surrender of Helen to her husband must have looked superb on the big screen: outlined against the sky as they rigidly stand, exuding hostility, on an open road, Agamemnon, Ulysses, and Menelaus, clad in their splendid armor of contrasting hues, look as statuesque as the Colossi of Memnon. So unforgettable a tableau reminds us how rarely these films capture the proud, disciplined spirit of Homer's glamorous warriors. The classic scene, on the other hand, where the armed Hector tenderly takes leave of his wife Andromache is strangely mishandled, so that their son is frightened not, as in Homer, by a great nodding plume on Hector's helmet but rather by an ordinary broom-style pate brush that could double as a tidy whisk.

Among the major liberties taken with Homer's plot is the collapsing of Hector's death with Achilles', so that Paris' arrow strikes just as Achilles, who scarcely has time to gloat, begins to drag Hector's corpse. Ulysses, however, is given a great line at Achilles' fall: "So dies Greek courage, but not Greek cunning." As the Greeks mope in their tents, Ulysses pitches his plan to them. They're skeptical: "What are you dreaming of, Ulysses?" He replies, "I'm dreaming of my wife, the good, constant Penelope, and in my dreams I see myself returning to her with all the treasures of Troy." Why couldn't the screenplay maintain this quality of dialogue?

The Trojan horse is sprightly and snappy-looking, its rear legs thrust back like those of a champion purebred dog. Our trusty sound engineers again deserve kudos for the raspy, creaking sound of its wheels. "Beware the Greeks bearing gifts," says Helen, looking down from the city wall. This line from the *Aeneid* belongs to Laocoön, but he didn't make it into the screenplay. The thought obviously doesn't go very deep with Helen anyway, since she immediately changes her mind and turns pro-horse. The contrarian Cassandra, of course, wants it burned and lobbies her parents about it. Even though it's night, Priam orders the thing immediately dragged into the city, which strains credulity.

The very prolonged shot of the majestically moving horse, spotlit against the dark sky and coming directly at us through the huge metal doors and towering pylon of Troy, must have been overwhelming on the wide screen. This is great cinema, and Steiner's score here is wonderfully funereal, music for a death march. Now all the Trojans, starved for a party, rush toward the horse, and the orgy begins. We get the usual biblical Golden Calf scene, where girls in short skirts do the hula or are carried around on platters. There's also body surfing in the mosh pit under the imposingly tall horse and then a rather quickly devised amusement of dangling on vine-covered rope swings attached to its belly. Wine is quaffed from helmets until everyone passes out.

When the Greek SWAT team rappels down from the horse and opens the gates, the scraping seems like a thunderclap in the heavy silence. The enemy pours in. "Troy is lost," Priam very simply says. The sack of the city is fairly good, with rope trains of women led along to enslavement with tied hands, and wagons piled with booty rolling out the gates before the fire begins. We see Cassandra brutally seized by Ajax while she is praying at Athena's shrine, but it's difficult to understand why Pyrrhus' gruesome, impious murder of Priam at the palace altar (recited even by the player in *Hamlet*) is always missing from these films, since a king's fate symbolizes that of the nation.

Somehow, in the middle of this mess, the fleeing Paris and Helen manage to run smack into Menelaus. A test of arms occurs, and Paris naturally falls only because he is stabbed from behind by a cowardly Greek. The last image of Troy is of the horse outlined against rising clouds of smoke, as chaos swirls below—another beautifully composed scene that must have been astonishing in the theater. The story ends there, except for a farewell shot that seems borrowed from *Queen Christina* (1933), where Greta Garbo stares mournfully out to sea. On the stern of a ship taking her back to Greece, the melancholy Helen is clearly thinking of her lost love. But barely a trace of the tragic destruction of an entire civilization seems to have left its mark on her smooth, rosy cheeks.

By odd synchronicity, a month after the NBC *Odyssey* was broadcast, Jean-Luc Godard's classic 1963 film, *Contempt* (*Le Mépris*), based on an Alberto Moravia novel, was re-released in restored form in the United States, to the ecstatic plaudits of critics. It was the avant-garde director's first experience with CinemaScope, the eye-seducing medium of the 1950s ancient epics. The producers of *Contempt* were Joseph E. Levine and Carlo Ponti (who produced *Ulysses*).

Like Fellini's *8½* and Truffaut's *Day for Night* (1973), *Contempt* is a movie about making a movie—in this case, of the *Odyssey*. Rugged Jack Palance, speaking in English (like Kirk Douglas as Ulysses), plays a pushy American movie producer, Jeremiah Prokosch, who descends on Rome like an angry god to deal with the project's thorny problems. Asked why he hired a German director (Godard's idol, the legendary Fritz Lang, playing himself), the producer invokes Heinrich Schliemann by name and declares, "The *Odyssey* needs a German director because the Germans discovered Troy."

Palance's character wants new scenes invented for the *Odyssey* screenplay and hires a serious, intellectual writer, Paul (Michel Piccoli), to do them. The men's first, tense encounter, mediated by an attractive female translator, occurs as Prokosch impatiently prowls the deserted Cinecittà lot. Surreal, intercut classical images flash before us: chalky white plaster casts, with garishly painted details (red eyes, blue lips, gold hair), of a kouros, Athena, Poseidon, the Apollo Belvedere, the Capitoline Venus, and Homer himself, presiding forlornly in a sunny meadow. Whether Godard is suggesting that the classics are dead and that, for better or worse, we have lost our link with the past, or whether he is portraying modern individuals as emotionally frozen and petrified, as in Alain Resnais' sculpture-filled *Last Year at Marienbad* (1961), the effect of *Contempt*'s kitschy statuary is somewhat ridiculous. Compare, in contrast, Truffaut's stunningly successful use of a statue evoking a Greek Cycladic idol in the garden of *Jules and Jim* (1961) to mirror the weathered beauty and sexual mystery of Jeanne Moreau.

Attractions and rivalries among the characters of *Contempt* begin to parallel those of the *Odyssey*. The writer's young wife, Camille (Brigitte Bardot), becomes the central point of an erotic triangle: feeling that Paul has in effect prostituted her by forcing her into the producer's sports car, she turns against her husband and eventually abandons him. As their marriage chills, Paul muses about Homer: "Maybe Ulysses is really fed up with Penelope, and that's why he goes to war." There are scattered rereadings of the poem throughout the film: the *Odyssey* is about "a wife not loving her husband," or Ulysses is gone for so long because "he doesn't want to get home." Even the producer tries his hand: "I rewrote the *Odyssey* last night," announces Prokosch at one point. The poem becomes a prism through which the film's shifting relationships are examined. The cynical director Lang has his own, more impersonal take on the material. He remarks, "The world of Homer was a real world that developed in harmony with nature. Homer's reality is what it is. Take it or leave it."

While the principal characters dance and squabble, the actual filming of the *Odyssey* is under way. A rather limply unathletic Ulysses, wearing a sad-looking, off-the-shoulder, plaid smock, is seen padding around at the periphery of things; sometimes he has a bow and arrow and sometimes a sword, which in *Contempt*'s final shot he lifts skyward as he gazes, paralyzed, across the flat sea. Far more dynamic is the saucy script girl in short shorts and a striped halter top. "Act one, scene one!" she barks, whacking the clapper-board labeled "ODYSSEY" in front of the camera lens. Casting is still in flux: *Laugh-In*-like auditions for a floozy-type Nausikaä go on in an empty theater (interesting but not nearly as well done as the scene in Fellini's *8½* where Marcello Mastroianni as the philandering director auditions actresses for the roles of his wife and mistress, as his real wife steams nearby).

Contempt is full of ironic play with classical minutiae. Having a fit in a screening room, the producer kicks a stack of film cans and pretends to hurl one like a discus—like Myron's statue but also like Odysseus on Phaeacia. Later, he hands Paul a book of Roman paintings—"to help with the *Odyssey*"—that Camille will listlessly leaf through. In their chicly furnished apartment, Paul slouches around in a white towel wrapped like a Roman toga (another borrowing from

8½), while Camille, announcing her future plans to sleep alone on the Italian-moderne red couch, perversely covers her blonde mane with a helmet-like black wig that critics see as an allusion to Godard's estranged wife, actress Anna Karina, but that could also evoke the "thinking," untouchable virgin goddess, Athena. The plucky, multilingual woman translator also has Minervan mental qualities.

As a *rewriter*, Paul the reluctant script doctor resembles Homer the bard, who reshaped the heroic lays of the Bronze Age Aegean. *Contempt* opens with a massive CinemaScope camera sliding down its track on a Mediterranean village street and turning to loom over us like one-eyed Polyphemus, a monstrous invader from infernal Hollywood. "The Cyclops scene" is explicitly announced on set later in the film, but what we actually see is a glum Camille in sunglasses (self-blinded?) moving away in a rowboat with Prokosch, anxiously watched by Paul from a cliff. Is she the Cyclops' stolen sheep? Helen eloping with Paris? Or an impatient Penelope who sails for adventure while, in a modern sex reversal, her husband waits? The producer who kicks things about and aggressively guns his red sports car around corners is like Antinous, the cock-of-the-walk suitor who finally wins his unfaithful Penelope.

The luxurious, Olympian hilltop house on Capri where jealousies simmer recalls both the emperor Tiberius' dissolute villa on that island and, in its broad steps and bare platform roof, the ruined temple of Apollo at oracular Delphi. The pistol which Paul secretly begins to carry but which the plot stops him from using is like Odysseus' bow, held in reserve for future vengeance. Fate or the gods intervene instead: Prokosch and Camille, bound for Rome in the sports car, collide with a gasoline truck and are killed. (Another gasoline truck as *deus ex machina* saves the hero from airborne destruction in *North by Northwest* [1959], directed by the New Wave's ultimate auteur, Alfred Hitchcock.) As in the traffic-clogged *Week-End* (1967), Godard presents highway accidents as modern shipwrecks, like those barely survived by tenacious Odysseus.

Brigitte Bardot has been a persistent presence in our Homeric tour. A bubbly ingenue in *Helen of Troy,* she is in full, sulky flower in *Contempt,* where she has become the archetypal sex bomb still imitated by Claudia Schiffer and Pamela Anderson Lee. But Bardot also has an unexpected connection to *Ulysses*. In Venice on a break from shooting that film, Kirk Douglas saw "the most gorgeous creature—long, silky blond hair, beautiful breasts, never-ending legs—running toward me in a bikini, a sight I will remember long after my eyes fail me."[2]

The then-obscure, seventeen-year-old Bardot had met Douglas when she was playing a bit part in *Act of Love*, the film he completed in France before leaving for Rome to do *Ulysses*. Seeing her for that visionary moment in Venice, he sensed her future stardom. In the gratuitous seminude scenes demanded by the producers of *Contempt*, the camera caresses Bardot's glossy curves as if she were an Arcadian landscape. Fusing Penelope with Circe and Calypso, she ultimately embodies immortal Aphrodite, the great goddess of love herself.

1. *The Ragman's Son: An Autobiography* (New York, 1988), p. 210.
2. Ibid., p. 211, *n*. 1.

SEX, GENDER, WOMEN

19

SEX QUEST IN TOM OF FINLAND

A typical Tom of Finland drawing of a flirtatious hitchhiker flagging an interested motorcyclist. Tom's dashing, glamorously leather-clad muscle men had an enormous influence on the style and sexual personae of gay men in the 1970s, following the birth of the gay liberation movement.

The swaggering sexual personae of Tom of Finland's world demonstrate the intimate intertwining of art and pornography, which moralists of both the Right and the Left have tried to drive apart. Tom's sculptured physiques descend, via modern muscle magazines, from Michelangelo's homoerotic dreams, where the male chest and biceps

[From *Tom of Finland XXL*, collected works, ed. Dian Hanson (Taschen, 2009).]

were extravagantly enlarged and complicated. Michelangelo in turn was inspired by Greco-Roman nudes, marble fragments like the massive, twisting Belvedere Torso then being excavated in Rome. Thus Tom's erotic designs have an ancient lineage: he is meditating on one of the great themes of Western culture, the pagan glorification of the ideal male body, imagined as a sharp-contoured glyph of heroic human will.

Tom's images are usually all foreground, with background minimal or missing. His assertive, theatrical figures fill the page and threaten to escape it. We are plunged into a mental landscape where the sex impulse represents pure energy and eternal youth. There is no fatigue or hesitation; resistance is merely a game to inflame desire. Subordination is never degradation, as it so often is in the Marquis de Sade, whose passive victims become non-persons, like meat fed through a grinder. In Tom of Finland, in contrast, the bottom partner retains his monumentality and explosive charge. Surrender is not annihilation but exhilarating play.

Uniforms, a bequest of Tom's army service in wartime Europe, symbolize social hierarchies melted and subverted by mischievous biology. They represent laws and limits undone or mastered by the greater tyranny of lust. When Nazi regalia are shockingly evoked, we are forced to weigh basic ethics and tragic historical memory against the brute seduction of absolute power. Tom's Aryan projections (including his somewhat Europeanized blacks) draw on the thunder-and-lightning Nordic myths that the Nazis mixed with Rosicrucian mysticism. His half-clad hitchhikers or bully motorcyclists are like roadside hallucinations, impish divinities suddenly springing up from woods and streams.

But there is no *Sturm und Drang* or Michelangelesque angst in Tom's emotional atmosphere. On the contrary, we are charmed and disarmed by his infectious wry humor. His prankish predators and their transient playthings are joyous and ebullient, as they rollick in a privileged zone that is marvelously free of the censoring superego of parents or God and where even policemen forget their mission and join the fun. As if by merciless revolution, the elders, with their sluggish prudence, have been swept from the earth. At first glance, Tom's tangled, orgiastic tableaux sometimes look like nostalgic memories of schoolyard wrestling, with murky desires brazenly externalized.

A case could be made from a conservative viewpoint that Tom's work is illustration, not art; that his draftsmanship, often based on photos, can be fussy or pat; and that his faces are generic, even sentimental, and lack subtext. Critical appreciation of Tom's totally figurative work—which first broke into major museum status in the U.S. through tributes by his gifted admirer, the photographer Robert Mapplethorpe—was retarded not simply because of Tom's extreme gay content but because his creative maturation coincided with the hegemony of radical abstraction in art. I would strongly argue, in Tom's defense, that photorealism is central to the twentieth-century era of cinema and advertising and that his fantastic action figures, recalling the superheroes of comic books, belong to the graphic tradition of animation—an ever-expanding genre that may be currently eclipsing the fine arts in prestige and influence.

Tom's square-jawed faces, with their glinting eyes and fixed smiles, are masks, denoting a class or clan rather than an individual. Early Greek *kouroi* (sculptures of nude young athletes and warriors) also sported an unvarying and ambiguous "Archaic" smile, shared by female figures. The Archaic smile can be interpreted (as I have done elsewhere) as a motif of springtime freshness, of nature's new beginnings. Tom's dashing ephebi, with their ripening pectorals and swollen buttocks, have internalized the fertility principle which is normally the province of women, who rarely appear in Tom's pictures save as waspish soubrettes or crones.

Tom of Finland was crucial in the development of my own thinking about art and gender. He armed me as a dissident feminist for my long war against the puritan ideologues and philistines who co-opted American feminism in the 1970s and who perversely turned against the 1960s sexual revolution: their reactionary movement would reach its peak in the 1980s in the fanatical anti-pornography crusades of Catharine MacKinnon and Andrea Dworkin. Anyone familiar with Tom's exuberant gay wonderland would have found as patently ridiculous as I did the feminist mantra that pornography is nothing but an instrument of political intimidation by which men threaten women with rape or, even more absurd, that pornography actually *causes* rape.

There is no doubt, however, that in Tom's work, the penis is power. Stunningly exaggerated (as in Aubrey Beardsley's witty rococo drawings), it is less a political weapon or club than a primitive totem, the ecstatic focus of a ritual cult. Tom's flaunted, mammoth phalli, thick and fibrous, are like serpentine vines or trees, brimming with sap. They are Dionysian maypoles around which his sparring characters collect and carouse. Everything bursts with vitality, including Tom's impossibly wedge-shaped torsos, where brawny shoulders broaden like oaks from slim hips. Gloved in super-tight clothing, the body itself is tumescent.

Tom's taunting sexual marauders are like Vikings or Goths, opportunistic adventurers who still roam or work in the open, while most men are hopelessly chained to office and home. His leathermen, draped in living, breathing animal skins, are wed to nature. Tom's typical scenarios of hunt and capture have atavistic analogies in ancient and tribal ritual—particularly his bondage, flagellation, and crucifixion scenes, where nipples are wrenched or the teeming scrotum gripped and stretched. And his stockade-like panoramas of trampling boots recall Minoan murals of ritual bull-dancing, where the celebrant risked mutilation or death beneath the hooves of a beast worshipped for its pugnacious virility. But in Tom's utopia, every wound is magically healed, and no scars remain.

The state of constant excitation and erection in Tom's dynamic universe is his vision of the sacred and numinous. A theologian might speculate that Tom's sadomasochistic reverie contains its own punishments, that heaven is always answered by hell. But Tom's imperial satyriasis is his protest against boredom and ennui, produced by the modern industrial and technocratic withdrawal from nature. Tom cannot be accused of blind idolatry of the liberated body: his pictures show a theater of eyes, a mass voyeurism where consciousness itself has become penetrating and inflamed. And there is a deeply emotional dimension to his variations on the mythic motif of battling and reconciling twin brothers—for Tom's personae often look like siblings in a wary dance of alienation and attraction.

In masculinizing the gay persona, Tom broke, for good or ill, with the cultural legacy of the brilliant Oscar Wilde, who promoted and flamboyantly embodied the androgynous aesthete. What is durably avant-garde in Tom, now that frank depictions of homosexuality (partly thanks to him) have become so common, is his unsettling treatment of male bonding, a foundational social principle that feminism has foolishly ignored. Tom's surreal, random encounters show the male gang or team in operation—forming, disintegrating, and regrouping through ruthless realignments and power reversals. This cruel, compulsive pattern enabled men to escape control by women (mothers and wives) and to push history and civilization forward. But the emotional cost may be chronic loneliness, a subliminal melancholy overridden by action, achievement, or mere display. In Tom of Finland's world of epic quest, with its bruising jousts and fleeting alliances, pugilistic sex becomes the medium through which rogue men regain their lost freedom.

20

WOMEN AND LAW

Before Brazil's Supreme Federal Court in the governmental Plaza of the Three Powers at Brasilia sits an imposing statue of Justice, her eyes blindfolded, her breasts bare, and her hands gently but firmly holding a sword in her lap, as an enthroned medieval Madonna cradles the Christ child. Carved in 1961 from a rugged block of creamy granite from Petrópolis by Alfredo Ceschiatti, the statue invokes the ancient allegorical personification of justice as a Roman goddess, Iustitia. Before her came Dike, the Greek goddess of justice who supervised human laws, just as her mother Themis, holding aloft a scale and brandishing a sword, represented divine law.

This symbolic tradition began in Egypt, where the goddess Ma'at monitored and maintained the physical and moral equilibrium of the universe. The hearts of the Egyptian dead were weighed on a scale, balanced by the "Feather of Ma'at." The sacred scale also appeared in Babylonian astrology and survives today in the constellation of Libra. Brilliantly, Ceschiatti has combined the sword and scale of Justice, whose feminine shoulders slope into robust arms of Cubist angularity: her strong hands, one facing up and the other down, seem to test the weight of her formidable blade, which represents the power of the state to punish.

[Preface for Gunter Axt, *Histórias de Vida: Mulheres do Direito, mulheres no Ministério Público*, vol. iii (Life stories: Women of law, women in public ministry), seventeen interviews with women serving as independent public prosecutors in Brazil (Florianópolis, Brazil, 2015).]

The ancient scale of Themis dramatized the systematic and scientific weighing of evidence, the triumph of cool reason over explosive emotion and rigid prejudice. This is the great theme of Aeschylus' *Oresteia,* where pitiless female Furies, stormy nature spirits driven by vengeance, yield to the new institutions of civilization, represented by the Athenian court of law on the Areopagus. The warrior goddess Athena, lacking a mother, casts the deciding ballot for the surrender of primordial female power and the triumph of masculine reason, aspiring toward the abstract and impersonal.

Ceschiatti has strangely flattened the head of Justice, as if he is alluding to the bust of Nefertiti, with her conceptually swollen wig-crown, or to the Meso-American Chac Mool, who oversaw with alert eyes the ritual of blood sacrifice, guaranteeing the rise of the sun. Justice is receiving pressure and illumination from above, in a new era led by mind rather than passion. After the chaotic impulsiveness of tribalism and clan warfare, the codification of law brings a higher standard and a system of measured due process. The ceremonial slowness of law makes space for thought.

The iconic blindfold of Justice, signifying the impartiality of the law toward wealth, fame, or power, was not an ancient motif but first appeared in the Northern European Renaissance. A Marxist analysis, with its reflex cynicism, would insist that law is always a product of political and economic exploitation and that law, as inherently oppressive, serves only a ruling elite. But idealism, however sabotaged by untidy reality, is a fundamental human value that separates us from the animal realm.

Today there is a new conundrum facing blindfolded Justice: should gender be visible or invisible to the law? Should women, in pursuing the noble goal of equality, be treated exactly the same as men, or should women be granted special privileges and protections under the law? And if the latter, is the basis for that gender distinction biological or cultural? This argument, which has split feminism, will not be resolved soon.

Despite the majestic deification of Justice, real-life women throughout most of world history were rarely able to exercise the power of law for their own benefit, except if they inherited royal authority from a father or borrowed it from a dead husband. More often, women were the victims of law, rather than its agents. In literature, we see the Antigone of Sophocles persecuted by the draconian Creon; the biblical Mary Magdalene and Hester Prynne in Nathaniel Hawthorne ostracized for adultery; Joan of Arc tried and condemned by male inquisitors; Hedda Gabler in Ibsen prompted to suicide by her claustrophobic entrapment by Judge Brack.

Woman as apostle and practitioner of law, as attorney or judge, is a pioneering modern phenomenon in which Brazil played an early role. Shakespeare, whose admiration of forceful, articulate women may have been partly inspired by the pugnacious Queen Elizabeth I, prefigured this development in *The Merchant of Venice,* where his resourceful heroine Portia disguises herself as a male law clerk to thwart the cruel contract of the usurer Shylock in court. Not until Hollywood movies, however, would most of the general public be introduced to the decisive persona of the woman lawyer, who has mastered the rules and strategies of what was once an exclusively male game.

In the United States, after women won the right to vote via a constitutional amendment in 1920, there was a surge of women entering the male professions. This was in my view the best and most productive period in feminism—when women openly expressed admiration for male achievement and merely demanded the opportunity to equal or surpass it. Many movies of studio-era classic Hollywood showed high-powered professional women at work, even if the plot-lines often focused on the conflicts faced by a successful woman in reconciling her job with the emotional needs of her husband and marriage—a difficult issue still troubling women today.

Rosalind Russell played a fast-talking newspaper reporter in *His Girl Friday* (1940) and a judge in *Design for Scandal* (1941) and *Tell It to the Judge* (1949). Katharine Hepburn played a famous, multilingual journalist (based on Dorothy Thompson) in *Woman of the Year* (1942) and a boldly assertive lawyer defending women's rights in *Adam's Rib* (1949), where she battles her husband, an assistant district attorney (Spencer Tracy), in the courtroom. Hepburn's tremendous authority and crystalline command of rhetoric before the jury (in a script specially written for her by Ruth Gordon and Garson Kanin) remain an inspiring model for women lawyers everywhere.

In the period following World War Two, the victorious but exhausted U.S. reverted to a reactionary culture of domesticity, and movies centered on professional women became much rarer. In *Witness for the Prosecution* (1957), for example, woman again undermines rather than reinforces the law: taking the witness stand, the disturbingly glamorous Marlene Dietrich is devious and serpentine, another beguiling Eve. It would be a long time before women lawyers returned to the movie screen. In *Lipstick* (1976), released shortly after the reawakening of feminism in the late 1960s, Anne Bancroft plays a tough prosecutor initiating and leading a criminal trial for the rape of a fashion model (Margaux Hemingway). In *Legal Eagles* (1986), a young attorney played by the vivacious Debra Winger clashes with an assistant district attorney (Robert Redford) in the courtroom. In Pedro Almodóvar's *Women on the Verge of a Nervous Breakdown* (1988), a film dubber played by Carmen Maura discovers that her lover is about to run away with a rudely unsympathetic feminist lawyer.

However, the most important role for a woman lawyer since *Adam's Rib* was certainly that of the assistant district attorney played by Kelly McGillis in *The Accused* (1988). Jodie Foster won her first Academy Award for Best Actress for playing a rape victim whose case is investigated and prosecuted by McGillis. The movie was based on actual events that had occurred in 1983 in the Portuguese-American community in working-class New Bedford, Massachusetts, once one of the leading whaling ports in the world. A young mother, Cheryl Araujo, was gang-raped by four Portuguese immigrants on a billiards table in a tavern. The subsequent successful trial of the rapists, televised live, was a national spectacle, prefiguring the 1994–95 double-murder trial of famous athlete O. J. Simpson, during which the woman chief prosecutor, Marcia Clark, was catapulted into media stardom.

As they became more common in real life, woman lawyers faded from the movie screen, but they multiplied on television, as in *L.A. Law* (1986–94), a major hit series about a Los Angeles law firm. In *Ally McBeal* (1997–2002), Calista Flockhart (who later married Har-

rison Ford) played a lawyer perpetually perplexed by romantic melodramas. In *Sex and the City* (1998–2004), a series about professional
women in Manhattan that attained worldwide popularity, a sharp-
tongued woman lawyer, Miranda Hobbes (Cynthia Nixon), was vexed
by the usual problems with intimate relationships with men. *Judging
Amy* (1999–2005) focused on a young woman judge presiding over
family court, while in *Boston Legal* (2004–08), Candice Bergen played
an acerbic woman litigator and co-founder of a high-profile Boston
law firm.

The status of women under the law has been a long saga of gains,
losses, and recoveries. At the dawn of civilization in ancient Mesopotamia, a new urban culture brought a greater sophistication, allowing women to enjoy more rights than they did later. In Sumeria,
upper-class women could transact business and sell household slaves.
However, adultery was punished by death for women only. After the
Babylonian conquest of Sumeria, women under the Code of Hammu-
rabi had fewer rights but could still buy and sell, inherit and bequeath
property, and participate in court cases as plaintiff, defendant, or witness, and even serve as judges.

In Egypt, legal rights were principally determined by social class
rather than gender. But women of different social levels had equality
with men. Egyptian women could own houses and land and could
participate in litigation. In Judaea, in contrast, women's lives were
strictly circumscribed by patriarchy, as enforced by religion. Hebrew
husbands could be polygamous, while wives had to be monogamous.
Wives addressed their husbands as "lord and master," echoing an
honorific used by slaves. A husband could divorce his wife, but not
vice versa. Hebrew women could not inherit property, except if there
was no living male heir.

In Athens at the height of classical culture, women had no rights
of citizenship and were defined by the law only in relationship to a
father or husband, who acted as guardian. Nevertheless, a husband
could not spend the dowry of his wife, to which she maintained her
right. Except for small commercial transactions permitted to working-
class entrepreneurs such as vegetable sellers, Athenian women could

not enter contracts. Neither could they inherit the crucial possession of land, which went directly to sons or grandsons, bypassing daughters. In the comedy of Aristophanes, *Women of the Assembly* (391 B.C.), Athenian women masquerading as men take over the government and pass laws to liberate women and establish a communistic paradise of shared wealth and universal social welfare. Strangely, Sparta, the mortal enemy of Athens and a militaristic city-state that created nothing of enduring cultural significance, granted far higher status and visibility to its women, who were renowned throughout Greece as competitive athletes.

During the Republic, the ancient Romans revered law as a fundamental moral principle of the universe. The Twelve Tables, the first code of law in Rome, was also the earliest surviving work of Roman literature. The *paterfamilias,* a head of family who might be a son after the death of a father, acted as a judge with absolute legal authority and power of life and death over family members, who had no avenue of appeal. The identity of Roman women of the Republic was subsumed in clan: men had three names, while women were known only by a feminized version of their clan name; sisters, like clones, bore the number of their birth order. Roman matrons, remarkable for their force of personality, did have certain property rights, but Roman women were given minimal education and could not hold public office.

Under Christianity, women were tainted daughters of Eve, as defined by the incremental complexities of medieval canon law. Unreliable and inferior beings, women were categorized with children and the mentally defective, and they could not own property or enter into contracts. A Christian husband, exercising the punitive dominion of Adam after the Fall, was the guardian of his wife, whose property automatically became his. Women could not testify in court or act as witnesses.

In Old China, women had no legal rights and could not own land or inherit property. Only concubines enjoyed special privileges. However, mothers-in-law in China have often had near dictatorial power in the home. The Communist Party of China made female emancipation a central principle of modernization. In 1953, the Electoral Law of the People's Republic of China granted women the right to vote and to hold political office.

In Japan as in China, Confucianism emphasized the group over the individual, a tradition that tended to suppress concern for women's rights. Japan had a matrilineal system until the militaristic samurai period. Until the reopening of Japan to the West in the nineteenth century, Japanese women had no legal standing and could not own property. World War Two, with its catastrophic destruction of Japanese cities, ended feudalism in Japan. The postwar Allied (and largely American) occupation of Japan introduced a parliamentary system as well as Western-style women's rights. In 1947, Japan passed a Labor Standards Act that guaranteed equal pay for women—sixteen years before the U.S. passed a similar law.

Feminism as a political movement began in the United States and Britain, which shared a thousand-year tradition of common law, based on custom and judicial precedents (as opposed to civil law, based on legislative statutes, which came to Brazil from Europe). Under common law, a woman lost all property rights upon marriage, and her legal identity was dissolved into that of her husband.

The first manifesto of feminism was published by a British writer who was inspired by the French Revolution: in *A Vindication of the Rights of Woman* (1792), Mary Wollstonecraft called for women to be granted the vote and to be educated for entrance into the professions. She fiercely protested the crippled legal status of married women, who had no rights even regarding custody of their children. At age 38, Wollstonecraft died from an infection following the birth of her daughter Mary, who would eventually marry the Romantic poet Percy Bysshe Shelley and write the classic novel of Gothic horror, *Frankenstein*.

Feminism as organized activism emerged from the abolitionist movement among Quakers in England and the United States. It was in Quaker "meetings" (worship services) and anti-slavery societies that women were first permitted and encouraged to engage in public speaking, traditionally regarded as improper and even scandalous for respectable ladies (who should avoid exposure to men's eyes). There was a strong Quaker presence in the campaign for "woman suf-frage" (the right to vote) from Lucretia Mott and Susan B. Anthony to Alice Paul. The first convention for women's rights, held in the small upstate town of Seneca Falls, New York, in 1848, issued a revolution-ary document declaring that "all men and women are created equal" and that any laws opposing such equality are contrary to the great "law of Nature" and therefore have "no validity."

Later in the nineteenth century, the American women's move-ment became distracted by the Temperance crusade, which pres-sured the government to ban the manufacture and sale of alcohol. Susan B. Anthony and Elizabeth Cady Stanton were very active in this puritanical campaign, as was Carrie Nation, a tall vigilante who posed for photos with the frightening hatchet that she used to smash beer barrels. The Women's Christian Temperance Union (1874) and the Anti-Saloon League (1893) eventually succeeded in their goal: in 1919, Prohibition became national law in the U.S. via a constitutional amendment. Fourteen years later, Prohibition was repealed: it had been a total failure that had merely created an underground network for smuggling, laying the foundation for the international drug traf-ficking of today.

With its authoritarian intrusion into matters of private choice, the Temperance crusade would be paralleled by the acrimonious and sometimes hysterical campaign against pornography in the 1980s by feminists Andrea Dworkin and Catharine MacKinnon, a law profes-sor and the daughter of a longtime judge on the U.S. Court of Appeals in Washington, D.C. Dworkin and MacKinnon wrote an ordinance for city governments that would ban the sale and distribution of pornog-raphy, which they arbitrarily defined as a violation of the civil rights of women. Dworkin and MacKinnon wanted to outlaw even main-stream men's magazines like *Playboy* and *Penthouse*. Their ordinance, passed into law by the cities of Minneapolis and Indianapolis, was struck down on appeal by higher courts as a violation of free speech rights, guaranteed under the First Amendment of the U.S. Constitu-tion. However, the ordinance was adopted in Canada, where it compli-cated and sometimes halted the import of books about sex, ironically including those of Dworkin.

In the 1920s, after women had won the right to vote in the United States and United Kingdom, organized feminism disappeared. When Simone de Beauvoir began writing her epic work, *The Second Sex* (published in 1949), she was regarded as hopelessly old-fashioned by fellow intellectuals in Paris. De Beauvoir's deeply researched and philosophical book would have a delayed impact. In 1963, Betty Friedan, a well-educated American magazine writer, published an angry, highly personal book that became a surprise bestseller: *The Feminine Mystique* expressed the discontents of affluent, middle-class women with their lack of professional opportunities and their imprisonment in the stay-at-home roles of wife and mother.

In 1966, Friedan co-founded the National Organization for Women (NOW), the first group devoted to political action for women's rights in over four decades. However, younger feminists, some of them lesbian, brought a more confrontational political style from the civil rights and antiwar movements of the 1960s. By 1970, Friedan was alienated from NOW, which in her view had become anti-man, anti-marriage, and anti-family, as well as too focused on lesbianism (which she called "the lavender menace"), all of which she correctly prophesied would drive mainstream women away from feminism. The manifesto of radical feminism was *The Dialectic of Sex* (1970) by Shulamith Firestone, who used terminology drawn from Marx and Freud to call for cybernetic reproduction to replace pregnancy and for collectives to raise children, thus abolishing traditional family structure.

Two major public issues caused an uproar around the newly reborn women's movement. In 1972, the U.S. Congress, urged by NOW, passed an Equal Rights Amendment, banning discrimination by federal or state law "on account of sex." Within a year, the ERA was ratified by 30 of the required 38 states. However, a "STOP ERA" movement was launched by a conservative mother and lawyer, Phyllis Schlafly, who argued that the amendment would harm women in key areas, such as alimony, child custody, and the military draft (from which women are exempt). By 1982, the official time limit, already extended for four years by Congress, had expired, and the ERA was dead. Furthermore, Schlafly's vigorous campaign had mobilized conservatives nationwide (including evangelical Christians), leading to a huge revival of conservative ideology and activism, which continues today.

The second uproar was about abortion. In 1973, the U.S. Supreme Court ruled, on privacy grounds, that a Texas law outlawing abortion was unconstitutional. Before this, individual states had the right to determine their own abortion laws. Now abortion (in the first three months of pregnancy) became a nationwide right. This case of *Roe v. Wade* would inflame passions in the U.S. for the next half-century. It pit the Catholic Church and evangelical Christians against feminism and turned abortion into the number one issue still motivating liberal voters during U.S. presidential campaigns (because the president appoints justices to the Supreme Court, which can overturn *Roe v. Wade*). Planned Parenthood Federation, vilified and picketed by conservatives, controversially receives government funding to offer family planning and abortion services to women, some of whom lack medical insurance. The ancestor of Planned Parenthood was the American Birth Control League, founded in 1921 by Margaret Sanger, who had been arrested and put on trial after she opened a birth control clinic in Brooklyn in 1916.

Since the late 1980s, the dominant approach in feminist theory, in both the U.S. and abroad, has been derived from the post-structuralism of Michel Foucault and his disciple Judith Butler, an American academic. The premise of this system, with its contorted jargon, is that gender is an illusion of language, through which all of reality is refracted. We can know nothing about ourselves or the world except through language, which is inherently slippery. The body itself does not exist except as a passive object of shadowy social control. Gender is always in flux in an ahistorical arena of subjective performance. It is difficult to understand how feminism is aided by a theoretical system so divorced from the problems and practicalities faced by most women in everyday life. The refusal by post-structuralist feminists to study, respect, or even acknowledge nature and biology will inevitably limit the reach of their self-referential discourse to a narrow elite.

Today, the major issues facing feminism are these: is woman a victim, mutilated by the horrors of history, or is she a capable and resilient agent, responsible for her own actions and desires? To what degree should the state act to further the crucial advance of women in society? Are legally enforced quotas and other preferential remedies authentically progressive, or are they reactionary, paternalistic, and infantilizing? Should women, having escaped control by fathers and husbands, now transfer that humiliating dependency onto the laby-rinthine bureaucracy of the state? Or should women, as a testament to their own strength and courage, value freedom above all, despite its pain and risk?

21

ON JEWISH-AMERICAN FEMINISTS

ADAM KIRSCH: You are always alert to the ethnic and class issues within white feminism; you credit your Italian background with giving you a different perspective on sex and gender from, say, Catharine MacKinnon. In this vein, why do you think so many of the prominent American feminists of the last fifty years have been Jewish women—including many of the people you argue with and about, from Betty Friedan to Gloria Steinem to Naomi Wolf? Is there something about Jewishness that is conducive to feminism?

CAMILLE PAGLIA: Second-wave feminism, to which Betty Friedan gave birth with her co-founding of the National Organization for Women in 1966, was strongly powered by a fiery social activism whose roots can be traced to the unionizing movement of the early twentieth century. One of the classic protest songs in my "Art of Song Lyric" course is "The Death of Harry Simms," about the 1932 shooting of 20-year-old Jewish labor leader Harry Simms Hersh in the battle for unionization of the Kentucky coal mines. I have described my principal mentors, poet Milton Kessler in college and critic Harold Bloom in graduate school, as more like visionary rabbis than professors. I have repeatedly acknowledged my debt to Jewish-American culture. For example, in my long

["Camille Paglia on Jews and Feminism: A dialogue with Adam Kirsch about her new collection *Free Women, Free Men,*" *Tablet Magazine,* March 9, 2017.]

1991 attack on post-structuralism, "Junk Bonds and Corporate Raiders," I wrote: "It was from Jews (beginning at T. Aaron Levy Junior High School) that I learned how to analyze politics, law, business, and medicine, how to decipher the power dynamics of family relationships, and how to plan pragmatic strategies of social activism."

In response to your question, I don't think it's so much the conduciveness of Jewishness to feminism as it is the readiness and ability of Jewish-American women to aggressively speak out and confront, without fear of loss of "respectability," as it was defined and enforced by the WASP establishment code that once governed U.S. business, politics, and education. The Jewish marriage contract is unusual in guaranteeing women's rights, suggesting the power that Jewish women have always wielded in the home and family. When I was growing up in Syracuse in the stiflingly conformist late 1950s and early 1960s, I was highly impressed by the bold and even abrasive vocal style (then called "the Jewish seagull") that was often employed by Jewish women, and there can be no doubt that I imitated and absorbed it. By the early 1990s, I was being called "the academic Joan Rivers"— Rivers hugely influenced me, including my onstage style.

Beyond that, Jewish-Americans, with their Torah-inspired zeal for legal studies, regularly challenged the status quo in ways that Italian-Americans rarely did. For nearly two millennia, Italians had been scattered in tight-knit tribal villages; even after Italy became a state again in the late nineteenth century, Italians regarded it as a distant sham. None of my immigrant family would dream of challenging the dictatorial authority or mysterious operations of the state, which occupied a nebulous, external realm, unreal in comparison to the intricate unit of the extended family. (Even the dead had infinitely more reality to an Italian family! Recreational cemetery visits were routine.) Nor would Italian-Americans of that era question a doctor's diagnosis or indeed ask any questions at all in a medical office or hospital. What I got from Jewish-American culture was a revolutionary fervor for political and institutional reform, totally outside the otherwise wonderfully rich legacy of rural Italian tradition. When I was at Harpur College (SUNY Binghamton) in the mid-1960s, all the outspoken student radical leaders were Jews from metropolitan New York. Indeed, one of the most iconic images from that period is the *LIFE* magazine photograph of Columbia student David Shapiro wearing hip dark glasses while insolently smoking a cigar at the president's desk during the student uprising of 1968. Thus the prominent Jewish presence in second-wave feminism must simply be regarded as yet another form of modern Jewish progressivism.

22

PORTRAYALS OF MIDDLE EASTERN WOMEN IN WESTERN CULTURE

For three millennia, the relationship between Europe and the Middle East has been marked by periodic alternations between bitter conflict and profound mutual influence. Academic theory of the past half-century has blamed modern Western imperialism and colonialism for generating belittling stereotypes of "Orientalism": Europe, assuming a dominant interpretative position, aligned itself with reason, morality, and civilization, while identifying the Middle East with mystery, duplicity, and barbarism. Particularly compromised have been the image and reputation of Middle Eastern women, who have been persistently portrayed in strangely contradictory terms as the silent, submissive wife, veiled from head to foot, or as the belly dancer or odalisque, sensual and half naked.

The proliferation of misunderstandings between Europe and the Middle East can be traced all the way back to antiquity, long before the birth of Islam. With its ambivalent, sometimes voyeuristic attraction to the "exotic," Western culture has wavered in confusion between dual fantasies of the Middle East, both of which had some basis in historical reality. The first is grounded in the ascetic conservatism of the nomadic Bedouin tribes, whose pastoral, polygamous lifestyle replicated that of the Hebrew patriarchs of the Judeo-Christian Old Testa-

[Foreword for Birgitte C. Huitfeldt, *Usensurert: Midtøstens kvinner/Ti møter* (Uncensored: Middle Eastern women/ten ways), ten interviews with Middle Eastern women (Oslo, Norway, 2017).]

ment. The second arose from the lavish luxury and decadence of the great pagan empires, which boasted highly sophisticated cities like Babylon, Persepolis, Alexandria, Antioch, and Constantinople. Imperialism is no recent invention.

In its reformist focus on expanding career opportunities and improving workplace conditions and access to political power for women, second-wave feminism has embraced an economic materialism and rigid secularism that cannot always be easily reconciled with other complex value-systems in the non-Western world. Today, many talented and ambitious professional women of the Middle East are actively searching for their own unique balance between modernity and tradition, which may often include religious faith as well as strong family ties. Western feminists, in their well-intentioned zeal to help and to "liberate," must proceed with caution and respect and must not permit their utilitarian social agenda to become yet another arrogant imperialism, imposing relatively recent liberal assumptions as if they were eternal human universals.

Women in Egypt seem to have enjoyed a higher status, including property rights, than most women elsewhere in the ancient world. In the Old Kingdom, as demonstrated by the vivid painted-limestone tomb effigies of Prince Rahotep seated with his wife Nofret (Fourth Dynasty), royal men and women were depicted as equal in size and therefore symbolically equal in importance—as would strikingly not be the case in later Egyptian art. Several extraordinary royal women appeared during the Eighteenth Dynasty of the New Kingdom whose names were erased from history until they were rediscovered by modern archaeology: Queen Hatshepsut, who seized power and ruled as pharaoh, with a male headdress and ceremonial beard; Queen Tiye, strong-willed mother of the rebel monotheist pharaoh, Akhenaten; and Queen Nefertiti, Akhenaten's elegant wife, who may well have exercised political power in place of her sickly and reclusive husband, a dreamy idealist who was more a poet than a warrior.

The most famous or rather notorious Middle Eastern queen remains Cleopatra, whose ancestry was mainly Macedonian Greek: she was the last ruler of the Ptolemy dynasty installed in Egypt by Alexander the Great nearly 300 years earlier. Although evidently not particularly beautiful, she was a shrewd diplomat and witty conversationalist who knew many languages. Two Roman leaders of quite different personality and temperament fell in love with Cleopatra: the intellectual, puritanical Julius Caesar and the convivial, hedonistic Mark Antony. A year after their humiliating defeat by Octavian Caesar (the future emperor Augustus) at a naval battle off the Greek coast at Actium, Mark Antony and Cleopatra committed suicide in Egypt. Had Cleopatra won that battle, the balance of power in the Mediterranean might have shifted from Europe to the Middle East for the next 500 years.

Patricians of the old Roman Republic, with their strict code of modesty, simplicity, and gravitas, denounced the luxury and sensuality of the Middle East, typified by the elaborate jewelry, cosmetics, and transparent, body-revealing linen garments of Egyptian aristocrats like Cleopatra and her court. In Shakespeare's *Antony and Cleopatra* (based on Plutarch), Cleopatra is dismissed by conservative Romans as a whore. In the *Aeneid*, which he began to write shortly after her death, Vergil portrayed Cleopatra as the tragic Dido, a historical figure who was queen of Tyre, a wealthy port city of Phoenicia (modern Lebanon). Dido led a migration to North Africa, where she founded the great city of Carthage (modern Tunisia), destined to be Rome's mortal enemy during the Punic Wars. Vergil presents Dido as a commanding and confident presence, a visionary architect as well as a queen.

Like the Romans, the Greeks opposed their own ethic of masculine discipline, embodied in competitive athletics and war to that of the "effeminate," overly emotional men of the Middle East, who wore jewelry, fine fabrics, perfume, and eye makeup (kohl, used in desert climates to reduce sun glare and prevent infection). As early as the *Iliad*, Homer's rugged Mycenaean Greeks disdain the Trojan prince Paris, Helen's lover and abductor, as a pampered dandy who shrinks from hand-to-hand combat and slays from a distance with bow and arrow. Troy (whose ruins have been found in Hissarlik near the Dardanelles strait in northwestern Turkey) was already perceived as a more pleasure-oriented Middle Eastern capital. The East-West distinction can even be seen in the formal modes of Greek music: in his *Republic,* Plato wants to banish the soft, relaxed, and seductive Lydian mode from his ideal state, whose anthem should properly be the vigorous, stirring Dorian mode, implicitly masculine. The Dorians were warlike peoples who had descended with iron swords into the Greek peninsula from the north at the end of the Bronze Age; the kingdom of Lydia, in contrast, occupied the western third of ancient Anatolia (modern Turkey in Asia Minor).

In their civic mythology, the Athenians preserved the legend of an army of masculine women archers, the Amazons, invading and attacking Athens from the east. The story appears again in Shakespeare's classic comedy, *A Midsummer Night's Dream,* where the hero Theseus, duke of Athens, is marrying his former enemy, Hippolyta, queen of the Amazons. Scholars have identified Scythia, a region bordering the Black Sea in Southern Russia, as the probable homeland of the Amazons. That the Greeks perceived women from the East as being fiercer and more intimidating or dangerous than European women is suggested by the legend of the sorceress Medea, who helps the Greek hero Jason steal the Golden Fleece and who later kills their children in romantic revenge. Colchis, Medea's native land, is located on the Black Sea in modern Georgia, at the Eurasian borderline. Possibly related to the myth of the Golden Fleece may be the stupendous use of heavy gold in Scythian art, as recovered by archaeologists from burial mounds.

Greece was again invaded and nearly conquered by the East during the Persian Wars (492–49 B.C.), the most sustained and pivotal confrontation between East and West until the medieval Crusades. The victory of the small but determined Greek forces against the overwhelmingly larger armies of Darius and Xerxes, emperors of Persia (modern Iraq and Iran), triggered an enormous surge of pride that produced the Golden Age of Athenian culture. Aeschylus' *The Persians* (472 B.C.), the oldest play surviving from antiquity, takes place at the Persian court in Susa and consists of a series of laments for the humiliating defeat of the Persian grand armada, whose massive, three-tiered ships were crushed in the straits of Salamis and whose expert archers were helpless against the Greek hoplites with their shields and spears. A central figure is Xerxes' mother, Atossa, whose powerful speeches make her the first fully developed Middle Eastern woman character in literature. The historian Herodotus says of Atossa, the daughter of Cyrus the Great, that she suffered from a bleeding lump in her breast; the tumor (extracted by a Greek slave) is considered to be the first documented case of breast cancer in medical history. A crowned head carved of lapis lazuli in the National Museum of Iran in Tehran is sometimes identified as a portrait of Atossa.

Confined to the gynaeceum (women's quarters) of their homes, women played virtually no public role except that of priestess during the Golden Age of Periclean Athens. There was only one prominent woman, a foreigner and hetaera (courtesan)—Aspasia, the mistress of Pericles. Highly educated and articulate, she was rumored to have written Pericles' famous funeral oration during the Peloponnesian War. It is extremely significant that Aspasia came from Miletus, an old city in Ionia in western Anatolia that was mentioned by Homer and that became a center of Pre-Socratic philosophy and early science. Similarly, the lyric poet Sappho, who was hailed as the greatest of all poets throughout the thousand-year Greco-Roman era, lived and worked in a sophisticated literary culture in the city of Mytilene on the island of Lesbos off the Anatolian coast (modern Mitilini, Lesvos, northwest of Izmir). The brilliant examples of Sappho and Aspasia demonstrate that upper-class women on the Middle Eastern coast of the Aegean Sea had far more access to culture and social position than did women on the Greek mainland, even in classical Athens at its height.

The female principle was given great emphasis in the religion of ancient Anatolia, as shown in its multiple goddess cults. Cybele, whose priests castrated themselves and dressed in her robes, emerged from Phrygia (central Turkey) to importance throughout the Mediterranean basin. A black meteorite representing Cybele as Magna Mater (the Great Mother) was brought from Anatolia to Rome as a protective idol during the Second Punic War. The popularity of Cybele was paralleled by that of the Egyptian mother goddess Isis, to whom temples were built in Rome. Later depictions of Mary with the baby Jesus in her lap were directly influenced by traditional portrayals of Isis holding the baby Horus. Another major goddess of Anatolia was the so-called Artemis of Ephesus (an Ionian city visited by St. Paul that would play a pivotal role in the spread of Christianity). The immense temple of Artemis, built by the fabulously wealthy Croesus, king of Lydia, was one of the Seven Wonders of the World. This deity was probably originally a fertility goddess, as suggested in surviving sculpture by the many strange breast-like sacs hanging from her mummiform torso.

The birth and evolution of Judeo-Christian religious doctrine were heavily influenced by opposition to the pagan goddess cults of the ancient Middle East. Inanna, goddess of love and war, is invoked at the start of *Gilgamesh,* an epic from Sumer (modern southern Iraq) that predates Homer and is considered to be the oldest known story in the world: the hero-king Gilgamesh is celebrated for his construction of Inanna's temple at Uruq (modern Warka, Iraq). Inanna's dramatic combination of sex with aggression or physical force, which would be repeated in her descendants, the Akkadian Ishtar and the Phoenician Astarte, separates the Middle Eastern goddesses from the Greco-Roman pantheon, where the roles of love and war are split between Aphrodite/Venus and Athena/Minerva.

Inanna was also a patron of prostitutes, whose ambiguous but possibly official association with the great temple of Ishtar at Babylon horrified the Hebrews during their 59-year Babylonian Exile, following their deportation from Judah after its conquest by King Nebuchadnezzar in the sixth century B.C. The memory of that culture shock would last for centuries and would take lurid, nearly cinematic form in the apocalyptic vision of St. John in the Book of Revelation ending the New Testament: the ultimate challenge to the Judeo-Christian God is the Whore of Babylon, riding a monstrous seven-headed beast (representing the seven hills of pagan Rome, the new Babylon) and holding a gold cup filled with "the filthiness of her fornication" (presumably indiscriminately harvested semen). The glamorous urban exhibitionism of aristocratic Babylonian women must have seemed sinfully decadent to the sexually conservative Hebrews, pastoralist and agrarian, with their body-shrouding wool tunics, cloaks, and flowing head-gear, designed to block the desert sun and heat.

The father god of the Old Testament is a bodiless spirit who transcends the gross material world of nature, with which pagan antiquity identified omnipotent mother goddesses. Eve, seduced by a devious serpent in a garden, was probably originally a Middle Eastern nature-goddess whose emblem was the serpent. The description in the Book of Genesis of a perpetually fertile Garden of Eden may have been inspired by the lush gardens and flowering orchards created by the marvelous gigantic irrigation projects of ancient Mesopotamia. It has been suggested that a probable location of the Bible's mythic garden was between the Tigris and Euphrates rivers in northern Iraq near the Iran border. An intriguing tale in the Apocrypha of the Bible claims that Adam divorced his first wife, Lilith, because she demanded the dominant position in sexual intercourse: Lilith was the name of a Babylonian wind-demoness.

The virtuous women of the Bible, like Sarah, Ruth, and Mary, are modest and self-sacrificing, charitably elevating the needs of others. A quite different type of Middle Eastern woman from outside the Judeo-Christian system was represented by the Queen of Sheba, who enamors King Solomon when she arrives in Jerusalem with a great caravan of camels carrying gold, jewels, and spices. It is thought that the location of wealthy Sheba was modern Yemen in southwestern Arabia. Many other strong-willed Middle Eastern women appear, however briefly, in history and legend: Semiramis (Sammu-Ramat), a ninth-century B.C. Assyrian queen, said by Herodotus to have built the famous river embankments in Babylon; Turandokht, an imperious Persian princess of the seventh century B.C. whose story was transferred to China in Puccini's opera *Turandot;* the empress Theodora, wife of Justinian (sixth century A.D.) and the most powerful and politically engaged woman in the annals of the Byzantine Empire, based in Constantinople (modern Istanbul).

After the fall of the Western Roman Empire in the fifth century A.D., there was a reversion to feudalism in Europe and an ebbing of international travel and contacts. The next major era began in the seventh century, shortly after the death of the prophet Mohammed, as Muslim invaders from Arabia conquered Egypt and Palestine, including the city of Jerusalem. European attitudes toward Islam and Muslim culture in general were forged in incomprehension and hostility from the start: the medieval Crusades to reclaim the Holy Land for Christianity (1095–1291) began a pattern, often called "the clash of civilizations," that has been seen by some as still operating as recently as the invasion of Iraq by allied forces led by the United States during the Second Gulf War (2003–11). However, Islam itself has historically been expansionist by ideology and policy, spreading west through North Africa to Spain and east through the Indian subcontinent to Indonesia.

Little was known or even rumored about Muslim life until the Ottoman Turks conquered Constantinople in 1453 and overthrew the Eastern Roman Empire, with its ancient Christian creed: the great basilica of Hagia Sophia became a mosque, flanked by four tall minarets. The immense and autocratic Ottoman Empire, which would last for nearly 600 years until it was cut up into sometimes illogical ad hoc new nations by the victorious European powers after World War One, is the ultimate source of many of the lurid fantasies or misconceptions about Middle Eastern women that fill Western literature, art, and movies. Orientalism in most of its forms is a lingering bequest of the Ottoman era.

The Ottoman-Venetian wars, which began in the fifteenth century and erupted sporadically until the early eighteenth century, disseminated rumors and aroused curiosity about Turkish life and customs. In his book, *Turkish History*, which described his captivity by Turks during the 1470s, the Venetian Giovanni Maria Angiolello gave one of the first descriptions of the imperial harem at the Ottoman sultan's vast Topkapi Palace in Istanbul. A general European awareness of the ongoing Ottoman military threat is evidenced in Shakespeare's *Othello*, which begins in Venice but quickly transports its characters to the island of Cyprus, where Othello commands the Venetian forces countering an attack by the Turkish fleet. It would be a Venetian bombardment in 1687 that ignited a Turkish gunpowder arsenal on the Athenian acropolis and nearly destroyed the Parthenon.

Orientalism as we know it began to take shape in the early eighteenth century, when the first European translation of *The Thousand and One Nights*, a collection of Middle Eastern and Indian folk tales, was published by Antoine Galland in twelve volumes (1704–17), to huge success. This book, also called *Arabian Nights*, contains the tales of Aladdin, Ali Baba, and Sinbad the Sailor that have become part of world literature and popular culture. The central character, dominating and structuring the narrative frame, is a woman—Scheherazade, who postpones execution by (and then enamors) a despotic sultan through her mesmerizing power of story-telling. It has been speculated that Scheherazade may have been modeled on Al-Khayzuran bint Atta, a Yemen-born slave who married a sultan and gave birth to two Abbasid caliphs in eighth-century Persia: one was Harun al-Rashid, who turned Baghdad into a glittering capital city. The magic and mystery of the *Arabian Nights* were beautifully captured by Rimsky Korsakov's haunting tone poem, *Scheherazade* (1888), which was used as the score for the Ballets Russes production of *Scheherazade,* starring Nijinsky as the Golden Slave, in Paris in 1910.

French culture seemed particularly receptive to Middle Eastern themes, perhaps partly because of France's longtime involvement with Algeria, which had been conquered by Muslims in the eighth century A.D. In 1671, Jean Chardin, son of a wealthy Parisian merchant, published a description of the coronation of the shah of Persia, which he had witnessed on his travels through the Middle East. After further years of wide-ranging exploration, Chardin published *Travels in Persia* (1686), which was so well-received that it went through several expanded editions. Racine wrote a fact-based play, *Bajazet* (1672), about perilous machinations at the Ottoman court in Constantinople. In 1721, Montesquieu, inspired by Chardin, published an epistolary novel, *Persian Letters*, in which two Persian noblemen leave the polygamous seraglio to travel through France. Giovanni Paolo Marana's *Letters Writ by a Turkish Spy* (1734), influenced by Montesquieu's book, intrigued European readers further with tales from the Middle East. Lady Mary Wortley Montagu, wife of the British ambassador to the Ottoman sultanate, lived in Istanbul for two years (1716–18) and sent a first-hand report to friends of a hammam (Turkish bath), where groups of women bathed scandalously nude; however, like virtually all outsiders, she was unable to penetrate the imperial harem and could only relay what she had heard rumored. Nevertheless, when Lady Mary's book, *Letters from Turkey,* was published in 1763 after her death, it made a sensation throughout Europe. Mozart's opera, *Abduction from the Seraglio* (1782), partly borrowed from a prior libretto, illustrated an increasing appetite for titillating sexual innuendo about harem life under Ottoman rule.

Napoleon's 1798 expedition to Egypt was a military fiasco but a cultural triumph: the teams of scholars and cartographers whom he had brought with him collected a huge amount of information that, after its laborious processing in France, inaugurated the field of Egyptology. Among the chief French achievements was the discovery of the Rosetta Stone, leading to Champollion's decipherment of Egyptian hieroglyphics. There was a wave of Egyptomania across Europe, influencing jewelry, clothing, furniture, architecture, and tombstones.

Lord Byron was instrumental in shaping a vision of the Middle East as a realm of the exotic. His verse drama, *The Tragedy of Sardanapalus* (1821), depicted the fall of Nineveh, as the last king of the Assyrian Empire destroys his palace and treasure, along with his concubines and himself, in an apocalyptic conflagration. Delacroix's tableau painting, *The Death of Saradanapalus* (1827), inspired by Byron's poem, is a masterpiece of High Romantic theater, overflowing with sex and sadism. In his picaresque poem, *Don Juan,* Byron shows his charmingly boyish protagonist thrust into female clothing by a masterful sultana, Gulbeyaz, and then smuggled into the imperial harem for sexual mischief.

Byron joined the Greek war of independence against the Ottomans: he even had his portrait painted while wearing a luxurious flowing turban with Orientalizing Albanian dress. His death at age 36 from a fever at Missolonghi, Greece, shocked the world. Two major paintings by Delacroix were inspired by the Greek rebellion: *The Massacre at Chios* (1824), where the Turks are shown as cruel villains slaughtering women and children as well as combatants, and *Greece Expiring on the Ruins of Missolonghi* (1826), which mourns a punishing Turkish siege. (Over 20,000 civilians may have died in the atrocity on the island of Chios.) Victor Hugo's *Les Orientales* (1829), a collection of poems inspired by the Greek uprising, similarly portrays the Turks as barbarians.

The most indelible images in art of the Ottoman imperial harem were certainly created by Ingres, the primary figure of nineteenth-century neoclassicism, following Jacques-Louis David. Ingres' *Grand Odalisque* (1814) embodies the ultimate sexual fantasy about the inhabitants of the harem. A naked odalisque (meaning "woman of the *oda*," Turkish for "room") lounges with passive indolence, undoubtedly enhanced by her opium pipe, which sits to one side. She is turned half away, so that we contemplate her strangely elongated, pear-like hips and buttocks from behind, even as her sullen eyes meet ours over her languid shoulder. A piquant erotic touch is the exposure of the soles of her feet, which are as soft and pampered as a baby's: this privileged prisoner of the harem has never walked anywhere; her identity is defined by horizontals, like the opulent divans and patterned rugs from which she rarely rises.

Ingres' odalisque is so light-skinned that it is natural for us to assume that the artist has projected his own European racial preferences or assumptions into the picture. But no: the Turkish sultans did indeed favor light-skinned Circassian or Georgian concubines, slaves purchased as adolescents from the mountainous Caucasus region of Southern Russia. Ingres' opium too is authentic: both the sultans and their female flock partook heavily of pleasure-inducing opium of the highest quality (often in pill form), refined from Asia Minor's plentiful fields of white poppies. More than 40 years later, Ingres' sensual vision of the Ottoman harem remained unchanged, as he executed his other famous painting on this theme, *The Turkish Bath* (1862). Its tondo form (used for the Madonna by Michelangelo and Raphael) makes it resemble a secret peephole, as we voyeuristically peer into a packed, humid, all-female womb-world, where nudity and intimacy have lesbian overtones. It is important to stress that the hammam, which descended from the Roman baths (*thermae*) of late Byzantium and Constantinople, never had pools or tubs of water during the Muslim era: standing water was thought to be infested with evil spirits. Instead, water was poured from silver or gold bowls held aloft by attendants, who used loofah sponges to briskly rub and cleanse the bather, seated on a stool. Lady Mary Wortley Montagu, who refused to remove her stiff corset in the Istanbul hammam, found the scrubbing unpleasantly harsh.

Among other notable Orientalizing works of the nineteenth century were Flaubert's novel, *Salammbo* (1862), which depicts ancient Carthage with a Hollywood-like luridness of sex and violence, and Verdi's *Aida* (1871), which was commissioned by Ismail Pasha, the khedive (viceroy) of Egypt, for the new Cairo Opera House and which portrays ancient Egypt as a hotbed of tyranny and treachery. But in the late nineteenth century, a new persona of the Middle Eastern woman gradually emerged: replacing the passive, recumbent odalisque of the sequestered harem was the belly-dancer, hyperkinetic and spellbinding, a virtuoso performer commanding an audience and shattering Judeo-Christian sexual taboos. Interest in the novelty of belly-dancing was provoked by the appearance of real Middle Eastern women dancers at the gigantic, massively popular industrial expositions held from mid-century on in London, Paris, Philadelphia, and Chicago, where a wide range of international cultures were represented in exhibits and performances. Of three dancers called "Little Egypt," by far the most famous was Farida Mazar Spyropoulos (a Syrian married to a Greek), who performed in the "Street in Cairo" exhibit of the World's Columbian Exposition in Chicago in 1893 and who successfully toured Europe afterward.

A glamorous image of the Middle Eastern dancer as merciless femme fatale took root in late-nineteenth-century French and British culture and helped create the perverse ambiance of decadent aestheticism, which spilled over into Vienna before World War One and into Weimar Germany after it. The persona was incarnated in Salome, who was identified by the ancient Jewish historian Josephus but who remains unnamed in the Bible, where she is described in the Books of St. Mark and St. Matthew as having been instigated by her malevolent mother Herodias to demand the head of John the Baptist as a reward for dancing before her stepfather, Herod Antipas, tetrarch of Galilee. At the 1876 Salon in Paris, the Symbolist painter Gustave Moreau exhibited two parallel works that had an electrifying impact on the writers and artists who saw them: *Salome Dancing Before Herod* and a watercolor, *The Apparition,* where the seductively bejeweled dancer seems immobilized on her toes by a hallucination of John's bloody head, hanging in midair in a bursting corona. It is said that Moreau was inspired by a head and halo that he had copied from a Japanese print at the Palais de l'Industrie in Paris in 1869.

Gustave Flaubert, already working on his story, "Herodias" (the last thing that he wrote), visited the Salon and saw and admired the two Moreau art works. Before she dances, the Salome of Flaubert's "Herodias" removes her veil—a new motif in her legend. Flaubert's interest in Salome actually began during his childhood in Rouen, where the tympanum of one of three front doors of the cathedral (whose facade was repeatedly painted by Monet) contains a fascinating medieval bas-relief of Salome acrobatically dancing on her hands, as an executioner lifts his sword over the praying St. John. During his extensive travels in Egypt, Palestine, Syria, and Turkey (1849–51), Flaubert had been deeply impressed by the Middle Eastern women dancers, particularly Kuchuk Hanem (a native of Damascus performing in Egypt), with whom he evidently had an intense sexual affair.

Another French writer, Joris-Karl Huysmans, stunned by Moreau's paintings at the Salon, inserted a very long and ecstatically detailed ode to *The Apparition* in his novel *À Rebours* (1884), which would be called "the breviary of the Decadence" and which became the unnamed evil book that corrupts Oscar Wilde's Dorian Gray. In 1877, *The Apparition* was exhibited at London's Grosvenor Gallery, where Wilde surely saw it, because he published a review of the British paintings displayed in the Gallery at that time. Wilde saw the painting again at the Louvre in 1884, the same year that *À Rebours* was released. Wilde's biographer, Richard Ellmann, states that the Salome chapter of *À Rebours* had "a staggering effect" on him. The result was the play *Salome*, which Wilde wrote in French in 1891. An English translation, illustrated with stylishly erotic black-and-white Art Nouveau drawings by Aubrey Beardsley, was released in 1894. Wilde's heroine is a dreamy fantasist and aggressive fetishist whose dance of the seven veils becomes a symbol of art itself. A premiere production of *Salome* starring Sarah Bernhardt was shut down during rehearsals by London authorities in 1892 because biblical stories were prohibited onstage. Wilde never saw the play performed: the first production opened in Paris in 1896, while he was in prison.

With her fluent Middle Eastern movements and daring semi-nudity, Salome became a vehicle for the liberation of the female body from prudish Victorian inhibitions and restrictions, including the suffocating cage of the corset. Several American women leaders of the modern dance movement were attracted to Salome. Loie Fuller performed an innocent, childlike version of *Salome*, with music by Gabriel Pierné, at the Comédie Parisienne in Paris in 1895. Maud Allan, clad in a shockingly revealing pearl brassiere, opened her production of *The Vision of Salome* (based on Wilde's play) in Vienna in 1906. She did hundreds of performances and became known as "The Salome Dancer." Allan's dance of the seven veils was her dramatic climax, as it also was for Richard Strauss in his opera, *Salome*, which premiered in 1905 and has become canonical to the repertory. Strauss had seen Wilde's play in Max Reinhardt's 1902 production in Berlin and had begun concentrated composition of the opera the following year. Salome was everywhere in this period, even in the exotic dancing of Mata Hari, the Dutch adventuress who was executed as a spy in France in 1917. Theda Bara, Hollywood's first "vamp" (man-destroying vampire), starred in a sexually suggestive 1918 movie version of *Salome* (now lost) that caused a conservative backlash in the United States. In Billy Wilder's classic film noir, *Sunset Boulevard* (1950), the aging, reclusive silent-film star Norma Desmond is obsessed with Salome, about whom she is writing a voluminous script as a vehicle for her comeback. Norma literally becomes Salome—replicating her femme fatale role by murdering her lover and then, in the final seconds of the film, dancing seductively toward the camera as she puts her spell on us, the audience.

In the dynamically populist new genre of cinema, the Middle East became symbolic of an alternate reality, breaking the Western code of logic, morality, and even space and time. The use of ancient Middle Eastern legends and locales for displays of pagan sensuality was already evident in D. W. Griffith's multi-layered epic, *Intolerance* (1916), which depicts the decadence and fall of ancient Babylon, and in *Cleopatra* (1917), where Theda Bara, near-nude in a glittering metallic brassiere ingeniously coiled like a serpent, hypnotizes her male conquests with her penetrating gaze. Hollywood's super-heated projection of sex and sin into Middle Eastern antiquity, piously followed in the script by Judeo-Christian salvation and purification, was a commercial strategy to boost ticket sales while evading the punitive censorship of civil and religious authorities. This clever tactic—showing as much flesh as possible before ending with a moral message—can be seen from the era of silent films through the wide-screen Technicolor epics of the 1950s. For example, in *The Egyptian* (1954), based on a 1945 novel by the Finnish writer Mika Waltari, an idealistic doctor during the reign of Akhenaten is destroyed by a heartless, ravishingly charismatic prostitute from Babylon but attains enlightenment through the doomed pharaoh's prophetic vision of monotheism. In Cecil B. DeMille's *The Ten Commandments* (1956), renegade Hebrews reverting to idolatry stage a wild, orgiastic party around the Golden Calf, until Moses descends from Mount Sinai to hurl the stone tablets of the law at them, as the earth cracks open with hellfire.

Hollywood's other mode of representing the Middle East, as in the classic silent film, *The Thief of Bagdad* (1924), starring the athletic Douglas Fairbanks, was as a fairy-tale realm of magical wonders, where carpets fly and genies pop out of golden lamps. Even when the supernatural was de-emphasized or excluded, as in *Arabian Nights* (1942), where Scheherazade is played by Maria Montez, or in *Ali Baba and the Forty Thieves* (1944), the Middle East is represented as a fluid, opaque, and subliminally menacing zone where cruelty, torture, and slavery are the norm. Female roles are limited to kidnapped princess, harem inmate, or sorceress. In 1992, despite decades of second-wave feminism and multiculturalism, there was little variation in the traditional tropes in Walt Disney Pictures' animated musical, *Aladdin*, which was a gigantic commercial blockbuster, earning well over a half-billion dollars worldwide.

After over a century of movie-making, it is remarkable how rarely Middle Eastern women have been featured in major productions of the Western film industry. In David Lean's *Lawrence of Arabia* (1962), for example, which treats Bedouin tribal life with attention and respect, women are virtually invisible, barely glimpsed as silhouettes or heard ululating in a distant wadi as their men ride to war. In *Justine* (1969), set in the 1930s and based on novelist Laurence Durrell's *Alexandria*

Quartet, Anouk Aimée (her stage name) plays the title role of a mysterious Jewish woman who is married to an Egyptian Copt and who is secretly involved in smuggling weapons to the Zionist underground in British Palestine. Terrorism was again the theme in *Black Sunday* (1977), where the Swiss actress Marthe Keller plays a Palestinian conspirator on a suicide mission to blow up the crowded football stadium where the president of the United States is attending the Super Bowl. However, the ancient and enduring values of Middle Eastern culture, with its family loyalty, ceremonial hospitality, and religious contemplativeness, have been neglected or poorly portrayed by Hollywood. There are two exceptions in epic Bible films: Yvonne De Carlo playing Sephora, the self-possessed eldest daughter of the nomadic sheik of Midian who becomes Moses' devoted wife in *The Ten Commandments;* and Haya Harareet (an Israeli born in Haifa in British Palestine) as a Jewish slave of the House of Hur who falls in love with her master, played by Charlton Heston, in *Ben-Hur* (1959). With admirable reserve and dignity, both actresses project a quiet strength and womanly grace that seem distinctly pre-modern.

Today, as the stereotypes of Orientalism are fast receding, the women of the Middle East will no longer accept definition or representation by others. They have found their voice and will speak for themselves.

23

ON AYN RAND

Many people have noticed the very real parallels between Ayn Rand and me. A *New Yorker* profile of Rand several years ago in fact called her "the Camille Paglia of the 1960s."

Ayn Rand was the kind of bold female thinker who should immediately have been a centerpiece of women's studies programs, if the latter were genuinely about women rather than about a cliched, bleeding-heart, victim-obsessed, liberal ideology that dislikes all concrete female achievement. Like me, Rand believed in personal responsibility and self-transformation as the keys to modern woman's advance.

Rand's influence fell on the generation just before mine: in the conformist 1950s, her command to think for yourself was brilliantly energizing. When I was a college student (1964–68), I barely heard of her and didn't read her, and neither did my friends. Our influences were Marshall McLuhan, Norman O. Brown, Leslie Fiedler, Allen Ginsberg, and Andy Warhol.

When my first book finally got published in 1990, a major Rand revival was under way. I was asked about her so often at my book-signings and lectures that I researched her for the first time. To my astonishment, I found passages in her books that amazingly resemble my own writing: this is certainly due to the fact that we were simi-

[In response to a reader question ("You remind me a lot of Ayn Rand"),
"Ask Camille," Salon.com, October 28, 1998.]

larly inspired by the same writers, notably Nietzsche and the High Romantics.

The main differences between us: first, Rand is more of a rationalist, while I have a mystical 1960s bent (I'm interested in astrology, palmistry, ESP, the *I Ching*, etc.). Second, Rand disdains religious belief as childish, while I respect all religions on metaphysical grounds, even though I am an atheist. Third, Rand, like Simone de Beauvoir, is an intellectual of daunting high seriousness, while I think comedy is the sign of a balanced perspective on life. As a culture warrior, I have used humor and satire as the most devastating weapons in my arsenal!

24

THE DEATH OF HELEN GURLEY BROWN

Helen Gurley Brown was a pioneer and prophet of the sexual revolution who triumphed over the American puritans attacking her from both the Right and the Left. Inspired by Hugh Hefner's *Playboy*, which jettisoned Christian guilt to re-wed sex to the pleasure principle, Brown was determined to liberate women from the masks of simpering modesty imposed on them by the postwar cult of neo-Victorian domesticity. In doing so, she resurrected the daring verve of women of the Jazz Age who had taken up free love along with the vote.

Born in the Ozark Mountains of Arkansas and later transplanted by her impoverished, widowed mother to Los Angeles, Brown worked her way up the secretarial ladder to become a highly successful advertising copy writer. It was her self-help book, *Sex and the Single Girl*, published in 1962 when she was 40, that propelled her to fame. Selling millions of copies around the world, the book became a film starring Natalie Wood that helped break down the censorship of the Hollywood studio code.

Brown became a major player in media when she was named editor of the venerable but pallid *Cosmopolitan* magazine in 1965. She went boldly sexy with her decolleté cover girls, all shot by Francesco Scavullo as vampy tigresses reminiscent of the bikini-clad Ursula Andress fiercely emerging from the sea in *Dr. No*. These flamboy-

["Helen Gurley Brown: The geisha fought the man-haters—and won, says
Camille Paglia," News Review, *The Sunday Times* (London), August 19, 2012.
After Brown's death. This is the original text, cut down in print for space.]

ant icons represented a new kind of female sensuality for the U.S.—
aggressive, confident, and vaguely European.

But the feminist movement, which was revived with Betty Friedan's
co-founding of the National Organization for Women in 1966, targeted Helen Gurley Brown as an archenemy. Kate Millett, who led a
feminist posse invading the *Cosmo* offices in 1970 (Brown was forced
back against a radiator), accused her of "reactionary politics," above all
for her celebration of "man-hunting" and seduction. *Cosmo's* fashion-
magazine look was a major irritant: the beauty and fashion industries
were automatically condemned as oppressive to women.

Thus at the very dawn of second-wave feminism, a cultural split
had opened up between grimly fundamentalist vigilantes like Millett
and other young women (like myself) who were avid fans of popular
culture. European art films had become increasingly sexually explicit,
while fashion magazines in the era of Diana Vreeland were documenting the dynamism of Mod London, with its hip new faces of the
international youthquake.

On TV talk shows in the 1970s, the petite Brown was a frequent
charming presence, speaking self-deprecatingly of herself as a homely
"mouseburger" who had to work extra hard to advance in life. She was
a stellar model of an ambitious businesswoman and entrepreneur. No
insult flung at her by feminists rattled her or provoked a catty reply.
Brown became a heroine to me for her grit and tenacity in fighting off
her humorless critics.

In the 1970s, feminists were attacking even the exhilarating *Charlie's Angels* TV series as sexist exploitation. My dissident wing of feminism, pro-pop and pro-sex, was being crushed and silenced before it
could even get off the ground. It was not until the 1990s that, thanks
to Madonna's racy music videos, pro-sex feminism finally overthrew
the Stalinist commissars of the feminist establishment. By 1998, the
TV series *Sex and the City* debuted and swept around the world as a
generational expression of female sexual freedom, fulfilling Brown's
vision of smart, energetic, sophisticated career women.

Kate Millett, on the other hand, faded into obscurity, despite her
enshrinement on a 1970 cover of *Time* magazine. But the damage she
did remains: her book *Sexual Politics* started the still entrenched style

of trashing great male authors and artists for their hidden sexism. As a graduate student, I saw Millett in action in 1970 at a sparsely attended workshop called "Free? Women" at the Yale Law School. I found her to be a morose philistine, extrapolating her personal grievances into universal issues—exactly as was done by Gloria Steinem, with her painfully chaotic childhood. These women were already locked into a doctrinal catechism. Male-bashing had become their addictive reflex: men were responsible for all the evil of history, and women were their victims.

Helen Gurley Brown most offended feminists for her tenderness toward men. She said of her husband, "I look after him like a geisha girl." Dismissed at the time as a confession of subservience, this declaration, coming from such a powerful professional woman, actually contains its own wisdom. It says in effect that men need nurturance and that a woman's love can supply it.

Helen Gurley Brown was a great lady and a fearless bulldog. She has beaten them all!

25

LEGENDS OF DIANA

Is Diana dead or alive? I write from a galaxy far, far away, where we know Diana only as a media image, a dancing hologram. In the U.S., we never see the royals' charity openings and walkabouts, and we are spared the debate over whether the monarchy embodies high national ideals or is merely a parasitic anachronism. Similarly, we knew little of the wrangle over Diana's memorial fountain, from its commissioning to its recent unveiling as a mediocre sump of diarrheic waters and malignly algae-slick stones.

Hence for me, as surely for thousands around the world, Diana remains teasingly alive. Though seven years have passed since the terrible accident in the Alma tunnel, the sudden extinguishing of so bright a light still seems unreal, preposterous.

Americans have largely ignored the tell-all books about Diana by unchivalrous butlers, bodyguards, and companions. But the steady stream of allegations about her infatuations or dalliances has certainly dimmed her reputation. After the release of Andrew Morton's block-buster 1992 book (when I first wrote about her cultural significance), popular sentiment completely supported Diana as the abandoned wife, a pensive princess in her gilded cage.

["Legends That Keep Diana Alive: The cultural critic Camille Paglia was the first to identify Diana's iconic status back in 1992. Now, writing for the first time since the princess's death seven years ago, she defines her eternal allure," News Review, *The Sunday Times* (U.K.), August 29, 2004. Commissioned for the seventh anniversary of Diana's death.]

But as time passed, one began to wonder whether Diana could sustain romance of any kind, due to insecurities that she herself traced to an unsettled childhood. It was hard to imagine how that merry prankster and mistress of worthy causes could be subject to such punishing mood-swings. The round-the-clock communications and solicitude evidently required for her maintenance demanded a heroism if not masochism in her patient allies.

I am reminded of what the critic Thomas Wentworth Higginson wrote to his wife of his first meeting in 1870 with the reclusive Emily Dickinson: "I never was with any one who drained my nerve power so much. Without touching her, she drew from me. I am glad not to live near her." Lucky man to have lived before the era of late-night nuisance phone calls.

Diana had a burning but erratic energy like that of the great Hollywood stars, who gave deeply but fed off their fans. The greatly gifted are sometimes vampiric. But Diana will always remain a sympathetic figure because of the extraordinary circumstances that cruelly thrust her into a global spotlight with only the most rudimentary preparation or support. Like a heliotropic plant, she turned toward warmth and light, which unfortunately were the blinding flashes of cameras.

"Atavistic religious emotions," which I once described in the modern cult of celebrity typified by Diana, certainly erupted after her death. Intermingled with labyrinthine conspiracy theories have been apocalyptic New Age fantasies spread by the Web. Visions of Diana were reported from Kosovo to Althorp. A statue of Diana in the robes of the Virgin Mary was exhibited in Liverpool. A paparazzo was immolated in a grisly suicide. The Alma bridge, it was claimed, was built at a site of pagan sacrifice and ritual combat for the Merovingian kings. The tunnel replicated an ancient underground chamber, and it all tied up with the Holy Grail. Through a bizarre "Lourdes effect," pilgrims have been dipping holy water from Diana's polluted fountain in Hyde Park.

Diana will have eternal life through her resurrection in the innumerable documentaries that are on regular rotation on U.S. television and elsewhere. Their roster of dazzling images is annually expanded by increments, as happened with bardic lays after the fall of Troy. What these programs indisputably show is that the photogenic Diana made an immense contribution to world visual culture, in my view exceeding the work of painters and sculptors as well as most filmmakers in the same period.

Diana's ability to command the moment, to make dramatic use of a sliver of time, was close to genius. She used minimal exposure to maximum effect. Working within the constraints of royal ceremony, she combined an impetuous, coltish physicality with high glamour and a flirtatious, seductive allure. Her early taste in clothing, all Sloane set ruffles and tweeds, was conventional. But during the 1980s, she discovered fashion as it discovered her. Her metamorphosis from plump, shy Di to a confident, chic woman of the world was a coming-of-age drama, like a *Bildungsroman*.

My all-time favorite of Diana's charismatic fashion epiphanies occurred at the Serpentine Gallery on the night in 1994 when Charles was confessing infidelity on TV. Clad in a svelte, off-the-shoulders, pleated black chiffon cocktail dress with a floating side panel, Diana fairly leapt from her car with mischievous ebullience and majestically bore down, with mannishly outthrust arm, on Lord Palumbo in the receiving line. To compensate for their quite different heights, the charging princess in her black stockings and stiletto heels made a deft diagonal dip, then a dynamic swoop into full-frontal camera range. It was a classic scene in twentieth-century performance, whose only equal is in film. I think, for example, of Bette Davis (also in a daringly shoulder-baring evening dress) whirling on the stairs at the cocktail party in *All About Eve* to say with a dark smile, "Fasten your seat belts—it's going to be a bumpy night!"

My least favorite of Diana's fashion sallies was her crisply athletic diving shows off the Al Fayed yacht in the final weeks of her life. Perhaps her sleek, animal-skin pattern bathing suits were a homage to her friend Gianni Versace, who had recently been murdered in Miami. But so gaudy (and borderline Eurotrash) a style made her look like a pampered odalisque rather than the mother of the future king. If she meant to upstage Camilla Parker-Bowles (then celebrating her 50th birthday at Highgrove House), there was something forced and excessive in her gestures of freedom and defiance. Vacationing aimlessly in the Mediterranean, she was an uprooted English rose. Her unseemly end, in flight from the Ritz after botched dinner plans, parallels the one suffered by the possessed ballerina (played by Moira Shearer) in *The Red Shoes*—dancing to her death off a parapet onto the railroad tracks at Monte Carlo.

Many things about Diana's career were movie-like. Her fairy-tale wedding, for example, has become a rear-view *Rashomon*. She felt like "a lamb to the slaughter," she later confessed. Now when clips of the wedding are replayed, we too see a horror show of doubt and fear, with shadowy rivals skulking in the pews. Whenever I watch Diana's story unfold on TV, I irrationally pray, as when watching *Gone with the Wind*, for a happy ending.

On occasion, I have felt something ghostly or preternatural about Diana and her memory. At a historical costume exhibit at the Philadelphia Museum of Art two months after her death, I joined the throngs gazing with uneasy admiration at a strapless white crepe-silk sheath that had belonged to Diana and been auctioned at Christie's that June. Hung on a stark frame, it was a mold of her long, lithe body. The installation was strangely isolated and elevated, like a gallows. Also on view, from the museum's permanent collection, was the wedding dress worn by Princess Grace of Monaco, a Philadelphia native and another blonde victim of a mysterious car crash far from her homeland.

Two summers ago, on a laborious trek to Frank Lloyd Wright's landmark Fallingwater in the mountains near Pittsburgh, I took a side trip to nearby Kentuck Knob, another private house designed by Wright on a heavily wooded hill. To my astonishment, it was now owned and occupied by Lord Palumbo. As my tour group stared at the souvenir photos of Diana with Palumbo, our guide said, "We never see him. We only smell the trail of his cigar smoke." I shivered. It was as if Palumbo had become the fugitive priest of the goddess Diana in her sacred grove at Nemi in the Alban Hills.

A final tale: In 1999, I made a first holiday visit to the British Virgin Islands. After a sensational sunset dinner of conch salad at a beachside restaurant on a far corner of Tortola, my party gradually became aware of the lyrics being pumped out by a steel-drum band on the patio. "Diana came to the BVI," they sang (referring to her two visits with her sons to Necker Island). But the refrain, repeated over and over in an incongruously jolly manner, was: "Her mother gave her a bloody foot."

There can be no better evidence of how Diana has been absorbed into world myth. The "bloody foot" is a severed chicken claw, used to cast a hex in voodoo. The islanders' song shockingly conflated the Queen with the jealous stepmothers and wicked queens of fairy tales. It was as if Diana, like Snow White, were merely asleep, drugged by a poisoned apple. The crushed Mercedes was the glass coffin in which the wounded Diana was on tragic display. It symbolized her life of total visibility, which she both courted and loathed.

What is her legacy? New generations will never experience the wrenching highs and lows of Diana's public life as her contemporaries did. Her saga will become archaeological, like the love stories of Victoria and Albert or Edward VII and Wallis Simpson. In the long term, Diana's legacy will be embodied in her sons, who must redeem their mother while honoring their father. But for now, what Diana left is the stateless system of paparazzi, which she did not invent but ratcheted up to dizzily lucrative heights. These jet-borne entrepreneurs plying their ruthless trade have become our canonical image-makers. But since there are no celebrities left of Diana's stature, we are mesmerized by a vacuum.

26

DECONSTRUCTING THE DEMISE
OF MARTHA STEWART

INGRID SISCHY: Camille, can you bake?

CAMILLE PAGLIA: *[laughs]* I don't bake, no. My specialty is large hunks of highly spiced meat. I'm good at making great pots of things like pot roasts and stews—like medieval banquet dishes for Viking warriors—but that's as far as I go. I belong to that '60s generation that revolted against Betty Crocker. To me, Betty Crocker was a vicious oppressor, so baking isn't part of my repertoire. I do admire Martha Stewart, however, for having updated the image of mistress of the household. She had a profound impact on American taste and design from the moment her books appeared in the 1980s. She kind of infiltrated the culture under the radar.

IS: When did you first become aware of Stewart?

CP: I was attending a cousin's wedding in upstate New York in the mid-'80s. It was theatrically staged at a remote country inn, and at the reception there were tables heaped with all sorts of produce—cabbage, chard, rutabagas, and so on. I remember saying, "What are all these *groceries* doing here?" [*Sischy laughs*] I had no idea that this was a Martha Stewart concept—natural

[Paglia in conversation with editor-in-chief Ingrid Sischy,
"Did the Homemaker Heroine Cook Her Own Goose?," *Interview*, June 2004.]

accents for bucolic country weddings. Her power of imagination and her ability to stimulate imagination in others—not the upper-middle-class elite but the middle and working class— was extraordinary. These were women who wanted to make their homes and family events occasions for beauty and pleasure. As an Italian-American, I had an immediate vibe with Martha Stewart. Despite her embrace of the tony WASP style and her early erasure of her family's immigrant past, I felt she had a kind of cultivated Mediterranean sensibility that was sorely needed in the U.S.

IS: The whole other argument says women felt inadequate because the image Martha Stewart was projecting was of "the perfect woman"—who has a great job and family, who is successful at work and yet still gets the perfect light-blue frosting on the cupcake. That made many women who could not get the damned frosting right or who didn't want to bake or cook feel inadequate. To them Stewart was the opposite of empowering: she was taking women backwards.

CP: But it was lower-middle-class women who created the Martha Stewart cult. Martha came to general attention after her 1994 appearance on *Oprah*, where the audience was jammed with her fans and their baffled husbands and where she inspired a rock-star hysteria. The resentment you're speaking of came from ambitious upper-middle-class women of my generation who had rejected the things that Stewart was espousing and who had pursued careers. For decades after Betty Friedan's 1963 book, *The Feminine Mystique*, feminism had disparaged and diminished the lives of women who wanted to be "merely" homemakers. Martha Stewart allowed these women to view the creation of an environment as an art form. Later the whole project became maniacal—she got lost in her fictive world like the Wizard of Oz.

IS: Compare Martha Stewart to Julia Child, the popular chef whose style was so loose and empathetic. I always loved how Child dropped a turkey on TV, wiped it off, took a sip of a drink, and just kept going.

CP: Well, Julia Child is Martha Stewart's primary precursor and a monumental figure in American culture. But Child actually came from the classy, privileged background that Martha, the daughter of Polish immigrants, aspired to. It's very ironic that Martha turned into "Miss Perfect," a brittle hallucination of what she thought the genteel lifestyle was, when Julia Child has the cordial, relaxed manner of the true elite—those to whom wealth and position came naturally. Child has the hearty, horsey, up-and-at-'em style of the old Seven Sisters colleges. It descends from the British upper class and their country manors, where there would be holes in the leather furniture and the little old man trotting around with a trowel and dirty gaiters turned out to be the duke. There's a lack of pretension. I think Martha made a pivotal error when she transplanted her primary residence to the Hamptons. That's when she lost her bearings. She had re-created the nature-centered British country house at her Connecticut home on Turkey Hill. But the Hamptons are all about status and wealth. She wanted to be a celebrity player. The Martha of the '90s began to be seen as a snobbish socialite who hobnobbed with Hillary Clinton. But that wasn't the Martha who originally attracted her mass audience—a group that has never lost its loyalty to her.

IS: Many people saw a smugness in Stewart emerging with the legal troubles caused by the sale of her IM Clone shares. Before her trial, which wrapped in March, she seemed to project the attitude that she was above the law. Some of those who are still loyal to her feel that she's been given a rough rap, perhaps due to a spirit of anti-feminism. In fact, some feminists claim that the case against Stewart is a feminist issue, that if a powerful man had been accused of this relatively minor crime, it never would have received the attention it has.

CP: I reject that reasoning. If you're going to define yourself as a public personality, then you should know—like Madonna or Jennifer Lopez—that you're going to take your lumps when you make a misstep. Martha Stewart marketed herself as an icon in ways that none of those TYCO or Enron execs did. She intruded herself and her vision into people's homes. Her image was part of her product. She entered into people's psychology and dream lives and manipulated them—hence the weird reaction. People are disillusioned.

IS: It's fascinating how the spectacle of Stewart's rise and fall, and possible rise again, seems to have caught the whole country's imagination.

CP: Yes. I loved that *Saturday Night Live* sketch the day after Martha's conviction. There was a riot by white middle-class suburban women screaming and rushing back and forth with garden hoes and spades and breaking windows. [*Sischy laughs*] It was hysterical, because usually when a jury votes to convict, it's the inner city that explodes.

IS: And now after the fall? What happens when a perfect figure like Stewart is exposed as flawed?

CP: The hospitable smile now seems false. My own view of Martha Stewart as a morally responsible human being has certainly altered. But her body of work remains unchanged. It's the same thing with a lot of great movie stars or artists—when they're revealed as demanding, infantile egomaniacs, some people are turned off. I detest that debunking style of biography—Elvis Presley lolled in bed and ate hamburgers; Picasso mistreated his girlfriends. It's a very reductive, vulgar way of treating major cultural figures. Nice, giving people are rarely stars. Great stars are monsters! [*Sischy laughs*] I recently saw Martha Stewart's first book, *Entertaining* [1980], at a friend's house, and it's still amazing—a gorgeous feast for the senses. Her books have staying power.

IS: It was hard to look away during the weeks of the trial. Initially, I found myself wondering why someone with all those image consultants would insist on carrying such an expensive Birkin bag from Hermès to the trial. Obviously, she wasn't going to stop wearing the things she loved or had worked for. It was her own way of holding herself together and keeping her dignity.

CP: When the scandal first broke, I was amazed at Martha's inability to handle it. I had always thought that she was a publicity genius, but no. The way she stonewalled the host during her cooking segment on the CBS morning show became an instant joke. Instead of just graciously saying, "This is a very distressing matter that I can't talk about but hope will be resolved quickly," Martha kept chopping her cabbage and dismissed the whole issue as "ridiculousness." That's when I lost confidence in her. She was an officer of the Stock Exchange and a former stockbroker! Her casualness about professional ethics was shocking. Then I was amazed by her inability to speak directly to the public, to take her fans into her confidence. She's so over-controlled she couldn't improvise. If she had just approached the problem in an honest, regretful manner and not tried to steamroll the feds, things might have turned out differently.

IS: It's all rooted in the problem of the idea of perfection. We know perfection is unattainable, but her whole empire was based on it. This is a drama about being human and admitting mistakes.

CP: Yes, you're right. She had a dream of perfection, as if she had a godlike power to remake human life into an Arcadian fantasy. Everything she touched turned to gold. By the time she became a billionaire, she had delusions of grandeur. It's a classic case of hubris.

IS: The first time I heard the word "hubris" was in history class about the Greeks. It concerned Clytemnestra in *Agamemnon,* and the lesson was: fight evil, don't become the source of it. What else does Martha's tale teach us?

CP: It shows us where women are in society today. Throughout history it's been mostly men—Achilles, Oedipus Rex—who've had the position or power to be guilty of hubris. It's rare that women have risen high enough to make hubris possible. And rarer still have been women achievers in finance. Martha Stewart is a pioneer, a captain of industry like the swashbuckling entrepreneurs of the Gilded Age. She's a worthy successor to

Henry Ford and John D. Rockefeller. Hence my sorrow at her self-induced fall. There's a grandeur to this story—finally women have advanced far enough to be as guilty of hubris as men.

IS: Is it your gut feeling that Martha Stewart, like others who have faced public shaming, will have a whole other chapter in her stardom after she completes her sentence?

CP: If Martha genuinely repents or even convincingly mimes repentance, she'll have another act. But something has stunted her power of self-analysis. She's as hunkered down in her private world as the brooding press lord in *Citizen Kane*.

IS: So, Camille, my last question: with Martha Stewart "going away," how about you going on the tube in her place?

CP: [*Paglia laughs*] Listen, I've already appeared on the TV Food Network!

IS: Chopping or deconstructing?

CP: In 1995, Bill Boggs took me to Papaya King on upper Broadway to sample the hot dogs. They filmed me ordering the dogs and passing judgment. I also did a segment in the studio where I sautéed clams with garlic.

IS: I hear an empire calling. Just make sure your finances are in order, alright? [*Both laugh*]

CP: Okay, Ingrid!

27

FEMINISM AND TRANSGENDERISM

JONATHAN V. LAST: I keep waiting for the showdown between feminism and transgenderism, but it always keeps slipping beneath the horizon. I've been looking at how the La Leche League—which stood at the crossroads of feminism once upon a time—has in the last couple years bowed completely to the transgender project. Their central text is (for now) *The Womanly Art of Breastfeeding*, but they've officially changed their stance to include men and fathers who breastfeed. The actual wording of their policy is wonderful: "It is now recognized that some men are able to breastfeed." Left unsaid, one supposes, is the corollary that some women are biologically unable to breastfeed. Though this would go against the League's founding principles, one supposes. What does one make of all of this?

CAMILLE PAGLIA: Feminists have clashed with transgender activists much more publicly in the U.K. than here. For example, there was an acrimonious organized campaign, including a petition with 3,000 claimed signatures, to cancel a lecture by Germaine Greer two years ago at Cardiff University because of her "offensive" views of transgenderism. Greer, a literary scholar who was one of the great pioneers of second-wave feminism, has

[Jonathan V. Last, interview, "Camille Paglia: On Trump, Democrats, Transgenderism, and Islamist Terror," interview with Jonathan V. Last, *The Weekly Standard*, www.weeklystandard.com, June 15, 2017.]

always denied that men who have undergone sex-reassignment surgery are actually "women." Her Cardiff lecture (on "Women and Power" in the twentieth century) did eventually go forward, under heavy security.

In 2014, *Gender Hurts,* a book by radical Australian feminist Sheila Jeffreys, created heated controversy in the U.K. Jeffreys identifies transsexualism with misogyny and describes it as a form of "mutilation." She and her feminist allies encountered prolonged difficulties in securing a London speaking venue because of threats and agitation by transgender activists. Finally, Conway Hall was made available: Jeffrey's forceful, detailed lecture there in July of last year is fully available on YouTube. She argues, among other things, that the pharmaceutical industry, having lost income when routine estrogen therapy for menopausal women was abandoned because of its health risks, has been promoting the relatively new idea of transgenderism in order to create a permanent class of customers who will need to take prescribed hormones for life.

Although I describe myself as transgender (I was donning flamboyant male costumes from early childhood on), I am highly skeptical about the current transgender wave, which I think has been produced by far more complicated psychological and sociological factors than current gender discourse allows. Furthermore, I condemn the escalating prescription of puberty blockers (whose long-term effects are unknown) for children, which I regard as a criminal violation of human rights.

It is certainly ironic how liberals who posture as defenders of science when it comes to global warming (a sentimental myth unsupported by evidence) flee all reference to biology when it comes to gender. Biology has been programmatically excluded from women's studies and gender studies programs for almost 50 years now. Thus very few current gender studies professors and theorists, here and abroad, are intellectually or scientifically prepared to teach their subjects.

The cold biological truth is that sex changes are impossible. Every single cell of the human body (except for blood) remains coded with one's birth gender for life. Intersex ambiguities can occur, but they are developmental anomalies that represent a tiny proportion of all human births.

In a democracy, everyone, no matter how nonconformist or eccentric, should be free from harassment or abuse. But at the same time, no one deserves special rights, protections, or privileges on the basis of that eccentricity. The categories "trans-man" and "trans-woman" are highly accurate and deserving of respect. But like Germaine Greer and Sheila Jeffreys, I reject state-sponsored coercion to call someone a woman or a man simply on the basis of his or her subjective feeling about it. We may well take the path of good will and defer to courtesy on such occasions, but it is our choice alone.

As for the La Leche League, they are hardly prepared to take up the cudgels in the bruising culture wars. Awash with the milk of human kindness, they are probably stuck in nurturance mode. Naturally, they snap to attention at the sound of squalling babies, no matter what their age. It's up to literature professors and writers to defend the integrity of English, which like all languages changes slowly and organically over time. But with so many humanities departments swallowed up in the post-structuralist tar pit, the glorious medium of English may have to fight the gender commissars on its own.

28

MOVIES, ART, AND SEX WAR

It's open sex war—a grisly death match that neither men nor women will win.

Ever since *The New York Times* opened the floodgates last October with its report about producer Harvey Weinstein's atrocious history of sexual harassment, there has been a torrent of accusations, ranging from the trivial to the criminal, against powerful men in all walks of life.

But no profession has been more shockingly exposed and damaged than the entertainment industry, which has posed for so long as a bastion of enlightened liberalism. Despite years of pious lip service to feminism at award shows, the fabled "casting couch" of studio-era Hollywood clearly remains stubbornly in place.

The big question is whether the present wave of revelations, often consisting of unsubstantiated allegations from decades ago, will aid women's ambitions in the long run or whether it is already creating further problems by reviving ancient stereotypes of women as hysterical, volatile, and vindictive.

My philosophy of equity feminism demands removal of all barriers to women's advancement in the political and professional realms. However, I oppose special protections for women in the workplace. Treating women as more vulnerable, virtuous, or credible than men is reactionary, regressive, and ultimately counterproductive.

["Camille Paglia on Movies, #MeToo and Modern Sexuality: 'Endless, Bitter Rancor Lies Ahead'" *The Hollywood Reporter,* February 27, 2018.]

Complaints to the human resources department after the fact are no substitute for women themselves drawing the line against offensive behavior—on the spot and in the moment. Working-class women are often so dependent on their jobs that they cannot fight back, but there is no excuse for well-educated, middle-class women to elevate career advantage or fear of social embarrassment over their own dignity and self-respect as human beings. Speak up now, or shut up later! Modern democracy is predicated on principles of due process and the presumption of innocence.

The performing arts may be inherently susceptible to sexual tensions and trespasses. During the months of preparation for stage or movie productions, day and night blur, as individuals must melt into an ensemble, a foster family that will disperse as quickly as it cohered. Like athletes, performers are body-focused, keyed to fine-tuning of muscle reflexes and sensory awareness. But unlike athletes, performers must explore and channel emotions of explosive intensity. To impose rigid sex codes devised for the genteel bourgeois office on the dynamic performing arts will inevitably limit rapport, spontaneity, improvisation, and perhaps creativity itself.

Similarly, ethical values and guidelines that should structure the social realm of business and politics do not automatically transfer to art, which occupies the contemplative realm shared by philosophy and religion. Great art has often been made by bad people. So what? Expecting the artist to be a good person was a sentimental canard of Victorian moralism, rejected by the "art for art's sake" movement led by Charles Baudelaire and Oscar Wilde. Indeed, as I demonstrated in my first book, *Sexual Personae*, the impulse or compulsion toward art making is often grounded in ruthless aggression and combat—which is partly why there have been so few great women artists.

Take director Roman Polanski, for example, whose private life has evidently been squalid and contemptible. The Academy of Motion Picture Arts and Sciences, founded as a guardian of industry reputation in 1927, would be perfectly justified in expelling him. But no sin or crime by Polanski the man will ever reduce the towering achievement of Polanski the artist, from his starkly low-budget *Knife in the*

Water (the first foreign film I saw in college) through masterworks like *Repulsion, Rosemary's Baby,* and *Chinatown.*

The case of Woody Allen, who began his career as a comedy writer and stand-up comedian, is quite different. Polanski's chilly world-view descends from European avant-garde movements like Surrealism and existentialism. In a sinister cameo in *Chinatown,* Polanski sliced open Jack Nicholson's nose with a switchblade knife. Allen, however, in his onscreen persona of lovable nebbish, seductively ingratiated himself with audiences. Hence the current wave of disillusion with Allen and his many fine films emanates from a sense of deception and betrayal, including among some actors who once felt honored to work with him.

It was overwhelmingly men who created the machines and ultra-efficient systems of the industrial revolution, which in turn emancipated women. For the first time in history, women have gained economic independence and no longer must depend on fathers or husbands for survival. But many women seem surprised and unnerved by the competitive, pitiless forces that drive the modern professions, which were shaped by entrepreneurial male bonding. It remains to be seen whether those deep patterns of mutually bruising male teamwork, which may date from the Stone Age, can be altered to accommodate female sensitivities without reducing productivity and progress.

Women's discontent and confusion are being worsened by the postmodernist rhetoric of academe, which asserts that gender is a social construct and that biological sex differences don't exist or don't matter. Speaking from my lifelong transgender perspective, I find such claims absurd. That most men and women on the planet experience and process sexuality differently, in both mind and body, is blatantly obvious to any sensible person.

The modern sexual revolution began in the Jazz Age of the 1920s, when African-American dance liberated the body and when scandalous Hollywood movies glorified illicit romance. For all its idealistic good intentions, today's #MeToo movement, with its indiscriminate catalog of victims, is taking us back to the Victorian archetypes of early silent film, where mustache-twirling villains tied damsels in distress to railroad tracks.

A Catholic backlash to Norma Shearer's free love frolics and Mae West's wicked double entendres finally forced strict compliance with the infamous studio production code in 1934. But ironically, those censorious rules launched Hollywood's supreme era, when sex had to be conveyed by suggestion and innuendo, swept by thrilling surges of romantic music.

The witty, stylish, emancipated women of 1930s and '40s movies liked and admired men and did not denigrate them. Carole Lombard, Myrna Loy, Lena Horne, Rosalind Russell, and Ingrid Bergman had it all together onscreen in ways that make today's sermonizing women stars seem taut and strident. In the 1950s and '60s, austere European art films attained a stunning sexual sophistication via magnetic stars like Jeanne Moreau, Delphine Seyrig, and Catherine Deneuve.

The movies have always shown how elemental passions boil beneath the thin veneer of civilization. By their power of intimate close-up, movies reveal the subtleties of facial expression and the ambiguities of mood and motivation that inform the alluring rituals of sexual attraction.

But movies are receding. Many young people, locked to their miniaturized cellphones, no longer value patient scrutiny of a colossal projected image. Furthermore, as texting has become the default discourse for an entire generation, the ability to read real-life facial expressions and body language is alarmingly atrophying.

Endless sexual miscommunication and bitter rancor lie ahead. But thanks to the miracle of technology, most of the great movies of Hollywood history are now easily accessible—a collective epic of complex emotion that once magnificently captured the magic and mystique of sex.

LITERATURE

29

THE UNBRIDLED LUST FOR BLURBS

Two pressing ethical issues need to be addressed by the publishing industry. First is the solicitation of advance blurbs for new books, a corrupt practice that chiefly afflicts the United States and that has grown wildly out of control over the past twenty years. This, in turn, has led to extravagant over-reliance on sending out costly unsolicited manuscripts.

Pre-publication endorsements have long outlived their usefulness. No informed person takes them seriously because of their tainted history of shameless cronyism and grotesque hyperbole. A string of breathless blurbs on a book is ultimately counterproductive, since it betrays the publisher's lack of confidence in the project, as well as the tin ear and general ineptitude of the publicity department. And the luminaries who turn out inflated blurb after blurb are hacks who give prostitution a bad name.

As an unknown and unpublished writer with a long, quirky manuscript, I had little power to influence the elegant production of my first book, *Sexual Personae,* released by Yale Press in 1990. I did make my feelings known about the loathsomeness of advance blurbs, but I don't know whether that affected the press's decision to use just a single dust-jacket endorsement—from my dissertation director, Harold Bloom. What I find objectionable is log-rolling and influence-peddling among a network of cronies whose personal associations aren't honestly revealed in blurb or text. In the case of *Sexual Personae,* the very

["My Say," guest editorial, *Publishers Weekly,* June 3, 1996.]

first words of the acknowledgments page explicitly cite Bloom for his support through two decades of career disasters.

Thanks to the success of *Sexual Personae,* I am now able to demand that my book contracts contain a clause forbidding the use of advance blurbs. I appeal to other authors and their agents to do likewise. Advance blurbing is legitimate, in my opinion, when the endorser is paying homage to some longstanding artistic or intellectual influence. Publishers' use of excerpts from book reviews in the public domain for ads and paperback editions is, of course, both desirable and proper.

The unbridled lust for provocative advance blurbs has led to a second horror—the dunning of potential endorsers with an avalanche of promotional mailings. Since my relatively recent arrival on the scene, I have become all too aware of the maniacal internal engines of American publishing. Because my work touches on so many subjects, I have had to fight back mountains of sometimes tediously inappropriate material, which has overwhelmed the limited facilities of my small university and generally made life hell.

A recent exasperating incident was the last straw. After a harried morning of teaching, I stopped by my office to find a gigantic package from a major New York publisher enthroned on my chair, an unsolicited manuscript so massive that it had pierced the packaging, scattering its ashy innards all over the rug. Furious, I immediately called the editor and vice president who had sent it and denounced him for his intrusion into my professional life, as well as for his thoughtless exploitation of staff, his and mine, who must do all the actual copying, packing, and transportation of these monstrous parcels, dispatched at the whim of an impractical literary elite.

Slamming the phone down, I then called the company president and left a heated message condemning this folly and extravagance. In a period of economic constraints, unsolicited manuscripts are a criminal waste of publishers' assets, which should be diverted instead into authors' royalties and appallingly low staff salaries. A letter of inquiry containing a return reply postcard can cheaply determine whether someone wants to review a manuscript or not. Unsolicited manuscripts kill trees, choke the mails, infuriate recipients, and swell landfills.

Smart, shrewd publicity does not rely on phony or extorted blurbs. I am fortunate to have had three bestselling books produced by a brilliant collaborative team at Vintage Books. When there is a shrinking audience for serious books, it is vital for publishers to attract, develop, and support a cultivated and sophisticated staff. Too many publishers lurch between sloth and frenzy in their quest for the big, splashy bestseller. But there is no substitute for taste, imagination, scruples, and good old-fashioned common sense.

30

TEACHING SHAKESPEARE TO ACTORS

Who wrote Shakespeare's plays? An actor. No aristocrat, such as Sir Francis Bacon or the earl of Oxford, could have produced these nearly forty plays, which show such intimate knowledge of the demands and dynamics of ensemble performance. When Shakespeare was active in London, theater was borderline disreputable, denounced from the pulpit by Puritan preachers. Because of issues of public hygiene and crowd control, municipal authorities eventually forced the theaters outside the city limits—to the South Bank of the Thames, where Shakespeare's company built the Globe Theatre. While aristocrats attended plays and even sponsored theater companies, they could never have inhabited and learned from that brash underworld, from its cramped, ramshackle back-stages to the volatile streets and seedy inns and taverns. Shakespeare was a popular entertainer who knew how to work a crowd. His daring shifts in tone, juxtaposing comedy with tragedy; his deft weaving of a main plot with multiple subplots; his restless oscillation from talk to action to song and dance: this fast pace and variety-show format were the tricks of a veteran actor adept at seizing the attention of the chattering groundlings who milled around the jutting stage of open-air theaters.

My approach to teaching Shakespeare departs from the norm because most of my four decades as a classroom teacher have been spent at art schools—first Bennington College and then the Philadel-

[From *Living with Shakespeare: Essays by Writers, Actors, and Directors*, ed. Susannah Carson (2013).]

phia College of Performing Arts, which became the University of the Arts after a merger with its neighbor, the Philadelphia College of Art. Many of my students have been theater majors, some already with a professional resumé. In the United States, Shakespeare is usually taught as a reading experience, but my Shakespeare course is closer to a practicum, even though students neither recite nor perform in it. I approach the plays from a production angle, with stress on the range of interpretive choices available to an actor in each speech or scene. More academically structured universities have often offered Shakespeare as a large lecture course breaking out into weekly seminars led by graduate students. Students would be generally expected to read a play a week, thus sampling a third of the Shakespeare canon over one semester. That forced-march syllabus may be useful for English majors, but it does not work for actors, who must engage with the text on a far more concrete level. In guiding actors through Shakespeare, the teacher operates like an auto mechanic, taking an engine apart and showing how it goes back together again. Each internal function and connection must be grasped tangibly, as a sensory datum and not just a mental construct. Thus five Shakespeare plays have proved to be more than enough in my course, and it is still a struggle to cover them adequately. My goal is to give the actors a portable system for engaging with any of the plays, should they have the good fortune to encounter them in their careers. After two opening lecture classes, where I survey the transition from the Middle Ages to the Renaissance in art, science, economics, and politics, I turn to sequential line-by-line analysis of the plays, which occupies the rest of the semester.

Though they may have read one or several Shakespeare plays in high school, most young American actors basically come to Shakespeare cold. He is an import, trailing arty clouds of glory. In Great Britain, in contrast, Shakespeare represents history and tradition, stretching a thousand years back to early medieval kings and warriors. Many of his characters, from Lear and Macbeth to Richard II and Henry V, step straight out of royal annals, though Shakespeare enlarged, invented, and re-imagined at will. Despite ominous slippage these days through competition from mass media and video games, most British audiences know Shakespeare's plays well, having seen and performed in them at school and town events since childhood. Sophisticated theatergoers in Britain are finely attuned to every innovation, even the fleeting shading of a syllable. In the United States, no Shakespeare production, even on a college campus, can assume that more than a fraction of the audience is thoroughly familiar with the play or understands most of the dialogue. Hence the American actor has an immense responsibility for communication to the audience—a task hampered by the possibility that he or she may never have seen a live performance of Shakespeare. There are three major areas that deserve special attention from actors studying Shakespeare: language, action, and politics.

LANGUAGE

Confronted with students of widely varied academic backgrounds, a teacher must break through the sometimes paralyzing reverence that surrounds Shakespeare in the United States. His often archaic vocabulary, encrusted with editorial footnotes, can be intimidating, especially to young actors working out dialogue. Thus one must stress that Shakespeare was writing at the dawn of modern English, when the language was still in flux. He was making up words and usages as he went along, so successfully that many of them ended up in dictionaries, when those were first codified in the eighteenth century. What this suggests is that much of Shakespeare's audience too may have had only a dim idea of what was happening onstage. His actors conveyed thought and emotion through tone, rhythm, and gesture. It was a period that valued virtuoso shows of verbal facility for their own sake; characters in Shakespeare are sometimes seized by torrents of words so urgent and turbulent that the speaker seems possessed. Furthermore, Shakespeare often engineers lively and at times comic effects by bouncing plain, blunt Anglo-Saxon monosyllables off the fancy polysyllabic vocabulary, derived from Greek and Latin, that had been brought to Britain by the Norman conquest.

Some American directors, as reported by my students, make the actors annotate Shakespeare's blank verse, so that they know they are playing poetry. I am highly skeptical and even disapproving of this practice, except for actors who already have prior training in poetry or Latin, where meter is parsed. It may be profitable in England, where poetry has streamed in an unbroken line since Chaucer, but I fail to see how concern about the blank verse can do anything but disorient and unnerve American actors. The power of language in Shakespeare's plays resides more in variation than in regularity. There is a robust physicality and even muscularity in his speeches, which can be as jagged and syncopated as jazz. Indeed, I recommend that actors playing Shakespeare should look to music for inspiration. Some of Shakespeare's voices are lilting, melodious, or flutelike; others are relentlessly hammering and percussive; still others are rough, insolent, and zigzagging, like a bebop saxophone. To avoid monotonously "reciting" lines, the actor could borrow musical techniques such as dynamics (soft/loud) or modulations in tempo, including overt hesitations—following the way people in real life pause and grope for words. The actor must appear to be *thinking,* an impression aided by lively eye movements.

Where sensitivity to poetry is required, however, is for Shakespeare's all-pervasive imagery. As literary critics noted long ago, each Shakespeare play can be regarded as an extended poem with its own set of emblematic images, whose recurrence produces a chiming effect that works subliminally on the audience. Examples are the four elements of earth, air, water, and fire in *Antony and Cleopatra;* the master metaphor of the "garden" in *Hamlet,* with its attendant adjectives like "green" and "rank" (meaning rotten or malodorous); and the chillingly ubiquitous "nothing" in *King Lear*—a blank zero prefiguring the wasteland of modernist alienation. The production dramaturge should assist the actors in rehearsal in identifying these key words, which are sometimes the emotional or conceptual heart of a speech. They are always universals that transcend time and place. Although postmodernists myopically deny that universals exist, these basic terms of human experience animate all great art and give it global reach. Whenever a key word occurs in a given Shakespeare speech, the actor might consider subtly highlighting it, so that it hangs or floats over the audience, who through their own life record of pain and pleasure gain a moment of clarity and access into the play's deepest themes. It may be helpful for the dramaturge to present one or two of Shakespeare's sonnets in workshop to demonstrate the evocative power of concise imagery. Best for this purpose is certainly Sonnet 73 ("That time of year thou mayst in me behold"), with its vivid metaphors of tree, sun, and fire.

In Shakespeare's plays, quality of language equals quality of character. There is a stable, centered simplicity and nobility to the speech of his admirable, ethical characters. For example, here are the faithful Cordelia's virtually first words in *King Lear*: "Love, and be silent" (I.i.53).[1] This economical aside, with its enduring spiritual resonance, comes as a refreshing contrast to the glib, sycophantish babble that we have just heard from her treacherous sisters, Goneril and Regan. Improvisational eloquence under conditions of high stress proves substance and courage, as in Mark Antony's passionate oration over the corpse of Julius Caesar in the mobbed Roman Forum or Othello's defense at a midnight Venetian war council of his secret marriage to the young Desdemona, a mesmerizing speech whose journey through fabulous memory defuses the menacing atmosphere.

Syntax (sentence structure) is a primary indicator of mental health or psychological coherence in Shakespeare. The actor must be alert to syntactical obstructions or fractures which signal confusion, anxiety, or imminent breakdown. Claudius' first speech in *Hamlet*, for example, is disrupted and contorted by guilt as he tries to refer to Gertrude, the wife he took from the brother he murdered: the subject, verb, and direct object of his sentence are cleft apart and strewn dismembered over seven lines. Hamlet's brooding first soliloquy also degenerates from philosophical heights to syntactical chaos as he is compulsively flooded with lurid pictures of his mother's allegedly bestial sex life. When the villainous Richard III wakes up from troubled dreams before the climactic battle at Bosworth Field, where he will be defeated and killed, his speech heaves and lurches into sputtering fragments, sharply contrasting with the calm, steady, resolute address to the troops delivered by his opponent, the Earl of Richmond and future Henry VII, founder of the House of Tudor that will produce Elizabeth I. But sometimes complicated or serpentine syntax in Shakespeare arises from public rather than private ills, as in Horatio's opaque review in tortured legalese of the festering dispute with Norway that threatens war with Denmark.

ACTION

Shakespeare's bursts of action, alternating with passages of reflection and character development, seem perfectly normal to modern audiences schooled on war movies and TV crime dramas. But for a prolonged period, Shakespeare's violence, along with his trafficking in shock and horror, damaged his reputation in France, where elite taste was formed by Racine's neoclassic tragedies in the seventeenth century. In ancient Greek tragedy, action was reported by messenger speeches but never shown, even when traumatic events, such as Jocasta's suicide and Oedipus' self-blinding, have just occurred in a bedchamber on the other side of the palace doors. A cool, contemplative, philosophical distance, embodied in choral commentaries, was considered essential. Brutal business in Shakespeare, such as Hamlet stabbing Polonius through a tapestry in the Queen's bedroom or the Duke of Cornwall stomping out the pinioned Gloucester's eyes in *King Lear*, struck French critics as crude and vulgar.

High-impact physical expressiveness is a crucial component of Shakespeare's aesthetic, a masculine choreography that was sometimes neglected in sedate and tony productions of the late nineteenth and early twentieth centuries. Standards changed for both actors and audiences with the arrival of social realist theater in the 1930s, whose raw, proletarian style inspired the Actors Studio in New York and the "kitchen-sink" school of postwar London. Today, action is so accepted and expected that a required course in stage combat may be built into the theater curriculum (as at the University of the Arts, where women actors too must take it). Once identified with stunt work, action has risen in prestige over the past forty years because of the global influence of Asian martial arts movies. Explosions of action in Shakespeare are sometimes spiritually purgative, releasing the accumulated tensions of the play: this cathartic effect can be seen in the finales of both *Hamlet* and *Macbeth,* where the protagonists escape from their doubt and fear through bravura swordplay, thus atoning for their errors and defiantly recovering their heroic stature before death.

American actors have a natural facility for action, as was observed with admiration by European audiences even during the silent film era. In the United States, posture and deportment are more relaxed, and sports have a higher cultural status than they do in Great Britain, where most literati still profess disdain for them. Thanks to their spontaneity and playfulness, American actors are also good at farce, buffoonery, and slapstick—one reason for the huge popularity of pratfalling comedian Jerry Lewis in reserved France. Where this may pose a minor problem for Shakespeare productions is in drunk scenes, such as that between Sir Toby Belch and Sir Andrew Aguecheek in *Twelfth Night* or between Caliban and Stephano in *The Tempest*. Characters reeling around onstage elicit such delighted and uproarious audience response (perhaps from relief at finding something recognizable amid Shakespeare's demanding language) that American actors may be tempted to overdo the clowning and selfishly play to the gallery.

Other aspects of Shakespeare's staging can be classified as action, which governs the disposition of the body. Because the Globe had no curtain, Shakespeare devised ingenious ways of getting the actors on and off stage (more evidence that the plays were not closet dramas composed in a nobleman's library). Daringly, he starts scenes and whole plays in the middle of conversations: two actors stroll onstage while talking in normal tones, forcing the audience to hush itself in order to overhear. Shakespeare expects the audience to make rapid intuitive judgments based on characters' manner and body language. For example, *Antony and Cleopatra* opens with a Roman, Philo, disparaging Antony as a sex-addled "fool" and the dark-skinned Cleopatra as a lustful "gypsy" and whore (I.i.10–13). But this cynical view is immediately contradicted by the movingly poetic endearments exchanged by the two fond lovers as they arrive from the opposite direction.

King Lear too opens with characters entering mid-conversation: the Earls of Gloucester and Kent are sharing worrisome political rumors when the subject takes a personal and indiscreet turn. Each production of *Lear* must decide how much, if any, of this humiliating talk is heard by Gloucester's bastard son, the embittered and soon malevolent Edmund. Some show of over-familiar, leaning-in body language seems implied in Gloucester's lines, as he tastelessly boasts to Kent about the "good sport" had with a nameless pretty wench at Edmund's accidental conception. Kent's discomfort at this coarse sniggering is blatant, as he vainly tries to restore a dignified tone. Ideally, the audience should probably read the body language of Gloucester and Kent exactly as Edmund is reading it: Gloucester's bumptious insensitivity met by Kent's embarrassed unease. Before we have even heard Edmund speak, therefore, we already have a clue about the formation of his sociopathic character, hardened by routine discrimination and abuse—a prime example of Shakespeare's prescient anticipation of modern social psychology.

Body language is similarly cued in the scene on the castle ramparts where Hamlet, trying to follow his father's ghost, is being physically held back by Horatio and Marcellus, who fear the ghost may be a demon. Presumably drawing his sword, Hamlet threatens to kill anyone who stands in his way. This agitated scene superbly demonstrates Shakespeare's great gift for staging. What the audience sees are two men rushing forward and then being thrown backward, beyond the sweeping circle made by Hamlet's sword as it is pulled from its scabbard. It is a visually stunning, nearly geometrical effect that could have been designed only by a man with many years of practical experience in live theater.

Another example of implicit body language is the scene where Ophelia, obeying her pompous father's command, returns Hamlet's gifts and love letters. The mere sight of her beauty rescues Hamlet from one of his most despairing soliloquies, and he addresses her with tender respect and hope for forgiveness: "Nymph, in thy orisons / Be all my sins remembered" (III.i.95–96). No matter how many times one has read or seen the play, it is hard to resist a fantasy of Hamlet and Ophelia's reconciliation at this moment. But it is not to be: Ophelia dutifully plows ahead on her father's agenda, and Hamlet reacts with pain and anger: "No no, / I never gave you aught" (III.i.95–96). His change of mood is so extreme that some physical recoil is surely signaled, even perhaps an abrupt jump backward. At some point in this harrowingly escalating scene, where Hamlet correctly guesses that Ophelia has become a tool of her father and that he is being spied upon, the precious mementoes probably fall to the floor between them, a symbol of their shattered romance and a foreshadowing of Ophelia's pitiful ruin.

POLITICS

The contemporary actor's search for motivation in a Shakespeare role is complicated by alien elements in the Renaissance world-view. Politically, Shakespeare was not a populist or democrat but a monarchist who believed that government was best led by a wise, strong ruler. The crown is a near-mystical symbol in his plays, which feature sporadic suspicions of the fickle mob. Freedom is the watchword of modern democracies, but Shakespeare's guiding principle was order. Lingering in popular memory were the thirty years of civil war that England had endured a century before. For both the Middle Ages and the Renaissance, hierarchy or "degree" in the political realm mirrored the perfection of God's cosmic master plan. A king, it was thought, ruled by divine right. Although Shakespeare himself may have tended toward the agnostic, there is a trace of that religious premise in his plays in the difficulties encountered by usurping kings like Macbeth or Claudius in asserting and maintaining authority. Kingship is conferred but also learned, as when Prince Hal matures into Henry V by abandoning his youthful hedonism and severing ties with the carousing Falstaff.

Nationalism, customarily portrayed today as a crucible of war, imperialism, and xenophobia, is a positive value in Shakespeare. Nation-states had emerged in the Middle Ages as a consolidation of dukedoms, an administrative streamlining that, at its best, expanded trade, advanced knowledge, and reduced provincialism. This progressive movement of history is the major theme of *King Lear*, where Lear's foolish choice to divide his kingdom (which he does not possess but holds in trust) plunges it backward toward chaos and barbarism, reducing the king himself to a nomad battered by the elements. Unless they know European history well, most American actors rarely notice the nationalistic motifs in Shakespeare. In *Lear*, for example, the invasion of Britain by France—even though it promises rescue by the forces of good (Cordelia is now queen of France)—creates patriotic conflicts for a British audience that Americans will not feel. Similarly, even a small detail such as Hamlet being dispatched to England to collect overdue tribute for Denmark would stir a flicker of atavistic indignation in British hearts. Nationalism resoundingly recurs in a different context at the finale of *Hamlet*, where the stage is scattered with royal corpses. The bracingly vigorous entrance of Fortinbras marks the occupation of Denmark by a foreign power. With the self-destruction of its ruling class, Denmark has lost its autonomy and become a subject state of Norway.

Hierarchy also structures family and gender relations in Shakespeare. Fathers were law-givers, and children were expected to obey. In *Romeo and Juliet*, Shakespeare's audience would have sided with Juliet's parents, who had the right to make marital decisions for a fourteen-year-old girl. The play's power resides precisely in Shakespeare's success in shifting the audience from its default position through the captivating lyricism of Romeo and Juliet's love. Because of our own reflex bias toward romantic free choice, it's important that a contemporary production not side so completely with the lovers as to warp the play: Juliet's hot-tempered father should not be portrayed as a pasteboard ogre, nor should the aristocratic Paris, his sound choice for Juliet, seem like a callow prig. In *The Tempest*, Prospero displays a sometimes disturbing control over his daughter Miranda and her suitor Ferdinand: he puts Miranda to sleep and freezes Ferdinand in place, like a statue. This problematic manipulation of consciousness is partially ameliorated by Prospero's status as a magician whose secret arts parallel Shakespeare's spellbinding power over an audience.

Shakespeare is repeatedly critical of rigid, uncomprehending fathers. One of the haunting mysteries of his plays is how often he deletes the mothers of his young heroines, who are left undefended against the errors of obtuse fathers. Miranda has thrived in her widowed father's watchful nurture, but Cordelia, Desdemona, and Ophelia suffer severely from the absence of a mother's sympathetic counsel and intervention. Ophelia, torn between her proper deference to her father and her love for Hamlet, tries to do the right thing and ends up destroying her own and Hamlet's lives. Shakespeare worsens

Ophelia's plight by sending her brother off to university in Paris and oddly even denying her a female confidante, like Juliet's jovial nurse or Desdemona's worldly-wise maid servant, Emilia. This terrible isolation, compounded by her father's death at Hamlet's hands, intensifies the emotional pressure on Ophelia and makes comprehensible her descent into delusion and madness, which Shakespeare pointedly contrasts with Hamlet's passing episodic depressions. A contemporary actor playing Ophelia must strike a delicate balance in portraying her tragedy without excess sentimentality. She is not simply a frail flower or hapless victim of rank injustice. Her father, Polonius, is arrogant and at times stupid—ignoring her hurt and need for comforting and callously broadcasting her secrets as mere data to whisk to the king—but he is solidly within his rights to determine Ophelia's affairs and protect her chastity. Ophelia makes a considered ethical choice, a courageous decision to renounce the man she loves.

The divergence of cultural assumptions between the Renaissance and today is nowhere clearer than in regard to marriage, which is glorified in Shakespeare's plays as a symbol of spiritual harmony and social order. His comedies sometimes end in a stampede of mass marriages, blessed by heaven and destined for fertile procreation. Marriage in our own time has lost much of its uniqueness and high value, partly because women now have access to jobs outside the home and can support themselves. Weddings remain popular as theatrical extravaganzas, but marriage has shrunk to just another lifestyle option, and the divorce rate has soared. Shakespeare's generation of poets, including John Donne and Edmund Spenser, was instrumental in the valorization of marriage, which had once primarily been an economic contract negotiated between a father and a prospective son-in-law. Medieval love poetry was addressed to a mistress or a distant, unattainable idol, not a wife.

The strong tilt toward marriage in Shakespeare's plays creates interpretive problems for contemporary actors. In *As You Like It*, for example, the witty and boldly enterprising Rosalind, who spends most of the play disguised as a boy, instantly falls in love with Orlando, an amiable lunk who seems nowhere near her level. He is athletic and sweet but slightly slow, like Joey (played by Matt LeBlanc) on the long-running hit TV show, *Friends*. Rosalind's infatuation with Orlando exemplifies Shakespeare's favorite theme of the quirky madness of love, but it must not seem as if she is adopting and training a large, goofy dog. Her ritual divestment of her male garb before her wedding restores the Renaissance gender code and magically generates an approving apparition of Hymen, the guardian spirit of marriage. Rosalind's inseparable friendship with her cousin Celia is one of the few places in Shakespeare's plays where any trace of homosexuality can arguably be detected. (Another is Antonio's quick attachment and unusual generosity to Sebastian in a subplot of *Twelfth Night*.) Although his celebrated contemporary, Christopher Marlowe, wrote openly about a gay king in *Edward II*, Shakespeare's plays are overwhelmingly committed to heterosexual love. In his private life, Shakespeare was evidently split: his love sonnets are directed to a forceful, dusky-skinned woman and a well-born, aimless, beautiful young man.

Shakespeare is very sensitive to the dignity of women. Sexually degrading remarks about women in his plays are automatically symptomatic of a twisted, corrupted character or of a temporary state of mental disease, as experienced by Hamlet and Lear in their darkest moments. Nevertheless, modern productions of *The Taming of the Shrew* must struggle with the issue of misogyny. The play has long been the focus of feminist ire, with only the dissident Germaine Greer, a Shakespeare scholar among her other public roles, willing to stoutly defend it. The bad-tempered and violent Kate the shrew (a sharp-toothed mole) cows her inept father and breathes fire at any man who crosses her. It is possible to interpret Kate's hostility as a frustrated product of her entrapment in a world lacking any outlet for women's talents and pent-up energies except marriage. Petruchio, who frankly admits his motive for marrying is mercenary (he's on the hunt for the fattest dowry), breaks down Kate's rebellious personality by treatment that today would be classified as spousal abuse—denying her food and sleep, letting her wallow in the mud, and generally humiliating her. The actor playing Kate is confronted at the finale with one of the thorniest challenges in the Shakespeare canon: a long public speech where she declares that women are "soft and weak" and must "serve, love, and obey" their husbands (V.i.176–77). After the rollicking humor of the play, modern productions are reluctant to end on a sour note, so the speech is now performed as if it is overtly satirical—whether that is true to Shakespeare's original conception or not.

The dramatis personae of Shakespeare's plays are always a mix of social classes. Because of Britain's still entrenched class system, with its sometimes cash-poor but highly visible landed aristocracy, British actors have little trouble in playing Shakespeare's upper-class roles. In the United States, in contrast, status is conferred solely by wealth, celebrity, or transient political power. Furthermore, since the 1960s, American authority figures, from politicians, ministers, and bankers to parents and teachers, have gradually adopted a less formal, remote, and dictatorial style. Young people today will often startlingly say that one or both of their parents are their "best friends." Dress codes have also relaxed with the spread of sportswear, sneakers, and proletarian blue jeans, even marketed by a mandarin heiress, Gloria Vanderbilt. It is now hard to appreciate why John F. Kennedy caused a sensation by not wearing a hat at his presidential inauguration in 1961.

Because of these broad social changes, American actors coming to Shakespeare have few or no direct models of hierarchical authority and class assertion. The audience must clearly perceive the class differences among Shakespeare's characters. Working-class women, for example, would paradoxically take up more space on stage than their upper-class counterparts: their movements are physically freer and their clothing looser, because designed for labor. Upper-class posture is reserved and contained, as if housed in an invisible bubble. Actors with prior training in classical ballet, which descends from the elegant seventeenth-century court, or continental equitation (called English riding in the United States) have a distinct advantage here. Even among young British women actors winning parts these days in productions of Shakespeare, Jane Austen, or Oscar Wilde, there is an irksome trend for mannish arm-swinging, which originated among the new sportswomen of the 1920s who took up golf and tennis. Until World War One, respectable ladies kept their elbows close to their bodies and their hands clasped gracefully above the waist or otherwise occupied with some object like a fine handkerchief—an accessory crucial to the plot of *Othello*. Nor did ladies flash their teeth or grin like Huckleberry Finn, another anachronism currently epidemic in period roles.

Manners are not superficial trivialities but the choreography of social class. Manners both define and limit character and must therefore be represented in the actor's process. Without attention to class distinctions and stratification, important plot elements in Shakespeare will be blurred or missed altogether. In *King Lear*, for example, it is a violation of propriety for Goneril, who is the Duchess of Albany, to be confiding private matters about her father and sister to her steward, Oswald. In *Twelfth Night*, the countess Olivia is too flirtatious with the duke's page, Cesario (Viola in drag), just as her own steward, Malvolio, is later too presumptuously forward with her. On the other hand, Shakespeare presents as evidence of Prince Hamlet's refreshing lack of snobbery his gracious affability to the visiting troupe of players as well as his easy cordiality with the gravedigger at work in the churchyard. Precedence and rank are pivotal in the banquet scene where Lady Macbeth, trying to divert notice from her husband's hysteria at Banquo's bloody ghost (which only he can see), abruptly orders everyone to leave: "Stand not upon the order of your going, / But go at once" (III.iv.137–138). The ugly lack of ceremony in this chaotic mass exit represents the breakdown of social cohesion in a Scotland ruled by a criminal.

Witty banter, the signature sound of the upper-class comedy of manners, comes easily to British actors, whose culture is oriented toward verbal panache, from Oxbridge debating societies to Question Time in the House of Commons, with its scathing sallies met by laughter and applause. American actors today are overexposed to snark, the dominant style in TV comedy. With its snidely ironic put-downs, snark lacks the arch competitive rhythm, like that of fencing, which has always characterized the thrusts, parries, and repartee of great high comedy. For help with Shakespeare's witty dialogue, I recommend to my theater students such classic film comedies as *The*

Philadelphia Story, All About Eve, and *The Importance of Being Earnest* (the 1952 version directed by Anthony Asquith), which show how epigrammatic lines can be crisply shaped, timed, and delivered. The Mid-Atlantic accent (midway between American and British) once heard among scions of prominent, affluent families such as Franklin D. Roosevelt and Katharine Hepburn, used to be taught to actors in theater school. It was perfect for high comedy but became too affected and artificial over time. However, Sigourney Weaver, playing an imperious Wall Street stockbroker in *Working Girl,* shows how that elite accent can be subtly modified for use by American actors playing upper-class roles.

* * *

Shakespeare's plays famously survive transfer into any locale and time period. They have been set, for example, in medieval Japan, Nazi Germany, a space colony, and a suburban high school. But this amazing flexibility does not necessarily give infinite latitude to high-concept directors. In *The Goodbye Girl,* Richard Dreyfuss hilariously plays an earnest young actor struggling with a narcissistic Off-Off-Broadway director who sees Richard III as a flaming queer. Radical experiments with Shakespeare make sense in Britain, where new angles on the fatiguingly familiar are welcomed. But in the United States, live professional productions of Shakespeare are so rare that, like it or not, they are thrust into an educational role. Actors of Shakespeare are exponents and defenders of a high culture that is steadily disappearing.

Because of the dominance of the Method in theater training here, American actors seeking their own "truth" are sometimes impatient with the technical refinements in which British actors, with their gift for understatement, are so skilled. Rehearsal is central to the Method actor as a laboratory where the ensemble merges through self-exploration. American culture, from Puritan diaries and Walt Whitman to Jackson Pollock and Norman Mailer, has always excelled in autobiography. But which is more important—the actor or the play? Shakespeare's plays are a world patrimony ultimately belonging to the audience, who deserve to see them with their historical distance and strangeness respected. The actor as spiritual quester is an archetype of our time. But when it comes to Shakespeare, the actor's mission may require abandoning the self rather than finding it.

1. Citations taken by editor Susannah Carson from the Royal Shakespeare Company edition of 2009, which was modernized from the First Folio.

31

SCHOLARS TALK WRITING:
CAMILLE PAGLIA

Rachel Toor: **Do you think of yourself primarily as a writer?**

Camille Paglia: Yes, I do, and that is how I am mainly known outside the U.S. From college on, my ambition was to establish the legitimacy of the genre now widely accepted as creative nonfiction.

How did you learn to write?

Like a medieval monk, I laboriously copied out passages that I admired from books and articles—I filled notebooks like that in college. And I made word lists to study later. Old-style bound dictionaries contained intricate etymologies that proved crucial to my mastery of English, one of the world's richest languages.

What have you done that has helped you reach an audience beyond academe? Did that involve unlearning things from grad school?

Good Lord, I certainly learned nothing about writing from grad school! My teacher was Yale's Sterling Library, that Gothic cathedral of scholarship. I was very drawn to the lucid simplicity of British classicists of the late nineteenth and early twentieth centuries, where one could hear a distinct speaking voice.

In my final years of grad school in the early 1970s, French post-

["Good Lord, I certainly learned nothing about writing from grad school!,"
Rachel Toor, Scholars Talk Writing series, *The Chronicle of Higher Education*,
November 9, 2015.]

structuralism was flooding into Yale, and I was appalled at its willful obscurantism and solipsism. After a talk by some preening Continental mandarin, I complained to a fellow student, "They're like high priests murmuring to each other." I deeply admire French literature, but that post-structuralist swerve was one of the stupidest and most disastrous things that American humanities departments ever did to themselves or to the great works of art that were in their custody. It was mass suicide, and the elite schools are now littered with rotting corpses.

How do you think about crafting your literary persona/e? What choices do you make when you're thinking about that?

I was very influenced by American colloquial speech and slang. My mother and all four of my grandparents were born in Italy, so English was a relatively recent acquisition for my family—brash and dynamic. I adored the punchy, pugnacious sound of American media—Ann Landers' column in the newspaper ("Wake up and smell the coffee!") or the raucous chatter of 1950s disc jockeys.

Like Andy Warhol, another product of immigrant culture, I was fascinated by the bold crassness and rhetorical hyperbole of American advertising and comic strips, with their exploding exclamation points. I still listen constantly to radio, at home or in the car—it's a central influence, especially sports shows where you hear working-class callers going off on hilarious tirades.

For scholarly essays, I erase myself as much as possible, but my default literary persona—the one people instantly recognize—is a barking, taunting, self-assertive American voice.

Is there anything you're afraid of, or that you struggle with (when it comes to writing)?

Yes, the actual writing! My system of composition has four parts. There's a long period of very enjoyable rumination, where I assemble information and jot ideas and phrases at random on legal-size notepaper—pages upon pages. Then as the deadline approaches, I study my notes and bracket or underline principal themes in colored ink to map out a skeletal general outline. Third comes the dreaded moment of writing—which is total torture! It's a terrible strain, and I'm literally tied up in knots of anxiety as I toil over it. Once a draft is blessedly complete, my fourth stage of reviewing and tweaking the text (which can go on for days, if there's time) is pure, serene pleasure—there's nothing I love more!

I must stress that all of my important writing, including my books, has been done in longhand, in the old, pre-digital way. I absolutely must have physical, muscular contact with pen and page. Body rhythm is fundamental to my best work. I may write interviews and columns for the Web directly on the computer, but nothing else.

What is your process for revision?

After every few scribbled pages, I trek to the computer and type it all up, so that I can see what the text will look like to the reader. My later tweaking is always done on printed-out text.

But my sole revisions are stylistic. My preparation for writing is so slow and extensive that I never revise per se, as others might understand it. For example, perhaps only twice in my entire career have I changed the position of a paragraph. The consecutive logic of my block-like paragraphs (as in Roman road-building) is always resolved at the outline stage, before I ever sit down to write. Revision for me is essentially condensation—that's where the Paglia voice suddenly emerges. By subtracting words, I force compression and speed on the text. Through long practice, I've achieved a distinct flow to my writing—a compulsive readability, even when the reader hates what I'm saying!

I learned condensation from two principal sources: the impudent, crisply written *Time* magazine of my childhood and the epigrams of Oscar Wilde, which I discovered collected in a secondhand book when I was an adolescent in Syracuse. My Wilde-inspired ability to strike off sharp one-liners was a major reason for my rise to national visibility in the 1990s. For example, when *Time* contacted me at deadline for comment on its Viagra cover story in 1998, I replied within minutes, "The erection is the last gasp of modern manhood." Any compendium of contemporary quotes usually has a ton of mine.

In addition to condensation, I also employ syncopation, modeled on the jazz-inflected Beat poetry that had a huge impact on me in college. When people try to parody my prose, this is what they miss— those subtle, jagged twists, turns, and tugs, whose ultimate source is music. In short, the secret of my writing is focus, planning, persistence, labor, and attention to detail.

Your thoughts on academic prose. Who are the academics whose style you love?

Cue the laugh track! What's to love in any living academic's style? You'd have to go all the way back to Jane Harrison, C. M. Bowra, and Rhys Carpenter to find an academic style I cherish. I've spent 25 years denouncing the bloated, pretentious prose spawned by poststructuralism. Enough said! Let the pigs roll in their own swill.

32

SHAKESPEARE'S
ANTONY AND CLEOPATRA

Shakespeare is one of the supreme political analysts in world history. Through the lens of drama he examines the forces of social consolidation and destruction that cyclically sweep through human life. He documents the bursts of energy and idealism that motivate heroic achievement, and he re-creates with chilling precision the practical give-and-take, the compromises and trade-offs, and the malicious machinations that dispirit and disillusion and often drive the noblest spirits from the political arena.

Antony and Cleopatra is, I would argue, the greatest of Shakespeare's political plays. Based on Plutarch's portrait of Mark Antony in *Parallel Lives* (which Shakespeare read in Sir Thomas North's 1579 translation), it evokes a pivotal point in European history, when control of the Mediterranean hung in the balance. Had Antony and Cleopatra defeated Octavius Caesar in the naval battle at Actium in 31 B.C., the political and cultural center would have shifted from Europe to Africa, changing the course of the next two millennia.

In our era of Romantic individualism, audiences tend to favor star-crossed lovers and to be colder to characters representing reason or duty. Despite his reputation as a bard of love, Shakespeare has a very clear sense of the eternal conflict between passion and realism. His

[Program notes commissioned for a production of *Antony and Cleopatra* starring Helen Mirren and Alan Rickman at the National Theatre in London, October 20–December 3, 1998.]

sober Caesar in *Antony and Cleopatra* lacks the ostentatious empathy of our therapy-minded television talk-show hosts, who are now so much imitated by smiling presidents and prime ministers. Caesar feels no one's pain.

But we cannot forget that this Caesar is the future Augustus, creator not just of the Roman Empire, with its expansionist military brutality, but the Pax Romana, a period of peace, prosperity, and legal codification in which Christianity would be born and spread. Shakespeare sees that Antony and Cleopatra, for all their personal magnetism and lust for life, lack the steadiness and self-discipline that we require in leaders, who are responsible for the public welfare and for the systematic administration of justice.

Antony and Cleopatra had a generally low reputation with most critics (save for the astute A. C. Bradley) until just after World War Two. Its series of startlingly short scenes, bouncing all over the Mediterranean, seemed confusing and inept. And its heroine, one of the few female protagonists in Shakespearean tragedy, seemed sexually loose and morally obtuse. In the Victorian period, in fact, when decorously feminine images of saintly self-sacrifice like Cordelia and Desdemona were the most venerated Shakespearean women, Cleopatra looked like a whore.

But Hollywood, as the paramount cultural presence of the twentieth century, radically changed the fortunes of this play. The movie camera, with its pans and close-ups as well as such film-editing techniques as the jump-cut, have reshaped our expectations about drama. We now feel the full power of Shakespeare's directorial conception in *Antony and Cleopatra*—his breathtakingly spacious establishment of the world-stage and his zooming intimacy with the erratic, up-and-down emotional intensities of his enamored stars.

Furthermore, Hollywood, in its restoration of the pagan pantheon, has reeducated the world about sexual woman. Shakespeare's willful, ambitious, moody, charismatic Cleopatra is familiar to us from her cinematic sisters, who have specialized in formidable femmes fatales. A constellation of modern personae passes before us when we see Cleopatra on stage, from Theda Bara and Marlene Dietrich to Ava Gardner, Elizabeth Taylor, and Sharon Stone.

The interpretive task facing the actress who plays Cleopatra is how to capture her multiform physicality, which Shakespeare presents as a principle of vitality comprehending far more than the sexual. Cleopatra as queen is identified with Isis, who as goddess of fertility brings life out of the sun-baked Nile mud. Cleopatra as hoyden has a charming prankishness, gamboling in the streets and offering spontaneity and fun to her Roman lovers from a more dour milieu. Cleopatra as virago is commander-in-chief of the Egyptian armed forces, as well as a rash pugilist quick with fists or dagger.

To bring all these elements together is a daunting challenge—even more so when we recall that it was a boy actor who premiered the role. Most modern actresses have gravitated toward one extreme or the other, playing Cleopatra either as a rowdy, capricious vixen (like Bizet's Carmen) or as a cerebral dignitary whose mood changes seem like passing fits of dyspepsia.

The real-life Cleopatra was not particularly beautiful, but she was known for her mastery of languages as well as for her shrewd conduct of foreign policy. Her fascinating uniqueness is shown by the fact that two quite different types of men fell in love with her—the stoical, censorious, teetotaling Julius Caesar and the flamboyant Mark Antony, with his hedonistic conviviality.

The question of female leadership is very much on our minds today, as we urge women to break through the "glass ceiling" to the apex of business and politics. *Antony and Cleopatra* makes us ponder how much femininity a woman can or should retain as she assumes command. Does a woman's overt sexuality strengthen or destabilize her hierarchical authority?

In the *Aeneid,* Vergil recast Antony and Cleopatra, who killed themselves a year after Actium, as the legendary Aeneas and Dido, whose adulterous love affair ended in the latter's suicide. The Phoenician queen, overseeing the construction of Carthage, is given Cleopatra's managerial flair. Aeneas, a Trojan refugee, falls under her spell just as Antony did with Cleopatra.

Like Vergil, Shakespeare shows woman as an obstruction to the male mandate of Roman destiny. "The personal is political," contemporary feminism likes to say. *Antony and Cleopatra* asks if a person charged with ultimate public responsibility can ever live fully as a private person. When does true love or sexual adventurism distract, delude, and disable? And in the case of Caesar, can we confidently trust the design of society to career administrators who elevate the material and the general over the emotional and the specific?—like those in our own century who see life as pure economics, unleavened by spirituality or art.

From the Roman point of view, Antony has become a dominatrix's boy toy. Is this the irrational, misogynous prejudice of patriarchy? Or is it a painfully accurate perception of men's sexual vulnerability to women? Most feminism has not seen how the boudoir and the harem become the nursery, where the weary male seeks swaddling, the all-forgiving tender touch of maternal consolation.

Antony and Cleopatra's love is magnificent but volcanic. It reaches great heights but sinks to terrible depths, which destroy the lovers as well as the political independence of Egypt. In seeking her own power, has Cleopatra, like Lady Macbeth or some American First Ladies, covertly used her man as proxy? Beloved by her maids and aides, perhaps Shakespeare's Cleopatra is guilty of governing by coterie: on the battlefield of world politics, the family model breaks down—which may be one reason women have yet to achieve equality in leadership.

Shakespeare's England had recently emerged from a long, bloody period of civil wars. The playwright was born and entered professional life during the reign of a headstrong queen who kept sexuality at sword's point. *Antony and Cleopatra* was first staged a few years after Elizabeth's death, when British politics seemed sunk in the cynical mire.

Our justifiable modern animus toward imperialism should not blind us to Shakespeare's quite different premises. Because he had seen, in the anxiety-ridden transition from the Elizabethan to the Jacobean eras, how a lack of direction and vision at the top spreads to the nation at large, Shakespeare's portrait of Caesar is more sympathetic and discerning than has usually been acknowledged. Shakespeare knew that the weakening and breakdown of social controls may at first seem to bring personal liberation and Dionysian ecstasy but can end in chaos—to which there is a predictable authoritarian reaction.

I have learned more about politics from *Antony and Cleopatra* than from any Marxist or post-structuralist critique of society. The play integrates a subtle Freudian view of unconscious impulse and instinct with florid Baroque grandeur, the glamorization of personality found in Italian opera or Rubens' historical paintings. Like Thucydides, Shakespeare elegiacally charts the waxing and waning of political hubris and the failure of lofty national dreams.

As a feminist, I find Shakespeare's harshest lesson to involve military preparedness. From Cleopatra's disastrous misjudgments at Actium—where she forced the veteran army man Antony to fight by sea—I draw my belief in the urgent need for massive reeducation of women politicians. Compassion and caretaking are not enough to lead a nation. Conservative women have more easily reached the top—like Margaret Thatcher, who decisively went to war to protect the Falklands. All women who seek power must deeply study the history and art of warfare.

Antony and Cleopatra balances the claims of nature and culture and explores the dark, swirling undercurrents in male and female sexuality. Shakespeare's plays seem to change over time because each period brings its own assumptions to them. Caesar and Cleopatra look larger or smaller depending on the weight we assign to order or freedom. But Antony, torn between Rome and Egypt, remains much the same, a complex, tragic portrait of humanity's irreconcilable differences.

33

TENNESSEE WILLIAMS AND
A STREETCAR NAMED DESIRE

1947, December 3
Tennessee Williams' *A Streetcar Named Desire* premieres at the
Ethel Barrymore Theater in New York

"Hey, there! Stella, Baby!"

Marlon Brando, carrying a "red-stained package" from the butcher and sporting blue-denim work clothes as the lordly, proletarian Stanley Kowalski, ambles insolently onstage at the opening of Tennessee Williams' *A Streetcar Named Desire*. "Bellowing" for his adoring yet tart-tongued wife, Stanley is the strutting male animal in his sexual prime. The setting is a seedy tenement in the multiracial French Quarter of New Orleans, whose picturesque verandas open to the humid air. Street sounds and sultry, insinuating jazz riffs float in and out.

The exotic location, boisterous energy, and eruptions of violence in *A Streetcar Named Desire* were a startling contrast to the tightly wound gentility of Williams' prior hit play, *The Glass Menagerie* (1944), whose fractured family is cloistered in a stuffy St. Louis flat. *Streetcar* exploded into the theater world at a time when Broadway was dominated by musical comedies and revivals. At the end of its premiere, the audience sat numb and then went wild, applauding for thirty minutes. Critical responses ranged from positive to rapturous, with dissent coming only from Wolcott Gibbs and Mary McCarthy. *Streetcar*

[Commissioned for *A New Literary History of America,* ed. Greil Marcus and Werner Sollors (Harvard University Press, 2009).]

won the Pulitzer Prize and other major awards and ran for two years in New York before touring the country. European productions won enormous acclaim, except in England, where the verdict was split.

Brando as Stanley was a volcanic force of nature. Leering, brooding, belching, mumbling, scratching himself, and smashing crockery on the floor, he exemplified a radical new style of naturalistic acting, "the Method," which Brando learned from Stella Adler and which would gain public attention through Lee Strasberg's Actors Studio in New York. Focusing on emotional truth and painful personal memory, the Method was developed in the 1930s by the leftist, ensemble-oriented Group Theater, which was following Konstantin Stanislavsky's precepts for productions of realist plays (such as Chekhov's) at the Moscow Art Theater. Brando, along with his friend Montgomery Clift, would transfer the Method into movie acting, as in the 1951 film of *Streetcar,* which was directed, like the play, by Elia Kazan. The repercussions from Brando's performance in that film are still being felt among contemporary American male actors, who often do Brando without being aware of it.

In its taboo-breaking style, *Streetcar* belonged to an oppositional strain that emerged in American culture following World War Two. The near-universal patriotism of the war years, galvanized to defeat German and Japanese imperialism, continued in mainstream American society and media for nearly two decades. But it was countered by an underground variously represented by abstract expressionism, bebop, and the Beats, as well as existentialism imported from Paris. There was a touch of the cynical hipster in Brando's impudent delivery of Stanley's brusque, satirically deadpan lines. Brando's raw primitivism was also a jolting departure from the slickness of the prettified glamour boys of the Hollywood studio, and it prefigured the youth rebellion of the 1950s, including rock 'n' roll—to whose iconography Brando would contribute through his role as the black-leather-clad leader of a motorcycle gang in a low-budget 1953 film, *The Wild One.*

The rude, crude Stanley Kowalski, with his iconic white t-shirt and his immigrant ethnicity, was evidently based on two men: a St. Louis factory worker of that name and a Mexican boxer, Pancho Gonzalez, who was one of Williams' butch lovers. Stanley has a tinge of "rough trade," a gay male staple—the street hustler, hot and dangerous. In *Streetcar*'s rowdy scenes of men playing poker, bowling, cursing, and brawling, Williams is gazing longingly at male bonding from his distant outsider's position. (An earlier title for the play, which was partly inspired by a Van Gogh painting of a billiard hall, was *The Poker Game*.) Williams was a small, effeminate gay man (his adult height was 5'6") who had been called "sissy" by neighborhood boys and "Miss Nancy" by his bullying, rejecting father. Williams would immortalize his father's bumptious authoritarianism in the garrulous, overbearing Big Daddy of *Cat on a Hot Tin Roof* (1955).

The shocking frankness with which *Streetcar* treated sex—as a searingly revolutionary force—was at odds with the dawning domesticity of the postwar era and looked forward instead to the 1960s sexual revolution. Williams drew much of his philosophy of sex from D. H. Lawrence, whose wife Frieda he visited in Taos, New Mexico, in 1939, when he was planning to write a play about Lawrence's death. What distinguishes Williams from other American playwrights of leftist social realism, such as Arthur Miller (whose *Death of a Salesman* made a sensation in 1949), is his florid Romantic emotionalism and love of beauty, as well as his Romantic reverence for barbaric, elemental nature. Emotional expressiveness is so central to Williams that Irene Selznick, the producer of *Streetcar*, refused to produce his next play, *The Rose Tattoo*, because she said it was an "opera," not a play.

Streetcar's historical background, embodied in the fluttery, flirtatious Blanche DuBois, is the decay of the agrarian Old South and the rise of gritty, prosaic urban industrialism. All of Williams' plays, until *The Night of the Iguana* in 1961, were set in the South. (The latter play takes place in a ramshackle hotel in Mexico.) Like William Faulkner, Williams portrays the psychological landscape of Southern decadence, with its guilt, squalor, and self-destructive fantasy. But Williams has greater faith in the sheer mesmerizing power of human personality. His major women characters are flamboyant, instinctive actresses— sometimes literally so, as with the aging movie star Alexandra del Lago in *Sweet Bird of Youth* (1959).

The ultra-theatrical Blanche is one of Williams' relentless, nonstop talkers. Other examples are Amanda Wingfield, the suffocatingly over-protective mother in *The Glass Menagerie,* and Violet Venable, a malign New Orleans aristocrat in the 1958 one-act play, *Suddenly Last Summer.* (Violet was played by Katharine Hepburn in the stunning movie of *Suddenly Last Summer,* directed by Joseph L. Mankiewicz and released in 1959.) All these women were inspired by Williams' own overpowering mother, with her pretensions of Southern refinement and her pathologically incessant talking, which one visitor described as a "nightmare."

Blanche is a dreamer who lives by language, the medium of the playwright's art. She creates poetry and illusion through her flights of rhetoric, which transform the harsh, bare environment. Blanche is literally a conduit of Romanticism: we hear that she taught Poe, Whitman, and Hawthorne to resistant high-school students in the country. It is through words alone that she re-creates the vanished world of Southern chivalry. She cries, "I don't want realism. I want magic!" Blanche's love of imagination and artifice clashes with the humdrum routine of the practical, utilitarian world, embodied in Stanley's curt, deflating minimalism. (Williams derives great humor from the two characters' competitive conversational rhythm.) As the play proceeds, the number and speed of words begin to increase and cloud the air, signaling Blanche's hallucinatory memories and descent into madness. Blanche's aggressive talking and baroque fantasies will live again in the caustic termagant Martha in Edward Albee's play, *Who's Afraid of Virginia Woolf?* (1962).

Williams said of his work, "I draw every character out of my very multiple split personality. My heroines always express the climate of my interior world at the time in which those characters were created." Elia Kazan claimed that Blanche DuBois *was* Tennessee Williams. She has his sexual hedonism, restlessness, and love of illusion, as well as his chronic alcoholism (he also abused pills). The enterprisingly nymphomaniac Blanche is Williams' champion in his self-proclaimed war against American puritanism. Williams attributed his mother's hysteria and his sister Rose's mental instability to sexual repression: "They were both victims of excessive propriety." (Rose, who was lobotomized at a state hospital in Missouri, was the model for Laura Wingfield in *The Glass Menagerie.*)

Like Blanche, Williams was uprooted from his Southern birth-place and became a refugee. He spent his first seven "idyllic" years in Mississippi before his family's traumatic move to St. Louis. He would live in sixteen different houses before he was fifteen. Williams became a compulsive traveler. Though a millionaire from the movie rights to his work, he lived in hotel rooms and would die alone in one. He said in his 1975 memoirs, "I live like a gypsy, I am a fugitive." Amid his bleak St. Louis surroundings, he developed a nostalgia for what he imagined to be the grace and elegance of the antebellum South. An enormous early influence on him in Mississippi was his family's black servant, Ozzie, who told him and his sister African-American and Native American folk tales.

Williams understood that the Southern claim of aristocracy, en-abled by the atrocity of slavery, was built on lies. Hence in *Streetcar* the ancestral DuBois plantation, lost to creditors, is called Belle Reve—that is, "beautiful dream." But the dream was always a patchwork of illogic: the French noun *rêve* is masculine, so the estate's name should properly be "Beau Reve." Williams had already used "Belle Reve" as the title of an adolescent poem where he fantasized about living on a Missouri plantation with his parents. The name was evidently sug-gested by a shrine of St. Louis snobbery, the Bellerive Country Club (meaning "beautiful riverbank"), where his mother strove for social acceptance and where, as a teenager, he would slip on a diving board and knock out all of his front teeth. (He had to wear dentures for the rest of his life.) Hence Bellerive/Belle Reve was a beckoning mirage that led to failure, humiliation, and mutilation.

The archetypal Southern belle whom Blanche so desperately plays, eighty years after the Civil War, would have been instantly recogniz-able to audiences from Scarlett O'Hara of *Gone with the Wind,* the blockbuster film (based on Margaret Mitchell's 1936 bestseller) that had been released in a tremendous burst of international publicity just eight years earlier. (Coincidentally, a British actress, Vivien Leigh, would win two Academy Awards for Best Actress for playing both Scar-lett O'Hara and Blanche DuBois.) Belle Reve is partly Tara, the family plantation for which Scarlett fights tax collectors and carpetbaggers. But it is also (as Williams attested) the cherry orchard in Chekhov's

1904 play of that name, a precious patrimony that is mortgaged and seized by vulgarians.

A residue of Williams' transsexual self-projection into the archly predatory Blanche is perhaps discernible in her seductive exchange with the newsboy, toward whom she directs such blatant come-ons as "You make my mouth water." Williams said that Blanche, soliciting the startled newsboy, has *become* Allan, her young gay husband, whom she shamed into suicide. *A Streetcar Named Desire* was unusually forthright about homosexuality at a time when the subject was bowdlerized or demonized by Hollywood movies. Homosexuality was explicitly forbidden under the Motion Picture Production Code: *These Three*, for example, a 1936 film based on Lillian Hellman's hit play, *The Children's Hour*, substituted a heterosexual triangle for the central plot motif of lesbianism, which was expunged.

Williams introduced homosexuality into *A Cat on a Hot Tin Roof*, where it is the motivation for Brick's marital reticence with the hot-blooded Maggie, and into *Suddenly Last Summer*, where the backstory focuses on a promiscuous gay aesthete, Sebastian Venable, who is slaughtered and cannibalized by a pack of poor Spanish boys whom he had solicited. (The Adonis archetype invoked here is part of Williams' use of Greek mythology, as in his 1957 play, *Orpheus Descending*.) Sebastian's sex tours were based on Williams' own in Mexico and Italy, where he pursued orgiastic anonymous sex and indulged what he called his "deviant satyriasis." When he got an "appetite" for blonds (a line he gives Sebastian), he would mull going north. Williams' 1950 novel, *The Roman Spring of Mrs. Stone*, fictionalized his own experiences with Italian gigolos the year after *Streetcar*'s huge success. (Mrs. Stone, his female proxy, would be played onscreen once again by Vivien Leigh in the 1961 movie.)

Williams was a bold pioneer for sexual candor: *Baby Doll*, for example, a lurid 1956 film based on his screenplay and directed by Elia Kazan, was condemned by the Catholic Legion of Decency. Yet Williams was denounced by gay activists after the gay liberation movement awoke following the 1969 Stonewall rebellion. He was accused of always linking homosexuality to guilt, self-punishment, degeneracy, and death—themes of the closeted era in which he had written his major plays. But he himself had been courageously and even recklessly open about being gay at a time when it could have proved personally and professionally costly. Though he loved New Orleans for its sexual tolerance and pleasure-seeking lifestyle, Williams never liked Mardi Gras and was always uncomfortable about drag queens, who he felt degraded women. With his taste for macho and even heterosexual men, he criticized the "swish" and "camp" style among pre-Stonewall gays.

The sex roles of *A Streetcar Named Desire,* Williams' greatest play, are certainly polarized by any conventional standard. The heterosexual electricity between Stanley and Stella across the gender divide is positively blinding. (Eyes repeatedly "go blind" in the stage directions at moments of sexual arousal.) In the 1970s, after his popularity had waned with the rise of younger playwrights, Williams told a gay interviewer that he did not want to ghettoize himself: "I wish to have a broad audience because the major thrust of my writing is not sexual orientation, it's social. I'm not about to limit myself to writing about gay people." With his empathy for the suffering yet dynamic individual, Williams produced not tendentious political potboilers but works of true universality, whose passionate characters have entered world literature.

34

DANCE OF THE SENSES:
NATURAL VISION AND PSYCHOTIC MYSTICISM
IN THEODORE ROETHKE

The poetry of Theodore Roethke springs almost entirely from his early, formative experiences in the Saginaw Valley of central Michigan. Although he traveled in Europe and taught for many years amid beautiful landscapes, from Pennsylvania's Delaware River Valley to the Green Mountains of southern Vermont to panoramic Puget Sound in Washington State, very little of what Roethke observed there found its way into his work until relatively late in his career. His finest poetry, which critics have called spiritual autobiography, was a journey of personal memory, a process of recovery of his vivid childhood impressions in Saginaw, to which both sides of his family had emigrated from Germany.

Roethke's love of the Michigan landscape was profound. In a college essay that he wrote as an undergraduate in Ann Arbor, he declared: "I can sense the moods of nature almost instinctively. Ever since I could walk, I have spent as much time as I could in the open. A perception of nature—no matter how delicate, how subtle, how evanescent,—remains with me forever. I am influenced too much,

[Keynote lecture of a conference celebrating the centenary of the birth of Theodore Roethke, held at the University of Michigan, Ann Arbor, on October 17, 2008. Published in *Michigan Quarterly Review*, Winter 2009.]

perhaps, by natural objects. I seem bound by the very room I'm in. . . .
When I get alone under an open sky where man isn't too evident,—
then I'm tremendously exalted and a thousand vivid ideas and sweet
visions flood my consciousness."[1]

Roethke described the Saginaw Valley as "very fertile flat country"
that lies "at the northern edge of what is now the central industrial area
of the United States."[2] There had been extensive ancient habitation in
the area by Native Americans, notably the Sauk and Chippewa tribes.
The young Roethke had a shoebox full of arrowheads he had found
along riverbanks. Once Saginaw became lumber country, emigrants
began trickling in—Mainers from New England, French-Canadians,
Irish, Germans, Italians, and Slavs. In East Prussia, Roethke's grandfather had been head forester of the estate of Bismarck's sister; his
grandmother, a housekeeper, was in charge of the estate's wine cellar. After a mysterious altercation with their employers, the couple
left first for Berlin and then America while Roethke's father was still
a baby. In Saginaw, the Roethke family began as market gardeners
selling produce and then expanded into flower-growing. The Roethke
sons, including Theodore Roethke's father, eventually owned one of
the biggest wholesale flower companies in the region and country.
There were twenty-five acres under cultivation, with a quarter of a million feet under glass. The Roethkes also owned an icehouse, a fenced
game preserve, and a patch of virgin forest outside town.

Roethke said about the greenhouses, in reference to their appearance in his second book, *The Lost Son and Other Poems* (1948): "They
were to me, I realize now, both heaven and hell, a kind of tropics created
in the savage climate of Michigan, where austere German-Americans
turned their love of order and their terrifying efficiency into something truly beautiful. It was a universe, several worlds, which, even as
a child, one worried about, and struggled to keep alive."[3] Similarly, in
a notebook entry from the mid-1940s, Roethke asked himself, "What
was the greenhouse? It was a jungle, and it was paradise; it was order
and disorder."[4]

Absorbing the dazzling sights and dank smells of the greenhouse,
the young Roethke stored up a wealth of sensory impressions for his
later work. Roethke's father, who was Prussian to his bones, was an

intimidating, godlike figure who nevertheless had an artistic streak: he experimented with breeds of roses and orchids, some of which he never sold. Roethke's identification of the palatial greenhouse with his colossus-like father is evident in this striking passage from the note-books: Roethke says, "I was born under a glass heel and have always lived there."[5]

Roethke's relationship to nature in Saginaw was therefore dual: there were the thick woods and teeming wetlands; the harsh winters, lush summers, and colorful autumns; but also the intricate world of horticulture—where nature is managed and subjected to the artificial forms and borderlines of civilization. Ultimately, the Roethke green-house, like the "stately pleasure-dome" of Coleridge's Xanadu, is a symbol of art itself—the poem's structure and transparency roofing a seething subject matter with its invisible roots. Roethke's vision of nature is close to Walt Whitman's—not in Whitman's epic sweep but rather in his microscopic attention to and compassion for the tiniest twigs and pebbles of the American landscape. As a craftsman of highly condensed lyrics, Roethke cited among his primary inspirations the Elizabethan song poets and the seventeenth-century Metaphysicals. British High Romanticism from William Blake on was also a major influence. The critic John Wain observed, "The greenhouse occupies the same place in Roethke's poetic evolution as the hills and dales of the Lake District do in Wordsworth's."[6]

Roethke's expansive natural vision seemed perfectly suited to the back-to-nature idealism of the 1960s. I was introduced to Roethke's work in college in the mid-1960s at the State University of New York at Binghamton. The poet Milton Kessler—the greatest teacher I ever had—had been a graduate student of Roethke's at the University of Washington. My entire introduction to contemporary poetry was through Kessler's intensely dramatic readings of Roethke, whose work had an enormous impact on me and marked me for life. Roethke rep-resented a stunning departure from the genteel and sanitized poems that had been assigned to us in high school—such as Robert Frost, who may have influenced Roethke but whose work I resented for what I felt to be its pious platitudes.

What Kessler highlighted in Roethke was his sensory engagement with his material, above all his kinesthetic robustness, illustrated by his famous poem, "My Papa's Waltz." But in the famous greenhouse poems too, there is a sense of Roethke's own powerful looming physical presence. Kessler talked about the unsettling disjunction between Roethke's huge size and the fineness of his perception, as in "Elegy for Jane," a strange and haunting poem where Roethke remembers a dead girl's "neckcurls, limp and damp as tendrils." There is a charged sense of danger and trespass. Interestingly, Roethke as a child had been small and sickly but had shot up to his bulky 6'2" height the year before he left for college.

It is the tangled multiplicity of the senses, including rank smells, that differentiates Roethke from most other poets of his time or indeed ours. (His departure point may have been the Metaphysical poets' constant theme of mortality and decay, which is also a pungent motif in Shakespeare's late tragedies.) Through his assertive rhythms and his subliminal assault on the nerves, Roethke's poetry achieves a seductive micro-muscular activation of the reader. Roethke certainly revolutionized my ideas about literature. My aesthetics had been formed by Oscar Wilde, that worshipper of beauty and high priest of the religion of art, whom I had discovered in high school via a British collection of his epigrams in a second-hand bookstore in Syracuse. Roethke was a revelation in adding the next term: the centrality of the senses in art. For art, I always argue, is not philosophy. Whatever ideas art may convey must be concretely embodied in material or sensory form. Hence the drift of high-profile poetry, post-Roethke, toward an abstruse philosophizing has, in my view, been both lamentable and self-destructive and has helped produce the present marginalization of contemporary poetry in the U.S.

Roethke compared teaching to dance: a class was a performance that, like dance, vanished "down the rathole" when it was over.[7] Judging from Milton Kessler's testimony about Roethke's flamboyant classroom style, there was definitely a kinesthetic dimension to his teaching. Roethke wrote, "Most teaching is visceral," and in his notebooks he said, "The teaching of poetry requires fanaticism."[8] In a letter to a cousin, he wrote about the teaching of literature, "The best teachers don't teach it as a 'subject' at all (as body of information, as 'culture', etc.) instead as experience. . . . [I]t is a constant effort to recover the creative powers lost in childhood." He felt that a teacher should use "every possible means to move students ahead intellectually and even at times, if you'll pardon the word, spiritually." It's a method "that makes great use of the associational forces of the mind."[9] Teaching, Roethke said in his notebooks, is "one of the few sacred relationships left in a crass secular world."[10]

In a collection called *Remembering Elizabeth Bishop,* the poet Henry Carlile recalled that Bishop, a virtuoso poet who (at least when I saw her read when I was in graduate school) was publicly discreet and reserved, "deplored" the influence of her fellow teacher Roethke on students at the University of Washington. Carlile alludes to Roethke's "spiritual bombast" and his "overwhelming, hyperbolic" style in the classroom: "His students worshiped him and imitated some of his worst mannerisms."[11] From the long list of topics and quotations from poetry recorded by one of his students from a single class, one can appreciate the huge range of Roethke's pedagogical method and the supple, associative play of his mind.[12]

Insofar as I adopted Milton Kessler's own eclectic, associative, Roethke-shaped teaching style for the whole of my own career, I must, if it is not too presumptuous, number myself among Roethke's spiritual grandchildren. My sense of connection with him was deepened by the fact that my first teaching job out of graduate school in the 1970s was at Bennington College, where Roethke taught in the mid-1940s. Shingle Cottage, which still housed a faculty poet when I was there, was hallowed ground because it was where Roethke had written his great greenhouse poems. (He had been encouraged in that project by the polymath critic, Kenneth Burke, who lived for half the week in a room upstairs.) I spent many convivial hours in that picturesque country house, where Roethke had, by his own testimony, danced in the nude at the height of inspiration!

So pivotal has Roethke always been to my understanding of modern poetry that I included three of his poems in *Break, Blow, Burn,* my book of commentaries on lyric poetry. The only other writers with three poems in that book are Shakespeare, John Donne, George Herbert, and Emily Dickinson. Perhaps not coincidentally, all four of those poets were among Roethke's claimed artistic ancestors. Imagine my unhappy surprise, therefore, when on my two national tours for that book—for the Pantheon hardback in 2005 and the Vintage paperback in 2006—I discovered that Roethke's reputation was no longer as I had remembered it. There were two persistent questions or comments most often made to me by interviewers or patrons at bookstore signings. The first was, "Why isn't Charles Bukowski in your book?" I doggedly replied that I had certainly intended to feature him very prominently to dramatize my protest against pretentious or middlebrow academic criticism. But to my distress, I could find no satisfactory complete Bukowski poem to endorse for the general reader.

The second most frequent comment, however, came as a complete shock. I was thanked for having featured Roethke in my book because, I was told again and again, he has slowly faded from attention and is no longer even well represented in poetry anthologies. Upon investigation, I was horrified to discover a dribbling out of scholarly books about Roethke over the past twenty years. For example, the massive Van Pelt Library at the University of Pennsylvania in Philadelphia owns only two books of Roethke criticism published in the 1990s—one in 1991 and the other in 1999. There has been nothing in the last decade. Furthermore, virtually all of the books on Roethke, from the 1960s on, were published by small or regional university presses—from Louisiana, Missouri, and Indiana to Washington State—with none produced by the bicoastal elite universities. Of course this situation is appalling and unacceptable. An American literary criticism that neglects Theodore Roethke has sunk into irrelevance and folly.

After pained reflection, I have identified what I would propose are three primary reasons for Roethke's apparent eclipse. First of all, the general politicization of literary criticism from the 1970s on may have eroded Roethke's position. Social crises and political events—the Great Depression, World War Two, the Cold War—made little or no impact on Roethke's poetry. Furthermore, it is hard to classify him according to the approved theoretical categories of class, race, and gender. There seems to be agreement even among sympathetic scholars (I am not one of them) that Roethke's views of women are sentimental and retrograde. The hovering spirit woman of "The Visitant,"

for example—one of my favorite poems in all of literature—belongs
to the pre-feminist period of archetype and myth, as explored by the
poet Robert Graves in *The White Goddess* (1948) or by the Jungian analyst Erich Neumann in his magnum opus, *The Great Mother* (1955).
The dethroning of the European tradition and the demythologization
of criticism have also unfortunately led to the erasure of myth critics
like Northrop Frye, whose magisterial *Anatomy of Criticism* (1957) was
still considered a landmark when I entered graduate school in 1968
but which now seems to have been completely forgotten.

One of the striking characteristics of Roethke's poetry is his portrait of nature as informed by magical presences, as in the German
folk songs and fairy tales that he loved in childhood. Roethke attributes a primitive state of consciousness not just to slugs and insects
but to fungi and mildew. Hence Roethke's world-view resembles that
of animism, the earliest stage in the history of world religions. The
critic Lynn Ross-Bryant notes an intriguing parallel between Roethke
and the Beat poet, Gary Snyder, who declared in his book, *Myths and
Texts*: "As poet I hold the most archaic values on earth. They go back
to the upper Paleolithic: the fertility of the soil, the magic of animals,
the power-vision in solitude, the terrifying initiation and rebirth, the
love and ecstasy of the dance, the common work of the tribe."[13] Yes,
Roethke, like Snyder, seeks ancient wisdom—whereas too many of
today's poets and critics are over-absorbed in the present and in the
narrow ideological conflicts of post-Enlightenment politics.

It might certainly seem, with the global rise of the environmental movement since the 1960s, that a nature poet such as Roethke
would be treasured. But environmentalist assumptions too have
become politicized. In today's debates, nature is projected as a victim of exploitation and despoliation, a hostage to unbridled capitalist
greed. But until very late in his work, there is no sense whatever in
Roethke that nature needs to be preserved or protected by man or that
it can suffer serious or permanent harm. Yes, nature can be directed,
tamed, pruned, and nurtured. (Roethke humorously spoke of his
family's constant fretting about fertilizer: "My father literally spent
weeks scouring the valley contracting with farmers for cow-dung.")[14]
But ultimately for Roethke, nature's generative forces are remote and

unknowable. The human in Roethke's world-view is simply a subset to nature.

When Wordsworth imagines his Lucy "Roll'd round . . . / With rocks, and stones, and trees," the human unit has been dissolved and absorbed into a vast dynamic of pure energy. There is an exhilarating sense of the sublime, which is also felt in Shelley's ode to the awesome peak of Mont Blanc. Roethke, in contrast, celebrates the small and particular; he shows a tender respect for the homely and specific that, I suspect, he may have learned from George Herbert and Emily Dickinson. Remarkable examples include such innovative compound phrases from Roethke's poem "Cuttings" as "sand-crumb" or "intricate stem-fur." Roethke's focus on the infinitesimal is nearly scientific. When Whitman embraces chaff or debris, he is trying to banish conventional distinctions between gold and dross, good and evil, clean and dirty. Hovering behind Whitman's epic, therefore, is a moral imperative, a critique of constricting definitions of race, gender, and sexual orientation. But with Roethke, there is no social critique but rather a mystical search for the hidden power within natural forms.

The degree to which Roethke was directly influenced by mystical literature has been much debated by critics. However, Neal Bowers definitively established, through a study of Roethke's notebooks as well as the record of his borrowings from the University of Washington library, that Roethke was very curious and knowledgeable about mysticism.[15] Evelyn Underhill's classic 1911 book, *Mysticism: A Study in the Nature and Development of Spiritual Consciousness,* struck a special chord with him, and he copied out her outline of the stages of the mystic's spiritual journey.

But what is unique in Roethke is that he has integrated the standard mystic vision of ecstatic unity with the cosmos with a darker, mustier, more realistic organicism. Roethke values precisely what cannot be sublimized or transcended. His natural vision, drawing on his practical observation of botany in action in the family greenhouse, triggers a dance of the senses—that Dionysian delirium which the nature-loving Ralph Waldo Emerson called for but, paralyzed by his own good taste, could not join. Roethke spoke openly of his cultivation of "Dionysian frenzy"—notably in the strange circular dance in the woods that began his overwhelming mystic experience and first mental breakdown while he was teaching at Michigan State College in East Lansing in 1935.[16]

The second reason I would propose for Roethke's present eclipse is related to the general loss in status of poetry criticism itself over the past three decades. From the 1950s through the 1960s, the professor-critics who specialized in poetry were at the top of the prestige ladder in English departments and in the humanities in general. Post-structuralism, which invaded U.S. universities via Johns Hopkins and Yale in the 1970s, changed all that. Post-structuralism, as I have long maintained, is helpless with poetry. It was designed for narrative forms like the short story and novel or nonfiction prose. Poetry, with its metaphors, symbolism, and body-centered rhythms, is beyond post-structuralism's reach.

Furthermore, the writing style encouraged by post-structuralism—extended, labyrinthine sentences, doubled-back, self-interrogating syntax, and arch flourishes of irony (imitating in English the aggressively anti-rationalist French of Derrida and Lacan)—changed basic notions of language. This development, I submit, gradually marginalized poets like Roethke who employ suggestive sensory effects to contemplate real things in nature—whose very existence post-structuralism, trapped in its own slippery rhetoric, denies. Roethke's syntax and vocabulary are based not on abstruse French precedents but on the Anglo-Saxon and Germanic substrate in English. This linguistic attraction or atavism reinforces the concreteness in Roethke's world-view. As American higher education, from the 1970s on, toppled the canon of Dead White European Males, the Anglo-American core in English departments was supplanted or minimized—and along with it a consciousness of the ancient and medieval etymology of English words, a complex lineage that is wittily evoked in our poetry by such masters of the language as Shakespeare and Emily Dickinson. Among Roethke's outstanding attributes is the tactility with which he employs the brusque texture of monosyllabic Anglo-Saxon and Old High German words—the barnyard element in English, a vestige of the agrarian past. Hence appreciation of Roethke, who is not an ironist and who uses words not simply as ciphers on a page but as resistant, mouth-filling things-in-themselves, has been undermined by the collapse in will and mission of English departments nationwide.

The third reason I would offer for Roethke's lack of attention in recent criticism is the shift in paradigms in psychology. Both Freud and Jung can be felt throughout Roethke's poetry. Whether Roethke actually read Freud or Jung is not the point. It has been reliably established that he had read Maude Bodkin's *Archetypal Patterns in Poetry* (1934), with its Jungian framework. And his use of Freudian psychobiography was very daring for poetry of the 1940s and directly influenced the new genre of Confessional poetry of the late 1950s and '60s. But I submit that it was the highly unusual *fusion* of Freud with Jung in Roethke's poetry that made his work so cutting-edge and increased his power for my baby-boom generation during the 1960s.

Another daring synthesis of Freud and Jung could be seen in the then highly controversial work of the leftist critic, Leslie Fiedler, beginning in the late 1940s and culminating in his 1960 opus, *Love and Death in the American Novel*. Freudian criticism remained under a cloud throughout the 1950s and well into the 1960s, when the New Criticism was at its height and when psychological interpretations of literature were still considered crude and déclassé. A speculative integration of Freud with Jung can also be seen in Norman O. Brown's transition from his Freudian *Life Against Death* (1959) to his mystical *Love's Body* (1966), with its disconnected sets of archetypal paradigms drawn from literature, religion, and philosophy.

In Roethke's poetry, the standard Freudian family romance of an omniscient, judgmental father-god and a sainted, self-sacrificing mother, combined with gnawing guilt over unruly sexual impulses, is combined with a Jungian cataloguing of the mythic archetypes of heroic quest and elemental nature. However, this extraordinary aspect of Roethke's work has slowly ceased to be visible because of ancillary cultural changes. In the early 1970s, just as psychoanalytic criticism and historiography seemed poised to receive academic recognition, French Freud was imported through the overwrought Jacques Lacan.

Simultaneously, in the real world, professional therapists were abandoning full-scale Freudian psychoanalysis, a protracted and expensive process that excavated childhood memories, and were moving toward more pragmatic protocols of psychological counseling, supplemented by medications. Over time, basic Freudian insights, including dream interpretation (a tremendous tool for interpreting symbolism in literature and art), have faded away. It's hard even to recall how Freudian references once suffused general culture, from the comedy routines of Lenny Bruce or Elaine May and Mike Nichols to pithy bestsellers like Dr. Eric Berne's *Games People Play* (1964), with its innovative transactional analysis. The Freudian style of lacerating or satirical self-examination is now gone amid a general trend, intensified by both post-structuralism and identity politics, toward blaming all psychological distress on oppressive external forces or conditions. Furthermore, Jung has been completely erased from academe, although his work continues to flourish off-campus in the New Age movement.

Hence the waning of both Freud and Jung has made Roethke's exquisite psychological effects much more difficult for readers to grasp. But another factor is operative in Roethke's psychological world. After his first hospitalization, Roethke was diagnosed as both a neurotic and a psychotic. It was his psychosis that was surely most fruitful for him as a poet. He liked to think of himself as the latest in a line of mad poets like Christopher Smart, John Clare, and William Blake. His was definitely not the madness of depressiveness and paralysis. Roethke mostly dwelled at the manic end of the schizophrenic spectrum, with its restless, roving energy and hallucinatory fantasy. Yet Roethke was not a true visionary like Blake, with his operatic private mythology of allegorical spiritual forces.

Roethke's psychotic component can be detected in his hushed sense of continuity or identification with the subhuman environment, particularly in a poem like "Root Cellar," with its uncanny riot of snaky shoots. It was once a well-known feature of schizophrenia that a patient would claim, "I am the wall"—an obliteration of the subject-object dichotomy that has been paralleled with peak moments of religious ecstasy, when saints feel a dissolution of the ego and an illumination of matter, transfigured by the Holy Spirit. Roethke said of the mystic episode preceding his first breakdown, "I knew how it felt to be a tree, a blade of grass, even a rabbit."[17] In his notebooks he wrote, "I can project myself easier into a flower than a person." And:

"I change into vegetables. First, a squash, then a turnip. . . . I become a cabbage, ready for the cleaver, the close knives." In another notebook entry, he wrote, "I wish I could photosynthesize."[18] Roethke's dissolution of human identity and his mapping of the humming energy-field of matter made him instantly comprehensible to the 1960s psychedelic generation—something which has never been documented, to my knowledge, in the critical literature on him.

Roethke's greenhouse poems replicate the quasi-religious way of seeing the world that so many members of my generation discovered through hallucinogens, some of them natural (like the mushrooms used in Mexican ritual) and some artificial, above all LSD, which at the time was being improbably touted as an agent of political transformation. Visions of physical and spiritual connectedness to plant and animal life were absolutely the norm during that period. Although I never took LSD (virtually everyone around me did), I identified strongly with the psychedelic world-view, which permeated Pop and Op Art, with their vibrating neon colors; movies like *Fantastic Voyage* (1966) and Stanley Kubrick's *2001: A Space Odyssey* (1968); and of course popular music. The Beatles' "Strawberry Fields Forever" and "Lucy in the Sky with Diamonds" are the most well-known psychedelic songs, but I would also mention the Electric Prunes' "I Had Too Much to Dream (Last Night)," Status Quo's "Pictures of Matchstick Men," and early Pink Floyd's "See Emily Play." Jimi Hendrix's song "Manic Depression" would have special relevance to Roethke. This psychedelic perspective was projected onto the walls of concerts and dances through swirling, multicolored amoeboid gels—an ambient reference to a Roethke-like congruence between microcosm and macrocosm.

Roethke, however, could reach his psychedelic altered consciousness merely by walking through the countryside and retrieving his childhood memories. Hence we might more accurately call his method psychotic mysticism. And here is yet another reason why Roethke's work seems to have temporarily receded. The young people of the '60s most influenced by psychedelics and therefore psychotic vision did not go on to graduate school, so there was a drastic loss of that radical perspective in arts criticism. Many psychedelic voyagers were also damaged by overzealous experimentation with drugs and lost the ability to communicate their spiritual discoveries to society. In medicine, furthermore, with the arrival of lithium, which suppresses the manic extreme in bipolar disorder, psychosis has virtually disappeared from modern life, with the exception of street people who resist being rounded up by social workers and put on a fixed schedule of medication.

The neutralization and elimination of psychosis, combined with the widespread use of designer antidepressants among the urban professional class in the U.S., may have unexpectedly impoverished the cultural world and most of all harmed poetry, both in its appreciation and its production. We are now left in poetry with the even, flattened sound of adjusted neurosis rather than the hectic or inflamed rambunctiousness of psychosis. The vibrancy of Roethke's psychotic mysticism, which is so wonderfully interwoven in his work with the English literary tradition, makes one ask, where have all the psychotic artists gone? I would suggest that they have abandoned poetry and have migrated into genres more amenable to hallucination— animation, video games, and science-fiction movies, with their spectacular computer-generated special effects. For example, the varied species of aliens and monsters in George Lucas' six-part *Star Wars* series are worthy successors of William Blake. Poetry, alas, has lost its psychotics!

In conclusion, renewed study of Theodore Roethke is precisely the way to reform and redirect literary studies, which are presently in disarray amid the slow implosion of post-structuralism and postmodernism. With his unerring instinct for universal themes and his plain use of common imagery—dog, fish, crow, crab, water, earth—Roethke is one of the most accessible of poets. He does not need the tortuous mediation of mandarin scholars to interpret and explain him. As the product of a family dedicated to unceasing manual labor, Roethke is completely without elitism. As a working poet, he shows aspiring writers how to gather and shape materials near to hand and how to develop and refine a unique voice that still preserves the great conversation among successive generations of poets.

Much of American and British poetry from Roethke's period has dated. But Roethke's major poems, written more than a half-century ago, still feel fresh and contemporary. Roethke's refusal to be drawn into political topicality has ironically aided his longevity. With young people increasingly drawn to environmental issues, the time seems right for poetry to realign itself with nature and to recover the prophetic power it once had in the 1960s. Let us all agree that a path to that reawakening lies through Theodore Roethke, a giant of American imagination.

1. Theodore Roethke, "Some Self-Analysis," in *On the Poet and His Craft: Selected Prose of Theodore Roethke*, ed. Ralph J. Mills, Jr. (Seattle and London, 1965), p. 4.

2. Roethke, "An American Poet Introduces Himself and His Poems," ibid., p. 7.

3. Ibid., pp. 8–9.

4. Theodore Roethke, *Straw for the Fire: From the Notebooks of Theodore Roethke 1943–63*, ed. David Wagoner (New York, 1974), p. 150.

5. Ibid.

6. John Wain, "The Monocle of My Sea-Faced Uncle," in *Theodore Roethke: Essays on the Poetry*, ed. Arnold Stein (Seattle and London, 1965), p. 61.

7. Quoted in Allan Seager, *The Glass House: The Life of Theodore Roethke* (New York, 1968), p. 139. "A class can be a dance," Roethke also said in "A Word to the Instructor," *On the Poet and His Craft*, p. 55.

8. Roethke, "The Teaching Poet," *On the Poet and His Craft*, p. 51; *Straw for the Fire*, p. 231.

9. Quoted in Seager, *The Glass House*, pp. 138–39. See also "poetry as experience" in "A Word to the Instructor," *On the Poet and His Craft*, p. 52.

10. Roethke, *Straw for the Fire*, p. 231.

11. *Remembering Elizabeth Bishop: An Oral Biography* (Amherst, MA, 1994), ed. Gary Fountain and Peter Brazeau, p. 209.

12. Quoted in Seager, *The Glass House*, pp. 180–84.

13. Quoted in *Theodore Roethke: Poetry of the Earth, Poet of the Spirit* (Port Washington, 1981), p. 19.

14. Quoted in Seager, *The Glass House*, p. 13.

15. See "Roethke's Mysticism," in Neal Bowers, *Theodore Roethke: From I to Otherwise* (Columbia, MO, 1982), pp. 2–46.

16. Quoted from unpublished transcript of interviews with Roethke for the film *In a Dark Time*, in Bowers, ibid., p. 10.

17. Quoted in Seager, *The Glass House*, p. 101.

18. Roethke, *Straw for the Fire*, pp. 93, 150.

35

FINAL CUT:
THE SELECTION PROCESS FOR
BREAK, BLOW, BURN

Break, Blow, Burn, my collection of close readings of forty-three poems, took five years to write. The first year was devoted to a search for material in public and academic libraries as well as bookstores. I was looking for poems in English from the last four centuries that I could wholeheartedly recommend to general readers, especially those who may not have read a poem since college. For decades, poetry has been a losing proposition for major trade publishers. I was convinced that there was still a potentially large audience for poetry who had drifted away for unclear reasons. That such an audience does in fact exist seemed proved by the success of *Break, Blow, Burn,* which may be the only book of poetry criticism that has ever reached the national bestseller list in the United States.

On my two book tours (for the Pantheon hardback in 2005 and the Vintage paperback in 2006), I was constantly asked by readers or interviewers why this or that famous poet was not included in *Break, Blow, Burn,* which begins with Shakespeare and ends with Joni Mitchell. At the prospectus stage of the project, I had assumed that most of the principal modern and contemporary poets would be well repre-

[*Arion,* Fall 2008.]

sented. But once launched on the task of gathering possible entries, I was shocked and disappointed by what I found. Poem after poem, when approached from the perspective of the general audience rather than that of academic criticism, shrank into inconsequence or pretension. Or poets whom I fondly remembered from my college and graduate school studies turned out to have produced impressive bodies of serious work but no single poem that could stand up as an artifact to the classic poems elsewhere in the book. The ultimate standard that I applied in my selection process was based on William Butler Yeats' "The Second Coming," a masterpiece of sinewy modern English.

Ezra Pound, because of his generous mentoring of and vast influence on other poets (such as T. S. Eliot and William Carlos Williams), should have been automatically included in *Break, Blow, Burn*. But to my dismay, I could not find a single usable Pound poem—just a monotonous series of showy, pointless, arcane allusions to prior literature. The equally influential W. H. Auden was high on my original list. But after reviewing Auden's collected poetry, I was stunned to discover how few of his poems can stand on their own in today's media-saturated cultural climate. Auden's most anthologized poem, "Musée des Beaux Arts," inspired by a Brueghel painting, felt dated in its portentous mannerisms. A homoerotic love poem by Auden that I had always planned to include begins, "Lay your sleeping head, my love, / Human on my faithless arm." But when I returned to it, I found the poem perilously top-heavy with that single fine sentence. Everything afterward dissolves into vague blather. It was perhaps the most painful example that I encountered of great openings not being sustained.

Surely the lucid and vivacious Marianne Moore, so hugely popular in her day, would have produced many poems to appeal to the general reader. However, while I was charmed by Moore's ingenious variety of formats, I became uncomfortable and impatient with her reflex jokiness, which began to seem like an avoidance of emotion. Nothing went very deep. Because I was so eager to get a good sports poem into *Break, Blow, Burn* (I never found one), I had high hopes for Moore's beloved odes to baseball. Alas, compared to today's high-impact, around-the-clock sports talk on radio and TV, Moore's baseball lingo came across as fussy and corny.

Elizabeth Bishop presented an opposite problem. Bishop is truly a poet's poet, a refined craftsman whose discreet, shapely poems carry a potent emotional charge beneath their transparent surface. I had expected a wealth of Bishop poems to choose from. With my eye on the general reader, I was keenly anticipating a cascade of sensuous tropical imagery drawn from Bishop's life in Brazil. But when I returned to her collected poems, the observed details to my surprise seemed oppressively clouded with sentimental self-projection. For example, I found Bishop's much-anthologized poem "The Fish" nearly unbearable due to her obtrusively simmering self-pity. (Wounded animal poems, typifying the anthropomorphic fallacy, have become an exasperating cliché over the past sixty years.) Even splendid, monumental Brazil evidently couldn't break into Bishop's weary bubble, which traveled with her wherever she went. It may be time to jettison depressiveness as a fashionable badge of creativity.

Charles Bukowski was another poet slated from the start to be prominently featured in *Break, Blow, Burn*. (Indeed, he proved to be the writer I was most asked about on my book tours.) I had planned to make the dissolute Bukowski a crown jewel, demonstrating the scornful rejection by my rowdy, raucous 1960s generation of the genteel proprieties of 1950s literary criticism, still faithfully practiced by the erudite but terminally prim Helen Vendler. I was looking for a funny, squalid street or barroom poem, preferably with boorish knockdown brawling and half-clad shady ladies. But as with Elizabeth Bishop, I could not find a single poem to endorse in good faith for the general reader. And Bukowski was staggeringly prolific: I ransacked shelf upon shelf of his work. But he obviously had little interest in disciplining or consolidating his garrulous, meandering poems. Frustrated, I fantasized about scissoring out juicy excerpts and taping together my own ideal Platonic form of a Bukowski poem. The missing Bukowski may be the surly Banquo's ghost of *Break, Blow, Burn*.

Feminist poetry proved a dispiriting dead end. Grimly ideological and message-driven, it preaches to the choir and has little crossover relevance for a general audience. Adrienne Rich's "Diving into the Wreck," a big anthology favorite, is symptomatic of the intractable artistic problem. A tremendously promising master metaphor—Rich uses deep-sea diving to dramatize modern women's confrontation with a declining patriarchal civilization—collapses into monotonous sermonizing and embarrassing bathos. The poem's clumsiness and redundancy are excruciating (risible "flippers," for example, loom large). I was more optimistic about finding a good feminist poem by Marge Piercy, who treats her woman-centric themes with spunky humor. Piercy's work is full of smart perceptions and sparkling turns of phrase, but her poems too often seem like casual venting—notes or first drafts rather than considered artifacts. I finally chose for *Break, Blow, Burn* two forceful, lively poems by Wanda Coleman and Rochelle Kraut that are not explicitly feminist but that express a mature and complex perspective on women's lives.

I had glowing memories of dozens of poets whom I had avidly read (or seen read in person) after my introduction to contemporary poetry in college in the mid-1960s: Denise Levertov, Randall Jarrell, Muriel Rukeyser, Robert Duncan, John Berryman, W. D. Snodgrass, Robert Creeley, John Ashbery, and Galway Kinnell, among many others. But when I returned to their work to find material for *Break, Blow, Burn,* I was mortified by my inability to identify a single important short poem to set before the general reader. Live readings seem to have beguiled and distracted too many writers from the more rigorous demands of the printed page—the medium that lasts and that speaks to posterity. All of the above poets deserve our great respect for their talent, skill, versatility, and commitment, but I would question how long their reputations will last in the absence of strong freestanding poems. Beyond that, I was puzzled and repelled by the stratospheric elevation in the critical canon given to John Ashbery in recent decades. "Self-Portrait in a Convex Mirror" (1974), Ashbery's most famous poem, is a florid exercise in strained significance that could and should have been compressed and radically reduced by two-thirds. Can there be any wonder that poetry has lost the cultural status it once enjoyed in the United States when an ingrown, overwrought, and pseudo-philosophical style such as Ashbery's is so universally praised and promoted?

Given my distaste for Ashbery's affectations, it would come as no surprise how much I detest the precious grandiloquence of marquee poets like Jorie Graham, who mirrors back to elite academics their own pedantic preoccupations and inflated sense of self. That Graham, with her fey locutions and tedious self-interrogations, is considered a "difficult" or intellectual poet is simply preposterous. Anointing by the Ivy League, of course, may be the kiss of death: Nobel Prize winner Seamus Heaney, another academic star, enjoys an exaggerated reputation for energetically well-crafted but middling poems that strike me as second- or third-hand Yeats. As for the so-called language poets, with their postmodernist game-playing, they are co-conspirators in the murder and marginalization of poetry in the United States.

For the contemporary poems in *Break, Blow, Burn,* my decisions were based solely on the quality of the poem and never on the fame of the poet. As I stumbled on a promising poem in my search, I photocopied it for later consideration. Once the finalists were assembled, I pored over them again and again to see if they could hold up to sequential re-reading. Did a poem retain its freshness and surprise? Some of my finds were soon dropped when I noted how a powerful opening was not sustained by the rest of the text. It was highly distressing to see what might have been a remarkable poem self-destruct or wither away, as if the poet failed to keep pressure on his or her own imagination—or perhaps to hold the poem back long enough to let it develop and ripen on its own.

An example of this latter problem is William Stafford's "The Color That Really Is." The poem begins stunningly: "The color that really is comes over a desert / after the sun goes down: blue, lavender, / purple . . . What if you saw all this in the day?" Stafford sees the rays of the sun as swords that "slice—life, death, disguise—through space!" These amazing, even shamanistic perceptions about existence are followed by an arresting second stanza sketching a stark scene of chilling specificity: the poet glimpses a woman's "terrible face" under the light of a casino table in Reno. That ravaged face reveals "what a desert was / if you lived there the way it is." The juxtaposition of sublime, visionary images with a gritty slice-of-life portrait is brilliant and daring. But then Stafford attaches a jarring finale—a stanza awkwardly inserting himself in a posture of mawkish piety: "Since then I pause every day to bow my head." What a waste!

Again and again, there were poems that had provocative or inspired first lines but that then fell flat, as if the poet were baffled about how to proceed. For example, Bill Knott's "More Best Jokes of the Delphic Oracle" (wonderfully sly title) begins, "I vow to live always at trash point." What satiric pleasures that bold line promises, but the poem never delivers. Sometimes an ambitious poem would find its natural architecture but then neglect smaller details of workmanship or tone. An example is Bob Kaufman's "To My Son Parker, Asleep in the Next Room." An African-American Beat poet, Kaufman, like his colleague Allen Ginsberg, was directly influenced by Walt Whitman. This memorable poem is an epic chant that surveys human history from "shaggy Neanderthals" marking "ochre walls in ice-formed caves" to artists and priests in far-flung cultures from Egypt and Assyria to China, Melanesia, and Peru. The rhythms are forceful and insistent and the images compellingly visual or visceral. The poem ends in an exalted if uneven coda celebrating freedom.

After working with Kaufman's poem, however, I became disillusioned by its needlessly simplistic politics: India is "holy," while Greece is "bloody"—as if India's soil has not been equally drenched in blood. And there are rote hits at "degenerate Rome" and "slave Europe." These angry value judgments, exalting all non-Caucasians over Europeans, have become so hackneyed through political correctness since the 1960s that they undermine the poem, whose ultimate theme is human aspiration and artistic achievement. The poet would have served his poem better with a more expansive, forgiving, and authentically Whitmanian vision. As is, it is too close to a rant. Kaufman's sadly self-limiting poem demonstrates how progressive American poetry began to isolate itself from general society in the last half of the twentieth century. When poets defensively cluster in a ghetto of homogeneous opinion, they lose contact with their larger audience. Great poetry never requires a political litmus test.

A poem that emerged from a quite different social milieu is Morris Bishop's "The Witch of East Seventy-Second Street," which was published in *The New Yorker* in 1953. Though my primary critical sympathy remains with the rude, rebellious Beat style, I find Bishop's poem far more effective than Kaufman's in reaching its artistic goal:

"I will put upon you the Telephone Curse," said the witch.
"The telephone will call when you are standing on a chair with a
        Chinese vase in either hand,
And when you answer, you will hear only the derisive popping of
        corks."
But I was armed so strong in honesty
Her threats passed by me like the idle wind.

"And I will put upon you the Curse of Dropping," said the witch.
"The dropping of tiny tacks, the dropping of food gobbets,
The escape of wet dishes from the eager-grasping hand,
The dropping of spectacles, stitches, final consonants, the
        abdomen."
I sneered, jeered, fleered; I flouted, scouted; I
        pooh-pooh-poohed.

"I will put upon you the Curse of Forgetting!" screamed the
        witch.
"Names, numbers, faces, old songs, old joy,
Words that once were magic, love, upward ways, the way home."
"No doubt the forgotten is well forgotten," said I.

"And I will put upon you the Curse of Remembering," bubbled
        the witch.
Terror struck my eyes, knees, heart;
And I took her charred contract
And signed in triplicate.

Catering with its chic uptown address, well-appointed decor, and so-phisticated whimsy to the affluent readers of the glossy *New Yorker*, "The Witch of East Seventy-Second Street" nevertheless manages to tap archetypal imagery for eerily unsettling effect. Poet and witch have an odd intimacy: she breaks into his ordered routine like an ambassador from elemental nature. Is she a malign proxy for mother or wife, as in fairy tales? She speaks in ominous parallelism, like the witches of *Macbeth*—four curses in four stanzas, culminating in the parodic "triplicate" business contract, "charred" by hellfire and signed by the defeated poet.

As with Jaques' melancholy speech about the seven ages of man in Shakespeare's *As You Like It,* human life is mapped as a series of losses, with the elderly regressing to an infantile state. The witch's "Curse of Dropping" attacks the body (fingers and hands stiffen; the belly sags), while her "Curse of Forgetting" attacks the mind (memory lapses, especially costly to poets with their bardic mission). Everything valuable in life—emotion as well as sensation—seems to recede. But the worst is the "Curse of Remembering," which overwhelms the mind with regrets. Remembering is too crushing a burden. Better to remain in the fenced preserve of quaint connoisseurship (the Chinese vases), into which modern technology can barely penetrate (the sputtering telephone). The poem presents the poet as isolated, refined, and removed from collective joys (the "popping of corks" at unattended parties), but open to attack from mythic forces. It's as if, with their active imagination, poets are the vulnerable point in modern civilization, where the archaic can invade and retake spiritual territory.

Bishop's poem, for all its virtues, finally seemed too arch or pat for *Break, Blow, Burn.* A poem that came very close to inclusion, however, was Gary Snyder's "Strategic Air Command." (I decided to use Snyder's "Old Pond" instead.)

> The hiss and flashing lights of a jet
> Pass near Jupiter in Virgo.
> He asks, how many satellites in the sky?
> Does anyone know where they all are?
> What are they doing, who watches them?
>
> Frost settles on the sleeping bags.
> The last embers of fire,
> One more cup of tea,
> At the edge of a high lake rimmed with snow.
>
> These cliffs and the stars
> Belong to the same universe.

This little air in between
Belongs to the twentieth century and its wars.

VIII, 82, Koip Peak, Sierra Nevada

Snyder's opposition of serene nature to ethically distorted society is classically High Romantic. The two men camping out in the Sierra Nevada mountains hear the "hiss" of a military jet, the serpent in the garden as well as an avatar of impersonal industrial mechanization. The jet's passage near the planet Jupiter in the constellation and astrological sign of Virgo suggests that male authority figures (as in William Blake) have become cruel or sterile. God's periodic encounter with a virgin (as in Yeats) can lead to a destructive new birth. The rogue satellites are the all-seeing eyes of government surveillance, agents of a global system of mutual hostility and fear.

The visitors seek a spartan simplicity. They have stripped down to essentials in order to purify themselves, like tea-drinking Buddhist monks at the "high lake rimmed with snow." The fading fire (as in Shakespeare's Sonnet 73) represents an elemental reality, like the frost settling on the sleeping bags, prefiguring the beds of the dead. The men's humble comforts, with their tactile immediacy, contrast with the jet's dehumanized perfection and arrogance. Earth, air, water, and fire: these endure, while political events flare up and disappear, like the jet. The poet contemplates the largeness of the universe, compared to the narrow band of the earth's atmosphere, where the jet, representing the war-torn twentieth century, cruises. Skeptical questions could certainly be asked: would Snyder return society to the preliterate nomadic era, when humans lived desperately hand to mouth and were helplessly vulnerable to accident and disease? But that does not invalidate his protest. The poem is prophetic: machines, dazzling artifices of the mind, may gradually be robbing humanity of free will, but nature is ultimately unreachable, unperturbed by human folly. Wars, like the jet's "flashing lights," are mere dying sparks in nature's harmony.

Because Allen Ginsberg had made such a huge impact on me in college, I confidently expected him to play a prominent role in *Break,*

Blow, Burn. But *Howl,* my favorite Ginsberg poem, proved thornily difficult to excerpt: the notorious opening section (starting "I saw the best minds of my generation destroyed by madness, starving hysterical naked") seemed too strident and unsupported on its own. Ginsberg's oft-anthologized "A Supermarket in California" was a possibility, but I found its prosy humor a bit too blatant. There was an obscure early Ginsberg poem, however, that obsessed me—"The Blue Angel." But its traditional format (six four-line stanzas) is so unrepresentative of Ginsberg's work as a whole that I felt it would mislead a general audience. Furthermore, because the theme is Marlene Dietrich, it might seem as if I had chosen the poem merely because it's about a movie star—a charge that might well have been true! (My first book, *Sexual Personae,* argued that cinema, prefigured in Plato, is the master principle of Western culture.)

The title refers to Dietrich's breakthrough 1930 film, *The Blue Angel,* where she plays a cabaret femme fatale. The poem begins: "Marlene Dietrich is singing a lament / for mechanical love." Ginsberg portrays Dietrich as "a life-sized toy, / the doll of eternity." She is a streamlined objet d'art: her hair is "shaped like an abstract hat / made out of white steel." But her face is ghoulishly "whitewashed and / immobile like a robot," with a "little white key" protruding from the temple. Her eyes, with their "dull blue pupils," are "blank / like a statue's in a museum."

Ginsberg's poem works on multiple levels—cultural, biological, and psychological. First of all, the Dietrich doll, like a surreal construction by Salvador Dalí (who did mock-ups of Mae West and Shirley Temple), represents the artificial projections of Hollywood, the studio-created stars whose machine-made images infatuated audiences around the globe. White-blonde Dietrich is a modernist abstraction, an *idea* of sex removed from the sensory. She is eternal because her celluloid image will never age.

More disturbingly, Ginsberg also portrays female sexuality as a brute, fascist imperative. That there is personal projection here seems proved first by a tagline identifying the poem as a dream that Ginsberg had in Paterson in 1950, and second by the despairing coda, introduced by a hasty dash: "—you'd think I would have thought a plan / to end the inner grind, / but not till I have found a man / to occupy my mind." A startlingly frank gay revelation for that repressed period. But after so vividly hallucinatory a poem, what strangely bland language. Here Ginsberg plainly suggests that his homosexuality was a route of escape from the drearily grinding occupation of his mental space by demanding, domineering women—above all his mother, whose mental breakdown and institutionalization he would memorialize in *Kaddish*. Walt Whitman's longings for a male comrade were couched in far more effusive and tender language. But in Ginsberg's poem, all of the drama and glamour belong to a pitiless female automaton.

Related questions: is Dietrich, with her "lament / for mechanical love," a personification of random, anonymous gay sex, with which Ginsberg was perhaps feeling fatigued or disillusioned? As a gay male icon at the time, was Dietrich a symbol of gay men's own enforced, artificial construction of self? Is Ginsberg implying that gay male love is a flight from real women—a jailbreak toward male identity and freedom? Woman's image here is godlike yet cold and terrifying (like Yeats' desert beast with its "blank and pitiless" gaze in "The Second Coming"). Dietrich sings, but she does not speak. Was poetry Ginsberg's way of reclaiming and liberating language?

Gay men's cultish attachment to movie stars in the closeted era before the 1969 Stonewall rebellion, which sparked the gay liberation movement, is also registered in a sprightly little untitled poem by Frank O'Hara that begins, "Lana Turner has collapsed!" O'Hara, who always wrote quickly, tossed it off on the Staten Island ferry on his way to a 1962 reading where he scandalized Robert Lowell by impudently reciting it. I was very tempted to use this increasingly popular poem in *Break, Blow, Burn* but decided instead to treat another O'Hara poem, "A Mexican Guitar," which has never to my knowledge received critical comment or even been publicly noticed.

At the time O'Hara wrote his Lana Turner poem, most intellectuals accepted European cinema as an art form but still dismissed Hollywood glamour movies as trash or kitsch. The "Method," ultra-serious and socially leftist, was the prestige style in acting. But splashy Hollywood movies, with their ferocious or suffering divas (Bette Davis, Judy Garland) and their frivolity and excess (Busby Berkeley, Carmen Miranda), were defiantly central to gay male "camp." Andy Warhol's hyper-colored silk screens of Elizabeth Taylor and Marilyn Monroe cheekily turned movie stars into Byzantine icons.

Angst-ridden, suicide-studded Confessional poetry was then at its height. Lana Turner, fresh from a series of lurid scandals, was a symbol of glitzy tabloid celebrity and not remotely an appropriate subject for a poem. "Lana Turner Collapses on Movie Set" was an actual headline, a version of which O'Hara evidently spotted on a New York newsstand. The poet describes the weird muddle of rain, snow, and city traffic through which he hurries, distracted. The headline, with its boldface visual clarity and exclamatory, telegraphic diction, breaks on him like an electrifying epiphany. The grey mediocrity of everyday life seems transformed, and the slippery ambiguities of language and definition in which a poet dwells are temporarily transcended. Lana Turner's soap opera traumas are like a ritual martyrdom, a sacrament avidly witnessed by her millions of fans. O'Hara's last line: "oh Lana Turner we love you get up." Who is "we"? Presumably gay men, who found themselves sympathetically bonding as fans with a vast audience of mainstream movie-lovers who normally ostracized them.

Lynn Emanuel's poem "Frying Trout While Drunk" is far more sober. Instead of the kinetic urban landscape of O'Hara's fancy-free sophisticates (the Lana Turner poem refers to "lots of parties" where the poet "acted perfectly disgraceful"), we are now in a crimped realm of psychological entrapment and wounded memory.

> Mother is drinking to forget a man
> Who could fill the woods with invitations:
> Come with me he whispered and she went
> In his Nash Rambler, its dash
> Where her knees turned green
> In the radium dials of the '50s.
> When I drink it is always 1953,
> Bacon wilting in the pan on Cook Street
> And mother, wrist deep in red water,
> Laying a trail from the sink
> To a glass of gin and back.
> She is a beautiful, unlucky woman

In love with a man of lechery so solid
You could build a table on it
And when you did the blues would come to visit.
I remember all of us awkwardly at dinner,
The dark slung across the porch,
And then mother's dress falling to the floor,
Buttons ticking like seeds spit on a plate.
When I drink I am too much like her—
The knife in one hand and in the other
The trout with a belly white as my wrist.
I have loved you all my life
She told him and it was true
In the same way that all her life
She drank, dedicated to the act itself,
She stood at this stove
And with the care of the very drunk
Handed him the plate.

As autobiography, if it is that, Emanuel's poem seems influenced by Robert Lowell's seminal *Life Studies* (1959). (I used a Lowell poem from that book, "Man and Wife," instead of this one.) Admirably condensed and finely written, "Frying Trout" distills an entire life of helpless observation and pained reflection. Food, drink, and sex are literally and symbolically intertwined. Everyday routine and rituals, such as cooking, are punctuated by erratic and impulsive breaches of convention. The daughter both admires and pities her mother and tries to understand her weaknesses and compromises, which she fears she has inherited via the time-dissolving act of drinking. The mother is betrayed and humiliated by her own desires and foolish trust. She accepts exploitation and betrayal as the price of sexual pleasure, a mime of love.

Emanuel's intense imagery, skillfully underplayed, is tremendously evocative. The knife and white-bellied trout suggest sex but also a masochistic vulnerability. Exquisitely caught details abound in quick scenarios: the mother's knees turning green in the car's radio light; bloody water trailing to a gin glass; buttons of a fallen dress "ticking like seeds spit on a plate." Flesh is fruit here, carelessly devoured. This poem patiently, methodically offers its story without sentimentality or melodrama. There is no flinching from harsh facts and yet no gratuitous self-dramatization either. Emanuel's technique is quiet, steady, and scrupulously exact. "Frying Trout While Drunk" is a tour de force of courageous truth-telling.

Two poems about women rockers nearly made the final cut. In "Marianne Faithfull's Cigarette," Gerry Gomez Pearlberg describes a scene of charged suspension and voyeurism. Spare and ritualistically structured, this poem has a cool Baudelairean perversity. Marianne Faithfull, "bored," is chain-smoking while a crew of daft academics is "talking, talking, talking." The poet is transfixed by the singer's discarded cigarette, branded with its "ring of lipstick." There is an idolatrous fetishism in her desire for the butt, but she asks someone else to fetch it. Abashed, she herself will not cross the aesthetic distance to the enthroned star, whose insouciance is wonderfully caught.

The poem becomes the words that the poet could not speak in the star's presence. I love the gap between the academics' inflated discourse and the squalid litter of Faithfull's red-smeared cigarettes—a tainted beauty that the fascinated poet tries to capture. However, I did not include Pearlberg's poem, which so perfectly captures my own cultic attitude toward stars (such as Elizabeth Taylor, Catherine Deneuve, or Daniela Mercury), because I was uncertain about its interest to a general audience. Furthermore, I had qualms about the finale: "Watching her light up was like seeing the Messiah. / Or Buddha's burning moment under leaves of cool desire." This is way too much. Faithfull's oblique, imperious divinity is already well caught by the poem. We don't need the Messiah and Buddha, with their centuries of accumulated associations, to come crashing in like colossi. All the poem needs at the end is a haiku effect, words floating off like smoke.

Alice Fulton's "You Can't Rhumboogie in a Ball and Chain" is a tribute to Janis Joplin. ("Ball 'n' Chain," a blues song by Big Mama Thornton, was Joplin's hallmark.) The first two stanazas are a knockout:

> You called the blues' loose black belly lover
> and in Port Arthur they called you pig-face.

The way you chugged booze straight, without a glass,
your brass-assed language, slingbacks with jeweled heel,
proclaimed you no kin to their muzzled blood.
No chiclet-toothed Baptist boyfriend for you.

Strung-out, street hustling showed men wouldn't buy you.
Once you clung to the legs of a lover,
let him drag you till your knees turned to blood,
mouth hardened to a thin scar on your face,
cracked under songs, screams, never left to heal.
Little Girl Blue, soul pressed against the glass.

The heavy sprung rhythms and eye-popping imagery, rattling the reader with hard consonants and alliteration, are reminiscent of the poet-priest Gerard Manley Hopkins, whose ecstatic techniques are deployed here for far earthier and more carnal purposes. Even Fulton's rugged slang scintillates. Through a series of sleazy snapshots, Joplin's pain and defiance and her bold explorations of the netherworld are rivetingly captured.

If it had continued at this sensational level, "You Can't Rhumboogie" would, in my view, have become a contemporary classic. But over the next four stanzas, the sense of urgent compression is lost. We get tantalizing glimpses of seedy diners, "nameless motels," and bad memories of senior proms, but the bruising shocks of the wonderful opening stanzas are repeated and done to death. "Blood" pops up in every stanza; there are simply too many traumas and tortures for the beleaguered reader to process. Instead of sympathizing with Joplin, we feel resentfully penned in a gore-spattered emergency room. While the powerful rhythms and images did all the work at the start, there's now a turn toward editorializing and psychoanalysis ("self-hatred laced your blood").

The final stanza is clever but makes too radical a shift in tone:

Like clerks we face your image in the glass,
suggest lovers, as accessories, heels.
"It's your shade, this blood dress," we say. "It's you."

Well, we've sure left Texas. That's Sylvia Plath coming through the door—a far more middle-class and coyly ironic voice. Fulton has unfortunately abandoned the proletarian percussiveness of her opening, which explodes with the vernacular.

David Young's "Occupational Hazards" still enchants and intrigues me. It draws its inspiration from riddles, fairy tales, children's songs, and emblematic chapbooks with roots in medieval allegory:

> *Butcher*
> If I want to go to pieces
> I can do that. When I try
> to pull myself together
> I get sausage.

> *Bakers*
> Can't be choosers. Rising
> from a white bed, from dreams
> of kings, bright cities, buttocks,
> to see the moon by daylight.

> *Tailor*
> It's not the way the needle
> drags the poor thread around.
> It's sewing the monster together,
> my misshapen son.

> *Gravediggers*
> To be the baker's dark opposite,
> to dig the anti-cake, to stow
> the sinking loaves in the unoven—
> then to be dancing on the job!

> *Woodcutter*
> Deep in my hands
> as far as I can go

the fallen trees
keep ringing.

The poet's pure pleasure in improvisational, associative play with language is registered in the mercurial puns and quirky metaphors. Young's catalog of occupations echoes the children's limerick "Rub-a-dub-dub, three men in a tub" ("The butcher, the baker, the candlestick-maker"). However, each vocation here—butcher, baker, tailor, gravedigger, woodcutter—can be read as an analogue to the practice of poetry.

The butcher going to pieces is the poet exploring his or her emotional extremes, out of which may come "sausage," the inner life ground up, processed, and strung together in linked stanzas. Such a life requires intestinal fortitude. Rising long before dawn, bakers (normally beggars) "can't be choosers"; like writers wrestling with their material, they are under compulsion to knead their sticky, shapeless dough. With a strangely active dream life, the bakers see metaphorically: "buttocks" and "moon" prefigure the raw white loaf (compare the slang term "buns" for buttocks; flashing one's buttocks is "mooning"). Poets, the "kings" of their own "bright cities," have a tactile intimacy with language, while their sources of inspiration range from the coarsely material to the celestial.

A tailor at work resembles the poet cutting, trimming, and stitching his verse. The needle is the sudden penetration of insight, while the flexible thread, assuring continuity and shape, is dragged in the rear as a secondary process. The result is "my misshapen son": art-making by men is an appropriation of female fertility. The end product, like Frankenstein's "monster" with his stitched-up face, may seem ugly or distorted (in an avant-garde era). But the artwork is the artist's true posterity, a child of the intellect rather than the body—a distinction made by Plato.

Young wittily says that the merry gravedigger ("the baker's dark opposite") must "dig the anti-cake" and "stow the sinking loaves in the unoven"—as if the bakery has gone through Alice's looking-glass and turned into a graveyard. Cake and corpses: this morbid mingling of sweets and rot is a brilliant conflation of motifs from *Hamlet,* with its jovial gravedigger and its satirical imagery of the murdered king's body served up as "funeral baked meats" at a too-hasty wedding banquet, where the main dish is the queen (*Hamlet* I.2.180). Meditating on elemental realities, the poet faces death and turns it into artistic sustenance and pleasure ("dancing on the job"). Finally, the woodcutter is the poet who ruthlessly topples his lofty forebears to clear mental space for himself. But their words still ring in his mind. They have seeped into his bones, to the deepest layers of his psyche. Poetry, a form of making, is a mission he cannot escape. The battered hands of the craftsman dictate to the soul.

I often regret not including David Young's marvelous poem in *Break, Blow, Burn.* But in perfect truth, I wondered if I could do it justice. It was weighed against May Swenson's "At East River," which has a similar list-like format and childlike sense of wonder. I ultimately went with Swenson because of her poem's intriguing parallelism with Wordsworth's panoramic sonnet about a modern metropolis tranquilly embraced by nature, "Composed Upon Westminster Bridge," which appears earlier in my book.

A. R. Ammons' "Mechanism" upset me severely and still does. This poem should have been the dramatic climax of *Break, Blow, Burn.* In fact, it should have been one of the greatest poems of the twentieth century. Its vision of complex systems operating simultaneously in human beings and animal nature is at the very highest level of artistic inspiration. But in execution, the poem is a shambles, with weak transitions and phrasings that veer from the derivative to the pedantic. "Mechanism" (available online, including at the Poetry Foundation Web site) is my primary exhibit for the isolation and self-destruction of American poetry over the past forty years:

> Honor a going thing, goldfinch, corporation, tree,
>   morality: any working order

The pretty goldfinch flitting in and out of the poem symbolizes nature unconscious of itself. Flashing through the cherry bushes in the last line, it carries a valedictory blessing like the ones in Wordsworth's "Tintern Abbey" and Wallace Stevens' early poem "Sunday Morning" (which ends with flocks of birds sinking "on extended wings").

But it is the doggedly philosophical late Stevens, notably in "The Auroras of Autumn" and "An Ordinary Evening in New Haven," who is exercising a baleful and crippling influence here on Ammons, as on so many other American poets of his generation, including John Ashbery. (Two examples of luminous early Stevens appear in *Break, Blow, Burn.*) Over time, Stevens' language tragically failed him. He ended his career with a laborious, plodding, skeletal style, employed in self-questioning poems of numbing length. Gorgeous images or lines still abound, but pompous, big-think gestures have become a crutch.

The obtrusive "ideas" in late Stevens have naturally provided grist for the ever-churning academic mill. But poetry is not philosophy. Philosophic discourse has its own noble medium as prose argumentation or dramatic dialogue. Poetry should not require academic translators to mediate between the poet and his or her audience. Poetry is a sensory mode where ideas are or should be fully embodied in emotion or in imagery grounded in the material world. Late Stevens suffers from spiritual anorexia; he shows the modernist sensibility stretched to the breaking point. Late Stevens is not a fruitful model for the future of poetry.

In Ammons' "Mechanism," Whitman's influence can be felt in the cosmic perspective and catalog of organic phenomena. But there isn't nearly enough specificity here. Whitman was able to invoke nature's largest, most turbulent forces along with the tiniest details of straw, seeds, or sea spray. Ammons was on the verge of a major conceptual breakthrough in his willingness to consider the intricacies of human organizations, corporations, and management as expressions of the nature-inspired drive toward order. Whitman's melting, all-embracing Romantic love is no longer enough for a modern high-tech world. Connecting sexual "courtship" to state-guaranteed "territorial rights," Ammons is using an anthropological lens to focus on the ancient birth of civilization itself in law and contract. And by conflating history, science, economy, and art, he would end the war between the artist and commercial society that began with the Industrial Revolution and that has resulted in the artist's pitiful marginalization in an era dominated by mass media.

"Mechanism" approaches a view of consciousness itself as a product of evolutionary biology. The minute chemistry of enzymes and platelets is made almost psychedelically visible. The poem makes us ponder huge questions: are we merely flitting goldfinches in nature's master plan? Is free will an illusion? Is art too a product of natural design? But the poem is fatally weakened by its abstruse diction, bombastic syntax, and factitious format. Why did Ammons choose those untidy, erratically staggered triads? They seem forced and arbitrary, out of sync with his own music. While David Young's cryptic "Occupational Hazards" uses a concrete, vigorous, living English that connects us to the sixteenth century, "Mechanism" relies on a clotted, undigested academese that strains at profundity.

And the poem is too long (sixteen stanzas). Shakespeare's sonnets, bridging his piercing emotional experiences with his wary social observations, demonstrate the beauty and power of high condensation. In his great sonnet, "Leda and the Swan," Yeats showed how a vast historical perspective could illuminate shattering contemporary events. Perhaps "Mechanism" should have been a sonnet, a worthy heir to Shakespeare and Yeats. But the poem shows the increasing distance of the poet from general society, which Ammons is analyzing but is no longer addressing in its own language. It prefigures what would happen to American poetry over the following decades, as the most ambitious poets became stranded in their own coteries and cultivated a self-blinding disdain for the surrounding culture.

36

WESTERN LOVE POETRY

In evaluating love poetry, we must ask first whether the language is private and original or formulaic and rhetorical. Is the poet speaking for him- or herself, or is the voice a persona? The poem, if commissioned by friend or patron, may be a projection into another's adventures, or it may be an improvised conflation of real and invented details. A love poem cannot be simplistically read as a literal, journalistic record of an event or relationship; there is always some fictive reshaping of reality for dramatic or psychological ends. A love poem is secondary rather than primary experience; as an imaginative construction, it invites detached contemplation of the spectacle of sex.

We must be particularly cautious when dealing with controversial forms of eroticism like homosexuality. Poems are unreliable historical evidence about any society; they may reflect the consciousness of only one exceptional person. Furthermore, homoerotic images or fantasies in poetry must not be confused with concrete homosexual practice. We may speak of tastes or tendencies in early poets but not of sexual orientation: this is a modern idea.

Love poetry is equally informed by artistic tradition and contemporary cultural assumptions. The pagan attitude toward the body and its pleasures was quite different from that of Christianity, which assigns sex to the fallen realm of nature. The richness of Western love poetry may thus arise in part from the dilemma of how to reconcile mind or

[From *The New Princeton Encyclopedia of Poetry and Poetics,*
ed. Alex Preminger and T. V. F. Brogan (1993).]

soul with body. Moreover, the generally higher social status of women in Western as opposed to Eastern culture has given love poetry added complexity or ambivalence: only women of strong personality could have inspired the tormented sagas of Catullus or Propertius. We must try to identify a poem's intended audience. In antiquity the love poet was usually addressing a coterie of friends or connoisseurs; since Romanticism, however, the poet speaks to him- or herself, with the reader seeming to overhear private thoughts. We must ask about pornographic material in love poetry whether it reflects the freer sensibilities of a different time or whether the poet set out to shock or challenge his contemporaries. Much love poetry is clearly testing the limits of decorous speech, partly to bring sexual desire under the scrutiny and control of imagination. In the great Western theme of the transience of time, vivid sensuous details illustrate the evanescence of youth and beauty; the poet has a godlike power to defeat time and bestow immortality upon the beloved through art. Romantic impediments give the poem a dramatic frame: the beloved may be indifferent, far away, married to someone else, dead, or of the wrong sex. However, difficulty or disaster in real life is converted into artistic opportunity by the poet, whose work profits from the intensification and exploration of negative emotion.

The history of European love poetry begins with the Greek lyric poets of the Archaic age (7th–6th centuries B.C.). Archilochus, Mimnermus, Sappho, and Alcaeus turn poetry away from the grand epic style toward the quiet personal voice, attentive to mood and emotion. Despite the fragmentary survival of Greek solo poetry, we see that it contains a new idea of love, which Homer shows as foolish or deceptive but never unhappy. Archilochus' account of the anguish of love is deepened by Sappho, whose poetry was honored by male writers and grammarians until the fall of Rome. Sappho and Alcaeus were active on Lesbos, an affluent island off the Aeolian coast of Asia Minor where aristocratic women apparently had more freedom than later in classical Athens. Sappho is primarily a love poet, uninterested in politics or metaphysics. The nature of her love has caused much controversy and many fabrications, some by major scholars. Sappho was married, and she had a daughter, but her poetry suggests that she fell in love with a series of beautiful girls, who moved in and out of her coterie (not a school, club, or cult). There is as yet no evidence, however, that she had physical relations with women. Even the ancients, who had her complete works, were divided about her sexuality.

Sappho shows that love poetry is how Western personality defines itself. The beloved is passionately perceived but also replaceable; he or she may exist primarily as a focus of the poet's consciousness. In "He seems to me a god" (fragment 31), Sappho describes her pain at the sight of a favorite girl sitting and laughing with a man. The lighthearted social scene becomes oppressively internal as the poet sinks into suffering: she cannot speak or see; she is overcome by fever, tremor, pallor. These symptoms of love become conventional and persist for more than a thousand years. In plain, concise language, Sappho analyzes her extreme state as if she were both actor and observer; she is candid and emotional yet dignified, austere, almost clinical. This poem, preserved for us by Longinus, is the first great psychological document of Western literature. Sappho's prayer to Aphrodite (fragment 1) converts cult-song into love poem. The goddess, amused at Sappho's desperate appeal for aid, teasingly reminds her of former infatuations and their inevitable end. Love is an endless cycle of pursuit, triumph, and ennui. The poem, seemingly so charming and transparent, is structured by a complex time scheme of past, present, and future, the ever-flowing stream of our emotional life. Sappho also wrote festive wedding songs and the first known description of a romantic moonlit night. She apparently invented the now commonplace adjective "bittersweet" for the mixed condition of love.

Early Greek love poetry is based on simple parallelism between human emotion and nature, which has a Mediterranean mildness. Love-sickness, like a storm, is sudden and passing. Imagery is vivid and luminous, as in haiku; there is nothing contorted or artificial. Anacreon earned a proverbial reputation for wine, women, and song: his love is not Sappho's spiritual crisis but the passing diversion of a bisexual bon vivant. Love poetry was little written in classical Athens, where lyric was absorbed into the tragic choral ode. Plato, who abandoned poetry for philosophy, left epigrams on the beauty of boys. The learned Alexandrian age revived love poetry as an art mode. Theocritus begins the long literary tradition of pastoral, where shepherds complain of unrequited love under sunny skies. Most of his *Idylls* contain the voices of rustic characters like homely Polyphemus, courting the scornful nymph Galatea, or Lycidas, a goatherd pining for a youth gone to sea. Aging Theocritus broods about his own love for fickle boys, whose blushes haunt him. In his *Epigrams,* Callimachus takes a lighter attitude toward love, to which he applies sporting metaphors of the hunt. In Medea's agonized passion for Jason in the *Argonautica,* Apollonius Rhodius tries to mesh love poetry with epic. Asclepiades adds new symbols to love tradition: Eros and arrow-darting Cupid. Meleager writes with equal relish of cruel boys and voluptuous women, such as Heliodora. His is a poignant, sensual poetry filled with the color and smell of flowers.

The *Greek Anthology* demonstrates the changes in Greek love poetry from the Alexandrian through Roman periods. As urban centers grow and speed up, nature metaphors recede. Trashy street life begins, and prostitutes, drag queens, randy tutors, and bathhouse masseuses crowd into view. Love poets become droll, jaded, less lyrical. Women are lusciously described but given no personalities or inner life. For the first time, love poetry incorporates ugliness, squalor, and disgust: Leonidas of Tarentum and Marcus Argentarius write of voracious sluts with special skills, and Antipater of Thessalonika coarsely derides scrawny old lechers. Boy-love is universal: Straton of Sardis, editor of an anthology of pederastic poems, celebrates the ripening phases of boys' genitals. By the early Byzantine period, however, we feel the impact of Christianity in more heartfelt sentiment but also in guilt and melancholy.

The Romans inherited a huge body of Greek love poetry. Catullus, the first Latin writer to adapt elegy for love themes, is obsessed with Lesbia, the glamorous noblewoman Clodia, promiscuously partying with midnight pickups. "I love and I hate": this tortured affair is the most complex contribution to love poetry since Sappho, whom Catullus admired and imitated. The poet painfully grapples with the ambiguities and ambivalences of being in love with an aggressive, willful Western woman. He also writes tender love poems to a boy, honey-sweet Juventius. There is no Roman love poetry between adult men. Propertius records a long, tangled involvement with capricious Cynthia, a fast-living new woman. There are sensual bed scenes, love-bites, brawls. After Cynthia dies (perhaps poisoned), the angry, humiliated poet sees her ghost over his bed. Tibullus writes of troubled love for two headstrong mistresses, adulterous Delia and greedy Nemesis, and one elusive boy, Marathus. In Vergil's *Eclogue 2*, the shepherd Corydon passionately laments his love-madness for Alexis, a proud, beautiful youth; the poem was traditionally taken as proof of Vergil's own homosexuality. Horace names a half dozen girls whom he playfully lusts for, but only the rosy boy Ligurinus moves him to tears and dreams. In the *Amores*, Ovid boasts of his sexual prowess and offers strategies for adultery. *The Art of Love* tells how to find and keep a lover, including sexual positions, naughty words, and feigned ecstasies. *The Remedies for Love* contains precepts for falling *out* of love. The love letters of the *Heroides* are rhetorical monologues of famous women (Phaedra, Medea) abandoned by cads. Juvenal shows imperial Rome teeming with effeminates, libertines, and pimps; love or trust is impossible. The Empress prowls the brothels; every good-looking boy is endangered by rich seducers; drunken wives grapple in public stunts. Martial casts himself as a facetious explorer of this lewd world where erections are measured and no girl says no. The *Dionysiaca*, Nonnus' late Greek epic, assembles fanciful erotic episodes from the life of Dionysus. Also extant are many Greek and Latin *priapeia*: obscene comic verses, attached to phallic statues of Priapus in field and garden, which threaten thieves with anal or oral rape.

In medieval romance, love as challenge, danger, or high ideal is central to chivalric quest. From the mid-12th century, woman replaces the feudal lord as center of the militaristic *chansons de geste*. French aristocratic taste was refined by the courtly love of the Occitan (Provençal) troubadours, who raised woman to spiritual dominance, something new in Western love poetry. Amorous intrigue now lures the hero: to consummate his adultery with Guinevere, Chrétien de Troyes' Lancelot bends the bars of her chamber, then bleeds into her bed. The symbolism of golden grail, bleeding lance, and broken sword of Chrétien's *Perceval* is sexual as well as religious. Wolfram von Eschenbach's German Parzival is vowed to purity, but adulterous Anfortas suffers a festering, incurable groin wound. Sexual temptations are specifically set to test a knight's virtue in the French romances *Yder* and *Hunbaut* and the Middle English *Sir Gawain and the Green Knight*. The adultery of Gottfried von Strassburg's Tristan and Isolde, with their steamy lovemaking, helped define Western romantic love as unhappy or doomed. The Trojan tale of faithful Troilus and treacherous Cressida was invented by Benoît de Sainte-Maure and transmitted to Boccaccio and Chaucer. Heavily influenced by Ovid, *The Romance of the Rose* (Guillaume de Lorris and Jean de Meun) uses dreamlike allegory and sexual symbols of flower, garden, and tower to chart love's assault. The pregnancy of the Rose is a first for European literary heroines. Abelard wrote famous love songs, now lost, to Heloise. Dante's youthful love poems to Beatrice in the *Vita nuova* begin in troubadour style, then modulate toward Christian mysticism. In the *Inferno*'s episode of Paolo and Francesca, seduced into adultery by reading a romance of Lancelot, Dante renounces his early affection for courtly love. Medieval Latin lyrics express homoerotic feeling between teacher and student in monastic communities. There are overtly pederastic poems from the 12th century and at least one apparently lesbian one, but no known vernacular or pastoral medieval poetry is homosexual. The goliardic *Carmina Burana* contains beautiful lyrics of the northern flowering of spring and love, as well as cheeky verses of carousing and wenching, some startlingly detailed. The French *fabliau*, a ribald verse-tale twice imitated by Chaucer, reacts against courtly love with bedroom pranks, barnyard drubbings, and an earthy stress on woman's hoary genitality. Villon, zestfully atumble with Parisian trollops, will later combine the devil-may-care goliard's pose with the fabliau's slangy comedy.

Renaissance epic further expands the romantic elements in chivalric adventure. Boiardo, Ariosto, and Tasso open quest to an armed heroine, a motif adopted by Spenser, whose *Faerie Queene*, emulating Ovid's *Metamorphoses*, copiously catalogues incidents of normal and deviant sex. Petrarch, combining troubadour lyricism with Dante's advanced psychology, creates the modern love poem. His Laura, unlike saintly Beatrice, is a real woman, not a symbol. Petrarch's nature, vibrating to the lover's emotions, will become the Romantic pathetic fallacy. His conceits, paradoxes, and images of fire and ice, which

spread in sonnet sequences throughout Europe, inspired and burdened Renaissance poets, who had to discard the convention of frigid
mistress and trembling wooer. Ronsard's sonnets, addressed to Cas-
sandre, Marie, and Hélène, first follow Petrarchan formulas, then
achieve a simpler, more musical, debonair style, exquisitely attuned
to nature. In the *Amoretti,* Spenser practices the sonnet (introduced
to England by Wyatt and Surrey), but his supreme love poem is the
Epithalamion, celebrating marriage. Like Michelangelo, Shakespeare
writes complex love poetry to a beautiful young man and a forceful
woman: the fair youth's homoerotic androgyny is reminiscent of
Shakespeare's soft, "lovely" Adonis and Marlowe's long-haired, white-
fleshed Leander, romanced by Neptune. Richard Barnfield's sonnets
and *Affectionate Shepherd* openly offer succulent sexual delights to a
boy called Ganymede, a common Renaissance allusion. The traditional allegory, based on the Song of Songs, of Christ the bridegroom
knocking at the soul's door, creates unmistakable homoeroticism in
Donne's Holy Sonnet XIV, George Herbert's "Love (III)," and spiritual stanzas by St. John of the Cross. In ardent poems to his fiancée,
later his wife, Donne, with Spenser, demonstrates the new prestige of
marriage: before this, no one wrote love poetry to his wife. Furthermore, Donne's erudition implies that his lady, better educated than
her medieval precursors, enjoys flattery of her intellect as well as of
her beauty. Aretino's sonnets daringly use vulgar street terms for acts
of love. Marino's *Adonis* makes baroque opera out of the ritualistic
stages of sexual gratification. Waller and Marvell use the *carpe diem*
argument to lure shy virgins into surrender; the Cavalier poets adopt
a flippant court attitude toward women and pleasure. Carew's "A Rap-
ture" turns Donne's ode to nakedness into a risqué tour of Celia's
nether parts. Libertines emerge in the late 17th century: Rochester, a
Restoration wit, writes bluntly of raw couplings with ladies, whores,
and boys. Milton's *Lycidas* revives the Classical style of homoerotic
pastoral lament. *Paradise Lost,* following Spenser and Donne, exalts
"wedded Love" over the sterile wantonness of "Harlots" and "Court
Amours" (4.750–70).

The Age of Reason, valuing self-control and witty detachment,
favored satire over love poetry. Rousseau's delicate sentiment and

pagan nature-worship created the fervent moods of "sensibility" and woman-revering Romanticism. Goethe, identifying femaleness with creativity, writes of happy sensual awakening in the *Roman Elegies* and jokes about sodomy with both sexes in the *Venetian Epigrams,* with its autoerotic acrobat Bettina; withheld pornographic verses imitate ancient *priapeia.* Schiller dedicates rhapsodic love poems to Laura, but his hymns to womanhood sentimentally polarize the sexes. Hölderlin addresses Diotima with generalized reverence and reserves his real feeling for Mother Earth. Blake calls for sexual freedom for women and for the end of guilt and shame. Burns composes rural Scottish ballads of bawdy or ill-starred love. Wordsworth's Lucy poems imagine woman reabsorbed into roiling nature. In *Christabel* Coleridge stages a virgin's seduction by a lesbian vampire, nature's emissary. The younger English Romantics fuse poetry with free love. In *Epipsychidion* Shelley is ruled by celestial women radiating intellectual light. Keats makes emotion primary; his maidens sensuously feed and sleep or wildly dance dominion over knights and kings. Byron's persona as a "mad, bad" seducer has been revised by modern revelations about his bisexuality. In the "Thyrza" poems, he woos and changes the sex of a favorite Cambridge choirboy; in *Don Juan* his blushing, girlish hero, forced into drag, catches the eye of a tempestuous lesbian sultana. Heine's love ballads are about squires, shepherd boys, hussars, and fisher maidens; later verses record erotic adventures of the famous poet wined and dined by lady admirers.

The French Romantics, turning art against nature in the hell of the modern city, make forbidden sex a central theme. Gautier celebrates the lonely, self-complete hermaphrodite. Baudelaire looses brazen whores upon syphilitic male martyrs; sex is torment, cursed by God. Baudelaire's heroic, defiant lesbians are hedonistically modernized by Verlaine and later rehellenized by Louÿs. In *Femmes* Verlaine uses vigorous street argot to describe the voluptuous sounds and smells of sex with women; in *Hombres* he lauds the brutal virility of young laborers, whom he possesses in their rough work clothes. He and Rimbaud co-wrote an ingenious sonnet about the anus. Mallarmé's leering faun embodies pagan eros; cold, virginal Herodias is woman as castrator. In contrast, Victorian poetry, as typified by the Brownings, exalts tenderness, fidelity, and devotion, the bonds of married love, preserved beyond the grave. Tennyson and the Pre-Raphaelites revive the medieval cult of idealized woman, supporting the Victorian view of woman's spirituality. Tennyson's heroines, like weary Mariana, love in mournful solitude. His *Idylls* retell Arthurian romance. *In Memoriam,* Tennyson's elaborate elegy for Hallam, is homoerotic in feeling. Rossetti's sirens are sultry, smoldering. Swinburne, inspired by Baudelaire, reintroduces sexual frankness into highbrow English literature. His Dolores and Faustine are promiscuous femmes fatales, immortal vampires; his Sappho, sadistically caressing Anactoria, boldly proclaims her poetic greatness. Whitman broke taboos in American poetry: he names body parts and depicts sex surging through fertile nature; he savors the erotic beauties of both male and female. Though he endorses sexual action and energy, Whitman appears to have been mostly solitary, troubled by homosexual desires, suggested in the "Calamus" section of *Leaves of Grass.* Reflecting the Victorian taste for bereavement, Hardy's early poetry features gloomy provincial tales of love lost: ghosts, graveyards, suicides, tearful partings. Homoerotic Greek idealism and epicene fin-de-siècle preciosity characterize the poems of Symonds, Carpenter, Hopkins, Wilde, Symons, and Dowson. Renée Vivien, the first poet to advertise her lesbianism, writes only of languid, ethereal beauty.

Love poetry of the 20th century is the most varied and sexually explicit since Classical literature. T. S. Eliot diagnoses the sexual sterility or passivity of modern man. Yet Neruda writes searing odes to physical passion, boiling with ecstatic elemental imagery. D. H. Lawrence similarly roots the sex impulse in the seasonal cycles of the animal world. Recalling long-ago, one-night pickups of handsome, athletic youths, Cavafy declares sex the creative source of his poetry. For Yeats, woman's haunting beauty is the heart of life's mystery; in "Leda and the Swan," rape is the metaphor for cataclysmic historical change. Rilke contemplates the philosophical dilemma of love, the pressure upon identity, the tension between fate and freedom. Valéry makes language erotic: the poet is Narcissus and, in *La Jeune Parque,* the oracle raped by her own inner god. Éluard sees woman erotically metamorphosing through the world, permeating him with her supernatural force. Lorca imagines operatic scenes of heterosexual seduction, rape, or mutilation, and in "Ode to Walt Whitman" denounces urban "pansies" for a visionary homosexuality grounded in living nature. Fascinated but repelled by strippers and whores, Hart Crane records squalid homosexual encounters in subway urinals. Amy Lowell vividly charts the works and days of a settled, sustaining lesbian relationship, while H. D. projects lesbian feeling into Greek personae, often male. Edna St. Vincent Millay is the first woman poet to claim a man's sexual freedom: her sassy, cynical lyrics of Jazz Age promiscuity with anonymous men are balanced by melancholy love poems to women. Auden blurred the genders in major poems to conceal their homosexual inspiration; his private verse is maliciously bawdy. William Carlos Williams is rare among modern poets in extolling married love and kitchen-centered domestic bliss.

For Dylan Thomas, youth's sexual energies drive upward from moldering, evergreen earth. Theodore Roethke presents woman as unknowable Muse, ruling nature's ghostly breezes and oozy sexual matrix. Delmore Schwartz hails Marilyn Monroe as a new Venus, blessing and redeeming "a nation haunted by Puritanism." The free-living Beat poets, emulating black hipster talk, broke poetic decorum about sex. Adopting Whitman's chanting form and pansexual theme, Allen Ginsberg playfully celebrates sodomy and master-slave scenarios. In "Marriage," Gregory Corso imagines the whole universe wedding and propagating while he ages, destitute and alone. The Confessional poets weave sex into autobiography. Robert Lowell lies on his marriage bed paralyzed, sedated, unmanned. Anne Sexton aggressively breaks the age-old taboo upon female speech by graphically exploring her own body in adultery and masturbation. Sylvia Plath launched contemporary feminist poetry with her sizzling accounts of modern marriage as hell. With its grisly mix of Nazi fantasy and Freudian family romance, "Daddy," after Yeats' "Leda," may be the love poem of the century. John Berryman's *Sonnets* records a passionate, adulterous affair with a new Laura, her platinum hair lit by the dashboard as they copulate in a car, the modern version of Dido's dark "cave." *Love and Fame* reviews Berryman's career as a "sexual athlete" specializing in quickie encounters. The sexual revolution of the 1960s heightened the new candor. Hippie poetry invoked Buddhist avatars for love's ecstasies. Denise Levertov and Carol Bergé reverse tradition by salaciously detailing the hairy, muscular male body. Diane di Prima finds sharp, fierce imagery for the violent carnality of sex. Charles Bukowski writes of eroticism without illusions in a tough, gritty world of scrappy women, drunks, rooming houses, and racetracks. Mark Strand mythically sees man helplessly passed from mother to wife to daughter: "I am the toy of women."

The 1960s also freed gay poetry from both underground and coterie. James Merrill, remembering mature love or youthful crisis, makes precise, discreet notations of dramatic place and time. Paul Goodman, Robert Duncan, Frank O'Hara, Thom Gunn, Harold Norse, and Mutsuo Takahashi intricately document the mechanics of homosexual contact for the first time since Imperial Rome: cruising, hustlers, sailors, bodybuilders, bikers, leather bars, bus terminals, toilets, glory holes. Gay male poetry is about energy, adventure, quest, danger; beauty and pleasure amid secrecy, shame, and pain. Lesbian poetry, in contrast, prefers tender, committed relationships and often burdens itself with moralistic political messages. Adrienne Rich and Judy Grahn describe intimate lesbian sex and express solidarity with victimized women of all social classes; Audre Lorde invokes African myths to enlarge female identity. Olga Broumas, linking dreamy sensation to Greek sun and sea, has produced the most artistically erotic lesbian lyrics. Eleanor Lerman's *Armed Love,* with its intellectual force and hallucinatory sexual ambiguities, remains the leading achievement of modern lesbian poetry, recapitulating the tormented history of Western love from Sappho and Catullus to Baudelaire.

37

"STAY, ILLUSION":
AMBIGUITY IN SHAKESPEARE'S *HAMLET*

Hamlet begins with a question: "Who's there?" It's midnight on the high, cold battlements of Elsinore, the Danish royal castle, and the guard is changing. The relief sentinel, the officer Barnardo, solicitously urges his fellow soldier, Francisco, to get to bed, but their first exchange is a hostile military challenge. The play's opening bristles with tension, uncertainty, and fear.

"Who's there?" could stand as an epigraph to *Hamlet*. Barnardo's question might be applied to many moments in the play—such as the traumatic scene in the queen's bed chamber where prince Hamlet stabs a bulging curtain and accidentally kills Polonius, the Lord Chamberlain, or the grisly scene set in a graveyard where Hamlet stares into the hollow eyes of Yorick's skull. "Who's there?" is also the theme of Hamlet's soliloquies, where he questions his own identity and mortality. And finally, "Who's there?" can possibly be understood as addressed to the audience itself—challenging our openness to the artist, whose work unfolds before us, and asking if and how we know ourselves.

The doubt and distrust on the dark battlements pervade the entire

[Lecture in a series on ambiguity in Western culture, Intellectual Heritage Program, Temple University, October 18, 2003. Published in *Ambiguity in the Western Mind* (2005), ed. Craig J. N. de Paulo et al.]

play, so that even small, enclosed spaces feel chill and gusty. Ambiguity blurs or qualifies every theme and character in *Hamlet*. No major work in literary history has been so contested in meaning or subjected to such a mass of alternative interpretations. Criticism has buried the play in questions, while stage and film productions continue to experiment with an astounding variety of readings and settings. No final answers are possible, because the text is embedded with contradictory material. The play seems to have changed every time we come back to it—a mysterious effect that intensifies as we ourselves age. Like Aeschylus' *Oresteia* and Sophocles' *Oedipus Rex*, *Hamlet* reflects back to us our hard-won experience of the great fundamentals of life, which are glimpsed but never fully grasped in youth.

The nagging, teeming questions of *Hamlet* include the following: Why does Hamlet delay and procrastinate in avenging his father the king's murder? Was queen Gertrude a co-conspirator in her husband's murder? Did she commit adultery with her brother-in-law Claudius before her husband's death? Why is Hamlet depressed at the start of the play? Why does he contemplate suicide? Is he mad or only feigning madness? If both, when is he faking, and when is he genuinely out of control?

What was Hamlet's relationship with his father? Is the king's ghost real? Is it a demon? Does Hamlet believe in God? If he is a Christian, is he Catholic or Protestant? Should Hamlet be king? Exactly how old is he? If he is 30, as the gravedigger claims, why is he still a student? Does he love Ophelia, and did he ever intend to marry her? Why does Hamlet mistrust and abuse women? Why does Ophelia choose her father and brother over Hamlet? What happened to Ophelia's mother? Why does Ophelia go mad? Is her death a suicide or an accident? Do Hamlet's friends—the intellectual Horatio and the sycophantish Rosencrantz and Guildenstern—have a sex life? If so, what is it? What are the Norwegian prince Fortinbras' motives and goals? Why does king Claudius permit the Norwegian army to cross through Denmark? What is the future of Denmark as a sovereign nation?

I will classify the ambiguities in *Hamlet* into three groups—philosophical, political, and psychological. To the philosophical category, I also assign questions of religious belief as well as language; to the political, matters of law and procedure; and to the psychological, issues of identity, emotion, and sexuality.

For a century, scholarship has connected the philosophical explorations in *Hamlet* to the play's position at a crucial juncture in the evolution of Western thought and science. A contemporary of Bacon, Shakespeare was writing between Montaigne and Descartes and between Copernicus and Galileo. Hamlet is a student at the University of Wittenburg, a center of the Protestant Reformation. It was in 1517 in Wittenburg that, according to popular legend, the dissident priest, Martin Luther, nailed his 95 theses to the cathedral door, a challenge to authority that dramatized the new, free, inquiring mind. Hamlet's questions go beyond organized religion and its residual medieval dogma to the very existence of God. Holy Scripture is not in his thoughts—at least not in the way that Bible study would become central to evangelical Protestantism from the seventeenth century on. Rather, the codes and assumptions of Christianity seem to be receding and dissolving.

In the immediate intellectual background of *Hamlet* (which is Shakespeare's adaptation of a medieval Scandinavian saga), the bold, questing individualism inspired by the Reformation was intensified by the skeptical spirit of Montaigne, who showed that a new literary genre—the essay—could be a vehicle of philosophical thought. The autobiographical candor and improvisational, associative form of Montaigne's essays can perhaps be felt in Hamlet's soliloquies, although scholars have debated how much Montaigne could or did directly affect Shakespeare. Insofar as Shakespeare belonged to an artistic London milieu that overlapped cultivated court circles, it seems quite possible that he was at least generally familiar with Montaigne's ideas—above all his first principle, "What do I know?," but also his relentless questioning of the traditional underpinnings of certainty and truth.

Hamlet scrutinizes virtually every aspect of human existence— from personal relationships and social organization to the fundamental nature of matter and being. The prince's most famous soliloquy begins, "To be, or not to be: that is the question" (III.i.56).[1] When Hora-

tio calls out to the ghost stalking the battlements, "Stay, illusion"—
that is, *"Stop!"*—he is also summarizing a major argument in Western
philosophy (I.i.127). Is reality nothing but flickering illusions—the
shadows projected on the wall of Plato's cave of prisoners—or does
some stable substratum remain, however it is transformed over
time? *Hamlet* frequently describes life with metaphors of "dream"
and "shadow" (II.ii.260–69). Though a supernatural visitation, the
ghost or "apparition" embodies the delusion of earthly appearances
(I.i.28). "Stay, illusion" also expresses the longing of the creative
artist—Shakespeare as well as the producer/director Hamlet who co-
writes the self-reflexive play-within-a-play—to linger in the realm of
imagination, which Hamlet calls "a fiction" and "a dream of passion"
(II.ii.562). Through art, life is seen not with scientific or philosophical
clarity but with deeper truth.

As attested by his soliloquies, Hamlet is an agnostic about theological issues such as the existence of a hell where sinners are punished and from which demons masquerading as ghosts may fly. At
one point, he acknowledges a transcendent being called "the Everlast-
ing" who has published a "canon" of interdictions, including a law
against suicide—the "self-slaughter" that Hamlet weighs at his darkest moment (I.ii.131–32). At times, he seems to envision a universe
of godless blankness, like the modernist waste land. Elsewhere, he
suggests there is an occult power that cannot be explained in secular
terms: "There are more things in heaven and earth, Horatio, / Than
are dreamt of in your philosophy" (I.v.166–67). By the end, Hamlet
feels "There's a divinity that shapes our ends," a fate inexplicably
at work in human lives (V.ii.10). Is that force Christian or pagan or
impersonally astrological? Its nature and operations are left ambiguous, even if its effects are felt in a play whose plot seems to lag and
surge, then sweep from scene to scene in a way that never ceases to
surprise us.

Pondering the link between soul and body, Hamlet wonders
whether consciousness survives death. "What dreams may come /
When we have shuffled off this mortal coil": the body, entwining or
strangling the soul, is shed like a snake skin at death (III.i.66–67).
Hamlet strives to reconcile humanity's divided nature—"how noble

in reason, . . . in action how like an angel, in apprehension how like a god"—with our gross materiality, "this quintessence of dust" (II.ii.312–17). "What is a man?" he asks elsewhere—simply a "beast" who is content "to sleep and feed"? (IV.iv.33–35.) If simply driven by material needs, we are slaves to the flesh and its impermanence. One of *Hamlet*'s obtrusive patterns is its morbid imagery of squalid decay—a common motif of seventeenth-century literature and Mannerist painting. The ubiquity and certainty of decay (one of the few certainties possible in this play) press on Hamlet amid the general implosion of events. In a world of "garbage," foul smells, and decay, objects and identities are continually fracturing—a slow disintegration where the opposite and fertile extreme in the regenerative cycle is either unperceived or undervalued (I.v.57).

Hamlet's theme of universal decay—often flagged by the word "rank," with its implication of putrid dampness—also affects the state of language. Words are Hamlet's vital instruments, his primary medium of engagement with life. This most brilliantly intelligent of all characters in world literature is shown walking onstage while reading a book. But words always betray him, either by dragging him down to despair or luring him outward, as on Elsinore's battlements, into dizzying doubts. (*Horatio:* "These are but wild and whirling words, my lord" [I.v.133].) Words in *Hamlet* are unreliable, slippery. And in the ethically compromised world of Denmark, they are corrupted by lies—the "forgeries" of Claudius and Polonius or the calculating flattery of Rosencrantz and Guildenstern and the unctuous courtier, Osric, which debase language and worsen Hamlet's sense of nausea (II.i.20).

Hamlet wants language to be an escape from subjectivity, but as he ostentatiously puns and quibbles, words seem to multiply on their own and cloud his mind. "Words, words, words," he says satirically of his reading (II.ii.194). As the Romantic poet Samuel Taylor Coleridge may have been the first to argue, Hamlet's mental activity disables him from acting as required in the real world: "the native hue of resolution / Is sicklied o'er with the pale cast of thought" (III.i.84–85). That is, action stimulates the blood, while reading and thinking drain it. When he tries to goad himself into resolution by seeking absolute proof of Claudius' guilt, Hamlet becomes enmeshed in contradiction: he is already convinced of the relativity of perception—illustrated when he contemptuously forces the busybody Polonius to see animal shapes in the mobile clouds (an image that Shakespeare's Mark Antony uses to describe his own search for coherent identity). Hamlet is trapped in a median realm of floating ambiguity and conflicting impulses—impelled by duty toward action while unable to renounce the alluring, infinite qualifications of ever-shifting language.

Now for the political ambiguities in *Hamlet*. As the play opens, there are undercurrents of political instability as well as popular unrest and anxiety in Denmark. Horatio almost immediately notes the political implications of the walking of the late king's ghost: "This bodes some strange eruption to our state"—an image suggesting both ulceration and the tell-tale unearthing of a corpse (I.i.69). On the battlements, the officer Marcellus questions Horatio about the recent frenzy of activity in Denmark portending war or fear of invasion—arms and ship manufacturing going on day and night, seven days a week. The common people are unsettled by these projects, whose purpose is unknown. Political decisions at the top, which have life-and-death consequences for the masses, are concealed. In a pre-media age, information must come distorted and secondhand via rumor and the grapevine. Hence Marcellus' interrogation of Horatio has a paranoid insistence: there are five questions in nine lines—"why," "why," "why," "what," and "who" (I.i.71–79).

Horatio's long response (a 28-line monologue) is one of the oddest passages in the play, presenting so knotty a problem to actors that it is sometimes shortened or cut out entirely in performance. It chronicles the political background and military rivalry between Denmark and Norway from the last generation to this. Perhaps mindful of the many law students in his London audience, Shakespeare surely intended it as a parody of legal language—abstract, contorted, labyrinthine, and self-interrupting. Norway forfeited land through a compact pledging a personal combat to the death between the Norwegian and Danish kings. That episode, which ended in Denmark's victory, is narrated in labored syntax and obscure locutions from which the current threat, young Fortinbras, son of the slain Norwegian king, bursts "hot and full" (I.i.96). Horatio's tangled exposition of Fortinbras' legal claim says in effect that it is meretricious but potent nonetheless. Thus in *Hamlet* law too distorts language, as it subordinates justice to glib verbal formulations.

"Something is rotten in the state of Denmark," says Marcellus in one of the play's signature lines (I.iv.90). The rot affects not only the state as a political and administrative entity but the state of the nation in spiritual and physical terms: the nation becomes a living organism in medical crisis. Throughout Shakespeare, kings embody or personify their nations and, like dukes, are addressed by the name of their lands. Hence in *King Lear*, the king of France is called "France" and the Duke of Burgundy "Burgundy." In *Hamlet*, as in *Oedipus Rex*, disease at the top trickles downward to all the body's parts. In Sophocles' Thebes, the crops are dying, and women are miscarrying: the pollution upon the land comes from the fact that an incestuous patricide sits on the throne, though he is unaware of his crimes. In *Hamlet*, the king is again a murderer, this time a fratricide, but his crime was committed in cold blood, and his nephew must expose and avenge it. Much of the political turbulence in *Hamlet* ultimately comes from the quaking of the king's uneasy conscience as well as the devious machinations by which he (unlike Oedipus) tries to stop the truth from outing.

Claudius' weak grip on power is betrayed by his raucous, all-night drinking parties, marked by trumpet blasts and gunfire, about which the stoical Horatio questions Hamlet (echoing the sentinels' earlier questioning of Horatio). Hamlet disapprovingly attributes the palace carousing to rowdy Danish tradition, but the audience is led to conclude that the king is drinking to numb himself and revive his flagging spirits. Certainly, Claudius is an awkward, imprudent, and self-absorbed ruler, as indicated at his first appearance by his nervous, distracted deference to a much younger inferior, Laertes. One of the political conundrums of the play is why, after only recently neutralizing Fortinbras' military threat through direct appeal to his aged uncle, the present king of Norway, Claudius allows the Norwegian army to cross Danish territory on the way to Poland, to which the Norwegians have staked yet another questionable claim. This easily overlooked detail puts Fortinbras in Denmark at the play's violent climax, where the entire Danish ruling class destroys itself, bringing Hamlet's dynasty to an end and leaving Denmark under Norwegian occupation.

The structure of Denmark's government, or rather the transmission of its power, is another unanswered question in *Hamlet*. The matter is left so tenuous that audiences and readers need help from program notes or scholarly explication. Whether Shakespeare intended this ambiguity remains arguable. Denmark's monarchy, unlike England's, is described as elective, but the mechanics of election, as well as the character of the electors, whether oligarchic or popular, are left vague. By murdering his brother, Claudius opened up space for his ambitions, but his election to the vacant throne was by no means certain, for Hamlet and other nobles would also presumably be candidates. Or is there a trace of matrilinearity in the ancient *Hamlet* tale, as some scholars have found in *Oedipus Rex*? Does Gertrude, like queen Jocasta, confer kingship through her marriage?

The question of succession was a major public anxiety during Shakespeare's lifetime. Elizabeth I, who assumed the throne in 1558, six years before Shakespeare was born, never married, despite determined wooing by a long list of aristocratic and royal suitors in England and Europe. When *Hamlet* was first staged some time in the late 1590s, it was already clear that Elizabeth, then in her sixties, would die without issue. Hence the English foresaw the end of the House of Tudor, a cataclysm possibly paralleled in the extinction of the Danish royal family in *Hamlet*. A justifiable fear throughout the history of monarchies worldwide has been that ambiguity in succession can lead to civil war—a plague on English society during the 32-year War of the Roses of the fifteenth century.

Denmark's elective monarchy in *Hamlet* might seem to avoid the succession problem inherent in royal dynasties, but Shakespeare shows it as equally susceptible to chaos because of its dependence on group thought or mass will. Throughout his plays, Shakespeare is often suspicious and even disdainful of the fickleness of popular emotion. Democracy for him means mob rule—a blind force tending toward anarchy. This is glimpsed in *Hamlet* when Laertes, protesting his father's killing and undignified, perfunctory funeral, leads a mob (the "rabble") who break through the palace gates and shout, "Laertes shall be king!" (IV.v.98–108.) In appeasing and defusing Laertes, Claudius hatches his second scheme against his nephew's life—the fencing match where Laertes' rapier will be poisoned. Earlier, Claudius explicitly acknowledges his fear of popular rebellion in conspiring for Hamlet to be murdered in England rather than at home in Denmark.

Does Hamlet have ambitions to be king? Although he sardonically jokes that he is gloomy because "I lack advancement," political ambition does not seem to figure large in his temperament (III.ii.347). As suggested by his delays and hesitations, he prefers the calm, contemplative life. Does he possess the qualities to be a good king? Or is he too impatient for the dull routine of practical affairs? Brooding or mercurial temperaments aren't the best fit for public life—a point occasionally raised in Great Britain over the past quarter century about Charles, Prince of Wales, an amateur painter and botanist. Hamlet is not a playboy prince, like Shakespeare's Prince Hal, who when he assumes the throne must exile his rollicking, fellow fun-lover, Falstaff. But Hamlet does suffer from chronic inhibitions and indecisiveness. Though he can act on impulse—as when he leaps aboard the pirate ship or into Ophelia's open grave—he spends most of the play buffeted or stymied by excess thought.

As a revenge play, a popular, sensationalistic genre in Elizabethan theater, *Hamlet* is also a mystery story or crime drama, paralleled by modern police and detective fiction descending from Edgar Allan Poe. A murder has occurred in Elsinore but been covered up, and Hamlet is the unwilling civilian drafted into service: he snoops around, follows clues, and conducts surveillance and entrapment (the play-within-the-play). Other legal issues in *Hamlet* include the miscarriage of justice when the king, who represents and enforces the law, is a murderer. There is also the vexed question of the disposition of Ophelia's remains: if she is judged to have committed suicide (she falls into a brook when a bough breaks while she is hanging garlands), then according to church law, she cannot be buried in sacred ground. The matter is ambiguous: a Doctor of Divinity sternly calls her death "doubtful" (V.i.229). In a compromise dictated by the king for his own political protection, her grave is dug in the churchyard, but she is given a truncated service—a harshness bitterly protested by her brother. Another ambiguity, played for farce, is the location of Polonius' body, which Hamlet has unceremoniously dragged offstage: can there be a crime if there is no corpse? The frantic courtiers are turned by the king into detectives who find the body only when Hamlet, sarcastically urging them to follow their noses and snuff the air, tips them off that he has stashed it under the palace stairs.

I group the psychological ambiguities in *Hamlet* into three areas. First is the question of identity. Is there an essential self, a fixed personality, or are human beings simply a collection of masks, exchanged at whim? Hamlet is afflicted and tormented by his own metamorphoses. He has an actor's facility to try on poses, toss verbal darts, and play with mood and tone—which is why he has such infectious rapport with the troupe of traveling players, whom he tutors in stagecraft. But acting for Hamlet can dangerously overlap deceit: he enjoys duping others and shows contempt for their gullibility (as in his weary exchanges with the gossipy, senile Polonius and the slavish Osric). Impersonation comes too easily to Hamlet, leaving him with feelings of disgust and misanthropy.

The soliloquies show Hamlet's search for identity as well as his despair at not finding it: ideas spiral out of control, and his mood darkens, as certain themes keep recurring, obsessively and compulsively. General reflections on existence and the cosmos always seem to circle back and be overwhelmed by Hamlet's family psychodramas. The persistence of these negative thoughts must be weighed in judging Hamlet's mental competence. Early on, he warns Horatio that he will "put an antic disposition on"—and we do recognize such moments, when Hamlet allows us to laugh with him at his naïve victims (I.v.172). But Shakespeare leaves other scenes ambiguous: when Hamlet, as described by Ophelia, appears with clothing disarrayed and looks her up and down with tragic sighs, is this another game, or has he temporarily lost his wits? His tumultuous confrontation with his mother in her bed chamber can be played several ways, but the text indicates a rising level of passion and recrimination peaking in hysteria and near-violence. The ghost who materializes is seen only by him and not his mother—as opposed to its two visits to the battlements, when there is a total of three witnesses aside from Hamlet. Gertrude is in little doubt: "Alas, he's mad," she says to herself, as if her son can no longer hear external voices (III.iv.106).

A second area of psychological ambiguity is generational relationships. To the original Hamlet story Shakespeare has added the imposing parallelism of fathers and sons: there are Hamlet Senior and Hamlet Junior; Fortinbras Senior and Fortinbras Junior; and Polonius and Laertes. The elder Hamlet and elder Fortinbras were blood rivals, just as the younger Hamlet suffers the rivalry (real or imagined) of the younger Fortinbras and Laertes. What relevance this theme might have had to Shakespeare's interaction with his own father has been discussed by scholars, but biographical evidence is slight. The play asks us to consider the charged issue of fatherhood and its legacy, particularly in families where the father has power and fame as well as a daunting record of achievement.

Hamlet admires his heroic father but feels overshadowed by him. (He was born on the very day that the king slew Fortinbras.) He is unable or unwilling to match that mythic and archaic level of dominant masculinity, devoted to the service of a competitive nationalism. Hamlet occupies the more sophisticated, cosmopolitan world of humanistic Europe. From the birth of psychoanalytic criticism in the early twentieth century, Hamlet's fervid, divinizing praise of his dead father was defined as ambivalent "over-estimation," concealing contrary impulses of hostility or even repressed homicidal wishes. The matching term in the Oedipus complex—incestuous desire for the mother—has also been detected in Hamlet's indecorous over-involvement with Gertrude's sex life, which he pictures with startlingly pornographic exactitude. Modern productions, beginning with John Barrymore, regularly give Oedipal inflections to the play. In strict Freudian terms, Hamlet's delay in exacting vengeance comes from his paralyzed recognition that his uncle has fulfilled the forbidden fantasies of his own unconscious—that is, killing his father and marrying his mother.

But *Hamlet* had a magnetic effect on audiences and readers alike for 300 years before Freudian theory, with all its insights. The ghost is an oppressive paternal presence. His aggressive demand for revenge is an energy-sapping burden that usurps Hamlet's life and identity. The son at first accepts his mission with enthusiasm because of his hatred for his uncle, but the duty soon becomes a tedious and demeaning irritation. The ghost makes him a prisoner of the past, a servant of the king's now canceled life.

Fortinbras, in contrast, seems to relish his role as his father's avenger. Hamlet sourly contrasts himself with Fortinbras and lacerates himself with debased female imagery: he, the prince of Denmark, is a "whore," a "drab," a "scullion" (a kitchen maid) (II.ii.597–99). What we see of Fortinbras is limited: his first entrance is in the last minute of the play, when the stage is strewn with corpses. If Fortinbras has self-doubts, we don't know them, though his manic militancy (like Shakespeare's Hotspur elsewhere) might be interpreted as an attempt to surpass his father by dramatizing the latter's failures.

Parental love as an ambiguous form of power and control is shown in Polonius' bullying behavior toward his son. The scene of Laertes' farewell before his return to university in Paris is usually played for humor: the greybeard Polonius taxes his smirking children with hoary old saws and bromides, whose lessons he himself fails to heed. Parental instruction is shown as boring but harmless. Far more disturbing is the scene where Polonius instructs his servant Reynaldo to spy on Laertes in Paris. In his ruthless thirst for information, Polonius tells Reynaldo to slander Laertes' character and then read the response of his auditors. Even the low-born servant is appalled by such wanton degradation of Laertes' public image and honor. This is another example of poisoned language operating in the play: Polonius spreads it like an epidemic to another country to taint his own son. Overbearing fatherly concern commits murder—this time of Laertes' reputation.

The third area of psychological ambiguity is love and sex, about which Hamlet is tortured throughout the play. Love is an illusion in which he cannot place faith, and he gratuitously savages both his mother and Ophelia for what he perceives as their betrayals— Gertrude for falling under Claudius' erotic spell, and Ophelia for behaving like a proper Renaissance girl and following her father's orders rather than the call of her own heart. Hamlet ends up denouncing all women as false—their thick "paintings" of makeup the false faces and fakery of actress-whores (III.i.144). (This was at a time when no women performed on the English stage: respectable ladies did not put themselves on public display.) The theme of women's crafty self-beautification belongs to the play's constant contrast between shadow and substance: woman traffics in illusion, and what she offers is a lie.

Sexual desire itself is delusive for Hamlet, who feels it entrammels the free mind in animality. The language of disgust spewed in his explosive rages is so extreme that commentators cannot agree on its meaning. As the only son of a royal house, it is Hamlet's obligation to procreate, but the play repeatedly obstructs and frustrates his natural relationship with Ophelia, which his mother blesses (as we learn after Ophelia's death) even while her father and brother hootingly proclaim their union impossible on political grounds. Hamlet himself is unable to sustain romantic love. His attachment to Ophelia cannot withstand his own self-involvement and self-hatred: the death force, in other words, conquers the life force in the play. But why? Is Denmark under a curse that blights the future?

The play systematically undermines Hamlet's hold on his own identity. All of his personal relationships, except with the steady, impassive Horatio, founder. Even his early friendships are corrupted by politics: Rosencrantz and Guildenstern, summoned by the king and queen to spy on Hamlet, make themselves tools to royal command. Hamlet jovially questions the pair about their sudden visit to court, but his attitude hardens when they refuse to admit the obvious truth. The interrogation is nearly an inquisition, with Hamlet taking the roles of detective and prosecutor, microscopically studying Rosencrantz and Guildenstern's ambiguities of response and body language and forcing them along a track of self-exposure until they are helpless. Hamlet learns to distrust emotions and social bonds, which the play shows as painfully fallible.

In *Hamlet*, illusions rule. As a landmark of Western literature, the play symbolizes the cultural shift from the orderly absolutes of the scholastic Middle Ages to the flux of the modern era, in which beliefs, disciplines, and institutions are continually remade, with the individual left to a vertigo of free choice. Major works of art whose appeal endures over centuries usually have some elusiveness or indeterminacy of form or content: the ambiguous qualities of Leonardo's *Mona Lisa,* for example, can also be seen in *Hamlet,* which seems to take place in Leonardo's *sfumato* or smoky shadows and where sex and emotion, as in the *Mona Lisa,* are cryptic.

Hamlet is a truth-seeker who wants to *be* and not *seem*—that is, to live without illusions. But in order to defeat illusions, he vainly tries to make them stay or stop. In that instant, their insubstantiality envelops him and his view of the material world. The play unfurls in a swirl of ambiguities, destabilizing person, thing, place, time, and action—which is why, like Heracleitus' river, *Hamlet* seems to change with each of our encounters with it. The play too is an illusion that, to our dismay and pleasure, will never stay.

1. All quotations from *Hamlet* are from *The Signet Classic Shakespeare,* general editor, Sylvan Barnet (New York, 1963).

38

COLUMBIA JOURNAL
INTERVIEW: WRITING

Mary Phillips-Sandy: *I wanted to start off with a really general question. What are you reading right now? And do you find yourself reading more fiction or nonfiction?*

Camille Paglia: I read almost entirely nonfiction, unfortunately, because of what I regard as the self-marginalization of fiction in America, at least following World War Two. I'm afraid I've made some rather extreme statements about this—that the cultural center in letters has migrated into nonfiction. I tend to read politics, ancient history, biography, that kind of thing.

MPS: *Who are some of your current favorite nonfiction writers?*

CP: I don't think I have any one or even several favorite writers of nonfiction—aside from myself, of course! I choose books for their topic rather than the writer. In fact, that's one of the problems I see. There's been a tremendous opportunity for young nonfiction writers over the last ten or fifteen years, but while there's often been a media stir over one figure or another, I don't notice that anyone has emerged that strongly from what used to be called Generation X to dominate the scene in terms of consistency or quality of work or uniqueness of voice. It could very well be that the Web—and I'm a great proponent

[Mary Phillips-Sandy, A *Columbia Journal* Interview, *Columbia: A Journal of Literature & Art,* Columbia University, Issue 39 (2004).]

of the Web and began writing for it early on—may have drained off a lot of the energy that young people used to devote to poetry writing or fiction or nonfiction.

MPS: *I've read your comments about academia in general, and higher education, and how a lack of a humanities foundation is failing our young people. I was wondering about your thoughts on specifically creative programs, like MFA creative writing programs. Are those useful to writers, do you think?*

CP: It's a good and bad thing. The good part of the MFA program is that it offers people a chance to spend quality time in the company of others interested in writing in a period when popular culture and mass media dominate the landscape. I'm a great admirer of mass media, but it has definitely driven serious writing to the edges. So going to an MFA program is a gift, I think, for many people—a golden opportunity to have like-minded aspiring professionals around them. To be able to talk about writing and deal with nothing but books is a literary oasis in the midst of a desert.

But the bad part, the downside, is that this is not the way writers have trained themselves for more than two millennia. In order to write, there has to be some direct experience of life, it seems to me. Jumping immediately from college into an MFA program is a perpetual student bubble that young people get trapped in. There's also a kind of slick professionalization that some teachers convey to their students—teachers who, especially in the last twenty years or so, belong to the postmodernist or pseudo-hip school of writing and may encourage their students to adopt these increasingly passé gestures as a way to get published or make a name for themselves. The absence of a topic to write about, because of a lack of experience of real life, leads to a self-cannibalization that's inevitable.

So I think the way a writer should be taught is through self-education—through absorbing as much literature as possible and through living independently—just going out and *living*. Doing things. There was a time when avant-garde artists earned rent money by unloading trucks or varnishing floors—manual labor that gave them a feel for life and an exposure to other types of people. Unfortunately, the students who go into writing programs, as well as the teachers themselves these days, are completely middle-class. It's as suffocating and bourgeois as a suburban shopping mall—and that cloistered culture becomes the totality of the students' experience. Now, I don't mean to paint with such a broad brush—there are countless hard-working, committed teachers who truly want to develop students' individual voices. But there's no sure way to develop such a voice without going out and encountering life head-on.

MPS: *Of course, the homogenization of MFA programs, as you say, is to some extent related to the cost of them.*

CP: Oh, yes, yes. That's a serious problem across higher education generally. All the elite schools, especially at the undergraduate level, are suffering from this. The parents' outlay of hundreds of thousands of dollars—and the schools' strenuous efforts to ensure "diversity" through scholarships—have created a strange kind of arch, fictitious world at the elite schools. Whenever I set foot on an Ivy League campus these days, it's like Disney World! It's a palpably self-enclosed realm. There was a time, following World War Two, when the only schools offering writing degrees were the progressive colleges like Bennington, where I taught for eight years. They were small schools, okay, not big universities. The casual, improvisational nature of those programs was, I think, a far more fertile atmosphere for development of the individual voice. These larger programs embedded within major universities—I can't imagine what that's like, trying to learn to write in that kind of artificial environment.

MPS: *What did you think about Stephen King, a pop-culture icon, winning the National Book Award? As a native Mainer, I was very proud, but many people in the publishing world were fairly upset about it.*

CP: Well, the number-one protester was my own mentor, Harold Bloom (who directed my doctoral dissertation at Yale). I was a bit disappointed with the dismissive position Harold took in his op-ed in *The Wall Street Journal*. I felt that it was unkind and unnecessary—at least before the ceremony took place. A case can indeed be made, from a traditional literary point of view, about deficiencies in King's prose style. But anyone who's been following popular culture for the past three decades has to realize that Stephen King's imagination has had tremendous cultural impact, and that ought to be honored by the cultural establishment in some way.

I think there's an analogy to Edgar Allan Poe here. In the 1830s and '40s, Poe was just a trashy newspaper writer with a low reputation. He was considered a ne'er-do-well, and the genteel literary establishment thought his prose style was execrable. No one took him seriously—his horror stories were considered sensationalistic and so on. Well, Poe's reputation was hugely elevated by one of his major fans, Charles Baudelaire, the French Romantic poet who translated Poe's work and laid the foundation for Poe's European reputation. In the late nineteenth and early twentieth centuries, the French criticized America for neglecting one of our greatest poets—they regarded Poe as a poet not just because he wrote poems but because of the power of imagination in his stories. And of course Poe had an enormous influence in terms of inventing the genre of detective fiction, revitalizing the short story as a genre, and transmitting Gothic fantasy to modern horror films.

So now we look back and see Edgar Allan Poe as a giant of literary imagination in the nineteenth century. I guess I would have expected Bloom to have considered the Poe precedent in his article—especially since it was Bloom who revolutionized literary Romantic studies by foregrounding the principle of creative imagination in Blake and Shelley. It's possible Bloom didn't realize how beloved King is as a cultural figure. Usually Bloom takes anti-establishment positions—he's had huge quarrels himself with the academic establishment. So I might have expected him to identify more with King, who's so productive and unpretentious. I personally think it was a fine gesture to give King that award.

MPS: *I'm thinking of the so-called chick-lit that sells incredibly well—* Bridget Jones's Diary, The Devil Wears Prada, *and* The Nanny Diaries. *As a feminist and as a critic, what do you think about these books and what they say about current reading?*

CP: Look, throughout the entire nineteenth century, the main consumers of novels tended to be women. So it doesn't particularly surprise or disturb me. Anything that gets people to read, including Oprah's Book Club, is positive. We are moving very rapidly toward a post-literate culture, where most information is being conveyed via the Web in very unreliable form. The entire practice of book reading itself is seriously threatened. After all, it's pretty much a blip in the history of culture. We thought it was going to last forever, but maybe it's not! So I can't get too worried about it—if young women who buy Prada are willing to buy a book with Prada in the title, I can't complain.

MPS: *What do you feel is the role of a writer in a society?*

CP: A writer is reflecting his or her own times and connecting it to the past and the future. I feel that a writer has an obligation to absorb *everything*, to take in every possible detail of everyday life as well as the social and political scene. And then to constantly be processing that into language, to try to adapt one's own private language to English as it evolves. I'm an enormous admirer of English, partly because I came from an Italian immigrant family. All four of my grandparents and my mother were born in Italy, so English is relatively new to my family. And I think it's one of the most superb instruments ever invented. It's an American writer's obligation to *use* that instrument, to find some way to sing with it, to make it fully expressive of the writer's individual consciousness.

A writer must always think about being read in the future. That's certainly one of my motivations. As I'm writing, I'm always thinking how to make what I'm writing relevant not only to contemporary readers but to someone looking at it ten, twenty, or thirty years from now. In order to do that, I carefully study works and passages of the past that I think still have resonance. The prose style of people writing in the 1920s, let's say—what in there has retained its power? What in it has dated? I'm constantly subjecting prose to that kind of test.

I am convinced that certain things remain constant in English. One of the terrible problems that's happened to writers of English in the last twenty years or so is that a French style of writing—very contorted, self-conscious, and effete—became fashionable through the exposure of American academics and the downtown New York art scene to translated versions of French theorists like Lacan and Derrida. You can find it in postmodernism everywhere, in fiction as well as academic books. It's derailed highbrow American writing—I mean seriously derailed it.

There's a distanced irony in French intellectual writing that's utterly inconsistent with the pragmatism of the American style. American English is very close to concrete reality—there are firm, vigorous speech rhythms in good American writing that come from a real person talking. The cliché in French theory is that there is no person behind the text, that the text exists on its own and that it's questioning, sabotaging, and dissolving itself. That kind of stuff—all that pretentious posturing that came over from Paris thirty years ago—is a recipe for suicide for any aspiring writer. The American writers who tried to write that way, servilely mimicking the French theorists, have completely lost their own voices. They cut their own throats as writers, so now they have no voice at all. It's just been done to death, and the people who practiced it have faded fast over the past decade. Their works are going to be consigned to the rubbish heap of history.

Coming from an immigrant family, I was fascinated by American voices. I heard the American style, with all its vitality, and I tried to absorb it. What I also try to do as a writer—and I would urge this on young writers—is never to have just one voice. I adapt my voice to situation, context, and audience. I have quite different voices when I'm writing for Salon.com or *The Wall Street Journal* or *The Times* in London.

When I pick up books today—fiction or nonfiction, except for works of history, which are often well-constructed if not particularly distinctive in terms of prose—I just don't see that people are spending much time on prose style in America. Great Britain is different: the British have a tremendous sense of literary style, sometimes to excess, so that it becomes glib or facile. Books from England can be all style and no substance! But in America, I don't see anyone, including famous writers, spending much time on their own prose. Joyce Carol Oates, for example—I can't believe she just throws that stuff out there! The number of books she writes and the blatant lack of attention that she pays to her prose style—I just don't get it. I don't understand how people can have such a tin ear for their own prose, and I don't know how readers can tolerate it. On the other hand, my favorite novel of the post–World War Two era is Patrick Dennis' *Auntie Mame.*

I urge anyone who's writing to study the dictionary, to analyze and really understand words and their history. That's a big problem with the young writers who have emerged in the last fifteen or twenty years, I think. They don't know English well enough—they don't have enough respect for English. They don't take care with individual sentences or paragraphs. It's like this blather, blather! It all seems thrown together, even things that are very arch and affected in the postmodernist way—sloppiness, slackness in diction and syntax and construction of the prose. Well, that's a very long answer.

MPS: *It's a good answer. As an aspiring writer, I think it's important to hear that answer.*

CP: I should add in regard to honing writing skills that, with the shift to e-mail, the art of letter-writing is probably gone forever. Historians have mentioned this as a potential future problem—letters are an enormous resource for historical research. But e-mail is a very instantaneous form of communication. It's fantastic—it's like sending bulletins from a spaceship. I mean, I love it, it's simplified my life in so many ways. But no one works on the *style* of an e-mail. I've realized that, over the years since I was very young, long letter-writing to friends was one of the ways that I was developing my own writing style. We're now in such a period of instant gratification that even a simple thing like that has deprived young writers of another forum for practice, for developing the craft.

In terms of my own career, I want to emphasize that even though I'm well-known now and have had three bestselling books, I was virtually unpublished until I was in my forties. In the early '80s, to add to my income while I was teaching part time, I was writing for alternative newspapers and little town weeklies. And I regard that as an important thing for writers to do. To write for every possible kind of venue, no matter how small the readership or pay. That's a problem today, especially with these high-profile writing programs: people are looking for prestige placement of their material. They don't think of writing as a craft that should be exercised wherever you can get an opening.

My philosophy is that writers should admire writers—period! It's good to go to an MFA program, but ultimately it's up to the individual writer to make a connection with the *dead* writers and be inspired by them. Writing is a living continuum. The more attention you pay to your own style, the more likely it is that you'll eventually break out of the pack. Writing right now is terribly sloppy. If a book isn't well-written, I'm just not interested. I see all this media praise for new books by celebrated writers or just-arrived figures, and I go to the bookstore thinking this must be an important book. Then I open it up and see page after page of weak, crappy, disconnected prose—which I'm never going to subject myself to. There's no reason for it! I'm just going to go home and turn on the television and watch a soap opera or old Hollywood movie. Very few contemporary American writers have a distinct voice any longer, an instantly recognizable voice—where you open the page and say, oh, yes, I know who wrote that.

The only way to go forward as a writer is to go backwards—to absorb everything that you most admire from twenty, fifty, or a hundred years ago. There's another thing I used to do as a student from adolescence through grad school: I would copy out passages I found especially striking in anything I encountered—whether it was fiction or nonfiction, contemporary or past. I have whole notebooks where I laboriously copied those things out and tried to understand the way they work. What makes them work in terms of structure, feeling, vocabulary, or rhetoric? Even an individual sentence—what's so fabulous about this sentence? I think if you pay that kind of attention to the basic mechanics of prose, over time your mastery of your craft will steadily improve, just like learning an instrument.

39

THE DEATH OF NORMAN MAILER

Norman Mailer's extensive obituaries this past week could not disguise the fact that his enormous fame was decades in the past and that very few young people (outside the writing community) had ever heard his name. Mailer was certainly a major player when I was in college and grad school. I didn't care about his novels—I don't care about *any* novels published after World War Two (Tennessee Williams is my main man)—but I was impressed by Mailer's visionary and sometimes hallucinatory first-person journalism. And I was directly inspired by his eclectic *Advertisements for Myself* (1959), which I took as a blueprint after my first books were attacked by the feminist establishment in the 1990s.

Mailer's "The Prisoner of Sex" (the original 1971 *Harper's* essay, not the book) was an important statement about men's sexual fears and desires. His jousting with Germaine Greer at the notorious Town Hall debate in New York that same year was a pivotal moment in the sex wars. I loved Greer and still do. And I also thought Jill Johnston (who disrupted the debate with lesbo stunts) was a cutting-edge thinker: I was devouring her *Village Voice* columns, which had evolved from dance reportage into provocative cultural commentary.

Feminism would have been far stronger had it been able to absorb Mailer's arguments about sex. If my own system seemed heterodox for so long, it's because I appear to have been one of the few feminists who could appreciate and integrate all three thinkers—Mailer, Greer,

[Salon.com column, November 13, 2007, and April 8, 2008.]

and Johnston. I'm sorry that Mailer, presumably cowed or pussy-whipped, abandoned the gender field. It would take Madonna, thanks to her influence on a generation of dissident young women, to bring authentically Dionysian '60s feminism back from the dead. That pro-sex wing of feminism (to which I belong) has of course resoundingly triumphed, to the hissy consternation of the puritans and the iconoclasts—those maleducated wordsmiths who don't know how to respond to or "read" erotic imagery.

Speaking of Madonna, one of the lousiest things Mailer ever wrote was his flimsy cover-story screed on her for *Esquire* in 1994. It was obvious Mailer knew absolutely nothing about Madonna and was just blowing smoke. I wonder if it's this debacle that Woody Hochswender, who had worked at *Esquire,* is describing in a startling letter following Roger Kimball's scathing Mailer critique, which is posted on that indispensable site, Arts & Letters Daily. Guess what—*Esquire*'s original proposal was for me to interview Madonna. Mailer was the sub!

Penthouse magazine had similarly tried to bring Madonna and me together, as had HBO, which proposed filming a *My Dinner with André* scenario of the two of us chatting in a restaurant. But Madonna, no conversationalist, always refused. When *Newsweek* asked her in a 1992 cover story whether she would like to meet me, she said, "First, I'd like to see her across the room and then I'd like to decide whether I want to approach her." (I said when I read it, "What is this, a sorority party?")

I attributed Madonna's skittishness at the time to her uncertainties about her education (she had dropped out of college after one semester to seek fame in New York). But nothing could be further from my respectful and indeed reverential attitude toward artists, particularly performing artists who must capitalize on their youth. The idea that Madonna somehow had to read *Sexual Personae* (a nightmarish assignment!) was of course preposterous. But so what—little is gained from such jacked-up personal encounters. Art and ideas must operate in their own realm.

—SALON.COM, NOVEMBER 13, 2007

Speaking of Madonna, Woody Hochswender (author of *The Buddha in Your Rearview Mirror*) wrote in to confirm that yes, Norman Mailer was indeed hired at mind-boggling expense by *Esquire* magazine to interview Madonna after she refused to be interviewed by me way back in 1994. The result was a cover story of astonishing emptiness and mediocrity. Hochswender says: "Editorial lapses of this sort are what have led to the downward spiral of men's magazines, once influential voices in our intellectual life."

—SALON.COM, APRIL 8, 2008

40

DISPATCHES FROM THE NEW FRONTIER: WRITING FOR THE INTERNET

BIRTH OF A MEDIUM

Although I had co-hosted public online chats for new Web sites like AOL, my work for the Internet began in earnest in November 1995 with the inaugural issue of Salon, the first general-interest Web-zine. As this essay goes to press, Salon's financial condition is shaky and its ultimate survival in doubt. It has always had to rely principally on advertising revenue, while its chief rival, Slate, is safely bankrolled by billionaire Bill Gates, founder of Microsoft, Inc.

For my first Salon piece, editor-in-chief David Talbot asked me to comment on conservative social critic William Bennett's recent attack on "trash TV" as a debasement of moral standards and a bad influence on the young. I charged Bennett in turn with elitism and argued that he seriously misunderstood popular culture: our rowdy daytime talk shows in fact reflect the actual tastes and raw comic energy of the mass audience, whose loyalties translate into sky-high ratings.

Salon was created during a newspaper strike by Talbot, then arts and features editor of the *San Francisco Examiner,* with a team of like-minded editors and reporters from the *Examiner* and KQED-TV. My professional association with him had begun four years earlier when

[From *Communication and Cyberspace: Social Interaction in an Electronic Environment,* 2nd ed., ed. Lance Strate et al. (2003).]

he interviewed me for the *Examiner*'s weekly magazine, *Image*, an entire issue of which he devoted to excerpts from my academic exposé, "Junk Bonds and Corporate Raiders," which had just appeared in the Spring 1991 issue of *Arion*, a classics journal at Boston University.

As a 1960s progressive who had co-written a study of the sexual revolution, Talbot sympathized with my thesis that liberal '60s principles had become distorted by political correctness in the 1980s, when campus speech codes were threatening free expression. As the son of a Hollywood actor (Lyle Talbot, the "king of B movies"), Talbot also appreciated my respect for popular culture, which my 1990 book, *Sexual Personae*, meshed with the fine-arts tradition and hailed as a pagan phenomenon connected to classical antiquity.

In 1990, I had begun writing op-ed pieces on hot-button current affairs for newspapers (an unusual forum at that time for humanities professors). Hence Talbot asked me to contribute to the *Examiner*: from late 1992 on, I wrote for him on Amy Fisher, the "Long Island Lolita"; comedienne Sandra Bernhard as the heir of Lenny Bruce; and Bill and Hillary Clinton, where I analyzed the pivotal role played by TV in the rise of an obscure Arkansas governor to the White House.

When Talbot left the *Examiner* to start Salon, I went with him. He envisioned international editions of Salon as well as an arts-and-ideas Salon TV show that was eventually contracted to Bravo. A Salon radio project was also later announced. For what seemed to be managerial as well as funding and personnel problems (the in-house staff, for example, may have been expanded too rapidly), none of these projects materialized. Reprints of Salon articles, however, do appear abroad via an international syndication service.

My first fleeting encounter with the Internet occurred in 1991 at the Massachusetts Institute of Technology after a lecture I gave called "Crisis in the American Universities." A visitor from the Boston area approached me at the podium and asked, "Are you aware that you're all over The WELL?" "What is The WELL?" I asked, completely baffled. He promised to send me some information.

A week later, a packet arrived at my office in Philadelphia. I brandished the thick print-out at my colleagues: "What IS this?" I sputtered. "Look—a person in Boston is arguing about my ideas with someone in Tennessee, and they're both arguing with someone else in San Francisco!" None of us in the humanities department could decipher the method or rationale of this peculiar document, nor did we guess that it was our first bulletin from a dawning communications revolution.

The co-creator of The WELL was Stewart Brand, founder of the *Whole Earth Catalog* (1968) and the *Whole Earth Review* (1985). Much later, when he interviewed me for the premiere 1993 issue of *Wired* (whose "patron saint" is Marshall McLuhan), I realized that he was another 1960s veteran actively reassessing American cultural history. The WELL had been launched in 1985 by Brand and Larry Brilliant as the first general cyber forum, turning the Internet away from its early orientation as a bulletin-board service for scientific and military exchanges. Like Salon, The WELL was based in Northern California and staffed by independent, tech-savvy thinkers outside both the academic and the East Coast media establishments. They shared my fatigue with the strident polarization of conservatism versus liberalism and were looking for something new, which did in fact materialize in the libertarianism and pro-sex feminism of the 1990s.

Brand recognized how deeply I had been influenced by McLuhan, who had been swept away in the 1970s by French and German theory. By the 1980s, popular culture was being routinely condemned from two sides: by conservatives on the grounds of immorality and vulgarity and by leftists on the grounds of sexism, racism, and economic exploitation, with capitalism stereotyped as a brutal tool of Western imperialism. Very little in the new academic approaches to media— abstract semiotics, the Frankfurt School, British Marxist cultural studies, or Franco-American postmodernism—made sense to me as a McLuhanite. Furthermore, there seemed to be a willful blindness to the role modern capitalism had played in enhancing individualism, raising the standard of living, and liberating women. And it was capitalism, via the technological marvel of the personal computer, that would make the Internet so powerful a vehicle of free thought and free speech around the world.

It was in fact via the Internet that the heirs of McLuhan, scattered across North America like defeated soldiers of a civil war, identified each other in the 1990s and regrouped. My commitment to the Internet is partly inspired by gratitude: it was The WELL, I later saw, that had helped spread the word about my controversial and long-delayed first book, a 700-page tome that its publisher (Yale University Press) did not expect would find a wide audience. In an era of political correctness, which had taken root on campus and in the major media, the Internet was operating like an invisible, subterranean resistance movement.

PROCESS AND PRACTICE

Since the mid-1990s, the Internet has caused a tremendous cultural shift whose most profound impact has been on young people. It will take another thirty years before the Internet's effects are clearly understood. The computer has literally reshaped the brain of those who grew up with it, just as television and rock music reshaped the brains of my baby-boom generation and made our thinking so different in form and content from that of writers and critics born just before World War Two.

College students, even in the Ivy League, may spend from two to five hours a night on the Internet. Most middle-aged professionals, including teachers, have yet to appreciate the scope or depth of what is happening. As late as 1997, for example, a prominent reporter at *The Boston Globe* tried to discourage my writing for Salon ("No one reads things on the Internet"); he exhorted me to focus on contributing to the major media instead. But one of my primary motivations in writing for Salon was to speak directly to young people, who have no loyalty to newspapers: today's college students were born in the 1980s, when newspapers, a major melting-pot medium for a century since the start of the immigration era, had already lost ground to television.

Campus literature departments were caught flat-footed by the sudden rise of the Internet. Throughout the 1990s, elite universities inflicted a cruel cognitive dissonance on their humanities students, who were forced to read antiquated French and German theory (based on premises and methodology predating World War Two), while cyberculture was exploding all around them. This was a principal factor in the decline in prestige and power of humanities departments in that period, when the number of literature majors steadily fell. The young knew perfectly well that the language of the future was now the computer and the Web.

Some theorists tried to shore up their system by redefining the Internet as a postmodern medium, but the idea was misconceived. The fragmentation or discontinuity they thought they saw was really the proliferation, multiplicity, and rapid pulses of electronic media that McLuhan correctly interpreted in physiological and neurological terms. Surfing the Web (significantly, a nature-sports metaphor) means catching its wave motion and feeling its tides and eddies. The Web has weather, particularly when news events unleash storms of popular sentiment. Though the body is quiet and dormant at the computer, the Web works by sensory overload, through which the surfer navigates along a zigzag track like a sailboat tacking at sea.

One reason I find writing for the Internet so fulfilling is that the Web's natural rhythms and strong, personal voices (contradicting the effete post-structuralist doctrine of the "death of the subject") seem to be in the direct line of the body-oriented, incantatory, anti-academic American poetry of the 1950s and '60s that influenced me heavily in college. Beat and Black Mountain poems were performance pieces meant to be recited. The fountainhead of this American style was Walt Whitman, whom Allen Ginsberg in particular invoked as an influence.

Whitman's "Leaves of Grass," as I see it, oddly prefigures Internet style: the poem's impressionistic sections and cascading verse-paragraphs resemble the way Salon articles are split into pages linked by provocative hypertext grabbers. My columns for Salon have consciously assimilated Whitman's salutations to the reader; his pluralist dwelling on social class; and his mix of street slang with oracular pronouncements. Whitman shows how to juxtapose the homely minutiae of everyday life with both contemporary politics and grand perspectives on nature.

But the key to Internet writing for me is visual, not verbal. Ever since computer operating systems progressed from half-mathematical ASCII to today's lively, colorful, high-resolution graphics HTML format, the Internet has become a mercurial hybrid of word, image, and sound. Television was the key, leading to the personal computer screen and thus the Internet. Nowhere in the world has TV been so dominant a cultural presence as here in the United States. Close to three generations of Americans have learned from childhood not just how to look at TV but how to live with it in virtually every room of the house (and now car).

More pertinently, only in the United States do commercials intrude at predictable intervals into newscasts, talk shows, sports, and drama. Elsewhere in the world, commercials are grouped at the start or end of programs, which thus may begin at odd times rather than on the hour or half-hour. Visitors to the United States sometimes become confused or lose focus when our commercials burst into a story line every few minutes.

I submit that the stop-start rhythm of a half-century of commercial TV viewing was Americans' basic training for Internet communication, active or passive (that is, writing or reading). "And now for a word from our sponsor," we used to hear; today it's "Hold that thought," as the host sternly stops even the most high-ranking guest mid-flight to cut away for a series of eye-assaulting commercials. The jump or truncation is an American specialty; it is precisely our suffusion in mass media that has allowed us to keep identity, thought, and mood intact as we vault over the alleged discontinuities of modern life that have proved so disabling to literati from T. S. Eliot and Samuel Beckett to the postmodernist theorists who drove aesthetics off the academic map for twenty-five years.

The puzzling failure of humanities professors to contribute in any substantial way thus far to the leading Web zines stems, I conjecture, from their long ambivalence about TV. Although prominent academics have made occasional appearances in Salon and Slate, they strangely fade away, retreating to the online special-interest groups where they resume the same professional conversation they have at conferences. Their lack of interest in addressing a general audience is remarkable in this period when the "public intellectual" (a questionable and overused term) is so much prized.

Some academics may feel that Internet writing, like the TV image, is evanescent, but the opposite is true. Ever since it switched from live to tape, TV is the great medium of the re-run, where nothing is ever lost; so with the Web, where the search engines not only net up every obscure, years-old crackpot rant like debris from the sea floor but where on the best-organized Web sites all past articles arc miraculously available by push-button access in their archives. The Web is an ever-expanding, if still ill-sorted and error-filled encyclopedia of Alexandrian dimensions.

Another reason for academics' reluctance to join the Web-zines may be the blinking marginalia of advertising logos that now adorn every Salon page. Perhaps academics feel that their text is swamped or compromised by so much visual distraction, like the banks of flashing bulbs at a casino or penny arcade. But I feel quite at home in this milieu, which replicates the jump-cuts and blizzard of special effects on commercial TV. Web pages crowned or rimmed by ads sometimes resemble medieval illuminated manuscripts, with their fantastic, embellished lettering, and also Art Nouveau books and prints, with their undulating borders of running tendrils.

My premises about advertising, in any case, are quite different from those of most academics. Like Andy Warhol, I always regarded ads, logos, and product packaging as an art form and probably for the same reason: as a child, I visually processed them as analogues to the lavish, polychrome iconography of the Italian Catholic church. (Warhol's Eastern European church was Byzantine and therefore even more ornate.) I remain fascinated by advertising slogans as folk poetry, which over time taught me how to speak in quotable "sound bites."

In writing for Salon, I regularly use many more voices and shifts of tone than I do in writing, for example, for *The Wall Street Journal*: my op-ed pieces for the latter are usually sober in tone and organized in a conventional, linear way, with a timely lead followed by factual evidence and a conclusion. In Salon, on the other hand, I've absorbed the hectoring personae of old-time radio and TV: the host, the stand-up comic, and the pitchman, a descendant of the carnival barker. Even when most of the column addresses serious issues, I often borrow its transitions from the evening talk-show form perfected by Johnny Carson on *The Tonight Show*, where a topical opening monologue yields to a series of guests and where the host may turn up in costume as cranky Aunt Blabby or that caped clairvoyant, Carnac the Magnificent.

The column began as a strict Q&A, a sequel to the parody "agony aunt" column, "Ask Camille," that I wrote for *Spy* magazine in 1993. As Salon reader questions, as well as my replies, got longer, however, the format broadened, so that the "host" voice opens, closes, and directs throughout. Another TV genre helping me organize material is the variety show, a form (descended from vaudeville) that was in its heyday in my adolescence but is now defunct due to sheer expense. At their height, *The Ed Sullivan Show* and *The Carol Burnett Show* struck a balance between mainstream offerings and controversial, cutting-edge acts. In writing my column, I try to draw in as many segments of the Web-reading public as possible—no easy task, since political junkies and pop fans, for example, now haunt their own ghettoized sites.

During the 2000 presidential campaign, I began weaving into the text longer passages than usual from reader letters on incendiary issues like gun control, so that the column began to resemble (as Talbot was the first to observe) a call-in AM radio show. In the media work that I have been invited to do over the past decade, the most dynamic has unquestionably been AM shows in the "drive-time" slots, when commuters are trapped in their cars and craving diversion and relief. The quarrelsome blare of AM radio, born in the obnoxious disc-jockey days of early Top 40 rock, is a truly modern voice, the embodiment of McLuhan's classification of radio as a "hot" medium. AM's abrasive high energy contrasts with the repressed mellifluousness of National Public Radio, geared to the velvety FM band. My Salon column consciously taps into AM's proletarian brashness rather than NPR's upper-middle-class gentility.

In writing for the Web, I've also found that text must be visually designed: its ideal basic architecture consists of sharply delineated, single-spaced paragraphs. While newspaper and magazine readers can flip through and scan the whole of an article before focusing in on it, the online reader typically sees no more than a half page at a time and would have to tediously scroll downward and jump by hypertext to successive pages to survey the whole. Because the eye of the online reader tires and needs refreshment, I build blank space into the article through regular paragraphing. I conceive of the text as floating blocks, much like the hovering rectangles in Mark Rothko's misty paintings. The paragraphs must be monumental and yet in motion.

The point-and-click method of advancing text produces a freeze-frame effect onscreen. These jumpy rhythms (finger-triggered by the mouse exactly as by the TV remote control) are positively new to reading experience and are so inconstant and improvisatory that they resemble syncopated jazz or jitterbug (once called "jump" music). At final-draft stage, I strip my paragraphs of excess words so that the sentences seem abrupt, which powers the text forward.

I also choose vocabulary that *looks* interesting on the page, which usually means juxtaposing blunt Anglo-Saxon nouns and high-action verbs with polysyllabic Greco-Roman abstractions. I use far more exclamation points, slang terms, alliterations, rhetorical questions, and expostulations than I would for a mainstream newspaper or magazine. Finally, I favor raucous sound effects, inspired by the reedy "honking" of alto-sax players. The text should be *palpable* and not just a remote stream of cyphers on a glassy wall.

Because of the blitzkrieg quality of Web bulletins—some of which notoriously turn out to be false—I strongly feel that Internet writing descends from the telegraph, that once high-tech innovation so vital to America's economic and political development as the frontier moved west. The wire services, which started up in the 1840s, reduced and condensed information to the atomized bits of Morse Code, a radical remaking of language that looked forward to modernism at its most minimalist. During the Civil War, telegraphed dispatches from the front transformed newspaper writing, not only creating the "inverted pyramid" protocol of news stories, where breaking news comes first, but drastically simplifying American English syntax and vocabulary.

There was as huge a gap in style between the punchy, telegraph-transformed, late-nineteenth-century newspapers and their more literary, periphrastic eighteenth-century precursors as exists today between mainstream or Web journalism and the still dismayingly turgid essays in academic journals like *PMLA* (quarterly of the Modern Language Association). While cast in more lucid prose, the leading articles on literature and culture even in the current *New Republic* or

New York Review of Books are often amazingly verbose, taking pages to make simple points: it's as if the thought processes of the authors and editors remain untouched by the media revolution of the past century. Internet text at its best is *streamlined*—a cardinal artistic principle of modernism extending beyond the Bauhaus to an American source, the late-nineteenth-century Chicago School of architecture.

Online articles that sustain reader attention beyond the first page are those, in my view, that take the telegraph as their ancestor. Simplification and acceleration are the principles. The Internet's residual telegraphic element has brought the frontier or battlefront into every wired home, so that any surfer can play dispatcher, flooded by urgent messages from all over the map. For this reason, I find the Drudge Report, almost universally disdained by upscale journalists, to be a unique and invaluable Internet resource. As a rough-hewn insurgent and outsider without institutional support, Matt Drudge, who styles himself after stentorian columnist Walter Winchell, provides constantly updated, siren-flashing news alerts and links to the world press, a format now widely imitated by other Web sites. Drudge's range of subjects has a tabloid flamboyance—from Washington and Hollywood scandals to earthquakes, airplane crashes, grisly crimes, and sentimental animal stories.

The Internet's flair for the "news flash" is something I try to capture in my columns—the on-street excitement that used to be generated by "extras" run off by urban dailies in the pre-TV era when big news broke between the morning and evening editions. The Internet democratizes the news, allowing the average citizen to get information straight off the wires before TV producers and print journalists can shape and doctor it. This unfiltered flow of information direct from stringers on location comes like a bolt of electricity into the private home.

In Salon, I also report on and weigh rumors, which I would never do for mainstream publications. Rumors have a life of their own and often are the first sign of a shift in popular thought, particularly in campaign years; a rumor is myth in the making. (The standard was set in the fifth century B.C. by Herodotus, who collected and analyzed rumors for his *Histories*.) An Internet column allows one to monitor and comment on contemporary life as it's actually happening. Since it's linked by hypertext to past columns and other sites, the text has an organic connection to the entire Web, an amplitude of reference analogous to the ponderous footnote material of print books that never appears, for reasons of space, in newspapers. Organic also is the Web-zine's ability to correct factual errors or typos in already posted articles—a luxury unavailable to print journalists, who are stuck forever with embarrassing mistakes (as when copy editors fresh from college maddeningly introduce grammar errors at deadline).

In topic sequence, my column has begun to resemble *Time* magazine, which I grew up with and virtually cut my teeth on in its classic era of superb reportage and acid-etched prose. Although *Time* has distressingly declined over the past fifteen years, it generally retains its old format, with high-impact national and international political news at the front, followed by science, sports, movies, books (much reduced), and celebrity gossip.

Time's revolutionary innovation was to package the week's news when the United States had just become a power on the international stage in the decade after World War One. And the magazine addressed a brand-new national audience, recently created by movies and radio. The Web-zines have gone one step further by expanding their readership internationally. E-mail responses to my column have come not just from Canada and England but from Iceland, Hungary, Russia, Chile, South Africa, Australia, and Japan. Because of this global reach, I carefully adjust my column so that American personalities, events, and places are discreetly identified for overseas readers.

A primary aim of mine has been to keep the column resolutely independent and non-partisan; hence I try to critique all invested positions. (For example, though a registered Democrat who voted for Bill Clinton twice, I have been scathing about the failures of the Clinton administration.) As a consequence, the column has had an unusually broad following. While negative mail is of course a constant for anyone who writes for a public forum, I am always surprised at the ideological and sociological range of supportive letters, which come from evangelical Christian home-schooling moms, conservative retired military officers, harried public-school teachers, anxious grad

students, cross-dressing bisexuals, movie-trivia fanatics, opera connoisseurs, and struggling young rock musicians. To bring all these
people together—many of whom lack the time or money for multiple
magazine and newspaper subscriptions—is a testament to the power
of the Web as a potentially universal medium.

MOBILIZATION UNDER FIRE: A CASE STUDY

Because Internet publication is unconstrained by traditional printing-
press deadlines, the Web-zines can dispense with a fixed production
schedule, an opportunity that Salon was the first to take advantage of.
Its rivals used to operate in slow motion, randomly dribbling out new
articles in late morning or the afternoon without regard for timeli-
ness or drama. That Salon's chief editors originally worked for a daily
(rather than a bimonthly, like Slate's editor) has certainly given Salon
a more militant intensity.

Each edition of Salon is finalized in San Francisco by the end of
the prior business day, Pacific time, though breaking news stories
can be inserted at any hour. The issue goes online around midnight,
East Coast time. Hence Salon is seen and read in the United Kingdom and Europe five hours before the workday begins in the United
States. Many times, I went to sleep in Philadelphia before my column
went online and awoke to find faxes and e-mail queries from the London press, who had been reading Salon at the start of their workday
(between 3:00 and 4:00 AM EST). Of the domestic newspapers, only
The New York Times (or, less so, *The Washington Post*) has that kind of
reach to European capitals.

The fluid press deadline newly created by the Web was never
clearer than in the tragic episode of the death of Diana in a car crash
in the early hours of August 31, 1997. This was a landmark in the early
history of Web journalism, where Salon, because of its quick reaction,
broke Web records in sheer volume of reader "hits."

That chronology should be documented as the first important example of a Web-zine outmaneuvering the print press. And in the process, Salon scooped and humiliated its rival, Slate, which had closed
its East Coast offices for the last week of August before Labor Day (the
staff presumably decamping to the Hamptons). In personal terms, this

was by far the most traumatic of all my media experiences, because I had been a longtime analyst of the Diana saga for both North American and British media.

The accident occurred just after midnight on a Saturday night in Paris. By chance, I was listening to the radio at home when the first news flash came just after 7:00 PM, Philadelphia time. The initial report said Diana was merely injured. Television responded immediately (as it had so memorably done for the assassination of John F. Kennedy in 1963), but already-scheduled network programming went on, interrupted by intermittent bulletins. More than two hours passed before all the networks and cable channels switched to continuous coverage. The top news stars were slow to appear on air because they had to return to the studio from their vacation retreats (the Hamptons again).

Just after 10:00 PM EST, the correspondents relayed the official announcement from a Paris hospital that the Princess of Wales had been declared dead. Hence U.S. residents heard the terrible news before they went to bed, whereas most of the British public, fast asleep in the middle of the night, still had no idea an accident had even occurred. The British woke up on Sunday morning to a stunning fait accompli, while many Americans had had three tense hours after news of the crash to prepare for the worst.

The accident occurred too late on Saturday night to make the Sunday newspapers in either the United Kingdom or the United States. On weekdays, the press deadline for major American dailies is between 5:00 and 6:00 PM, and it is much earlier on Saturdays. Hence it was not until Monday morning that newspapers could report on Diana's shocking death, which had occurred more than a full day earlier.

Into this press vacuum, when for over thirty hours there was nothing substantive for shocked people to read about the event, leapt Salon. The editors in San Francisco sprang into action ("like firehouse dogs," Talbot later said) as soon as Diana's death was announced on Saturday night. They immediately solicited reaction and commentary from within Salon's staff and outside it: the articles went online by stages from midday Sunday on and received a mammoth amount of traffic from all over the world. On following days, more pieces of reportage and background were added, and the epic Diana package remained flagged on Salon's main screen for weeks.

The perils attendant on Web publishing are illustrated by an unexpected reaction to my first remarks about the accident in Salon, where I lamented that Diana had been foolish to trust her safety and security to the Egyptian playboy Dodi Fayed (a point later substantiated by the inquest report). After the translated article was reprinted several days later in *Le Monde*, two rather menacing airmail letters from Paris arrived at my university office accusing me of fomenting anti-Muslim prejudice and propaganda. Despite the risk of incurring a fatwa, however, writing for Salon has been a golden opportunity to contribute to the World Wide Web at a pivotal point in its cultural development.

Whatever Salon's fate, it has already been enormously influential in creating the paradigm for online magazine publishing. Its graphic and tech design has been consistently cutting-edge. And its feature writers and columnists developed, through trial and error, the distinctive tone and style of online commentary, now imitated by Web sites across the political spectrum. In literary history, I submit, Salon can be compared to two bold and witty London periodicals, Richard Steele's *The Tatler* (1709–11) and Steele and Joseph Addison's *The Spectator* (1711–12; 1714). Despite their short lives, the *Tatler* and *Spectator* prefigured and helped beget the rhetorical forms and strategies of modern journalism.

ART

41

ON ANDY WARHOL

HUFFINGTON POST: You've referred to Andy Warhol as a hero, and yet his world-view seems to capture what you despise about contemporary culture with his blasé, bourgeois, insular, irreverent, too-cool-for-school attitude. Do you see Warhol in this way, and if so, why is he your hero?

CAMILLE PAGLIA: Warhol had an enormous impact on me as a college student in upstate New York in the 1960s. I have proudly called myself a "Warholite" ever since. It is baffling how Warhol could ever be called "bourgeois," because he was the product of a poor immigrant family in industrial Pittsburgh, and he boldly brought the dissident sexual underground into then-stuffy major museums in both Manhattan and Philadelphia. He surrounded himself with male hustlers, drug addicts, drag queens, and decadent, androgynous socialites. Warhol was openly gay long before the birth of the gay liberation movement. He was contemptuously ostracized as "swish" by closeted gay artists like Jasper Johns and Robert Rauschenberg in New York.

Neither would I accept the term "blasé" about Warhol, since that implies a far more sophisticated and affectedly fatigued persona than the one he projected. A colleague said that Warhol

[Priscilla Frank, interviewer, "Camille Paglia's *Glittering Images*: Controversial Writer Speaks on Warhol, Arts Funding, and *Star Wars*," *The Huffington Post*, November 7, 2012.]

pretended to be "the village idiot"—that is, a dysfunctional, marginalized, passive observer of society. Warhol's primary response to anything that interested him was "Wow"—the exact opposite of blasé. He was a voyeur who voraciously consumed mass media and who identified himself with the popular audience. Many of his early large-scale pictures were blow-ups of tabloid newspaper photos of automobile or airplane accidents. What he was demonstrating was the saturation of society by the sensationalistic visuals of modern media—a return to a primitive form of consciousness that pre-dated literacy.

To continue with the adjectives you have proposed, I see nothing "irreverent" in Warhol either. On the contrary, he transferred the religiosity of his youth in Eastern Rite Catholicism to his passionate reverence for Hollywood stars like Elizabeth Taylor and Marilyn Monroe, whom he turned into shimmering saints in an updated Byzantine style. "Marilyn Diptych," the subject of a chapter in my book, is really a giant icon screen like the one in Warhol's baptismal church in Pittsburgh. Similarly, those who see irony in Warhol's acrylic paintings of Campbell's Soup cans are simply imposing their own contemporary preconceptions backwards onto him. Warhol, who began his career as a commercial illustrator, loved brand-name logos and saw them as modern heraldry. Campbell's Soup cans were beautiful to him—exactly as they were to me as a child growing up in the sooty factory town of Endicott, New York. I used to cut out colorful logos from magazine ads and play with them like paper dolls.

Warhol's experimental films were also crucial in shaping my sensibility. I am not referring to the later, well-known feature-length color films directed by Paul Morrissey but to Warhol's grainy, improvised, black-and-white short films, which have strangely never been released on DVD (though they are available for viewing at the Andy Warhol Museum in Pittsburgh). The one that hit me like a thunderbolt in college was *Harlot* (1965), where a lounging drag queen in a blonde wig slowly peels and eats a banana, while hunky bystanders gradually shift position;

the soundtrack is simply offscreen banter in campy male voices. This parody of Hollywood sex queens—simultaneously trashy and sublimely cultic—seemed like a dream vision, revealing the deep structure of popular imagination, with its adulation of stars of both sexes. The last of Warhol's great films was *Chelsea Girls* (1966), a three-and-a-half-hour split-screen epic that mesmerizingly alternated between the banal and the surreal.

In short, Warhol's callow imitators may be blasé, bourgeois, insular, and irreverent, but *he* certainly was not.

42

MILLENNIUM MASTERWORKS:
THE *MONA LISA*

Leonardo da Vinci, *Mona Lisa*, 1503.
The Louvre, Paris.

Why does Leonardo da Vinci's *Mona Lisa* remain the most famous painting in the world? Its subject's thin smile has become synonymous with sexual mystery—with the secrecy, obliqueness, and heartbreaking elusiveness of woman.

[*The Sunday Times* (U.K.), April 18, 1999. Several sentences deleted in print for space have been restored.]

Hence the *Mona Lisa* represents everything that feminism cannot explain about woman's carnal magnetism, which for millennia has fascinated or repelled men across the spectrum of sexual orientation. Mona Lisa's silence is hypnotic and profound. She exists in another dimension, a twilight zone where anatomy is destiny. She is untouched by politics, careers, or social ambition.

Already renowned as a genius, Leonardo completed relatively few paintings. He was the prototypical Renaissance man with perhaps too many interests. His voluminous private notebooks were packed with botanical and anatomical drawings and with diagrams of mechanical devices real or fantastic.

The *Mona Lisa,* begun as a commissioned portrait in 1503, may be hauntingly juxtaposed to Leonardo's shocking notebook sketch of a fetus huddled in the womb, from which the wall has been peeled like the skin of an orange. It's as if Leonardo's Promethean intellect could not bear the baffling complexity of female procreative power.

Certainly, the *Mona Lisa* obsessed its maker, who could not let it go. The monastic (and probably gay-tending) Leonardo worked on it for four years and then carried it with him to France, where he died in 1519 in the employ of the king. Hence the presence of this Italian masterwork in the former royal palace of the Louvre, where the *Mona Lisa* is exhibited like a holy monstrance to which pilgrims flock from all over the world.

The lady of the painting is placidly posed in what was then a conventional way: she sits in a carved armchair with her back to what was normally a window. But at some point Leonardo removed the framing wall, so that she seems enthroned on a high, exposed parapet.

Her rippling, silky garments are like a soft nest from which rises the white expanse of her plush maternal bosom. Her figure, with its decorously crossed hands, forms a stable pyramid, but there is something unsettling about the heavy, egg-like head, which, if one looks long enough, seems to detach itself and swivel on a serpent's neck.

The *Mona Lisa* is subdued in color and misty with *sfumato*—the murky "smokiness" that Leonardo introduced to oil painting and that would spread to inky depths in Caravaggio and Rembrandt. Ambiguity cloaks the corners of the lady's browless, bulging eyes and mouth, so we must wonder what she is thinking. She is literally and figuratively veiled.

This face with its penetrating stare and smugly suggestive smile appears again and again in Leonardo's paintings—sometimes on women like St. Anne, the mother of Mary, and sometimes on men like Bacchus or St. John the Baptist. It may belong to the unwed peasant mother from whom the infant Leonardo was taken away, if we follow Freud's inspired guesses about the artist's tortured psyche.

The aesthete Walter Pater saw Mona Lisa as a "vampire," a dark goddess who had lived many lives through history. Marcel Duchamp drew a Dadaist mustache on her to signal her androgyny and his patricide, the disdain of impatient young artists with the burden of the past.

That the *Mona Lisa* as a vision of woman is not wholly benign is shown by the stark moonscape of rocks and water that opens out behind her. She may be content, but she promises us no pleasure gardens of love. She is ripe and florid yet closed and ungiving.

And the painting's distant horizon lines are oddly mismatched. Viewers who pause, transfixed, before this supreme European icon are subliminally feeling the ground give way, as they are propelled backward to the primeval, ruled by cruel mother nature.

43

PICASSO'S
GIRL BEFORE A MIRROR

Over the last twenty-five years, feminism has had a dual impact on the understanding and practice of art history. First, it has inspired a systematic effort to recover neglected female artists of the past and to focus special attention on those of the present. Second, it has subjected major male artists of the canon to a critical reassessment that makes gender issues central to their lives and work.

There is legitimate disagreement about the success of this enterprise. I feel that the hasty broadening of the canon, while laudably motivated, has too often produced an indifference to questions of quality, permanence, and historical accuracy. Furthermore, gender, however important, is not the ultimate determiner of art and thought, and it should not be used antagonistically and reductively to diminish great achievement. The ill effects of this latter feminist tendency can be seen in the shockingly widespread denigration of Degas, Picasso, and Duchamp, who have been labeled misogynist and overtly ostracized.

It is intolerable that a turbulent genius like Pablo Picasso, who is rivaled for invention and productivity only by Michelangelo in the history of world art, should be hauled up like a schoolboy and held to account for his untidy, bohemian sex life. Two hundred years ago, Romanticism definitively rejected the didactic neoclassical view that art must elevate and that the artist must set a moral example. Picasso's gargantuan oeuvre demonstrates not that he hated and demeaned

["Looking at Art: Picasso's Women," *ARTnews*, January 1996.]

women but that he was awed by and obsessed with female sexual power, which he observes, engages, and transmutes in all its modalities from motherhood to prostitution.

Two works in particular express for me Picasso's complex attitude of envy and admiration of woman's daunting autonomy. As one of the avant-garde masterpieces of the century, *Les Demoiselles d'Avignon* (1907) is familiar but still terrifying. In the pagan shrine of a brothel, five statuesque nude goddesses or priestesses, wearing tribal masks and staring blankly with cold, entranced eyes, welcome supplicant man into a fractured paradise garden of crystal shards and ashy fruit. Their breasts are hard and razor-edged, like armor plate; their legs are mannish and colossal, one a forbidding stump that seems part tenderloin, part cleaver. Low in the foreground looms, as a ruddy melon slice, the castrating blade of the crescent moon. This pleasure palace is a harem as inferno, from which no visitor escapes.

The second painting, *Girl Before a Mirror* (1932), has been widely reproduced but less discussed. Owned by the Museum of Modern Art, it has recently gained greater visibility through a somewhat free reproduction on imported coffee mugs. Since it shows woman not in her contemporary manifestation as successful careerist but rather in her most ancient archetype of solitary, pregnant divinity, we must wonder whether the painting's emerging popularity is not partly due to dissatisfaction and fatigue with feminism's increasingly strained redefinitions of gender.

Girl Before a Mirror is staged in another secret shrine, this time a boudoir where a woman, like Narcissus, gazes enamored at her own image in what seems to be a shadowy, rippling pool. The painting's calm grandeur comes from Picasso's conviction that he is apprehending woman's essence, something that current social constructionism—the theory that we are totally shaped by our environment—denies has ever existed. But academic theory is often wildly removed from everyday human reality. I submit that *Girl Before a Mirror* does indeed capture something universal and eternal about woman, which feminism, if it hopes to prosper beyond the millennium, must more honestly acknowledge.

A specific woman is recognizable in this painting: the sharp, clas-

Pablo Picasso, *Girl Before a Mirror*, 1932.
The Museum of Modern Art, New York.

sical nose and very modern, blonde bob belong to Marie-Thérèse Walter, who became the married Picasso's discreet mistress in 1927, after he spotted the athletic and voluptuous seventeen-year-old on a Paris street. We know her primarily from his many abstract, often convoluted paintings of her sleeping, as well as from a sculpture group of monumental archaic heads. Described as "sweet" and "placid," Marie-Thérèse bore Picasso a daughter in 1935; her influence waned with the decade. Forty years later, she committed suicide.

Girl Before a Mirror shows woman as Venus, Eve, Madonna, and witch. Creating and embracing her own reflection, she is like a painter gesturing toward an easel bearing an ovoid tondo rimmed with a rainbow. Behind her is a harlequin-pattern wallpaper, adorned not with the misty mauves of Picasso's Rose Period but with the garish, hallucinatory red and chrome-yellow borrowed from Gauguin by Matisse, who also likes to set his dreamy women against clashing decorative grids.

The patches, streaks, and halo of lime and apple-green represent the fertility of nature, also suggested by the dense, tapestry-like background. Picasso's Eve is herself the tree of knowledge, her breasts and swollen belly hanging like heavy fruit. She has become her own god, to whom she offers ritual homage amid kaleidoscopic walls of stained glass, reminiscent of the Sainte-Chapelle in Paris. We see into the magic circle of her womb with the X-ray eyes of the artist, who, like every man, is in exile, doomed to hover at the periphery of woman's solipsistic consciousness. For Picasso, even the sexually possessed woman is finally impenetrable.

The most stunning device in *Girl Before a Mirror* is the Cubist treatment of the face as sun and moon as well as evolving life phases. The cool, pure virgin becomes the mature, fleshy adult radiating sultry eroticism and daubed with rouge and mascara. Both see their future: a crone hooded in mourning violet and midnight-blue, Demeter weeping for lost Kore. The mirror as emblem of vanity is also a memento mori. The chalky, lidless skull of wintry mother nature is capped with a bloody shark fin, rising out of a Charybdis-like vortex of swirling waters.

The girl is garbed in a ribbed corset or flashy, flapper-era bathing suit. Its horizontal lines suggest both the layering of a landscape and the iron girders of a tower, which rises like an obelisk to a pyramid crowned with the mystic eye of the sun god. Her dark twin, with withered thorax and twiggy pubic pitchfork, also has a mystic eye or royal uraeus—a bulbous Spanish olive stuffed with pimiento, resembling both a bursting seed and fat male genitalia. Nature is shown as a self-regenerating cycle of birth and death. Woman clones herself. In this Annunciation, beneath a sliver of sky-blue window, woman originates, salutes, and accepts her biological destiny, spun out as a silky skein or web of arterial red draped across the picture.

As flat and ornamented as a Byzantine icon, *Girl Before a Mirror* is packed with mythological meanings and witty sexual puns. Feminism has yet to produce an artistic statement about woman equal to this in magnitude or poetic suggestiveness. Picasso's fascination with women was deeply rooted: compare the multiple faces of this painting to his 1895 pastel and 1923 oil of his brunette mother, Maria, in right and left profile. Picasso's blonde mistress had his mother's name and his mother's face, which ruled his inner world.

44

MORE MUSH FROM THE NEA

Last week, after Jane Alexander announced her resignation as its chairman, the National Endowment for the Arts released a 194-page report, "American Canvas," summarizing her four trying years of stewardship.

With her intelligence and classy poise, Ms. Alexander won respect from both sides in the protracted congressional battle over whether the NEA would live or die. She made budgetary concessions and deftly defused tensions, notably by dropping grants to individual artists to avoid controversies like those over homosexual sadomasochism and sacrilege in the photographs of Robert Mapplethorpe and Andres Serrano.

Alas, "American Canvas" is a clumsy, incoherent document that casts doubt on whether Ms. Alexander or her staff ever fully grasped the deepest issues in the attacks on the NEA. As a cultural historian and arts educator who favors expanded government support of the arts, I am appalled by this mushy, meandering, and visually ill-designed report, which can only confirm the worst suspicions of the agency's archconservative opponents.

By "American Canvas," the agency appears to mean not an American art work but an American duffel bag or circus tent: its photograph of two children admiring their painted clown faces in a hand mirror at a Los Angeles arts festival demonstrates the kind of narcissism and

[Review of "American Canvas," report by the National Endowment for the Arts at the departure of director Jane Alexander, *The Wall Street Journal*, October 24, 1997.]

fake populism that suffuse chatter about the arts in this country. Is recreational face-painting really the "cultural legacy" Ms. Alexander says we must "transmit" to the future?

Skewed summaries of the NEA report by *The New York Times* and *The Washington Post* took the politically correct party line that, in her tour of the fifty states and her six regional forums, Ms. Alexander had uncovered a pernicious elitism that separates artists from the communities they should serve.

This is sheer propaganda. The real problem facing the arts in America is not simply the dominance of mass media (which the report annoyingly sneers at) but the degeneration of standards in our Playskool model of primary education, in which everyone is an artist, without the discipline of technical mastery. Instead of protesting this feel-good relativism, Ms. Alexander endorses it (saying that we need "active participation rather than passive observation" in the arts)— which is exactly why she was never able to whip up public pressure on Congress.

The gravest problem with "American Canvas" is its cowardly refusal to engage the NEA's fierce critics, who deserve to have their morality-based arguments fairly recorded, digested, and answered. Ms. Alexander has squandered a splendid opportunity to present a substantive apologia for the arts and their high meaning in history.

But her report speaks with a forked tongue. It pays lip service to homespun traditional values while pushing the usual limousine-liberal agenda of soggy multiculturalism or "diversity" by quota, without true scholarship. It calls for "lasting works of art" yet reduces art to everyday "self-expression"—including birthday parties!

The report claims on one page that the arts "embody family activities and values" and yet, twenty pages later, scornfully attacks "the tyranny of the majority" in Charlotte, N.C., where an arts council was denied public funds for "supporting homosexuality," in a production of Tony Kushner's *Angels in America* (which the report elevates to "masterpiece" status). Whether independent, commercially successful plays need government subsidies is not considered.

As a professional actress, Ms. Alexander may have been too drawn to a free-form, hand-holding, ensemble model of the arts and less sympathetic to the slogging, unglamorous mission of restoration and conservation of fine-art objects and anthropological artifacts, which most Americans would deem worthy of government support. The report pictures but makes only passing reference to an American Indian "Tsimshian longhouse" and "historic adobe churches," which constitute our genuine national heritage.

The NEA got into trouble when it tried to underwrite original work by contemporary artists, selected by a cliquish, costly bureaucratic process. In a 1995 speech at Harvard's John F. Kennedy School of Government, another actress, Barbra Streisand, declared: "All great civilizations have supported the arts," Well, yes and no. Great civilizations only support arts that celebrate their greatness. With their eyes on personal glory, the pharaohs and Medici princes sure weren't commissioning "subversive" art.

Since Romanticism, much important art has been oppositional, critiquing political, religious, or artistic norms—which is why so many artists starved and won only posthumous fame. But let's get real: no self-respecting avant-garde artist should be on the government dole. Hollywood liberals who support cutting-edge work should be putting their ample money where their mouths are by endowing private arts foundations.

The NEA must serve the citizenry as a whole and cease operating as a partisan political tool. This report is strongest when it promotes the role of the arts in both rural and urban renewal—as is shown in Philadelphia by Mayor Ed Rendell's visionary plan for the Avenue of the Arts, where I teach.

But the report brazenly ignores the worst excesses of the art world—the cynical, university-bred jargon of post-structuralism and postmodernism, which has infected art magazines and exhibition catalogs and helped destroy public confidence in and appreciation of art. All of Jane Alexander's roses can't hide that skunk. In America, the Left as well as the Right—Stalinism as well as Puritanism—has abused art.

A better NEA strategy might have been to offer bold new proposals. For example, we need coast-to-coast educational radio stations devoted to classical music and jazz history. Aspiring young artists deserve college scholarships comparable to those given athletes. Economically disadvantaged students should be sent abroad on grand tours of European museums and archaeological sites in Mexico, Egypt, and India. Major folklore museums documenting American Indian culture must be built in every region of the country. Local libraries need massive revitalization and expansion as culture centers, sanctuaries from the mean streets and shopping malls.

The American people will support the NEA when the agency shows that it knows the difference between a wise investment and a politicized penny arcade.

45

DANCE: THE MOST FRAGILE OF THE ARTS

What attitude does mainstream America have toward dance, and why should dance professionals care? As someone who monitors the media closely, I have become increasingly disturbed about the low reputation of the fine arts with the mass audience to whom the powerful medium of political talk radio caters. Conservative hosts and callers regularly deride modern art as a scam and dismiss artists as frivolous, elitist, immoral, sacrilegious, and anti-American.

These attitudes have real-life consequences when local or state governments curtail or cancel arts funding outright as a wasteful extravagance. Even in Philadelphia, with its resident symphony orchestra and ballet and modern dance companies, City Hall last year shockingly eliminated its Office of Arts and Culture. Nationally, there has been an alarming trend for the cutting of arts programs from public schools, which disastrously affects working-class students whose families cannot afford private lessons.

Dance is the most fragile of the arts in that it cannot flourish in isolation or with long fallow periods. Any rupture is deeply destructive. Steady financing is critical to provide facilities, maintain companies, and nurture the living link between teacher and student down the generations.

Dance in the U.S. has never enjoyed the high prestige it has in Europe and Russia, where state and civic funding is a given. One reason

["Rants & Raves: How Can Dance Education Compete
with the Power of the Media?," *Dance Magazine,* July 2005.]

for this is that classical ballet, which descends from the royal court world, is gloriously embedded in national history. It is remarkable, for example, that even after the Bolsheviks toppled the czars, the socialist Soviet Union preserved ballet as the Russian people's cultural heritage.

America, in contrast, never had or wanted a titled aristocracy. Despite the waves of ethnic immigration since then, our cultural roots stubbornly remain in New England Puritanism, with its business-oriented practicality, sexual prudery, and suspicion of art and beauty. The Puritan residue in America still manifests itself in uneasiness about nudity and in periodic calls for censorship of art and entertainment. The frontier code of masculinity also survives, impugning the virility of male dancers and making it difficult to attract American boys to dance schools.

Popular dance, from jitterbug to disco and hip-hop, has a strong presence in the U.S. Tap, for example, which has massively revived, is respected by mainstream audiences for its dynamic, upbeat athleticism and its evocation of classic all-American movies. It's art dance that the general public has trouble with. Most people living outside the sophisticated metropolises or university centers will never see a professional production of live dance. Despite its tremendously loyal and knowledgeable core audience, serious dance simply doesn't exist for most Americans.

Unlike the visual arts, dance lacks the public relations vehicle of blockbuster museum shows to spread the word. We no longer have a Rudolf Nureyev or a Mikhail Baryshnikov in his prime, charismatic superstars whose offstage adventures were covered by glossy, general-interest magazines. Prime-time TV variety shows (such as *The Ed Sullivan Show* or *Omnibus*), which once showcased dance, are long gone. Public broadcasting features opera or popular shows like *Riverdance* but rarely airs productions of classical ballet or modern dance. Music videos have also waned since the 1980s, when Michael Jackson and the Graham-trained Madonna made news through dance.

As with many fields (including literary criticism), professionals may not realize the degree to which they are talking mainly to each other. Outreach is not just about fostering dance instruction but about spreading dance consciousness to the public at large. Dance education should be built into the educational curriculum, so that even those who will never set foot in a dance studio will have a basic knowledge of dance history.

What is desperately needed is a standardized middle-school or high-school-level elective that focuses on dance. Ideally multicultural in orientation, it would trace dance from its birth in religious ritual and folk dance to the evolution of classical ballet and modern dance styles. It would be useful to incorporate Asian martial arts into this survey to enlarge the common definition of dance.

The National Endowment for the Arts or a consortium of private foundations should commission the creation of a provisional dance history course, outlined in a handbook buttressed by video and Web resources. Sample syllabi could be adapted by school districts nationwide at minimal expense. But in the meantime, dance professionals themselves, perhaps through local lectures or newspaper articles, must seek ways to promote not just the technique but the vision of dance to their wider communities.

46

CONTROVERSY AT THE BROOKLYN MUSEUM

The frontier between politics and art was commandeered for the past two weeks by New York Mayor Rudy Giuliani in his attack on the "Sensation" show at the Brooklyn Museum of Art, a once dignified institution that has in my view disgraced itself by this detour into the tacky. Of the behavior of some museum curators and library directors, a Salon reader writes to ask "why liberals charged with the public trust go out of their way to incense the public."

The rote attacks on Giuliani have been deafening. While the mayor certainly exceeded his authority in demanding that the entire show be stopped (rather than simply denouncing individual works that did not merit public funding), I am frankly enjoying his assault on the arts establishment, which is in dire need of a shake-up. I have nothing but contempt for Brooklyn Museum director Arnold Lehman, who was hired two years ago and whose suitability for that position, on the basis of the present debacle, seems questionable.

"What a whiny slug!" I declared as Lehman nervously defended himself on TV. He struck me as an affected provincial oblivious to the fact that the zenith in campy collections of 1950s Tupperware and Formica kitchen tables was about, oh, fifteen years ago. The liberal casuists who sprang to unqualified defense of Lehman and his show (which includes not just Chris Ofili's dung-and-porn-adorned Madonna but a rotting cow's head and a formaldehyde-suspended bisected pig) seem

[Salon.com column, October 6, 1999.]

to have lost sight of the larger question: what should be the role and status of art in the United States?

Since the Puritan hegemony of three centuries ago, it has been a struggle for art to win acceptance here. Each of these incidents of religious desecration or of ostentatious decadent display (I speak as a sympathetic theorist of decadence in *Sexual Personae*) simply poisons the cultural atmosphere and ensures popular hostility to art and artists.

The price for this pointless provocation will be paid by schoolchildren whose arts programs are gutted for lack of funding. Sure enough, Republican presidential candidate Elizabeth Dole has just responded to the Brooklyn exhibit (which she calls "highly offensive") by calling for the complete abolition of the National Endowment for the Arts, which had nothing to do with this show.

As an arts educator, I think that the behavior of the Brooklyn Museum has been self-interested and shortsighted. I want to raise the prestige of art in this country; I want to expand opportunities for young artists and to radically increase funding for community arts projects. The entire future of American art is at stake.

How ironic that Jane Alexander rejoined her actor friends on the barricades last week to support the Brooklyn Museum, since in "American Canvas," her valedictory report as she left the NEA chairmanship two years ago, she sharply criticized the elitism separating American artists from the communities they should serve. The Brooklyn show is a perfect example of the improper diversion of public monies—in this case to aggrandize a single British collector, an obnoxious advertising executive of dubious taste.

At the end of the twentieth century, when popular culture has triumphed, the mission of museums must be to evangelize for art, to demonstrate art's higher meanings and continuing relevance to a mass audience that will otherwise be consumed in the blood-and-guts literalism of slasher films and shoot-'em-up action-adventures. The Brooklyn show illustrates the utter bankruptcy and sterility of the avant-garde, which collapsed thirty years ago and is now desperately grasping at straws to get a reaction, even of disgust, from an indifferent public.

Great works of art, like the monumental *Laocoön* (with its giant serpent strangling the agonized Trojan priest and his two sons), can be made out of Hellenistic sensationalism—coincidentally a focus of my advanced seminar in aesthetics this semester at the University of the Arts. But the most lurid works in the Brooklyn show are pure kitsch. If I want to see carcasses or body parts floating in formalde-hyde, I'll go to the Mütter Museum of the College of Physicians of Philadelphia—a spectacular and grisly nineteenth-century medical collection that I recommend to everyone.

Contemporary art, with its postmodernist gimmicks, is so divorced from science that Damien Hirst's high-school-project rot-and-fly cycle strikes some museum-goers as a profound revelation. (Wow, nature exists! Rise and shine, Manhattan!) We're back to Fellini's *La Dolce Vita*, which four decades ago showed the cul-de-sac of modern intel-lectualism in scenes where chic partygoers raptly listen to nature sounds on a tape recorder and where an erudite, angst-dazed father murders his children in their beds.

Let's get past this adolescent wallowing in slack "oppositional" art. The Romantic era of "subversive" gestures is over. As I have con-sistently maintained since my 1991 defense of photographer Robert Mapplethorpe in *Tikkun* (where I derided his sentimentalizing liberal supporters), no self-respecting avant-garde artist should be on the government dole. Free speech protections in the U.S. do not extend to financial support of "cutting-edge" new art by taxpayers. Commis-sioned projects—whether by the pharaohs, the Medici, the popes, or the French kings—always require the artist's subordination to the val-ues and publicity needs of the patron.

And I'm just as sick of Catholic-bashing as Giuliani himself. I may be an atheist, but I was raised in Italian Catholicism, and it remains my native culture. I oppose Mayor Giuliani's arbitrary and needlessly inflammatory use of city power to intimidate and harass an arts institu-tion, but I applaud the position he has taken against an arrogant, pre-tentious, parasitic arts establishment that has made a mockery of art and injured its reputation in the eyes of the nation at large. The Brook-lyn Museum has turned itself into Madame Tussaud's Waxworks—a collegiate carnival and tinny video game for desensitized poseurs who fiddle while Rome burns.

47

THE MAGIC OF IMAGES:
WORD AND PICTURE IN A MEDIA AGE

Education has failed to adjust to the massive transformation in Western culture since the rise of electronic media. The shift from the era of the printed book to that of television, with its immediacy and global reach, was prophesied by Marshall McLuhan in his revolutionary *Understanding Media,* which at its publication in 1964 spoke with visionary force to my generation of college students in the United States. But those of us who were in love with the dazzling, darting images of TV and movies, as well as with the surging rhythms of new rock music, had been given through public education a firm foundation in the word and the book. Decade by decade since the 1960s, popular culture, with its stunning commercial success, has gained strength until it now no longer is the brash alternative to organized religion or an effete literary establishment: it *is* the culture for American students, who outside urban centers have little exposure to the fine arts. I cannot speak for Canadian or European students, whom I have had little opportunity to observe closely over time. But because the U.S. is the driving media engine for the world, what happens there may well be a harbinger for the future of all industrialized nations.

Interest in and patience with long, complex books and poems have

[An expanded version of a lecture at a conference, "Living Literacies: What Does It Mean to Read and Write Now?," at York University, Toronto, November 15, 2002. Published in *Arion,* Winter 2004.]

alarmingly diminished not only among college students but college faculty in the U.S. It is difficult to imagine American students today, even at elite universities, gathering impromptu at midnight for a passionate discussion of big, challenging literary works like Dostoyevsky's *The Brothers Karamazov*—a scene I witnessed in a recreation room strewn with rock albums at my college dormitory in upstate New York in 1965. As a classroom teacher for over thirty years, I have become increasingly concerned about evidence of, if not cultural decline, then cultural dissipation since the 1960s, a decade that seemed to hold such heady promise of artistic and intellectual innovation. Young people today are flooded with disconnected images but lack a sympathetic instrument to analyze them as well as a historical frame of reference in which to situate them. I am reminded of an unnerving scene in Stanley Kubrick's epic film *2001: A Space Odyssey,* where an astronaut, his air hose cut by the master computer gone amok, spins helplessly off into space. The new generation, raised on TV and the personal computer but deprived of a solid primary education, has become unmoored from the mother ship of culture. Technology, like Kubrick's rogue computer, HAL, is the companionable servant turned ruthless master. The ironically self-referential or overtly politicized and jargon-ridden paradigms of higher education, far from helping the young to cope or develop, have worsened their vertigo and free fall. Today's students require not subversion of rationalist assumptions—the childhood legacy of intellectuals born in Europe between the two World Wars—but the most basic introduction to structure and chronology. Without that, they are riding the tail of a comet in a media starscape of explosive but evanescent images.

The extraordinary technological aptitude of the young comes partly from their now-instinctive ability to absorb information from the flickering TV screen, which evolved into the glassy monitor of the omnipresent personal computer. Television is reality for them: nothing exists unless it can be filmed or until it is rehashed onscreen by talking heads. The computer, with its multiplying forums for spontaneous free expression from e-mail to listservs and blogs, has increased facility and fluency of language but degraded sensitivity to the individual word and reduced respect for organized argument, the process

of deductive reasoning. The jump and jitter of U.S. commercial television have demonstrably reduced attention span in the young. The
Web too, with its addictive unfurling of hypertext, encourages restless
acceleration.

Knowing how to "read" images is a crucial skill in this media age,
but the style of cultural analysis currently prevalent in universities
is, in my view, counterproductive in its anti-media bias and intrusive
social agenda. It teaches students suspicion and paranoia and, with its
abstract European terminology, does not offer an authentic anthropology of the North American media environment in which they came to
consciousness. Post-structuralism and postmodernism do not understand magic or mystique, which are intrinsic to art and imagination.
It is no coincidence that since postmodernist terminology seeped into
the art world in the 1980s, the fine arts have receded as a major cultural
force. Creative energy is flowing instead into animation, video games,
and cyber-tech, where the young are pioneers. Character-driven feature films, on the other hand, have steadily fallen in quality since the
early 1990s, partly because of Hollywood's increasing use of computer
graphics imaging (CGI) and special effects, advanced technology that
threatens to displace the live performing arts.

Computer enhancement has spread to still photography in advertisements, fashion pictorials, and magazine covers, where the human
figure and face are subtly elongated or remodeled at will. Caricature
is our ruling mode. In the last decade in the U.S., there has also been
a relentless speeding up of editing techniques, using flashing, even
blinding, strobe-like effects that make it impossible for the eye to
linger over any image or even to fully absorb it. There has been a
reduction of spatial depth in image-making: one can no longer "read"
distance in digitally enhanced or holographic films, where detail has
a uniform, lapidary quality rather than the misty atmospherics of
receding planes, so familiar to us from post-Renaissance art based on
observation of nature. Movies have followed the TV model in neglecting background, the sophisticated craft of mise-en-scène. Distorting
lenses and camera angles producing warped, tunnel-like effects (as in
Mannerism or Expressionism) deny the premise of habitable human
space. Subtlety and variety in color tones have been lost: historical sto-

ries are routinely steeped in all-purpose sepia, while serious dramas and science-fiction films are often given a flat, muted, shadowless light, as if mankind has fled underground.

The visual environment for the young, in short, has become confused, fragmented, and unstable. Students now understand moving but not *still* images. The long, dreamy, contemplative takes of classic Hollywood studio movies or postwar European art films are long gone. Today's rapid-fire editing descends from Jean-Luc Godard, with his hand-held camera, and more directly from Godard's Anglo-American acolyte, Richard Lester, whose two Beatles movies have heavily influenced commercials, music videos, and independent films. Education must slow the images down, to provide a clear space for the eye. The relationship of eye movements to cognitive development has been studied since the 1890s, the groundwork for which was laid by investigation into physiological optics by Hermann von Helmholtz and Ernst Mach in the 1860s. Visual tracking and stability of gaze are major milestones in early infancy. The eyes are neurologically tied to the entire vestibular system: the conch-like inner ear facilitates hand-eye coordination and gives us direction and balance in the physical world. By processing depth cues, our eyes orient us in space and create and confirm our sense of individual agency. Those in whom eye movements and vestibular equilibrium are disrupted, I contend, cannot sense context and thus become passive to the world, which they do not see as an arena for action. Hence this perceptual problem may well have unwelcome political consequences.

Education must strengthen and discipline the process of visual attention. Today's young have a modest, flexible, chameleonlike ability to handle or deflect the overwhelming pressure of sensory stimuli, but perhaps at a cost to their sense of personal identity. They lack the foolish, belligerent confidence of my own generation, with its egomaniacal quest for the individual voice. In this age dominated by science and technology, the humanities curriculum should be a dynamic fusion of literature, art, and intellectual history. Because most of my career has been spent at arts colleges, I have been able to experiment with a wide range of images in the classroom. The slide lecture, with its integration of word and picture, is an ideal format for engaging students who are citizens of the media age. Discourse on art works should be open to all humanities faculty. No specialist "owns" the history of art, which ultimately belongs to the general audience.

My students at the University of the Arts—painters, sculptors, ceramicists, photographers, animators, Web and industrial designers, screenwriters, dancers, actors, musicians, composers, and so forth— come from an unusually wide range of backgrounds, from working farms to affluent suburbs or the inner city. I have gotten good pedagogical results over the past two decades with canonical works of art that can be approached from the point of view of iconography. This method of art-historical analysis, sometimes called iconology, was formalized in the 1920s and 1930s by Erwin Panofsky from earlier theorizing by Aby Warburg and was further developed by Rudolf Wittkower and Ernst Gombrich. Iconography requires the observational skills and fine attention to detail of literary New Criticism but sets the work into a larger social context, consistent with late-nineteenth- and early-twentieth-century German philology. To help focus scrutiny, one must find images in art that are more vivid than what the students see around them every day. The point is not just to show pictures but to seek a *commentary* that honors both aesthetics and history. This is an exercise in language: the teacher is an apostle of words, which help students find their bearings in dizzy media space.

Works that make the most immediate as well as the most lasting impact on undergraduates, I have found, usually have a magic, mythological, or intensely emotional aspect, along with a choreographic energy or clarity. Here is a quick overview of objects from the Western tradition that have proved consistently effective, as assessed by student performance on midterm and final exams. Among ancient artifacts, the bust of Queen Nefertiti, with its strange severity and elegance; the monumental Hellenistic sculpture group of the Trojan priest Laocoön and his two sons being strangled by serpents; and the Varvakeion Athena, our small Roman-era copy of the colossal, chryselephantine statue of the armed Athena from the Parthenon. The latter in particular, with its dense iconography of coiled serpent, winged Victory, triple-crested helmet, and aegis with gorgon's head medallion, seems to burn its way into student memory.

Images from the Middle Ages, aside from elegant French Madonnas and Notre Dame's gargoyles and flying buttresses, have proved less successful in my experience than the frankly carnal images of the Italian Renaissance. A dramatic contrast can be drawn between Donatello's sinuously homoerotic, bronze *David* and his late, carved-wood *Mary Magdalene,* with its painful gauntness and agonized posture of repentance. Two standards never lose their power in the classroom: Botticelli's *Birth of Venus,* where the nude goddess of love stands in the dreamy S-curve of a Gothic Madonna, and Leonardo's eerie *Mona Lisa,* with its ambiguous lady, barren landscape, and mismatched horizon lines. From Michelangelo's huge body of work, the deepest response, independent of the students' religious background, has been to his marble *Pietà*, where a ravishingly epicene dead Christ slips from the lap of a heavily shrouded, strikingly young Mary, and second to a surreally dual panel in the Sistine Chapel ceiling, *Temptation and Fall:* on one side of the robust tree wound by a fat, female-bodied serpent, sensual Eve reaches up for the forbidden fruit, while on the other, an avenging angel drives the anguished sinners out of paradise.

Because of its inherent theatricality, the Baroque works resoundingly well with undergraduates. Paramount exhibits are Bernini's designs for St. Peter's Basilica: the serpentine, 95-foot-high, bronze pillars of the *Baldacchino* (canopy) over the main altar; or the elevated chair of St. Peter—wood encased in bronze and framed by a spectacular *Glory,* a solar burst of gilded beams. Next is Bernini's Cornaro Chapel in Rome's Church of Santa Maria della Vittoria, with its opera-box stage setting, flamboyant columns of multicolored marble, and over the altar the wickedly witty marble-and-bronze sculpture group, *Ecstasy of St. Teresa,* where spiritual union and sexual orgasm occur simultaneously.

Nineteenth-century Romantic and realist painting offers a staggering range of image choices. Standouts in my classes have included the following: Géricault's *Raft of the Medusa,* a grisly intertwining of the living and the dead, bobbing on dark, swelling seas against a threatening sky. Delacroix's *Death of Sardanapalus,* inspired by a Byron poem, with its swirl of luxury and butchery around the impassive king of

Nineveh, who has torched his palace and capital. Turner's *The Burning of the Houses of Lords and Commons* (chronicling a disaster Turner witnessed in 1834), where nature conquers politics and the Thames itself seems aflame. (Of several views in this series, the version owned by the Cleveland Museum of Art is the best because most panoramic.) Manet's *A Bar at the Folies-Bergère,* a penetrating study of social class and exploitation amid the din and glitter of modern entertainment: we ourselves, thanks to a trick mirror, become the dissolute, predatory boulevardier being waited on by a wistful young woman lost in the harsh night world of the city.

Twentieth-century art is prolific in contrasting and competitive styles but less concerned with the completeness or autonomy of individual images. Two exceptions are Picasso's still intimidatingly avant-garde *Les Demoiselles d'Avignon,* with its brothel setting, contorted figures, and fractured space, and second, his monochrome mural, *Guernica,* the most powerful image of political protest since Goya, a devastating spectacle of fire, fear, and death. Also unfailingly useful are Hollywood glamour stills from the 1920s to the 1950s, which are drawn from a slide collection that I have helped build at the University of the Arts since 1990. I view these suave portrait photos, with their formal poses and mesmerizing luminosity, as true works of art in the main line of Western culture.

But an education in images should not simply be a standard art-survey course—though I would strongly defend the pedagogical value of survey courses, which are being unwisely marginalized or dismantled outright at many American colleges. Thanks to postmodernism, strict chronology and historical sweep and synthesis are no longer universally appreciated or considered fundamental to the graduate training of humanities professors. But chronology is crucial if we hope, as we must, to broaden the Western curriculum to world cultures. To maintain order, the choice of representative images will need to be stringently narrowed. I envision a syllabus based on *key images* that would give teachers great latitude to expand the verbal dimension of presentation, including an analysis of style as well as a narrative of personal response. I will give three examples of prototypical images for my proposed course plan. They would play on students' feeling for

mystery yet ground them in chronology and encourage them to evaluate historical evidence. The first example is from the Stone Age; the
second from the Byzantine era; the third from pre-Columbian Central
America.

*　*　*

Among and sometimes boldly *on* the prehistoric paintings of animals
found in the caves and rock shelters of southern France and northern
Spain are eerie stenciled hands captured in circles of color (Fig. 1).
Powdered minerals—white, black, brown, red, violet, or yellow—were
mixed with water and blown by the unknown artist through a reed
or hollow bone over his or her own hand. At the Castillo cave com-

(Fig. 1) Prehistoric stenciled handprint on the wall of the cave of Pech Merle at
Cabrerets (c. 25,000–16,000 B.C.), in the Midi-Pyrénées region of southern France

plex in Santander, Spain, is the so-called Frieze of Hands, a series of forty-four stenciled images—thirty-five left hands and nine right. In some cases, as at the Gargas cave in the French Pyrenees, mutilated hands appear with only the stumps of fingers. It is unclear whether the amputation was the result of frostbite or accident or had some ritual meaning of root, primal power.

These disembodied hands left on natural stone 25,000 years ago would make a tremendous impression on students who inhabit a clean, artificial media environment of hyperkinetic cyber images. The hand is the great symbol of man the tool-maker as well as man the writer. But in our super-mechanized era, many young people have lost a sense of the tangible and of the power of the hand. A flick of the finger changes TV channels, surfs the Web, or alters and deletes text files. Middle-class students raised in a high-tech, service-sector economy are several generations removed from the manual labor of factories or farms.

The saga of the discovery of the cave paintings can also show students how history is written and revised. The first cave found, at Altamira in northern Spain, was stumbled on by a hunter and his dog in 1868. The aristocratic estate owner, an amateur archaeologist, surveyed the cave but did not see the animals painted on the ceiling until, on a visit in 1879, his five-year-old daughter looked up and exclaimed at them. Controversy over dating of the paintings was prolonged: critics furiously rejected the hypothesis of their prehistoric origin and attributed them to forgers or Roman-era Celts. The discoveries of other cave paintings in Spain and the Dordogne from the 1890s on were also met with skepticism by the academic establishment. Funding for the early expeditions had to come from Prince Albert of Monaco. The most famous cave of them all, Lascaux, was found in 1940 by four adventurous schoolboys who tipped off their schoolmaster. Thus children, with their curiosity and freedom from preconception, have been instrumental in the revelation of man's primeval past.

Cave paintings re-create a subsistence world where human beings' very survival was at stake—a situation that can come again in war or after severe climatological change. Was the stenciled prehistoric hand a tribal badge or a symbol of possession and control over the painted animals?—whose real-life originals constituted a critical food supply in the Ice Age. Cave paintings usually follow strict realism: minutely varied species of horses, deer, bison, and mammoths, delicately painted with improvised brushes of grass or fur, can be identified. The fragility yet willed strength of human power symbolized by the stenciled hand is suggested by the sheer size of animals depicted. For example, seventeen images of the long-horned steppe bison (*Bison priscus*) appear in the cave at Lascaux: speedy climbers and leapers, they were 6'6" in height at their hump. If one were trapped or speared, it could provide up to 1,500 pounds of meat for an extended family. The fierce, prehistoric aurochs, whose descendants include the ox and the Spanish fighting bull, were of even greater size, sometimes weighing over 2,800 pounds. There are fifty-two aurochs depicted on the walls at Lascaux: one is eighteen feet long.

The prehistoric hand, whether personal signature or communal avowal of desire, is clearly a magic image with copious later parallels. It might be juxtaposed with other upraised hands, such as the gesture of peace and blessing made by Buddha and Jesus or the signal of formal address (*ad locutio,* representing the power of speech) of Roman orators and generals, as in the restored Prima Porta statue of Augustus Caesar or Constantine's fragmentary colossus in the Capitoline Museum. There is a constellation of associations with the "speaking" hand movements of South Asian dance, called *mudra* in India and even more intricately refined in classical Khmer dance (*aspara*) in Cambodia. Then there are the operatic gestures of fear and awe made by wind-blown saints in Baroque art as well as folk motifs of the magic hand, such as the archaic Mediterranean charm with two fingers extended, still worn by Italians to ward off the *malocchio* (evil eye).

*   *   *

My second exemplary image is the Byzantine icon, in an early medieval style that survives in Eastern rite or Greek and Russian Orthodox churches (Fig. 2). It was born in the great capital of Byzantium, renamed Constantinople (modern Istanbul). In late-medieval and early Renaissance Italy, this style was called *la maniera greca,* the Greek manner or style. Insofar as Byzantine religious art is commonly

(Fig. 2) Byzantine icon of *Christ Redeemer* (c. 1393–94) by the icon-painter
John Metropolitos, Gallery of Art, Skopje, Macedonia

reproduced on Christmas cards and museum-shop curios, the Byzantine style remains part of contemporary culture in Europe and North America. The classic icon is a rather stern, even glowering image of Jesus, Mary, or a saint set against a gold or blue background. It may be a mosaic panel bonded to a church wall or dome or a portable image painted in shiny egg tempera on wood. Icons were paraded in cities on feast days and carried into battle to protect the armies.

The figure in icons is always static and seen in strict frontality (in contrast to cave paintings, where animals are depicted only in profile). Space is compressed, and composition is shallow, with the figure pressed against the picture plane. Even when a floor is shown, figures seem to hover. The human dimension is inconsequential. The Byzantine emperor and his queen, clad in heavy brocade robes studded with jewels and pearls, may appear but primarily as a conduit to the divine. Usually floating somewhere in the image is a vertical or horizontal strip of Greek letters, a sacred name or fragment of Scripture. This elegant black calligraphy, outlined against gold, presents words as magic. It seems to show sound soaring through the air—a ritual incantation, an abstract idea being transformed into words. The Byzantine icon, therefore, is an ideal marriage of word and picture. Church and basilica, with their architecturally embedded images, were living books for the masses. The soaring Byzantine domes emblazoned with the enthroned Virgin or Christ Pantocrator ("Ruler of All") recall the painted ceiling of Lascaux's Great Hall of the Bulls, a rotunda that has been called "the Sistine Chapel of Prehistory."

The glittering Byzantine icon seizes student attention: its aggressive stare forces us to stare back. It also provides an excellent entrée to long, tangled lines of cultural history. Until the late nineteenth century, Byzantine art was dismissed as a degenerate or barbarous form of classical art. The ornate Byzantine style actually originates in the luxurious ostentation of the ancient pagan Near East—notably the great capitals of Alexandria and mercantile Antioch. The figures in Byzantine icons exist as head and hand: if the bodies seem stiffly imprisoned or encased in their robes, perhaps it's because their distant ancestors were Egyptian mummies. The watchful, wary eyes of Byzantine icons, which seem to drill through and see past the viewer, descend from mummy masks of Roman-era Egypt, such as those found in a Hawara cemetery in the Fayum oasis southwest of Cairo. These vividly painted encaustic (wax) portraits, set into linen body wrappings, show only the dead's bustlike head and shoulders. The individualism of Fayum faces descends from Roman culture, with its stress on realistic portraiture. Stone busts—originally clay death masks—of Roman ancestors were kept in the family atrium and carried in procession once a year. The Fayum figures' enlarged, almost bulging eyes and dilated pupils (sometimes described as "haunting" or "insomniac") reflect the mystical importance of the eye, identified with the god Horus, in Egyptian culture. The soulfulness of the Fayum portraits, whose originals were urban sophisticates in an anxious period of social change, survives in the ascetic faces of Byzantine saints: Osiris' promise of resurrection and eternal life has become Christ's.

The subject of Byzantine icons is inextricable from that of iconoclasm—the destruction of images because of their alleged solicitation to idolatry. Nothing could be more relevant to the dominance of images in our celebrity culture, which strives to turn us all into pagan idolators. Suspicion of or hostility to images persists in the American Puritan tradition, which surfaced at both extremes of the political spectrum in the 1980s: first, in the attempted legal suppression of sex magazines, including mainstream *Playboy* and *Penthouse,* by antipornography feminists Andrea Dworkin and Catharine MacKinnon; and second, in the attack by Christian conservatives on the National Endowment for the Arts for funding blasphemous, homoerotic, or sadomasochistic photographs by Andres Serrano and Robert Mapplethorpe. Literal iconoclasm was undertaken in Afghanistan in 2001 when the Taliban ordered the pulverizing by artillery fire of ancient colossi of Buddha, carved out of a cliff at Bamian.

Iconoclasm originates in the Old Testament's prohibition of making pictures—called "graven images" or "idols" in the Ten Commandments—of God, man, or animal. In Judeo-Christianity and its ancillary descendant, Islam (which forbids depiction of the figure in mosques), God is pure spirit and cannot be reduced to material form. During the bitter debate about this issue in early Christianity from the second century on, pagan image-making often won out, thanks to the momentum of Mediterranean cultural tradition. Protestant reformers such as Ulrich Zwingli and John Calvin were severe critics of the image-intoxicated style of late-medieval Roman Catholicism. There was smashing of church statues and stained-glass windows in the sixteenth and seventeenth centuries throughout Northern Europe, as there also was in England after Henry VIII's dissolution of the monasteries and during Cromwell's Puritan Revolution. The austere, white Protestant church in the seventeenth-century neoclassical style of Christopher Wren (the fount of American church design) is a temple to reason, with no images to distract the worshippers from Holy Scripture, the word of God.

Hence the battle in Western culture between word and picture can be traced over 2,500 years. The first outbreak of iconoclasm in the Byzantine Empire occurred in 726 A.D.: when Leo III, the emperor and pope, ordered that a beloved icon of Christ be removed from its place above the Chalke Gate, the main entrance to the imperial palace, there was a violent riot by women, whose leader was later martyred and canonized as St. Theodosia. An edict by Leo four years later reinforced his ban on the use of the figure in church art because images, in his view, were being blasphemously worshipped. Leo's son, the emperor Constantine V, convened a council in 754 that institutionalized iconoclasm; he attacked the monasteries and persecuted iconodules (venerators of icons). Many icons were destroyed outright: mosaic images were hacked from the walls and crosses put in their place. Women, particularly among the imperial family, were fervent iconodules. The banning of images in Byzantium lasted, with several breaks, for over a century until the restoration of the icons in 843, after the death of the last iconoclast emperor, Theophilos, the prior year.

Portable icons were carried along medieval trade routes into Russia. At the conquest of Constantinople by the Ottoman Turks in 1453, many of the city's precious objects were dispersed even further into Russia and Italy. There was long controversy among Russian theologians about whether the iconostasis (from *eikonostasion*, medieval Greek for "shrine"), a partition or picture screen separating the altar from the nave in an Orthodox church, detracted attention from the

Holy Eucharist as the center of the Christian service. The modern Orthodox iconostasis consists of fold-out screens with stacked registers (rows) of gilt wooden images of Christ, the Virgin, archangels, patriarchs, prophets, apostles, evangelists, and other saints, which the faithful read like posters. It resembles a modern newsstand, with its linear array of glossy magazine covers featuring celebrities and pop stars. A little area facing the front door in Russian Orthodox homes—*krasnyi ugolok,* the "red or beautiful corner"—was devoted to icon display. Bowing and crossing themselves, visitors saluted the icons even before greeting the host. Once again we detect female influence, since it was Russian women, who could not be ordained as priests, who created and tended the icon corners.

Byzantine icons hugely influenced European culture: their arrival in medieval Italy revived Italian art and, through their reinterpretation by Duccio di Buoninsegna and his student Simone Martini in Siena, began the evolution toward the Renaissance. I recommend three Byzantine icons in particular that might intrigue students: the tenth-century mosaic panel of St. John Chrysostom ("Golden Mouth") of Antioch in the north tympanum of Hagia Sophia in Istanbul; a twelfth-century tempera-on-wood icon of St. Gregory Thaumaturgus ("Wonder Worker") in the Hermitage Museum in St. Petersburg; and a thirteenth-century tempera-on-wood icon of St. Nicholas of Myra in Bari, where the saint's relics are preserved (this is the St. Nick later identified with Santa Claus). In each case, a fiery-eyed figure, ornately robed, is standing against a gold background inscribed with floating Greek letters. Each saint is holding a book, a Bible studded with jewels. He catches it in the crook of his arm and steadies it with a shrouded hand, as if it were too sacred or numinous to touch. A book, in other words, is represented as the burning source of spiritual power.

Finally, I would invoke one of my favorite works of art, Andy Warhol's *Marilyn Diptych* (Tate Gallery), which clearly demonstrates the childhood influence on Warhol of his family's Eastern rite church. It is a modern iconostasis: fifty images of Marilyn Monroe are lined up in registers on two large screens. On one, the orange-yellow riot of Marilyn's silk-screened images illustrates her cartoon-like stardom.

On the other, her photos have faded to smudged black and white, like newsprint washed by rain or tears. *Marilyn Diptych* suggests that in a media age, words melt away, and nothing is left but images.

*   *   *

My final exemplary image is that of the skull in pre-Columbian art (Fig. 3). This is another area of tremendous controversy: life-size crystal skulls continue to be touted on New Age Web sites as Aztec,

(Fig. 3) Turquoise- and shell-encrusted mask of Quetzalcoatl, the Aztec Feathered Serpent. The British Museum, London.

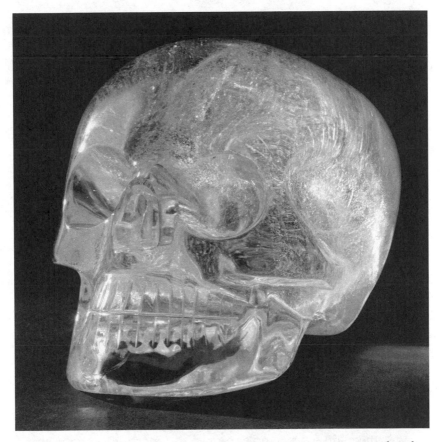

(Fig. 4) Rock crystal carving, claimed to be Aztec or Mixtec, Mexico (ca. 14th–15th centuries). Possibly European (late 19th century). The Museum of Mankind, London.

Mayan, or Incan artifacts that allegedly function as archaic magnets or radio receivers to capture cosmic energy and confer prophetic power (Fig. 4). These weird objects, I submit, would be highly useful for warning students of the still-unreliable state of Web resources. My commitment to the Web as a new frontier is unshaken. (I have been a columnist for Salon.com, with long breaks, from its inaugural issue in 1995.) Nevertheless, I still believe that only through prolonged, comparative study of books can one learn how to assess ambiguous or contradictory evidence and sort through the competing claims of putative authorities.

Though most major studies of Meso-American culture acknowledge the enormity of human sacrifice that occurred, particularly in the two centuries before the Spanish conquest, the issue has been de-emphasized over the past thirty years in the ideological campaign to convict Christopher Columbus of genocide. Otherwise well-produced picture books of Chichén Itzá, for example, the mammoth Mayan complex in the Yucatán, document the great step pyramid, the ball court, the domed observatory, and the temple of a thousand pillars crowned by a raffish Chac Mool statue holding a belly plate on which freshly extracted, still-quivering human hearts were laid. But it is difficult to find photographs, much less comprehensive ones, of Chichén Itzá's centrally situated Platform of the Skulls, where the severed heads of sacrificed prisoners, ritual victims, and even losing ballplayers were displayed on wooden racks to bake in the sun. Around that imposing stone platform, which I have personally inspected, runs a complex frieze of stone skulls still bearing remnants of bright red paint. The widespread view of the Maya as peaceable, compared to the bloodthirsty Aztecs, certainly needs adjustment.

Such platforms, called *tzompantli*, date from the prior Toltec era in Central Mexico and northern Yucatán. Among several eye-witness accounts by Spanish soldiers and priests in Cortés' expedition, one extravagantly estimated that 136,000 skulls were displayed on the *tzompantli* in the main Aztec temple complex of Tenochtitlán on the site of present-day Mexico City. A codex ink sketch by Friar Diego Duran shows tiers of skulls tightly strung like an abacus with rods piercing the cranium from ear to ear. In their orderly symmetries, these vanished skull racks resemble Byzantine icon screens as well as the tall magazine shelves of modern libraries. The grinning, pre-Columbian skull also appears in isolation on stone altars and on the heads, crowns, or trophy belts of ferocious earth goddesses like Coatlicue ("She of the Serpent Skirt"), who represents the cycle of fertility and death. Even more striking are unearthly masks worn by Aztec priests: an example in the British Museum, which may have belonged to king Montezuma himself, consists of the front half of a real human skull surfaced with mosaic and tied around the face; it was worn with an elaborate feather headdress. The finest of these mosaic masks are fac-

eted with brilliant turquoise jade, with detail work in red or white sea-
shells and obsidian, a black volcanic glass.

These authentic Aztec masks, which have circulated in Europe
since Cortés' first shipment of booty, undoubtedly inspired today's
notorious crystal skulls. At least fourteen crystal skulls, some transparent and others varying in hue from smoky brown to rose and ame-
thyst, are currently heralded by New Age spiritualists. Several were
once in major museum collections and loaned out for scholarly exhi-
bitions. In 1996, however, a BBC TV crew, in the course of making a
documentary, subjected a series of crystal skulls to scientific testing
and revealed that microscopic evidence of machine polishing showed
they were probably made in Germany some time since the nineteenth
century. Dismayed officials at the British Museum and Smithsonian
Institution immediately withdrew their crystal skulls from public display.

There is a Canadian connection here. The world's most celebrated crystal skull—the so-called Skull of Doom—is owned by Anna
Mitchell-Hedges, who lived as a child in Port Colborne, Ontario. Her
stepfather, a British-born adventurer, claimed she had discovered the
skull at a Mayan ruin in Belize on her seventeenth birthday in 1924.
From 1967 on, the skull, which weighs eleven and a half pounds, was
kept in a felt-lined case in her house in Kitchener, to which pilgrims
came from all over the world. A Toronto medium did work with the
Skull of Doom and reported on its prophecies in a 1985 book, *The
Skull Speaks*. The BBC producers traveled to Toronto to interview Mrs.
Mitchell-Hedges, but she did not allow the skull to be tested. Its present whereabouts are unknown.

Crystal skulls, fabricated or not, are splendid symbols of human
brainpower and vision. A skull, stripped of gender and identity, reduces the face to eyes and jaw—to seeing and speaking. Yet it has neither lips to shape syllables nor throat to generate breath. Images like
the Aztec skull can help students bridge the vast distance between the
archaeological past and futuristic cyberspace. But it is only language
that can make sense of the radical extremes in human history, from
the ecstatic spirituality of Byzantine icons to the gruesome barbarism

of Aztec ritual slaughter. It is language that *fleshes out* our skeletal outline of images and ideas. In a media age where books are no longer the primary medium for information storage and exchange, language must be reclaimed from the hucksters and the pedants and imaginatively reinforced. To save literature, educators must take command of the pre-rational world of images. The only antidote to the magic of images is the magic of words.

EDUCATION

48

FREE SPEECH AND THE MODERN CAMPUS

Our current controversies over free speech on campus actually represent the second set of battles in a culture war that erupted in the U.S. during the late 1980s and that subsided by the mid-1990s—its cessation probably due to the emergence of the World Wide Web as a vast, new forum for dissenting ideas. The openness of the Web scattered and partly dissipated the hostile energies that had been building and raging in the mainstream media about political correctness for nearly a decade. However, those problems have stubbornly returned, because they were never fully or honestly addressed by university administrations or faculty the first time around. Now a new generation of college students, born in the 1990s and never exposed to open public debate over free speech, has brought its own assumptions and expectations to the conflict.

As a veteran of more than four decades of college teaching, almost entirely at art schools, my primary disappointment is with American faculty, the overwhelming majority of whom failed from the start to acknowledge the seriousness of political correctness as an academic issue and who passively permitted a swollen campus bureaucracy, empowered by intrusive federal regulation, to usurp the faculty's historic responsibility and prerogative to shape the educational mission and to protect the free flow of ideas. The end result, I believe, is a violation of the free speech rights of students as well as faculty.

[Lecture at Free Speech Forum, Pennoni Honors College,
Drexel University, April 21, 2016.]

What is political correctness? As I see it, it is a predictable feature of the life cycle of modern revolutions, beginning with the French Revolution of 1789, which was inspired by the American Revolution of the prior decade but turned far more violent. A first generation of daring rebels overthrows a fossilized establishment and leaves the landscape littered with ruins. In the post-revolutionary era, the rebels begin to fight among themselves, which may lead to persecutions and assassinations. The victorious survivor then rules like the tyrants who were toppled in the first place. This is the phase of political correctness—when the vitality of the founding revolution is gone and when revolutionary principles have become merely slogans, verbal formulas enforced by apparatchiks, that is, party functionaries or administrators who kill great ideas by institutionalizing them.

What I have just sketched is the political psychobiography of the past 45 years of American university life. My premises, based on my own college experience at the dawn of the counterculture, are those of the radical Free Speech Movement that erupted at the University of California at Berkeley in the fall of 1964, my first semester at the State University of New York at Binghamton. The Berkeley protests were led by a New York–born Italian-American, Mario Savio, who had worked the prior summer in a voter-registration drive for disenfranchised African-Americans in Mississippi, where he and two colleagues were physically attacked for their activities. When Savio tried to raise money at Berkeley for a prominent unit of the civil rights movement, the Student Nonviolent Coordinating Committee, he was stopped by the university because of its official ban on political activity on campus.

The uprising at Berkeley climaxed in Savio's fiery speech from the steps of Sproul Hall, where he denounced the university administration. Of the 4,000 protestors in Sproul Plaza, 800 were arrested. That demonstration embodied the essence of 1960s activism: it challenged, rebuked, and curtailed authority in the pursuit of freedom and equality; it did not demand, as happens too often today, that authority be expanded to create special protections for groups reductively defined as weak or vulnerable or to create buffers to spare sensitive young feelings from offense. The progressive 1960s, predicated on assertive individualism and the liberation of natural energy from social controls, wanted less surveillance and paternalism, not more.

The entire political and cultural trajectory of the decades following World War Two in the U.S. was a movement away from the repressions of the Cold War stand-off with the Soviet Union, when the House Un-American Activities Committee of the U.S. House of Representatives searched for signs of Communist subversion in every area of American life. A conspicuous target was the Hollywood film industry, where many liberals had indeed been drawn to the Communist Party in the 1930s, before the atrocities of the Stalinist regime were known. To fend off further federal investigation, the major studios blacklisted many actors, screenwriters, and directors, some of whom, like a favorite director of mine, Joseph Losey, fled the country to find work in Europe. Pete Seeger, the leader of the politicized folk music movement whose roots were in the social activism of Appalachian coal-miners in the 1930s, was banned from performing on network TV in the U.S. in the 1950s and '60s.

There were sporadic landmark victories for free speech in the literary realm. In 1957, local police raided the City Lights Bookshop in San Francisco and arrested the manager and owner, Beat poet Lawrence Ferlinghetti, for selling an obscene book, Allen Ginsberg's epic protest poem, *Howl*. After a long, highly publicized trial, *Howl* was declared not obscene, and the charges were dropped. The Grove Press publishing house, owned by Barney Rosset, played a heroic role in the battle against censorship in the U.S. In 1953, Grove Press began publishing affordable, accessible paperbacks of the voluminous banned works of the Marquis de Sade, a major thinker about sex and society at the close of the Enlightenment. In 1959, the Grove Press edition of D. H. Lawrence's 1928 novel, *Lady Chatterly's Lover*, then banned in the U.S., was confiscated as obscene by the U.S. Postal Service. Rosset sued and won the case on federal appeal. In 1961, the publication by Grove Press of another banned book, Henry Miller's 1934 novel, *Tropic of Cancer*, led to 60 obscenity trials in the U.S. until in 1964 it was declared not obscene and its publication permitted.

One of the supreme symbols of newly militant free speech was Lenny Bruce, who with Mort Sahl transformed stand-up comedy from its innocuous vaudevillian roots into a medium of biting social and political commentary. Bruce's flaunting of profanity and scatology in his improvisational onstage act led to his arrest for obscenity in San Francisco in 1961, in Chicago in 1962, and in New York in 1964, where he and Howard Solomon, owner of the Café Au Go Go in Greenwich Village, were found guilty of obscenity and sentenced to jail. Two years later, while his conviction was still under appeal, Bruce died of a drug overdose at age 40.

This steady liberalizing trend was given huge impetus by the sexual revolution, which was launched in 1960 by the marketing of the first birth control pill. In Hollywood, the puritanical studio production code, which had been adopted in the early 1930s under pressure from conservative groups like the Legion of Decency and the United States Conference of Catholic Bishops, was gradually breaking down and was finally abandoned by the late 1960s. The new standard of sexual expression was defined by European art films, with their sophisticated scripts and frank nudity. Pop music pushed against community norms: in 1956, Elvis Presley's hip-swiveling gyrations were cut off by the TV camera as too sexual for *The Ed Sullivan Show*, which was then a national institution. As late as 1967, *The Ed Sullivan Show* was trying to censor the song lyrics of major bands like the Doors and the Rolling Stones, who were imitating the sexual explicitness of rural and urban African-American blues. (The Stones capitulated to Sullivan, but the Doors fought back—and were never invited on his show again.) Middle-class college students in the 1960s, including women, began freely using four-letter words that had rarely been heard in polite company, except briefly during the flapper fad of the 1920s. In the early 1970s, women for the first time boldly entered theaters showing pornography and helped make huge hits out of X-rated films like *Deep Throat, Behind the Green Door*, and *The Devil in Miss Jones*.

In short, free speech and free expression, no matter how offensive or shocking, were at the heart of the 1960s cultural revolution. Free speech was a primary weapon of the Left against the moralism and conformism of the Right. How then, we must ask, has campus leftism in the U.S. been so transformed that it now encourages, endorses, and celebrates the suppression of ideas, including those that question its own current agenda and orthodoxy?

My conclusions are based on my personal observation as a career academic. Despite the longstanding claim by conservatives that "tenured radicals" invaded the universities in the 1970s, I maintain that no authentic 1960s radicals, except for Todd Gitlin, the president of SDS (Students for a Democratic Society), entered the profession and attained success. If they entered graduate school, most of them dropped out. To enter grad school at all was in fact viewed as a sellout. For example, during my last semester in college in 1968, I was confronted near the fountain on the quad by the leader of the campus radicals, who denounced me for my plan to attend the Yale Graduate School. "Grad school isn't where it's happening!" he contemptuously informed me. "And if you go anywhere, you go to Buffalo!" As it happens, I had indeed applied to and been accepted at the State University of New York at Buffalo, where I would have happily worked with the psychoanalytic critic Norman Holland and the notorious leftist critic, Leslie Fiedler, whose controversial 1960 masterwork, *Love and Death in the American Novel,* had had a huge influence on me. Indeed, Fiedler had just become a folk hero of the counterculture the year before, when police raided his Buffalo house and arrested him for drug possession, a disastrous incident that he would chronicle in his 1969 book, *Being Busted.* At any rate, I had chosen Yale because of its great library, which I sorely needed for my research, but my fellow student's warning stung and shook me.

There can be no doubt that elite universities like the Ivy League at that period were in drastic need of reform. Their prevailing WASP (white Anglo-Saxon Protestant) style was not a hospitable climate for racial or ethnic minorities, including Jews and Italian-Americans. Medieval Anglo-Saxon was actually still a required first-year course for graduate students in English literature when I arrived at Yale in 1968. There had evidently just been a purge of gay male professors from the English department—it was rumored they had migrated up-country to all-female Smith College in Western Massachusetts. The English department had only one woman faculty member, a rather conservative medievalist. While women had been admitted to the graduate school for a century, undergraduate Yale College was still all-male and turned coeducational while I was there—which was a huge relief, because I was tired of being stared at like an exotic trespasser in the cavernous main reference room of Sterling Library. In my Anglo-Saxon class one day, the otherwise very affable young WASPy professor did a crass sexist stunt, also involving an ethnic slur against working-class Italian-Americans, that still shocks and disgusts me after all these years. We first-year students said nothing—there was no framework yet for critique or complaint.

To understand how political correctness was later able to sweep like a plague through U.S. humanities departments, it must be stressed that the prevalent approach to literature in Great Britain and the U.S. since the 1940s had been the New Criticism, which in its focus on textual explication minimized or totally excluded history and psychology. When Buffalo's Leslie Fiedler, who grounded literature in both history and psychology, including sex, gave a lecture at Yale while I was there, not one professor from the English department attended. Fiedler's insulting ostracism could not have been more obvious. Hard as it is to believe now, my doctoral dissertation, *Sexual Personae,* was the only dissertation on sex in the Yale Graduate School at the time. Asking questions about sex and gender was considered bad form. That, as well as my fervent interest in mass media and popular culture (which were regarded as frivolous), certainly complicated and nearly derailed my first search for a teaching job.

After the 1960s cultural revolution, it was clear that the humanities had become too insular and removed from social concerns and that they had to reincorporate a more historical perspective. There were many new subject areas of contemporary interest that needed to be added to the curriculum—sex and gender, film, African-American and Native American studies among them. But the entire humanities curriculum urgently demanded rethinking. The truly radical solution would have been to break down the departmental structure that artificially separated, for example, English departments from French departments and German departments. Bringing all literature together as one field would have created a much more open, flexible format to encourage interdisciplinary exploration, such as cross-fertilizations of literature with the visual arts and music. Furthermore, I wanted an authentic multiculturalism, a curriculum that affirmed the value and achievements of Western civilization but expanded globally to include other major civilizations, all of which would be studied in their chronological unfolding. Even though I am an atheist, I have always felt that comparative religion, a study of the great world religions over time, including all aspects of their art, architecture, rituals, and sacred texts, was the best way to teach authentic multiculturalism and achieve world understanding. Zen Buddhism was in the air in the 1960s as part of the legacy of the post-war Beat movement, and Hinduism entered the counterculture through the London scene, partly because of Ravi Shankar, a master of the sitar who performed at California's Monterey Pop Festival in 1967.

However, these boundary-dissolving expansions were unfortunately not the route taken by American academe in the 1970s. Instead, new highly politicized departments and programs were created virtually overnight—without the incremental construction of foundation and superstructure that had gone, for example, into the long development of the modern English department. The end result was a further balkanization in university structure, with each area governed as an autonomous fiefdom and with its ideological discourse frozen at the moment of that unit's creation. Administrators wanted these programs and fast—to demonstrate the institution's "relevance" and to head off outside criticism or protest that could hamper college applications and the influx of desirable tuition dollars. Basically, administrators threw money at these programs and let them find their own way. When Princeton University, perhaps the most cloistered and overtly sexist of the Ivy League schools, went coeducational after 200 years in 1969, it needed some women faculty to soften the look of the place. So it hastily shopped around for whatever women faculty could be rustled up, located them mostly in English departments at second-tier schools, brought them on board, and basically let them do whatever they wanted, with no particular design. (Hey, they're women—they can do women's studies!)

I maintain, from my dismayed observation at the time, that these new add-on programs were rarely if ever founded on authentic schol-arly principles; they were public relations gestures meant to stifle criticism of a bigoted past. In designing any women's studies pro-gram, for example, surely a basic requirement for students should be at least one course in basic biology, so that the role of hormones in human development could be investigated—and rejected, if neces-sary. But no, both women's studies and later gender studies evolved without reference to science and have thus ensured that their ideol-ogy remains partisan and one-dimensional, stressing the social con-struction of gender. Any other view is regarded as heresy and virtually never presented to students even as an alternative hypothesis.

Today's campus political correctness can ultimately be traced to the way those new programs, including African-American and Native American studies, were so hastily constructed in the 1970s, a process that not only compromised professional training in those fields over time but also isolated them in their own worlds and thus ultimately lessened their wider cultural impact. I believe that a better choice for academic reform would have been the decentralized British system traditionally followed at Oxford and Cambridge Universities, which offered large subject areas where a student could independently pur-sue his or her special interest. In any case, for every new department or program added to the U.S. curriculum, there should have been a central shared training track, introducing students to the methodol-ogy of research and historiography, based in logic and reasoning and the rigorous testing of conclusions based on evidence. Neglect of that crucial training has meant that too many college teachers, then and now, lack even the most superficial awareness of their own assump-tions and biases. Working on campus only with the like-minded, they treat dissent as a mortal offense that must be suppressed, because it threatens their entire career history and world-view. The ideology of those new programs and departments, predicated on victimology, has scarcely budged since the 1970s. This is a classic case of the deaden-ing institutionalization and fossilization of once genuinely revolution-ary ideas.

Let me give just one example of political correctness run amok in campus women's studies in the U.S. In 1991, a veteran instructor in

English and women's studies at the Schuylkill campus of Pennsylvania State University raised objections to the presence in her classroom of a print of Francisco Goya's famous late-eighteenth-century painting, *Naked Maja*. The traditional association of this work with the Duchess of Alba, played by Ava Gardner in a 1958 movie called *The Naked Maja*, has been questioned, but there is no doubt that the painting, now owned by the Prado in Madrid, is a landmark in the history of the nude in art and that it anticipated major nineteenth-century works like Manet's *Olympia*.

The instructor brought her case to a committee called the University Women's Commission, which supported her, and she was offered further assistance from a committee member, the campus Affirmative Action officer, who conveyed her belief that there were grounds for a complaint of sexual harassment, based on the "hostile workplace" clause in federal regulations. The university, responding to the complaint, offered to change the teacher's classroom, which she refused. She also refused an offer to move the painting to a less visible place in the classroom or to cover it while she was teaching. No, she was insistent that images of nude women must never be displayed in a classroom—which would of course gut quite a bit of major Western art since ancient Greece.

Finally, the *Naked Maja* was moved, along with four other classic art prints in the classroom, to the TV room of the student community center, where a sign was posted to alert unwary passerby that art was present—a kind of enter-at-your-own-risk warning. This action by the university seems to have been widely regarded as a prudent compromise instead of the shameful capitulation to political correctness that it was. There was a spate of amused publicity about the incident in the mainstream press, with criticism passingly voiced by prominent journalists like Nat Hentoff (a free speech warrior) and Robert Hughes, the longtime art critic of *Time* magazine. But the response from within the teaching profession was strikingly weak and limited. This was a moment for independent thinkers everywhere in American academe to condemn that puritanical exercise by a literature instructor who had made herself a dictator in the visual arts, a field about which she was conspicuously uninformed. All that she had was a rote ideology absorbed from anti-porn fanatics like the crusading feminist Andrea Dworkin, whose attempt to ban the sale of pornography (including mainstream men's magazines) in Minneapolis and Indianapolis had been struck down in federal district court in 1984 as an unconstitutional infringement of free speech rights. The instructor claimed that she was protecting future women students from the "chilly climate" created by the *Naked Maja*. But in a later published article about the controversy, she revealed that she herself was uncomfortable in the presence of the painting. She wrote, "I felt as though I were standing there naked, exposed and vulnerable." I'm sorry, but we simply cannot permit uncultivated neurotics to set the agenda for arts education in America.

Here we come to one of the most pernicious aspects of identity politics as it reshaped the American university—the confusion of teaching with social work. The issue of improper advocacy in the classroom has never been adequately addressed by the profession. Teaching and research must strive to remain objective and detached. The teacher as an individual citizen may and should have strong political convictions and activities outside the classroom, but in the classroom, he or she should never take ideological positions without at the same time frankly acknowledging them as opinion to the students and emphasizing that all students are completely free to hold and express their own opinions on any issue, no matter how contested, from abortion, homosexuality, and global warming to the existence of God or the veracity of Darwin's theory of evolution. Unfortunately, because of the failure of American colleges and universities to seek and support ideological diversity on their campuses, the humanities faculties have trended so far toward liberal Democrats (among whom I number myself) that they often seem naïvely unaware that any other beliefs are possible or credible.

The old-guard professors at the Yale Graduate School in the late 1960s may have been stuffy and genteel, but they were genuine scholars, passionately devoted to study and learning. They believed they had a moral obligation to seek the truth and to express it as accurately as they could. I remember it being said at the time that a scholar's career could be ruined by fudging a footnote. A tragic result of the era of identity politics in the humanities has been the collapse of rigorous scholarly standards, as well as an end to the high value once accorded to erudition, which no longer exists as a desirable or even possible attribute in job searches for new faculty.

Another problem in 1970s academe was a job recession in the humanities that arose just as deconstruction and post-structuralism arrived from Europe. The deconstructionist trend started when J. Hillis Miller moved from Johns Hopkins University to Yale and began bringing Jacques Derrida over from France for regular visits. The Derrida and Lacan fad was followed by the cult of Michel Foucault, who remains a deity in the humanities but whom I regard as a derivative game-player whose theories make no sense whatever about any period preceding the Enlightenment. The first time I witnessed a continental theorist discoursing with professors at a Yale event, I said in exasperation to a fellow student, "They're like high priests murmuring to each other." It is absurd that that elitist theoretical style, with its opaque and contorted jargon, was ever considered leftist, as it still is. Authentic leftism is populist, with a brutal directness of speech.

Post-structuralism, in asserting that language forms reality, is a reactionary reversal of the authentic revolutionary spirit of the 1960s, when the arts had turned toward a radical liberation of the body and a reengagement with the sensory realm. By treating language as the definitive force in the world—a foolish thesis that could easily be refuted by the dance, music, or visual arts majors in my classes—post-structuralism set the groundwork for the present campus impasse where offensive language is conflated with material injury and alleged to have a magical power to create reality. Furthermore, post-structuralism treats history as a false narrative and encourages a random, fragmented, impressionistic approach that has given students a fancy technique but little actual knowledge of history itself.

The woeful decline in quality of humanities scholarship was quite obvious during the five years of research I did for my art book, *Glittering Images*, which was released four years ago. I chose 29 images extending over 3,000 years since ancient Egypt and read through the major scholarly literature on each work of painting, sculpture, architecture, or film, beginning in the nineteenth century and continuing to the present. In the great period of German philology, writing about art had a tremendous range of both conception and detail. The impact of philology could be felt well into the twentieth century, as in the work of the great Marxist art historian, Arnold Hauser, whose magisterial *The Social History of Art,* published in 1951, had a huge impact on me in graduate school. Writing on art remained strong through the 1960s but began to weaken with the impact of postmodernism and post-structuralism in the 1970s and '80s. From the 1980s on, I was shocked by the drop-off. Yes, there was the occasional specialist whose work was rigorous and reliable, but there was none of the broad learning and expansive vision of early-twentieth-century art historians like Aby Warburg, Heinrich Wölfflin, and Erwin Panofsky. Even worse, humanities books of the past two decades are suffering from shrinking bibliographies, where young academics are revealing that they have systematically consulted few or no books published before the 1980s.

The problem of political correctness is intensified by the increasing fixation of humanities and even history departments on "presentism," that is, a preoccupation with our own modern period. Even the Renaissance is being redefined: it is now clumsily and in my view inaccurately called "Early Modern." Presentism is even afflicting major museums, when they repair and over-restore ancient objects so that they look brand-new. A year ago, for example, in conjunction with my current research project into Native American culture of the late Ice Age, I visited the National Museum of the American Indian, a beautiful modernistic building on the Mall in Washington, D.C. I had very high expectations—hence my surprise and horror at how vapid and unscholarly the exhibits were. The entire museum looks like a glorified gift shop, stocked with glossy fabrications, poster-board displays, light shows, and annoying recordings of vacuous happy talk. After a long search, I finally found something old and authentic—a small, sad picture-frame display of a handful of genuine arrowheads and unremarkable stone tools from the Washington area. I have found far better artifacts right here in the plowed fields of Southeastern Pennsylvania! The worst crime of political correctness is that it has allowed current ideologies to stunt our sense of the past and to reduce history to a litany of inflammatory grievances.

To break through the stalemate and reestablish free speech on campus, educators must first turn away from the sprawling cafeteria menu of over-specialized electives and return to broad survey courses based in world history and culture, proceeding chronologically from antiquity to modernism. Students desperately need a historical framework to understand both past and present.

Second, universities should sponsor regular public colloquia on major topics where both sides of sensitive, hot-button controversies are fully discussed. Any disruptions of free speech at such forums must be met with academic sanctions.

Third, it is my position, stemming from the 1960s sexual revolution that ended campus parietal rules, that colleges and universities must stay totally out of the private social lives of students. The intrusive paternalism of American colleges in this area is an unacceptable infringement of student rights. If a crime is committed on campus, it must be reported to the police. There is no such thing as a perfectly "safe space" in real life. Risk and danger are intrinsic to human existence.

As tuition costs rose stratospherically over the past quarter century, American colleges and universities shifted into a consumerist mode and have now become more like shopping malls than educational institutions—they don't want to upset the paying customers! But the entire college experience should be based on confronting new and disruptive ideas. Students must accept personal responsibility for their own choices and behavior, and university administrators must stop behaving like substitute parents and hovering therapists. The ultimate values at any university should be free thought and free speech.

49

ON CANONS

GUNTER AXT: Where do you place yourself in the tradition of thinkers who focus on the major canons of Western art?

CAMILLE PAGLIA: Canon-formation and canon-revision are the obligation of the true critic. Artistic tradition is like a magnificent flowering tree, whose vitality in its spreading branches must be traced to its roots. The postmodernist allegation that all canons are the product of political ideology is malicious propaganda. Membership in the canon is first determined by artists themselves. That is, we define the importance of an artist by his or her influence on *other* artists, either at that moment or (as with El Greco and Emily Dickinson) much later in time.

At the birth of second-wave feminism in the late 1960s, we were told that we would soon discover many "female Michelangelos"—the great women artists whose names had been erased from art history by sexist male scholars. A massive rewriting of the official canon was prophesied. Well, a half-century has gone by, and no woman artist even remotely near Michelangelo's titanic achievement has ever been found. Yes, we now know more about minor women artists, such as Artemisia Gentileschi or Mary Cassatt, but the old canon of art history remains essentially unchanged—because it was always based on artistic evolution, not politics. Women were indeed denied

[Interview with Gunter Axt, *CULT* magazine, São Paulo, Brazil, August 15, 2014.]

opportunities in workshop-centered crafts like sculpture, but in music composition, for example, middle-class women have had access to the piano at home for over two centuries. Yet there is still no female Mozart. As I argued in my first book, *Sexual Personae,* women have never invented a major new style in the arts because in order to create, you must first destroy—something most women are reluctant to do.

The centrality of canons can be seen in popular music. Seventeenth-century British ballads, preserved in America's Appalachian Mountains, were reinterpreted during the 1930s and '40s by the leftist folk singers Woody Guthrie and Pete Seeger. Guthrie's devoted disciple, Bob Dylan, then shaped the imagination of an entire generation and made an immense impact on other singers and bands worldwide. The canon in black music is equally obvious: West African motifs (with melismatic Muslim tonalities) survived under slavery in rural African-American blues and were transmitted through singers Robert Johnson and Howlin' Wolf to young musicians in the postwar British blues revival, such as the Yardbirds, the Rolling Stones, and Led Zeppelin. In Brazil, prolific canonical figures of genius status, such as Antonio Carlos Jobim and Dorival Caymmi, can be easily identified.

Critics should engage the public to dispute established canons and propose new ones. For example, I have waged war for decades against the widespread claim in the U.S. that Meryl Streep is the world's greatest actress. For me, Jane Fonda, with her emotional depth and lithe physical grace, is a far greater actress than Streep, whom I find mechanical, superficial, and pretentious. Indeed, in terms of cultural influence, there is no one more canonical than Marlene Dietrich, who created the sophisticated "hard glamour" seen everywhere in fashion magazines and who through her direct impact on Madonna has massively influenced women's assertive performance style and costume throughout the world.

50

THE RIGHT KIND OF MULTICULTURALISM

The field of archaeology is under a political cloud because of its allegedly racist and exploitative history. American Indians have protested the "desecration" of tribal burial grounds by archaeological digs. A longstanding argument rages about the legal ownership of antiquities acquired by museums through donation or purchase since the late eighteenth century.

The brief against archaeology for its physical predations has been extended to its interpretive system. Militant identity politics claims that no culture can be understood except by its natives, as if DNA gave insight. All scrutiny by outsiders is supposedly biased, self-interested, and reductive.

A related complaint comes from post-structuralism, specifically the work of Michel Foucault, whom Edward Said introduced to American literary criticism in his 1975 book, *Beginnings*. Said, a professor of literature at Columbia University and president of the Modern Language Association, adopted Foucault's view of oppressive power, operating in Western conceptual systems as a covert instrument of domination, in his 1978 book, *Orientalism*. Far less talented academics followed Said's lead in the dreary movement called New Historicism, which sees imperialism under every bush.

Erudite, cultivated, accomplished, and prolific, Said is a major scholar. Unfortunately, his sharp critiques of European interest in the

[*The Wall Street Journal,* September 30, 1999. Author's original title: "In Defense of Archaeology." Reprinted in *Archaeology Odyssey* magazine, May/June 2000.]

Near East focus on literature (which he sees as a mask for colonialism), to the exclusion of the visual arts and architecture. In his central books, Said gives dismayingly short shrift to the massive achievements of Egyptologists and Orientalists, fomenting a suspicion of and cynicism about archaeology that have spread through the humanities.

This is regrettable, since archaeology is a perfect model for multiculturalism in the classroom. During three decades as a college teacher, I have found that archaeology fascinates and unites students of different races, economic backgrounds, and academic preparation.

First, archaeology gives perspective, a vivid sense of the sweep of history—too often lacking in today's dumbed-down curriculum. Second, archaeology shows the fragility of culture. It illustrates how even the most powerful of nations succumbed to chaos and catastrophe or to the slow obliteration of nature and time.

The epidemic of violence in American high schools is, I suspect, partly a reaction to the banality of middle-class education, which is suffused with sentimental liberal humanitarianism. Anything not "nice" is edited out of history and culture—except, of course, when it can be blamed on white males. Archaeology, with its stunning panoramas of broken ruins, satisfies young people's lust for awe and destruction.

Third, archaeology introduces the young to the scientific method, presented in the guise of a mystery story. Greek philosophy and logic, revived at the Renaissance and refined in the seventeenth century, produced the archaeological technique of controlled excavation, measurement, documentation, identification, and categorization. Modern archaeology is one of the finest fruits of the Western Enlightenment.

Stratigraphy, the analysis of settlement layers or ash deposits, is a basic tool of archaeology, cutting through the past so it can be read like a book. Dumps, latrines, and cave floors are mined for microscopic study of seeds and pollen and for radiocarbon dating of wood, plant fibers, and textiles. Chewed bones and worn teeth reveal diet and diseases and help draw the map of migration patterns and trade routes. With saintly patience, archaeologists laboriously collect shattered potsherds and reassemble them like Cubist jigsaw puzzles.

Western technology has given archaeology a wealth of tools. Aerial survey reveals the faint traces of buildings, earthworks, and irrigation channels. Underwater archaeology, born after World War Two, recovers artifacts from lakes and seas via scuba diving, unmanned submersible vehicles, and side-scanning sonar.

Archaeology has restored human memory of vanished societies like that of Pakistan's prehistoric Indus River Valley civilization or that of the mighty Khmer Empire centered at Cambodia's Angkor Wat. We now know about the Olmec of Mexico, whose society began a thousand years before Christ, and the Maya of Central America, whose pyramids at Tikal were slowly buried in the tangled jungle.

In the 1880s, thanks to European archaeologists, Akhetaton, the utopian city on the Nile built by Akhenaten and Nefertiti and destroyed by their political rivals, was rediscovered at Tel el Amarna. In the 1890s, Sir Arthur Evans' excavations at the labyrinthine palace at Knossos revealed the greatness of Minoan Crete.

In the 1920s, C. Leonard Woolley excavated the forgotten Mesopotamian city of Ur, whose ornate treasures grace the University Museum in Philadelphia. In 1975, tens of thousands of cuneiform tablets found in Syria helped resurrect Ebla, a commercial capital of the third millennium B.C., and also deepened our understanding of biblical texts. Archaeologists are still at work on the tantalizing conundrum of the Etruscans, who heavily influenced Rome.

The British Museum is currently celebrating the bicentenary of the discovery of the Rosetta Stone, a second-century B.C. basalt slab whose tripartite inscription was the key to deciphering Egyptian hieroglyphics. The Rosetta Stone, found during Napoleon's invasion of Egypt when it was still an Ottoman province, is a symbol of Western intellectual virtuosity and achievement.

The modern disciplines of knowledge, far from being covert forms of social control as the leftist post-structuralists tediously claim, have rescued ancient objects and monuments from neglect and abuse and have enormously expanded the record of our species. Degree-granting programs in archaeology are few and beleaguered in the U.S. Funding for archaeology, at school and in the field, is as crucial as for space exploration. Archaeology is our voyage to the past, where we discover who we were and therefore who we are.

51

CANT AND FAD IN CLASSICS

VICTOR DAVIS HANSON AND JOHN HEATH,

WHO KILLED HOMER? THE DEMISE OF CLASSICAL EDUCATION

AND THE RECOVERY OF GREEK WISDOM

Bullets are still flying in the culture wars of the last decade, but the front has changed. As costs rise and as competition for students intensifies, administrators are taking increased control of curricular matters from the often bitterly factionalized faculties. By terminating or transferring vacated faculty positions and by relying on poorly paid part-time instructors, many institutions are being reshaped by purely economic criteria. Among humanities programs, classics departments have been the most vulnerable to drastic downsizing and outright annihilation.

Victor Davis Hanson is professor of Greek at California State University in Fresno, and John Heath is chairman of the classics department at Santa Clara University. In *Who Killed Homer?*—a murder-mystery title wittily echoing that of Christina Hoff Sommers' groundbreaking 1994 book, *Who Stole Feminism?*—Hanson and Heath demonstrate in riveting detail the actual scale of the threat to Greco-Roman studies in the United States.

["Ancients and Moderns," front-page lead review,
The Washington Post Book World, March 29, 1998.]

Who Killed Homer? is a blistering indictment not just of administrators, who must meet the bottom line, but of classicists themselves, who ignored the developing crisis over the past thirty years. Instead of reaching out to the general public to defend the classics, many professors withdrew into insular academic conferences and narrow, "obscurantist" scholarship saturated with French post-structuralism and postmodernism. Surveying recent academic critiques (my own exposés are briefly cited), Hanson and Heath suggest that the media's false portrayal of the culture wars as a quarrel between tolerant liberals and reactionary conservatives has helped the most ruthless campus careerists, who gained major professorships with huge salaries and reduced teaching loads by espousing a fashionable leftism.

Hanson and Heath eloquently assail the systematic denigration of Western culture in prevailing campus "trend, cant, and fad": "Why do few professors of Greek and Latin teach us that our present Western notions of constitutional government, free speech, individual rights, civilian control over the military, separation between religious and political authority, middle-class egalitarianism, private property, and free scientific inquiry are both vital to our present existence and derive from the ancient Greeks?"

Sternly rebutting the misleadingly rosy picture of classics studies given by such partisan figures as Garry Wills, Hanson and Heath show that, from 1962 to 1976, the number of high-school students studying Latin "plunged 80 percent" and has never recovered. Decline is also clear at the college level: "Of over one million B.A.'s awarded in 1994, only six hundred were granted in Classics." Yet classics professors themselves merrily spin on: since 1962, "twice as many scholars now publish 50 percent more material in twice as many journals."

"Our own Founding Fathers," Hanson and Heath point out, "helped establish an American cult of antiquity. . . . To walk through Washington, D.C., is to experience Graeco-Roman institutions, architecture, sculpture, and city-planning at first hand." They argue that enthusiasts and amateurs, not professional classicists, made the great breakthroughs in our understanding of the ancient world, from Heinrich Schliemann, the discoverer of Troy, to Milman Parry, who established the Homeric oral tradition, and Michael Ventris, who cracked the code of Linear B, the Minoan script.

A long chapter called "Thinking Like a Greek" intricately presents the "Greek paradigm," with its principles of democracy, rational thought, and the "free exchange of ideas." The material on Greek warfare is particularly fine: military history is shamefully neglected in contemporary education, to our future national peril. Another chapter, "Who Killed Homer—and Why?," asserts that the university has been hijacked by "therapeutics"—"diversity training, journal writing, gender and racial sensitivity, multiculturalism, situational ethics."

Hanson and Heath believe that interdisciplinary experiments, such as "Mediterranean Cultures" programs, have compromised scholarly standards for both professors and students, from whom deep, rigorous learning is no longer expected. In concealing the autocracy and brutality of non-Western societies, academic multiculturalism is "intellectually naive" and "hypocritical to the core." Many feminists' anti-male rhetoric has marred legitimate inquiry into the status of women in antiquity, and some gay-studies scholars have used their field for "self-projection of their gender preferences."

A sequence of appalling passages from recent classics books proves Hanson and Heath's thesis that current scholarship is shot through with "bad prose," "elitist vocabulary," and "vacuous jargon," which manage "to make Homer silly and absolutely dull." Documenting "the strange cycle of self-promotion," where "everything now is to be deconstructed except resumés," the book boldly names names—as, for example, that of Martha Nussbaum, a prominent University of Chicago professor whose career gets a long-overdue public scrutiny here that raises serious questions about high-echelon academe.

The remedies offered by Hanson and Heath are based on "classics as a core curriculum." They laud the intellectual challenge of the study of ancient Greek, where the verb has over 350 forms. They provide a thematic teaching guide to Homer and a reading list of recommended scholarly works of unimpeachable quality.

The authors' proposals for academic reform are intended to re-awaken a sense of professional ethics and to reorient universities toward undergraduate teaching. These include ending the exploitation of graduate students as "helot" teaching assistants; abolishing doctoral dissertations; dismantling tenure in favor of five-year contracts; and cutting off subsidies for pointless travel to conferences—which are underwritten by the tuition bills of unwitting parents and taxpayers.

Hanson and Heath are perhaps too focused on American abuses; some broader consideration of still-vital classical studies in Europe and Great Britain would have been useful. The authors' portrait of popular culture is excessively bleak, and I was distressed by their skepticism about psychoanalytic criticism and even undergraduate study of Egyptian art. However, *Who Killed Homer?* is the most substantive by far of the academic critiques that have appeared in the past fifteen years. This passionate protest, with its wealth of facts and its flights of savage indignation, is a must-read for anyone interested in the future of higher education in the United States.

52

INTOLERANCE AND DIVERSITY IN THREE CITIES: ANCIENT BABYLON, RENAISSANCE VENICE, AND NINETEENTH-CENTURY PHILADELPHIA

Tolerance and diversity emerged as ideal principles of campus discourse and governance forty years ago at the rise of identity politics, which empowered formerly marginalized groups such as women, gays, African-Americans, Latinos, Native Americans, and Asians. Once used relatively neutrally by historians and sociologists, these two terms now carry a distinct value judgment and even a punitive moralism. Insofar as both tolerance and diversity are usually the products of slow social forces in the wider culture, it is debatable to what degree they can be imposed from above by campus administrations or inculcated by professors. As a libertarian, I remain very concerned about the speech codes which, whether codified or ad hoc, have become a tool of enforcement of tolerance in American academe and which from my point of view threaten constitutionally guaranteed free expression.

An uneasy tension persists between identity politics and tolerance: that is, the more forcefully group identity is affirmed, the more likely that rivalry or conflict with other groups will be perpetuated. Condi-

[Lecture in series on "Justice, Tolerance and Diversity," Ethics/Religion and Society Program at Xavier University, Cincinnati, Ohio, April 5, 2013. Published in *Justice Through Diversity?*, ed. Michael J. Sweeney (2016).]

tions of true tolerance eventually lead to assimilation, through which a tremendous amount of cultural heritage may be lost, as is happening to my own generation of Italian-Americans and perhaps also to secular American Jews. What I want to show in this lecture about three cities separated by hundreds of years is how intolerance, with all its persecutions and rampant injustice, has sometimes led to the consolidation of group identity through fierce external pressures. In my three choices—ancient Babylon, Renaissance Venice, and nineteenth-century Philadelphia—geographical and economic factors played a crucial role in the achievement or suppression of diversity. In contrast to the Marxist assumptions of the 1930s-based Frankfurt School which currently pervade the humanities, I would submit that commerce has often played a *liberalizing* role, breaking up the static traditionalism of agrarian societies and reducing provincialism and xenophobia through the introduction of new ideas. Furthermore, religion, which is often treated with indifference or hostility on today's elite campuses, has been a defining force in ethnic history. (I am speaking here as an atheist.) At the end of this lecture, I will offer some personal reflections about tolerance and diversity in contemporary academe.

My first example is Babylon in ancient Mesopotamia, whose territory was roughly congruent with modern-day Iraq. Although it was a center of immense learning, especially in mathematics, astronomy, and medicine, Babylon as a symbol of sin and decadence has become imprinted on Western culture via the Bible, which records the highly intolerant eye-witness accounts of Hebrews deported to that city after the conquest of the kingdom of Judah and the destruction of Jerusalem in the sixth century B.C. The handicraft skills of thousands of Hebrews were needed and exploited by King Nebuchadnezzar in his systematic reconstruction of Babylon. The Babylonian Captivity of the Hebrews would last fifty-nine years (not seventy years as prophesied by the Book of Jeremiah), until they were freed after the invasion of Babylon by Persia. What the Book of Genesis attacks as the Tower of Babel was the sacred ziggurat of the god Marduk-Bel, a triumph of ancient engineering that soared over 270 feet high and was sheathed in shiny copper. Babylon is excoriated even in the last book of the New Testament, the Book of Revelation, where imperial Rome is portrayed as the bejeweled Whore of Babylon, the "Mother of Harlots" arrayed in purple and scarlet as she rides a seven-headed beast and holds a golden cup brimming with "the filthiness of her fornication."

It is hard to believe that the nondescript piles of melted mud brick spread across a desert fifty miles south of contemporary Baghdad were once a spectacular, palm-ringed metropolis whose hanging gardens were a wonder of the ancient world. Elite Babylonians were highly sophisticated in dress and manner: both sexes evidently wore cosmetics such as kohl eyeliner and anointed themselves with heavily perfumed oils. While it is probably not true, as the Greek historian Herodotus reported, that every Babylonian woman had to prostitute herself once in her lifetime in the Temple of Ishtar, it does seem as if prostitutes operated openly in the Temple grounds. Furthermore, the festivals of the war goddess Ishtar may have involved ritual public sex acts of some kind, perhaps even involving transsexuals. There can be no doubt that Judeo-Christian values, with their strict regulation of sexuality and hatred of idolatry, were partly formed in opposition to Babylonian paganism, which was organized around elaborate rituals for the dressing, feeding, and daily transfer of massive golden idols, in which the gods were thought literally to reside.

The culture shock of the Hebrews in big-city Babylon was partly due to their own pastoralist roots: they had been shepherds, herdsmen like the Arab Bedouin, who dressed modestly and followed a conservative code of stoicism, frugality, and sexual discipline. What the exiled Hebrews recorded as a babel of voices inflicted as a punishment by God was actually the immense ethnic diversity of Babylon, which was a fabulously wealthy trading center perfectly situated between the Mediterranean and the Persian Gulf. A huge variety of people and languages were always represented in the mixed population of Babylon, with its masses of immigrants, fugitives, deported laborers, and itinerant merchants.

Babylon's diversity began with its physical location in the 500-mile-long alluvial plain of the flood-prone Tigris and Euphrates rivers, which stream down from the snowy mountain ranges of Armenia. Babylonia was mythically fertile, a true Garden of Eden, but its sedimentary landscape lacked stone, timber, and metals. (Indeed it was precisely its lack of stone that would reduce Babylon to ruins by the time of imperial Rome. Babylon's clay bricks did not have the sturdiness of Egypt's abundant stone.) Babylon's tolerant outward orientation toward other peoples began in its economic need to exchange its surplus of crops for other basic resources. In other words, commerce was the basis of that industrious but open and pleasure-loving civilization. Furthermore, merchants, with their adventurous mobility, shrewd alertness, and pragmatic flexibility, provided a liberating counterpoint to the ponderous fixities of the bureaucrats and pedagogues whose obsessive list-making constitutes the bulk of the cuneiform tablets yet discovered in Mesopotamia. A massive system of canals, created and maintained by a sometimes dictatorial hierarchical government, provided reliable irrigation and efficient transport of goods. Babylon collapsed when its government weakened and could no longer effectively maintain the canals as they silted up. Furthermore, the soil became irretrievably salinized due to poor drainage on the flat plain, leading to abandonment of the land.

The Hebrews' experience in Babylon helped to consolidate their sense of cultural identity as well as their theology. In the Babylonian destruction of the Temple in Jerusalem, the Hebrews lost their hallowed place of worship but as a consequence developed in their exile a more refined concept of divinity that would eventually be absorbed by Christianity. Yahweh, a symbol of Hebrew nationalism, ceased to be the resident or patron of a building but became a spirit suffusing the universe, a living flame carried in all hearts.

As a coda to the story of Babylon, I would cite the 1916 silent film *Intolerance,* a three-and-a-half-hour epic conceived and directed by the controversial D. W. Griffith. With its giant set of the walls of Babylon, it was the most ambitious and expensive film yet made, featuring thousands of costumed extras. However, the film was a commercial failure, partly due to Griffith's stipulation that showings be accompanied by a symphony orchestra. *Intolerance* was Griffith's attempt at self-justification after the bitter national backlash over his prior film, *The Birth of a Nation* (1915), which remains infamous for its racist caricatures of African-Americans as well as its glorification of the Ku Klux Klan. *Intolerance* daringly or dizzyingly crosscuts among four story lines, each dealing with some aspect of historical bigotry, including the St. Bartholomew's Day massacre of 1572, when thousands of Protestant Huguenots were slaughtered by Roman Catholics in France. Griffith's ancient story focuses on the fall of Babylon to the Persians. Prince Belshazzar (whose ominous vision of a hand writing on the wall was interpreted by Daniel in the Bible) is presented as a devotee of Ishtar and a defender of religious tolerance, but he is fatally conspired against by the intolerant high priest of Bel, whose betrayal of Babylon leads to its destruction in flames.

My second example is Renaissance Venice, which because of its position at the north end of the Adriatic Sea had been a major trading center since the Middle Ages. Built for defensive purposes on a chain of marshy islands, Venice was physically separated from the mainland and was psychologically oriented less toward Italy than toward Constantinople, the great gateway between East and West. Venice consequently became one of the most culturally diverse cities in world history. Its central church, St. Mark's Basilica, is Byzantine in style, as was Venetian taste in general, with its luxurious ornateness. The Venetian instinct for pleasure, as embodied in its sensual art, would become increasingly sybaritic over time, especially as compared to the austere sensibility of the more intellectual Florentine Renaissance.

The constant presence of foreign (and often Levantine) merchants in Venice gave it a cosmopolitan character. At times, the Venetians tried to safeguard their ethnic identity by limiting itinerant merchants' stay to a fixed period of months or years and by banning them from bringing their families to the city, but such rules were often flouted. Ethnic tensions became blatant in Venice's official establishment of the Ghetto, in which Jews were compelled to reside after 1516. Jews had created and controlled the money-lending industry in the region of Venetia since the twelfth century. It was the religious tolerance of Venice that drew them and that eventually produced the largest population of Jews in Europe. Jews were usually permitted to practice their religion in Venice without state interference. In contrast, England had expelled the Jews in 1290; France had expelled them in 1306; Spain did the same in 1492, followed by Portugal in 1497. Lingering anti-Semitism in England was illustrated by Shakespeare's play, *The Mer-*

chant of Venice, where the fictitious Shylock makes cruel and arbitrary loan demands that would never have actually been permitted under Venetian law.

The word *ghetto,* which was revived in the twentieth century for the Nazi sequestration of Jews in Warsaw and for the urban blight of African-American neighborhoods, was derived from *geto,* the Italian word for "foundry": an abandoned fourteenth-century cannon factory had once occupied the Venetian island to which Jewish merchants and bankers were restricted. The high walls of the Ghetto were designed as much for the protection of the Jews as for their confinement. Resident Jews were responsible for paying four Christian sentries to keep watch at night, when the two gates were shut. No Jews except for doctors were allowed on the streets of Venice until the morning bell rang at St. Mark's. While Jews were originally required to wear a yellow badge in Venice, that was modified to yellow and then red head gear for most of the Renaissance. Jews were not permitted to own property, and they could not become Venetian citizens until the early nineteenth century. Overcrowding in the two districts of the Ghetto caused higher and higher buildings to be built (resembling modern apartment buildings), leading to occasional collapses on the spongy soil.

The Ghetto population itself was highly diverse, with a multiplicity of ethnicities and languages—Hebrew, Spanish, French, German, Polish, Greek, Turkish, and Judeo-Arabic, as well as many Italian dialects. There were eight splendidly designed and furnished synagogues in that limited space, each devoted to a single ethnicity; five have survived, restored but intact. The wealth of the Venetian Jews, as signaled by the lavish jewelry worn by strikingly beautiful women attending synagogue, was reported by a British traveler, Thomas Coryat, in a 1611 memoir published in London. That their own diversity presented a challenge to Venetian Jews was demonstrated by the energy and attention they continually devoted to adjusting the ethnic representation of the internal governing committees of the Ghetto.

Venetian power and glory would fade after the Portuguese discovery of the Cape of Good Hope in South Africa, which allowed merchant ships from Northern Europe to travel directly to Asia without passing through the Mediterranean and transferring cargo to slow overland caravans. Now supplanted by Lisbon as a rich commercial capital, Venice began its decline, which would turn into the eighteenth-century decadent hedonism of Casanova and then the city's humiliating dependence on tourism, captured in Thomas Mann's portrayal of the rotting, plague-filled resort during the Belle Époque in *Death in Venice*.

My third example is nineteenth-century Philadelphia. The "city of brotherly love" began as a Quaker refuge founded in 1682 by William Penn, who was escaping persecution of the Quakers in Britain. The city was laid out in mathematical squares between two great rivers, with north-south streets assigned numbers and east-west streets given tree names, reflecting the Quaker interest in botany as a symbol of harmonious nature. The Quaker ideal of tolerance drew immigrants to Philadelphia throughout the eighteenth century, but Quakers lost power within the city when their code of anti-militarism led them to abstain from any involvement with the American Revolution, so much of which occurred around Philadelphia. It was the Quaker commitment to social justice that led to Philadelphia becoming a center for abolitionism, which had begun among English Quakers. America's first anti-slavery society was formed in Philadelphia in 1833. The Quakers themselves were not immune to dissension: a major schism between Orthodox and Hicksite Quakers in the Northeastern United States led to the "Great Separation" of 1827 that was not healed until 1955.

Women had always been active and prominent in the Religious Society of Friends. Indeed, it was in Quaker meeting houses, with their absence of a hierarchical clergy, that women were first permitted and encouraged to gain experience in public speaking, which was considered improper and unfeminine for respectable ladies well into World War One. A New England–born Quaker resident of Philadelphia, Lucretia Coffin Mott, founded an anti-slavery society for women but was denied delegate status because of her gender at the World's Anti-Slavery Convention held in London in 1840. Mott's indignation led her to collaborate with Susan B. Anthony and Elizabeth Cady Stanton to organize a convention on women's rights, held at Seneca Falls, New York, in 1848, that produced the woman suffrage movement and marked the birth of modern feminism.

But there were contrary forces at work in nineteenth-century Philadelphia. In 1838, three days after the opening of Pennsylvania Hall, erected by the Pennsylvania Anti-Slavery Society as a headquarters for abolitionism, a mob attacked the building and burned it to the ground. A black church (Bethel AME) and the Quaker Shelter for Colored Orphans were burned the same night. There had already been race riots in the city several years earlier between Irish immigrants and African-Americans competing for the same jobs in manual labor. Hostility to working-class immigrants was building in the U.S. The Native American Party was founded in 1837 in Germantown, a historic seventeenth-century village outside Philadelphia that is now part of the city. The Nativist campaign against immigration would take rabidly anti-Catholic form. Samuel F. B. Morse, the Massachusetts-born inventor of the telegraph, ran unsuccessfully for mayor of New York on the Nativist ticket and published an incendiary 1835 tract (*Imminent Dangers to the Free Institutions of the United States Through Foreign Immigration*) denouncing the Jesuits as "a *secret* society" bent on subduing American democracy to the monarchical tyranny of "Popery," with newly formed Catholic schools as their diabolical wedge. Condemning Roman Catholicism as "intolerant and illiberal," Morse called for stringent naturalization reform to stop the incursion of "the priest-ridden slaves of Ireland and Germany."

Back in Philadelphia, there was a tremendous surge of hostility to Irish Catholics, who began arriving in the city even before the Great Potato Famine of 1845–49. Some of the animus came from Scots-Irish Protestants (mainly Presbyterians) from Northern Ireland. For much of the nineteenth century in Boston and New York as well as Philadelphia, the Irish were stereotyped and vilified as violent, dirty, coarse, clannish drunks. In 1842, the militant American Protestant Association was formed in Philadelphia. Two years later, there were anti-Catholic riots in the city that resulted in twenty deaths, one hundred injuries, and the burning to the ground of St. Michael's Church, St. Augustine's Church, and the Seminary of the Sisters of Charity. Mobs invaded Irish neighborhoods and burned a dozen homes. The militia was called out to restore order, and martial law was declared for a week. These civil disturbances would lead to the creation of a professionalized police force and to the 1854 consolidation of the city, which officially incorporated all districts, boroughs, and outlying towns in Philadelphia County.

Anti-Irish sentiment would linger into the early twentieth century, when the wealthy John B. Kelly, the self-made son of an immigrant from County Mayo, was snubbed by the Philadelphia social elite because he had begun his meteoric business career as an apprentice bricklayer. Although he had won six U.S. National Championships in rowing, the super-athletic Kelly was rejected from competing in the Diamond Sculls on the Thames at the Henley Royal Regatta in England because it was a written rule that no one could compete in the regatta "who is or has been by trade or employment for wages a mechanic, artisan, or labourer." In other words, Kelly was not a gentleman. But he became a hero to the Irish everywhere when, later that same year, he won a gold medal by beating the British sculling champion in the 1920 Summer Olympics in Antwerp, Belgium. A bronze statue of Kelly at his oars stands today in Philadelphia on the banks of the Schuylkill River where he trained. His daughter, Grace Kelly, who was excluded from the city's debutante balls because she was Irish Catholic, would have her revenge not only by marrying a prince of Monaco but by acidly playing the supercilious socialite role of Tracy Lord in *High Society,* a 1956 musical version of the 1940 classic MGM comedy, *The Philadelphia Story.*

Industrialization in the mid-nineteenth century led to the rapid transformation of Philadelphia, which physically expanded with the erection of factories for consumer goods and the construction of vast new neighborhoods of inexpensive two-story brick row houses for workers. Starting in the 1880s, a flood of job-seeking immigrants poured into the U.S. from Italy and Eastern Europe. Most of them were unskilled workers from a lower social level than the craftsmen and small merchants who had emigrated earlier from Northern Europe. Tensions rose even within the Jewish community because of ethnic differences. Earlier Jewish immigrants, like the Swiss-born Meyer Guggenheim, whose first job after his arrival in Philadelphia in 1847 was selling metal polish in the streets, were Sephardic or German Jews, while the new immigrants came from the rough farmlands of Poland and Russia. Guggenheim would go on to accumulate one of the greatest fortunes of the century by buying mining and smelting operations here and abroad and bequeathing them to his numerous, productive, and philanthropic children and grandchildren.

In the early nineteenth century, the genteel Protestant establishment of Philadelphia had been concentrated in banking and finance, but huge fortunes were now being made in railroads, coal, and manufacturing. This local aristocracy adopted a defensive posture toward the non-English-speaking immigrant hordes who were changing the character of the city, increasingly afflicted with noise and soot. Gilded Age families in Philadelphia began to migrate themselves, moving from their mansions in fashionable Rittenhouse Square in Center City to estates in the rolling countryside along the Main Line of the Pennsylvania Railroad heading west toward Pittsburgh and Chicago. There they built lavish country houses in the British manner, ironically often employing virtuoso Italian stonecutters, woodworkers, and gardeners. Many of those houses, which represented some of the most beautifully designed and situated domestic architecture in U.S. history, were demolished to make way for suburban developments following World War Two.

The aggressive Anglophilia of the Main Line elite was a calculated strategy against diversity, as was also the invention of country clubs in the Northeastern United States in the late nineteenth and early twentieth centuries. The country club, ostensibly devoted to golf and tennis, was a sanctuary for the preservation of WASP (white Anglo-Saxon Protestant) hegemony. A related development was the creation of associations tracing lineage to the colonial period, such as Sons of the American Revolution, founded in 1889; the Colonial Dames of America and the Daughters of the American Revolution, both founded in 1890; and the General Society of Mayflower Descendants, founded in 1897. These organizations, which were clearly a reaction to the rising tide of immigration, undertook to proclaim who the *real* Americans were, now under assault by grubby ethnic invaders.

Publication of the Social Register, starting in 1886 with the volume for New York, catalogued the important individuals and families in polite society in every major city, virtually all of whom were Protestants. Metropolitan men's clubs also arose in this period, allowing the leaders of finance, industry, and law to meet in leisurely, privileged access behind closed doors. Discrimination could be overt: it is reported that the original University Club in Cincinnati, founded in 1879, was dissolved seven years later during a controversy over the admission of a Jewish member. New England boarding schools and Ivy League universities became arenas for inter-city reinforcement of the WASP cultural code. The initial lack of diversity at those institutions is demonstrated by the fact that no Ivy League humanities department appointed a Jewish tenured professor until after World War Two.

Indeed, I can recall even upon my arrival at the Yale Graduate School in 1968 how charged the atmosphere was in the Yale English Department over faculty appointments, who remained mostly Protestant. Jewish professors still felt like an embattled minority, and there had just been a rumored purge of gay male teachers, who had all gone off to Smith College. I was jestingly questioned about the pronunciation of my Italian surname by the chairman of the English Department in what I felt to be an offensively condescending manner. When Yale named its first Italian-American president in 1978, it is no coincidence that he had always called himself A. Bartlett Giamatti—Bart for short—when his real first name was Angelo.

I could detail here incidents of overt discrimination or insulting treatment experienced by my immigrant family (all four of my grandparents and my mother were born in Italy) when they were transplanted to old Protestant upstate New York, the location of the Endicott-Johnson shoe factories where my grandfather and many other relatives were employed. Given this background, it might be assumed that I would welcome all campus initiatives to achieve tolerance and diversity, but I have certain reservations. Surely tolerance and diversity in regard to race, ethnicity, gender, and sexual orientation must also be extended toward ideological diversity, if colleges and universities are to succeed in their mission of fostering the free exchange of ideas. But from my own observation, as well as my participation in the long-running culture wars, little deviation is permitted from approved political positions, which are usually predicated on a utopian, big-government liberalism that bears little resemblance to the fiery, freedom-oriented liberalism of my student days in the 1960s. I for one am not entirely comfortable with a national environment in the humanities where I am surrounded by fellow Democrats who vote exactly the way I do (although in the last presidential election I rebelled by casting a protest vote for the Green Party).

Elite American colleges and universities have undermined their credibility and authority by their intolerance to conservative views, particularly in regard to ethical issues such as the debate over abortion, which has divided the nation for nearly a half-century. My militant pro-choice position, based on my libertarian principles, does not blind me to the great moral weight on the pro-life side, whose arguments should be honestly presented without prejudice to students. Furthermore, despite their claims of seeking and nurturing diversity among the student body, the elite universities still end up homogenizing everyone to the same bland, genteel Protestant style that I found so limiting and prejudicial when I arrived at Yale in the late 1960s. The costliness of the uniformity of thought imposed at elite universities over the past three decades—some have called it a "monoculture"—is now becoming manifest in the failure of major new intellectuals or culture critics to emerge among the young.

To create an atmosphere of tolerance on college campuses, the spectrum of permissible ideological opinion must be broadened, a reform that must begin at the classroom level. Second, it must be shown through a study of history that no group has ever had a monopoly on the truth and that virtually every political or social movement has been subject to factionalism and eventually fanaticism. Third, efforts must be made to undo, wherever they occur, power concentrations that impede free thought and free speech. Currently, those reside in the bureaucratic sprawl of campus administrations, which have eaten up budgets and slowly usurped faculty prerogatives. For it is ultimately well-meaning administrators, in their zeal to comply with sometimes intrusive government regulations, who have diverted tolerance and diversity from noble goals into dictates of social engineering that turn institutions from the organically dynamic to the soullessly mechanical.

53

ON GENIUS

The idea of artistic genius descends from paganism: the Romans saw a "genius" or generative spirit dwelling in a man or house or natural locale. The classical Greeks envisioned a semi-divine "daimon" that guided a man's path through life; it descended in turn from the mysterious forces of nature propitiated by early Greek religion.

Although the Greeks venerated Homer and honored tragedians, painters, and sculptors, it was the Italian Renaissance that invented artistic genius as we understand it: the prototype was the brooding, misanthropic Michelangelo, a titanic creator in many genres. Romanticism, with its flamboyant personae from Beethoven to Byron, revived the Renaissance model and laid the groundwork for modern pop stars.

Yes, indeed, the word "genius" has been lamentably overused. Today, when there are so few major artistic innovations, our idea of greatness has shriveled—helped along by shallow postmodernist academics who disguise their own mediocrity by denying that greatness has ever existed at all.

Geniuses there certainly have been in this century—Pablo Picasso, Igor Stravinsky, James Joyce, Martha Graham. Claims could also be made for Duke Ellington, Miles Davis, Alfred Hitchcock, Jackson Pollock, Ingmar Bergman, and Bob Dylan. And there are scores of performers we must call "brilliant" in dance, theater, opera, and film. A

[In response to a reader letter saying the terms "brilliant" and "masterpiece" are now "vague from misuse over time" and asking for Paglia's "theory of genius," Salon.com column, February 3, 1999.]

"masterpiece," on the other hand, should be a large, definitive statement but may be too difficult to make in this commercialized era of fragmented, niche audiences.

If critical coinage seems debased, it's partly because criticism has waned along with the high arts over the past thirty-five years. Criticism is now dully content-driven on and off campus: aesthetics have been superseded by strident politics and mushy therapeutics. Cultural energy has moved into other areas like technology and the Internet, where fluid interactive communications are antithetical to perfection of a finalized object.

As for the hypothesis of "unconscious" genius: yes, I believe that the initial inspiration and primary ideas of much important work have come from an obscure, subliminal area of the artist's dream life. The drive to express is often rooted in the artist's need to work out and to clarify painful internal conflicts. The material form of paper, paint, sound, or gesture externalizes, fixes, and exorcises, as in ancient pagan ritual. (My theory of art was partly influenced by the Cambridge School of Anthropology, notably Sir James George Frazer and Jane Harrison.)

But unconscious impulse is not enough: there must be a strong foundation in the discipline of the genre. Dante was dogged by nightmares, visions, guilt, and a lust for vengeance, yet he also possessed the formalizing framework of medieval scholasticism. Dante surely heard his intricate terza rima stanzas taking shape in his head and may have sometimes felt as if he were taking dictation. There is some form-making faculty buried deep in the creative mind—but it must be nurtured through practice and hard work.

54

THE MIGHTY RIVER OF CLASSICS:
TRADITION AND INNOVATION IN
MODERN EDUCATION

In Samuel Taylor Coleridge's poem "Kubla Khan," one of the classic texts of English Romanticism, a "sacred river" runs for miles, "meandering with a mazy motion" through a paradise realm and then falls down through caverns to "a sunless sea." The river continues underground, then reappears as a "mighty fountain," a geyser forced up with such power that boulders are tossed in the air like "chaffy grain." The river now runs overland, only to fall again beneath the earth and disappear.

Though his setting is imperial China, Coleridge calls his river the "Alph," probably after the Alpheus, a river in the Greek Peloponnesus that flows past the sacred precinct of Olympia and was thought to pass in a single pure stream through the Mediterranean Sea until it reappeared as the fountain of Arethusa on an island in the harbor of Syracuse in Sicily. According to legend, the river god Alpheus had fallen in love with the nymph Arethusa, and when he pursued her, the virgin goddess Artemis protected her by changing her into a fountain.

By shortening "Alpheus" to "Alph," Coleridge also evokes the Chris-

[Lecture at a conference, "Jesuit Humanism: Faith, Justice, and Empiricism in the Liberal Arts," at Santa Clara University, Santa Clara, California, May 5, 2001. Published in *Arion*, Fall 2001.]

tian use of the first and last letters of the alphabet as a symbol for God, who is the "Alpha and Omega," the first and the last, a paradox often illustrated in the wall decorations or mosaics of churches. Coleridge's alternately "mazy" and "mighty" Alpheus seems to me an excellent metaphor for the classical tradition in Western culture, which flows down like a river from antiquity and sometimes seems to disappear underground. But despite constant prophecies of its extinction, it always reappears, forced up again with renewed power.

We are in yet another period when the validity of the classics as the foundation of Western learning and education is being questioned and when there are many signs of erosion—as in the reduction or outright elimination of Latin language courses in public high schools and classics departments in American universities and when the amount of classroom time devoted to the classics in freshman survey and composition courses has in many institutions drastically diminished. There are several reasons for this. The demand after the 1960s cultural revolution for contemporary "relevance" in the curriculum produced a relaxing of academic methods and demands and a proliferation of courses oriented toward the present. Popular culture has entered the classroom as teaching tool as well as subject—a phenomenon toward which there are quite different views. I myself, as a product of the 1960s, feel that popular culture has massively shaped American society over the past 150 years and that students, who have been immersed for their lifetimes in pop, need a map to it—to understand its evolution, technology, modus operandi, and persistent themes. On the other hand, an education that has tipped toward popular culture at the expense of the past threatens to become frivolous, faddish, and merely reactive. There is a way to teach or discuss popular culture, I would argue, that can be integrated with and can reinforce the classics, since so much of Hollywood's use of sex and violence—from molten sex goddesses to larger-than-life action-adventure heroes—can be seen as an analogy to and even as a direct survival of classical mythology.

A second reason for the turn from classics in the past quarter-century is the new interest in multiculturalism, which also originates in the 1960s. Veterans of World War Two had come home with direct experience of Europe, the Pacific islands, the Philippines, and Japan, but in the domestic preoccupations of the postwar period and in the exacerbation of political tensions in the Cold War stalemate with the Soviet Union, with nuclear warfare hanging in the balance, a certain xenophobia took over, so that the rest of the world was sometimes regarded as picturesque to visit but always improvable if it would only Americanize. In the 1950s and 1960s, the civil rights movement and labor activism for migrant workers put the theme of racial and class justice front and center. When the controversy over the Vietnamese war split the generations, the patriotism of protestors was often questioned, partly because leftism from the mid-nineteenth century on has indeed been programmatically internationalist. Proletarian solidarity was premised by Marxism to cut across national boundaries, even though the working class from common observation has always been fervently patriotic. In cultural terms, the 1960s were also permeated by Asian influences, coming from Zen Buddhism, an interest of the West Coast branch of the 1950s Beat movement, and then Hinduism as well.

Multiculturalism is in theory a noble cause that aims to broaden perspective in the U.S., which because of its physical position between two oceans can tend toward the smugly isolationist. It is no coincidence that much of the primary impetus toward multiculturalism began in California, because of its Hispanic heritage and its pattern of immigration from Mexico, Latin America, and the Pacific rim. What poisoned the debate over educational reform, however, was that so many of the proposals for multicultural change were explicitly political, using a leftist frame of reference that polarized the campuses. Shortcuts were resorted to to get quick results in democratizing the curriculum: the number of texts by dead white European males was reduced to make room for those by women or people of color, sometimes without due regard for whether the substitute texts, which were often contemporary, had the same cultural weight or substance as what they replaced.

Indeed, for some in this movement, questions of quality were fundamentally elitist, having been created, it was alleged, by a cabal of imperialist white males to perpetuate their own power. The actual mechanics of canon-formation over time were either unknown or ignored: in point of fact, major writers and artists have rarely possessed or were significant beneficiaries of power in the political sense; in most cases (as in that of the embittered Dante) they were eccentrics or social failures. Second, only sporadically, as in Victorian England, can it be shown that major art was primarily a political vehicle—and even then, it had little effect on the curriculum, which was still based on the classics. When scrutinized over a time-span of thousands of years, canon-formation, a process always fluid and open to dispute, is more intimately linked to artistic impact than to political ideology. We declare something is important and assign it to the curriculum when we find evidence of its influence on *other* artists. In other words, the canon is really about artistic or intellectual fertility; it is the dynasty of works that have generated other works. To return to my river metaphor, art is a cascade down the centuries, like the cataracts that mark the changes of level of the descending Nile.

The laudable mission of multiculturalism also unfortunately got entangled with academic careerism. Job creation, recruitment, and promotion became attached to multiculturalism. Some established academics were so resistant to change that as universities sought diversity in the student body and curriculum, an add-on strategy was hastily adopted. New programs and departments multiplied so that diversity was achieved not by genuinely revising the curriculum but by turning the campus into a crazy quilt of competitive fiefdoms.

Furthermore, the nascent multicultural programs were more allied with campus administrators than with the older professors with their classical erudition. A host of assistant deanships were created nationwide whose positions and budgets were wed to particular campus constituencies and which therefore fostered divisiveness rather than reconciliation. Over the past thirty years, American education at both the primary and secondary levels has been deformed by a steady expansion of bureaucracy that not only drains resources and usurps prerogatives that belong to the faculty but that sometimes encourages administrators to be more committed to external public relations than to internal academic quality.

In this first decade of the new millennium, I have yet to be persuaded that college students are graduating even from the elite schools with deeper or broader knowledge. They are certainly well-tutored in sentiment—that is, in how to project approved attitudes of liberal tolerance, though how well these will survive the test of adult life remains to be seen. Too much academic writing in multiculturalism, whether about the Americas or the Indian subcontinent or the modern Mideast, has been filtered through post-structuralism—which is ironically just about as Eurocentric and elitist a technique as can be imagined. Furthermore, too many proponents of multiculturalism have adopted the social realist or Stalinist view of art as an instrument of indoctrination, deploying positive social messages as a prelude to political action. However, on the other extreme, those most intellectually prepared to give multiculturalism a scholarly system—the professors of ancient history and classics—frequently did not respond to the demand for change except as a challenge to their survival. They set no counterproposal before the nation and lost the opportunity to take control of the momentum of reform.

The grand sequence of the classical tradition, which extends in various strands through the Middle Ages and Renaissance to the scientific Enlightenment and modern era, is actually a master paradigm for how to structure an authentically multicultural curriculum on a global scale. All students abroad as well as in the U.S. need to learn the general contours of the world's major artistic and cultural traditions. These long channels of lineage can best be understood as streams— mighty rivers that are fed by tributaries and that are a confluence of mixed and varied material. The great rivers of cultural tradition are nearly always powered by religion, even when they slow down and spread out into the secular delta of modern life.

Thus my premise in understanding art and culture is always *continuity*. From Egyptian and Greek sculpture to Hollywood movies and rock music, I believe in creative influence over time. I categorically reject the view of culture as disconnected fragments or as the breakage of meaning—an insular fiction fostered by depressive intellectuals who lack the long view and whose ability to weigh or negotiate historical evidence is questionable. The modernist delusion of fragmentation can be traced to T. S. Eliot's poem *The Waste Land*, published in 1922 in the aftermath of the disaster of World War One. Its use in the chic postmodernism of the closing decades of the twentieth century descended from European writers and intellectuals in crisis after World War Two. Lamentably, this outdated and provincial point of view has been given canonical status by those who evidently cannot see the patterns in culture and who have imposed their own limitations on hapless students.

Even in manifest destruction, I see construction or the possibility of cultural recovery and transformation. A superb example is a church in Rome, Santa Maria sopra Minerva, a medieval church with a Renaissance facade. Built in the thirteenth century in the Gothic style—the only one of its kind in Rome—it sits on the foundations of an ancient Roman temple to the virgin goddess Minerva. That in turn was built over a sanctuary to the mother goddess Isis, whose cult had spread from Egypt to Greece by the fourth century B.C. and from there throughout the Hellenized Mediterranean. Isis worship was very popular with the masses in ancient Rome, though it was intermittently opposed by religious conservatives. Everywhere in the rites of Isis, the sacred waters of the Nile were used; a cistern to store them has been excavated at the remains of the Isis shrine in the buried city of Pompeii.

The passage in just this one building of Santa Maria sopra Minerva from Isis to Minerva to Mary, who is both virgin and mother, encapsulates the entire cultural history of the West. Such examples of cultural overlaying can and should be found for every major tradition in the world. In this age of mass media, when students are swamped by the present, it is a teacher's obligation not to tear down or deconstruct our artistic and intellectual heritage but to reveal the invisible foundations or hidden roots of the present.

In 1665 an Egyptian obelisk, clearly belonging to the original sanctuary of Isis, was dug up in the garden of the Dominican monastery at Santa Maria sopra Minerva. Pope Alexander VII asked Gianlorenzo Bernini, the genius of the Italian Baroque, to design a pedestal for it so that the obelisk could be displayed in the street in front of the church. Possibly after consulting with the renowned Jesuit scholar, Athanasius Kircher, who would publish a treatise on the hieroglyphics of this obelisk in 1666, Bernini produced one of his most charming works. Today the obelisk, carried on the back of a muscular elephant beckoning toward passersby with its trunk, remains one of the most beloved works of public art in Rome.

When they were unearthed during the rebuilding and expansion of the city of Rome during the Renaissance and afterward, obelisks, four-sided pillars capped by a pyramid, were interpreted as symbols of divine illumination. Like the tendrilous Gothic spires of Northern European cathedrals whose stone seems to dissolve in midair, obelisks carried the eye and mind skyward, toward a realm of greater permanence. In Baroque Rome they were usually crowned with a bronze crucifix, signifying the triumph of Christianity over pagan religion. In ancient Egypt too, obelisks, which were hewn by virtuoso engineering in the quarry as single, fragile blocks of stone, also signified a yearning for ultimate reality as they soared toward the divine disc of the sun.

The obelisk, therefore, in its simple, clean, sharp-edged geometry, can be seen to embody a long line or current of idealism in the Western tradition that connects pagan with Christian thought. It is precisely that idealism that I find missing in contemporary higher education, which in its laudable movement toward secularism—that is, freedom from sectarian coercion or dogma—has ended up with a chaotic, diffuse humanities curriculum that is too often simplistic in content and spiritually empty, despite its claims to be the agent of social good.

Many members of my 1960s generation followed the High Romantic pattern of critiquing politics and rejecting organized religion—both of which were viewed as forms of outmoded masculine authority. But the Sixties counterculture, like Romanticism, retained a religious perspective and sense of the sacred by honoring nature: hence the poet Percy Bysshe Shelley, who was expelled from Oxford University for writing a manifesto in defense of atheism, could write an ecstatic ode to the highest mountain in Europe, "Mont Blanc," with its awesome spectacle of cold, brute power. American Romantics like Ralph Waldo Emerson and Walt Whitman explored religious traditions outside the West, specifically Hinduism, which was assimilated into 1960s music as well as the Transcendental Meditation movement. But the Roman-

tic comprehensiveness of Sixties consciousness was almost immediately lost by the 1970s, the hedonistic disco era.

Massive drug-taking in the Sixties, notably psychedelics used
to gain visionary insights, became a substitute for serious spiritual
inquiry and took a great toll personally and psychologically on some
who, urged on by new-minted gurus like Timothy Leary, chose to
become dropouts from the career system and public realm and thus
were unable to effect authentic and enduring change. But I respect
those psychedelic explorers of inner space who destroyed themselves
in a genuine quest for truth. On the other hand, I lament the tragic
waste, for these were the idealists of my generation, the ones who
should have been the real educational reformers of our time.

The religious impulse and cosmic perspective of the Sixties shifted
not into education but in diminished and sentimentalized form into
the New Age movement, which has become a highly commercialized farrago of self-help therapies, mystical lore, and sometimes quite
beautiful, atmospheric trance music, Asian or Celtic in mood. New
Age, another creation of the West Coast, is syncretistic in the way it
fuses Asian and European influences, but as an approach to life, it is
all-accepting and undemanding, suspending guilt and judgment. It
offers a psychology without conflict, and a subjective ethics without
challenge or moral responsibility.

Elements of New Age sensibility seem to have entered American
Catholicism, which in the 1950s was already moving away from its
déclassé ethnic roots and Protestantizing itself through a startling
drabness of church architecture and décor. The folk songs, Protestant
hymns, affable sermons, and literal hand-holding in today's suburban
Catholic churches illustrate mellow New Age principles of inclusion
and harmony and reinforce the casualness of the vernacular Mass
and the slackness of unpoetic contemporary translations of Scripture.
Priests, meanwhile, are now being trained to be social workers; theology and learning per se are no longer as heavily emphasized. The
priest, with his public performance of the mysterious Latin Mass, was
once an embodiment of learning for ordinary people. Latin, which
I still believe to be the basis of most strong writing in English, was
intrinsic to a priest's official identity and gave churchgoers a moving

sense of historical continuity with classical antiquity, when the Christian story began. The priest, in other words, was an educator, just as university education began in the Middle Ages as training for priests.

In the wake of the 1960s cultural revolution, organized religion in America has clearly tempered its authoritarianism and tried to make itself more user-friendly. But in this welcome process, which posits the parish as a happy family, what has been lost is the sense of theology as intellectual history, complex and daunting. Jesuit colleges, following the mandate of early Jesuit missionaries to learn native languages and customs, tended to be hospitable to the post-Sixties movement for multiculturalism. But I am not aware of Jesuit voices taking a leading role on either side of the public debate over post-structuralism, which seeped into American universities in the 1970s and early 1980s and has in my view damaged the humanities in ways that it will take a half-century to repair. Surely Jesuit professors, with their scholarly training and tradition of disputation, could have been in the vanguard of engaging post-structuralism in its own terms as a putative philosophy and freeing nascent multiculturalism from its grip. Certainly the response to the theory trend by the professoriat at secular institutions was too slow and feeble, so by the time the general alarm sounded, it was too late.

Nothing has been more deleterious than the common error that post-structuralism is a product of 1960s leftism and therefore an agent of progressive political change. This misconception was made possible only because authentic American radicals of the Sixties rarely if ever entered or completed graduate school in the humanities or made their way up the academic ladder. Post-structuralism was two generations older; it was a product of the school of Saussure, a system of linguistic theory predating World War Two and subscribed to by French intellectuals who were heavily influenced by the pessimistic modernism of Samuel Beckett. The American Sixties believed in social reform, in individual identity, in emotional intensity, and in nature; post-structuralism believes in none of these things. It asserts that there are no "facts"; that language constructs or mediates all reality; that political power is created and sustained through language; and that, conversely, an alteration in language will somehow produce political change. Post-structuralism is simply a new version of verbalism—the excessive preoccupation with words—that has repeatedly plagued the history of Western education, even in ancient Rome. The Sixties cultural revolution, as energized by mass media, was grounded in the sensory—and it should have produced a massive reform of education in this era of cutting-edge science and technology by moving the humanities curriculum forcibly toward the arts. That leftist politics *can* be synthesized with traditional erudition and passionate respect for the arts is proved by Arnold Hauser's Marxist study, *The Social History of Art,* a magnificent magnum opus in the tradition of German philology.

America is presently suffering from an effete, cynical pseudo-intellectuality in the universities, a manic rotation of superficial news cycles in the media, and a generalized hypochondria in the professional middle class, as shown by its preoccupation with stress-related ailments and disorders, buffered by tranquilizers. From a distance, this affluent society, with its avalanche of high-tech toys, must look as if it can barely survive the anxieties of freedom. In a secular society where commerce is king and where the fine arts have never been deeply rooted, it is up to professional educators to provide the sustaining material of culture. But when they themselves cannot agree on what constitutes a basic body of knowledge for the young, then education disintegrates and the humanities are inevitably marginalized—disdained and ignored by average Americans busy with their daily lives.

At the University of the Arts in 1990, I collaborated with Lily Yeh, a professor of painting and art history and a social activist born in China, to create an experimental course called "East and West," the notes for which were published in my first essay collection in 1992. We sought to identify the major themes in Western and Asian tradition that could provide the foundation for a curriculum not just for American but for global education. I certainly expected to see more evidence over the past decade that college teachers understood the urgent need to address the general public about educational reform. But American humanities departments have been amazingly stagnant in this period, demoralized in some cases by factionalism or by financial pressure. Few new ideas have emerged, and no rising major critics or scholars are visible on the horizon. Bread-and-butter issues have come to the fore, such as the long-overdue recognition by the profession of the outrageous exploitation of part-time teachers and graduate students.

Radical change would be needed for the universities to shift to a truly global curriculum. But the Western classical tradition would nevertheless retain centrality because of the sheer massiveness of its documentation, as well as the unrivaled interrelationship of its artistic genres. In my own experience over thirty years as a teacher in a wide variety of schools—including, when I was a struggling adjunct, adult night classes at a helicopter factory in Connecticut—I have found that archaeology captures students' attention. They are transfixed by material about the destruction of great civilizations. Because they inhabit a superefficient world of plastics and stainless steel, where the old and worn simply disappears, they find particularly sobering images of the catastrophic effects of *time*. The contemplation of ruins, in all their decay and devastation, was basic to European education in the eighteenth century. Engravings of the broken, half-buried remnants of the Roman Forum, then an overgrown pasture for herds of sheep and goats, provided a melancholy object lesson on human vanity and mortality.

Archaeology is a fusion of the arts and sciences, of theoretical speculation and engagement with the stubbornly concrete material world. It is in the recovery, identification, and conservation of objects from the past that the West has distinguished itself. My proposed reform of education would put the world's major religious traditions at the center of the curriculum and present them in an Old Historicist, multi-tiered way as a combination of ritual, text, artifact, and architecture. Through archaeology conjoined with anthropology—and here I am deeply influenced by the early-twentieth-century Cambridge School of classical anthropology—religion can be taught in a non-doctrinaire way that expands and develops the student's mind and opens up the distant past without smothering it with contemporary assumptions and political projects.

Occupying the center of Rome's spacious Piazza Navona, whose oval shape follows that of the ancient stadium of the emperor Domitian, is another splendid monument by Bernini, the Fountain of the Four Rivers, commissioned by Pope Innocent X and built between 1648 and 1651. A mammoth Egyptian obelisk, ringed at its base with papal insignia, rests on the grotto of a hollow travertine mountain in front of the church of Sant'Agnese. At the foot of the mountain sit, gushing spouts of water, colossal sculptures of the four great rivers of the world: the Danube, representing Europe; the Ganges, representing Asia; Argentina's Rio de la Plata, representing the Americas; and the Nile, representing Africa. Carved around the fountain are allegorical inscriptions by that omnipresent Jesuit scholar, Athanasius Kircher, whose treatise on this recently unearthed obelisk was published in the Holy Year 1650.

Bernini's stunning design for the Nile sculpture seems to me a great metaphor for culture in general and particularly for European culture, which descends from the warring tribes and empires of the ancient Near East. The Nile is depicted as a burly, nude, adult man wrapping a shroud around his head—signifying that the source of the Nile in central Africa was still unknown. These pagan river gods ringing a North African obelisk before a Catholic church represent the mighty force of tradition feeding and irrigating the present. But the Nile god's masking shroud suggests that all earthly knowledge is partial and contingent. This is no discovery by modern theorists but a basic perception of most major philosophers since Heracleitus, the pre-Socratic who said you cannot step into the same river twice.

The Baroque era, in which St. Ignatius' Society of Jesus flourished, produced a public art that teaches without condescension, that translates big ideas into passionate, theatrical, accessible form. Counter-Reformation Baroque, in which religion was turned into grand opera, has more in common with Hollywood than with the wizened creeds of our current campuses. Bernini's Fountain of the Four Rivers, fusing pagan and Christian and incorporating the entire known world, is multiculturalism at its best. It presents culture as massive and monumental yet at the same time in perpetual flux. It is a perfect symbol for enlightened education, whose energies must be constantly renewed by the interplay and confluence of tradition and innovation.

55

THE NORTH AMERICAN
INTELLECTUAL TRADITION

A war still rages over the legacy of the 1960s. For many conservatives that decade, which began in the 1950s spirit and whose cycle
of excess was triggered by the assassination of John F. Kennedy in
1963, is responsible for the worst aspects of contemporary culture,
from sexual promiscuity and epidemic divorce to rampant drug use
and debased educational standards.

The immense variety of 1960s experience has been abbreviated
into several stock formulas: leftist political activism, emerging from
the civil rights movement and sparking the women's and the gay liberation movements; the nature-worshipping counterculture of drug-
taking hippies, influenced by Asian religions that have thinned out
into today's New Age sensibility; and finally what might be called
urban mod, the kaleidoscope of Pop Art, multimedia innovations
in dance and film, and a technicolor explosion of theatrical fashion,
originating in London's Carnaby Street and Portobello Road. It's this
last category that I identify with as a disciple of Andy Warhol and his
gender-bending circle of poets, musicians, and filmmakers.

What seems to have been forgotten is that there were major intellectual breakthroughs in the 1960s, thanks to North American writers
of an older generation. A schism or rupture in continuity occurred,

[The Second Annual Marshall McLuhan Lecture, Fordham University,
co-sponsored by the Canadian Consulate, February 17, 2000.
Published in *Explorations in Media Ecology* I, no. 1 (2002).]

since the young people most influenced by those breakthroughs did not on the whole enter the professional system and their insights were dissipated into the general society. A cultural vacuum was created that would be filled in the 1970s by French post-structuralism and German critical theory of the Frankfurt School. Those approaches would dominate American literature departments for the next quarter century, devastating the humanities and reducing their prestige and power in the world at large.

It's time for a recovery and systematic reassessment of the North American thinkers whose work, I believe, will endure over time when the French and German schools have been discarded. Marshall McLuhan, Leslie Fiedler, and Norman O. Brown are the triad I would substitute for the big three of French theory—Jacques Lacan, Jacques Derrida, and Michel Foucault—whose work in my view is specific to postwar European culture and whose ideas do not, I maintain, transfer successfully into the Anglo-American tradition.

McLuhan, Fiedler, and Brown were steeped in literature, classical to modern. They understood the way the creative imagination works, and they extended those insights into speculation about history and society. They themselves creatively reshaped traditions and cross-fertilized disciplines, juxtaposing the old and new to make unexpected connections that remain fresh. Most importantly, their influence on others was positive and fruitful. McLuhan, Fiedler, and Brown did not impose their system on acolytes but liberated a whole generation of students to think freely and to discover their *own* voices. Their independence fostered independence in others. Lacan, Derrida, and Foucault, in contrast, hang so heavily on their admirers that only strong, already formed figures like the cultivated scholar Edward Said can use them without being strangled by them. French post-structuralism, like the Frankfurt School, whose antiquated pre–World War Two assumptions dictate so much current media study, grinds up texts and subjects and makes them all sound drearily alike. And at this point, as we survey the scholarship of the last three decades, it should be tragically obvious that very few, if any, genuinely major books were produced by the British and American critics who fell under the spell of European theory.

I feel fortunate indeed that Marshall McLuhan published his central work, *Understanding Media*, in the very year—1964—that I entered college at the State University of New York at Binghamton. McLuhan's ideas were to pervade the cultural atmosphere. Leslie Fiedler's *Love and Death in the American Novel*, as well as Norman O. Brown's *Life Against Death: The Psychoanalytic Meaning of History* (which McLuhan cites in his bibliography), had appeared just five years before.

This was a time when "theory" meant *Anatomy of Criticism*, the magisterial work published in 1957 by McLuhan's rival at the University of Toronto, Northrop Frye. In chapters subtitled "Theory of Modes," "Theory of Symbols," "Theory of Myths," and "Theory of Genres," Frye demonstrated what vital theory should look like—hypotheses and conclusions based on hard evidence, on a wealth of scholarly detail presented in a lucid, accessible style. I will not include Frye here because, as a literary critic rather than an intellectual per se, he rarely addressed contemporary social or political issues outside of education—and he also disliked and rejected mass media.

McLuhan's pioneering examination of the ongoing revolution wrought by electronic media in Gutenberg's print culture demonstrated how history could be reinterpreted with terms bridging high and popular culture. There was a breathtaking sweep to his vision and a charming aptitude for the startling example. McLuhan's irreverent, aphoristic wit was perfectly attuned to the brash spirit of my generation, with its absurdist "happenings" and its taste for zinging one-liners—in both the acerbic satiric style of comedian Lenny Bruce and the gnomic, oracular manner of Zen sages and Hindu gurus.

Understanding Media, which had a tremendous impact on me at a pivotal moment in my development, is a landmark of cultural analysis. In its invigorating interplay of high art and popular culture, technology, and commerce, we see an epic panorama of Western culture. Greek myth, Shakespeare, William Blake, James Joyce, Pablo Picasso, and Margaret Mead mingle with the Marx Brothers amid an Alice in Wonderland swirl of clocks, comic books, alphabets, telephones, and typewriters. Architecture, Roman roads, automobiles, sports, dance, jazz, movies, radio, TV, paper currency, clothing—all the elements of culture meet, merge, and bounce away again. In its picaresque form and carnivalesque tone, *Understanding Media* resembles a work like Petronius Arbiter's *Satyricon,* which gives a vivid picture of first-century Neronian Rome in multifarious language, from elite banter to working-class slang. McLuhan achieves here what semioticians only claim to do. He finds the interpretive key to our supercharged and overloaded cultural environment, and his swift rhythms, playful tone, and deft touch make academic semiotics look ponderous, pretentious, and pointlessly abstract.

In *The Mechanical Bride: Folk Lore of Industrial Man,* published in 1951, McLuhan brought his training as a literary critic to bear on the iconography of modern advertisements, reproduced in a graphic style that seems amazingly contemporary. The rest of the world has finally caught up to that book. But McLuhan never displays the condescending irony of postmodernist appropriation, with its fatiguingly arch self-consciousness. Like Andy Warhol, who began his career as a commercial illustrator, I have loved advertisements since childhood, when they conflated in my mind with the Catholic iconography of stained-glass windows and the mythological tableaux of paintings and sculptures in picture books. In 1960, I surprised my ninth-grade teacher with a term project consisting of clipped-out ads and running commentary—exactly the style, little did I know, of McLuhan's *Mechanical Bride.* Hence my grateful appreciation of that book when I finally saw it—with its merry profusion of Betty Grable posters, pulp-fiction dust jackets, and magazine ads for lightbulbs, diamonds, whiskey, mouthwash, girdles, soap flakes, cars, Coca-Cola, and cod liver oil.

Leslie Fiedler used his profound knowledge of literature to become the forefather of today's academic multiculturalism. He presciently dwelled on the outsider—the Native American, the black, the homosexual, and even the maturely sexual woman, whom nineteenth-century American literature caricatured or excluded. Fiedler knew how to apply his liberal progressive ideals without deforming the texts under study. He did not *indict* literature, whatever its ethically disturbing content, nor did he define art as an oppressive tool of unjust power in the reductive way now so familiar. Fiedler's opening of the literary canon to science fiction or to sentimental nineteenth- and twentieth-century novels, like Margaret Mitchell's *Gone with the Wind,* raised hackles in the academic establishment. I was a graduate student at Yale University in 1970 when Fiedler came to speak on the topic "Teaching Literature in the '70s." Not a single member of the English department came to hear him. But I admired Fiedler's combination of Jungian archetypes with dark Freudian insights into personality, and I would borrow from it for my own work.

Norman O. Brown, with his background in classical studies, moved out of his field to daringly apply Freudian principles to a massive rereading of Western history. *Life Against Death* is one of the great nonfiction works of the twentieth century. It is what Michel Foucault longed to achieve but never did. The long, sinuous lines of argumentation—paragraph by paragraph and chapter by chapter—make *Life Against Death* a tour de force of North American thought. Brown weaves material from Greek philosophy and Christian theology with modern psychology and economic theory to show the conflicts and repressions in human life. He stunningly juxtaposes Jonathan Swift's so-called "excremental vision" with Martin Luther's devil-haunted Protestantism and the birth of modern capitalism. Brown shows the link between ideas and physiology, projection and body-image. Compared to *Life Against Death*, Herbert Marcuse's *Eros and Civilization* (1955), one of the centerpieces of the Frankfurt School, seemed overschematic yet blobby and imprecise to me in college, and I continue to question the inflated reputation of Marcuse as well as his Frankfurt colleague, Theodor Adorno.

My argument is that the North American intellectuals, typified by McLuhan, Fiedler, and Brown, achieved a new fusion of ideas—a sensory pragmatism or engagement with concrete experience, rooted in the body, and at the same time a visionary celebration of what might be called artistic meta-space—that is, the fictive realm of art, fantasy, and belief portrayed by William Blake in his hallucinatory epic poems that oddly prefigure our own cyberspace.

North American philosophers from the late nineteenth century on turned away from the metaphysical preoccupations and increasingly dour world-view of European thinkers. The term "pragmatism" was first used by Charles Peirce in 1878 but was developed by William James, who significantly began his career as a lecturer in anatomy and physiology and only later entered psychology and philosophy. In other words, James' foundation as a thinker was in the human body. In James' later portrait of consciousness as an active agent and in his method of testing an idea by defining its "sensations" and asking about its "reactions" or practical effects, we see anticipated Marshall McLuhan's identification of modern media as "extensions" of the human senses and, second, McLuhan's practice of analyzing technology by focusing on its "effects" in the individual or group. In *Understanding Media,* for example, McLuhan says, "Environments are not passive wrappings but active processes."[1]

John Dewey, whose critique of authority has had immense influence on modern education, also never lost sight of the biological element in human behavior. Dewey's theories are grounded in the senses through consideration of "motor-activity" or physical energy. In his philosophy of "instrumentalism," related to pragmatism, change is a constant in life, but our response should not be doubt or despair, the radical subjectivity of European thought. Dewey is committed to social improvement and experiment, active strategies always subject to review and revision. This resembles McLuhan's view of the whirlwind of modern society, where each invention or solution makes another obsolete. The entire cultural system is in a state of dynamic transformation.

Dewey's focus on educational reform also prefigures McLuhan's attentiveness to how the young struggle to process information in a media-saturated age. The French post-structuralists, in contrast, deconstruct and expose the institutions and organization of modern knowledge without thinking about how they would improve matters outside their already highly educated coterie. In fact, they would reject the idea of improvement or reform as bourgeois.

Dewey's faith in democracy is another departure from French and German theory, with its Marxist premises. McLuhan was implacably opposed to Marxism because he clearly saw how capitalism has enhanced modern individualism, unleashed creativity, and promoted social mobility. Dewey's democratic ideals also connect to Leslie Fiedler, who published in the Old Left *Partisan Review* but whose vision of a pluralist, populist America descends more directly from Walt

Whitman's dream of all-embracing inclusiveness in the wake of the Civil War. McLuhan's interests overlapped with Marxism in the area of institutional analysis: he hated bureaucracy and was one of the first, for example, to condemn the centralization and over-specialization of the contemporary university.

The final late-nineteenth-century American thinker who prefigured our triad is the economist Thorstein Veblen, who is explicitly cited as an influence by Norman O. Brown in *Life Against Death*. In his 1899 classic, *The Theory of the Leisure Class*, Veblen speculated about the psychological forces at work in the formation and activity of social institutions in a way that, in Brown's view, anticipated Freud. This American line of thought, which extrapolates from observation of actual human behavior rather than, in the French way, the dissection of verbal formulas, can be seen passing from Veblen to the eminent Canadian-American sociologist Erving Goffman, whose 1956 work, *The Presentation of Self in Everyday Life* (cited in a later book by Brown), examines the creation and daily operation of social roles. Goffman's book, a primary text for my 1960s generation, was extensively borrowed from without due acknowledgment by Foucault, and it is Goffman's theories that one often hears flowing from the mouths of credulous Foucauldians.

The primacy of the body in the North American intellectual tradition is one of our great distinctions. McLuhan's classification of different eras as "acoustic" or "visual" as well as his emphasis on the "haptic"—that is, the sense of touch—meshes beautifully with the actual practice of the arts. Exploration of the body as a vehicle of thought and emotion is everywhere in the American arts, from the late nineteenth century on. It's in Isadora Duncan's freeing of the body through flowing drapery and lyrical, improvisatory dance. It's in Martha Graham's creation of the vocabulary of modern dance through study of muscle contractions and visceral spasms and in the orientation of her movement by gravity toward the earth. It's in the ferociously concentrated rehearsal technique of Lee Strasberg's interpretation of the Stanislavsky "Method" in the Actors Studio. It's in the Black Mountain school of poetry's search for a new kind of rhythm and declamation following the organic pulses and respirations of the body. And it's in the percussiveness of our glorious popular music, from ragtime and Dixieland jazz through rhythm and blues to rock 'n' roll—the master art form of the 1960s that united us all.

It is a scandal that American humanities professors are still forcing unprepared undergraduates to read turgid French and German theorists rather than the linked triad of McLuhan, Fiedler, and Brown as interpreters of postwar reality. The philosophic tradition behind the post-structuralists was bankrupt even before their books arrived on these shores. European philosophy collapsed after Kierkegaard and Nietzsche. In their pessimism about objective reality as well as in their nihilistic politics, Husserl and Heidegger, Foucault's precursors, were responding to specifically European problems, which would end in the disaster of two world wars.

From our distant view at the dawn of a new millennium, surely it should be apparent that the despairing introversion of European philosophy in the late nineteenth and early twentieth centuries happened precisely as mass media were rising to power in the wake of the industrial revolution. Mass communication, the gift of technology, was giving the people their voice and a public forum for their tastes, which always offend the educated elite. Marxist theory has never been able to adjust to the astounding success of the capitalist mass media, but snobbish, censorious, and now hackneyed Marxist formulations like "commodification" are still being drilled into students by followers of the Frankfurt School.

A fundamental problem with the post-structuralists is that they were narrowly French thinkers who were struggling with the limitations of French discourse as, significantly, French political power was waning around the world. Americans who had absorbed McLuhan, Fiedler, and Brown had no need of post-structuralism, which is monotonously based on Saussurean linguistics, with its view of reality as mediated through language. Continental French speakers, with their rationalist Cartesian heritage, may have needed a Saussurean critique, but English speakers do not. That critique is already contained in English literature itself, as it developed from the Middle English of Chaucer down to the avant-garde verbal experiments of James Joyce—whom both McLuhan and Brown studied and wrote about.

The encyclopedic episodes of Joyce's *Ulysses* (1922) contain the whole history of language and rhetoric and make Saussure both unnecessary and irrelevant.

English is one of the richest and most complex languages in the world. It is a living art form down to its tiniest parts, which McLuhan recognized in his lifelong devotion to word lists and etymology. There are multiple layers in English—the foundation of concrete Anglo-Saxon monosyllables with the Greco-Roman overlay of abstract polysyllables brought by the Norman invasion, with its own lingering bequest of aristocratic household terms. In his plays, written at the birth of modern English, Shakespeare was the first to exploit those levels for serious and comic effects. Immersion in English literature, as it cascaded down the centuries, gives one a philosophic range because of the profusion of English word choices. Two, three, or four words might be possible, emerging from different roots and periods: diction is determined by context. Hence English speakers develop a sense of social context—a hyperawareness of the dramatic situation to which words must be fit.

The North American intellectual tradition began in my view in the mid-nineteenth century with the encounter of Romanticism, coming from British poetry, with the assertive, pragmatic English spoken by North Americans—the plain style, originally Protestant, in the United States as well as Canada, with its strong, no-nonsense Scottish immigrants. It's Romanticism, incidentally, that Michel Foucault somehow completely missed in his bizarrely incomplete picture of modern intellectual history after the Enlightenment, which he was by no means the first to critique. McLuhan from his schooldays was steeped in the history of English poetry, and it remained his first love. Moreover, he heard his mother, a professional performer, recite poetry at home, so he had a keen sense of oratory and the folkloric oral tradition. At Cambridge University, he studied with the founders of the New Criticism, I. A. Richards and William Empson, and he adapted the technique of textual explication for his media work: McLuhan modernized the New Criticism by showing how close reading transfers to fields other than literature.

The writer who did most to unite Romanticism with the North

American plain style was Ralph Waldo Emerson, a poet and public lecturer who drew on the sermon genre but altered its climactic structure for aphorism, which often dissolves his essays into fragments. It is partly to Emerson that I trace McLuhan's intellectual lineage: McLuhan's aphorisms, or as we now say, "sound bites," were his public signature and may have interfered, to his dismay, with his production of conventional books and essays.

It is to Emerson that Norman O. Brown's strange 1966 book, *Love's Body*, should be traced. Brown's thematic chapter titles ("Liberty," "Trinity," "Unity," "Boundary") sound like Emerson's titles in *Nature*, and Brown's disconnected passages of packed, vatic utterances and quotations are like Emersonian prose-poems. There are precedents in Emerson to McLuhan's concern with the "extension of consciousness," with circuits, "integral patterns," and the "total inclusive field" of experience and perception. For example, Emerson says in "Circles," "The eye is the first circle; the horizon which it forms is the second." Or notoriously in *Nature* in 1836, "I become a transparent eyeball; I am nothing; I see all; the currents of the Universal Being circulate through me."

McLuhan's two-way charting of technological advance and obsolescence is anticipated in Emerson's observation in "Self-Reliance" in 1840: "Society never advances. It recedes as fast on one side as it gains on the other. . . . For everything that is given something is taken. Society acquires new arts and loses old instincts." Emerson goes on to draw a Romantic analogy between nature and culture: "Society is a wave. The wave moves onward, but the water of which it is composed does not."

Indeed it is the respect accorded to *nature* that I define as a primary characteristic of the North American intellectual tradition. The claustrophobic world of post-structuralism sees nothing but oppressive society operating on passive, helpless mankind. Nature at its wildest and most sublime rarely impinges on Paris—and when it does, as in the once-a-millennium storm winds that swept over France in late December 1999, ten thousand trees fall and the Cathedral of Notre Dame itself begins to crumble. We in North America, with its powerful, ever-changing weather systems, its vast geography, and monumental landmarks like Niagara Falls and the Grand Canyon, know that nature is the ever-present ground of all human thought and action.

Marshall McLuhan's vastness of perception partly came, as his biographer Philip Marchand notes, from his origins in Alberta with its prairie landscape—exactly the kind of landscape, I would add, that inspired an American genius, the Wisconsin-born architect Frank Lloyd Wright, with his "prairie style" that has revolutionized residential design. Leslie Fiedler too, though born and toughened in urban Newark, New Jersey, became a big-sky Northerner whose work would bring American nature together with American history, ethnicity, and sexuality. Fiedler attended graduate school in the north country at the University of Wisconsin—where McLuhan had briefly taught in his first job in 1936. Fiedler began his career at Montana State University, where he taught from 1941 to 1964, after which he became an eminence for 35 years at the State University of New York at Buffalo, one of the snowiest cities in America. Norman O. Brown, interestingly enough, also attended graduate school at the University of Wisconsin at the same time, receiving his Ph.D. a year after Fiedler received his. I too, despite my immigrant Italian lineage, claim the feisty independence of the northerner: I was born, grew up, and attended college in the snow belt of upstate Central New York. I was raised, I like to say, breathing cold, clear Canadian air.

Marshall McLuhan, Leslie Fiedler, and Norman O. Brown, born within six years of each other (from 1911 to 1917), became models of the public intellectual for the baby-boom generation born just after World War Two. Although an academic at a major university, McLuhan was always an outsider who became a citizen of the world, appearing on talk shows, advising business groups, and always trying to address a general audience. Fiedler too believed that a critic must speak the common language to the widest possible audience. Fiedler became a culture hero to campus radicals everywhere when, because of his sponsorship of a student group advocating legalization of marijuana, he was arrested in 1967 and convicted, though he escaped a prison term when the charges were dropped for lack of evidence. The police raid on Fiedler's Buffalo house was one of the most sensational events of my college years in Binghamton. In one stroke, Fiedler broke the genteel code of American academe. Norman O. Brown made memorable appearances to student groups (though I never saw him) and seemed to give his Dionysian imprimatur to the sexual revolution—for which he certainly lost credibility in the scholarly community.

The North American synthesis of the pragmatic and the visionary in the works of McLuhan, Fiedler, and Brown is uniquely suited to analyze the swiftly changing present of our age of technology. Mass media and communication, which have been developed and refined in the United States since the nineteenth-century rise of tabloid-style mass-market newspapers, cannot be fully understood with European models. Media domination, as we have known it since television captured the nation in the 1950s, is still unknown in Europe, where at-home Internet use too has at this date barely begun.

McLuhan himself was not the wholesale fan of pop culture that many think him; he called TV "a vile drug," for example, and relegated it to lesser rooms of the house. McLuhan forecast what my generation lived, from transistor radios and stereo headphones to today's one hundred cable channels. But we baby boomers had the advantage of a traditional education in history and great books. I agree with social critic Neil Postman that we should be very concerned about the cultural quandary of American children raised on banal TV shows and violent movies. But the antidote, as I see it, is not to curb the rowdy pagan energies of pop but to reconstruct the counterbalancing citadel of primary education, which has so shockingly deteriorated over the past three decades.

As for secondary education, it must be purged of desiccated European formulas, which burden and disable the student mind. We need to recover North American paradigms and metaphors, to restore the North American idiom to academic discourse. Media and Internet communications are a Jamesian and Joycean "stream of consciousness," fluid and mercurial, and our young people—from the brilliant Web entrepreneurs to the pirate hackers who harass institutions and disrupt e-commerce—occupy a radically different mental space than the valley of death of pre- and postwar Europe.

As I know from my own work with the online magazine Salon, with its international readership, McLuhan's "global village" has come to pass. The Web's power of rapid response to breaking news events is making daily newspapers and even network TV seem slow and cumbersome. Every day, the Web is fulfilling the 1960s dream of expanded perception or cosmic consciousness.

In concluding this call for a reawakening of North American sensibility, let me cite Emerson's exhortation in his 1837 lecture "The American Scholar": "We have listened too long to the courtly muses of Europe," he declares. Of Americans, Emerson vows, "We will walk on our own feet; we will work with our own hands; we will speak our own minds."

1. McLuhan, "Preface to the Third Printing," *Understanding Media: The Extensions of Man* (1964), p. 7.

56

ERICH NEUMANN:
THEORIST OF THE GREAT MOTHER

How should the humanities be taught, and how should scholars in the humanities be trained? These pivotal questions confront universities today amid signs of spreading agreement that the three-decade era of post-structuralism and postmodernism is over.

It remains my position—as detailed in my long review-essay, "Junk Bonds and Corporate Raiders," published in *Arion* in 1991— that Jacques Derrida, Jacques Lacan, and Michel Foucault were false gods, created and promoted by secular academics who might have been expected to be more skeptical of authority. As it became institutionalized in the undergraduate and graduate curriculum, post-structuralism hardened into dogma, and many humanities professors lost the ability to respect, assess, or even recognize any hypothesis or system outside their own frame of reference. Such insularity has little to do with genuine intellectualism and is more akin to religious fundamentalism.

Most seriously, post-structuralism did manifest damage to two generations of students who deserved a generous and expansive introduction to the richness of the humanities and who were instead force-fed with cynicism and cant. I fail to see that American students are

[A slightly expanded version of a lecture in the Otto and Ilse Mainzer Lecture Series, sponsored by Deutsches Haus at New York University, November 10, 2005. Published in *Arion*, Winter 2006.]

emerging today even from elite universities with a broad or discerning knowledge of arts and letters. Nor has post-structuralism produced any major new critics—certainly none of the towering scholarly stature once typical of prominent professors who had been educated in the first half of the twentieth century.

The issue I address here is what kind of thinkers or theorists should be set before students as models of progressive yet responsible scholarship. How does one cultivate sensibility or develop scholarly aptitude and judgment? Which writers prove most fruitful over time by stimulating new work in an original voice rather than by simply coercing sycophantic replication?

During my college years, I regarded the declining New Criticism, based on close reading of literary texts, as too limited for the forces—social, historical, psychological, and sexual—then converging in the 1960s, and I began searching for alternate templates. I was drawn to maverick writers who had broken through disciplinary boundaries—Marshall McLuhan, Leslie Fiedler, Norman O. Brown, Alan Watts.

In graduate school, I ransacked the library in my quest for inspiration: it was a kind of archaeological excavation. Today, because of online catalogs and specialty Web sites, information can be targeted with pinpoint accuracy and accessed with stunning speed. Hence I doubt whether that kind of untidy, often grimy engagement with neglected old books will ever appeal again to young scholars. But it was through the laborious handling of concrete books that I learned how to survey material, weigh evidence, and spot innovative categorizations or nuggets of brilliant insight. Many times, the biggest surprises revealed themselves off-topic on neighboring shelves.

One of my central, galvanizing discoveries was Erich Neumann, who was born in Berlin in 1905 and who wrote in German throughout his life. He was a product, I would argue, of the final phase of the great period of German classical philology, which was animated by an ideal of profound erudition. Neumann's higher education and maturation belonged to the Weimar cultural milieu, with its daring, heady spirit yet underlying economic instability and rising political tension. Neumann pursued graduate study in philosophy at the University of Erlangen in Nuremburg and received his Ph.D. in 1927. Researching eighteenth-century Hasidism and cabalism, he chose as the subject of his dissertation Johann Arnold Kanne, a Christian philosopher who had been influenced by Jewish mysticism. In his subtitle, Neumann called Kanne "a neglected Romantic."

Increasingly intrigued by psychoanalysis, Neumann began medical studies at Friedrich Wilhelm University in Berlin. He passed his examinations in 1933 but was unable to obtain an internship because of the race laws affecting Jews. Decades later, when he was already internationally famous, the university granted him a belated medical degree. Neumann had an early interest in the arts: he wrote poetry as well as a long novel, *Der Anfang* (The Beginning). He undertook a critical study of Kafka's novels in 1932, when Kafka was still a minor figure.

Though Freud made a deep impact on him, the pivotal figure in Neumann's career would be Carl Jung, whom he met and studied with in Zurich in 1934. Neumann (thirty years younger) eventually became Jung's anointed intellectual heir. The relationship between these two prolific writers was close yet ambivalent because of Jung's sporadic anti-Semitism. Neumann and his wife Julia, who had joined Zionist organizations in their teenage years, emigrated to Palestine in 1934. There Neumann began his lifelong practice as a Jungian psychologist in Tel Aviv. His wife too became an analyst (and, oddly, earned a high reputation as a professional palm reader). Neumann later became president of the Israel Association of Analytical Psychologists.

During World War Two, when communications were disrupted, Neumann suffered severely from his lack of contact with European colleagues. But from 1948 to the end of his life (he died of kidney cancer at the age of 55 in 1960), he frequently traveled to and lectured in Europe, notably at conferences of the Eranos Society in Ascona, Switzerland. (Other attendees at the Eranos conferences included Mircea Eliade, Herbert Read, Heinrich Zimmer, and Carl Kerényi.) Princeton University Press published Neumann's wide-ranging lectures on art and psychology as four volumes of essays in its Bollingen Series.

Neumann's first published book was *Depth Psychology and a New Ethic* (1949), which interpreted the "scapegoating" of the Nazi era as a projection of repressed cultural and psychological forces. In the same year appeared his first magnum opus, *The Origins and History of Consciousness*, with a foreword by Jung. In this book, my personal favorite of his works, Neumann argues that each individual's psychological growth recapitulates the history of humanity. He charts what he calls "the mythological stages in the evolution of consciousness": the creation myth, the hero myth, and the transformation myth, identified with the Egyptian god Osiris. Here he also presents his idiosyncratic theory of centroversion in ego formation—a blend of extraversion and introversion.

The massive volume for which Neumann is most renowned, however, is *The Great Mother: An Analysis of the Archetype,* a study of the Magna Mater that was evidently first published as a 1955 translation into English by Ralph Manheim. (The dedication reads: "To C. G. Jung, Friend and Master in his Eightieth Year.") In such evocatively titled chapters as "The Primordial Goddess," "The Great Round," "The Lady of the Plants," and "The Lady of the Beasts" (all ancient epithets), Neumann traces the genealogy and symbolism of goddess figures in world culture. Though *Origins* is well-illustrated, *The Great Mother* is a visual feast, a truly essential text with 74 figures and 185 plates of pictures of prehistoric and tribal artifacts of mother goddesses, juxtaposed with striking sculptures and paintings from classical antiquity through the Renaissance. The core of these images came from the Eranos Archive for Symbolic Research, assembled by Olga Froebe-Kapteyn, the free-thinking founder of the Eranos Society who was an early disciple of Jung.

Other substantial writings by Neumann include two monographs, *Amor and Psyche,* a Jungian reading of a myth in Apuleius' *The Golden Ass* (1952), and *The Archetypal World of Henry Moore* (first published as an English translation by R. F. C. Hull in 1959), a study of the British artist's monumental sculptures of women. The latter is another of my favorite Neumann works: Moore supplied some of his own private, previously unpublished photos for the book, and Neumann supplemented them with comparative images of French Neolithic, Egyptian, Cypriote, Mayan, Peruvian, and African objects. Neumann pointedly calls Moore's mother-and-child groups "fatherless" and sees them as prophetic evidence of cultural change: "Today a new shift of values is beginning, and with the gradual decay of the patriarchal canon we can discern a new emergence of the matriarchal world in the consciousness of Western man."

Though he dismissed Freud's *Totem and Taboo* as "ethnologically untenable," Neumann hailed Freud as a "Moses" who had led his people out of "servitude": "Freud opened the way for the liberation of man from the oppression of the old father figure, to which he himself remained deeply fixated." But Freud saw too late that an "earth mother" had preceded the "Father-God": "He never discovered the decisive significance of the mother in the destiny of the individual and of mankind." Neumann found greater variety and flexibility in Jung's system, with its spiritual metaphors drawn from alchemy, the occult, and the *I Ching*. In a tribute to Jung published in 1955, he insisted that Jung had surpassed Freud: "What now emerged was the primal psychic world of mankind, the world of mythology, the world of primitive man and of all those myriad forms of religion and art in which man is visibly gripped and carried away by the suprapersonal power that sustains and nourishes all creative development. The human psyche stood revealed as a creative force in the here and now." Neumann implied that the therapeutic Freud was too fixed on social adaptation and that he trapped patients in their private past.

The narrowness of Freud's view of women, based on a limited sample of late-nineteenth-century types, has often been denounced and became an easy excuse in some quarters of mainstream feminism to dismiss his revolutionary work wholesale. I would maintain that Freud's gender theory, however problematic, was ultimately irrelevant to his mapping of the psyche and the dream life, which radically transformed modern art and thought. Jung's relations with women, including his unstable mother, were blatantly conflicted, but a remarkable number of the first Jungian analysts were forceful, articulate women, who supplied what they found missing in his theories. Neumann's work belongs to that successor generation, among whom there was considerable mutual influence.

Neumann laid out what he theorized to be four fundamental stages in women's psychological development. The first is an undifferentiated matrix or psychic unity where the ego and the unconscious are still fused. He called this stage "matriarchal" and symbolized it as the uroboros, an ancient symbol of a snake biting its tail, both devouring and giving birth to itself, an image of either solipsism or fertility. In the second stage, there is spiritual invasion and domination by the Great Father archetype (associated with rationalism and monotheism), who is perceived as a destroyer or rapist. A gloss here might be William Blake's peculiar, haunting poem, "The Sick Rose," where a ruthlessly phallic "invisible worm . . . flies in the night / In the howling storm" to "destroy" a virginal rose's passively self-enclosed "bed / Of crimson joy." In the engraved plates of *The Songs of Innocence and of Experience* (1789, 1794), Blake, like Neumann, is picturing an unfolding series of spiritual and psychosexual states.

In his third developmental stage, Neumann embodies the masculine in a normative individual, a rescuing hero who liberates the young woman from the controlling father but yokes her to conventional marriage under new male authority. Sex roles are polarized, with masculinity and femininity mutually exclusive. Neumann's fourth and final stage has feminist implications: here the mature woman discovers her authentic self and voice. As she borrows from the masculine, sex roles are blurred.

I hope I have outlined Neumann's four stages accurately. This is not in fact the aspect of his work that most drew or influenced me. General theories of female psychology quickly lost favor after the resurgence of the women's movement in the late 1960s. They appeared arbitrary and reactionary insofar as they reflected a conception of women preceding their massive entrance into the professions. Issues relating specifically to motherhood were now avoided and gradually abandoned—at some cost to feminism in the long run. While women's groups lobbied on and off campus for such practical matters as daycare and flex time, biology and reproduction would be purged from discussion in most women's studies programs—or rather they were reduced to the single, still hotly contested matter of abortion rights (which as a feminist I fully support).

If one were to judge by the women's studies curriculum at most American colleges and universities over the past three decades, motherhood seemed permanently relegated to that distant past when the only roles open to women were wife or nun. The symbiosis of mothers and daughters was addressed in early women's studies because of its potential transmission of negative stereotypes; analysis was generally confined to social dynamics, with little or no consideration of biological factors. Contemporary motherhood faded completely in post-structuralism, which ideologically excludes nature and biology from its discourse and which sees nothing impinging on human life except oppressive political power. By the late 1980s and '90s, with the arrival of queer theory, an offshoot of post-structuralism, gender itself was declared to be entirely fictive, nothing but a series of language-mediated gestures.

Jungian approaches have regrettably played no role whatsoever in high-profile academic feminism. Principal reasons for this include Jung's religious orientation (his father was a Protestant minister) and his passion for nature. British and American academic feminists took up French Freud via the pretentiously convoluted Lacan instead. But Jung belongs in any humanities program that claims to be teaching "theory": his archetypes constitute the universal tropes and basic structures of epic, drama, folklore, and fairy tale. Erich Neumann's work, above all, assimilates or smoothly dovetails with major literature and art. Post-structuralism, on the other hand, which is predicated on the Francocentric linguistics of Ferdinand de Saussure, can claim success only with self-reflexive literature—that is, writing that is self-referential or self-canceling in the ironic modernist way. Post-structuralism has nothing useful to say about the great religious and mythological themes that have dominated the history of world art.

There has been heavy Jungian influence on feminism outside the academy, however. Jung is a cardinal progenitor of the New Age movement, which developed from two important strands of 1960s thought—the back-to-nature imperative (which can be classified as vestigially Romantic) and multiculturalism, notably relating to East Asian and Native American religions. (I would identify my own work as New Age in this sense; I am an atheist who reveres the symbol systems of world religions.) Part of the Jungian legacy is the feminist goddess cult, an almost entirely off-campus phenomenon that may have peaked in the 1980s but is still flourishing less visibly today.

The goddess has attracted different degrees of belief. In some cases, she is a metaphor—a symbol for "the goddess within," the liberated female spirit. Leading examples of this approach are Sylvia Brinton Perera's *Descent to the Goddess: A Way of Initiation for Women* (1981), which celebrates the Sumerian goddess Inanna-Ishtar, and Jean Shinoda Bolen's *Goddesses in Everywoman: Archetypes in Women's Lives* (1984; 20th anniversary edition, 2004). In other cases, the goddess is literally worshipped, through witch-cult or druidism, as a pagan substitute for the patriarchal judgmentalism of main-line Judeo-Christianity, with its anti-nature and anti-sex biases. One liberal theological branch of feminism has attempted to correct or reform Christianity by implanting it with female paradigms ("Our Father" becomes "Our Mother").

Goddess feminism went seriously wrong in accepting and promoting an error first made by the Swiss writer Johann Jakob Bachofen in his 1861 book, *Das Mutterrecht* (Mother Right). The worldwide ubiquity of prehistoric goddess artifacts led Bachofen to wrongly conclude that early societies were matriarchies, literally governed by women. His theory received wide circulation via the great British scholar of classical antiquity, Jane Harrison, who taught at Cambridge University from 1898 to 1922. I love Harrison's books and have been specifically influenced by her theme of the chthonic (I say "chthonian"), an uncanny motif of earth cult. But she was simply mistaken about the existence of prehistoric matriarchy, for which no evidence has ever been found.

When the matriarchal hypothesis resurfaced in Jungian feminism, it had turned into Arcadian soap opera: once upon a time, there were peaceful, prosperous, egalitarian, goddess-worshipping societies, happily thriving for eons until they were viciously overthrown by men— those greedy aggressors who invented violence, war, oppressive social hierarchies, and the unjust economic disparities we suffer from today. This naïve view of political history was promulgated in innumerable feminist books over two decades (and is still detectable in some eco-feminist denunciations of the capitalist exploitation of nature). Riane Eisler's *The Chalice and the Blade* (1987), for example, has achieved near-canonical status despite its partisan sentimentalism and flimsy historical claims. It may even have influenced Dan Brown's internationally bestselling mystery novel, *The Da Vinci Code* (2003), which alleges a suppressed tradition of woman power in early and medieval Christianity.

A principal evangelist for matriarchy was the Lithuanian archaeologist Marija Gimbutas, who taught at UCLA. It is unfortunate that Gimbutas took as her Jungian mentor not the scholarly Erich Neumann but the popularizing Joseph Campbell, who had been a colleague of Neumann's in the Swiss Eranos conferences and who edited six volumes of the Eranos Yearbooks. A teacher for thirty-eight years at Sarah Lawrence College, Campbell became known to the public through his 1949 bestseller, *The Hero with a Thousand Faces* (which evidently inspired George Lucas' film saga, *Star Wars*), and through a 1988 public television series, *The Power of Myth,* where he was interviewed by Bill Moyers. Campbell encountered Bachofen's theory of matriarchy in Jane Harrison and uncritically adopted and transmitted it. Later, Campbell officially endorsed Gimbutas by writing the foreword to her 1989 book, *The Language of the Goddess.* Both are deceased, but their alliance is memorialized today in the Joseph Campbell and Marija Gimbutas Library at California's Pacifica Graduate Institute.

The ancient Great Mother was a dangerously dual figure, both benevolent and terrifying, like the Hindu goddess Kali. Neumann saw this clearly, but Campbell and the goddess's feminist boosters did not: they sanitized and simplified, stripping away the goddess's troublesome residue of the archaic and barbaric. Neumann cited and praised Bachofen's pioneering work in prehistory but was careful to note that the latter's idea of matriarchy (as Neumann puts it in *The Great Mother*) must be "understood psychologically rather than sociologically." While quoting Bachofen in *The Origins and History of Consciousness,* Neumann insists that the matriarchal stage "refers to a structural layer and not to any historical epoch." Such fine distinctions are precisely why I admire Neumann—because he scrupulously tempers speculation with evidence. This vexed issue of matriarchy, which remains one of the most dubious strains in feminism, is of special importance to me because it provoked some of my earliest public clashes with fellow feminists when I began teaching in the early 1970s.

I would propose that Erich Neumann is the key for a future incorporation of Jung with academic feminism. But gender inquiry is only one aspect of Neumann's work. I regard him as an accomplished culture critic whose synthesis of art, history, and psychology offers a more promising direction for culture studies than the current approved academic models, which are mainly derived from British or German Marxism (such as the Frankfurt School). Authentic cultural criticism requires saturation in scholarship as well as a power of sympathetic imagination. Neumann's manipulation of material is improvisational rather than schematic, though he does draft illustrative psychic graphs that will inevitably seem quirky or bogus to the non-Jungian. But there is neither moralism nor a political agenda operating in his work.

Because of the deftness with which he deploys archaeological and etymological evidence, Neumann belongs, in my view, to the 150-year-long dynasty of German scholars following the idealizing Winckelmann, such as Hermann Usener, Werner Jaeger, and Ulrich von Wilamowitz-Moellendorff, who bitterly warred over the character and methodology of classical studies. I would call Neumann a historicist, except that the term "historicism" has been tainted by German nationalism and imperialism, with which the Zionist Neumann obviously had no connection. In his gravitation toward Hellenistic and Oriental (that is, Near Eastern) studies, which began to boom in the late nineteenth century, Neumann is in the line of Jacob Burckhardt and Friedrich Nietzsche, who had controversially expanded the definition of Greek culture beyond serene Athenian high classicism.

Neumann always has a keen sense of historical context even as he weaves his eclectic details into a dense tapestry. He appropriates but not to fragment and destabilize, in the postmodernist way. In resituating facts, he retains their historical weight and gives them a psychological aura. Neumann accepts chronology and acknowledges cause and effect in history—which post-structuralism does not. But he also perceives deep cycles and repetitions, as do Vico, Nietzsche, and Yeats, so that history and nature become dimly analogous. I found this hybrid perspective in Neumann very appealing. I strongly believe in a mensurable time line, but it is not ascendant and progressive, in the Victorian way. My book, *Sexual Personae* (the title of which invokes Jung's concept of "persona," that is, the social mask), portrays art and history as an unstoppable, near-compulsive sequence of growth, loss, and revival.

Neumann's meshing of European with world cultures continues and extends Jung's enterprise, whose syncretistic anthropology can be traced to Sir James George Frazer's *The Golden Bough.* Frazer's epic work, published in twelve volumes from 1890 to 1912, had a huge impact on the first generation of modern writers and artists, the most famous example being T. S. Eliot's apocalyptic 1922 poem, *The Waste Land.* I would call Neumann's philology Frazerian. Like Frazer (whose "mass of ethnological material" he cites), Neumann creates a vast, dreamlike prose-poem, with startling and sometimes bizarre material floating in and out.

Neumann's scholarship is an art form partly because it emanates from his deep knowledge of and intimacy with the arts. He is the supreme exemplar of the Jungian flair for the visual image. Freud, in contrast, saw language as primary: he characterized the contents of the unconscious as entirely verbal; hence his device of the interminable "talking cure" to unravel neurosis. In Freud's linguistic analysis of dreaming, every detail resolves into wordplay, whereas Jung treats dreams as visions, which may be symbolic but are potent in their own right.

Neumann found revelation and inspiration in art. In his essay, "The 'Great Experience,'" he says that effective art provides "a streaming moment, as flowing and ungraspable as the vitality of life itself": "The infinite abundance of the art of humanity presupposes a corresponding abundance of human responses." He speaks of "human openness and readiness to receive 'great art' or alternatively to remain closed and unmoved by it" (the latter being dismayingly rampant in recent academe).

With notable catholicity (rare at the time), Neumann embraced both classical and avant-garde modern art. His essays teem with allusions to the visual arts of every period—Giotto, Bosch, Grünewald, Titian, Rembrandt, El Greco, Goya, Hokusai, the Impressionists, Van Gogh, Cézanne, Rousseau, Picasso, de Chirico, Klee, Chagall, Giacometti, Dalí. Also conversant with music, Neumann devotes an essay to Mozart's *The Magic Flute* and elsewhere cites such composers as Bach, Beethoven, Verdi, and Wagner. His literary taste is similarly cultivated—Shakespeare, Cervantes, Goethe, Balzac, Poe, Baudelaire, Melville, Dostoyevsky, Zola, Thomas Mann, James Joyce.

For Neumann, art exists as form, materials, and technique and not just content—to which art has too often been reduced in Freudian interpretations. Freud's analysis of the psychodrama of the modern bourgeois family was unsurpassed, but his discussions of art were uneven. Although he collected archaeological artifacts, Freud had little feeling for the visual arts or for music, and he tended to read the art work as a neurotic symptom. Neumann's article, "Leonardo da Vinci and the Mother Archetype," pays due homage to Freud's important 1910 essay on Leonardo but is in fact a vigorous rebuttal. Neumann disputes Freud's account of the "pathological" genesis of Leonardo's art and asserts that Freud distorted facts about Leonardo's childhood. For Neumann, Leonardo is "a Western phenomenon," like Goethe an example of the titanic Western artist properly raised to "hero" status, as in Michelangelo and Beethoven. In the Jungian way, Neumann sees the creative man as "bisexual," even "feminine," because of his high "receptivity." Neumann wonderfully evokes Leonardo's "loneliness" and compares it to Nietzsche's. This essay alone would be enough to establish Neumann's virtuosity as a culture critic.

Freud's adoption by Lacanian post-structuralism compounded his basic problem—that is, his overestimation of language in our neurological makeup. The brain has many chambers: *Homo sapiens* also thinks in flashing images, which have become primary in what I have elsewhere called our modern Age of Hollywood. Erich Neumann was exquisitely attuned to the evolution and permutations of artistic style; he also had an awareness of the spirituality of art as well as a sophisticated understanding of the creative process—a subject too much neglected today. Furthermore, Neumann's time frame vastly exceeds that of post-structuralism. Foucault, for example, was focused on the Enlightenment and its sequelae in Europe and North America; he knew little about world cultures or even about European classical antiquity until late in his career.

Any major theory of culture must begin with prehistory and the development of agrarian society out of the nomadic. Here is where the Jungian approach, with its attentiveness to nature, demonstrates its superiority to the strict social constructionism of post-structuralism. The deletion of nature from academic gender studies has been disastrous. Sex and gender cannot be understood without some reference, however qualified, to biology, hormones, and animal instinct. And to erase nature from the humanities curriculum not only inhibits students' appreciation of a tremendous amount of great, nature-inspired poetry and painting but also disables them even from being able to process the daily news in our uncertain world of devastating tsunamis and hurricanes.

A passage from Erich Neumann's superb essay, "Art and Time," displays his scope and quality of mind:

> How can the individual, how can our culture, integrate Christianity and antiquity, China and India, the primitive and the modern, the prophet and the atomic physicist, into *one* humanity? Yet that is just what the individual and our culture must do. Though wars rage and peoples exterminate one another in our atavistic world, the reality living within us tends, whether we know it or not, whether we wish to admit it or not, toward a universal humanism.

This is a stirring manifesto for a new, comprehensive scholarship, a marriage of art and science as well as an enlightened multiculturalism.

While writing this lecture for the Mainzer Series, I found (through the magic of the Web) a rivetingly detailed article on Erich Neumann's life and career by the Israeli journalist Aviva Lori which was published earlier this year [January 28, 2005] in the daily newspaper *Ha'aretz*. It was commissioned to coincide with a symposium held at Kibbutz Givat Haim Ihud to honor the centenary of Neumann's birth. To my surprise and delight, a conference about Neumann, sponsored by the Austrian Association of Analytical Psychology, was also held in Vienna last August to mark that centenary. It appears that the Zeitgeist—a force that Neumann says drives creative artists—is preparing the way for a Neumann revival.

57

SLIPPERY SCHOLARSHIP

JOHN BOSWELL, *SAME-SEX UNIONS*
IN PREMODERN EUROPE

In 1980, John Boswell came to attention with a long scholarly book, *Christianity, Social Tolerance, and Homosexuality: Gay People in Western Europe from the Beginning of the Christian Era to the Fourteenth Century*, which won the American Book Award. Even those who did not read it may have been aware of the controversy over the appearance of the contemporary word "gay" in a book about the Middle Ages, a usage criticized by some as anachronistic and tendentious.

As the first openly gay professor to win tenure at an Ivy League university, Boswell made history. Many substantive questions raised about his work have been eclipsed by his general celebrity in a period when gay studies began to enter college curricula. Since his big book, Boswell has published *The Kindness of Strangers* (about the medieval treatment of children) and been awarded the A. Whitney Griswold Professorship of History, as well as chairmanship of the history department at Yale.

In his new book, *Same-Sex Unions in Premodern Europe*, Boswell, conceding to his scholarly opponents, abandons his earlier reliance on the word "gay." This retreat has scarcely been noticed in the extraordi-

[Front-page review, *The Washington Post Book World*, July 17, 1994.]

nary notoriety the book has inspired even before publication. Boswell's thesis—that homosexual marriages were sanctioned and routinely conducted by the medieval Catholic Church—was aired on network television, publicized nationally in the *Doonesbury* comic strip, and promoted in a full page of a major magazine by his commercial-press editor, who is hardly qualified to vouch for the book's arcane scholarship.

Evaluation of serious academic books does not normally occur in such an atmosphere of highly politicized pressure. Boswell states that *Same-Sex Unions* is directed toward "readers with no particular expertise in any of the specialties" in which he claims "mastery." But no one without special knowledge could be expected to absorb, or even comfortably read, a text so crammed with labyrinthine footnotes and ostentatiously untransliterated extracts from ancient Greek and Old Church Slavonic.

The credibility of Boswell's book rests on three points. First is the authenticity of the medieval manuscripts containing the disputed liturgies, to whose existence in European archives Boswell says he was alerted by "a correspondent who prefers not to be named." Second is the accuracy of translation of those manuscripts. Third is the interpretation of the texts.

I have no reason to doubt issues one and two. Boswell has told reporters he daily photographed the relevant manuscript pages, lest they be sabotaged. I also accept his claim of fluency in many languages. However, in my opinion, this book, like *Christianity, Social Tolerance, and Homosexuality,* demonstrates that Boswell lacks advanced skills in several major areas, notably intellectual history and textual analysis. The embattled complexities of medieval theology and the ambiguous nuances of language and metaphor familiar to us from great literature seem beyond his grasp. Speculative reasoning is not his strong suit.

Boswell argues that homosexual marriages of some kind were widely accepted in classical antiquity and that the medieval church simply continued the pagan practice. But his weak, disorganized, and anecdotal material on Greek and Roman culture never proves such marriages existed outside the imperial Roman smart set, whose cynical "Dolce Vita" decadence he does not see. Furthermore, he disproportionately stresses evidence from isolated or marginal regions, such as post-Minoan Crete, Scythia, Albania, or Serbia, all of which had unique and sometimes bizarre local traditions.

Insisting that heterosexual marriage had no prestige and was "primarily a property arrangement" in antiquity, he repeatedly portrays Achilles and Patroclus as lovers (a Hellenistic fantasy not in Homer), while shockingly never mentioning Odysseus and Penelope, one of the most famous marital bonds in literary history. Animus against or skepticism about heterosexual marriage runs through the book: Boswell dubiously claims, in a careless unsubstantiated note, that "more than half of all spouses commit adultery" in the United States.

The question of pagan survivals in Christianity is a fascinating one, but Boswell neglects the most obvious facts critical for his larger argument. Gnosticism and Neoplatonism are never dealt with. Addressing the ambivalent Judeo-Christian attitude toward sexuality, he shows no understanding of basic philosophic problems of body and soul, matter and spirit. He simplistically views opposition to homosexuality as motivated only by prudery or bigotry, never morality. He fails to see that the development of canon law and church hierarchy had complex intellectual consequences in the West, beyond his favorite, somewhat sentimental notions of oppression and intolerance.

Boswell's treatment of the Middle Ages, ostensibly his specialty, is strangely unpersuasive. Surely, bonding ceremonies are of special interest to feudalism—a word that occurs just once here, and only in a footnote. Boswell has no feeling or sympathy for military or political relationships, which distorts his portrait of medieval society. Indeed, he seems grotesquely incapable of imagining any enthusiasm or intimate bond among men that is not overtly or covertly homosexual.

The subliminal sexual tension and process of sublimation in asceticism and monasticism, also prominent in Asian religions, are never honestly examined. Despite sporadic qualifications, Boswell repeatedly implies a genital subtext to intense spiritual alliances, even when his supporting manuscripts make clearly uncarnal invocations to martyred paired saints, who died in the service of Christ. Conversely, he under-interprets the profane excesses of corrupt Renaissance clergy, who may well have conducted illicit ceremonies of all kinds, including Black Masses.

Boswell's style, here as in *Christianity, Social Tolerance, and Homosexuality*, is to pack an enormous amount of dry, irrelevant bibliographic material into scores of footnotes, building a pretentious barricade around his thin and vacillating central presentation. Meanwhile, crucial research is often avoided. For example, one would expect a historian discussing medieval sexuality to at least cursorily consider the enormous "courtly love" tradition, with its inherent perversities, but that is relegated to a footnote, which glibly lists, without explanation, 23 books and articles for us to read. Boswell's knowledge of psychology or general sexual history seems minimal, confined to a handful of chic, narrow academic books cited from the 1980s.

Whatever medieval ceremonies of union he may have found, Boswell has not remotely established that they were originally homosexual in our romantic sense. Their real meaning has yet to be determined. Sacrilegious misuse of such ceremonies may indeed have occurred, leading to their banning, but historians are unjustified in extrapolating backwards and reducing fragmentary evidence to its lowest common denominator. The cause of gay rights, which I support, is not helped by this kind of slippery, self-interested scholarship, where propaganda and casuistry impede the objective search for truth.

58

MAKING THE GRADE:
THE GAY STUDIES GHETTO

That there has been a collapse of gay political leadership in America in the past three years is obvious to most observers. The major gay activist organizations have lurched through acrimonious personnel turnovers, while the openly gay congressional representatives and executive appointees in Washington have failed to achieve national stature, through their own lack of statesmanlike dignity and authority. None of them saw the stunning Republican sweep of the November 1994 election coming, nor have they yet acknowledged the part their strategic misjudgments played in alienating the electorate from progressive issues in general and the Democratic Party in particular. Their inability to learn from their mistakes bodes ill for the gay movement in a period when, worldwide, there is a shift toward economic conservatism and religious fundamentalism.

In the future, parochialism and conventionalism in gay thinking must be caught and corrected before they have such disastrous political consequences. Let's start with gay studies, which is the biggest ghetto in the making in the current cultural landscape. If gay studies means taking oral histories from aging pre-Stonewall gays or writing honest, detailed, responsibly researched accounts of lost moments in gay experience, then I'm for it. Recent examples of the latter would be

[Last Word column, *The Advocate*, September 5, 1995.]

Lillian Faderman's *Odd Girls and Twilight Lovers,* Robert Aldrich's *The Seduction of the Mediterranean,* and George Chauncey's *Gay New York.*

But if gay studies means distorting history, literature, and art with anachronistic contemporary agendas or using elitist, labyrinthine, jargon-infested post-structuralist theory to suppress or deny scientific facts about gender, then I'm against it. Not only are these abuses very common in gay studies, but they are exactly what has won unscrupulous opportunists the highest rewards of academe: top appointments at leading universities with stratospheric salaries. Authentic leftists—indeed, all ethical persons across the political spectrum—must oppose corruption and fraud wherever they occur.

The great cause of gay rights is not served by tolerating mediocrity, pretension, and deceit. The best work in gay studies remains that informed by rigorous traditional standards of historiography and criticism as well as by clear-sighted, unbiased observation of the larger, non-gay world. Without a sympathetic sense of social life as a whole, writers of any specialized interest risk loss of perspective. When human sexuality is the topic, such narrowness is fatal. I call on young gay intellectuals to renounce gay studies as a lifetime preoccupation and to hone their skills instead on old-style, high-level history of ideas. Classical philology, as it was practiced by the magisterial nineteenth-century German scholars, for example, had precision, deep learning, and interdisciplinary breadth.

Only long immersion in the vast, 2,500-year-old treasury of still-relevant scholarship can prepare one to detect the shoddiness and sleight of hand in the work of a prominent, openly gay professor of history at Yale University. I speak of the late John Boswell, whose prizewinning *Christianity, Social Tolerance, and Homosexuality* is full of weak evidence and questionable conclusions but whose last book, *Same-Sex Unions in Premodern Europe,* is a shocking piece of propaganda, cunningly mined with traps to mislead the general reader. While some reviews of the latter were strongly skeptical (I reviewed it negatively for *The Washington Post*), most of the gay and mainstream press fell gullibly for it hook, line, and sinker. But the grim truth about Boswell is starting to emerge, as even the politically correct *New York*

Times admitted in June in a disillusioned article marking the book's one-year anniversary.

If gays do not stand for truth, they stand for nothing. When I see t-shirts for sale at a gay resort listing Emily Dickinson, Virginia Woolf, Eleanor Roosevelt, Amelia Earhart, Janis Joplin, and Madonna as "gay," I am embarrassed by the childish credulity and disrespect for facts that are now widespread in the gay scene. This sort of heavy-handed mistreatment of the subtleties of complex biographies is no better than hysterical superstition.

Similarly, there is wild overpraise of misogynous Michel Foucault by literary academics, who naïvely attribute to their gay idol break-through insights that have been common coin since Romanticism and the birth of modern sociology in the 1890s. Queer theory cannot go on trafficking in inflated reputations, such as those of Eve Kosof-sky Sedgwick and Judith Butler, glib game-players and cloistered careerists whose evident lack of hard knowledge of history, anthropology, psychology, and science makes their writing about sex absurd.

The gay studies sections of bookstores are bulging. But who is browsing in them except gays? Gay writers and thinkers are stunting their own development if they address only a gay audience. It's time to rejoin the mainstream. I don't seek sanitization and normalization: I stand with the prostitutes, boy lovers, drag queens, and transgendered. But gays, who are vulnerable to abrupt changes in political climate, must have disciplined free minds to see the present and past without sentimentality or fear.

59

GAY IDEOLOGY IN PUBLIC SCHOOLS

Spin the gay bottle! Pin the tail on the gay donkey! Welcome to the wild and wonderful world of American public education.

The prestigious Oak Hill Middle School of Newton, Mass., has posted, for the edification of its 11- to 13-year-old students, the photos of fourteen major gay figures of the ancient and modern world.

The purpose? To show that "it's OK to be gay" and that "gay is good," school officials told *The Boston Globe*. The female art teacher who created the bulletin-board exhibit declared, "Kids commit suicide over their sexuality; it's up to us to take this issue from under the covers, and say, 'It's OK, it's normal.'"

Who made the Newton gay hit parade? Not just professed gays like Marcel Proust, Andy Warhol, James Baldwin, and Newton's own Congressman Barney Frank, but Alexander the Great, Michelangelo, Leonardo da Vinci, William Shakespeare, Walt Whitman—and Eleanor Roosevelt. "If kids question how the wife of a president could be gay, good," declared the teacher, who defined her professional goal as "teaching tolerance and respect."

But wouldn't students be better off if their teachers fed them facts rather than propaganda? Proclaiming Eleanor Roosevelt gay is not only goofy but malicious. It reduces a bold, dynamic woman whose entire achievement was in the public realm to gossip and speculation about her most guarded private life.

["It Wasn't Romeo and Julian" (their headline),
The Wall Street Journal, February 22, 1999.]

Only in puritanical Anglo-American culture could kisses and hugs (the acts with which Mrs. Roosevelt is charged) be transformed into salacious evidence for prosecution and conviction. False accusations in seventeenth-century Salem got you hanged as a witch. False accusations in twentieth-century Newton get you hoisted as a gay saint.

As a specialist in the history of the arts, I am outraged at the coarse political exploitation and distortion of art, a trend that began twenty-five years ago on our college campuses. That Michelangelo, Leonardo, and Walt Whitman were attracted to young men, I have no doubt. But those phenomenally productive geniuses were obsessively solitary characters who may have diverted their sexual energies into art. In the absence of hard information, to call them "gay" is ethically wrong. And to introduce major artists to schoolchildren via sexual scandal rather than through the art itself is a perversion of education.

Those who promote Shakespeare's homosexuality for their own ideological agenda conveniently overlook the fact that none of his thirty-seven plays address homosexuality or allude to it except in negative terms. (Is Iago, with his evil fixation on Othello, now to be a gay role model?) On the contrary, Shakespeare is world-famous for his celebration of heterosexual love, as in the eternally popular *Romeo and Juliet*.

There are two romantic objects of Shakespeare's sonnets, conventionally called the Dark Lady and the Fair Youth, but it is not at all clear that physical consummation occurred with the latter. In fact, in Sonnet 20, Shakespeare remarks that his friend's penis is an obstruction to their union and elsewhere explicitly urges him to marry.

Sexual orientation is fluid and ambiguous, and homosexuality has multiple causes. It certainly is not inborn, as was claimed by several small, flawed studies of the early 1990s. The intrusion of militant gay activism into primary schools does more harm than good by encouraging adolescents to define themselves prematurely as gay, when in fact most teens are wracked by instability, insecurity, and doubt.

Questionable and overblown statistics about teen suicide (like those about rape a few years ago) are being rankly abused. In most cases, the suicide attempts are probably due not to homophobic persecution but to troubled family relations—which may be the source of the social maladjustment and homosexual impulses in the first place. Trumpeting gayness in adolescents short-circuits their psychological inquiry and growth.

Many pressing civil-liberties issues remain to be resolved for gays—the right to serve with honor in the military, for example, or the extension of equal benefits to domestic partners. But the kind of arrogant cultural imperialism shown in Newton—where "tolerance and respect" would clearly not be accorded to a fundamentalist Christian or Hindu who declared homosexuality immoral—can only create a backlash empowering the religious far Right.

Preachers of the Left and preachers of the Right must stay out of our public schools. "Self-esteem" is not the purpose of education. Teachers should stop posing as therapists and do-gooders and get back to introducing the huge expanse of art, literature, history, and science to American students, who desperately need cultural enrichment and intellectual development.

60

THE DEATH OF CLAUDE LÉVI-STRAUSS

I was appalled at the sentimental rubbish filling the air about Claude Lévi-Strauss after his death was announced last week. *The New York Times,* for example, first posted an alert calling him "the father of modern anthropology" (a claim demonstrating breathtaking oblivi-ousness to the roots of anthropology in the late nineteenth and early twentieth centuries) and then published a lengthy, laudatory obituary that was a string of misleading, inaccurate, or incomplete statements. It is ludicrous to claim that Lévi-Strauss singlehandedly transformed our ideas about the "primitive" or that before him there had been no concern with universals or abstract ideas in anthropology.

Beyond that, Lévi-Strauss' binary formulations (like "the raw and the cooked") were a simplistic cookie-cutter device borrowed from the dated linguistics of Ferdinand de Saussure, the granddaddy of now mercifully moribund post-structuralism, which destroyed American humanities departments in the 1980s. Lévi-Strauss' work was as much a fanciful, showy mish-mash as that of Joseph Campbell, who at least had the erudite and intuitive Carl Jung behind him. When as a Yale graduate student I ransacked that great temple, Sterling Library, in search of paradigms for reintegrating literary criticism with history, I found literally nothing in Lévi-Strauss that I felt had scholarly solidity.

In contrast, the twelve volumes of Sir James George Frazer's *The Golden Bough* (1890–1915), interweaving European antiquity with tribal societies, were a model of intriguing specificity wed to speculative

[Salon.com column, November 10, 2009.]

imagination. Though many details in Frazer have been contradicted or superseded, the work of his Cambridge school of classical anthropology (another of whose ornaments was the great Jane Harrison) will remain inspirational for enterprising students seeking escape from today's sterile academic climate.

61

THE COLUMBINE HIGH SCHOOL MASSACRE

Last week's horrifying massacre at Columbine High School in a suburb of Denver has brought widespread attention to clique-formation in high school—a pitiless process that has remained amazingly consistent for the past sixty years. The arrogant jocks and debs still sublimely sail over the cowering nerds and wallflowers, who compensate by organizing their own pecking order, in minute gradations of status painfully obvious to everyone.

"We are hierarchical animals," I declared in my first book. Rousseauist liberals and armchair leftists (like Michel Foucault) think hierarchy is imposed on free-flowing human innocence by unjust external forces, like the government and the police. But hierarchy is self-generated on every occasion by any group, especially in a philosophical vacuum. As an atheist, I acknowledge that religion may be socially necessary as an ethical counterweight to natural human ferocity. The primitive marauding impulse can emerge very swiftly in the alienated young.

Guns are not the problem in America, where nature is still so near. These shocking incidents of school violence are ultimately rooted in the massive social breakdown of the industrial revolution, which disrupted the ancient patterns of clan and community. Our middle-class culture is affluent but spiritually empty. The attractive houses of the

[Salon.com column, April 28, 1999.
Reprinted in *The Guardian* (U.K.), May 1, 1999.]

Columbine killers are mere shells, seething with the poisons of the isolated nuclear family and its byzantine denials.

Alas, the Columbine bloodbath already seems to be the rationale for increased surveillance of young people, who are now exhorted to snitch on each other to the authorities. The brooding apartness of Leonardo da Vinci, Lord Byron, or Emily Brontë; the shrinking shyness of John Keats; the passive-aggressive reclusiveness of Emily Dickinson; the erratic moodiness of Edgar Allan Poe or Charles Baudelaire—all will now be defined as antisocial, potentially dangerous behavior not to be tolerated by the omnipotent group, which will dispatch counselors of every stripe to coerce conformity. The totalitarian brave new world is upon us.

For me, the lesson of Columbine is that primary and secondary education, as it gradually expanded over the past century, has massive systemic problems. We are warehousing students from childhood to early adulthood, channeling them toward middle-class professional jobs that they may or may not want. Young, male, hormonally driven energy is trapped and stultified by school, with its sterile regimentation into cubical classrooms and cramped rows of seats.

I found naggingly unsettling the aggressively upbeat, we're-all-family public discourse of the Columbine faculty and staff, particularly when juxtaposed with the bland, sometimes indistinguishably WASPy faces of the students themselves. The conflict between individualism and the norm can be brutal: bourgeois "niceness" is its own imperialism. Fantasies of student revenge go way back to *Carrie* (1976), Brian De Palma's film version of Stephen King's novel, where a tormented teen unleashes her occult force to incinerate her high school. The rock revolution began with a pounding Bill Haley song blared over the credits of *Blackboard Jungle* (1955), with its juvenile delinquents on the rampage against teachers and authority.

Today's busy, busy, busy high-school education seems to prepare young people for nothing. There are too many posh cars in the parking lot and too much stress on extracurricular activities. Just as I have argued for lowering the age of sexual consent to fourteen, so do I now propose that young people be allowed to leave school at fourteen—as they did during the immigrant era, when families needed every wage to survive. Unfortunately, in our service-sector economy, entry-level manual labor is no longer widely available.

At home, American teenagers are being simultaneously babied and neglected, while at school they have become, in effect, prisoners of the state. Primary school should be stripped down to the bare bones of grammar, art, history, math, and science. We need to offer optional vocational and technical schools geared to concrete training in a craft or trade. Practical, skills-based knowledge gives students a sense of mastery, even if they don't stay in that profession. A wide range of careers might be pedagogically developed, such as horticulture and landscape design; house construction; electric and plumbing; auto-motive and aviation mechanics; restaurant culinary arts; banking, accounting, investment, and small business management.

The mental energy presently being recreationally diverted by teens to the Internet and to violent video games (one of the last arenas for masculine action, however imaginary) is clearly not being absorbed by school. We have a gigantic educational assembly line that coercively processes students and treats them with Ritalin or therapy if they can't sit still in the cage. The American high school as social scene clearly spawns internecine furies in sexually stunted young men—who are emotionally divorced from their parents but too passive to run away, so that they turn their inchoate family hatreds on their peers. Like the brainy rich-kid criminals Leopold and Loeb (see the 1959 film, *Com-pulsion*), the Columbine killers were looking for meaning and chose the immortality of infamy, the cold ninth circle of the damned.

62

VOCATIONAL EDUCATION AND REVALORIZATION OF THE TRADES

Education has returned to the front pages: in the wake of the most recent school shootings, state legislatures are debating bills outlawing bullying, while the president of the University of California, concerned about low academic performance by minorities, has called for dropping the SAT exam as a criterion for college admission—as if that would solve the problem instead of merely masking it. Authoritarian intrusion and social engineering seem to be the order of the day.

The entire American school system needs to be stringently reexamined from primary grades through college. If high school has turned into a seething arena of boredom and competitive tension erupting in mayhem, it's partly because (as I said after the Columbine massacre two years ago) modern schools have become airless dungeons for active young men at their most hormonally driven period of life.

Forcing restless teens of both sexes to sit like robots in regimented rows in crowded classrooms for the better part of each day is a pointless, sadistic exercise except for those with their sights on office jobs. This school system is not even 200 years old, yet most people treat it as if the burning bush floated it down from Mount Sinai. Too often, school has become a form of mental and physical oppression.

Exactly what is being taught? Certainly not wisdom or perspective on life. Can anyone honestly claim that current high-school students know more about history, science, language, and the arts than stu-

[Salon.com column, March 21, 2001.]

dents forty years ago? As for college students, the shallowness of their training in the humanities has become all too evident as graduates of the elite schools have entered the professions and the media over the past twenty years.

A gigantic, self-perpetuating school system is forcing students along a pre-professional track whether they want it or not. Perhaps as many as half the college students currently in the elite schools may not really want to be there but have just numbly followed along in the track of their parents' and peers' social expectations. They have no other options. If our pampered students have the best of all possible worlds, why are so many of them binge drinking and anesthetizing themselves with brain-wrecking designer drugs?

As I've argued in the past, there's no way that the daughter of prosperous, successful, white upper-middle-class parents could decide to drop out of an Ivy League school in her sophomore year to get married and be a stay-at-home mom. She would be upbraided and shamed, accused of "wasting" her education and betraying her "real" talents—and embarrassing her status-conscious parents.

Similarly, it's scarcely imaginable that the son of such a family could opt for the career of auto mechanic or trucker instead of physician, lawyer, or businessman. There was a time when most high schools offered shop classes and when technical institutions gave practical preparation in the trades to non-college-bound students. As the service sector expanded in the U.S. economy after World War Two, such choices became fewer.

The boys who are collecting guns and fantasizing about shooting up their schools need a more constructive outlet for their energy—which working with their hands would partly satisfy. As for the misfits who are being "bullied" into homicidal rampages, those who find school life unbearable or useless should be permitted to leave at age fourteen (as was legal during the immigrant era) to try to live life on their own. Let them return to school when and if they so desire; the presence in the classroom of adult students would infinitely improve both primary and secondary education, since it's grade segregation by age that perpetuates and aggravates the tyranny of social cliques.

You say that the young are far too immature to survive at fourteen? Well, that's proof positive that they've been infantilized by their parents in this unctuously caretaking yet flagrantly permissive culture that denies middle-class students adulthood until they are in their twenties and later—long after their bodies are ready to mate and reproduce. The Western career system is institutionalized neurosis, elevating professional training over spiritual development and forcing the young to put emotional and physical satisfaction on painful hold.

The trades need to be revalorized. Young men and women should be encouraged to consider careers outside the effete, word-obsessed, office-bound professions. Construction, plumbing, electrical wiring, forestry, landscaping, horticulture: such pursuits allow free movement and require a training of the body as well as the mind.

POLITICS

Color caricature by Zach Trenholm of Camille Paglia as no-nonsense schoolmarm scolding Presidents Saddam Hussein and George W. Bush before the U.S. invasion of Iraq. Published with The Salon Interview: Camille Paglia, Salon.com, February 7, 2003.

63

NO TO THE INVASION OF IRAQ

Camille Paglia is a rarity in the increasingly polarized world of public intellectuals, a high-profile thinker and writer who is not readily identified with any political camp or party line. She burst onto the scene in 1990 following the publication of her book, *Sexual Personae*. Paglia was a rough-trade feminist not afraid to challenge the orthodoxy of the women's movement or its reigning sisterhood; a professor from a small college with no qualms about torching the Parisian academic trends then enthralling Ivy League humanities departments; a self-proclaimed "Democratic libertarian" who voted twice for Bill Clinton and then loudly denounced him for bringing shame to his office.

Given Paglia's originality and unpredictability, we had no idea what to expect when we phoned her earlier this week for her opinions on the Bush administration's looming war with Iraq. Paglia proudly describes herself as a Dionysian child of the '60s, a generation not known for its martial spirit. And yet, during her long run as a Salon columnist, she developed an enthusiastic following among conservatives, including retired and active military personnel, for her eloquent tributes to family, tradition, country, and uniformed service, as well as her stop-your-blubbering take on modern American life.

Paglia retired her Salon column last year to focus on teaching—she is the University Professor of Humanities and Media Studies at

[Editor-in-Chief David Talbot, The Salon Interview: Camille Paglia. "Bad Omen: Why the *Columbia* disaster should make Bush think twice about rushing to war with Iraq," Salon.com, February 7, 2003.]

the University of the Arts in Philadelphia—and to finish her fifth book, a study of poetry that will be published by Pantheon Books. She returns in the Salon Interview to reveal her opinions on Iraq for the first time. "The foreign press has asked me repeatedly to comment on Iraq, and I've said I don't think it's right as an American citizen to do that. I said I should reserve my criticisms of the administration for home consumption," said Paglia. "That's why I'm talking to you now."

What is your position on the increasingly likely U.S. invasion of Iraq?

Well, first of all, I'm on the record as being pro-military and in insisting that military matters and international affairs were neglected throughout the period of the Clinton administration—which partly led to the present dilemma. The first attack on the World Trade Center in 1993 should have been a wake-up call for everyone. However, I'm extremely upset about our rush to war at the present moment. If there truly were an authentic international coalition that had been carefully built, and if the administration had demonstrated sensitivity to the fragility of international relations, I'd be 100 percent in favor of an allied military expedition to go into Iraq and find and dispose of all weapons of mass destruction.

But most members of the current administration seem to have little sense that there's an enormous, complex world beyond our borders. The president himself has never traveled much in his life. They seem to think the universe consists of America and then everyone else—small-potatoes people who can be steamrolled. And I'm absolutely appalled at the lack of acknowledgment of the cost to ordinary Iraqi citizens of any incursion by us, especially aerial bombardment. Most of the Iraqi armed forces are pathetically unprepared to respond to a military confrontation with us. These are mostly poor people who have a profession and a dignity within their country, and they're not necessarily totally behind Saddam Hussein's ambition to dominate his region. There's just no way that Saddam's threat is equal to that of Hitler leading up to World War Two. Hitler had amassed an enormous military machine and was actively seeking world domination. We don't need to invade Iraq. Saddam can be bottled up with aggressive surveillance and pinpoint airstrikes on military installations.

As we speak, I have a terrible sense of foreboding, because last weekend a stunning omen occurred in this country. Anyone who thinks symbolically had to be shocked by the explosion of the *Columbia* shuttle, disintegrating in the air and strewing its parts and human remains over Texas—the president's home state! So many times in antiquity, the emperors of Persia or other proud empires went to the oracles to ask for advice about going to war. Roman generals summoned soothsayers to read the entrails before a battle. If there was ever a sign for a president and his administration to rethink what they're doing, this was it. I mean, no sooner had Bush announced that the war was "weeks, not months" away and gone off for a peaceful weekend at Camp David than this catastrophe occurred in the skies over Texas.

From the point of view of the Muslim streets, surely it looks like the hand of Allah has intervened, as with the attack on the World Trade Center. No one in the Western world would have believed that those mighty towers could fall within an hour and a half—two of the proudest constructions in American history. And neither would anyone have predicted this eerie coincidence—that the president's own state would become the burial ground for the *Columbia* mission.

Including one small town where the debris fell called Palestine, Texas.

Yes, exactly! What weird irony with an Israeli astronaut on board who had bombed Iraq twenty years ago. To me this dreadful accident is a graphic illustration of the limitations of modern technology—of the smallest detail that can go wrong and end up thwarting the most fail-safe plan. So I think that history will look back on this as a key moment. Kings throughout history have been shaken by signals like this from beyond: Think twice about what you're doing. If a Roman general tripped on the threshold before a battle, he'd call it off.

The Bush administration is not known for thinking twice—they pride themselves on their certitude, a certitude that strikes many as arrogant.

I'd call them parochial rather than arrogant. Last summer, Bush's tone was certainly arrogant, but he's quieted his rhetoric since then. I don't know who got to him, his father or the elders around him. Talk about destabilizing the world! "Regime change" and "you're with us or against us" and so on—impatient, off-the-cuff rants that tore the fabric of international relations. You don't unilaterally demand the overthrow of a government of a sovereign nation, for heaven's sake. It turns our own presidents into targets. As for [Defense Secretary Donald] Rumsfeld, I think he's some kind of hot dog. It's as if he's trying to pump up his testosterone, to operate on some constant, hyper-adrenaline level, to show "I can still hack it, man!" I was of two minds about Rumsfeld's snide comment about "old Europe." On the one hand, I love to see France put in its place, because of course it no longer is the center of the world but keeps insisting that it is. On the other hand, this is yet another example of the ham-handedness of this administration in world relations.

I think that Bush administration officials are genuinely convinced of the rightness of their positions, although their biblical piety is cloying. I think they do intend the best for the American people. It's not just a covert grab for oil to placate corporate interests. But I also think that their current course of action in Iraq is disastrous for long-term world safety. After 9/11, what should have been perfectly clear is that we need a long, slow process of reeducating the peoples of the world, to try to convince Muslims of the fundamental benevolence of American intentions. And we had most of the world behind us in the days after 9/11, except for the Muslim extremists. We desperately need the world's cooperation, from police agencies to informers. Above all, we need moderate Muslims to turn out the homicidal fanatics in their midst.

Do you think the Bush administration's focus on Saddam is a diversion from this global campaign against terrorism?

The real diversion is from other global hot spots. If we get bogged down in Iraq, China might think it's a good moment to retake Taiwan. Saddam is an amoral thug, but he's not the principal danger to American security. The real problem is a shadowy, international network of young, radical Islamic men. And we have played right into their hands since last summer by coming across as a bullying world power, threatening war with Iraq and acting completely callous to the result-ing human carnage and death of innocent civilians. What privileges American over Iraqi lives? Why does the *chance* of American casual-ties through random terrorism outweigh the certain reality of Iraqi devastation in a crushing invasion?

But don't you think if Saddam were to succeed in his longtime goal of building an operational arsenal of doomsday weapons, that he would then provide an umbrella for this network of terrorists to carry out its plots against the West?

But how are we going to counter that threat? Are we going to bomb laboratories and facilities storing dangerous chemicals and release them in the air near population centers? Are we going to poison Bagh-dad? This is as barbarous as what we're opposing in Saddam. We need to be going in the opposite direction—to lower global tensions. This constant uncertainty is bad for everyone. It's bad for the economy, it's bad for people's psychic health, and it's going to endanger Americans around the world. How are we ever going to do business around the world and function in a global market, when any American traveling abroad is subject to assassination?

We know so little about Iraq in this country. It's enormous, and yet most Americans can't even find it on the map. I love to listen to talk radio and have been doing it for years. But I'm frightened by what I'm hearing these days from commentators like Sean Hannity, whose program I listen to when I'm driving home from school. He's conservative, but I'm not—I'm a libertarian Democrat who voted for Ralph Nader. These days I can't believe what I'm hearing, the gung-ho passion for war, the lofty sense of moral certitude, the complete obliviousness to the world outside our borders. How many people has Hannity known who aren't Americans? Has he ever been anywhere in the world? His knowledge of world history and culture seems thin at best. This is increasingly our problem as a nation—we can't see beyond ourselves. It shows the abject failure of public education.

But there are a number of people with a more sophisticated view of the world who also endorse war with Iraq—people like Christopher

Hitchens or *New Yorker* editor David Remnick, who just came out in favor of attacking Saddam.

I do believe that Saddam is a menace and that he must be confronted. But the Bush administration is operating under an artificial timetable. There's no reason not to give diplomacy and expanded inspections ample time to work. We need the support of the world community, not just for this crisis but the next one.

I tried to be open-minded about Bush's case for war. I waited for him to present the evidence for an imminent threat to the U.S. But months passed, and they hemmed and hawed. It was words, words, words. Do they think the American people are fools? That we can't be trusted to understand a *casus belli*? There was a shiftiness, a sleight of hand, a kind of blustery bravado and smugness: "Well, we know, but we just can't tell you, because it would compromise national security." Give me a break—we're about to go to war and kill or maim thousands of innocent people. Americans will die too. And they couldn't lay all their cards on the table?

[Rep.] Charles Rangel is quite right that the burden will be borne by a lower social class. The American elite don't view military service as prestigious for their sons and daughters, whom they groom for white-collar professions. In England, however, serving in the military is part of aristocratic and royal tradition.

Rangel and others in the Democratic Party have raised sharp objections to Bush's war plans, but what do you think in general of the Democrats' response on this issue, have they presented a coherent alternative?

I'm disgusted at the Democratic Party—what a bunch of weasels. The senators laid down flat in the weeks before the Fall election and voted without a full debate over Iraq. That was the moment for a searching national discussion, no matter what the outcome. And since the Democrats rolled over, of course Bush was right to proceed—they gave him carte blanche.

The Democrats should have provided the geopolitical analysis that the Republicans were avoiding. In countries like Turkey that have reluctantly agreed to let U.S. forces use their territory as a staging ground, for example, there's a sharp disconnect between these government decisions and what the mass of people think and feel. And we don't need that—a situation where moderate governments are overthrown by a rising tide of Islamic radicalism.

I have a long view of history—my orientation is archaeological because I'm always thinking in terms of ancient Greece and Rome, ancient Persia and Egypt. People are much too complacent in the West—though their comfort level has been shaken (as I predicted long ago in Salon) by the stock market drop. Most professional people in the West do not understand the power of Islamic fundamentalism. Westerners dismissed Iran's Ayatollah Khomeini—"Oh, how medieval; our modern culture will triumph over that!" But guess what: ever since Khomeini, Islamic fundamentalism has been spreading and spreading right to our front door.

It's similar to early Christianity. Christianity began as a religion of the poor and dispossessed—farmers, fishermen, Bedouin shepherds. There's a great lure to that kind of simplicity and rigor—the discipline, the call to action. There's a kind of rapturous idealism to it. No one thought in the first century after Christ that this slave religion would triumph over the urbane sophisticates of the ancient Roman world. Taking the long view, I think Islamic radicalism is the true threat, not Saddam Hussein's arsenal. At the worst, Saddam's biological or chemical weapons could take out a neighborhood or send a drifting poison cloud through a city. But what I'm talking about is a movement so massive it could bring down the West—the entire civilization of the West. No one thought that imperial Egypt or Rome would fall—but they did.

So do you agree with Oriana Fallaci's characterization of the war on terrorism as a clash of civilizations?

Before 9/11, I would never have believed it, but I do now. For years I was saying that the study of world religions in higher education will lead us toward mutual understanding and world peace and so on and so forth. Well, the attack on the World Trade Center opened my eyes.

After a decade of government neglect of this issue, we now face an entire generation of ruthless young Islamic men who have been radicalized. The solution is not to bomb Baghdad but to win over the Muslim center, which has been alarmingly passive. We need a cultural war—one certainly enforced by targeted military strikes and espionage directed at terror cells and leaders, like the Predator attack on that jeep in Yemen. Boom! Perfect—out of nowhere comes a missile that takes them out. Fantastic! We need small, mobile units of special forces deployed everywhere, stealth operatives—kidnapping terrorists and debriefing and neutralizing them. Undercover activity is the way to go. But this kind of conventional war that Bush has planned for Iraq won't get to the root of the problem. All Bush is doing is shifting moderate Muslims in sympathy toward the radical extreme.

There may be an apparent immediate victory in Iraq, but we'll be winning the battle and losing the war. The real war is for the hearts and minds of the Islamic world. We don't want a world where Americans can't travel abroad without fearing for their lives—or even within our borders, where a small cell of fanatics can blow up a railway station or bridge or tunnel.

You mentioned that you don't think much of Rumsfeld—how about the other members of the Bush foreign policy and national security team. What do you think about Condi Rice, for instance?

I've been a longtime admirer of Condoleezza Rice, because I like her articulateness and style—her toughness and rigor. However, she might be a great national security advisor, but I'm not sure she has the touch and finesse that are needed for international relations. I like how she huddles with Bush to watch football and hash out strategy. She's got a military mind. I love her steeliness, but there's something a little harsh in her view of the world. She lacks the human touch. There's something a little off-putting about someone who has no evident romantic relationships, who sees life as basically a chessboard. One of the great moments in American politics would be if Cheney is out as VP the next time around, and Bush puts Rice—a black woman—on the ticket. That would put Hillary in her place! (*laughs*)

What do you think of Colin Powell's role these days?

It's not very clear, is it? It goes back and forth. He's caught in the middle, so that his public image has become blurred. His language is usually so bland and vacuous that he's drowned out by Rumsfeld. By the time Powell made his presentation of hard evidence to the U.N. Security Council this week, he had a credibility problem. His words no longer had the weight they once had. The administration should have been publishing reconnaissance photos six months ago. After all this build-up, I was hoping to see something more formidable than amateurish peekaboo games by Saddam's underlings.

It doesn't seem that Rice or any other member of the Bush inner team has spent any real time in the Mideast.

No, they have no visceral feeling for the people of that complex region. The Middle East has been a seething crucible for thousands of years. All the borderlines there are provisional—they're always being drawn and redrawn. So this is madness—even trying to sustain Iraq as a national entity after destroying Saddam's tyranny. Iraq is just a self-serving idea that the British had at the end of the Ottoman Empire. It's a cauldron of warring tribesmen. Clinton never understood this either—about the Mideast or the Balkans. He just wanted everyone to get along. What naïveté! The fierce animosities, the blood memory in those parts of the world. I understand it from my family background in Italy. We have long memories: things that happened decades or centuries ago are as vivid as today—it's tribal memory. That's what the Bush administration is missing about Iraq. They think that destroying Saddam will create a nation of happy Iraqis.

Another thing is that Saddam thinks of himself as the heir of Babylon and Assyria. Most Americans don't understand the pride that he and his people have in that history. They want to revive it. It's exactly the way Americans take pride in our roots and our founding fathers and want to spread American values around the world. It looks illogical to the Arab world when we say, "Well, of course we have thousands of nuclear weapons, but you can't have any." They don't see why the

U.S. thinks it can decide which sovereign nations should have nuclear weapons and which cannot.

What do you think of the ambitious scenario put forth by many intellectual hawks in and around the Bush administration, who predict that by destroying Saddam, the U.S. can reorder the entire Middle East chessboard, making it a haven for Western-style democracy?

It's a utopian fantasy that will have a high price in bloodshed. We already have one democracy over there, Israel—and it's being shattered by wave after wave of atrocities. War on Iraq may destabilize pro-American regimes there. Who knows how long the Saudi regime can survive the aftereffects of a war?

Of course some of these hawks would say, "Who cares if the Saudi regime falls—they're corrupt and their society breeds terrorism and they're not trustworthy allies."

Yes, but who's going to take over Arabia—the strongest alternative is the radical Muslims. What if Egypt goes? The dream of the radical Islamic movement is to topple all of the secular, pro-West governments in the Middle East. Americans may say, "Oh, that can never happen." Well, yes it can—because of the discipline and rigor of these radical, self-contained belief systems.

How will war with Iraq affect the volatile Israel-Palestine powder keg?

For years in my Salon column, I questioned the automatic way the American government gave billions of dollars a year to Israel without putting pressure on Israeli policy toward the displaced Palestinians. The American major media were cowardly in avoiding the issue. The best time to have created a Palestinian state was twenty years ago. But at this point the situation is probably too inflamed. So the American media's inertness "enabled" the Israeli government, allowing it to stay addicted to our profligate funding. Hence compromises were not made when peaceful relations between Israel and the Palestinians were possible. The suicide bombings of the past two years have disillusioned me with the Palestinian cause. Now I believe we have an ethical obligation to support Israel.

If our incursion into Iraq succeeds, it will clearly strengthen Israel. But if it doesn't, and there's a domino effect of destabilized Mideastern governments, then Israel is in mortal danger. It's so foolish to add more negative energy to that explosive chemical mix in the Mideast. Why give Islamic militants one more major grievance against us? This one will be even more massive than the U.S. leaving military bases on Saudi soil after the Gulf War, which added fuel to bin Laden's crusade to radicalize young Muslims.

What do you think of the antiwar movement that is taking shape in the U.S.?

Well, I had great hopes for it but am discouraged. I turned on C-SPAN with great excitement to watch the big march in Washington last month. But talk about shooting yourself in the foot! Several speakers were good, but most of them tried to drag all sorts of extraneous issues into it—calling Bush a "moron," accusing America of imperialistic ambitions, "No blood for oil"—all these clichés. When fringe, paleo-leftist voices take over the platform, it drives away the moderate, mainstream people in this country who have nagging doubts about this war. I just don't believe the polls claiming overwhelming public support for the war. I'm skeptical about the way the pollsters are asking the questions. I don't know anyone who's wholeheartedly for this war.

Whatever support the administration would have going into the war might prove fleeting if there are significant casualties, or the occupation proves costly and messy, don't you think?

Yes, but I don't want it ever to get to that point. You know, we've been bombing Iraq for years, because of the conditions imposed on Saddam after the last Gulf War—the no-fly zones and so on. In effect, we've been in a state of war for over a decade there. It's not like we've been ignoring Saddam and merrily letting him do whatever he wants.

If we do go to war, I pray it's a brief incursion. But this idea of occupying Iraq! When we need those billions here. Our medical care system is staggering, inner-city education is still a mess, the elderly are in straitened circumstances, and Social Security is in jeopardy, and we're going to spend all this money not only in bombing Iraq but then building it again from the rubble and governing it? This is madness!

Why aren't more public figures speaking out about the war, both pro and con, outside of the usual circles? I mean, on the antiwar side, of course, we have some high-profile Hollywood liberals like Sean Penn and Susan Sarandon.

Yes, that's one of the problems. Of course actors have a right and even obligation to speak out. But so many of them—not Sarandon, whom I respect—come across as witless or knee-jerk. They question Bush's intelligence, or they sneer and snort. They don't sound fully mature; they don't sound like they've fully considered the complexity of the positions that any president and his administration have to take. The infestation of the issue by posturing celebrities and the usual suspects on the fruitcake far Left make people think, "I don't want to be one of them."

And then there are the intellectuals like Susan Sontag and Noam Chomsky who've made a career abroad out of anti-Americanism. Sontag's made no secret of her lifelong adulation of all things European. My take is different: my immigrant family escaped poverty in Italy, and so I look at America in a very positive, celebratory way. So I'm reluctant to become part of this easy chorus of anti-Americanism.

I also don't want to do anything to undermine national morale, if we are indeed going to war. It's wrong to be divisive when families have parents or children in danger on the front lines. I don't want to add to their grief.

Do you think war is a certainty at this point?

I'm still hoping against hope that somehow backstage pressure on Saddam from Arab regimes will finally force him to accept exile in some plush pleasure spot. It's so late in the day now. The media should have been focusing six months ago on who the Iraqi people are, on the history and dynamics of the region.

If I could, I would assign everyone to watch *Gone with the Wind*—which is dismissed these days as an apologia for slavery. But that movie beautifully demonstrates the horrors of war. Everyone is so wildly enthused for war at the start, but Ashley Wilkes says, "Most of the miseries of the world were caused by wars. And when the wars were over, no one ever knew what they were about." The movie shows the destruction of a civilization, the slaughter of a whole generation of young men, and people reduced to squalid, animal-like subsistence conditions. And that's what's missing right now, as we prepare to march off to Baghdad—a recognition of the horrors and tragic waste of war.

64

LANGUAGE AND THE LEFT

For twenty years the language of the American Left has become increasingly debased. Progressive politics is now too often merely empty rhetoric, divorced from the everyday life of the people for whom liberals claim to speak.

If the Democratic Party is to recover from its cataclysmic defeat in the November 1994 election, attention must be paid to the quality and tone of its public pronouncements. First, there must be an immediate moratorium on the saccharine Victorian scenarios of suffering-but-noble beggars, waifs, and cripples on which Democrats have over-relied in their speeches to prove their "compassion" versus Republican "callousness." This strategy of portraying the GOP as the Marie Antoinette party of the arrogant rich has been ineffective since the 1968 election, when Richard M. Nixon won the presidency with the support of disaffected middle-class Democrats with working-class roots. As the Democratic Party lost its traditional proletarian base, its superstructure became dominated in the '70s and '80s by a white upper-middle-class professional elite whose contact with laborers was nil and whose victim-centered language about the working class was condescending and paternalistic. To this day, leading Democrats constantly project a nauseating caricature of themselves as saintly Lady Bountifuls ministering to the helpless, pathetically grateful serfs.

As a libertarian Democrat who hopes to vote for Bill Clinton again, I wish my party would clean up its act. Democrats have become unc-

[Last Word column, *The Advocate*, March 7, 1995.]

tuous sentimentalists and Orwellian thought-police, abusing and deadening language with cliché and cant. The decline of progressive politics was shown by the fact that it was liberals who supported the totalitarian campus speech codes while conservatives defended free speech—a complete reversal of their positions in the McCarthyite 1950s.

All fear of "offensive" speech is bourgeois and reactionary. Historically, profane or bawdy language was common in both the upper and the lower classes, who lived together in rural areas amid the untidy facts of nature. Notions of propriety and decorum come to the fore in urbanized periods ruled by an expanding middle class, which is obsessed with cleanliness, respectability, and conformism. Bland euphemisms and circumlocutions abound, as when Victorians spoke of a pregnant woman as being "in an interesting condition."

Working-class style is far more aggressive and vigorous than that of the effete, self-censored wordsmiths who emote at us from the rostra of the Democratic Party and its special-interest groups. Today's Democrats have become hypocrites and pharisees, a smug, clubby establishment concerned with showy, sanctimonious rituals rather than self-critique.

Liberals' addiction to melodramas of victimhood has been particularly counterproductive in the national debate over abortion. While I support abortion rights, I loathe the grotesquely inflammatory language used for fifteen years by many abortion organizations, which portray their opponents as "fanatics" and "right-wing extremists . . . fanning the flames of pro-choice hatred." Pro-life activists, in this view, are never motivated by ethics; they are "opponents of women's empowerment" determined to "deny women their basic rights." (I quote from recent mailings by Planned Parenthood, to which I belong.)

The hysterical Manichaean language of abortion leaders who starkly see the world as a battle between good and evil has polarized the nation. Those women have wasted untold millions of dollars in shrill advertising campaigns whose propaganda has prevented liberals from recognizing the genuinely moral forces that drive most of the pro-life movement. It is not surprising that, having manipulated their Washington cronies into using fascist tactics to curb legitimate pro-life protests, feminist leaders have now left clinics (not designed as fortresses) vulnerable to murderous attacks by lunatic commandos.

The moment when authentic liberalism turned delusional may well have been the Anita Bryant controversy of 1977, when a perky, all-American, over-the-hill singer who hawked orange juice was hounded and destroyed because she said, amid a Florida fight over gay rights, that the Bible condemns homosexuality. The latter point—which seems to me as an atheist historically incontrovertible—was never honestly dealt with by liberals. For years, Christian ministers addressing the issue on talk shows were screamed at and silenced by gays, egged on by liberal hosts. That strategy of intimidation was stupidly shortsighted, since religious fundamentalism was gaining ground worldwide.

The ignominious defeat of Anita Bryant intoxicated liberal activists with their new rhetorical style of cheap derision, which they were to use again and again. Short-circuiting serious inquiry and real thought, it was to lead them into disastrously underestimating the Roman Catholic hierarchy, Dan Quayle, Rush Limbaugh, and Newt Gingrich, all of whom were spokesmen for profound changes in the culture. There is reason for concern about a new regime of utilitarian politics that overvalues sectarian piety and devalues art. But liberals cannot offer a promising alternative until they analyze their own systematic failures.

CAMP INSENSITIVITY

By CAMILLE PAGLIA

Whereas the American corporate and academic landscape has been overrun by sensitivity police, who by workshop, focus group, grievance committee, litigation, inquisition and general nagging seek to drill into the population a neurotic fear of giving offense; and whereas perpetuation of this process will blur the sense of reality

Martin Kozlowski

and undermine the leadership potential of the young by turning them into sniveling, cowering, jelly-brained sentimentalists, we announce that applications and/or abductions are being accepted for Camille Paglia's Three-Day Insensitivity Training Boot Camp, to be held on the coldest weekend this fall on a high, piney cliff in the Adirondacks, with a schedule as follows.

* · * · *

Friday

"Toughen up!" Welcoming harangue by Miss Jane of "The Beverly Hillbillies."

Group song: "Wimps and Wusses Begone!" General backslapping.

Lunch: Red-hot Texas chili.

Lecture: "Why Rush Limbaugh has done more for American intellectual life than the entire Ivy League."

Exercise: Boxing lessons.

Music: Early Rolling Stones.

Sauna: Purification ritual.

Song: "We're Going to Wash False Compassion Right Out of Our Hair!"

Dinner: Roast boar with flagons of Viking ale. No forks. Cigars.

Speech: "Tobacco as noble Indian herb and magic inspirer of art and thought."

Movie: "All About Eve." Watch Bette Davis reduce Manhattan to rubble!

* * *

Saturday

Cold shower. Breakfast: Flapjacks and grits.

Lecture: "The history of satire from Aristophanes and Jonathan Swift to Oscar Wilde and Lenny Bruce."

Video: "Howard Stern Hosts Lesbian Dial-a-Date."

Lunch: Jalapeño casserole and passion fruit flambé.

Entertainment: Beat the piñata of Karl Marx.

Lecture: Katharine Hepburn, "Pain Builds the Character."

Video: "Great Women Comedians of Scathing Wit: Joan Rivers, Joy Behar and Sandra Bernhard."

Exercise: Snappy comebacks and put-downs.

Music: Southern rock.

Dinner: Torch-lit roast-pig luau.

Movie: "Lawrence of Arabia". See the desert! Behold the power of nature, and get over your silly self!

* * *

Sunday

Service honoring the European Enlightenment, creator of the modern world.

Brunch: Grilled organ meats and Cajun crawfish.

Video: "Drudgery," an enactment by the Royal Shakespeare Company of women's grueling daily lives before capitalism.

Exercise: Write 99 Hillary Clinton jokes and find them funny.

Lecture: Boadicea, "Why we need a strong military."

Picnic: Buffalo burgers and raw onions.

Commencement: Vince Lombardi, "Get off your duff and hit the line hard!" Jessye Norman leads graduates in contrapuntal chant: "I don't have to be nice!" "I will stand on my own!" "Humor is health!"

Ms. Paglia's book on Alfred Hitchcock's "The Birds" was just released by the British Film Institute.

["Camp Insensitivity," illustration by Martin Kozlowski, editorial page, *The Wall Street Journal,* July 30, 1998.]

BILL CLINTON: THE HORMONAL PRESIDENT

Why does Bill Clinton seem to bob and weave, drift and circle on policy issues? His strength—a supersensitive attunement to mercurial public opinion—is also his weakness. He values intuition and spontaneity over steadiness and consistency. The reason so many men viscerally detest Clinton is that he is "womanish," as the word was negatively used in the pre-feminist era. He is as moody, capricious, flirtatious, and teary-eyed as fickle females were alleged to be in their mysterious monthly cycle.

A gifted politician if a sometimes weak leader, Clinton has true charisma, a magic aura hovering around major historical figures and screen stars. This makes him a seductive television presence at a time when an ability to manipulate the media is, for better or worse, the primary tool for communication with the electorate. Charisma, as I analyzed it in *Sexual Personae,* is always androgynous. By subtly shifting between male and female, the charismatic personality has mass appeal to both sexes in the transsexual theatricality of public life.

In his quest for identity, Clinton has been haunted by two key personae, John F. Kennedy and Elvis Presley, whom he has tried to co-opt and conflate, with mixed results. Elvis is the sensual, soulful Southern boy who bridged white and black popular culture. With their full faces and fleshy cheeks, Elvis and Clinton (an activist of the

[Last Word column, *The Advocate,* June 25, 1996.]

enlightened New South) do appear to come from the same, perhaps racially mixed stock.

But Clinton, donning shades to blow his sax on talk shows, seems to work too hard to please. He lacks Elvis' relaxed animal beauty and imperious athleticism. Painfully chubby as a child, Clinton remains awkward and lumberingly bottom-heavy. Even as a jogger, he chugs. His presentation as president is much improved from early on, when ill-fitting suits, goofy arm dangling, and prickly, flyaway hair were the rule. With his pasty, chapped skin, thin upper lip, and nervous dry mouth, the chatty, affable Clinton can't capture the Elvis of aggressive flamboyance and brooding Byronic menace. As lover boy and candy man, laying on sweet talk with a trowel, Clinton more resembles the copycat crop of lightweight Elvises such as Fabian, Frankie Avalon, and Bobby Rydell—pretty, adolescent Adonises with creamy skin and pompadour locks.

Jack Kennedy's dashing precedent has bedeviled several generations of politicians, from Canada's Pierre Trudeau to England's Tony Blair. No one has yet duplicated Kennedy's suave blend of brash Irish vitality, crisp wit, sharp tailoring, and cock-of-the-walk strut. In the past, Clinton longed to imitate the predatory lady-killing of the Kennedy men, but he genuinely likes women more and enjoys their company. Indeed, one of Clinton's problems is that he craves women's approval and is addicted to their attention. Hence the feminist establishment leads him around by the nose, as in the very expensive and poorly conceived Violence Against Women Act. Clinton's strong mother and lack of a positive father figure made him appreciative of assertive women and uneasy with conventionally masculine men—which directly led to his naïve bungling of the gays-in-the-military issue. And too many of his top male appointees look like Milquetoasts or runts of the litter.

Clinton's ambivalence about authority produced his habit of skipping law school classes and (thanks to a photographic memory) cramming for exams, analogous to his sporadic binge eating. Without the long discipline of clock time, Clinton is a scheduler's nightmare, chronically late. From the start, Clinton's relationship with Hillary Rodham was that of naughty Huck Finn and the schoolmarm, who keeps her charming rascal in line. Hillary does not need to throw lamps at her husband; she whips him with words, with the sheer terror of her cold fury.

Workaholic and yet procrastinating, Clinton is in love with process, with squeezing, lubricating, wringing, and milking the hidden organs of power. He gorges on facts, yet is paralyzed by decision-making. His graceful hands, with their waxy, tendrilous fingers, betray his feminine openness and irresolution. He is indifferent to the fixed coordinates of policy. He prefers endless jawing, chewing the fat. His emotional diffuseness and volatility, which endear him to a public remarkably forgiving of his mistakes, are curbed and regimented only by Hillary.

Like the gender-blending Walt Whitman, Clinton wants an indiscriminate, all-inclusive democracy in which masculine judgment is suspended and female nurturance fills the cosmos. Unlike dour Bob Dole, rigid with testosterone poisoning, Clinton is a brilliant improviser, coasting ecstatically on the liquid responsiveness of his audience. Like the actor who lives in performance, he is in constant psychic flow. Sexually, he has never fully jelled. The White House is currently bimbo-free, in my opinion, only because of the president's chaste homoerotic bonding with cutesy George Stephanopoulos, the human pincushion and chief court catamite. What is Clinton's position on gay rights or any other issue? Look up at the clouds, for the answer is blowing in the wind.

67

SARAH PALIN: COUNTRY WOMAN

In the U.S., the ultimate glass ceiling has been fiendishly complicated for women by the unique peculiarity that our president must also serve as commander-in-chief of the armed forces. Women have risen to the top in other countries by securing the leadership of their parties and then being routinely promoted to prime minister when that party won at the polls. But a woman candidate for president of the U.S. must show a potential capacity for military affairs and decision-making. Our president also symbolically represents the entire history of the nation—a half-mystical role often filled elsewhere by a revered if politically powerless monarch.

As a dissident feminist, I have been arguing since my arrival on the scene nearly twenty years ago that young American women aspiring to political power should be studying military history rather than taking women's studies courses, with their rote agenda of never-ending grievances. I have repeatedly said that the politician who came closest in my view to the persona of the first woman president was Senator Dianne Feinstein, whose steady nerves in crisis were demonstrated when she came to national attention after the mayor and a gay supervisor were murdered in their City Hall offices in San Francisco. Hillary Clinton, with her schizophrenic alteration of personae, has never seemed presidential to me—and certainly not in her bland and over-praised farewell speech at the Democratic convention (which

[Salon.com column, September 10, 2008, eleven days after Sarah Palin was introduced by Republican presidential nominee John McCain.]

skittered from slow, pompous condescension to trademark stridency to unseemly haste).

Feinstein, with her deep knowledge of military matters, has true gravitas and knows how to shrewdly thrust and parry with pesky TV interviewers. But her style is reserved, discreet, mandarin. The gun-toting Sarah Palin is like Annie Oakley, a brash ambassador from America's pioneer past. She immediately reminded me of the frontier women of the Western states, which first granted women the right to vote after the Civil War—long before the federal amendment guaranteeing universal woman suffrage was passed in 1919. Frontier women faced the same harsh challenges and had to tackle the same chores as men did—which is why men could regard them as equals, unlike the genteel, corseted ladies of the Eastern Seaboard, which fought granting women the vote right to the bitter end.

It is certainly premature to predict how the Palin saga will go. I may not agree a jot with her about basic principles, but I have immensely enjoyed Palin's boffo performances at her debut and at the Republican convention, where she astonishingly dealt with multiple technical malfunctions without missing a beat. A feminism which cannot admire the bravura under high pressure of the first woman governor of a frontier state isn't worth a warm bucket of spit.

Perhaps Palin seemed perfectly normal to me because she resembles so many women I grew up around in the snow belt of upstate New York. For example, there were the robust and hearty farmwomen of Oxford, a charming village where my father taught high school when I was a child. We first lived in an apartment on the top floor of a farmhouse on a working dairy farm. Our landlady, who was as physically imposing as her husband, was an all-American version of the Italian immigrant women of my grandmother's generation—agrarian powerhouses who could do anything and who had trumpet-like voices that could pierce stone walls.

Here's one episode. My father and his visiting brother, a dapper barber by trade, were standing outside having a smoke when a great noise came from the nearby barn. A calf had escaped. Our landlady yelled, "Stop her!" as the calf came careening at full speed toward my father and uncle, who both instinctively stepped back as the calf galloped through the mud between them. Irate, our landlady trudged past them to the upper pasture, cornered the calf, and carried that massive animal back to the barn in her arms. As she walked by my father and uncle, she exclaimed in amused disgust, *"Men!"*

Now that's the Sarah Palin brand of can-do, no-excuses, moose-hunting feminism—a world away from the whining, sniping, wearily ironic mode of the establishment feminism represented by Gloria Steinem, a Hillary Clinton supporter whose shameless Democratic partisanship over the past four decades has severely limited American feminism and not allowed it to become the big tent it can and should be. Sarah Palin, if her reputation survives the punishing next two months, may be breaking down those barriers. Feminism, which should be about equal rights and equal opportunity, should not be a closed club requiring an ideological litmus test for membership.

Here's another example of the physical fortitude and indomitable spirit that Palin as an Alaskan sportswoman seems to represent right now. Last year, Toronto's *Globe and Mail* reprinted this remarkable obituary from 1905:

ABIGAIL BECKER

Farmer and homemaker born in Frontenac County,
Upper Canada, on March 14, 1830

A tall, handsome woman "who feared God greatly and the living or dead not at all," she married a widower with six children and settled in a trapper's cabin on Long Point, Lake Erie. On Nov. 23, 1854, with her husband away, she single-handedly rescued the crew of the schooner *Conductor* of Buffalo, which had run aground in a storm. The crew had clung to the frozen rigging all night, not daring to enter the raging surf. In the early morning, she waded chin-high into the water (she could not swim) and helped seven men reach shore. She was awarded medals for heroism and received $350 collected by the people of Buffalo, plus a handwritten letter from Queen Victoria that

was accompanied by £50, all of which went toward
buying a farm. She lost her husband to a storm,
raised 17 children alone and died at Walsingham Centre, Ont.

Frontier women were far bolder and hardier than today's pampered,
petulant bourgeois feminists, always looking to blame their complaints about life on someone else.

68

DONALD TRUMP: VIKING DRAGON

Zap! If momentum were a surge of electromagnetic energy, Donald Trump against all odds has it now. The appalled GOP voters he is losing seem overwhelmed in number by independents and crossover Democrats increasingly attracted by his bumptious, raucous, smash-the-cucumber-frames style. While it's both riveting and exhilarating to watch a fossilized American political party being blown up and remade, it's also highly worrisome that a man with no prior political experience and little perceptible patience for serious study seems on a fast track to the White House. In a powder-keg world, erratic impulsiveness is far down the list of optimal presidential traits.

But the Democratic strategists who prophesy a Hillary landslide over Trump are blowing smoke. Hillary is a stodgily predictable product of the voluminous briefing books handed to her by a vast palace staff of researchers and pollsters—a staggeringly expensive luxury not enjoyed by her frugal, unmaterialistic opponent, Bernie Sanders (my candidate). Trump, in contrast, is his own publicist, a quick-draw scrapper and go-for-the-jugular brawler. He is a master of the unexpected (as the Egyptian commander Achillas calls Julius Caesar in the Liz Taylor *Cleopatra*). The massive size of Hillary's imperialist operation makes her seem slow and heavy. Trump is like a raffish buccaneer, leaping about the rigging like the breezy Douglas Fairbanks or Errol Flynn, while Hillary is the stiff, sequestered admiral of a bullion-

[Salon.com column, May 19, 2016, two weeks after Donald Trump became the presumptive Republican nominee.]

laden armada of Spanish galleons, a low-in-the-water easy mark as they creak and sway amid the rolling swells.

The drums had been beating for weeks about a major *New York Times* exposé in the works that would demolish Trump once and for all by revealing his sordid lifetime of misogyny. When it finally appeared as a splashy front-page story this past Sunday (originally titled "Crossing the Line: Trump's Private Conduct with Women"), I was off in the woods pursuing my Native American research. On Monday, after seeing countless exultant references to this virtuoso takedown, I finally read the article—and laughed out loud throughout. Can there be any finer demonstration of the insularity and mediocrity of today's Manhattan prestige media? Wow, millionaire workaholic Donald Trump chased young, beautiful, willing women and liked to boast about it. Jail him now! Meanwhile, *The New York Times* remains mute about Bill Clinton's long record of crude groping and grosser assaults—not one example of which could be found to taint Trump.

Blame for this fiasco falls squarely upon the *New York Times* editors who delegated to two far too young journalists, Michael Barbaro and Megan Twohey, the complex task of probing the glitzy, exhibitionistic world of late-twentieth-century beauty pageants, gambling casinos, strip clubs, and luxury resorts. Neither Barbaro, a 2002 graduate of Yale, nor Twohey, a 1998 graduate of Georgetown University, had any frame of reference for sexual analysis aside from the rote political correctness that has saturated elite American campuses for nearly forty years. Their prim, priggish formulations in this awkwardly disconnected article demonstrate the embarrassing lack of sophistication that passes for theoretical expertise among their overpaid and undereducated professors.

When I saw the reporters' defensive interview on Monday with CNN anchors Kate Bolduan and John Berman, I felt sorry for the earnest, owlish Barbaro, who seems like a nice fellow who has simply wandered out of his depth. But Twohey, with her snippy, bright and shiny careerism, took a page from the slippery Hillary playbook in the way she blatheringly evaded any direct answer to a pointed question about how Rowanne Brewer Lane's pleasantly flirtatious first meeting with Trump at a crowded 1990 pool party at Mar-a-Lago ended up being called "a debasing face-to-face encounter" in the *Times*. The hidden agenda of advocacy journalism has rarely been caught so red-handed.

The supreme irony of the *Times'* vacuous coverage is that the early 1990s banquet-hall photograph of the unmarried Rowanne Brewer and Donald Trump illustrating it is the sexiest picture published in the mainstream media in years. Not since Melissa Forde's brilliant 2012 Instagram portraits of a pensive Rihanna smoking a cigarillo as she lounged half-nude in a fur-trimmed parka next to a fireplace have I seen anything so charismatically sensual.

Small and blurry in the print edition, the Brewer-Trump photo in online digital format positively pops with you-are-there luminosity. Her midnight-blue evening dress opulently cradling her bare shoulders, Rowanne is all flowing, glossy hair, ample, cascading bosom, and radiant, lushly crimson Rita Hayworth smile. The hovering Trump, bedecked with the phallic tongue of a violet Celtic floral tie, is in Viking mode, looking like a triumphant dragon on the thrusting prow of a long boat. "To the victor belong the spoils!" I said to myself in admiration, as seductive images from Babylon to Paris flashed through my mind. Yes, here is all the sizzling glory of hormonal sex differentiation, which the grim commissars of campus gender studies will never wipe out!

Hey, none of this should make Trump president. But I applaud this accidental contribution by the blundering *New York Times* to the visual archive of modern sex. We've been in a long, dry-gulch period of dully politicized sex, which is now sputtering out into round-the-clock crusades for transgender bathrooms—knuckle-rapping morality repackaged as hygiene. An entire generation has been born and raised since the last big epiphany of molten onscreen sexuality—Sharon Stone's epochal and ravishingly enigmatic performance in *Basic Instinct* (1992). Maybe we need Trump the movie mogul most of all. Forget all that Capitol Hill and Foggy Bottom tsuris—let's steer Trump to Hollywood!

RELIGION

69

JESUS AND THE BIBLE

I'm a right-wing, pro-life, Christian, Republican extremist. In your column, you said you were an atheist. The Old Testament of the Bible predicted the coming of Jesus as the Savior of all mankind, and all of those detailed predictions, written hundreds of years before, came to pass. What if the Bible is true? Where would you spend eternity? Thanks and may God bless you.

Thank you for your challenging question. I respect the Bible as one of the world's greatest books, based on a magnificent body of oral poetry. It is a fundamental text that everyone, atheist or believer, should know. It speaks profoundly to everyone at each stage of life. And of course its hero sagas, from Moses to Christ, have been absorbed into the Western fine arts tradition.

But I do not accept the Bible as divinely inspired. Indeed, most scholars would agree that the New Testament was purposefully written as a point-by-point response to the Old Testament to prove that Jesus was indeed the Messiah whose arrival had been forecast for centuries. Therefore the details of Jesus' life and experiences were tailored and shaped to echo the language and imagery of the Old Testament.

Personally, I do believe there was a historical Jesus. The evidence is fragmentary but to me convincing that a charismatic, itinerant preacher of his name was swept up into the cruel politics of the Roman occupation of fractious, rebellious Judaea. Furthermore, as a literary

[Reader question (name deleted), Salon.com column, January 14, 2009.]

critic, I hear a very distinct speaking voice in the sayings attributed to Jesus. This was a brilliant poet who was able to find simple, universal metaphors (a coin, a tree, a mustard seed) to convey spiritual truths to the masses. He was also a performing artist with startling improvisational gifts. Whether or not he himself thought he was the Messiah is unclear. A solid general education today should include Siddhartha (the Buddha), Jesus, and Mohammed, all of whom radically changed the world.

In regard to your question about eternity, I am a naturalist who reveres the cosmos and the vast organic cycle. Despite their superior consciousness, human beings, like plants and animals, simply decay to revitalize the earth. I see nothing depressing in that; on the contrary, it is an affirmation of the life force. My philosophy is very similar to that of Amerindians, who saw godlike forces in every rocky outcropping and storm. I also like the attitude of feisty, progressive Katharine Hepburn, who said, "I don't fear death. It must be like a long sleep— delicious!"

70

THAT OLD-TIME RELIGION

'Tis the season to think about religion. The highly commercialized holidays blanket the cultural landscape in America from mid-November
to New Year's Day. Believers and nonbelievers alike are assaulted from
every direction by Christmas carols and relentlessly cheerful Yuletide decorations. For many gays, end-of-year family gatherings force
a more somber assessment of the individual's relationship to clan,
country, and faith.

In the general wreckage of gay activism as practiced by an arrogant
elite in the '80s and early '90s, religion remains a supreme problem.
Leftism, from the French Revolution to this day, has never managed to
woo the working class away from religion. On the contrary, religion is
most powerful among the poor and dispossessed, to whom it gives a
philosophical system and cosmic view, vast, consoling, and beautiful.

If, as Karl Marx claimed, religion is "the opium of the people,"
keeping them in a docile state of passive acceptance of their suffering, it is also the visionary drug of artists, spurring them to brilliant
and enduring achievements in pictures, words, and music. Any honest educator outside the airless ghetto of post-structuralism has to
acknowledge the intricate interrelationship of art and religion, ever
since humans first traced animal shapes on the walls of caves.

Gay activists' open hostility to religion has been a political and
intellectual disaster, galvanizing the Christian far Right to mobilize
at the grassroots level of town councils and school boards. Civil rights

[Last Word column, *The Advocate*, December 26, 1995.]

leaders such as Gandhi and Martin Luther King succeeded by appealing to spiritual rather than secular values. During the '60s rebellion
against organized religion, I rejected the authoritarian dogma, sexual
rules, and artistic censorship of American Catholicism. As a professed
atheist, however, I have never lost respect for religion, which remains
far more sustaining than secular humanism for far more people.

A good test of the relative weight of religion and gay activism
occurred in early October when Pope John Paul II held four open-air
Masses in metropolitan New York and Baltimore. The gay press made
loud noises about planned protests. The result? A papal triumph—
and a big gay fizzle. Much of the gigantic crowd welcoming the pope
in rain-soaked Central Park consisted of devout Hispanics. A sunrise
concert was given by Roberta Flack, Natalie Cole, and the Boys Choir
of Harlem. In his sermon to this exuberant, multiracial congregation,
the conservative pope called for international cooperation to help the
poor.

Amid heavy media coverage, a major gay protest went virtually
unreported, even by the usually obsequiously pro-gay *New York Times*.
Six men cleverly invaded Saks Fifth Avenue and unfurled a long
white banner from a sixth-floor window facing St. Patrick's Cathedral,
where a huge crowd waited for the pope to arrive to recite the rosary.
The sign read, CONDOMS SAVE LIVES. Gay newspapers reported a
child asking, "What's that, Dad?" and her father replying, "Those are
bad people." When police arrested the protesters and tore down the
banner, the crowd cheered.

This incident unfortunately illustrates the prevailing mediocrity
and hypocrisy of gay activist thinking. First of all, considering how
many gay men are still having unprotected sex after a decade of
"safe sex" education, that sign belongs on the Stonewall Inn, not at
St. Patrick's. Second, the "lives" that religion saves are spiritual not
physical—a crucial distinction Plato himself pioneered. Third, only
cultural illiterates, given this splendid opportunity for public theater,
could come up with such a dull, feeble slogan, redolent of reactionary
'50's Betty Crocker caretaking.

Gay activists' obsession with bits of latex sealed in desensualized
foil packets (which they want to force into public schools) is a de-

fense mechanism to avoid thinking about their own contaminated flesh. Catholic theology is more complex, taking in both Jesus' ministry to the lepers—who represent any diseased, despised, or ostracized group—and the doctrine of original sin, which symbolizes our shared mortality, a universal condition. Gay activists' rage against the church is displaced guilt. It is certainly not the church, which counsels premarital chastity and heterosexual monogamy, that spread AIDS around the world.

True radicals committed to revolutionary principles should be able to find a more thrilling poetry for their banners. Mottos I would have liked to see fly on violet satin over St. Patrick's: PENIS POWER; LONG LIVE GAY LOVE; PARADISE NOW; SYMPATHY FOR THE DEVIL; FLESH AND FANTASY; THERE IS NO GOD; EAT OF MY BODY; SEX IS SACRED; ART, PLEASURE, SEX; DIONYSUS LIVES; BRING BACK BABYLON; PAGANS UNITE; DISOBEY AUTHORITY; FREE YOUR MIND.

Until gay activism gets over its adolescent scorn for religion, gays will continue to lose ground in the culture wars. The great world religions contain thousands of years of accumulated human experience and spiritual symbolism. To compete with that wealth, gays must take ideas more seriously and directly engage the general discourse. Modern reform, from Martin Luther to Rousseau and Marx, shows that all fundamental change begins in the mind. Right now it's that old-time religion, not liberal activism, that has won the people's hearts.

71

CULTS AND COSMIC CONSCIOUSNESS: RELIGIOUS VISION IN THE AMERICAN 1960S

1. ECLIPSE BY POLITICS

Commentary on the 1960s has been massive. Law and politics in that turbulent decade are well-documented but remain controversial, and the same thing can be said of contemporary innovations in mass media and the arts. One major area remains ambiguous or poorly assimilated, however—the new religious vision, which for a tantalizing moment in the American Sixties brought East and West together in a progressive cultural synthesis. Its promise was never completely fulfilled, for reasons I will try to sketch here. But the depth and authenticity of that spiritual shift need to be more widely acknowledged.

A political model currently governs interpretations of the Sixties because of the enduring reform movements born in that period, including environmentalism, feminism, and gay liberation. Their mobilizing energy, as well as the organizational style that would also be adopted by antiwar protests, initially came from the civil rights movement sparked by the U.S. Supreme Court's 1954 decision declaring segregation in public schools unconstitutional. In that crusade, it must be remembered, ordained Protestant ministers such as Martin

[An expanded version of a lecture delivered on March 26, 2002, at Yale University, sponsored by the Institute for the Advanced Study of Religion at Yale. Published in *Arion*, Winter 2003.]

Luther King, Jr., played a leading role, as they also had in nineteenth-century abolitionism. The civil rights movement, with its hymns and anthems, appealed not just to secular standards of social justice but to a higher moral code.

Political expression on the Left in the American Sixties was split. Radical activists such as Students for a Democratic Society (1960–68) drew their ideology from Marxism, with its explicit atheism. But demonstrations with a large hippie contingent often mixed politics with occultism—magic and witchcraft along with costumes and symbolism drawn from Native American religion, Hinduism, and Buddhism. For example, at the mammoth antiwar protest near Washington, D.C., in October 1967, Yippies performed a mock-exorcism to levitate the Pentagon and cast out its demons. Not since early nineteenth-century Romanticism had there been such a strange mix of revolutionary politics with ecstatic nature-worship and sex-charged self-transformation. It is precisely this phantasmagoric religious vision that distinguishes the New Left of the American 1960s from the Old Left of the American 1930s and from France's failed leftist insurgency of 1968, both of which were conventionally Marxist in their indifference or antagonism to religion.

Members of the Sixties counterculture were passionately committed to political reform, yet they were also seeking the truth about life outside religious and social institutions. Despite their ambivalence toward authority, however, they often sought gurus—mentors or guides, who sometimes proved fallible. One problem was that the more the mind was opened to what was commonly called "cosmic consciousness" (a hippie rubric of the Sixties), the less meaningful politics or social structure became, melting into the Void. Civil rights and political reform are in fact Western ideals: Hinduism and Buddhism, by extinguishing the ego and urging acceptance of ultimate reality, see suffering and injustice as essential conditions of life that cannot be changed but only endured. Alteration of consciousness—"blowing your mind"—became an end or value in itself in the Sixties. Drugs remade the Western world-view by shattering conventions of time, space, and personal identity. Unfortunately, revelation was sometimes indistinguishable from delusion. The neurological risks of long-term drug use were denied or underestimated: the most daring Sixties questers lost the ability to articulate and transmit their spiritual legacy to posterity.

The source material in this area is voluminous but uneven in quality, partly because Sixties chronicles at their most colorful often rely on anecdote and hearsay. Hence, much of the present essay is provisional. My aim is to trace lines of influence and to suggest historical parallels—an overview that might aid teachers in the U.S. and abroad who are interested in developing interdisciplinary courses about the Sixties.

2. CULTS ANCIENT AND MODERN

Tens of thousands of young people in the American Sixties drifted or broke away from parents to explore alternative world-views and life-styles. A minority actually joined communes or cults. These varied in philosophy and regime from the mild to the extreme. The true cults that proliferated in the American Sixties and early Seventies resemble those of the Hellenistic and imperial Roman eras. Such phenomena are symptoms of cultural fracturing in cosmopolitan periods of rapid expansion and mobility. Consisting of small groups of the disaffected or rootless, cults are sects that may or may not evolve into full religions. Hence, the cult phenomenon even at its most bizarre demonstrates the sociological dynamic of the birth of religions, as they flare up, coalesce, and strengthen or sputter out and vanish. A cult is a foster family that requires complete severance from past connections—kin, spouses, friends. Membership in cults may begin with a sudden conversion experience where an individual feels that ultimate truth has been glimpsed. This may lead to zealotry, the conviction that the cult view is the only possible view, which therefore must be promulgated to the benighted or is too refined to be understood by others. A persecution complex and siege mentality may result: cult members feel that the world is the enemy and that only martyrdom will vindicate their faith.

During the Hellenistic and imperial Roman periods, transnational mystery religions competed with the established state religions of the Olympian or civic gods, whose official worship was public and often located in city centers. The mammoth dissemination of Olympian images in sculptures and artifacts has resulted in Greco-Roman religion, from the excavation of Rome at the Renaissance, being portrayed by neoclassicism as stabler or more uniform than it was. Mystery religions, which generally produced fewer and less monumental stone or chryselephantine idols, offered personal salvation through initiation into an enlightened group bound by some special secret, often involving the promise of an afterlife, a recompense for present miseries. Hence mystery religions had great appeal to the powerless and dispossessed.

The major Mediterranean mystery religions—of Dionysus, Demeter, Isis, and Mithras—anticipated, influenced, or vied with Christianity. Compared to the sometimes dryly contractual veneration of the Olympians, mystery religion was characterized by a worshipper's powerful identification with and emotional connection to the god. Christianity, based on the teachings of Jesus of Nazareth, one of many itinerant preachers in Palestine, emerged from a proliferation of splinter sects in Judaism, among which were the Essenes, who left the famous Dead Sea Scrolls in jars found just after World War Two in caves near Qumran in Israel. The Essenes, ascetic and celibate hermits with an apocalyptic theology, were a cult by any modern definition. The American Sixties, I submit, had a climate of spiritual crisis and political unrest similar to that of ancient Palestine, then under Roman occupation. But this time the nascent religions faltered under the pitiless scrutiny of modern media. Few prophets or messiahs could survive the deglamorizing eye of the invasive TV camera.

Yet a major source of cultic energies in twentieth-century America was the entertainment industry: the Hollywood studio system, cohering during and just after World War One, projected its manufactured stars as simulacra of the pagan pantheon. Frenzied fans (a word derived from the Latin *fanatici,* for maddened worshippers of Cybele) had already been generated by grand opera in the late-seventeenth and eighteenth centuries, when castrati sang female roles and were the dizzy object of coterie speculation and intrigue. Modern mass media immensely extended and broadened that phenomenon. Outbursts of quasi-religious emotion could be seen in the hysterical response of female fans to Rudolph Valentino, Frank Sinatra, Elvis Presley, and the Beatles. Eroticism mixed with death is archetypally potent: there were nearly riots by distraught mourners after Valentino's death from a perforated ulcer at age thirty-one in 1926. The rumor that Elvis lives is still stubbornly planted in the culture, as if he were a demigod who could conquer natural law. Tabloids have touted Presley's canonization as the first Protestant saint. The same myth of surviving death is attached to rock star Jim Morrison, whose Paris grave has become a magnet for hippies of many nations.

Cultism of this demonstrative kind is persistently associated with androgynous young men, half sweet, half surly, who like Adonis are sometimes linked with mother figures. Presley, for example, sank into depression and never fully recovered from his mother's unexpected death at age forty-six in 1958; after long substance abuse, he died prematurely at age forty-two in 1977. Rock music, even at its most macho, has repeatedly produced pretty, long-haired boys who mesmerize both sexes and who hauntingly resemble ancient sculptures of Antinous, the beautiful, ill-fated youth beloved by the Roman emperor Hadrian. It's no coincidence that it was Paul McCartney, the "cutest" and most girlish of the Beatles, who inspired a false rumor that swept the world in 1969 that he was dead. Beatles songs and album covers were feverishly scrutinized for clues and coded messages: I myself contributed to this pandemonium by calling a New Haven radio station to identify mortuary lines from *King Lear* submerged in the climactic cacophony of "I Am the Walrus." In cultic experience, death is sexy. The hapless McCartney had become Adonis, the dying god of fertility myth who was the epicene prototype for the deified Antinous: after Antinous drowned in the Nile in 130 A.D., the grief-stricken Hadrian had him memorialized in shrines all over the Mediterranean, where ravishing cult statues often showed the pensive youth crowned with the grapes and vines of Dionysus.

The evangelical fervor felt by many heretical young people in the 1960s was powered by rock music, which at that moment was becoming an art form. The big beat came from late-'40s and '50s African-American rhythm and blues. But the titanic, all-enveloping sound of rock was produced by powerful, new amplification technology that subordinated the mind and activated the body in a way more extreme than anything seen in Western culture since the ancient Roman Bacchanalia. Through the sensory assault of that thunderous music, a whole generation tapped into natural energies, tangible proof of humanity's link to the cosmos.

"Flower power," the pacifist Sixties credo, was a sentimentalized, neo-Romantic version of earth cult, which underlay the ancient worship of Dionysus. In the *Bacchae*, Euripides saw nature's frightful, destructive side, but that perception was gradually lost over time. *Bacchanalia* is the Latin term for the Dionysian ritual *orgia* (root of the English word "orgy"), where celebrants maddened by drink, drugs, and wildly rhythmic music went into ecstasy (*ecstasis*, "standing outside of"), abandoning or transcending their ordinary selves. Hence the association of Dionysus (called *Lusios*, the "Liberator") with theater. The Bacchanalia arrived in southern Italy from Greece in the fifth century B.C. and eventually spread to Rome. Celebrants decked with myrtle and ivy danced to flutes and cymbals through city parks and woods in festivities that became notorious for open sexual promiscuity and opportunistic crime. After repeated outbreaks following the Second Punic War, the Bacchanalia were declared a threat to public order and officially suppressed by the Roman Senate in 186 B.C. But their influence persisted, as attested by Dionysian designs on sarcophagi and the walls of private villas. In the ruins of Pompeii, the hedonistic resort destroyed by a volcanic eruption in 79 A.D., there is evidence that the Bacchanalia had evolved into private sex clubs. This process of secularization, where sex divorced from cosmology becomes permissively recreational, can also be seen in the transition from the hippie Sixties to the manic Seventies and early Eighties: sex detached from Romantic nature cult withdrew to glitzy urban discos, bathhouses, and sex clubs like Plato's Retreat.

3. NEW MESSIAHS AND CULTURAL POLARIZATION

What we think of as the 1960s was really concentrated into the half-dozen years after the assassination of John F. Kennedy in 1963. Cultural changes exploded and burnt themselves out with tremendous speed. The religious impulse of the Sixties has been obscured by a series of scandals that began mid-decade and spilled into the 1970s—communes that failed, charismatic leaders who turned psychotic, cults that ended in crime and murder. The sensational chain of events began with the dismissal in 1963 of Timothy Leary and his colleague Richard Alpert from psychology lectureships at Harvard for experimenting with LSD on student volunteers. This episode first brought LSD to public attention. An Irish Catholic turned self-described prophet, Leary envisioned a world network of "psychedelic churches" whose Vatican would be his League for Spiritual Discovery (acronym: LSD), headquartered in Millbrook, New York, until it was closed after a 1966 police raid led by Dutchess County assistant prosecutor G. Gordon Liddy. Though registered as a religious institution, the League was noted for its sex parties—reportedly a frequent attraction of Leary's Harvard offices as well.

The optimistic Sixties saga degenerated into horrifying incidents of group psychology gone wrong. Most notorious is the case of Charles Manson, a drifter who became a fixture of San Francisco's Haight-Ashbury district during its famous 1967 "Summer of Love" and who gathered a group of fanatical devotees, hippie girls who thought he was both Jesus Christ and the devil. Though barely 5'2" tall, Manson had hypnotic powers as a cult leader. He became patriarch of the "Family," a commune on a ranch near Los Angeles where heavy use of a cornucopia of drugs was promoted and ritualistic group sex practiced. A student of the Bible, Manson believed that the Book of Revelation prophesied the Beatles: modern pop culture, in other words, had an apocalyptic religious meaning. In August 1969, Manson dispatched a hit squad to slaughter seven people in two nights, including the actress Sharon Tate, living in a rented house in the Hollywood Hills. The details still shock: in jailhouse confessions, Manson's girls boasted of the "sexual release" they felt in their Maenadic frenzy as they plunged their knives into their victims. Tate, eight months pregnant, was stabbed sixteen times and a male companion fifty-one times.

By the 1970s, cults seemed increasingly psychopathic. Radical political cells like the bomb-making Weathermen or the Symbionese Liberation Army, who kidnapped Patty Hearst in 1974 and whose emblem was a talismanic seven-headed cobra, began to merge in popular perception with nominally religious groups like Jim Jones' People's Temple, whose mostly black congregation was drawn from San Francisco at the height of the hippie era. Jones was a social worker and political activist who claimed to be the reincarnation of Jesus, Buddha, Akhenaten, and Lenin and who eventually emigrated with his followers to a commune called Jonestown in the Guyana jungle. After a shootout that killed a visiting U.S. congressman in 1978, Jones ordered mass suicide by cyanide-laced punch: 914 people were found dead, including 280 children.

In the 1990s, interest in the swinging Sixties revived among curious young people at the same time as an acrimonious debate about the Sixties legacy intensified with the election of the first baby-boom president, Bill Clinton. Thus, a coincidental upsurge of cult incidents also triggered memories of the Manson era. In 1993, a Christian commune of Branch Davidians near Waco, Texas, was destroyed by fire, with the loss of eighty-one lives, after a four-month siege by agencies of the federal government. The Davidians were a branch of Seventh-Day Adventists with roots in the 1930s. Their leader, David Koresh, called himself "Yahweh" and kept a harem. In 1997, thirty-nine bodies, all wearing Nike sneakers and draped in purple shrouds, were found in a house near San Diego, California. An obscure cult led by Marshall Applewhite, the son of a Presbyterian minister, had committed mass suicide in the expectation of ascent to heaven, signaled by the Hale-Bopp comet. The cult followed a strict code of celibacy: Applewhite and seven other men had been surgically castrated to avoid homosexual temptation.

These sensational cases further distorted and distanced the religious dimension of the Sixties. Though there are cults abroad—the Armageddon-style Solar Temple that resulted in fifty-three suicides in Switzerland in 1994 or the Aum Shinrikyo group who released sarin gas in the Tokyo subway in 1995, killing twelve and injuring 5,000—it is primarily in American culture that the Sixties drama of idealism and disillusion has been played out. The Sixties lost credibility through their own manifest excesses, which produced the counterreaction of Christian fundamentalism. The American evangelical and pentecostal movements, already stirring again in the early 1960s, gained great momentum. In 1968, Richard Nixon won the White House on a law-and-order platform; by 1976, a "born-again" Southern Baptist, Jimmy Carter, was elected president.

The Sixties were the breeding ground for the depressingly formulaic political and cultural pattern of the last thirty-five years—a rigid polarization of liberals and conservatives, with each group striking predictable postures and mouthing sanctimonious platitudes. Gradations of political thought have been lost. One reason is that liberals have shown continual disrespect for religion, thereby allowing conservatives to take the high road and claim to be God's agents in defending traditional values. Liberals have forgotten the religious ferment on the Left in the Sixties, so that progressive politics has too often become a sterile instrument of government manipulation, as if social-welfare agencies and federal programs could bring salvation. Memories of the Sixties have been censored out of embarrassment, since the flakiest of Sixties happenings seemed to delegitimize the period's political ideals.

On the other hand, it could be argued that there are traces of Sixties religiosity in the liberalism of recent decades. An obvious example is the Arcadian matriarchal myth of "the Goddess" that emerged in feminism and lesbian separatism in the 1970s and still flourishes in innumerable books still in print. A second example is the puritanical feminist ideology typified in the 1980s by Catharine MacKinnon and Andrea Dworkin, who allied with far Right Christians in an anti-pornography crusade that threatened First Amendment liberties. With its ironclad dogma and inquisitional style, the "political correctness" of the 1980s should be regarded as a cult that brainwashed even sophisticated journalists until their deprogramming in the pro-sex 1990s. A third example is post-structuralism, which has infested American humanities departments since the late 1970s: the uncritical academic adulation of Jacques Derrida, Jacques Lacan, and Michel Foucault is an insular and self-referential cult that treats pointlessly cryptic texts as Holy Writ.

Religion has always been central to American identity: affiliation with or flight from family faith remains a primary term of our self-description. America, of course, began in religious dissidence: many early Northeastern colonists, such as the Pilgrims, were seventeenth-century Separatists who had seceded from the Church of England. Psychic repressions perhaps produced by Protestant rationalism and intolerance of dissent among the Massachusetts Puritans erupted in the Salem witch-trials (1692), whose lurid imagery of sex and demonism oddly resembles that of modern popular culture. The compulsive cycle of sexual license and puritan backlash remains a deep-seated pattern in American culture.

The 1960s' combination of spirituality with progressive politics was prefigured by the reformist world-view of the Quakers (the Religious Society of Friends), who emigrated to America in the seventeenth century after persecution in England. The Quakers rejected materialism, authority, and hierarchy and espoused pacifism, social activism, sexual egalitarianism, and liberty of conscience. The Shakers (a slang term that described their ecstatic transports) were English Quakers who emigrated to America for religious freedom in the late eighteenth century. Nineteenth-century Shaker communities were known for their code of celibacy and communal property as well as their plain style of furniture and crafts that would influence minimalist modern design.

The Mennonites, another sect in search of religious freedom, were Dutch and Swiss Anabaptists who fled to Germany and then to America in the late seventeenth century. Their most conservative branch, the Amish, still live in rural central Pennsylvania and reject electricity, automobiles, and contemporary clothing. The most successful of America's nonconformist sects, Mormonism (the Church of Jesus Christ of Latter-Day Saints), was founded by a self-proclaimed prophet, Joseph Smith, in upstate New York in 1830 and eventually found refuge in Utah. (The Mormons clashed with the federal government in 1852 when they adopted the Old Testament practice of polygamy, later renounced.) There were many, short-lived utopian communities in the nineteenth century, such as Brook Farm (1841–47) and the "new Eden" of Fruitlands (1843–44), both established by Transcendentalists in Massachusetts. In Central New York, the Oneida Community (1848–81) were Christian Perfectionists who advocated communal property and open marriage.

Hence the religious dissidence and secessionist tendencies of the

1960s were simply a new version of a long American tradition. The decade's politics loom large partly because demonstrations, unlike inner journeys, were photographable and indeed often staged for the camera. Today's young people learn about the Sixties through a welter of video clips of JFK's limousine in Dallas, Vietnamese firefights, and hippies draped in buckskin and love beads. Furthermore, the most fervent of the decade's spiritual questers followed Timothy Leary's advice to "Turn on, tune in, and drop out" and removed themselves from career tracks and institutions, which they felt were too corrupt to reform. The testimony of those radical explorers of inner space has largely been lost: they ruined their minds and bodies by overrelying on drugs as a shortcut to religious illumination.

The absence of those Sixties seekers from the arena of general cultural criticism can be seen in the series of unresolved controversies in the last two decades over the issue of blasphemy in art. With the triumph of avant-garde modernism by the mid-twentieth century, few ambitious young artists would dare to show religious work. Though museum collections are rich with religious masterpieces from the Middle Ages through the nineteenth century, major American museums and urban art galleries ignore contemporary religious art—thus ensuring, thanks to the absence of strong practitioners, that it remains at the level of kitsch. And the art world itself has suffered: with deeper themes excised, it slid into a shallow, jokey postmodernism that reduced art to ideology and treated art works as vehicles of approved social messages.

By the 1980s, during the conservative administrations of Ronald Reagan, an artist's path to instant success was to satirize or profane Christian iconography. Warfare erupted in 1989 over *Piss Christ,* a misty photograph by the American Andres Serrano of a wood and plastic crucifix submerged in a Plexiglas tank of his own urine, and then a decade later over a 1996 collage of the Virgin Mary by the British-Nigerian Chris Ofili, who adorned the Madonna with a breast of elephant dung and ringed her with pasted-on photos of female genitalia clipped from pornographic magazines. The Ofili painting made hardly a ripple in London but caused an explosion in the U.S. in 1999 when it was exhibited, with a deplorable lack of basic curatorial support, by the Brooklyn Museum. The uproar in all such cases was fomented by grandstanding politicians with agendas of their own: New York mayor Rudy Giuliani, for example, outrageously moved to cut off the Brooklyn Museum's public funding. Nevertheless, the ultimate responsibility for this continuing rancor rests with the arts community, who are fixed in an elitist mind-set that automatically defines religion as reactionary and unenlightened. Federal funding of the arts, already minuscule in the U.S., has been even further diminished because of the needlessly offensive way that religion has been treated in such incidents.

This cultural stalemate was aggravated, I contend, by the disappearance of voices from the Sixties religious revolution. Even counterculture agnostics had respected the cosmic expansiveness of religious vision. There was also widespread ecumenical interest at the time in harmonizing world religions. The primary guide in this new syncretism was Carl Jung, who was the son of a Protestant minister and who began to study Asian thought in depth after his break with Freud in 1913. Jung's theory of the collective unconscious was partly derived from the Hindu concept of *samskaras,* the residue of past lifetimes. His interdisciplinary interpretation of culture was also influenced by Sir James George Frazer's multi-volumed work of classical anthropology, *The Golden Bough* (1890–1915). Jung revealed the poetry and philosophy in the rituals and iconography of world religions. But Jungian thought had little impact on post-Sixties American academe, thanks to the invasion of European theory. French post-structuralism, the Frankfurt School, and British cultural studies all follow the Marxist line that religion is "the opiate of the masses." The end result was that, by the Eighties, the claim that great art has a spiritual meaning was no longer taken seriously—and was positively perilous to anyone seeking employment or promotion in the humanities departments of major American universities.

4. TRANSCENDENTALISM AND ASIAN RELIGION

That the spiritual awakening of the 1960s belonged to a long series of religious revivals in America was argued by William G. McLoughlin in his splendid 1978 book, *Revivals, Awakenings, and Reform.* McLoughlin's point was taken up again by Robert S. Ellwood in *The Sixties Spiritual Awakening* (1994), but general discussion of the Sixties remains unchanged. The resistance of received opinion is too strong: the Right refuses to acknowledge anything positive in the Sixties legacy, while the Left rejects religion wholesale.

In the Great Awakening of the mid-eighteenth century, the Congregational minister Jonathan Edwards lit up the Connecticut Valley with his call for a renewal of Calvinist belief. Edwards viewed the ease and slackness of contemporary religious practice as a falling off from the disciplined vigor of New England's Puritan forefathers. His terrifying 1741 "Fire Sermon" ("Sinners in the Hands of an Angry God") stressed man's contemptible weakness. But the 1960s' spiritual awakening, as a program of rebellious liberalization, more resembled Transcendentalism (1835–60), which was influenced by British Romanticism and German idealism. Its leading figure, Ralph Waldo Emerson, had been a Unitarian minister (descended from a line of clerics) but resigned his post because he could not accept the doctrine of transubstantiation in the Eucharist. More generally, Emerson was repelled by the passionlessness and rote formulas of genteel churchgoing. His suave father, a Boston minister, had had the social success that Emerson spurned.

Emerson was reserved and austere, not unlike the Romantic poet, William Wordsworth, who had a similar reverence for nature. Emerson transferred his family's religious vocation to the Romantic cult of nature, a pagan pantheism. His holistic vision of nature, like that of his friend Henry David Thoreau, prefigures 1960s ecology: indeed, Thoreau's *Walden* (1854), a journal of his experiment in monastic living in the woods near Boston, became a canonical text for the Sixties counterculture.

The most intriguing of the parallels between New England Transcendentalism and 1960s thought is Emerson's interest in Asian literature—mainly Hindu sacred texts (the *Bhagavad Gita* and the *Upanishads*) and Confucius' maxims. India's religious literature had been unknown to the West until the first European translation of the *Bhagavad Gita* appeared in 1785, when Sanskrit studies had just begun.

The titles Emerson gave to his poems "Brahma" and "Maya" were inexplicable to most readers at the time. (Brahma is the Hindu creator god; Maya is the veil of illusion.) "Brahma," first published in 1857, was the butt of so many satirical lampoons that Emerson's publisher begged him, to no avail, to drop it from the 1876 edition of his selected poems. In his seminal essays (1836–41), Emerson refers to God as the "Over-Soul," a translation of the Sanskrit word *atman*, meaning "supreme and universal soul." Emerson's "Over-Soul" would be reinterpreted by Friedrich Nietzsche as the *Übermensch*, which translators often misleadingly render in English as "Superman."

Emerson's study of Hindu literature, which intensified after his first wife's death, was documented by Arthur Christy, a professor at Columbia University, in his 1932 book, *The Orient in American Transcendentalism*. Christy inspected borrowing records at the Boston Athenaeum and Harvard College Library, as well as Emerson's journals and marginalia, to trace his considerable reading history of Asian texts. By contrast, Harvard Library records showed no sign that the undergraduate Thoreau ever withdrew books on Eastern religion. His transforming knowledge of it came entirely from his casual reading in Emerson's personal library, through which he was guided by Emerson's second wife. Among the other Transcendentalists, Bronson Alcott was most interested in Hindu philosophy, which he had explored while working as a Philadelphia schoolteacher in the 1830s.

Emerson the sage was the main draw in the Transcendentalist circle. Harvard students and other young people flocked to hear him speak or made pilgrimages to his home in Concord. His warm rapport with and encouragement of the young came from his own conflicts with authority, from which evolved his doctrine of American individualism and self-reliance. Emerson's charismatic appeal as an antiestablishment mentor could be compared to that of the early Timothy Leary, who warned, "Don't trust anyone over thirty." (As a college student in 1966, I witnessed the mob scene around Leary when I traveled with other students from Binghamton to Cornell University to hear him speak about LSD and his new League for Spiritual Discovery.)

In *Leaves of Grass* (1855), Walt Whitman absorbed British Romantic poetry as well as Emerson's poems and essays, with their disparate

Asian influences. Whitman's sprawling, pagan epic (expanded over succeeding decades) openly challenged Judeo-Christianity. After William Blake's allegorical long poems, *Leaves of Grass* is Western literature's closest approximation to the dynamic form and visionary style of Hindu sacred literature, with its cosmic scale. Whitman's poem would have tremendous influence on the 1960s via Fifties Beat poetry, in particular Allen Ginsberg's prophetic protest poem, *Howl* (1956), which imitates Whitman's long, incantatory lines. Ginsberg regularly paid homage to Whitman, as in his amusing 1955 poem, "A Supermarket in California," which addresses Whitman by name.

The limitations in Emersonian Transcendentalism are suggested by the reservations expressed by both Emerson and Thoreau to the sexual material in *Leaves of Grass,* which, despite their great admiration for the poem, they felt to be crude flaws. Emerson, who had always disliked the bawdiness in Shakespeare's plays, actually advised Whitman to purge sexual references from later editions of *Leaves of Grass.* In this respect, the Romantic nature cult of Emerson and Thoreau betrays their Puritan lineage. They see nature in clean, rigorous terms but cannot tolerate or encompass nature's stormier energies—the theme of Herman Melville's *Moby-Dick* (1851). Significantly, though he enjoyed choosing hymns for Sunday services, Emerson did not much care for music. Despite the call for ecstasy in his poem "Bacchus," he was evidently made uncomfortable by music's heady rhythms and emotional stimulation. It was the American 1960s that would complete Transcendentalism—through the new, barbaric medium of rock.

5. AMERICAN STRAINS OF ASIAN RELIGION IN THE TWENTIETH CENTURY

The pervasive presence of Asian religion in the bohemian underground in the U.S. after World War Two was unparalleled in avant-garde and existentialist Paris during the same period. Anti-clericalism—hostility to priests and church hierarchy—has been entrenched among the European intelligentsia since the Enlightenment, partly because the Roman Catholic Church was once an active force in politics and economics and, in the period of the Papal States, was a nation in its own right.

The defiant rejection of organized religion by Beat poets and artists was a substantial part of their legacy to the 1960s counterculture. Their hip appropriation of Asian thought is illustrated by the title of Jack Kerouac's 1958 autobiographical novel, *The Dharma Bums* (*dharma* is a Hindu and Buddhist term for natural truth or right living). Though most of the Beats merely dabbled in Asian religion, they borrowed enough to help their second-generation fans critique Western intellectual assumptions. Ginsberg, Kerouac, and the other Beats who drifted to San Francisco in the 1950s learned about Zen Buddhism from the poet Gary Snyder, a rugged, Thoreau-style naturalist from Oregon who would later live in a monastery in Japan. (A leading character in *The Dharma Bums* is based on Snyder.) Buddhist references percolated from the Beats into anti-academic poetry of other schools from the 1950s to the early 1970s.

A Zen Institute was established in New York in 1930; San Francisco's Zen Center began in 1959. But American interest in Zen was primarily stimulated by two nonfiction writers, Daisetz T. Suzuki (1870–1966), a Japanese Buddhist scholar, and Alan Watts (1915–73), who was born in England. In the 1950s, Suzuki lectured extensively on Mahayana Buddhism in the U.S., including as a visiting professor at Columbia University. Watts was an Anglican priest with a master's degree in theology who had had an interest in Asian thought and culture since adolescence. His first book on Buddhism, *The Spirit of Zen,* was published in 1936 after he had met Suzuki in London earlier that year. Watts was the Episcopal chaplain at Northwestern University near Chicago during World War Two and then moved to the West Coast, where he taught at the School of Asian Studies in San Francisco and joined the Los Angeles Vedanta Society, devoted to Vedanta Hinduism. Watts' many books, such as *The Way of Zen* (1957) and *Psychotherapy East and West* (1961), were widely available as vividly bound paperbacks in the Sixties. Though Watts has sometimes been dismissed as a popularizer, I can attest that his comparative studies of Asian and Western culture had a great impact on me as a student. In 1966, he spent several days at my college, where he lectured on "Narcotics and Hallucinogenic Drugs" and "Differing Views of the Self and Its Relation to Nature."

It was Watts' reference to "cosmic consciousness" in his 1962 book, *The Joyous Cosmology,* that put it into the cultural atmosphere of the time. The term had been coined by a Canadian psychiatrist, Richard Maurice Bucke, in a very odd, spiritualistic book, *Cosmic Consciousness: A Study in the Evolution of the Human Mind* (1901). While superintendent of an asylum for the clinically insane, Bucke had begun to question the standard categories of Western logic and science. In 1894, he read a paper called "Cosmic Consciousness" to a meeting of the American Medico-Psychological Association in Philadelphia. In his book, Bucke attempted to fuse Asian and Western religion by juxtaposing somewhat quirky profiles of figures like Buddha, Jesus, Dante, William Blake, and Walt Whitman. Such extraordinary individuals, Bucke felt, exuded a palpable magnetic aura because they had attained spiritual illumination.

The Hinduism of the American 1960s had several sources. Allen Ginsberg modeled his prophetic persona on Blake as well as on visionary rabbis in his own Jewish tradition. Though introduced to Buddhism by Gary Snyder, the gay, bookish Ginsberg had none of Snyder's athletic asceticism. Chatty and omnivorous, Ginsberg celebrated appetite and excess in food and sex. By the Sixties, he had transformed himself into a genial Hindu guru. Playfully brandishing finger-cymbals and a squeezebox and sometimes dressed in Hindu robes, the bearded Ginsberg was a constant, mantra-chanting presence at major demonstrations. He turned political theater into vaudeville—much like the Yippies, who nominated a pig for president in 1968.

Hinduism had had an organized basis in the U.S. since the 1890s, following the visit of Swami Vivekenanda, a disciple of the legendary Indian spiritual leader, Ramakrishna, to the Parliament of Religions at the World's Columbian Exposition held in Chicago in 1893. Vivekenanda (1863–1902) founded the American Vedanta Society in New York City, from which numerous branches opened around the country. Until after World War Two, however, American interest in Hinduism was mainly confined to urban centers and was connected in the popular mind with kooks, charlatans, and Hollywood actors. Aldous Huxley, who had moved to California, studied Vedanta Hinduism with Swami Prabhavananda in the 1940s and was a member of the Los Angeles Vedanta Society. Another British expatriate, Christopher Isherwood, edited a book about the Society, *Vedanta for Modern Man* (1951). The openly gay Isherwood, whose autobiographical *Berlin Stories* about decadent 1930s Germany inspired *I Am a Camera* and *Cabaret*, had converted to Hinduism after moving to Los Angeles.

The groundwork for the Asian trend of the American Sixties was probably laid by Paramahansa Yogananda (1893–1952), the first yoga master to teach full-time in the West. Born in Bengal, Yogananda established the international headquarters of his Self-Realization Fellowship in Los Angeles in 1925. He lectured to packed audiences, including at Carnegie Hall, and met President Calvin Coolidge at the White House. His *Autobiography of a Yogi* (1946) had an enormous impact, not least for the numinous, Christlike cover photo of the white-robed, boyishly beardless guru with long hair flowing over his shoulders. The director of Forest Lawn Memorial Park, where Yogananda was buried, stated in an affidavit that there was "no physical disintegration" in his body twenty days after death, "a phenomenal state of immutability."

A singular figure of lesser influence was "Avatar" Meher Baba (1894–1969), who arrived in the U.S. in 1952 and opened a center in South Carolina. Baba was an author and teacher born to a Zoroastrian family in India. Mute from the 1920s on, perhaps as the result of being struck on the head years earlier, he communicated by smiles, gestures, and an alphabet board. He worked with the poor and insane in India in the 1940s. Baba's sometimes nebulous philosophy of "spiritual value" and world harmony, resembling that of Yogananda, prefigured New Age. In the Sixties, he strongly condemned the use of LSD and other drugs as a route to enlightenment.

The major Asian cult of the Sixties was Transcendental Meditation, founded in India as the Spiritual Regeneration Movement by Maharishi Mahesh Yogi in 1957. The Maharishi brought TM to Hawaii in 1959, from which it spread to North America and Europe. His practice of deep relaxation, whose aim is "bliss," was based on ancient Vedic literature that he claimed to have learned from his master, Shri Guru Deva. At the start, TM had more cult-like characteristics, such as a personal secret mantra imparted by master to student. The Maharishi was at times accused of claiming godlike powers. By the mid-1970s, TM was more professionally organized as a business, with certified trainers teaching the system at stress-relief centers throughout the U.S. In 1974, TM bought the campus of a Presbyterian college in Iowa and opened the Maharishi University of Management. TM currently claims five million followers worldwide. Deepak Chopra, the New Age motivational speaker and bestselling author who became a media star through his visibility on Oprah Winfrey's TV show, was a disciple of the Maharishi but broke with him and TM in 1993.

Several cults caused much public concern in the Sixties and Seventies because of their hold on young people. The Hare Krishna movement—the International Society of Krishna Consciousness, which claims to have been founded in the sixteenth century—is still in operation, with headquarters in Mayapur, India. Its followers became notorious for their shaved heads, saffron robes and beads, and aggressive behavior on street corners as they sang, shook rattles and tambourines, and pushed pamphlets. Their ascetic founder, Swami Prabhupada (1896–1977), had begun preaching in India in the 1950s and moved to New York in 1965. There he wrote books and conducted mass chanting of Hindu phrases in Tompkins Square Park— provocative activity at the time. In 1966, he began publishing *Back to Godhead* magazine and incorporated his organization, which required disciples to renounce meat, alcohol, gambling, and extramarital sex. He then took the Society to San Francisco, where it drew an enormous hippie following, particularly among those addicted to drugs. His disciples carried the message to London and Berlin; at the Society's peak, there were 108 centers worldwide. The movement won much publicity at the 1970 release of George Harrison's song, "My Sweet Lord," with its "Hare Krishna" refrain. The Hare Krishnas were pursued with huge fanfare by Ted Patrick, a "deprogrammer" who forcibly rescued young people from cults and returned them to worried parents. A former staff member for then Governor Ronald Reagan in California, Patrick inaccurately warned that the Krishnas were a cult as dangerous as Charles Manson's.

The Divine Light Mission was brought to the U.S. in 1971 by thirteen-year-old Maharaj Ji, whose father had founded the organization in India in the 1920s. Its Sikh and Hindu philosophy required vegetarianism, celibacy, and meditation. American hippies searching for gurus in India in the Sixties had appealed to Maharaj Ji, who claimed to be the successor of Jesus and Buddha, to visit America. The Divine Mission's Denver commune would become its world headquarters: it claimed 480 centers in thirty-eight countries. By 1973, there were thirty-eight ashrams in the U.S. with 40,000 followers. The organization began to unravel later in the 1970s when Maharaj Ji's taste for luxury cars and mansions was exposed. When he married, he incurred the wrath of the Divine Mission's power behind the throne—his mother, who returned to India and tried to supplant him with his brother.

As the Hindu boom subsided in the 1970s, neo-Christian sects like Jim Jones' People's Temple rose to prominence. The Children of God, founded in 1968 as Teens for Christ by "Moses" David Berg in Huntington Beach, California, were negligible in number but came to public attention when they loudly prophesied that the U.S. would be destroyed by Comet Kohoutek in January 1974. The group continues under the name "The Family" and is regularly excoriated by conservative Christian watchdog groups for its practice of free love (called "Flirty Fishing") as well as its heretical beliefs that Jesus was sexually active and that God is a woman.

The most important neo-Christian sect of the Seventies was the Holy Spirit Association for the Unification of World Christianity, founded by the Reverend Sun Myong Moon in Seoul in 1954. Missionaries of the Unification Church were at work in the U.S. from 1959 on, but there was little publicity until Moon arrived in 1971. Moon was born in 1920 into a farming family in what is now North Korea. He was raised by Confucian principles until his parents became Presbyterians in 1930. In 1935, Moon claimed, Jesus appeared in a vision to summon him to ministry. Because of his staunch anti-communism (he had been imprisoned by Korean Communists), he was welcomed by Republican legislators in the U.S. and was hosted by President Richard Nixon in the White House. In 1981, however, Moon was charged with tax evasion and would eventually spend thirteen months in prison.

Though massive advertisements for the Unification Church still appear in major world newspapers, the zenith of Moon's organization was 1982, when he sponsored a mass wedding of 2,075 couples in Madison Square Garden. The grooms wore badges declaring "World Peace Through Ideal Family," upholding conservative family values against the sexual anarchy of the psychedelic Sixties and disco Seventies. However, most Americans, as evidenced by the slang term "Moonies" for its members, continue to regard the Unification Church as just another Asian cult. Moon's Christian theology is unorthodox: he preaches, for example, that Jesus was illegitimate, the product of an affair between Mary and her cousin's husband, Zachariah.

6. HINDUISM AND 1960S MUSIC

A main aperture through which Hinduism flowed into the Sixties was popular music, which adapted the non-Western harmonics of raga and experimented with the sitar, the long-necked Indian lute. George Harrison, the Beatles' lead guitarist, was not the first British musician to experiment with the sitar, but he deserves principal credit for popularizing it in Anglo-American rock music. Jangling sitar riffs were a ubiquitous lyrical motif in late-Sixties music. At the opening of songs, the sitar was equivalent in meaning and effect to the European church bell, summoning the faithful to worship.

The first Western album of Indian music, a collaboration between Yehudi Menuhin and sarod master Ali Akbar Khan, was released in 1955. In the late Fifties, Khan's brother-in-law, Ravi Shankar, gave sitar concerts in Europe and the U.S. By 1959, Shankar had influenced jazz compositions by Miles Davis and John Coltrane. By the mid-Sixties, the sitar sound had traveled far afield into folk music circles in Great Britain, New York, and San Francisco.

Harrison's interest in India began during production of the Beatles' second movie, *Help!* (1965), with its slapstick Hindu subplot. He was intrigued by the sitar used in an Indian restaurant scene filmed in London. While beach scenes were being filmed in the Bahamas, the Beatles were approached by a man in orange robes who handed them a signed copy of his book on yoga. It was Swami Vishnudevanda, the founder of Sivananda Yoga. Intrigued, Harrison began to study Hinduism. He then traveled to India to study the sitar with Ravi Shankar, who gave him a copy of Yogananda's *Autobiography of a Yogi*. It was Harrison who invited Shankar to perform at the seminal 1967 Monterey Pop Music Festival in California, where the sitar's artistic kinship to the electric guitar was dramatically demonstrated. (See the 1969 documentary, *Monterey Pop*.) The sitar's cultural impact on the late Sixties paralleled that of the Javanese gamelan on late-nineteenth-century music. Debussy was fascinated by the gamelan (a percussive instrument with gong and bells) when he heard it played at the Paris Universal Exposition in 1889. Through him, the gamelan's Asian harmonics transformed French and British classical music for the next half-century.

In 1967, Patti Boyd Harrison, George's wife, took the Beatles to a lecture in London by the Maharishi Mahesh Yogi. The Beatles fell under the Maharishi's spell and began to dress in quasi-Hindu style, with chic Nehru jackets and mod paisley fabrics, which revolutionized fashion around the world. In 1968, the Beatles flew to India to meditate at the Maharishi's ashram in Rishikesh. But their flirtation with Hinduism ended abruptly in bitter disillusion: the Maharishi ruined his saintly reputation by reportedly making sexual advances to another celebrity pilgrim, Mia Farrow, who was there with her studious sister Prudence. The Beatles and the Farrows decamped in high dudgeon. A record of that adventure is contained in two Beatles songs on the 1968 *White Album*: "Dear Prudence" and "Sexy Sadie" ("You made a fool of everyone"), a transsexual tribute to the Maharishi's seductive charms. Farrow confirmed the rumored details about the Maharishi's blunder in her 1998 autobiography, *What Falls Away*. However, it was thanks to the Beatles' cross-fertilization of Hinduism with rock that the Swami Satchidananda, seated in white robes on the stage, would give the prayer invocation that opened the 1969 Woodstock Music Festival.

In addition to the sitar, or an electric guitar strung and played to sound like one, the style of "acid rock" that originated in the San Francisco hippie scene can arguably be considered to have religious intonations. Acid rock helped promulgate the Sixties concept of cosmic consciousness. Even those (like me) who did not take drugs were radicalized by the power and expansiveness of that shimmering music, with its unfixed keys, sonic distortions, ominous drone, wandering melodic lines, and twangy, floating, evaporating notes. The leading San Francisco acid-rock bands were Jefferson Airplane, the Grateful Dead, Quicksilver Messenger Service, and Big Brother and the Holding Company. Psychedelic effects were used in Los Angeles by the Byrds and the Doors and in England by the Yardbirds, Jeff Beck, the Jimi Hendrix Experience, the Beatles, the Rolling Stones, Donovan, the Kinks, and early Pink Floyd. The drugged mood of this "trippy" style was revived in British trance music (called "trip-hop") in the early 1990s as a development of the rave scene.

Because it consists of transient instrumental effects, psychedelic music has received far less attention than folk and folk-rock with overtly political lyrics, whose manifest content is easier to analyze. This is yet another factor impeding general recognition of the Sixties' religious legacy. Though the Beats left their mark in novels and poems, the counterculture was less interested in constructing self-contained artifacts. The enduring achievements of the Sixties generation were in music, modern dance, experimental film and video, Pop and Conceptual Art, and performance art, which swallowed up poetry. Literature is strikingly underrepresented. Literary surveys of the Sixties overrely on the work of figures like Norman Mailer, whose brilliant career began in the late Forties. The major critics and theorists of the Sixties—Marshall McLuhan, Leslie Fiedler, Norman O. Brown—also belong to an earlier generation. Hermann Hesse, whose novels *Siddhartha* (1922), about the early life of Buddha, and *Steppenwolf* (1927) were Sixties cult classics, was born in 1877. Except for Tom Wolfe's New Journalism, most Sixties culture crystallized outside the book.

The gap in the Sixties' artistic and intellectual legacy partly occurred because too many young people followed their elementary understanding of Asian religion by making sensory experience primary. Shunning schedules and routine, they sought the "eternal Now," dramatized by the otherworldliness of psychedelic rock. Furthermore, the sexual revolution, which began in 1960 with the commercial release of Enovid, the first reliable oral contraceptive in history, finally overwhelmed the Sixties' spiritual quest. Beat interpretations of Asian thought tended to exaggerate its sexual component. In 1958, Alan

Watts criticized "Beat Zen" for its "anything goes" attitude toward sex. Similarly, hipsters often carelessly reduced Hinduism to the erotic acrobatics of Tantric yoga or Vatsyayana's Kama Sutra (c. 250 A.D.). But sexual codes have been very strict throughout India's history: at no time was promiscuity endorsed. The yoni and lingam (monumental stone genitalia in Hindu shrines) or the voluptuous copulating couples on the facades of Hindu temples belonged to a fertility cult where sexual intercourse symbolized the natural cycle of birth and death.

"Make love, not war" was a Sixties rubric. Free love had been endorsed by radical Romantics like Percy Bysshe Shelley who sought to shatter the bonds of bourgeois marriage. A cheeky promiscuity was also affected by urban flappers in the 1920s, which was energized by the hyperactive dance rhythms of the Jazz Age as well as the seditious mood of underground speakeasies. But free love was never achieved on a massive scale until the 1960s, when random sexual connection was blithely assigned a spiritual and redemptive meaning. "Getting it on" meant freeing mind and body to strike a blow against residual American puritanism. By the hedonistic Seventies, spirituality had been abandoned, a change marked by the shift in drugs from communal, "mellow" marijuana and visionary LSD to edgy, expensive, hoarded cocaine, which sharpened competition and enhanced the ego sense of power and mastery. Sexual liberation, as should now be obvious, had its high costs, which we are still sorting out: sexual diseases, a soaring divorce rate, and a pandemic sexualization of media images with uncertain consequences for children. Self-presentation by early teenagers, for example, has become strikingly eroticized, leading to premature sexual pressures and demands.

Feeling trapped by a corporate and technological society, Sixties rebels tried to empower sex as a quick route to reconnection with nature. The Sixties dreamed of limitless sex without consequence—a bouncy, open-ended, Technicolor film with a rock soundtrack. Many genuine hippies dropped out of college to join communes, bake bread, and have babies. Others of the Sixties generation who entered the professions often defied or delayed the procreative principle that was at the heart of ancient mystery cult. Two new models of sexual liberation who emerged in the 1970s were the liberated woman, who put career before marriage and family, and the post-Stonewall gay man, in whose paradise of pleasures even lesbians were no longer welcome. Reproductive rights, establishing women's control over their own bodies, were always a major issue in feminism, but over the next quarter century would become an obsessive preoccupation, determining campaign politics and judicial appointments. Feminism inextricably identified itself with abortion—with termination of life rather than fertility. (I am speaking as a militantly pro-choice feminist.) Feminism's foregrounding of abortion, which caused national turmoil and limited its outreach as a populist movement, was one consequence of the loss of Sixties cosmic consciousness by the 1970s.

For gay men, free love detached from all reference to nature meant that, by the Eighties, their ruling theorist would be social constructionist Michel Foucault rather than the nature-revering Whitman or Ginsberg. Despite a Seventies fad for the virile lumberjack look, the erotic ideal in the gay male world has reverted over time to the ruthless master type of the Greek beautiful boy, Antinous reborn: the shaved, sculpted, callipygian ephebe whose perfection is heartbreakingly transient.

7. PSYCHEDELIC DRUGS

"Sex, drugs, and rock and roll" was the fast-track reality for a significant segment, working-class as well as middle-class, of the Sixties generation. Drugs melted defenses and broke barriers, creating a momentary sense of unity with mankind and the world. They functioned as magic elixirs for the missing initiatory rituals in an increasingly transient society. In the matter of drugs, I must stress, I was merely an observer: as an Italian-American, I am a product of Mediterranean wine culture, where intoxicants are integrated with cuisine. As a libertarian, I favor legalization of drugs, not because I approve of their use but because in my view government should have no power to dictate what individuals do with their bodies. On the other hand, I am painfully aware of the tragic toll that drugs took on my generation. This was one of the great cultural disasters of American history. I warn my students that recreational drugs—now a toxic cocktail of black-market tranquilizers—may give short-term gains but impair long-term achievement.

Nevertheless, it was drugs, abused until they turned on their takers, that helped trigger the spiritual explosion of the Sixties. Getting high—as in the magnificent, rumbling Byrds song "Eight Miles High"—was to elevate perspective. Aspiring beyond materialism and conformity, young people manufactured their own martyrdom. They pushed their nervous systems to the limit, until social forms seemed to dissolve. What they saw was sublime—the High Romantic vision of creative nature, its vast energies twisting and turning along a continuum from the brain to the stars. That cosmic consciousness is precisely what is lacking in too many of today's writers and academics, especially followers of post-structuralism and postmodernism, cynical systems that are blind to nature.

The association of drugs with the avant-garde began with British High Romanticism. Samuel Taylor Coleridge's great "mystery" poems of the 1790s ("Kubla Khan," "Christabel," and "The Rime of the Ancient Mariner") were partly inspired by his experiences with opium, present in laudanum, a common pain medication to which he had been addicted since childhood. In *Artificial Paradises* (1860), his response to Thomas De Quincey's *Confessions of an English Opium Eater* (1821), Baudelaire described the hallucinations of his experiments with hashish mixed with opium. In late-nineteenth-century America, white middle-class women took "patent medicines" containing morphine, a derivative of opium, for their "nerves" or "female ailments." In the same period, opium dens were common in Chinese immigrant communities around San Francisco. Opium, extracted from the seedpod of the opium poppy, had arrived in China from India via Burma in the seventeenth century; by the next century, China was the center of a flourishing international opium trade. Non-prescription possession of opium and cocaine was banned in the U.S. by the Harrison Narcotics Act of 1914, which helped create organized crime. Drugs, like alcohol during Prohibition, would be eagerly supplied by an underground economy.

William James first studied the connection between drugs and mystic vision that would become so basic a tenet of the 1960s. In his 1901–02 Edinburgh lectures, published as *The Varieties of Religious Experience,* James described his experiments with nitrous oxide, which he believed duplicated the altered perception reported by saints in their visions of God or angels. James skeptically viewed foundational religious figures as obsessives afflicted with "nervous instability."

Havelock Ellis was more sympathetic: in an 1898 article, "Mescal: A New Artificial Paradise," he described ritual use among Southwestern American Indians of mescal, obtained from the button of a cactus plant. He himself had experimented with mescal in London. Aldous Huxley cited Ellis' essay in *The Doors of Perception* (1954), where he described his own experiment with mescaline (a synthetic version of the chemical agent in mescal) the prior year at his Hollywood home. (Huxley's title, based on a Blake maxim, inspired the name of the Los Angeles art-rock band, the Doors.) Huxley's partner in taking mescaline was Humphrey Osmond, a British research psychiatrist attending a convention of the American Psychological Association in Los Angeles. It is Osmond who invented the term "psychedelic" for the effect of hallucinogens on the brain. Later transmogrified into "psychedelia," it remains the best word for the garish mental adventurism and extremism of the Sixties.

The Beats used peyote, derived from mescal buttons. Snyder first tried peyote while studying American Indian culture at Reed College in 1948. It had been used since the Aztecs, who chewed the buttons or steeped them in a bitter tea. Ginsberg took peyote in New York in 1951 and Kerouac at Big Sur, California, the following year. Peyote use was common in bohemian Greenwich Village by 1957; mescaline arrived there the next year. In 1960, the Native American Church of North America won the legal right (revoked in 1990) to use peyote in its religious rituals. "Magic" mushrooms (" 'shrooms" for short) containing psychotropic psilocybin were also used by the Beats: Ginsberg, Kerouac, and Neal Cassady had been given them by Timothy Leary in 1960 after his return from summer vacation in Mexico, where he had first tried them. Before he began investigating LSD, Leary called his program the Harvard Psilocybin Project.

The Sixties' premiere drugs, however, were marijuana and LSD.

Marijuana entered the U.S. in the early twentieth century with migrant Mexican farm workers in Texas. The hemp plant from which it comes was introduced to North America in the sixteenth century by the Spanish, who used it for fiber for rope and ship rigging. Before World War One, New Orleans was a major port for marijuana shipments from Mexico and Cuba. Marijuana use, then confined to the working class, spread through the rural South and was brought by blacks to Midwestern and Northeastern cities during the Great Migration for factory jobs during and after World War One. It was in the urban centers that marijuana became associated with music and the underground—a hip marriage that would last through the Sixties and beyond. The Beats, who made a cult of bebop jazz (a style evolving from the late 1930s through the mid-1950s), imitated black musicians' habit of smoking "reefer." Marijuana was then used by white folk musicians and spread across the country via leftist circles. It was through folk music (cf. Bob Dylan's line, "Everybody must get stoned," from "Rainy Day Woman") that marijuana was transmitted to college students in the Sixties—the first time it had entered the middle class. For white users in the Fifties and Sixties, therefore, marijuana had the aura of creativity and progressive politics.

LSD-25 (lysergic acid diethylamide; hence the term "acid") was synthesized from rye fungus in 1938 by Dr. Albert Hofmann, a biochemist at Sandoz Pharmaceuticals in Basel, Switzerland. Hofmann discovered the chemical's hallucinogenic effects when he inhaled it by accident in 1943. Because it seemed to mimic the warped sense of space and time in psychosis, LSD was first viewed as a promising mental-research drug. Humphrey Osmond tested it in Saskatchewan as a potential treatment for alcoholism. LSD also seemed to reproduce the effects of peyote in ancient Mesoamerican rituals. In 1949, Dr. Max Rinkel brought LSD from Sandoz to the U.S., where he began experiments in Boston. ("Sandoz" lingered as a code term for LSD in the U.K., as in the Animals' 1965 song, "A Girl Named Sandoz.") The CIA conducted its own tests on LSD from 1951 through the decade.

LSD was being used in Greenwich Village by 1961 and was available on the East and West Coasts the next year. By the summer of 1964, it was widespread in the San Francisco Bay area, where it confused the political climate on the Left. (See Mark Kitchell's first-rate 1990 documentary, *Berkeley in the Sixties*.) Within a year, LSD had become a major street drug in cities nationally. It was popularized by a 1964 book by Timothy Leary and Richard Alpert, *The Psychedelic Experience*. The book's subtitle, *A Manual Based on the Tibetan Book of the Dead*, showed the religious cast that drug-taking was acquiring. As a student volunteer at a California veterans hospital, novelist Ken Kesey first took LSD in 1959 (the same year that Ginsberg did) and later conducted "Acid Test" parties at his home in the hills near San Francisco. Neal Cassady was part of these carnivalesque gatherings, which evolved into the Merry Pranksters, a free-form hippie group that toured the U.S. in a Day-Glo-painted 1939 school bus. By the late Sixties, Kesey (who was jailed for five months for marijuana offenses) was denouncing LSD. His recantation resembled that of Alpert, who went to India in 1967 and became Baba Ram Dass, a drug-free Hindu guru.

Hyperbolic claims were made for LSD in the Sixties. For example, Walter Houston Clark, a friend of Leary, predicted in a 1969 book, *Chemical Ecstasy: Psychedelic Drugs and Religion*, that LSD's intellectual effect on civilization would equal that of "the Copernican revolution." In his 1970 bestseller, *The Greening of America*, Yale Law School professor Charles Reich similarly celebrated marijuana as an indispensable "truth-serum" that exposed society as "unreal." Drug taking was also a gesture of rebellion against Western commercialism: marijuana— called "weed" or "mother nature" to highlight its organic character— was the intoxicant of choice for those who rejected the businessman's martinis or scotch and sodas. On the West Coast in particular, drug takers savored psychedelics' associations with the "vision quest" of tribal shamans. In *The Teachings of Don Juan* (1968), the first of several bestsellers, Carlos Castaneda claimed, without substantiation, that he had received spiritual instruction in peyote from a Yaqui Indian shaman in Mexico. By establishing continuity or solidarity with Native American and pre-Columbian societies, drugs became an affirmation of multiculturalism as well as a vehicle of religious revelation.

The psychedelic "trip" into inner space replicated the shaman's magic journey, from which he returned with secret knowledge for his tribe. This myth of a spiritual journey was a motif of premodern societies from Central Asia to the Amazon River basin. It is possible that hallucinatory shamanism was widespread in Native American cultures because it was brought from Siberia by the Indians' North Asian ancestors when they emigrated across the Bering Strait. ("Shaman" is a Ural-Altaic word.) Furthermore, North America, in contrast to Africa, for example, is especially fertile in hallucinogenic plants. Even the species of strong tobacco (*Nicotiana rustica*) used in Native American rituals had hallucinogenic properties.

Many ritual practices, such as fasting and marathon drumming, have been used throughout history to induce trance and facilitate divination. In some cases, techniques of flagellation or mutilation resemble those of the modern s&m scene, whose devotees claim to attain a beatific state. Mushrooms eaten by Siberian shamans caused convulsions. Hallucinogens, perhaps mushrooms, were used by worshippers in the Eleusinian Mysteries. Possessed by Apollo, the Delphic oracle went into paroxysms after intoxication by fumes from a cleft in the earth. Fault lines have recently been identified in the bedrock at Delphi by an archaeologist and geologist, who speculate that the priestess was maddened by oozing petrochemical vapors like ethylene (prized by modern glue-sniffers). Drugs were also used in medieval European witchcraft. The iconic Halloween image of the witch flying on a broomstick is another version of the shaman's visionary journey: ritual staffs were smeared with a greenish hallucinogenic ointment and "ridden," to autoerotic effect.

The massive drug taking in the Sixties, promoted by arts leaders and pop stars, redefined the culture and set the stage for the decade's religious vision. But shamanistic drug taking in tribal societies took place within small communities unified by a coherent belief system. Hippies and college students casually sampling hallucinogens were relative strangers and brought with them a mélange of private turmoils and family psychodramas. What they shared was a yearning humanitarianism—and rock music, which urged the liberation of sexual desire. Sex was portrayed as a revolutionary agent: the establishment, like the walls of Jericho, would fall before eros unbound. This overestimation of sex—the faith that sexual energy freed of social controls is inherently benign—was one reason for the dissipation of the authentic spiritual discoveries made by the Sixties generation. A philosophy of random contacts and "good vibrations" built little that could be passed on to the next generation. At its mildest, the Sixties cult of sex and drugs led to a frivolous dilettantism, youthful high jinks like the Florida spring flings of the Fifties. At its worst, however, there was permanent damage that has never been systematically assessed. In retrospect, it is clear, for example, that the meteoric literary careers of Allen Ginsberg and Ken Kesey were sadly truncated by drug abuse.

8. MYSTICISM AND SOCIAL CHANGE

Social regroupings dramatized the generational change of the Sixties—the mass gatherings of demonstrations, rock festivals, happenings, and love-ins, which began in temperate California. For example, the "Human Be-In," subtitled "A Gathering of the Tribes," which was held in 1967 in San Francisco's Golden Gate Park, attracted 25,000 people. It fused politics with pop music and Asian religiosity: the leading San Francisco acid-rock bands performed; among the speakers (many in Hindu garb) were Alan Watts, Timothy Leary, and Beat poets Gary Snyder, Allen Ginsberg, and Lawrence Ferlinghetti.

While the political sentiments of young people at such events were progressive, there was often little understanding of the slow process and banal practicalities of legislation, administration, and financial accounting. Repelled by the expanding bureaucracies of the 1950s, the Sixties counterculture was suspicious of hierarchy and embraced a simplistic egalitarianism predicated on quick fixes. The basic principle of the counterculture began as communality but ended as the horde, the most primitive entity in social history. The horde is prey to superstition and panic. It looks for leaders but ruthlessly slays them, then reveres them as ancestral spirits. As a survival response to its own flood of anarchic energies, the horde automatically generates cults and cultic belief.

The Sixties horde that was a benign extended family of music-loving stargazers at the Woodstock Music Festival in August 1969 turned into a restless, bickering mob four months later at the Altamont Festival, where a murder was committed in front of the stage. The

Sixties never completed its search for new structures of social affiliation. Fifties liberalism was integrationist, but Sixties leftism, despite its claims of inclusiveness, disintegrated into the separatism of identity politics, with ghettoizing reclassifications and hypersensitive divisions by race, gender, and sexual orientation. The Sixties code of "do your own thing" encouraged individualism but produced fragmentation. Similarly, the Sixties global religious vision, inspired by fleeting contact with Hinduism and Buddhism, would broaden yet dissipate into the thousand cults of the present New Age movement.

Cults multiply when institutional religion has lost fervor and become distracted by empty ritual. Early Christianity, for example, began as a rural rebellion against the fossilized Temple bureaucracy in Jerusalem. In 1950s America, the political and professional elite were still heavily WASP. Prosperous congregations were overly concerned with social status at church or at its annex, the country club. Roman Catholicism, searching for social credibility, was steadily purging itself of immigrant working-class ethnicity, a process of genteel self-Protestantization in music, ceremony, and decor that in middle-class parishes is now virtually complete. Many of those attracted to cults in the Sixties and early Seventies were escaping mainline denominations where bland propriety was coupled with sexual repression. It is a striking fact that few young African-Americans joined cults: surely the reason was that the gospel tradition, rooted in the South, invited emotional and physical expressiveness, stimulated by strongly rhythmic music. Dance, universal in pagan cults, had been banned in Christian churches in late antiquity. Its presence in Southern church tradition is a priceless vestige of West African tribal religion.

The social changes from the Fifties to the Sixties resemble, in compressed and accelerated form, those of the Hellenistic era following the conquests of Alexander the Great. In the three centuries of the Alexandrian age, the old city-states declined, and mercantile metropolises flourished. Hellenism—that is, Athenian high culture—spread throughout the Mediterranean world via a bustling commercial network that marketed Greek art works (often in shoddy knockoffs) as status symbols for the nouveau riche. The Romans had always clothed their provincial Italian mythology in borrowed Greek glory. As it transformed itself from republic to empire, Rome created a massive zone of cultural and religious exchanges extending from the Near East and North Africa to Northern Europe. Cosmopolitanism of this kind is usually produced by vibrant commercialism buttressed by military might. But when politics have overexpanded, there is a loss of psychological security; hence the rise of cults, which reinforce the borders of individual identity.

No sooner did the U.S. displace Great Britain and France to attain superpower status after World War Two than a surge of mysticism overtook the next American generation. The children born in the postwar baby boom, who would reach college age in the Sixties, had been conceived with a jolt of military energy and were reared in a climate of national confidence. But they intuitively absorbed the hidden conflicts of the Fifties, with its surface tranquility masking the anxieties of an older generation whose life experiences had been economic depression and war. Mainstream Fifties values promoted duty and uniformity, as if to recover the reassurance of known limits. Trade always opens up travel and tourism. The international network of Roman roads (so well-constructed that some are still in use) resembles that of the U.S. interstate highway system, launched in the 1950s as a national defense plan for emergency evacuation. Ironically, improved transportation weakens regionalism and nationalism too. Multiculturalism was spurred by the jet plane, which got Ravi Shankar so quickly to Monterey or the Beatles to India and back.

What commercialized Hellenism was for the Greco-Roman era, popular culture was for the American Fifties and Sixties. Hellenism was an artistic and philosophic system embedded with pagan mythology. The unifying language of youth culture from the mid-1950s on was new media—TV, teen movies, and rock 'n' roll, broadcast by a vast number of privately owned AM radio stations (then unparalleled in Europe) and received on portable transistors. America's pop Hellenism spread to England in the 1950s and bounced back in the Sixties via the British invasion. Popular culture remains a major American export, so vital and dominant that it has rightly been called cultural imperialism. Television has indeed turned the world, as Marshall McLuhan prophesied, into a global village. However, the general style of American mass media, rooted in nineteenth-century tabloids and early Hollywood, has always been luridly Hellenistic—extravagant, emotional, and sensationalistic, with a predilection for sex and violence.

Mass media inflamed the mind, while the institutional framework was being rigidified. A major social shift of the postwar period in America was the massive expansion of colleges and universities. In the two decades following the G.I. Bill, which subsidized higher education for veterans, college became an entitlement—still not the case in other nations. By the 1980s, America was in the grip of an overpriced, self-perpetuating education industry whose principal product is brand names and social status rather than humanistic cultivation. Fifties prosperity meant that middle-class young Americans did not have to go to work immediately after high school, as their parents had done. The down side was that adulthood, including marriage, was indefinitely postponed.

Despite their material comforts and privileges, therefore, middle-class students of the American Sixties were also captives, hostages confined at their hormonal height in institutional frames without the venerable history or in-group identification of tony British schools. Classes became like warehouses, with students stacked in primary-school rows—unlike European universities, where student-teacher contact is either in tutorial or in unmonitored public lectures. Supervision of student behavior on American campuses was intrusive and authoritarian—another feature without parallel in Europe. When I was a freshman in 1964, colleges still acted *in loco parentis* (in place of the parent). Parietal rules were strictly enforced: at my public university, women students had to sign in at 11:00 PM, while men could roam free. Hence the late Fifties and Sixties were a period of high excitation yet repressive containment.

The paternalistic regimentation of American colleges was nearly military and thus can be viewed as a vestige of the national mobilization of World War Two. Students were conscripts who often dressed in army-navy surplus, and the new brick dormitories of residential campuses resembled factories or army barracks—all the more ironic since college matriculation brought exemption from the draft. There have been town-gown problems since the goliardic carousing of the Middle Ages, but the frictions of the Sixties were highly politicized. As the Sixties counterculture spread, campuses became tense garrison towns, like the frontier outposts of the Roman legions, who occupied well-appointed camps of precise, geometrical design.

Roman soldiers were drawn not simply from Italy but from all over the empire. They were stationed far from home for years and decades—in forts in the Sahara, on the Danube, or at Hadrian's Wall in northern Britain. They were notorious devotees of cults, above all that of Mithras, the bull-slayer, with his androgynous face, lanky hair, Phrygian beret, and blousy Persian trousers. Merchants, with their internationalist orientation, were another group who venerated Mithras, a Zoroastrian demigod representing the principle of light and truth. Mithraists, like early Christians, gathered in secrecy in small, cave-like rooms to memorialize a great act of ritual bloodshed. Amid the ruins of Roman camps in England and Germany, cult objects and idols from Egypt, Syria, and Anatolia are still being found. Cultic practice on the Roman frontier, I submit, paralleled that on American campuses in the Sixties, when there was a syncretistic mix of drugs, Asian religion, and pop idolatry.

Cults arise when the official gods seem weak or fickle or subject to fate themselves. The cult phenomenon in the U.S. escalated after the assassination of John F. Kennedy in 1963—the president who vowed to surpass the Soviet Union's 1957 Sputnik satellite by putting a man on the moon by the end of the 1960s. The baby-boom generation was the first to grow up in the shadow of nuclear war. In elementary school, we were shepherded into dim hallways for civil defense drills requiring us to crouch down and cover our eyes. We were taught to fear not a rain of bombs from manned warplanes but rather a single, slim, strangely omnipotent object that could find its way over thousands of miles to unleash a monstrous fire cloud that would melt the nation in a split second.

The Sixties generation, in other words, had been injected with a mystical sense of awe and doom about the sky. This is one possible reason for the sudden popularity and ubiquity of astrology, which for most of the twentieth century had been a fringe practice associated with eccentrics in Greenwich Village and West Hollywood. Zodiac and Tarot symbolism permeated the Sixties, from jewelry and album covers to wall posters. "Aquarius," the signature song of *Hair* ("An American Tribal Love-Rock Musical," 1967) and a hit single for the Fifth Dimension in 1969, assumed public knowledge of astrological lore in its imagery of the moon in the seventh house and Jupiter's alignment with Mars. With genuine poetry, the song also invoked "Mystic crystal revelation / And the mind's true liberation."

Astrology, for better or worse, was emblematic of the religious vision of the Sixties. It countered the Fifties' paranoia about nuclear apocalypse with the promise of a humanitarian Aquarian age. Astrology is intertwined with the West's pagan heritage. Despite unstinting efforts from antiquity, Judeo-Christianity has never succeeded in wiping astrology out. First refined by the Chaldean magi of Babylonia, astrology was widely practiced in the Hellenistic and imperial Roman periods, when elusive fortune was personified as female Tyche—chance or Lady Luck. Different branches of astrology still flourish in India and China. Like the *I Ching,* a Chinese book of divination widely used in the Sixties, astrology reverently connects man to nature—the link that Judeo-Christianity has always tried to sever. Astrology is not the fatalistic determinism to which its opponents reduce it; on the contrary, it is a study of nature's rhythms and cycles, to which humanity like the tides is subject.

This is yet another area where Sixties drugs took their toll. Those most attracted to astrology lost their ability to defend it. Scientists rightly dismissive of superstition refuse to acknowledge that astrology anticipated modern theories about circadian biorhythms or cycles of solar flares whose electromagnetic storms disrupt telecommunications. The science community's customary approach of derision and debunking has been futile and counterproductive: an immense alternative culture survived the collapse of the Sixties and has steadily spread to this day under the name "New Age"—which discreetly elides its astrological reference to the Age of Aquarius.

9. THE RISE OF NEW AGE

The New Age movement began to form in the late 1970s, gained visibility in the 1980s, and became an international commercial success in the 1990s. Because it is unstructured and decentralized, New Age has been underestimated as a force competing with mainline religions. It is a constellation of beliefs loosely drawn from Asian religion, European paganism, and Native American nature-cult. Its ethics can be described as non-judgmental humanism. The one common theme in New Age is cosmic consciousness, which it inherited from the Sixties.

New Age is a marvel of Alexandrian syncretism. It is often impressionistic and soft-focus, seeking "spirituality" rather than the discipline of orthodox religion. Its followers run the gamut from harried office workers seeking stress relief through yoga and meditation to "neo-pagan" white witches rendezvousing on the moors to celebrate the summer solstice. Specialty shops and mail-order catalogs supply the ritual paraphernalia of New Age—amulets and talismans, healing crystals, angel icons, incense, candles, aromatherapy bath salts, massage rollers, table fountains, wind chimes, and recordings of trance music in Asian or Celtic moods.

A principal distinction between Sixties and early-Seventies cults and their New Age successors is that the Sixties sought the release of primal energy through the shattering of social conventions. *Paradise Now,* the title of the Living Theater's infamous 1968 performance piece, where nude actors infiltrated the audience, says it all. The Sixties wanted to embrace and reclaim the senses, to plunge fully into matter, like the festival-goers wallowing in the mud at Woodstock. New Age, however, has smoothly adjusted to the stubborn persistence of the social structures that the Sixties failed to budge. An analogy might be the introspective period just before and after the destruction of Jerusalem in 70 A.D., when the Roman Empire seemed insuperable. New Age is much more concerned with the afterlife—past lives, reincarnation, astral projection.

New Age sees a spiritual universe permeating or transcending the visible, material one. This idea descends from nineteenth-century spiritualism, a late Romantic stream that has flowed like an undercurrent through Anglo-American culture beneath the official history of literary and artistic modernism. Harold Bloom has argued, in his 1992 book of the same name, that "the American religion" (typified today by what he tartly calls "California Orphism") has always been a version of gnosticism, which defines matter as evil and urges the soul's emancipation from earthly limitation. The gnostic cults of second-century Christianity and Jewish mysticism were influenced by Hellenistic mystery religions as well as Plato's dualism of mind versus matter. In gnosticism, as in New Age, it is matter itself, rather than society, that chains the soul. The 1960s, in contrast, hammered by the concrete power of rock music, grandiosely valorized sex and redefined heaven as present sensual ecstasy. The Sixties at their most radical collapsed spirit into matter. Psychedelic voyagers claimed to corroborate the Zen insight, "I am that," when feeling themselves flowing into and "becoming" the chair or wall—a perception commonly reported by schizophrenics. In Sixties Pop Art, even mundane or commercial objects like soup cans or sponges become luminously animate.

The American ancestry of New Age began in the nineteenth century with two women who did their central work at virtually the same moment—Mary Baker Eddy, a New Englander, and Helena Blavatsky, who was born in Russia and moved to the U.S. in 1873. Eddy (1821–1910) believed she had recovered from chronic invalidism through New Thought, the mental-health philosophy of Phineas Parkhurst Quimby, with whom she studied in Maine. In the 1840s, Quimby had fused Hindu and Buddhist concepts from Transcendentalism with hypnotherapy, based on Anton Mesmer's eighteenth-century theory of "animal magnetism." For Quimby and Eddy, the material world is an illusion, and illness has no real existence. However, Quimby rejected Christianity, as Eddy did not. Her seminal book, *Science and Health* (1875), was shortly followed by her founding of the Church of Christ, Scientist, which focuses on the parables and miracles of Jesus. For Christian Science, only divine power, not physicians or medicine, can heal.

The line from Eddy to New Age can clearly be seen in the alternative medicine movement of the 1980s and 1990s, which restored the

Asian concepts that Eddy had erased from Quimby. Andrew Weil, a graduate of the Harvard Medical School who had studied the effects of marijuana, claimed in his 1972 book, *The Natural Mind,* that altered consciousness is necessary for healing. From his clinic at the University of Arizona, he criticizes commercial pharmaceuticals as toxic and calls for "integrative medicine," a Sixties-style holistic approach combining the best of East and West. After his split from the Maharishi, Deepak Chopra also became identified with alternative medicine. From the Chopra Center, his headquarters at the La Costa Resort near San Diego, he promulgates ayurveda, a traditional Hindu medicine that claims disease can be cured by opening the organism to cosmic energy. Chopra also alleges that his mind technique can stem aging and bring success and wealth.

Other leading figures of this movement are Marianne Williamson, a bestselling author and inspirational speaker who first won a following in Los Angeles in the early 1980s; Bernie Siegel, a surgeon trained at Yale-New Haven Hospital who claims that "creative visualization" can cure disease; and Caroline Myss, a lapsed Catholic and "medical intuitive" who divines illness by reading a patient's "energy field" and who advocates healing through acupressure, reflexology, and "therapeutic touch." Both of Williamson's parents were liberal Jewish lawyers in Houston. Her books are Jungian in orientation but feature secular, multicultural prayers. Her major influence remains *A Course in Miracles* (1976), which she read after having a breakdown in her twenties.

The three volumes of *A Course in Miracles* were allegedly dictated by Jesus over seven years to Helen Cohn Schucman (1909–81), a psychologist at Columbia-Presbyterian Medical Center in New York. A colleague, William Thetford, did the typing from her notebooks. Schucman's father was Jewish and Lutheran, while her mother had had contact with Theosophy and Christian Science. At twelve, Schucman visited Lourdes with her family; at thirteen, influenced by their devout black maid, she was baptized a Baptist. *A Course in Miracles* was published by the Foundation for Inner Peace in Mill Valley, California. Its original name in New York was the Foundation for Para-Sensory Investigation, reflecting the longstanding interest of its director, Judith

Skutch Whitson, in parapsychology. The *Course* asserts that the universe is pure love and that sin does not exist. Though non-sectarian, it descends from Eddy in its Christian vestiges: our sole guide should be an internal "Voice" identified as our "inner Jesus."

The second of the nineteenth-century women progenitors of New Age was the occultist Helena Blavatsky (1831–91), who won an enormous international following. Her fame recalled but exceeded that of Emanuel Swedenborg, an eighteenth-century Swedish philosopher censured by Blake for his spiritualistic readings of the Bible. Madame Blavatsky claimed to have acquired secret knowledge through seven years of study in Tibet. In New York in 1875, she and Henry Steele Olcott founded the Theosophical Society, which combined Hindu and Buddhist concepts with the Western esoteric tradition. (Theosophy, meaning "divine wisdom," was associated with the seventeenth-century German mystic, Jacob Boehme, who taught that God is immanent in nature.) A Blavatsky ally, G. R. S. Mead, translated the *Corpus Hermeticum*, a densely symbolic work of Greco-Egyptian gnosticism from the third century A.D. When its manuscript was rediscovered at the Italian Renaissance, the *Corpus Hermeticum* was incorrectly identified with Neoplatonism and boosted the fashion for magic, alchemy, and astrology.

In her two major works, *Isis Unveiled* (1877) and *The Secret Doctrine* (1888), Madame Blavatsky tried to unify world religions by their shared mysticism. Her work also belongs to the nineteenth-century Egyptian Revival (spurred by Napoleon's invasion of Egypt), with its romanticized views of Egypt's magic arts. In 1878, Madame Blavatsky went to India and later made Madras the international headquarters of her Theosophical Society. A substantive result of her presence in India would be the renewal of interest in ancient Sanskrit religious texts, which were translated and disseminated around the world, providing the raw material for the twentieth century's spiritual healing movements as well as the Western practice of yoga.

Though she rejected the spookhouse spiritualism of mediums and séances, Madame Blavatsky lost credibility in the West because of her histrionic poses as a high priestess with healing powers. But her Theosophical Society would influence Gandhi, Nehru, and the movement for Indian nationalism. Blavatsky's anointed successor, Annie Besant, was a lapsed Catholic and former Fabian socialist. Despite having written *The Gospel of Atheism* (1877), Besant converted to Theosophy in 1889. In 1909, she declared that a fourteen-year-old Indian boy, Jiddu Krishnamurti (spotted at a beach by her pedophiliac colleague, Charles Webster Leadbeater), was the messianic Buddha. In 1929, Krishnamurti denied he was the messiah and dissolved the Order of the Star of the East, the cult that had been built around him. But he continued to teach his theosophical system of "self-awareness." In 1969, Krishnamurti moved to Ojai, California, to establish the Krishnamurti Foundation; he died there in 1986.

Another figure directly influenced by Madame Blavatsky was Edgar Cayce (1877–1945), a clairvoyant born in Kentucky who toured the U.S. for 40 years doing "life readings" and promoting his belief in reincarnation. Dismissed as a charlatan by mainstream journalists, Cayce prepared the way for 1960s occultists and '70s and '80s channelers like Jane Roberts ("Seth") and J. Z. Knight ("Ramtha"), as well as for today's New Age psychics and mind-readers.

The nineteenth-century fin de siècle in Europe and the U.S. was teeming with spiritualistic sodalities, publications, and art images, part of the Romantic legacy of demonic archetypes from a glorified Satan to spellbinding femmes fatales. The most prominent British organization was the Hermetic Order of the Golden Dawn, founded by three Freemasons interested in Rosicrucian thought. The Order's Isis Urania Temple opened in London in 1888. One member was William Butler Yeats, who believed that his wife was a medium and who used Rosicrucian and astrological symbolism in his poetry. The Rosicrucians, also called Illuminati, claimed their esoteric order was founded in ancient Egypt and was brought to Europe by knightly crusaders; however, it probably dates from the seventeenth century. Its cabalistic and Hermetic imagery includes the rose, cross, swastika, and pyramid. (The Nazis borrowed the swastika from the Rosicrucians because of its association with medieval chivalry.) There had been interchanges in eighteenth-century England between the Rosicrucians and Freemasonry, a secret, ceremonial order with roots in medieval guilds—though it too claimed descent from Egypt, Babylon, and Jerusalem. Leading figures of the American Revolution, such as Benjamin Franklin and George Washington, were Masons, whose anti-clerical creed was a coolly intellectual Deism.

A member of the Golden Dawn would have great impact on the 1960s: the Satanist Aleister Crowley (1875–1947), who joined the order in 1898. Crowley rebelled against his affluent British family, who were Plymouth Brethren, a puritanical, originally Irish Protestant sect. Throughout his flamboyant career, Crowley combined Asian mysticism with Western occultism and black magic. After the Golden Dawn self-destructed in quarrels in 1900, he began traveling the world— Mexico, India, Burma, and Ceylon, where he learned yoga. He took mescaline in 1910. He wrote many books, among them *Diary of a Dope Fiend* (1922) and *Magick in Theory and Practice* (1929). Crowley advocated total sexual freedom, including orgies and bestiality. He called himself "The Great Beast" and took the Anti-Christ's apocalyptic 666 as his personal number. From 1912, Crowley led a German cult, the Ordo Templi Orientis, that opened branches in the U.S. His politics were pro-Nazi—a dismaying detail usually lost in his legend.

Crowley's influence fell heavily on the late 1960s and '70s. Biographies of Crowley had been published in England in 1958 and 1959; his autobiography, *The Confessions of Aleister Crowley* (1929–30), was re-released in 1969. The Beatles inserted Crowley's face (back row, second from left) in the cartoon cover collage of their landmark *Sgt. Pepper* album (1967). It is rumored that the title song's first line ("It was twenty years ago today") alludes to Crowley's death in 1947. Because of its descent from blues—called the "devil's music" in the American South—rock already had a voodoo element lingering from Afro-Caribbean cults. But the Satanism in classic Rolling Stones songs and the magic pentagrams on Led Zeppelin's album covers and stage costumes came from Crowley. Jimmy Page, Zeppelin's virtuoso lead guitarist, collected Crowley memorabilia and bought his mansion, Boleskine House, on Scotland's Loch Ness. The fad for backwards messages in rock songs, which the Beatles popularized, is said (on what authority I cannot confirm) to have been inspired by Crowley, who lauded the practice of reverse reading of scripture in medieval Satanic rituals. Crowley admirers in 1970s rock included David Bowie and heavy-metal musicians like Ozzy Osbourne, whose song, "Mr. Crowley" ("You waited on Satan's call"), appeared on his first solo album after leaving Black Sabbath.

Sixties Satanism was nurtured in California by Anton Szandor LaVey (born Howard Levey in Illinois). The author of *The Satanic Bible* (1970), LaVey had been practicing Crowley-style Black Arts since the 1950s. An advocate of Crowley's creed of radical sexual liberation, he proclaimed "indulgence" to be the master Satanic principle. In 1966, LaVey founded the Church of Satan at his home in San Francisco, an all-black Victorian house where he conducted black masses with perkily nude women in lavish, tribal animal masks (photos survive). Contrary to rumor, LaVey did not, according to his daughter, appear as Satan in Roman Polanski's occult hit film, *Rosemary's Baby* (1968), nor did he have any connection with it whatever. Celebrities and libertines (Mick Jagger reportedly among them) did visit LaVey's "Black House," which may have once been a hotel. One of the most brilliant songs of the 1970s, the Eagles' "Hotel California," is said to have been inspired by rites at LaVey's house, whose address was 6114 California Street.

A startling and little-known example of Crowley's enduring influence is the Church of Scientology, founded in 1954 by science-fiction writer L. Ron Hubbard, one of the main shapers of New Age thought. Hubbard had met Crowley at the latter's Los Angeles temple in 1945. Hubbard's son has revealed that his father claimed to be Crowley's successor: Hubbard told him that Scientology was born on the day that Crowley died. The drills used by Scientologists to cleanse and clarify the mind are evidently a reinterpretation of Crowley's singular fusion of Asian meditation with Satanic ritualism, which sharpens the all-conquering will. The guiding premise of Hubbard's mega-bestseller, *Dianetics: The Modern Science of Mental Health* (1950), is that morality and spirituality can be scientifically analyzed and managed—as if guilt and remorse, in the Crowley way, are mere baggage to be jettisoned. Scientology, which attracts celebrities like John Travolta and Tom Cruise, has been pursued by the IRS for its tax-exempt status as a religion. Scientology's religiosity can be detected in its theory of reincarnation: the "process" allegedly eradicates negative thoughts and experiences predating our life in the womb.

After Madame Blavatsky, the most important architect of Sixties to New Age thought was George Gurdjieff (1866–1949). Gurdjieff was a half-Greek Armenian who arrived in Moscow in 1913 and claimed to have spent twenty years gathering esoteric spiritualist knowledge from Mecca to Tibet. As a refugee in France after the Russian Revolution, Gurdjieff created his "Fourth Way," a mixture of Tantric Buddhism, Hinduism, and Sufi mysticism. Based on a method called "the Work," it uses free movement and sacred dances along with intense group sessions where masks are stripped off to achieve a higher awareness. Gurdjieff's Institute for the Harmonious Development of Man, relocated in 1922 to Paris, originated the "transformational" technique of encounter sessions that would be widely adopted in the U.S. and serve in the vanguard of the sexual revolution. Gurdjieff demonstrated his dances in the U.S. in 1924 but spent most of his life in France. Branches of the Gurdjieff Foundation opened in New York in 1953 and in San Francisco in 1958.

Gurdjieff's influence can be seen in the Esalen Institute, established in 1962 at Big Sur, California, by two psychology graduates of Stanford University. Eventually, 100 Esalen Centers (named after an Indian tribe) opened around the U.S. Its headquarters, nestled in the mountains at natural hot springs overlooking the sea, remains the symbol of the enterprise, which combines Asian religious concepts with Western humanistic psychology. Esalen is a pure example of the Sixties spirit in its explicit mission to fuse comparative religion with art and ecology. Its workshops, based on the Gurdjieff group session, drew a long list of writers and thinkers in the Sixties, including Alan Watts and Aldous Huxley. Esalen's continued exploration of mystical issues is shown by recent conferences at its Big Sur site—"Survival of Bodily Death" (2001) and "Subtle Energies and Uncharted Realms of the Mind" (2000).

Traces of the Gurdjieff encounter session can be found in EST (Erhard Seminar Training), founded in San Francisco in 1971 by Werner Erhard, a used-car salesman from Philadelphia. Erhard was Jewish but had been raised as an Episcopalian; he oddly gave himself a German name in adulthood. In the late 1960s, Erhard investigated Scientology and studied Zen with Alan Watts in Sausalito. He claimed to have gone to India to consult gurus like Swami Muktananda and Satya Sai Baba. In EST, Erhard gave the workshop format the fervor of a Protestant revival meeting and framed it with the language of Asian meditation and spiritual discovery. Participants in EST's Large Group Awareness Training were supposed to get "It"—Watts' term for the moment of revelation. Marathon eight-hour sessions, in which they were confined and harassed, supposedly led to the breakdown of conventional ego, after which they were in effect born again. Erhard said he wanted "to blow the Mind" in the Sixties way. Explicitly anti-Christian in philosophy, EST was generally regarded as a cult, but it was a private, for-profit organization. Its students were not runaways or hippies but prosperous professionals. In 1991, amid tax problems and unsavory family rumors, Erhard left the country.

In its focus on public meetings, EST resembled Alcoholics Anonymous, the model for today's twelve-step programs for recovery from drug or sex addiction, with their glossary of pat terms like "enabling," "co-dependency," and "interventions." AA has religious undertones: partly inspired by the Oxford Group, a Christian fellowship of British origins, it was founded in 1935 by "Bill W," a New Englander saved from alcoholism by visions of divine white light. AA members still profess faith in a "Higher Power" and practice public confession as well as missionary outreach. In the 1960s, the Oxford Group, under a new name, sponsored the saccharine "Up with People" to foster wholesome behavior among increasingly rebellious American teens.

There was a confluence in the Sixties of revisionist trends in psychology with "body work"—exercises or manipulations to release "blocked" energy, a concept directly or indirectly borrowed from kundalini yoga, with its symbolic spinal chakras. (The latter word entered the American vocabulary in the 1980s through the New Age proselytizing of actress Shirley MacLaine.) In the early 1950s, Abraham Maslow, an American influenced by the German school of Gestalt psychology (which focuses on present adjustment rather than past conflicts), developed his theory of "self-actualization," from which the contemporary obsession with "self-esteem" evolved. The term seems to echo Yogananda's "self-realization." Maslow was an early associate of Esalen but criticized it for its lack of a library, which he felt limited its definition of enhanced consciousness. He described his system as the "Third Force," following the first two of Freud and behaviorism. He later advocated a "Fourth Force," a Sixties synthesis of transpersonal psychology with Asian mysticism.

Like Maslow, psychotherapist Carl Rogers sought "wholeness" of the person. Intriguingly, Rogers began his career as a theology student and Vermont pastor but afterward turned to clinical psychology. An admirer of John Dewey's progressive education theories, he pioneered "client-centered" or "non-directive" therapy, which suspended and even questionably reversed the hierarchical relationship of doctor to patient. Among Rogers' books was *Encounter Groups* (1970), with its obvious Gurdjieff lineage. Christian conservatives regularly, and probably with some justice, attack the self-actualization or human potential school of psychology for its "pagan" stress on personal needs and desires at the expense of moral reasoning and responsibility. For many people, humanistic psychology has indeed become a substitute for religion.

The Sixties trend to look to the body for salvation was anticipated in the writings of Wilhelm Reich (1892–1957), an Austrian psychiatrist of the Gestalt school who worked and quarreled with Freud, then moved to New York in 1939 to escape the Nazis. Rejecting Freud's theory of the social origin of neurosis, Reich envisioned "orgone energy" surging through the universe and the human body. In *The Function of the Orgasm* (1927), a sober book with a titillating title that was widely available as a paperback in the 1960s, he argued for the biological necessity of sexual "discharge" of that energy—thus providing a rationale for pagan pansexuality. Reich's work recalls passages about Romantic nature in Emerson and Whitman, and his energy principle resembles that of kundalini yoga as well as the power of the Christian Holy Spirit. Reich founded an Orgone Institute in 1942. However, when he marketed a coffin-like "orgone box" to capture orgone energy at home, he was charged with fraud and sentenced to two years in prison, where he died.

While still in Europe in the 1930s, Reich had become interested in the physical-culture work of Elsa Gindler in Berlin. Around 1910, Gindler (1885–1961) developed a psychotherapy based on dance movements and correction of breathing: it resembled Chinese tai chi as well as the Alexander technique, used by actors and singers to free the voice from tension and fear. Gindler's ideas were brought to the U.S. by her student, Charlotte Selver, who began teaching at Esalen in 1963. The Sensory Awareness Foundation, dedicated to Gindler and Selver's work, was established at Mill Valley, California, in 1971. Another important teacher at Esalen was Ida Rolf (1896–1979), who earned a doctorate in biological chemistry from Columbia University in 1920 and began exploring the body's internalization of stress in the 1940s. Rolf combined aspects of yoga with the Alexander technique to create "rolfing," a sometimes brutal reshaping of the muscles to release painful memories and resentments. The Guild for Structural Integration, based in Boulder, Colorado, is still dedicated to Rolf's mission.

The principle of self-actualization in most methods of body work is closer to Sixties Dionysianism than to New Age gnosticism. That is, body work assumes not that the aspiring soul must be freed from the opaquely material body but that spiritual maladies can collect and calcify in the body, clogging its vital connection to the macrocosm. Body work, like rock and its forebear, rhythm and blues, wants to "kick out the jams," so that we can freely vibrate to nature's music.

10. CONCLUSION

The New Age movement deserves respect for its attunement to nature and its search for meaning at a time when neither nature nor meaning is valued in discourse in the humanities. New Age has a core of perennial wisdom. It exalts the brotherhood of man, encourages contemplation, and finds beauty in the moment. But too much cultural energy has been absorbed by New Age over the past twenty years to the detriment of the fine arts, which frittered away their authority in their dalliance with trendy political tag lines. Despite its appeals to the archaic, New Age is fuzzily ahistorical. It lacks an analytic edge: with its soothing promises and feel-good therapies, New Age induces a benevolent relaxation that may be disabling in the face of aggression. In a world of terrorism, New Agers can only take to the hills and leave their scriptures in jars at Esalen.

There was a massive failure by American universities to address the spiritual cravings of the post-Sixties period. The present cultural landscape is bleak: mainline religions torn between their liberal and conservative wings; a snobbishly secular intelligentsia; an alternately cynical or naïvely credulous media; and a mass of neo-pagan cults and superstitions seething beneath the surface. All-night radio features call-ins about crop-circles, UFOs, and abduction by aliens, science-fiction themes popularized by Swiss writer Erich von Däniken's 1968 international bestseller, *Chariot of the Gods* (which attributes archaeological monuments to extraterrestrials). Prime-time TV programs are regularly devoted to seers like Rosemary Altea, James Van Praagh, and John Edward, who claim to hear messages from dead relatives hovering around audience members.

These developments are alarming. Science—its objectivity impugned by post-structuralism and postmodernism—is desperately needed to sort out the mystical muddle of New Age, but it cannot do so without understanding. J. B. Rhine's inconclusive 1936 experiments in parapsychology at Duke University, for example, have been only erratically followed up. Claims of telepathy have yet to be systematically compared to known animal communication or to bird migrations linked to the earth's magnetism. These matters have been left to tabloids and talk shows, which have no apparatus of testing. There is nothing supernatural or occult—only natural phenomena that science has yet to chart or explain.

What is to be done? Higher education needs to be worthy of its name. My proposal is the same that I have made since co-creating the course "East and West" with artist and community activist Lily Yeh at the University of the Arts in 1990. The core curriculum for global education should be comparative religion. Study of the major world religions (including Islam) is the key to politics as well as art. As an atheist who worships only nature, I view religions as vast symbol-systems far more challenging and complex than post-structuralism, with its myopic focus on social structures. Post-structuralism has no metaphysics and is therefore incapable of spirituality or sublimity. There has been wave after wave of influences from Asian religion over the century and a half since Emerson and Madame Blavatsky, but the resultant New Age movement is choked with debris—with trivia, silliness, mumbo-jumbo, flimflam, and outright falsehoods. The first step in any solution is a return to origins—to the primary texts of sacred literature, supported by art history and archaeology.

The religious impulse of the Sixties must be rescued from the wreckage and redeemed. The exposure to Hinduism and Buddhism that my generation had to get haphazardly from contemporary literature and music should be formalized and standardized for basic education. What students need to negotiate their way through the New Age fog is scholarly knowledge of ancient and medieval history, from early pagan nature cults through the embattled consolidation of Christian theology. Teaching religion as culture rather than as morality also gives students the intellectual freedom to find the ethical principles at the heart of every religion.

72

RELIGION AND THE ARTS IN AMERICA

At this moment in America, religion and politics are at a flash point. Conservative Christians deplore the left-wing bias of the mainstream media and the saturation of popular culture by sex and violence and are promoting strategies such as faith-based home-schooling to protect children from the chaotic moral relativism of a secular society. Liberals in turn condemn the meddling by Christian fundamentalists in politics, notably in regard to abortion and gay civil rights or the Mideast, where biblical assumptions, it is claimed, have shaped U.S. policy. There is vicious mutual recrimination, with believers caricatured as paranoid, apocalyptic crusaders who view America's global mission as divinely inspired, while liberals are portrayed as narcissistic hedonists and godless elitists, relics of the unpatriotic, permissive 1960s.

A primary arena for the conservative-liberal wars has been the arts. While leading conservative voices defend the traditional Anglo-American literary canon, which has been under challenge and in flux for forty years, American conservatives on the whole, outside of the *New Criterion* magazine, have shown little interest in the arts, except to promulgate a didactic theory of art as moral improvement that was discarded with the Victorian era at the birth of modernism. Liberals, on the other hand, have been too content with the high visibility of

[The Cornerstone Arts Lecture, Colorado College, Colorado Springs, February 6, 2007. Broadcast by C-SPAN, American Perspectives series. Published in *Arion*, Spring-Summer 2007.]

the arts in metropolitan centers, which comprise only a fraction of America. Furthermore, liberals have been complacent about the viability of secular humanism as a sustaining creed for the young. And liberals have done little to reverse the scandalous decline in urban public education or to protest the crazed system of our grotesquely overpriced, cafeteria-style higher education, which for thirty years has been infested by sterile post-structuralism and postmodernism. The state of the humanities in the U.S. can be measured by present achievement: would anyone seriously argue that the fine arts or even popular culture is enjoying a period of high originality and creativity? American genius currently resides in technology and design. The younger generation, with its mastery of video games and its facility for ever-evolving gadgetry like video cell phones and iPods, has massively shifted to the Web for information and entertainment.

I would argue that the route to a renaissance of the American fine arts lies through religion. Let me make my premises clear: I am a professed atheist and a pro-choice libertarian Democrat. But based on my college experiences in the 1960s, when interest in Hinduism and Buddhism was intense, I have been calling for nearly two decades for massive educational reform that would put the study of comparative religion at the center of the university curriculum. Though I shared the exasperation of my generation with the moralism and prudery of organized religion, I view each world religion, including Judeo-Christianity and Islam, as a complex symbol system, a metaphysical lens through which we can see the vastness and sublimity of the universe. Knowledge of the Bible, one of the West's foundational texts, is dangerously waning among aspiring young artists and writers. When a society becomes all-consumed in the provincial minutiae of partisan politics (as has happened in the U.S. over the past twenty years), all perspective is lost. Great art can be made out of love for religion as well as rebellion against it. But a totally secularized society with contempt for religion sinks into materialism and self-absorption and gradually goes slack, without leaving an artistic legacy.

The position of the fine arts in America has rarely been secure. This is a practical, commercial nation where the arts have often been seen as wasteful, frivolous, or unmanly. In Europe, the arts are heavily subsidized by the government because art literally embodies the history of the people and the nation, whose roots are pre-modern and in some cases ancient. Even in the old Soviet Union, the Communist regime supported classical ballet. America is relatively young, and it has never had an aristocracy—the elite class that typically commissions the fine arts and dictates taste. In Europe, the Catholic Church was also a major patron of the arts from the Middle Ages through the Renaissance and Counter-Reformation. Partly because of the omnipresent Greco-Roman heritage, furthermore, continental European attitudes toward nudity in art are far more relaxed. In Europe, voluptuous nudes in painting and sculpture and on public buildings, fountains, and bridges are a mundane fact of life.

Conservatives often speak of the U.S. as a Judeo-Christian nation, a formulation that many people, including myself, find troublesome because of the absorption by our population, over the past century and a half, of so many immigrants of other faiths. The earliest colonization of America by Europeans was certainly Christian, and in New England specifically Protestant. The Spanish Catholic settlements in Florida and California, as well as the French missions in the Great Lakes and central New York, were eventually abandoned. Maryland, established in 1634 as a refuge for English Catholics, was the exception, and out of it would come the dominance of the bishops of Baltimore on American Catholic doctrine.

The Puritans who arrived in New England in the early seventeenth century brought with them the Calvinist hostility or indifference to the visual arts. A motivating principle of the sixteenth-century Protestant Reformation was its correction of Roman Catholicism's heavy use of images in medieval churches—in statues, paintings, and stained-glass windows. The Protestant reformers reasserted the Ten Commandments' ban on graven images, idolatrous objects that seduce the soul away from the immaterial divine. The Puritans, a separatist sect that seceded from the too-Catholic Church of England, followed the Reformation imperative of putting the Bible at the center of their faith. Through direct study of the Bible, made possible by Gutenberg's invention of the printing press in the fifteenth century, believers opened a personal dialogue with God. This focus on text and close reading helped inspire the American literary tradition. Both poetry and prose, in the form of diaries, were stimulated by the Puritan practice of introspection: a Puritan had to constantly scrutinize his or her conscience and look for God's hand in the common and uncommon events of life. Oratory, embodied in Sunday sermons, was very strong. Literary historian Perry Miller identified the jeremiad or hellfire sermon as an innately American form, the most famous example of which is Jonathan Edwards' sermon "Sinners in the Hands of an Angry God," which was delivered in Connecticut in 1741 during the religious revival called the Great Awakening. This enthusiastic style of denunciation and call to repentance can still be heard on evangelical television programs, and it is echoed in the fulminations of politically conservative talk radio (which I have been listening to with alternating admiration and consternation for over fifteen years).

The visual arts, on the other hand, were neglected and suppressed under the Puritans. The Puritan suspicion of ornamentation is symbolized in the sober black dress of the Pilgrim Fathers depicted every year in the Thanksgiving decorations of American schools and shops. The Puritans' attitude toward art was conditioned by utilitarian principles of frugality and propriety: art had no inherent purpose except as entertainment, a distraction from duty and ethical action. The Puritans did appreciate beauty in nature, which was "read" like a book for signs of God's providence. The social environment in England from which the Puritans had emigrated to America (either directly or indirectly via the Netherlands) was overtly iconoclastic. Destruction of church art was massive during the Reformation in Switzerland and Germany as well as England, where destruction of churches, priories, and abbeys followed Henry VIII's severance of the English church from control by the Roman Catholic hierarchy in the 1530s. Crowds smashed medieval stained-glass windows and intricately carved wooden altar screens and decapitated the statues of saints carved on church facades. Walls were whitewashed to cover sacred murals. Politically incited damage to churches was even more severe during the English Civil Wars (1642–51), when Puritan soldiers dispatched by Parliament attacked even the cathedral at Canterbury, which Richard Culmer, Cromwell's general and the leader of the ravagers, called "a stable for idols." Puritan iconoclasm was a pointed contrast to the image mania of the contemporary Counter-Reformation, the Vatican's campaign to defeat Protestantism that would fill Southern Europe with grandiose Baroque art.

The first serious body of painting in America was eighteenth-century portraiture, documentary works commissioned to mark social status. Professional theater also began in the eighteenth century in the Southern colonies and New York City, although a vestige of the battles waged by the English Puritans against the theater world in Shakespeare's time survived in the laws prohibiting stage plays that were passed during the two decades before the American Revolution in Massachusetts, Rhode Island, and Pennsylvania. Though American drama and the visual arts may have languished in the wake of Puritanism, music was tremendously energized. The first book published in the American colonies was the *Bay Psalm Book,* which was released in 1640 in Massachusetts and went through twenty-seven editions. As a collection of psalms for singing in church, it belonged to a century-long line of British and Scottish psalters. Before the Reformation, hymns for the Catholic Mass were in Latin and were sung only by the clergy, not the laity. But Martin Luther, a priest and poet who admired German folk song, felt that hymns should be couched in the vernacular and should be sung by the entire congregation of worshippers. This emphasis on congregational singing is one of Protestantism's defining features—imitated in recent decades, with varying success, by American Catholic parishes. Through its defiance of medieval religious authority, Protestantism helped produce modern individualism. Yet Protestant church services also promoted community and social cohesion. The intertwining of capitalism and Protestantism since the Renaissance has been extensively studied. But perhaps the congregational esprit of church-going may also have been a factor in the Protestant success in shaping modern business practices and corporate culture.

The Protestant reformers were bitterly split, however, over the issue of music in church. Luther encouraged the composition of new hymns and was the author of a famous one—"A Mighty Fortress Is Our God" ("Ein' Feste Burg Ist Unser Gott"). In contrast, John Calvin, the father of American Puritanism, maintained that only the word of God should be heard in church; hence songs had to strictly follow the biblical psalms. Like his fellow reformer, Ulrich Zwingli, Calvin opposed the use of organs or any instruments in church: organs were systematically destroyed by Protestant radicals. Furthermore, Calvin condemned the complex polyphonic music endorsed by the more artistic Luther. Calvin rejected harmony or part-singing, so that the Holy Scripture could be heard with perfect clarity. Thus the American style of Protestant church song, based on Calvin's principles, was simple, slow, serious, and cast in unaccompanied unison. That intense, focused group sound has descended through the centuries and can be heard in the majestic hymns that have been adopted as stirring anthems by American civil rights groups, such as "Amazing Grace" and "We Shall Overcome."

The Quakers, who were pivotal to the abolitionist movement against slavery, were even more restrictive about such matters: they frowned on music altogether, even at home, because they believed it encouraged thoughtlessness and frivolity. But the German and Dutch who emigrated to America from the late seventeenth to the mid-eighteenth centuries held the more expansive Lutheran view of church music. The German influence was especially strong in Philadelphia, to which German Pietists imported a church organ in 1694. By the start of the nineteenth century, hymn writing exploded in America. Over the next hundred years, hymns of tremendous quality poured out from both men and women writers. In many cases, they were simply lyrics—pure poetry that was attached to old melodies. A famous example from the Civil War is Julia Ward Howe's "Battle Hymn of the Republic," which Howe wrote overnight in a fever of inspiration after visiting a Union Army camp near Washington, where she heard the soldiers singing "John Brown's Body," a tribute to the executed abolitionist rebel. Several other songs would become political hymns to the nation, such as "My Country 'Tis of Thee," written in 1832 by a Baptist minister, Samuel Francis Smith, and "America the Beautiful," a lyric written by Katharine Lee Bates, a native of Massachusetts whose father was a Congregationalist pastor. Bates saw the Rockies for the first time when she taught here at Colorado College in 1893. She wrote

"America the Beautiful" after a wagon trip to the top of Pike's Peak. When it was published in 1899, it became instantly famous and has often been described as America's true national anthem. The huge nineteenth-century corpus of Protestant songs became part of common American culture for people of all faiths—thus the tragic power of that final scene on the sinking *Titanic* in 1912, when the ship's band struck up the hymn, "Nearer My God to Thee."

Hymnody should be viewed as a genre of the fine arts and be added to the basic college curriculum. One of the most brilliant products of American creative imagination, hymnody has had a massive global impact through popular music. Wherever rock 'n' roll is played, a shadow of its gospel roots remains. Rock, which emerged in the 1950s from urban black rhythm and blues of the late 1940s, had several sources, including percussive West African polyrhythms and British and Scots-Irish folk ballads. But a principal influence was the ecstatic, prophesying, body-shaking style of congregational singing in the camp meetings of religious revivalists from the late eighteenth century on. All gospel music, including Negro spirituals, descends from those extravaganzas, which drew thousands of people to open-air worship services in woods and groves.

The most influential camp meeting occurred at Cane Ridge in Bourbon County, Kentucky, in 1804. For three days and well past midnight, a crowd estimated to be between twenty and thirty thousand sang and shouted with a great noise that was heard for miles around. Worshippers transported by extreme emotion jerked, writhed, fell to the ground in convulsions, or went catatonic. This Kentucky Revival, called the Second Great Awakening, spread through the inland regions of the South and eventually reached western Pennsylvania. But the movement never flourished in the North because of its harsher weather.

Collections of gospel music for use in revivals were published to huge success throughout the nineteenth century—from *Gospel Melodies* (1821) and *Spiritual Songs for Social Worship* (1832) to Ira D. Sankey's volumes of *Gospel Hymns and Sacred Songs* (1875–91). A defining characteristic of such songs is their subjectivity—that is, their use of the first-person pronoun to assert an intimate relationship with Jesus—as in "Abide with Me," "I Need Thee Every Hour," "Jesus Loves Me," "He Leadeth Me," "I Love to Tell the Story," or the rousing "Give Me That Old-Time Religion." Out of this gospel tradition also came Negro spirituals, which would powerfully counter the degraded stereotypes of African-Americans circulated by minstrel shows. Spirituals began on the antebellum plantations, where Bible stories were ingeniously adapted to carry coded political messages, as in "Go Down, Moses," a dream of liberation where Pharaoh represents the white slave-owner in collusion with American law. A major addition to the gospel repertory was *Slave Songs of the United States,* published in 1867. In the 1870s, an African-American choir, the Jubilee Singers of Fisk University in Tennessee, traveled the country performing Negro spirituals in a concert setting to help endow black educational institutions. The songs made a sensation, not only for their melodious beauty and religious fervor but for their residual African elements, such as bluesy flat notes and off-beats, the syncopation that would later surface in jazz.

The brilliant folk hymns of nineteenth-century camp meetings were inherited by modern revivals, such as the Billy Graham Crusade. In popular music, the spasmodic undulations and ecstatic cries of camp-meeting worshippers were borrowed by performers like Little Richard, Elvis Presley, and the late, great James Brown, whose career began in gospel and who became the "godfather of soul" as well as of funk, reggae, and rap. Gospel music, passionate and histrionic, with its electrifying dynamics, is America's grand opera. The omnipresence of gospel here partly explains the weakness of rock music composed in other nations—except where there has been direct influence by American rhythm and blues, as in Great Britain and Australia. The continuing impact of gospel music on young African-Americans in church may also account for the current greater vitality of hip-hop as opposed to hard rock, which has been in creative crisis for well over a decade.

There was a second great confluence of religion with the arts in nineteenth-century America. The Bible, in its poetic and indeed Shakespearean King James translation rather than in today's flat, pedestrian versions, had a huge formative influence on the language, imagery, symbolism, and allegory of such major writers as James Fenimore Cooper, Nathaniel Hawthorne, Ralph Waldo Emerson, Emily Dickinson, Walt Whitman, and Herman Melville. The American literary renaissance was produced by the intersection of the nation's residual Calvinism with British Romanticism, which was hostile to organized religion but which had transferred its concept of spirituality to nature. Pantheism helped inspire transcendentalism, which was suffused with aspects of Hinduism by Ralph Waldo Emerson (a refugee from strict Unitarianism). This view of nature, which saw God as immanent in creation, was spectacularly embodied in the nineteenth-century Hudson River School of landscape painting. In such works as Thomas Cole's *River in the Catskills* or Frederic Church's *Niagara*, these artists showed America's mountains and monumental cataracts glowing with the numinous.

Catholic immigration in the nineteenth century brought a radically different aesthetic to church architecture and decor. The typical American church had been in the Protestant plain style, white and rectangular with a steeple that formed the picturesque apex of countless villages—a design bequeathed by the British architects Sir Christopher Wren and James Gibbs. Originally, American churches were often simply a meeting house (a word still retained in Quaker practice). Also used for local government, the meeting house was a boxy space with exposed timbers and benches but no ornamentation—a template that was borrowed by town halls across the nation. Catholic taste was far more lavish. The influx of Irish immigrants in the 1830s and '40s—which caused anti-Catholic violence (including the burning of churches in Philadelphia)—was soon registered in New York's St. Patrick's Cathedral, designed by James Renwick and constructed from 1850 to 1877. With its soaring spires, delicate stonework, and stained-glass windows, it exemplified the current Gothic Revival—a grand style that was also adopted by Episcopalian churches in America.

Polish and Italian Catholics arrived en masse in the closing decades of the nineteenth century. Eastern European parish churches followed the ornate Byzantine model. Italian-American churches, as was customary in the old country, installed a profusion of polychrome statuary. That flamboyant style continued until after World War Two, when the German branch of the Liturgical Movement for Catholic reform introduced a stripped-down modernist design, with concrete construction, open spaces, and little imagery except for abstract crucifixes. This development (blandly formulaic at its worst) resulted in a genteel Protestantizing of American Catholicism, which erased all traces of working-class ethnicity. When aging Catholic churches were renovated in the 1950s and '60s, the saints' statues were displaced or banished altogether. I mourn this loss, which has impoverished the cultural environment for young people: my interest in the arts was first kindled in childhood by the gorgeous stained-glass windows and theatrical statuary of my baptismal church, St. Antony of Padua in Endicott, New York. Perhaps America's rising Hispanic population will restore the great imagistic style of Latin Catholicism.

Though there was a long tradition of censorship in Roman Catholicism, typified by its voluminous *Index Librorum Prohibitorum* ("Index of Prohibited Books"), American Catholics made few attempts to influence public policy during the nineteenth century. That role was taken up with gusto by the Protestant-led temperance movement, which called for a ban on the public sale of alcohol—a long campaign that finally succeeded with the ratification in 1920 of the Eighteenth Amendment to the U.S. Constitution, which began thirteen years of Prohibition. Major groups in the temperance movement, which included leading feminists like Susan B. Anthony and Elizabeth Cady Stanton, were the Women's Christian Temperance Union and the Anti-Saloon League, which was heavily financially subsidized by Methodists and Baptists. Episcopalians, in contrast, kept their distance from the temperance crusade.

Catholic surveillance of American public life would come with the rise of Hollywood. At the start of the studio era, movies were still viewed as vulgar. In the Roaring Twenties, the Jazz Age, there was a new rule-breaking energy and sexual adventurism in urban areas. Responding to audience demand, movies began pushing the limits with bare flesh and sexual innuendo. Small communities across the U.S. felt they were being invaded by an alien cultural force. Resistance came from a collaboration between the Catholic Church and local Protestant women's groups, speaking from the perspective of concerned mothers. There were tinges of anti-Semitism in this protest, because so many of Hollywood's early producers and financiers were Jewish. A series of guidelines was instituted in moviemaking throughout the 1920s, but compliance remained uneven. The Motion Picture Production Code, written by a Jesuit priest, was adopted by Hollywood in 1930 but laxly enforced by the Hays Office. Finally, in 1933, a conference of U.S. bishops created the Catholic League of Decency (later renamed the National League of Decency) and threatened a nationwide boycott. Hollywood responded by appointing a tough Irish Catholic, Joseph Ignatius Breen, to administer the Code, which he did through the Breen Office for the next twenty years. The Code, which wasn't officially abandoned until 1967, required scripts to follow a moral formula: crime had to be punished and marriage respected, with homosexuality and miscegenation forbidden.

Though long disbanded, the Legion of Decency lingers on today in our lettered rating system for movies—G, PG, PG-13, R, NC-17. The Legion attached descending grades of A, B, or C to each film released in the U.S. When I was a child, the group was still a formidable force. After Mass one Sunday, I was transfixed by the official list, posted in the church foyer, that showed the Legion of Decency had slapped a C on the 1956 film *Baby Doll*, meaning it was "Condemned" and that no Catholic could see it without pain of sin. The title, *Baby Doll*, seemed inscribed in smoking, red-hot letters from hell! The film, based on an over-the-top Tennessee Williams tale about Southern decadence, was being provocatively advertised by kiddy-porn images of blonde Carroll Baker lounging in a nightie and sucking her thumb. It was forty years before I finally had a chance to see *Baby Doll* on cable TV in the 1990s. It still retains its mythic, subversive significance for me. Indeed, *Baby Doll* is emblematic of the quarrel between religion and the arts in America.

As avant-garde modernism triumphed in the first half of the twentieth century, it was only the movies that addressed or expressed the religious convictions of the mass audience. With few exceptions, most modern artists and intellectuals were agnostics or atheists, above all in Europe, where anti-clericalism has raged since the Enlightenment. In its search for ticket sales, Hollywood returned again and again to the spectacular Bible epic, one of my favorite genres. Cecil B. DeMille, for example, made *The Ten Commandments* twice, in 1923 as a silent film and then as a wide-screen Technicolor extravaganza released in 1956. The latter is regularly broadcast on religious holidays and remains a masterpiece of heroic narrative and archaeological re-creation of upper-class Egyptian life. The bestselling American religious novel of the nineteenth century was General Lew Wallace's *Ben-Hur: A Tale of the Christ,* published in 1880 and widely imitated. *Ben-Hur* was also made into two films, the first a 1925 silent and the second yet another wide-screen masterpiece, released in 1959. The dynamic star of both *The Ten Commandments* and *Ben-Hur* was Charlton Heston, who afterward became a conservative activist and president of the National Rifle Association.

Because of the divergence between religion and the prestige fine arts in the twentieth century, overtly religious art became weaker and weaker. One of the most disseminated images of the twentieth century was Warner Sallman's *Head of Christ,* a 1940 American oil painting inspired by Victorian precedents that showed a long-haired Jesus bathed in light and gazing raptly toward heaven. In his intriguing 1996 book, *Icons of American Protestantism,* David Morgan notes that *Head of Christ* was reproduced five hundred million times over the next four decades. The image was beloved among evangelicals but not mainline Protestants. Many critics, even believers, rejected the painting as sentimental kitsch and denounced its portrayal of Christ as "effeminate" as well as overly Nordic Caucasian. (Sallman was in fact the son of Scandinavian immigrants.) *Head of Christ* shows Jesus as the gentle, benevolent Good Shepherd—the forgiving friend with whom born-again Christians, such as President Jimmy Carter, claim to walk and talk.

If there were few open conflicts in America between religion and the fine arts through most of the twentieth century, it was simply because the two realms rarely overlapped. But that uneasy truce ended with the culture wars of the 1980s and '90s. Under the conservative presidencies of Ronald Reagan, whose goal was to reduce big government, there was close scrutiny of cultural agencies. Considerable impetus came from William Bennett, the new director of the National Endowment for the Humanities, whose budget he cut; when Bennett was appointed Secretary of Education, he was succeeded as director of the NEH by Lynne Cheney, wife of the future vice president, Richard B. Cheney. She targeted deconstruction on campus and liberal bias in government-funded public broadcasting programs. A focus of controversy soon became the National Endowment for the Arts, whose authorization was approved in 1964 by President Lyndon Johnson but which had to struggle for congressional funding from the start, with vehement opposition even to its creation coming from Strom Thurmond, the conservative senator from South Carolina.

A variety of groups mobilized outside government in the 1980s to counter what was perceived as a moral degeneration in the media environment. These included Dr. James Dobson's Focus on the Family, the Rev. Louis Sheldon's Coalition for Traditional Values, and Pat Robertson's Christian Coalition. In 1985, the Parents Music Resource Center, led by Tipper Gore (wife of then-Senator Al Gore of Tennessee), lobbied in Senate hearings for content labeling of popular music because of concerns about sex and violence. In 1985, evangelical Protestant organizations, led by the Rev. Jerry Falwell, founder of the Moral Majority, and the Rev. Donald Wildmon, founder of the National Federation for Decency (renamed the American Family Association), allied with anti-pornography feminists (whom I strongly opposed) to pressure 7-Eleven and other national chains of convenience stores to ban the sale of *Playboy* and *Penthouse* magazines. That effort succeeded but may have been a pyrrhic victory insofar as it immediately stimulated the market for pornographic videos, introduced into homes by the then-new technology of the VCR. In 1988, Wildmon's lobbying led to the introduction in the U.S. House of Representatives of a resolution (sponsored by conservative Southern California Congressman William E. Dannemeyer) calling for Universal Studios to cancel the release of Martin Scorsese's "morally objectionable" film, *The Last Temptation of Christ*. The resolution was referred to committee and never reached the floor for a vote.

Wildmon's activities expanded to the fine arts when, in 1989, his group publicized an apparent example of blasphemy in an exhibition that had been partly funded (in the amount of $70,000) by the National Endowment for the Arts. The show had opened at the

Southeastern Center for Contemporary Art in Winston-Salem, North Carolina, in conservative Senator Jesse Helms' home state, and after a short tour closed in Richmond, Virginia. The point of contention was New York artist Andres Serrano's *Piss Christ*—a five-foot-high blow-up of a misty photograph of a back-lit plastic crucifix immersed in a Plexiglas vat of the artist's urine. Without that slangy and perhaps gratuitously confrontational title, of course, no one would have known how the photo's golden glow had been produced. The outcry over *Piss Christ* began with local letters to the editor and spread to Congress, where New York Senator Alphonse D'Amato called Serrano's photo "filth" and "garbage" and punctuated his remarks by tearing up the exhibit catalog and flinging the pieces to the Senate floor.

Another bitter controversy broke out that year over an exhibit of Robert Mapplethorpe's openly gay and sadomasochistic photographs: this show was assembled by the Institute of Contemporary Art in Philadelphia and was partly funded (in the amount of $30,000) by the National Endowment for the Arts. There were no problems in Philadelphia, but negative publicity exploded just before the Mapplethorpe show was to open in Washington's venerable Corcoran Gallery of Art, located only a block from the White House. The director preemptively canceled the exhibit, an arbitrary move that caused outrage in the art world (she resigned under fire by the end of the year). The Mapplethorpe show was quickly taken by a local progressive venue, the Washington Project for the Arts, where it drew huge crowds. When it moved to the Cincinnati Contemporary Arts Center, however, there were serious repercussions: police entered the gallery, and the director was charged with obscenity. He was put on trial but later acquitted by a jury.

Political activism on the left was unusually intense in the 1980s because of the AIDS epidemic, which the Reagan administration was accused of having initially ignored. Mapplethorpe, who had died of AIDS at age 42 in 1989, was viewed as an apostle of sexual liberation. As an admirer of Mapplethorpe, I argued at the time that this was a sentimental misreading of his work, whose dark, punitive hierarchies were partly a residue of his childhood Catholicism. Another seething ex-Catholic, Madonna, was also challenging taboos at the time: in

1989, her music video for "Like a Prayer," which showed her receiving the stigmata, making love to the animated statue of a black saint, and dancing in her slip in front of a field of burning crosses, caused Pepsi-Cola to cancel her $5 million endorsement contract.

Though work offensive to organized religion constituted only a fraction of the projects annually supported by the National Endowment for the Arts, conservative demands for the total abolition of that agency escalated. The NEA's administrators and peer-review panels were denounced for left-wing bias and anti-Americanism. As a career teacher at arts colleges, I was very concerned about the stereotyping of artists as parasitic nihilists that was beginning to take hold in the popular mind in America. While most people in the arts community viewed the Serrano and Mapplethorpe controversies as assaults on free speech, I saw them as primarily an argument about public funding. I feel that no genuinely avant-garde artist should be taking money from the government—a view also expressed at the time by the legendary Beat poet Lawrence Ferlinghetti (another Italian-American). Mapplethorpe, certainly, was no struggling artist—he was rich and famous by the time of his death. And I would question whether Mapplethorpe's cool, elegant torture and mutilation scenarios were an ideal advertisement for gay male life.

After acrimonious congressional debate, the National Endowment for the Arts managed to survive, but it was now regulated by an obscenity clause; grants to individual artists also decreased. Though controversy has subsided, the NEA disturbingly remains at the top of every list of government agencies that many citizens across the nation want abolished. What I found agonizing about the Serrano-Mapplethorpe episodes was that they ruined any prospect for vastly *increased* federal support for the arts in this country and furthermore that they would inevitably undermine arts funding at the state and local levels, where budgets are limited. Dance companies are particularly vulnerable, because they require high-quality rehearsal space and depend on a sustained continuity of teacher and student.

Almost a decade passed in America without a major conflict between government and the arts. In 1999, however, the Brooklyn Museum of Art mounted an exhibit called "Sensation: Emerging

British Artists from the Saatchi Collection." When this show had appeared two years earlier at the Royal Academy of Arts in London, controversy had mainly focused on a large image of an infamous child murderess, which was vandalized with ink and eggs. The work that caused trouble in the U.S., however, was the British-Nigerian artist Chris Ofili's mixed-media painting, *The Holy Virgin Mary*: it depicted a black-skinned Madonna with a protruding breast sculpted of lacquered elephant dung from the London zoo; two other lumps of dung supported the painting's base. In England, no one objected to the Ofili work. But in New York City, with its huge constituency of ethnic Catholics, there was an immediate reaction, fomented by the New York–based Catholic League for Religious and Civil Liberties, whose vocal president is William A. Donohue. Yet another Italian-American Catholic politician, Mayor Rudy Giuliani, expressed outrage—before the show had even opened. At a fiery press conference, Giuliani, who had not yet seen the Ofili painting, called it "sick" and "disgusting." The mayor unilaterally impounded the Brooklyn Museum's city funding and threatened to evict it from its century-old lease. This extreme political intrusion diverted the discussion from one of art to that of censorship.

While the director of the Metropolitan Museum of Art, Philippe de Montebello, wrote a *New York Times* op-ed criticizing the handling of the show by Arnold Lehman, the director of the Brooklyn Museum, most people in the arts community instantly rallied to the latter's side. But unease remained, especially after Lehman openly lied to the press about the pivotal financial role played in the show by Charles Saatchi, a British advertising executive notorious for his speculation in the art market. A direct intervention was made at the Brooklyn Museum by a 72-year-old devout Catholic, who evaded security guards to squeeze washable white paint all over Ofili's painting—an act that some viewed as racist but that oddly paralleled the whitewashing of Catholic images by early Protestant iconoclasts. The man, who told police he had attacked the painting because it was "blasphemous," was charged with violating the city's ordinance against graffiti.

When the controversy first erupted, I publicly questioned the double standard operative in the art world in regard to artists' manipulation of religious iconography: desecration of Catholic symbols was tolerated in American museums in ways that would never be permitted if the themes were Jewish or Muslim. Second, I denounced the total failure of curatorial support of "Sensation" at the Brooklyn Museum, which simply passively mounted the London show. Much of the misunderstanding of the Ofili painting might have been avoided if the museum had framed it with historical context about, first, African Christian and particularly Ethiopian art; second, tribal African fertility cults; third, the Catholic doctrine of the Virgin Birth; and fourth, the long Southern European tradition of black Madonnas. Commentary by the tabloid press and furious conservatives who had never seen the painting referred to dung being "thrown" or "flung" at the Madonna, which was completely false. But with all candor, no defense of this painting could have totally exonerated it from scandal, since Ofili had provocatively pasted around Mary a cloud of small cutouts of female genitalia culled from pornography magazines. From a distance, they looked like butterflies or hovering angels, emissaries of nature rather than the Christian God. That there was indeed unprofessional indifference to curatorship in this case would be confirmed just last year [in 2006] when Arnold Lehman shockingly demoted his principal curators in a reorganization of the Brooklyn Museum that demonstrated the unscholarly diversion of the institution from public education toward commercial buzz.

The automatic defense of the Brooklyn Museum during the "Sensation" imbroglio sometimes betrayed a dismaying snobbery by liberal middle-class professionals who were openly disdainful of the religious values of the working class whom liberals always claim to protect. Supporters of the arts who gleefully cheer when a religious symbol is maltreated act as if that response authenticates their avant-garde credentials. But here's the bad news: the avant-garde is *dead*. It was killed over forty years ago by Pop Art and by one of my heroes, Andy Warhol, a decadent Catholic. The era of vigorous oppositional art inaugurated 200 years ago by Romanticism is long gone. The controversies over Andres Serrano, Robert Mapplethorpe, and Chris Ofili were just fading sparks of an old cause. It is presumptuous and even delusional to imagine that goading a squawk out of the Catholic

League permits anyone to borrow the glory of the great avant-garde rebels of the past, whose transgressions were personally costly. It's time to move on.

For the fine arts to revive, they must recover their spiritual center. Profaning the iconography of other people's faiths is boring and adolescent. The New Age movement, to which I belong, was a distillation of the 1960s' multicultural attraction to world religions, but it has failed thus far to produce important work in the visual arts. The search for spiritual meaning has been registering in popular culture instead through science fiction, as in George Lucas' *Star Wars* saga, with its evocative master myth of the "Force." But technology for its own sake is never enough. It will always require supplementation through cultivation in the arts.

To fully appreciate world art, one must learn how to respond to religious expression in all its forms. Art began as religion in prehistory. It does not require belief to be moved by a sacred shrine, icon, or scripture. Hence art lovers, even when as citizens they stoutly defend democratic institutions against religious intrusion, should always speak with respect of religion. Conservatives, on the other hand, need to expand their parched and narrow view of culture. Every vibrant civilization welcomes and nurtures the arts.

Progressives must start recognizing the spiritual poverty of contemporary secular humanism and reexamine the way that liberalism too often now automatically defines human aspiration and human happiness in reductively economic terms. If conservatives are serious about educational standards, they must support the teaching of art history in primary school—which means conservatives have to get over their phobia about the nude, which has been a symbol of Western art and Western individualism and freedom since the Greeks invented democracy. Without compromise, we are heading for a soulless future. But when set against the vast historical panorama, religion and art—whether in marriage or divorce—can reinvigorate American culture.

73

RESOLVED:

RELIGION BELONGS IN THE CURRICULUM

Madame President, Madame Speaker, ladies and gentlemen:

Perhaps the most pressing issue is not whether religion belongs in the university curriculum but rather what religion is already being taught *now* to college students coast to coast in the U.S. And that religion, I submit, is a toxic brew of paternalistic neo-Victorian philanthropy and dogmatic political correctness—a sanctimonious creed promulgated and enforced with missionary zeal by a priestly caste of college administrators and faculty censors in unholy alliance with intrusive federal bureaucrats.

Although I am an atheist, I have argued for over twenty-five years that true multiculturalism would make scholarly study of comparative religion the core curriculum of university humanities programs everywhere. No society or civilization can be understood without reference to its religious roots. Every student should graduate with a basic familiarity with the history, sacred texts, codes, rituals, and shrines of the major world religions—Hinduism, Buddhism, Judeo-Christianity, and Islam. Indeed, what could be more urgent, in this time of terrorism, than to know exactly what the Quran says about jihad and how those verses have been interpreted in multiple ways in Muslim tradition?

[Opening Statement for the Resolution, Yale Political Union, Sudler Hall Auditorium, William L. Harkness Hall, Yale University, April 11, 2017.]

Universities as we know them began as schools for clerics in the Middle Ages. The academic robes and regalia we don for commencement ceremonies still invoke that medieval religious past, when scholarship arose from devout study of scripture and the conservation and copying of manuscripts. At their founding, Harvard, Yale, and Princeton were each affiliated with rivalrous branches of American Protestantism—Calvinist, Congregationalist, and Presbyterian respectively. Attendance at daily chapel was required for students in Yale College until 1926. Not until 2005 did Yale sever Battell Chapel from its historic link to the Congregational Church, now the United Church of Christ. But the grand cathedral of Sterling Memorial Library remains, a neo-Gothic temple of learning where a devout medieval scholar stands with quill and scroll in a stone niche between the main doors and where, above the ornate altar of the circulation desk, Alma Mater reigns with blue globe in hand like the Madonna. And we must ask: has the divestment by the elite schools of their religious associations in fact produced better educated or more sophisticated and creative graduates?

My profound respect for religion is partly based on my college experiences during the 1960s counterculture. Many members of my baby-boom generation turned away from the dictatorial organized religions of their childhood but actively sought spirituality in other directions. Among our role models were the Beat poets of the 1950s, who had been heavily influenced by Zen Buddhism. The poet Gary Snyder sporadically studied for years in a monastery in Japan. Allen Ginsberg, who went to India with Snyder, incorporated Hindu chanting with political protest at innumerable demonstrations and festivals during the 1960s. The sitar master Ravi Shankar performed at the Monterey Pop Festival in California in 1967, an event also notable for the explosive national debut of Janis Joplin. The Beatles made a famous, abortive pilgrimage to India, but George Harrison remained a lifelong disciple of the Hare Krishna movement. Psychedelics like peyote, hallucinogenic mushrooms, and LSD were widely used (although never by me) to duplicate the vision quests of Native American shamans in the deserts of the Southwest and Mexico. Spiritual aspiration, with a goal of cosmic consciousness, was a high ideal among that decade's hippies, who rejected the materialism and status-mongering of the Western career system. The idealistic comprehensiveness of the 1960s world-view has been completely forgotten: passionate commitment to protest and social reform was wedded to spirituality, outside the hierarchical framework of traditional faiths.

During graduate school at Yale (from 1968 to 1972), I did exhaustive research in the book tower of Sterling Library in ancient and modern religion as well as cultural anthropology, as it had developed along with the consolidation of archaeology as a scholarly discipline in the late nineteenth century. My work has always been aligned with the New Age movement of the 1970s, when now-neglected Jungian myth-criticism (originally inspired by Sir James George Frazer's synoptic *The Golden Bough*) spread beyond academe into increasingly commercialized lifestyle applications like yoga classes, aromatherapy, and acupuncture treatments. The major theme of my first book, *Sexual Personae,* which was an expansion of my Yale doctoral dissertation, is explicitly religious: I argue that Judeo-Christianity never did defeat paganism, which went underground during the Middle Ages and erupted at three key moments: the Renaissance, Romanticism, and modern popular culture, as signaled by the pantheon of charismatic stars invented by studio-era Hollywood and classic rock music. My commitment to religious inquiry continues today: my ongoing research project of the past nine years has been the nature religion of Native American peoples of the Northeastern United States after the withdrawal of the continental glacier over 10,000 years ago.

The New Age movement, with its spiritual goals, globalist scope, and interdisciplinary flexibility, failed to transform academe as it should have, because the most radical and free-thinking students of my era did not go on to graduate school, which remained stultifyingly conservative in most of the elite schools, with their genteel Old WASP style—that is, white Anglo-Saxon Protestant. When revolution arrived in American universities of the 1970s, it came in the form of bureaucratic fiat, as administrators primarily concerned with public relations imposed identity politics virtually overnight in the form of far too rapidly constructed new departments, such as women's studies and African-American studies, which in my view was not a progressive but a reactionary development that perpetuated the fragmented, insular structure of the pre-1960s university and that simultaneously flash-froze and institutionalized a single, then-current brand of political ideology. I was calling, in contrast, for an end to the entire artificial, balkanized departmental structure of the modern university in favor of restoration of large, general topics of concentration, such as history, literature, and art, which would permit free movement into any new area of urgent interest.

This new, overt politicization of academe in the 1970s was accompanied in humanities departments by the arrival of continental theory—deconstruction and post-structuralism, which first flowered in the U.S. at Yale, brought here from Johns Hopkins University by J. Hillis Miller while I was still a graduate student. These needlessly abstruse and elitist methodologies were predicated on old-school European Marxism, with its atheistic premises. The American literary critics who were such quick converts to deconstruction and post-structuralism had virtually never done the kind of wide reading in history, economics, and political science that one should expect from proponents of Marxism. Literary theory became a new secular religion, where reverent murmuring of the names Lacan, Derrida, and Foucault instantly conferred saintly prestige. Those theorists who prostrated themselves before false European gods have much to answer for: they drastically weakened, undermined, and marginalized the humanities in the U.S. As they now steadily move on into affluent retirement, they have left the profession in ruins.

As I wrote in a long exposé of post-structuralism over a quarter century ago, "Better Jehovah than Foucault." Let me repeat that: *"Better Jehovah than Foucault."* Veneration of Jehovah brings vast historical sweep and a great literary work—the Bible—with it. Veneration of Foucault (who never admitted how much he had borrowed from others—from Emile Durkheim to Erving Goffman) traps the mind in simplistic, cynical formulas about social reality, applicable only to the past two and a half centuries of the post-Enlightenment. The high level of intellect, conceptual analysis, and rigorous argumentation in the collected body of ancient Talmudic disputation and medieval Christian theology far exceeds anything in the slick, game-playing Foucault.

Go to YouTube, and listen to the heart-rending beauty of public recitation of the Quran sung by gifted imams to hundreds of thousands
of weeping worshippers at Mecca—and then you will recognize the
grotesque smallness of today's smug and glib post-structuralists.

Religion cannot be reduced to cheap stereotypes, as is too often
done these days by my fellow liberal Democrats, who equate believers
with the glum morality police or dismiss them as a naïve, unwashed
hoi polloi in fly-over country. All art began as religion, an enterprise
born in fear to map and propitiate the mysterious powers of the universe. Religions are complex symbol-systems that use ancient techniques of the oral tradition, such as paradox and metaphor, to convey
basic truths about human existence. Today's shallow literary theorists,
mired in their own subjectivity, deny there are any universals, but all
human beings must confront eternal forces of time, fate, and mortality, which have always been the preoccupation of great art. The sayings
of Buddha and the parables of Jesus have universal resonance and
should be regarded as foundational to world literature.

Religion is a higher poetry, requiring a leap of faith that exposes
the limitations of language far more effectively than deconstruction
has ever done. Second, religion is a metaphysics, which is completely
lacking from the Marxist system, which sees nothing but society. I
respect Marxist analysis: the great Marxist scholar Arnold Hauser's
magnificent magnum opus, *The Social History of Art*, was one of my
central influences in graduate school. But applied Marxism is blind to
nature and incapable of understanding grand emotions like awe and
wonder or electrifying peak experiences of the sublime or numinous.

Third, religion is a psychology, encouraging vital attributes of candor and resilience through unsparing self-scrutiny. The diaries of New
England Puritans, with their stark clarity and precision, are considered by many to be the first great works of American literature. Self-
examination is intrinsic to Yom Kippur, the Jewish Day of Atonement,
and the holy month of Muslim Ramadan, as well as the Roman Catholic sacrament of confession and penance.

Although he did not write extensively about religion, Karl Marx
made a famous remark in an early book where he called religion "the
opium of the masses"—by which he meant that Christianity's prom-

ise of salvation and resurrection in a heavenly afterlife were "illusions" that kept the working class from revolting against an unjust social system in the here and now. State atheism would become official in the twentieth century for Communist regimes from the Soviet Union under Lenin and Stalin to China under Mao Zedong.

Marx's unqualified materialism, which depicts human life as entirely determined by social and economic conditions, was a reaction against what he perceived as the excessive idealism of German philosophy of the late eighteenth and early nineteenth centuries. That the exclusive Marxist focus on society and politics is not in fact psychologically sustaining seems suggested by the astonishing wave of hysteria, rage, and depression that has been reported among many of my fellow Democrats after the last national election—reactions which we are still told have failed to subside in some quarters even after the passage of six months.

Social reform is an ethical imperative, but society itself, in any form, can never be the whole picture of human life and thought. If Marxism continues to be the ghost haunting the current campus creed of political correctness, then the only way to achieve balance is by building world religions into the curriculum, so that Marxist materialism can be countered by alternative historical designs of spirituality.

The Romantic poet Percy Bysshe Shelley was a radical whose 1811 pamphlet, *The Necessity of Atheism,* led to his expulsion from Oxford University. Until the mid-nineteenth century, Oxford and Cambridge Universities required undergraduates at both matriculation and graduation to sign formal assent to the *Thirty-Nine Articles* of the Anglican Church. In his great sonnet, "Ozymandias," Shelley prophesies the fall of all European tyrants, prefigured in the ruined colossus of the imperialist pharaoh, Rameses II. But Shelley's radicalism was maturely backed by a vision of a force much larger than politics—nature, expressed by the infinite, grinding sands of time—and by his supreme faith in the human power of art, signified by the capable hand and discerning eye of the anonymous slave artisan who sculpted the statue of arrogant pharaoh. But both nature and art are missing from the modern Marxist world-view, which reflexively and outrageously subordinates art to ideology.

In conclusion, Madame Speaker, there are five points that support my defense of the resolution:

1. By juxtaposing multiple belief systems, comparative religion is the true multiculturalism, demonstrating the range and complexity of human societies through history.

2. By presenting traditions of disputation of religious law and precept, comparative religion demonstrates and teaches powerful analytic techniques of interpretation and argument.

3. By its expansive metaphysics, comparative religion frees the mind from parochial entrapment in the immediate social environment.

4. By its allusive use of symbol and poetry, comparative religion develops artistic imagination and responsiveness.

5. By its stress on personal responsibility for the condition of the soul, comparative religion confers a balanced and emotionally sustaining perspective on life that releases the individual from irrational blame of others.

Madame Speaker, I thank the Yale Political Union for its fourth invitation and the opportunity to participate in this important debate.

74

ST. TERESA OF AVILA

There have been two St. Teresas in my life.

The first, Thérèse of Lisieux, a sweet-tempered nineteenth-century French nun who died at age 24, was to my dismay hugely popular in the American Catholic Church of my youth, and she remains so. Pretty statues of her as the Little Flower of Jesus, meekly standing with her arms full of roses, are everywhere.

I was introduced to another St. Teresa and quite another kind of statue in college. Bernini's *The Ecstasy of St. Teresa* is a canonical masterwork of the flamboyant Baroque.

It shows Teresa of Avila, the formidable sixteenth-century Spanish Carmelite nun, lofted by an orgasmic cloud while a flirtatious angel pierces her through the heart. The sculpture's fusion of spiritual and carnal love draws on erotic metaphors from the Song of Solomon.

St. Teresa of Avila, the first woman ever made by papal decree a Doctor of the Church, has been a tremendous role model for me.

Born to wealth, Teresa defied her father by running away to join a convent. Though troubled by illness, she became renowned for her mystic visions, so frequent and powerful that some accused her of satanism.

Teresa was a prolific author and reformer whose influence spread far beyond Spain. As a leader of the Discalced or Barefoot Carmelites,

[Recorded on December 2, 1999, at WHYY studios in Philadelphia and broadcast at 11:00 PM on New Year's Eve as the final broadcast of the year by BBC Radio 4 in the U.K.]

she called for a return to piety and ascetism. With modern managerial skill, she founded a chain of convents and friaries, despite bitter opposition from thc church hierarchy.

Ultimately, she triumphed over derision and defamation to become one of the giants of the Counter-Reformation.

Thérèse of Lisieux, modest, feminine, and obedient, was pre-feminist woman. But Teresa of Avila, bold, fiery, and tenacious, is for me a woman of the future, blending practical realism with passionate idealism.

APPENDICES

ILLUSTRATIONS

A MEDIA CHRONICLE

Color slide of Camille Paglia at age 8 in her Napoleon Bonaparte costume for Halloween, 1955, in Oxford, New York. She was obsessed with Jacques-Louis David's paintings of Napoleon in Courvoisier ads for Napoleon Cognac in *Time* magazine. All of her flamboyant Halloween costumes were sewn and constructed by her parents from pictures she found in books and magazines. The costume consisted of a black frock coat crossed by a red sash; red knee breeches; a lace jabot above a white vest; and a bicorne hat (black fabric over cardboard) adorned with a tricolor cockade. Gold ribbon was used for the hat trim and epaulets. The plastic sword with its brilliant ruby pommel was a Prince Valiant medieval two-edged short sword in a red metal scabbard, ecstatically purchased by her on the boardwalk in Atlantic City.

Red and black poster for appearance by Camille Paglia at the Yale Political Union, Law School Auditorium, Yale University, October 10, 1996. She gave the keynote address supporting the resolution, "Resolved: America Needs a Female President." The debate was taped for TV by C-SPAN and broadcast nationally.

A MEDIA CHRONICLE

"Camille Paglia Speaks on the Image of the Androgyne," *Quadrille,* Winter 1976 (quarterly of Bennington College, Bennington, Vermont). Report of September 21, 1976, lecture in Usdan Gallery by Literature and Languages faculty member Camille Paglia, discussing her research into the androgyne in literature and art (the theme of *Sexual Personae,* her doctoral dissertation at Yale University). "In her prefatory remarks Ms. Paglia stated: 'As a feminist scholar I use the androgyne as a kind of lens through which to examine masculinity and femininity in a condensed way." She described her method as "experimental" and "interdisciplinary," combining psychology, art history, and anthropology. Paglia analyzed examples of the androgyne from classical antiquity and the Renaissance and ended with figures from popular culture: Yul Brynner, Diana Ross, Gracie Allen, and French actress Stéphane Audran. Paglia showed rare Parisian color film stills of Audran and analyzed her make-up, couture, speech, and body language to demonstrate that "she is the objet d'art which has no sex."

Paglia, review, "The Way She Was: My night with Streisand," *The New Republic,* July 18 and 25, 1994. Barbra Streisand's concert at Madison Square Garden, her first live performance in New York City in 27 years.

Paglia, "The Stones," cover story, *The Boston Phoenix,* August 26, 1994. Review of the Rolling Stones' second show (at RFK Stadium, Washington, D.C.), launching their 1994–95 world tour. "Keith Richards is the modern Coleridge, an authentic tormented genius whose blues-based influence on modern music has been incalculable. . . . Fundamentally a rhythm guitarist, Richards specializes in the resonant deep structure of rock. His characteristic sound is a thick central texture of strummed, synchronized riffs, tightly oriented toward Charlie Watts' crisp, slamming drum shot and Bill Wyman's swift, rumbling, ringing bass line."

Variety, Film Reviews, August 29–September 4, 1994. *It's Pat* (spin-off from *Saturday Night Live*): "In the pic's only really funny bit, *Sexual Personae* author Camille Paglia deftly playing (and parodying) herself, appears on camera to comment on the significance of Pat's androgyny." [Paglia rewrote her dialogue in the original shooting script by Julia Sweeney, Jim Emerson, and Stephen Hibbert. In the film, Paglia's *Sexual Personae* is brandished by a gang leader who accosts Pat on the street.]

Suzanne Ramljak, interview on gender and art, *Sculpture* magazine, September–October 1994. *SR:* "You have managed to challenge and offend both the right and left factions. That's quite an achievement." *CP:* "I do that deliberately. An intellectual should be challenging: otherwise you are simply partisan. An intellectual cannot belong to any one thing. People from Europe always understand this: they find me interesting and stimulating because I'm not trying to change anyone's mind. I'm just trying to make everyone conscious of their own assumptions. I'm forcing people to examine the process of their own decision-making. People aren't very comfortable with this. People don't want to think for themselves. That was the whole thing in the '60s: think for yourself."

Melanie Wells, "Woman as Goddess: Camille Paglia Celebrates the Return of Striptease," *Penthouse,* October 1994. Paglia takes a woman reporter on a tour of three Manhattan strip clubs to demonstrate the inaccuracy of Hollywood movies about the behavior of male patrons: the Paradise Club (cheap beer); Flash Dancers (a "middle-of-the-road topless bar"); and Stringfellow's Pure Platinum (high-end with men in

Armani suits). Pull quote: "The feminist line is, strippers are victims. But women are far from that. Women *rule*." Photo of Paglia amid a bevy of strippers in the Stringfellow's dressing room. At Paglia's suggestion, *Penthouse* faxed and mailed the article plus a letter from her ("Hey, ladies! Wake up to the real world!") to the directors of women's studies programs at eight elite schools, including Harvard, Princeton, and Yale. A cover letter from *Penthouse* editor-in-chief Peter Bloch said the material "calls your attention to dramatic changes in the approach young women are taking to feminism in the 1990s." The *Penthouse* press release from Markham/Novell Communications was headlined: "Feminist Author Camille Paglia Chides Women's Studies Leaders; Urges Them to Visit Strip Clubs."

John Gallagher, "Attack of the 50-Foot Lesbian: Camille Paglia reigns as America's most controversial, intellectual, and intimidating gay woman," cover story, *The Advocate*, October 18, 1994.

"O.J.: Has the Trial Become a Way of Life?" Roundtable, *The Boston Phoenix*, October 28, 1994. Paglia ("Nicole as Objet d'Art") criticizes censored reporting of the trial of O. J. Simpson for the murder of his wife Nicole Brown Simpson and Ronald Goldman: "Early on, the major media made the mistake of taking the feminist high road. . . . But the tabloids went right to the heart of it. They went for the sex, while the major media did a lot of hand-wringing. . . . The tabloids were truer to Nicole's essence, to her personality. We have the tabloids to thank for the fact that Nicole has emerged as such a strong presence. The tabloids bought up every available photograph of her. Those incredible [Mexican beach and Los Angeles party] pictures! . . . I'd never heard of Nicole Simpson before she was dead, but suddenly she emerged as a charismatic figure. . . . The tabloids are gaining enormous power in this country because they tell the truth."

Paglia, interviewer, "The Sex Symbol and the Feminist," in-depth interview with Raquel Welch at her Beverly Hills home, cover story, *Tatler* (U.K.), November 1994. Welch had requested Paglia's assignment.

Leslie Stackel, interview, *High Times,* November 1994. Paglia criticizes "yuppie feminism": "We're rising on the career track. But the whole insight of the Sixties has been lost here. Ultimately, the social identity of people seeking status, money, and position is a false identity." About the legalization of drugs: "I am totally a radical libertarian. I believe the government has no right to ban any drug and that every single person has the right to decide what he or she wants to put into his or her body. . . . I never took LSD, but my worldview is that of the psychedelic era. What I do is psychedelic. There's something very lurid about my writing. It's hallucinatory."

Colin Richardson, interview with Paglia, "My Life as a Drag Queen," *Gay Times* (U.K.), November 1994.

Paglia, "The Real Lesson of *Oleanna:* David Mamet's play is now a film, and while deftly exposing the complexity of sexual harassment cases, it also takes on another subject long overdue for study: education," *The Los Angeles Times,* November 6, 1994.

James Martin, S.J., "An Interview: Camille Paglia," cover story, *America* (published by the Jesuits of the U.S. and Canada), November 12, 1994. "I feel *very* Italian Catholic. But I don't feel Christian, I have to say that." [Paglia may be the only person to have ever been featured in both *Penthouse* and a national Jesuit magazine—within a month of each other.]

Stewart Brand, interview with Paglia, "Scream of Consciousness," *Utne Reader,* November/December 1994. Reprint from premiere issue of *Wired,* March/April 1993. Brand's first question is about Marshall McLuhan, whom Paglia calls "one of the great prophets of our time."

Sarah Mowen, "Who'd Be a Bond Girl?," *Harper's Bazaar* (U.K.), December 1994. Paglia lauds the Bond girls (long condemned as sexist by feminists) as "fantastic images of women very powerful, physically active, and very sexy," showing "the limits of current feminist rhetoric."

Paglia, review of *Crossing the Threshold of Hope* by Pope John Paul II, *The New Republic*, December 26, 1994.

Jeannie Williams, News & Views, *USA Today*, January 24, 1995. On the New York Film Critics Circle Awards dinner: "Two big talkers met their matches as author Camille Paglia gave Quentin Tarantino his *Pulp Fiction* screenplay award. 'I'm the bad girl of letters, he's the bad boy of cinema,' Paglia said."

Paglia, interviewer, "When Camille Met Tim," cover story, *Esquire*, February 1995. Cover line: "Tim Allen Talks Tough with Camille Paglia." Paglia visits Allen on the set of *Home Improvement*, his ABC TV show, at Disney Studios in Burbank, California.

@times Auditorium event, sponsored by *The New York Times* from Times Square, February 9, 1995, moderated by David Rampe, new media editor at @times. Paglia (at home) replies to live online questions. "Juanabee asks: Camille, have you always had an opinion on everything?" Paglia replies: "As my friends and students know, I have been opinionated my whole life. When such people are young, we are an annoyance, big pains in the behind. But as we age, like Bette Davis or Katharine Hepburn, we become beloved cranks—dotty old ladies. Such is my fate."

Paglia, "Annie Oakley," for *The New York Times Syndication Special* for Women's History Month, March 1995. "In our troubled era of seething office politics and grim sexual-harassment tribunals, Annie Oakley remains a great liberating archetype from America's pioneer past. She had the practicality and blunt realism of working-class life, unpretentious and close to nature. . . . Oakley showed that female pride and self-definition can be achieved in harmonious partnership with men, whom we must stop treating as the enemy."

Paglia article, "Dear Mr. Data, You Made Me Love You: An appreciation of the almost-human android and the actor who made him simply irresistible," large-format special *Star Trek* collector's issue of *TV*

Guide, Spring 1995. At Paglia's suggestion, her mistily atmospheric photo by Kate Swan and Jason Beaupre imitates Judy Garland mooning over a photo of Clark Gable ("Dear Mr. Gable/You Made Me Love You") in *Broadway Melody of 1938*.

John Dugdale, "Feuds Corner: Susan Sontag vs. Camille Paglia," *The Sunday Times* (U.K.), April 16, 1995. Sontag about Paglia in 1993: "She should go join a rock band. Are people impressed by this shamelessness? We used to think Norman Mailer was bad, but she makes Mailer look like Jane Austen. The vindictiveness, the vulgarity, the aggression—she is repulsive to me." Dugdale cites "the hilarious essay 'Sontag, Bloody Sontag'" in Paglia's just-published *Vamps & Tramps*.

Judith Newman, "These Boots Apparently Think They're the Energizer Bunny," *The New York Times,* April 16, 1995. Interview with Nancy Sinatra about her posing at age 54 for the May issue of *Playboy* magazine. Sinatra says, "As a feminist, I feel very good about being my age and doing this. But I'm with Camille Paglia on this whole issue. Saying *Playboy* exploits women is like saying the Metropolitan Museum of Art exploits women, as far as I'm concerned. What's wrong with beautiful pictures of the nude female body?"

"Camille Paglia: A wild interview," The *Playboy* Interview, *Playboy,* May 1995. Cover story and centerfold: "Nancy Sinatra: She Does It Her Way."

Amy Fine Collins, "Fashion's Footman," profile of shoe designer Manolo Blahnik, *Vanity Fair,* May 1995. Blahnik: "And Camille Paglia. I read her book in the hospital. She's my American fantasy. That woman is fire!"

Paglia, "On Nudity," Last Word column, *The Advocate,* May 2, 1995.

UB Reporter, State University of New York at Buffalo, May 4, 1995. Paglia opens "Fiedler Fest" at the Center for the Arts, celebrating Buffalo's "resident literary intellectual Leslie Fiedler, the Samuel L. Clemens Professor of English." Paglia described how a radical student leader at Harpur College denounced her for going to Yale: "He said, 'If you're going on to grad school, there's only one place to go—Buffalo.'" Fiedler and other radical thinkers on the faculty made UB "the Alexandria of the '60s for student radicals," Paglia said. Citing Plato's theory of intellectual procreation, she called herself "a child of Leslie Fiedler and proud of it." Paglia described her admiration of Fiedler when, as a graduate student, she attended his talk at Yale about the future of literary studies and was outraged that the entire English department faculty boycotted the event.

"In This Corner . . . ," *San Jose Mercury News*, May 30, 1995. "Don't put Gloria Steinem and Camille Paglia in the same room. Asked about alleged anti-feminist Paglia in the latest *Interview* magazine, classic feminist Steinem began by comparing her to Supreme Court Justice Clarence Thomas as 'someone who was helped by a movement they weren't a part of, but then discovered they could be rewarded for opposing it.' Steinem says she considers Paglia worse than Thomas because Paglia blames women for their problems. And she said Paglia is even worse than arch-conservative Pat Robertson. At least 'he knows what the women's movement is doing.'"

Paglia, "Sex in the Classroom," Last Word column, *The Advocate*, June 27, 1995. Pull quote: "Sex must be liberated from preachers of the Left as well as preachers of the Right."

Claudia Roth Pierpont, "Twilight of the Goddess," profile of Ayn Rand, *The New Yorker*, July 24, 1995. Full-page photo of Rand by Arnold Newman with caption: "The Camille Paglia of the early sixties: Rand, wearing her signature pin, in 1964."

Dominic Wells, "Boys Keep Swinging," interview with David Bowie and Brian Eno, *Time Out* (London), August 23–30, 1995. *Bowie:* "I nearly sampled Camille Paglia on this album, but she never returned my calls! She kept sending messages through her assistant saying, 'Is this really David Bowie, and if it is, is it important?' [*laughs*], and

I just gave up! So I replaced her line with me." *Eno:* "Sounds pretty much like her." [Paglia considers this 1994 incident one of the major fiascos of her career. Her New York publisher conveyed a message that had been left for her: "David Bowie wants your telephone number." Paglia burst out laughing and hooted, "Oh, *right!* David Bowie wants my phone number! That takes the cake!" Despite repeated urging from her publisher, Paglia refused to take it seriously and assumed it was a hoax. It was not until many years afterward that she stumbled on this Bowie interview on the Web and was utterly horrified. Much later, when she was doing columns for *Interview* magazine, editor-in-chief Ingrid Sischy mentioned that she would be seeing Bowie at a Hamptons party that weekend. Paglia related the entire saga and begged her to convey Paglia's consternation and profound apologies to Bowie.]

Virginia Postrel, interview, "Interview with the Vamp: Why Camille Paglia hates affirmative action, defends Rush Limbaugh, and respects Ayn Rand," *Reason*, August/September 1995. Reprinted in *Feminist Interpretations of Ayn Rand* (1999), ed. Mimi Reisel Gladstein and Chris Matthew Sciabarra.

Paglia, review, *Virtually Normal: An Argument about Homosexuality* by Andrew Sullivan, *The Washington Post Book World,* September 10, 1995.

Laura Ziv, "Tough Your Way to the Top," *Marie Claire,* September 1995. "Players are also those people who make it through the school of hard knocks. 'You've got to be able to take things on the chin,' says the fierce and iconoclastic Camille Paglia. 'There's no way to climb up the ladder without taking the negatives that go along with success—like criticism, envy, and sabotage.' "

Constitution Hall, ACLU (American Civil Liberties Union), America Online auditorium event, September 19, 1995. Paglia (at home) replies to live online questions, moderated by Phil Gutis, national media relations director of the ACLU. *Gutis:* "Alright, I'll open with the first question: Why in the world, Camille, did you choose the screen name Volsci?" *Paglia:* "The Volscians were the fiercest tribe in ancient Italy. My mother was born in that region. Vergil named his great [Volscian] Amazon warrior in the *Aeneid* 'Camilla' and the name has been in my family for generations."

Paglia, "Learning to Hit: The unbridled muscularity of Texas football could teach simpering females something about defending their turf," *Texas Business* magazine, October 1995. Of legendary Dallas Cowboys quarterback Roger Staubach: "I thought Staubach was sensational—a focused, intense, true leader as well as a sharp passer and nifty runner. His years as a naval officer gave Staubach class, but he could flare up with populist verve. Stabbing his finger in the faces of sidelined Los Angeles Rams, he once shouted, 'We'll see you [bleep, bleep] chokers in the playoffs!' That's my kind of guy."

Letters to the editor, *The New Republic,* November 13, 1995. Paglia praises Naomi Wolf's "courageous essay" on the ethics of abortion ("Our Bodies, Our Souls," October 16) as an important contribution to "the reform movement within feminism."

Paglia, interviewer, "Howard Stern: The *Advocate* Interview," cover story, *The Advocate,* November 28, 1995.

Paglia, "Angels on Our Shoulder," *Allure,* December 1995. Paglia's "fantasy script" for *Charlie's Angels* (long condemned as sexist by feminists): "The Angels go undercover at a Mississippi women's prison. . . . Kelly, in a hairnet and décolleté white smock, blends in with the cafeteria staff to serve creamed chipped beef on toast points to shuffling lines of sullen inmates. . . . After earthquakes and a mudslide drop metropolitan Los Angeles into the sea, the Angels shrug philosophically and set off for New York City, where they go undercover in a disco."

Paglia, "The Good Witch," tribute to recently deceased Elizabeth Montgomery, *The New York Times Magazine,* December 31, 1995. "As Samantha Stephens, the witch-turned-suburban-housewife in *Bewitched* [ABC TV, 1964–72], Elizabeth Montgomery, a sunny, spunky, vaguely tomboyish blonde, was a transition from Doris Day, the marriage-minded virgin of 1950s movies to Mary Tyler Moore, the independent but vulnerable career woman of 1970s television."

Paglia, "The First Drag Queen," article on Hillary Clinton commissioned for Salon.com, January 28, 1996. Reprinted as "America's First Drag Queen: Camille Paglia on the Enigma of Hillary Clinton," cover story, *Friday Review, The Guardian* (U.K.), February 2, 1996. *The New Republic* then requested an expansion of the article for a cover-story package on Hillary. That article, "Ice Queen, Drag Queen: A psychological biography," was published to great controversy on March 4, 1996, under the general cover headline, "Hillary Unmasked." It juxtaposes Hillary's cheery Christmas TV tour of the White House (with its surprise gingerbread replica of her childhood home and oddly exposed bedroom) with her arrival at a federal court building to testify under subpoena before a grand jury: "She is wearing, quite improbably, a long black velvet coat trimmed with royalist gold brocade. . . . Then, like Mary Queen of Scots on her way to the scaffold, she sweeps away for her grueling four-hour rendezvous with independent counsel Kenneth W. Starr." Paglia connects Hillary's college nickname, "Sister Frigidaire," to the snowman that Hillary spontaneously describes (on the Christmas TV tour) on the Rodham front lawn—"the only one that never melted till spring." "What we see in the present, superbly poised First Lady is a consummate theatrical artifact whose stages of self-development from butch to femme were motivated by unalloyed political ambition. She is the drag queen of modern politics, a bewitching symbol of professional women's sometimes confused search for identity in this era of unlimited options." Reprinted by *The Independent Monthly* (Australia), June 1996.

Paglia, review, *Cultural Selection: Why Some Achievements Survive the Test of Time—and Others Don't* by Gary Taylor, *The Washington Post Book World,* April 7, 1996.

Gerry Kroll, *Ab Fab Gab,* cover story on Jennifer Saunders and Joanne Lumley, *The Advocate,* April 16, 1996. Paglia asked about their hit TV series, *Absolutely Fabulous:* "Every kind of liberal piety is spat upon. I think it is *absolutely* a gay male sensibility. Edina and Patsy represent the gay male idea of life, based on pleasure and enjoyment and satisfying the appetites of the flesh. What I adore about *Absolutely Fabulous* is the wickedly malicious humor, the over-the-top high camp that is the distinguishing mark of the gay male world."

Karen Springen, "The Biology of Beauty: What science has discovered about sex appeal," cover story, *Newsweek,* June 3, 1996. Round-table of feminists (including Naomi Wolf) and scholars. Paglia: "I am delighted by the recent resurgence in evolutionary biology, which is forcing science back onto the feminist agenda, where it has been disgracefully absent. We are half-animal beings, driven by instinctual forces that we can only dimly know. Science is our best hope of understanding the strange alchemy of lust that so disrupts our social lives. Supreme moments in the history of civilization, as in ancient Egypt, classical Athens or Renaissance Florence, were always accompanied by the worship of beauty. Feminism is shot through with puritanical Judeo-Christian assumptions, which exalt the soul over the body and moralistically devalue the physical realm. Today the human hunger for beauty is satisfied by the much maligned fashion magazines, which are glorious art for the masses."

"*Guitar World* Presents: 'All That Glitters': 25 Years of Led Zeppelin's 'Stairway to Heaven,'" ed. Tom Gogola. "Camille Paglia Decodes the Majestically Incomprehensible Lyrics of 'Stairway to Heaven'" (a tart line-by-line commentary). Special supplement, "Free Led Zep Mini Mag" in plastic bag packaged with June 1996 issue of *Guitar World:* "A celebration of the mother of all classic rock songs, with interviews, an in-depth lesson, lyric analysis, and more."

David Sheff, interview, "Camille Paglia: Fame & Lust on the Net," *Yahoo! Internet Life* magazine, September 1996. Cover line: "Camille

Paglia's Net Rant." Pull quote: "The Internet was crucial to my success." "Right after *Sexual Personae* came out, I was speaking, and
someone asked if I knew I was all over The WELL. I didn't even know
what The WELL was. He sent me reams of material reprinted from
there—intelligent, serious discussion based on my writings and lectures. I was flabbergasted. Someone from Boston was discussing my
work with someone from Tennessee with someone in California. The
established media were ignoring me, threatened by my ideas, but the
people in cyberspace were devouring them, analyzing them, debating them. . . . It happened because of the kind of thinking in *Sexual
Personae,* a book that is like cyberspace. The book is a reflection of
the way the Internet's collective mind works. Ideas are exchanged at
a million miles an hour, and every conceivable connection is made—
from TV sitcoms to David Bowie to McLuhan to Cindy Crawford. . . .
I consider myself the first Internet intellectual."

Paglia, "Designing Men," Last Word column, *The Advocate,* September 3, 1996. "A persistent libel says gay fashion designers hate women
and want to mock them. . . . The idea runs implicitly through Susan
Faludi's poisonous attack on Christian Lacroix" in *Backlash.*

Paglia, live chat with reader questions for *George* Magazine Online,
sponsored by AOL.com, September 11, 1996. (Paglia was replying from
home.) "*Question:* What do you think is the cause of the increased
incidence of male impotence? *ProfCP:* Men are shrinking, I've told
you all this a thousand times! When will you wake up? Testosterone
needs encouragement in order to operate at peak intensity! This is
why my third bestseller, *Vamps & Tramps,* opened with a celebration
of the penis! . . .
    "*Question:* Is John F. Kennedy, Jr. [co-founder and editor-in-chief
of *George*] as good-looking in person as in print? *ProfCP:* I have to say
that he is an Adonis—and I have never used the term in my life—I
mean, aside from referring to the real Adonis of Greek antiquity, of
course. His skin is the most beautiful dusky color—it's the Bouvier
heritage, probably. And he was so nice, it was unbelievable."

Paglia, "Risqué Business: It's Frederick's of Hollywood's 50th birthday this month, and the catalog is still required reading," *Los Angeles Magazine*, October 1996.

Paglia, "Hats Off to Classic Rock," *Guitar World*, November 1996.

Paglia, front-page review, *The Prospect Before Her: A History of Women in Western Europe*, Volume One 1500–1800, by Olwen Hufton, *The Washington Post Book World*, November 17, 1996.

Paglia, "Amelia Earhart: The Lady Vanishes," in "Heroine Worship: Inventing an Idolatry in the Age of Female Icons: A special issue," *The New York Times Magazine*, November 24, 1996.

Karl French, *Screen Violence: An Anthology* (1996), interview with Paglia about violence in popular culture.

"Can You Take Some Advice, Kid?," *LIFE* magazine, photo portfolio by Brian Lanker of public figures with their mentors, December 1996. Includes Jonathan Winters and Robin Williams, Cissy Houston and daughter Whitney Houston, Harold Bloom and Paglia. Bloom calls Paglia "self-begotten—Camille mentored herself." Photos of Paglia humorously harassing Bloom from behind on a couch backed by a wall of books at his New York town house.

Paglia, "The Internet & Sexual Personae," *Forbes ASAP* magazine, December 2, 1996. "I owe the Internet a lot. It is significant that my arrival on the scene coincided with a sudden leap forward in the availability of this technology. . . . The Internet, totally unknown to me, was spreading my ideas nationwide along a grapevine of dissenters and freethinkers who were tired of both the rigidities of American politics (then stuck in a sterile liberal-versus-conservative mode) and the censorship and conformism on campus and in feminism. My libertarian philosophy, as well as my pro-sex, pro-art, pro-popular culture positions, struck a chord with the radical individualists and space cowboys who were the pioneers of the Net. This is an excellent example of how the new personalized technology has broken the tyranny of the East Coast literary and media establishment. Ideas can no longer be controlled by an incestuous elite or the accidents of geography. . . . The long effort by feminist zealots to ban the porn trade has failed. The Internet proves that the sexual imagination cannot be policed: shut it down in one place, and it will bubble up somewhere else."

"For immediate release: New column by Camille Paglia debuts in Salon," press release from Salon, January 8, 1997: "Intellectual flame-thrower Camille Paglia launches a new column in Salon (www .salonmagazine.com) on Monday, January 13, editor David Talbot announced today. . . . 'We're excited about providing Camille Paglia a regular forum on the Internet—a medium that is perfectly suited for her slashing and uncompromising style,' said Talbot. 'Paglia cuts through encrusted thinking on the right, left and center. . . . Paglia has written several features for Salon, including a passionate defense of TV talk shows that appeared in the Web site's debut issue ["Talking Trash: In Defense of TV Talk Shows," November 12, 1995]. . . . Salon was recently named the Number One Web site of 1996 by *Time* magazine."

Paglia, "Pop Shots: A brief, annotated, slightly wacky, wholly subjective guide to the most fabulous moments in fashion history," *New York* magazine, February 24, 1997. Commentary on a photo gallery of stars, including Barbra Streisand, Jim Morrison, Françoise Hardy, Jane Fonda in *Klute,* Lauren Hutton, Diane Keaton, Donna Mills, Pat Benatar, Linda Evangelista, Sharon Stone, and En Vogue. Paglia: "Fashion is the glittering kaleidoscope of modern sexual personae. Ever since the industrial revolution raised the standard of living and expanded the options of middle-class women, fashion has provided dream visions of alternative selves that were once available only to the aristocracy. . . . The finest fashion photography will certainly outlast most of what the traditional arts have produced in the past two decades of shallow irony and message-heavy agitprop. . . . Fashion is a branch of the visual and performing arts. It is a glorious feast of color, form, dance, and gesture."

Stephen Holden, "On Black Films and Breezy Lesbians," *The New York Times*, March 5, 1997. *The Watermelon Woman*, written and directed by Cheryl Dunyé, "a breezy, faux-cinéma-vérité account of a black lesbian filmmaker researching the life of an obscure actress from the 1930s." Among "several wonderful comic asides" is Camille Paglia "in a self-parodying cameo appearance as herself."

Paglia, "Happy and at Home in the Halfway House: American suburbia," Arcadia column, *Financial Times* (U.K.), March 15–16, 1997. Describes the towering white and purple-black cumulus clouds of her childhood in upstate New York. "My youth in the snow belt has addicted me to weather, which I study and monitor as if it conveyed divine messages. When I stay too long in the city, I feel exiled from elemental realities. I must see the clouds and read their moods. And like my superstitious pagan ancestors, I uneasily scrutinize each phase of the moon."

Paglia, "The Big Night: The people cry out to the Academy gods: More cleavage and glitz! Less [Billy] Crystal!," Salon.com, March 25, 1997. "Oh, memories of Oscar of yore! . . . At last the Oscars begin, and I go into my usual frenzy of fury at the short shrift given to the stars' limousine-and-red-carpet arrival—a traditional, sacred ritual for which Angelenos begin lining up at dawn. Why the hell does the Academy think a billion people tune in around the globe? . . . Why in Dietrich's name must we tolerate these endless shenanigans by smug, corny hosts?—at the expense of the stars who are the true raison d'être of the evening. I and every drag queen from Rome to Rio want to see gowns, gowns, and glamour! What's the point of designers and jewelers lavishing all that luxury on nominees if we can't see the bloody stuff in all its glory?"

Ginia Bellafante, "Bewitching Teen Heroines: They're all over the dial, speaking out, cracking wise and casting spells," *Time* magazine, May 5, 1997. On popular new TV series like *Sabrina, the Teenage Witch* and *Buffy the Vampire Slayer*, which have succeeded "because they have avoided coming off as dramatized infomercials for the National

Organization for Women." Bellafante says the lead characters are "the product of a Camille Paglia feminism" based on "the very pragmatic idea that women can be smart and successful" while still embracing fashion and sex.

Paglia, interviewer, "It All Comes Back to Family: At Home with Mario Puzo," *The New York Times*, May 8, 1997. Paglia visits the 76-year-old author of *The Godfather* at his house in Bay Shore, New York.

Paglia, "The Death of Diana, Princess of Wales: A gift wasted," *The Irish Times*, September 6, 1997. Reprinted from Paglia's two-part conversation with managing editor Andrew Ross in Salon.com: "From Huntress to Hunted," August 31, and "They Destroyed Her," September 2, 1997. Diana had died at 4:00 AM in Paris on August 31. Also appeared as "A Gift Diana Squandered" in *The Guardian* (U.K.). "She began to waste her enormous gift. At one point she had said a fulfilling job was better than a man to give your life meaning. I wish she had pursued that avenue, because she met a very tacky end—to die in the car of a gigolo playboy in flight from the Ritz."

Ros Wynne-Jones, interview, "The Goddess: Camille Paglia, the academic thinker, was the first to identify Diana's divine symbolism," *The Independent on Sunday* (U.K.), September 7, 1997. About the process of deification of "Diana the icon": "The British have such a tradition of mediums and séances and haunted theaters, it can only be a matter of time before someone is cured by Diana."

"Paglia Takes on Feminist Philistines," Page Six, *The New York Post*, September 9, 1997. Paglia to speak at a "Fetish for Freedom" fundraiser for Feminists for Free Expression held at Mother, "a downtown dominatrix hangout" in Manhattan. Also on the program: Candida Royalle and Betty Dodson. " 'We're the authentic spirit of women's lib. We believe in laughter, sex, fun, music, and art,' said Paglia. 'The rest are prudes.' . . . Paglia's least favorite feminist seems to be Susan Faludi, author of *Backlash: The Undeclared War Against Women*—'She has no culture. She's a philistine.' "

"Narrative Threads: Some women of note on the emotional significance of clothing," *Fashions of the Times* supplement, *The New York
Times*, Fall 1997. "What in your wardrobe are you most attached
to—and why?" Among those polled: Helen Gurley Brown, Donna
Karan, Ivana Trump, Wendy Wasserstein, Queen Latifah, and Cindy
Sherman. Paglia replied: "My doctrine of Amazon feminism is best
expressed by the fierce, buttery-soft black leather ankle boots that I
bought in London in 1994 and debuted on the guerrilla cover photograph of my book *Vamps & Tramps*. . . . I inherited an Italian reverence for the fine art of leather-working; my family, which emigrated
from a region of Italy known for that trade, came to upstate New York
to work in the Endicott-Johnson shoe factories."

"All Hail the Bitch Goddess: Camille Paglia and Glenn Belverio (The
Artist Formerly Known as Glennda Orgasm) pay homage to the Queen
of Camp, Jacqueline Susann," a dialogue in honor of the re-release of
Jacqueline Susann's *Valley of the Dolls* (1966) by Grove Press, Salon
.com, November 17, 1997. *GB:* "It's about time that tribute is being paid
to Jacqueline Susann, because so much of pop culture is informed by
what she did." *CP:* "For me, *Valley of the Dolls*, like *Auntie Mame*, is one
of the great books of the postwar era. There are very few so-called 'serious' novels following World War Two that mean anything to me. I just
don't identify at all with any of those major heavy-hitters of fiction—
Bellow, Malamud, Grass, Pynchon, and so on."

John Strausbaugh and Queen Itchie, interview, "The Lesbionic Woman: Camille Paglia Speaks. We Listen," cover story, *The New York Press*,
November 26–December 2, 1997. Attacks the current leftist press in
New York for political correctness, above all the *Village Voice*, which
she read "religiously" in the 1960s and '70s but which was now "an
empty shell of itself" and "an apologist for the academic establishment, . . . taking the side of the tenured professors of Harvard, Yale,
Princeton against an outside voice like mine. . . . In the '60s it was
like 'Show us the weird books, show us the odd things. We want the
thing that destroys everything we've experienced so far.' Kafka said,
'A book should be an ax for the frozen sea within us.' I came out

of a period when eccentricity was glorified and going your own way was glorified. . . . The idea that a [post-structuralist] 'theorist' is an intellectual—a theorist is the *opposite* of an intellectual. A theorist is a fundamentalist, the equivalent of a fundamentalist Christian from the Bible Belt."

Joanna Coles, interview, "Enter the Amazon," *The Guardian* (U.K.), November 27, 1997. "She is America's most famous social philosopher, the anti-feminist feminist, the agent provocateur of academe." " 'I'm an equity feminist,' she shouts above the restaurant clatter. 'I want equality for women in the eyes of the law, but I oppose special protections—they're reactionary. . . . I worry about the kids today, the shrinking down of the cultural scene. There's too much irony now, everything's cool and people are afraid to be enthusiastic. In the Sixties, we were not afraid to make fools of ourselves. I'm always blundering! I'm always saying too much, knocking things over!' "

Edward J. Sozanski, "Museum canvasses area personalities for anniversary exhibition," *The Philadelphia Inquirer,* December 3, 1997. "The Museum of American Art of the Pennsylvania Academy of the Fine Arts opens 'Philadelphia's Choice,' paintings and sculptures chosen from the museum's permanent collection [in its storage vault] by 17 area residents." "Paglia picked three military portraits": Philip Alexius de László's General John J. Pershing, Thomas Sully's Major Thomas Biddle, and "a sword-bearing figure in a kimono called *Fantasie* by Charles Sprague Pearce." Quoted from Paglia's statement: "Military portraits, beginning with David's paintings of Napoleon, have inspired me since childhood. In my classification of sexual personae, they are glamorous Apollonian icons of the Western will to power."

Jenn Shreve, interview, "Animal House: Camille Paglia comments on the sexual politics of the Clinton White House," Salon.com, January 22, 1998. *Shreve:* "People are alleging that the president is a sex addict—is this true?" *Paglia:* "First of all, I want to get on the record that I am a Clinton supporter in political terms. But I was probably the only leading feminist to have believed Paula Jones from the start—

from the very moment she emerged in 1994. I felt that the charges that Anita Hill made were far less grave than the ones Paula Jones made against Clinton. . . .

"So I don't think his problem is sex addiction but just a normal, rather immature man's desire to be petted. He sure doesn't get the petting he needs from Hillary. Hillary got him to the White House, but she doesn't pet him. The moment his daughter is gone—and here's one of his most shameless appeals for popular approval—out comes the dog! He even walked out with the dog yesterday. That's the most pathetic part of this. He's desperate for a woman who will pet him and instead he gets a dog!"

Paul Johnson and Camille Paglia, "The Epic Film *Titanic* Hits Our Screens and Poses an Important Question About Our Values Today: Would we still put women and children first in the lifeboats?," *The Daily Mail* (U.K.), January 24, 1998 (the day after *Titanic* opened). Johnson says yes, and Paglia says no. Paglia: "At the very moment women were agitating for the right to vote in order to enter the political arena with men, an archaic standard was invoked on the *Titanic* that placed women in a special protected class. . . . If I were captain of a sinking ocean liner with too few lifeboats, I would assign places to younger people first, without respect to gender. By what logic do we prevent the death of an elderly woman, for example, while consigning to the watery depths a young man who has not yet tasted a full life?"

Paglia, Salon.com column, February 3, 1998. Response to reader question about Bill Clinton's "sexual appetite": "Exactly what drives Clinton's appetites? Fatherless, he was reared in matriarchy. He reveres women but fears their all-engulfing power. His feisty, florid, ribald mother Virginia—so strong that even the dominatrix Barbra Streisand fell under her influence—would be succeeded by her rival and opposite, the male-willed Hillary Rodham, a fanatically focused, high-minded Puritan who took Bill under her wing as a lovable but ever-straying son, whom she molds like clay but can't control outside her atelier.

"Clinton's crimes are incestuous: he makes the whole world his family and then seduces and pollutes it, person by person. Remember how then Governor Clinton, hot and sweaty from jogging, jovially stained Jim McDougal's expensive new leather chair?—something his Whitewater partner never forgot. . . . Clinton is a tactile, not a phallic president. His favorite gropes are at funerals, where he can give long, warm, tearful bear hugs to endless lines of ladies without scandal. He needs Hillary to structure him and give him spine, or he'd melt into a butter puddle of lip-smacking schmooziness. Look at how inept he was in reintroducing his yappy new puppy to the affronted presidential cat on the White House lawn after the last family vacation. 'Hillary will deal with that naughty dog!' I muttered peevishly."

Paglia, "A Call for Lustiness: Just say no to the sex police," *Time* magazine, cover story on Paula Jones' charges against Bill Clinton, March 23, 1998. "Liberal Democrats, who supported Anita Hill against Clarence Thomas in 1991, are waking up to the police state that their rigid rules have created."

Paglia, "Camille Does the Oscars: Winslet blooms, Madonna clunks, Stone styles: A Paglia's-eye-view of the Academy Awards," Salon.com, March 24, 1998. "Kate Winslet of *Titanic* is truly titanic in her magnificent green dress, which makes her look like the Grand Duchess Anastasia at a medieval tournament. She should get the Oscar for best bust. Anyone with those floaters doesn't need a lifeboat. I thought we'd gotten rid of Meg Ryan, but no, there she is bounding chirpily down the red carpet with her new face tucks and a skin sheen as blinding as a Maine lighthouse. God, she revolts me. Cher hoves into sight wearing what seems to be a beige lampshade cut like a tornado eggbeater on her head. Not exactly widow's weeds. She sure got over Sonny's death fast."

Paglia, "The Feminist Fault Line on Clinton," *The Boston Sunday Globe*, March 29, 1998. "The recent allegations of sexual misconduct swirling around President Clinton have driven feminist leaders such as Gloria Steinem and Patricia Ireland, president of the National Organization for Women, to desperate contortions of twisted logic. . . . As a registered Democrat who twice voted for Clinton (and who is deeply troubled by his private behavior toward women), I have long opposed the backstage collusion of feminist leaders with the superstructure of the Democratic party."

Bruce Handy, *The Viagra Craze*, cover story, *Time* magazine, May 4, 1998. Paglia: "The erection is the last gasp of modern manhood."

Paglia, "A Stranger in the Night: Camille Paglia on Frank Sinatra and his women," *The Guardian* (U.K.), May 19, 1998 (after Sinatra's death). "Women allured but remained a conundrum to him. . . . Like many Latin Catholic men, he seems to have suffered from the Madonna-whore complex. . . . The only woman who broke Sinatra's heart, however, was the Southern spitfire Ava Gardner, who shared his taste for indefatigable, boozing nightlife. . . . If Ava resembled anyone in Western history, it was Clodia, the glamorous, fast-track Roman aristocrat whom the poet Catullus accused of treachery and promiscuity. 'I hate and I love!' cried Catullus, in the agony of humiliation."

Paglia, "Judy Garland as a Force of Nature," *The New York Times*, June 14, 1998. Calls Garland "a personality on the grand scale who makes our current crop of pop stars look lightweight and evanescent." Discusses Garland's "wavering between male and female timbres" as evidence that "singing was her search for gender." This article was reprinted in the book enclosed in a Judy Garland four-CD box set and video, released by 32 Records in October 1998.

Paglia, "Making Marilyn of Monica: She displays '90s confusion of youth," *The Boston Sunday Globe*, June 14, 1998. Splashy spread of California beach photos of Monica Lewinsky by Herb Ritts in *Vanity Fair*. States that Lewinsky was "exploited for back-door, mechanical sexual servicing by the most powerful politician in the world" and "never accorded the honor or the benefits of a real mistress." Lewinsky "is not atypical of affluent American girls" today, "alternately blank and manipulative, insecure and aggressive." They have been "overprotected by peace and prosperity" and "seem removed from reality": "the horrors of history happened to someone else."

Paglia, "Spellbound by Beauty," *The Daily Telegraph* (U.K.), June 27, 1998. "Alfred Hitchcock has been accused of treating female characters—and his leading ladies—badly. Camille Paglia says he was misunderstood." Excerpt from cover story in *W, The Waterstone's Magazine*. Reprinted in *The Globe and Mail*, August 21, 1998.

Ginia Bellafante, "Feminism: It's all about me!," *Time* magazine cover story, June 29, 1998. Cover headline, "Is Feminism Dead?," with hovering heads of Susan B. Anthony, Betty Friedan, Gloria Steinem, and Ally McBeal (Calista Flockhart). "Ally McBeal and Bridget Jones are the products of what could be called the Camille Paglia syndrome. In her landmark 1990 book, *Sexual Personae,* author Paglia used intellect to analyze art, history, and literature from classical times to the nineteenth century and argue that it is men who are the weaker sex."

Paglia, "Hitch's Women" (on Alfred Hitchcock), cover story, *W, The Waterstone's Magazine* (U.K.), 14, Summer 1998.

"The Hitchcock House of Horrors: The mother, the shower, the knife," *The Guardian*, July 17, 1998. Roundtable of writers and movie stars about Hitchcock's *Psycho*. Paglia: "I was a schoolgirl in Syracuse, New York, when *Psycho* came out. It was a turning point for an entire generation. . . . The 1950s in America were very stable, very conformist, and the movie was a terrorizing break in the security of that era. . . . There had been horror films, ghost stories like *The House on Haunted Hill*, but never on this level. . . . Now that we look back, we can see Hitchcock was a prophet, that he was seeing something about to happen in the 1960s. . . . *Psycho* wasn't taken seriously by the critics. . . . That moment was a high point of European art cinema, so compared to statements made by Bergman or Antonioni, it seemed like a vulgar potboiler. And over time, we realize that Hitchcock's works have lasted. Young people have no feeling for those great art films, which don't have the staying power. But Alfred Hitchcock goes on and on."

Malcolm Johnson, "Strange, Fascinating 'Henry Fool' Is Hal Hartley's Best Film Yet," *The Hartford Courant,* July 17, 1998. " 'Henry Fool' is the name of a literary blowhard, a would-be Kerouac and ego-swollen drifter who finds an acolyte in a poor, bullied garbage man named Simon Grim. . . . Through his constant extolling of the commitments that must be made by poets, Henry turns the hopeless Simon into an international celebrity, a poet damned by the Right and embraced by Camille Paglia (who hilariously parodies herself on camera)." [Paglia rewrote her dialogue in the original script by director Hal Hartley.]

"Behavior, Beliefs, and Betrayal," *The Los Angeles Times,* August 20, 1998. "The *Times* asked women writers to talk about what messages were sent to women and girls by President Clinton's admission Monday night [about misleading the nation for seven months about his affair with Monica Lewinsky] and his wife's public reaction to it." Paglia: "Women are groupies or nannies. If you are a wife, you will be sent out to lie like a rug. If you are a daughter, you will be used as a family values stage prop." The *Times* headlined this paragraph "Mops, Props, and Nannies."

Angela Phillips, interview, "At War with the Sisters," "The *Guardian* Profile: Camille Paglia. Is she the Emma Peel of the women's movement—duffing up the right-on 'feminazis' on behalf of bad girls everywhere? Or is she, as they would say, peddling outdated, simplistic views completely out of touch with the Nineties?" *The Guardian* (U.K.), September 19, 1998. Pull quote: "I have always been convinced that I was right. I don't come from a line of self-doubters." "Camille Paglia's longtime friend Robert Caserio says, 'She doesn't want dialogue, she wants conflict. She sees dialogue as a sentimental term for coercion.' "

Paglia, "The New Morality," *Penthouse,* October 1998. *Penthouse* requested an expansion of CP's "A Call for Lustiness" in *Time* magazine, March 23, 1998.

"You ask the questions (Such as: Camille Paglia, feminist icon, how do you feel about being described as a misogynist?)," *The Wednesday*

Review, The Independent (U.K.), October 7, 1998. *"Why do you think some people find you scary?* Because I think for myself and don't seek approval. Most people are trapped by habit and fear."

Bryan Appleyard, interview, "Mouthtrap: Camille Paglia, fastest-talking feminist in the West, speaks her mind," *The Sunday Times Magazine* (U.K.), October 18, 1998. Jack DeWitt, Paglia's friend and colleague at the University of the Arts: "Her hyperboles are, in her mind, understatements. Values and beliefs are not, for her, intellectual games. They may not be a matter of life and death, but they are certainly a matter of life."

Leslie Felperin, interview, "Beauty and the Beasts: Camille Paglia on nature and civilization in Hitchcock's *The Birds*," *Sight & Sound,* October 1998. Paglia: "The main problem with so much feminist film criticism, as well as post-structuralism and postmodernism, is that they're obsessed with words. Film critics for the past 25 years have tried to impose verbal categories on film. But film works choreographically; it uses body language, for which Hitchcock had tremendous feeling. . . . I was very impressed in his silent films by his skill in photographing crowds. My theory is that because his father was a greengrocer, Hitchcock in his early years directly experienced the crowds in London moving in surging rhythms. So he learned how to show crowds moving through the streets or going down subway stairs—as in the title sequence of *North by Northwest,* with its crowds rushing across the screen. Hitchcock has the ability of a great stage or opera director to manage groups of people. Italians can do these giant, Fellini-like crowd scenes, but you don't expect that from someone emerging from British culture. The sense of space is so constrained in England that people learn to live within narrow borders. . . .

"One of my favorite scenes in *The Birds* is the one at the jungle gym near the schoolhouse. Tippi Hedren is anxiously smoking and looking over one shoulder, while over the other we see crows beginning to land on the jungle gym. For me, the jungle gym is a symbol of civilization—the framework, the grid—and the birds are nature. Soon the jungle gym is heaving and rippling with birds, which look very evil, very dark and almost shapeless. Then you have Hedren sitting there smoking in this amazingly sophisticated manner, fantastically elegant. That combination—the primitive horror of the rippling black birds, and the beauty of the woman staring off alone, with no male, staring off into space, very composed—is to me a symbolic depiction of human life, both nature and culture. I took from Hitchcock this view of the frame of culture, the invisible skeleton of civilized life. I regard myself as someone who is climbing and groping and trying to find the rungs of the invisible jungle gym of contemporary society and Western culture. It's an enormously important image to me."

"Bombs Away: More views of the president, the impeachment, and the bombing of Baghdad," *The New York Press,* December 23–29, 1998. Roundtable about bombings ordered by Bill Clinton. Paglia: "I was outraged by the timing of the bombing of Iraq. It was so absolutely tied to the onrushing impeachment debate the next day in the House of Representatives. As far as I'm concerned, this was proof positive that the missile raids Clinton ordered from Martha's Vineyard in August were similarly tied to political events. . . . Where was the Left? . . . Utter silence. . . . Meanwhile, in London, protestors threw red paint symbolizing blood on the Foreign Ministry. There were attacks on the U.S. embassy in Syria and riots in Moscow—in *Amsterdam* there were riots against the bombing! In *Amsterdam!*"

Paglia, "Millennium Reputations: Which are the most overrated authors, or books, of the past 1,000 years?," *The Sunday Telegraph* (U.K.), February 14, 1999. Paglia nominates Samuel Beckett, whose work is "shot through with callow wordplay and oafish low comedy, the defense mechanism of clammy, adolescent males squirming before the complexity of biology." States that the "cultural chasm between generations of intellectuals" is shown by attitudes toward Beckett. Michel Foucault and Susan Sontag are "on the record as Beckett worshippers," but Paglia's post-war generation sought "sensuality and passionate engagement" in art: "Hence Dionysian rock 'n' roll, based in African-American rhythm and blues, is our pagan ode to life."

Ros Wynne-Jones, interview, "Hitchcock's Birds," *The Express* (U.K.), February 27, 1999. "As we celebrate the centenary of the birth of Alfred Hitchcock, Camille Paglia talks to Ros Wynne-Jones about his portrayal of women. Was he really a misogynist?"

Paglia, "Camille Does the Oscars," Salon.com, March 22, 1999. "Whitney Houston is fabulously elegant in a slim white gown and early 1930s hair, but Mariah Carey, heavily girdled in a white dress with a broad halter strap, looks like a St. Pauli beer-garden waitress missing her tray of suds. The two hold hands as they wail a nominated song, while a columnar gold drape unfurls behind them like a rushing fountain or a Morris Louis tapestry painting. But less definitely isn't more at this show: suddenly the two gals are attacked by a gospel choir so badly filmed as they descend symmetrical staircases that they look like a giant flock of deranged geese. . . .

"At last an adrenaline rush as Sophia Loren, her massive, buttressed bosom leading like the prow of a battleship, comes out to introduce the clip for the Italian film, *Life Is Beautiful*. She looks a bit like Anouk Aimée these days. What star power! Loren puts all the smirky ingénues to shame. When Andie MacDowell schleps out after Loren, I literally have to turn my head away. Can't American actresses get their damned act together? . . . An x-rated joke about 'beavers' is an odd segue into the dreaded Anne Heche, whom I thought we got rid of last year in *Psycho*. Heche's radio mike, clamped to her bodice, keeps flickering out, but whether this is accidental isn't clear. Cutting-edge technology poisoned by her mushroom-like clamminess? Ellen DeGeneres, another victim clamped to the Heche bodice, had a similar fate. . . .

"Renée Zellweger, a minor actress who somehow ended up on the cover of *Vanity Fair* last year, clunks out hobbled by an elaborate purple-and-gold gown that she hasn't the foggiest clue about how to wear. 'What a big bag of oats!' I cry with disgust. Doesn't she have any gay guy friends to shop with? Someone should slap that girl up and down Rodeo Drive until she learns what fashion is. . . . I close my eyes when Nicolas Cage appears, since I can't stand his eternal pose of beady-eyed earnestness. . . .

"Val Kilmer walks out, leading a gorgeous bay horse, who has more beauty and style than three-quarters of tonight's actresses. Its splendid black-and-silver saddle and tack deserve the award for best costume. Then the horse turns its ass to the audience—which may be the perfect comment about the evening. . . . Dreary, hunch-shouldered Helen Hunt is back. 'She looks like Jan Brady,' Alison remarks. 'She looks like Patty Hearst,' I reply. Oh, I'm so tired of that generic kind of pallid, decorous WASP anemia. Take her away!"

Paglia, "Propelled by Earhart's Soaring Spirit," *The Los Angeles Times,* March 24, 1999, article on Amelia Earhart for Women's History Month.

Paglia, "Madonna and Her Sensational New Look," *Harpers & Queen* (U.K.), May 1999. "Camille Paglia interprets her latest guise—the Geisha." Photos by Patrick Demarchelier. Paglia: "Madonna Dominatrix, grandly making her queen's progress through costume history, has now entered her Japanese period. . . . Madonna has a positive genius for sexual personae."

Paglia, double book review, "Back to the Barricades," *The New York Times Book Review,* May 9, 1999. Christine Wallace, *Germaine Greer: Untamed Shrew,* and Germaine Greer, *The Whole Woman.*

Paglia, "Overrated and Underrated" special issue, *American Heritage* magazine, May/June 1999. "Most Overrated Feminist: Gloria Steinem"; "Most Underrated Feminist: Faye Wattleton." Paglia describes Wattleton's "brilliant" performance at the Senate Judiciary Committee's hearings on the nomination of David Souter to the Supreme Court.

Leslie Fiedler, "Hubbell Acceptance Speech," in Steven G. Kellman and Irving Malin, eds., *Leslie Fiedler and American Culture* (1999). Fiedler's 1994 speech on receiving the Jay B. Hubbell Medal for Lifetime Achievement in American Literary Studies, awarded by the American Literature Section of the Modern Language Association of

America. Fiedler: "Even more disturbingly, I am now routinely quoted in jargon-ridden, reader-unfriendly works I cannot bring myself to read, and am listed honorifically in the kind of footnotes and bibliographies I have always eschewed. But most disturbingly of all, as a result (in a culture where nothing fails like success) some younger, future-oriented critics have begun to speak of me as old-fashioned, a member of a moribund establishment. I was, however, heartened when Camille Paglia, the most future-oriented of them all, the *enfant terrible,* in fact, of her generation, as I was of mine, was moved by a new edition of *Love and Death in the American Novel,* to write, 'Fiedler created an American intellectual style that was truncated by the invasion of faddish French theory in the '70s and '80s. Let's turn back to Fiedler and begin again.' Her words not merely reassure me that I am, still, not P.C. They also make me aware that whatever I have written about has always been from an essentially American point of view and in an essentially American voice; and that therefore I am in the deepest sense an 'Americanist.'"

"Camille Does the Movies," National Film Theatre, British Film Institute, June 2–17, 1999. Film series chosen by Paglia, who introduced seven films in person: *Darling, Butterfield 8, The Philadelphia Story, All About Eve, Orphée, The Ten Commandments, La Dolce Vita, Auntie Mame, Suddenly Last Summer, Persona, Accident, Valley of the Dolls* (shown with *Glennda and Camille Do Downtown*), and *Niagara.* Accompanied by representatives of the BFI, Paglia lectured on *Persona* at screenings in the north of England, including Sheffield. From her keynote statement in the BFI's program brochure for June 1999: "Films for me are life experiences. They have formed the way I see the world, and they have populated my mind with mythic personae. As a scholar and critic, I can trace my guiding ideas, emotions, and tastes to the first films I saw in early childhood (such as Walt Disney's *Snow White* and *Fantasia*)."

Paglia, "Camille Paglia Tells Why Kids Want to Blow Up the World," conversation with Ingrid Sischy, *Interview* magazine, July 1999. "One of the biggest problems is that there has been a suppression of the masculine in our culture, and not just because feminism has been questioning it, but because there is no room in our service-sector economy for anything genuinely masculine."

Paglia, "Letter from Philadelphia" (featured series), *The Times Literary Supplement* (U.K.), July 16, 1999. From the Center City performing arts district to Termini Bakery and Pat's King of Steaks in Italian-American South Philadelphia.

Paglia, "Smashed Wine Bottles, Hairpin Bends, Formidable Brassieres, and My Other Favorite Moments," *The Observer Review* (U.K.), August 8, 1999. For the Alfred Hitchcock centenary: Paglia's favorite scenes in Hitchock films.

Paglia, Salon.com column, September 7, 1999. "My summer report begins with my enormous sense of satisfaction and relief over the renewal of public attention to the Waco disaster, which was so foul an affront to American civil liberties. The abortive investigation into the 1993 incident, in which more than 80 members of David Koresh's Branch Davidian religious sect died in a fire at their Texas compound, is currently being blamed on the FBI's withholding of crucial information from Attorney General Janet Reno, who had just assumed office.

"But the major media, with their strongly liberal bias, are equally guilty, for in trying to protect the new Democratic president, Bill Clinton, they let Reno get away scot-free with her blatant mismanagement of the Waco stand-off. At the quickly convened congressional hearing into Waco in 1993, Reno's self-righteous invocation of the child-abuse card deserved to be derided and rejected by the media, who were already in a state of collective amnesia over the appalling spectacle of government tanks knocking down the buildings of a private citizen.

"Where were America's leftists after Waco? Diddling their thumbs in their urban and campus coteries, as usual. The shocking absence of protest about this incident drove the issues underground. It reemerged two years later on the lunatic far Right, in Timothy McVeigh's bombing of the federal office building in Oklahoma City on the anniversary of Waco, at a cost of 168 lives.

"This is a good example of what I have described as the principle of rightward drift in populist thought. When authentic critique is silenced or censored on the Left, issues drift subliminally to the Right, where they burst out again full-formed as fascist violence. Government authority was illegitimately used at Waco—and one fascism begot another."

Paglia, Salon.com column, September 20, 1999. "The recent repeat TV airings of *Titanic* (1998) have enraged me anew about the injustice done to Kate Winslet, who deserved the Oscar for her emotional bravura and physical fortitude in that film. The tense footage of Winslet carrying an ax as she fights her way through the cold flood of seawater in a dusky corridor will be one of the few canonical moments of 1990s cinema, equal to cigarette-flaunting, leg-crossing Sharon Stone's flouting of the police from her interrogation throne in *Basic Instinct* (1992). Retchingly vanilla Helen Hunt, who walked off with Winslet's Oscar, goes on piling up undeserved awards, as at last week's Emmys. But a quarter century from now, when people are still admiring Winslet in *Titanic,* no one will remember who the hell Helen Hunt was. Hollywood, get your priorities straight: please reward artistic merit, not popularity in your chummy entertainment elite."

"The New Gate," *Suddenly Susan,* NBC TV situation-comedy, Season 4, Episode 1, aired September 20, 1999. Susan Keane (Brooke Shields) is a magazine writer in San Francisco dismayed by the arrival of a new boss, Ian Maxtone-Graham (Eric Idle of Monty Python), who plans to turn the magazine into an upscale men's publication. Ian says, "You've heard of Camille Paglia. . . . Paglia says, 'Sex sells.'" Susan briefly quits after being assigned to write what she sees as a sleazy sex piece.

Paglia, Salon.com column, December 8, 1999. "I was delighted to hear that Matt Drudge is leaving his Fox News Channel talk show, since I've longed for him to focus full attention on his historic creation, the Drudge Report, which at its best is an effervescent mix of politics, science news, crime stories, Hollywood gossip, and plain old-fashioned scandal. Last week was a classic Drudge moment: into the humdrum monotony of midday came blazing on the Drudge site a just-posted Reuters article entitled 'Daredevil jumps off Rio Christ in Bond-style stunt.' In the magnificent color photo of the 98-foot-tall colossus of Cristo Redentor on Corcovado Mountain overlooking the misty green slopes of Rio de Janeiro, an Austrian parachutist who had fired a cable from a crossbow over the statue's arm at dawn could be seen about to jump from its outstretched hand. (He had left flowers on the shoulder of the Christ 'as a mark of respect.') Thank you, Matt Drudge, for a sublime moment of beauty and awe. Art has migrated from the museums to the Web."

Paglia, Salon.com column, February 23, 2000. "In the three weeks since my last column, Hillary Rodham Clinton has been up hill and down dale, beating the bushes in upstate New York to try to convince someone somewhere that she is a woman of substance rather than a raisin-eyed, carrot-nosed, twig-armed, straw-stuffed mannequin trundled in on a go-cart by the mentally bereft powerbrokers of the state Democratic Party." This passage was picked up by the wire services and startlingly reprinted all over the world. As a native of upstate New York, Paglia was outraged by Hillary's upstate "listening tour," as she ran for Senate in a state where she had never lived (pushing out Bronx-born U.S. Representative Nita Lowey in the process). Cocooned by the Secret Service, Hillary was insulated from unscripted engagement with either voters or the media.

In response to a flood of reader letters supporting Paglia's protest about Kate Winslet losing the Academy Award for Best Actress for *Titanic*: "The Winslet Brigade is taking arms across the globe. I issue an appeal to my fellow warriors: whoever first sees Helen Hunt in public, whether at the grocery store or on the red carpet, please sing out, 'Give back Kate Winslet's Oscar!'"

Paglia, reply, "What Will, or Should Be, the Purpose of Art in This New Century?," *The Art Newspaper* (U.K.), March 2000.

"I'm Peter, Hear Me Roar," *Family Guy,* Fox Broadcasting Company animated TV series, Season 2, Episode 8, aired March 28, 2000. Peter's sexist joke at work leads to a sexual harassment lawsuit and a clash with feminist attorney Gloria Ironbox (voiced by Candice Bergen). For sensitivity training, he is forced to undergo a week at a women's retreat. Peter tells his wife he doesn't want to leave a feminist banquet because "Gloria Ironbox and Camille Paglia are gonna whip it out to see whose is bigger."

Paglia, *The Sunday Telegraph* (U.K.), June 25, 2000. "Revised Editions: Which authors, or books, do not enjoy the standing they deserve?" Series on "underrated reputations." Paglia nominates Rod Serling, whom she calls "the true heir of Edgar Allan Poe": as a Jew, Serling was "an alien" in conservative upstate New York, and his early experiences inspired his political liberalism and his searing defense of the individual against dogma and conformism." Paglia says that "in artistic style," Serling was "a clairvoyant surrealist."

Paglia, "Women Behind the Throne: Today's female politicians can learn a lot from the women of the eighteenth century French court" (on Madame Pompadour and Madame du Barry), *Cigar Aficionado* magazine, June 2000. "Our first female president, who may still be in diapers, will need to study all the achievements and missteps of prominent women from Hatshepsut and Cleopatra to Elizabeth Dole and Hillary Clinton, all of whom have lurched from pothole to pothole on the rocky road to high office."

Heather Findlay, "Paglia 101: Confessions of a campus radical," cover story, *Girlfriends* magazine, September 2000.

Paglia, Salon.com column, October 25, 2000. "As a libertarian, I must also express my opposition yet again to hate crimes legislation, which is not progressive but authoritarian. The government should enforce and even reduce existent laws, not pile on more and more regulation and surveillance, which increase the size and intrusiveness of the state. Hate-crimes bills formalize ideological inquiries into motive that smack of the totalitarian thought police. In a democracy, government has no business singling out one or several groups as more worthy of protection than any other individual or group. Justice should be blind."

Paglia, Salon.com column, November 15, 2000. After a lecture on "The Internet Revolution" at the Chicago Humanities Festival: "My quick visit to Chicago impressed me anew with this pressing national question: Why can't the U.S. guarantee a first-rate, fast-food hot dog to every citizen? . . . The taxi rides in and out of the city were tantalizing torture as an endless series of beckoning, neon-lit, hot dog emporia flew by. The classic American hot dog fell in prestige after the health-food movement of the late 1960s and '70s and can still be savored in its original glory only in scattered regions of the U.S. I lamented this cultural disaster in a feature I did with host Bill Boggs for 'Talking Food' on the TV Food Network in 1995, where we sampled sizzling hot dogs at the upper Broadway branch of Papaya King in New York City."

Paglia, column, in conversation with Ingrid Sischy, "Blonde by Choice," *Interview* magazine, December 2000. "Camille Paglia, Professor of Blonde." Paglia: "As an Italian-American, I have to say that blondeness has been one of the most oppressive themes of my entire life! My Italian immigrant family were aliens in upstate New York, which was still very conservative and Protestant. These local pressures were reinforced by the national messages about blondes coming from ads and the media. It was the period when Doris Day, Debbie Reynolds, and then Sandra Dee absolutely *ruled*. . . . I think blondeness in America is certainly politically reactionary insofar as it posits the supremacy of the old WASP elite."

Paglia, Salon.com column, December 6, 2000. "At a moment of maximum tension in the election standoff [Al Gore's Florida recount after the November 2000 presidential election], the Drudge Report posted a newswire alert about a massive outbreak of solar flares and the possible disruption of world telecommunications and power grids. I view Matt Drudge's pioneering Web site as performance art, a surrealist collage and Warholian series of hour-by-hour Polaroids of modern culture. His startling solar flares posting was literally hair-raising, reminding me of Ulysses' speech about 'degree' in Shakespeare's *Troilus and Cressida:* 'But when the planets / In evil mixture to disorder wander, / What plagues, and what portents, what mutiny, / What raging of the sea, shaking of earth, / Commotion in the winds, frights, changes, horrors, / Divert and crack, rend and deracinate / The unity and married calm of states / Quite from their fixture?' (I.iii.94–101)."

Paglia, Salon.com column, January 17, 2001 (three days before the first inauguration of George W. Bush): "If only one had the exhilarating sense of new beginnings that normally comes with a changing of the guard. But out of some strange psychological stagnancy, Bush has lazily surrounded himself with advisors and appointees from long-gone Republican administrations. It's baffling why someone who urgently needs to prove to the world that he has a political identity separate from that of his president father wouldn't make a more vigorous effort to bring in fresh blood. Bush has simply played into the hands of critics who claim he wasn't ready for the presidency. . . .

"But a bland, bumbling Bush may be better for this country than the hysterical chameleon and monstrous panderer that Democratic nominee Al Gore turned into last year. Given the upsurge in partisan warfare and racial animosity fomented in Florida by Democratic operatives after the election, I wish history could be rewritten: if only we could return to the height of the Monica Lewinsky crisis in 1998 and this time firmly force Clinton out. The Democratic establishment was cowardly and irresponsible in backing off from insisting that Clinton resign. The nation would have been spared two horrendous years of inquests, divisiveness, and legislative paralysis.

"Furthermore, Vice President Al Gore could have assumed the presidency before being overwhelmed by a national campaign and unraveling before our eyes. Had he risen to the presidency by default in 1998, Gore would have gained in stature and experience in the job and, without the burden of the Clinton scandals, might have been easily reelected."

Paglia, Salon.com column, February 28, 2001. "That feminism, despite the triumph in the 1990s of the pro-sex wing to which I belong, is not yet out of the woods is shown by the garish visibility of Eve Ensler and her *Vagina Monologues,* which have apparently spawned copy-cat cells on many campuses. . . . With her obsession with male evil and her claimed history of physical abuse and mental breakdowns, Ensler is the new Andrea Dworkin, minus Medusan hair and rumpled farm overalls. Wasn't one Dworkin quite enough?

"Today's genteel ladies would learn a lot more about life if they would cut the crap and get out of their gilded ghettos. A day at a potato farm or crab-picking plant would do a hell of a lot more for them than an evening at Madison Square Garden with Eve Ensler and her pack of giddy celebrity lemmings in hot-pink suits. . . .

"Here's my kind of role model: Antoinette Cannuli, the Sicilian matriarch of Cannuli's House of Pork in Philadelphia's Italian Market. She was profiled by Rita Giordano in the January 31 *Philadelphia Inquirer* under this headline: 'Vendor is a tough customer: At age 91, South Ninth Street's oldest merchant stays busy. And she still takes no guff.' Celeste Morello, an expert on South Philadelphia, says of Antoinette, who goes to work in her white coat every day at the family butcher shop, 'She is the boss, and the most macho guy in the place shakes when she starts in.'

> During the Depression, Antoinette was helping out at her husband's butcher shop when a customer wouldn't pay the full price for an order of chopped goat. The man told her what she could do with the meat. It wasn't nice. "I had a leg of lamb," Antoinette recalled. "I went boof! Right over the counter. He was bleeding." When she was 14, she insisted on getting a paying job and began work at a Philadelphia tailor shop. Her first day, the boss came by—and gave her a pat on the bottom. "I went Pow, right in the face! I said, 'You touch me again and I'll poke your eyes out!'"

"The energy and ferocity of Italian women, whose power came from the land itself, are the ultimate source of my take-charge philosophy of sexual harassment, which emphasizes personal responsibility rather than external regulation and paternalistic oversight. Too many women have confused feminism, which should be about equal opportunity, with the preservation of bourgeois niceties. Antoinette Cannuli's code of life has infinitely more wisdom than what American students are getting from their politicized textbooks."

"Happy Birthday, Bob: An appreciation of Dylan at 60," *Rolling Stone* magazine, June 7, 2001. "Birthday tributes" from a roundtable including Joni Mitchell, Tom Petty, Bono, and Lucinda Williams. Paglia: "Despite his pose as a Woody Guthrie–type country drifter, Dylan was a total product of Jewish culture, where the word is sacred. In his three surrealistic electric albums of 1965–66 (which remain massive influences on my thinking and writing), Dylan betrayed his wide reading, sensitivity to language, mastery of irony and satire, and acute observation of society. . . . Dylan is a perfect role model to present to aspiring artists. As a young man, he had blazing vision and tenacity. He rejected creature comforts and lived on pure will and instinct. He catered to no one but preserved his testy eccentricity and defiance. And his best work shows how creative imagination operates—in a hallucinatory stream of sensations and emotions that perhaps even the embattled artist does not fully understand."

"Encyclopaedia Anderson," *The New Yorker,* July 16, 2001. The Encyclopaedia Britannica commissions articles on American cities and towns: Laurie Anderson on New York, David Mamet on Chicago, Camille Paglia on Syracuse, and Annie Proulx on Rock Springs, Wyoming.

"Camille Paglia's Top 25 Wicked Women in History," *Talk* magazine, September 2001. Photos with thumbnail profiles.

Paglia's blurb for new Broadway Books edition of Patrick Dennis' *Auntie Mame* (2001): "*Auntie Mame* is the American *Alice in Wonderland.* It is also, incidentally, one of the most important books in my life. Its witty Wildean phrases ring in my mind, and its flamboyant characters still enamor me. Like Tennessee Williams, Patrick Dennis caught the boldness, vitality, and iridescent theatricality of modern American personality. In Mame's mercurial metamorphoses we see American optimism and self-invention writ large."

Murray Dubin, "Newsmakers: 'Sopranos' and its fans are criticized," *The Philadelphia Inquirer,* November 3, 2001. "Author and cultural critic Camille Paglia skewered *The Sopranos* and the critics who have acclaimed it at a lecture at Penn Thursday night. . . . 'It's a travesty. It's a debased characterization of Italians.' " Paglia described the storyline about a mob boss consulting a psychiatrist: "No Italian I know wants to be seen as a victim." She attacked New York media critics for being "full of designer Marxism" and "having no interest in the working class."

"Camille Paglia Gets in Tony Soprano's Face," *The Pennsylvania Gazette* (University of Pennsylvania alumni magazine), January/February 2002. Panel discussion, "Tony Soprano, the Media, and Popular Culture," the Gay Talese Lecture Series at Kelly Writers House. Paglia attacked "the haute bourgeoisie in New York" for overpraise of *The Sopranos,* which she said was "a cryptic version of dealing with race issues": "Italian-Americans are literally the last group that people are free to libel."

Paglia, column, in conversation with Ingrid Sischy, "Winning and Losing," *Interview* magazine, April 2002. *IS:* "If you were producing the Oscars, what would you do?" *CP:* "Well, I think the Oscar organizers are stupidly undercutting what should be the big moment of people getting out of their cars. Why don't producers of pre-show coverage realize that people are tuning in for that? Everyone around the world would watch the stars' arrival, as in the old days, as they grandly pause to wave to the crowd. If I could, I'd lead a rebel movement to get TV to pay full attention to the fashion and limo parade. Nothing but that—cinema verité for two hours, with stable cameras and no choppy cutting or yakking reporters. . . . Ceremony and procession are ancient ritual forms. The Oscars' red carpet should be pure spectacle, an epic extravaganza. . . . The restoration of Oscars night to prestige as performance art was achieved by Sharon Stone in 1994. She stepped from the car swathed in this gorgeous, almost Hindu, black veil, and she just stood there—thanks to her modeling experience—and *glittered*. From that moment forward, everyone went berserk. In fact, for a few years, actresses were laden down with so many jewels and chokers that they looked like camels hauling treasure across the Sahara."

Richard Corliss, "Girls Just Wanna Have Guns: Thrillers with female stars are hot. But is playing victim-heroes a victory for women?," *Time* magazine, April 22, 2002. Paglia: "The problem with current women-in-peril films is they've got the peril but not the deep emotional resonance. They're driven by gimmicky, high-concept plots. But the center of great women's pictures is the long close-up of a woman's soulful, suffering face as her eyes brim with tears. Today's actresses are too buff and brittle to take that kind of scrutiny. Too many know how to do everything but play real women."

Alessandra Stanley and Constance L. Hays, "Martha Stewart's To-Do List May Include Image Polishing," *The New York Times,* June 23, 2002. Camille Paglia wrote after the Stewarts' divorce: "She cut her hair. Now she's a self-complete man/woman on her estate, run by invisible serfs."

Paglia, "Gisela Richter: 1882–1972," in *Invisible Giants: 50 Americans Who Shaped the Nation but Missed the History Books* (2002). "Gisela Richter has inspired me since I first encountered her work on Greek sculpture in college. Like Jane Harrison, the pioneering British classical anthropologist, Richter belonged to a fertile period when enterprising women of great distinction accepted and honored the highest scholarly standards of the male tradition. I admire Richter for her clarity and rigor of mind; her fineness of sensibility and connoisseurship; her attention to detail and her power of observation and deduction; her mastery of form and design. She revered art and viewed herself as its custodian and transmitter to a wider public."

Paglia, "American Babylon" (on New York City), Foreword, *Sex in the City: An Illustrated History* by Alison Maddex (2002).

Thom Jones, "Expanding the Western Mind: Camille Paglia interview," *Urthona: Journal of Buddhism and the Arts* (U.K.) 17 (2002).

Paglia, "The Left Has Lost Its Way and Lost Its Voice," *The Times* (U.K.), August 17, 2002. "The language of leftism is out of date. It desperately needs reconstruction and revitalization, if the Left is ever to regain its proper status as a voice of ethical critique of materialistic modern society. . . . Leftist analysis has been slow to adjust to the massive expansion of the service sector after the Second World War."

Paglia, interviewer, "Interview: Donna Mills," *Interview* magazine, November 2002. Paglia tells Mills: "When the history of feminism is rewritten accurately, Joan Collins' performance as Alexis Carrington on *Dynasty* and yours as Abby Cunningham on *Knots Landing* will be seen as the pivotal roles in popular culture that had a revolutionary impact on women's behavior and self-image. You showed women around the world how to integrate power in the workplace with female sexual power. Joan's persona is very European, but you're the one who created the realistic American version." Mills' sleek, chic, short-skirted power suit became standard business dress for professional women for twenty years.

Paglia, "A Rock Meets a Hard Place," *Golf Digest*, April 2003. Controversy over women being barred from membership at Augusta, home of the Masters Tournament. "Two stubbornly insular groups faced off in the clash between Augusta National Golf Club and the National Council of Women's Organizations, each with its own rigid preconceptions and an unassailable faith in its own moral superiority."

Paglia, "How Far Will Good Intentions Take Hillary?," review of Hillary Clinton's *Living History*, *The Times* (U.K.), June 13, 2003. "Hillary seems to believe that good intentions excuse all. . . . Among other blind spots is the vexed issue of Bill's alleged indiscretions, which Hillary dismisses as agitprop by diabolical foes jealous of her husband's Christlike aspiration to transform earthly life. . . . The book is at its best when Hillary is rueful or self-satirizing. . . . Despite, or perhaps because of, the book's omissions and shadings of fact, Hillary does emerge from it as a credible presidential candidate."

Emily Nussbaum, "Misogyny Plus Girl Power: Original-Recipe Angels," *The New York Times,* June 29, 2003. Review of TV Land documentary on *Charlie's Angels:* "The presentation is unrepentantly rah-rah, with Camille Paglia popping up to remark that 'All of the feminist nags in the world are never going to make that particular show go away.'"

Debbie Stoller, "Fruit for Thought," interview with Paglia, *BUST* magazine, Summer 2003. Stoller asks why, except for Paglia, "feminists haven't had very much to say about gay men." Paglia replies: "Part of the reason is that there was such a parting of the ways in the '70s. Stonewall was enormously liberating in 1969, but the sense of community—of shared adventure and conflict—that lesbians and gay men had had up to that point was gone. By the mid-'70s, the number of men's bars exploded, and when open sex began in the back rooms, the doors of the gay men's bars closed in lesbians' faces. Not a lot of lesbians wanted to be there anyway. Feminism—which I was totally committed to from the start—headed off in this rabid anti-art, anti-pop direction. It left me marooned and isolated. . . . To me it was a real social cataclysm. I think it was culturally impoverishing in many ways that have yet to be assessed. . . . Feminism was navel-gazing with consciousness-raising sessions, trying to plumb the depths of personal victimization. And it was also starry-eyed—looking up at some grand theoretical system about all of history being nothing but male-dominated oppression. So I think that caused a split. Gay men were off partying where disco music was developing out of black culture, while you got awful, sappy music at women's bars. I saw disco as a tremendous cosmic vision of the world—a major form in music history that was absolutely entwined with the sexual revolution. But it was gay men who were pushing that forward, not lesbians. Feminist women were becoming Stalinists, cultural reactionaries. That's where the division started."

"Matt Drudge Gets Personal with Camille Paglia," dialogue about the Drudge Report by Drudge, Paglia, and editor Maer Roshan, *Radar*, Summer 2003. Paglia to Drudge: "There's something retro about your persona. It's like the pre–World War Two generation of reporters— those unpretentious, working-class guys who hung around saloons and used rough language. Now they've all been replaced with these effete Ivy League elitists who swarm over the current media. Nerds— utterly dull and insipid. . . . Your fascination with weather and nature is really interesting to me. You have this sublime mix. There will be all these sordid, squalid tabloid stories—a sex scandal or some hideous crime—and then all of a sudden you'll insert a huge image of a hurricane heading across the Atlantic toward Florida."

Paglia, interview, in Elizabeth G. Messina, *In Our Own Voices: Multidisciplinary Perspectives on Italian and Italian-American Women* (2003).

Paglia, column, in conversation with Ingrid Sischy, "Daring Duos and Daring Doers," special issue, *Interview* magazine, October 2003. *IS:* "This month let's start by your telling me what you think of when you hear the word 'daring.'" *CP:* "The first thing that comes to mind is my earliest role models—Katharine Hepburn and Amelia Earhart. In my teens, I thought Earhart embodied everything that women had been denied. In 1932, she became the first woman to fly solo across the treacherous Atlantic. Her airplane was flimsy, and navigation equipment was primitive. In exactly the same year, Hepburn made a huge splash on Broadway playing an Amazon in *The Warrior's Husband*. She entered by bounding downstairs onstage with a dead stag over her shoulder! Hepburn's athletic physicality broke every rule in terms of women's body language, which had been genteel and contained. Men, of course, wrote the book on daring. Testosterone goes up and down, but when it's really pumping, it pushes them to test limits and put their bodies on the line. Guys are constantly doing crazy things to form their identity—falling to their deaths while walking on a balcony railing when they're drunk, or lying down in the middle of a highway while trucks race by. How many women do that?"

IS: "Some people might call that behavior stupid rather than daring." *CP:* "Exactly—that's the whole point! Stupidity and daring are intertwined. The species moves forward and outward through acts of profound stupidity, which can be inseparable from genius. One of the most notorious sentences in my book, *Sexual Personae,* is, 'There is no female Mozart because there is no female Jack the Ripper.' Women track in the sensible middle, while men veer to radical extremes."

Editor-in-Chief Kerry Lauerman, interview, "Camille Speaks!: Paglia returns to cast a withering eye on Clark ('what a phony!'), Kerry ('the hair!'), Madonna ('a monster'), bloggers—and the 'delusional narcissists' in the White House who led an out-of-his-depth president into a disastrous war," Salon.com, October 29, 2003. "The last time we spoke with Paglia, in February, at the onset of war, she spoke of 'a terrible sense of foreboding' about what would come next. We pick up the conversation from there."

KL: You talked the last time about being "extremely upset about our rush to war." Has it played out as you would have predicted?

CP: How to start! This Iraq adventure is a political, cultural, and moral disaster for the United States. Every sign was there to read, but the Bush administration is run by blinkered people who are driven by ideology and who do not feel the largeness of the world and its multiplicity of religions, ethnicities, and customs. Despite the multicultural ambitions of higher education in the last 25 years, there has been a massive failure in public education. Media negligence also played a huge role in this cataclysm.

Throughout all of last year, as the war drums were beating, the media did not do its job in informing the American people about the complexities of Mideastern history or of the assumptions of world Islam. For example, it should have laid out the dark saga of foolish decision-making by the European powers as they cut up the Ottoman Empire after World War One and unleashed the territorial disputes and animosities that still plague us. With more historical perspective during the debate over Iraq, I don't think the polls would have been as high as they were.

I also blame the media for failing to inform the American people about the ancient history of Mesopotamia and of the vision of Saddam Hussein—who was just a Podunk tyrant who was no threat to the continental U.S.—to revive the greatness of Babylon. If that had been understood, maybe more people would have suspected that all that bluster about stockpiled weapons of mass destruction was hot air. Of course it was in Saddam's regional interest as a macho man to imply that he had this mountain of armaments, that he could strike the West at any moment. The Egyptian pharaohs were always pounding their chests and boasting in exactly the same way. U.S. intelligence was so naïve to have fallen for that, hook, line, and sinker!

Another sin by the media was their failure to publicize the immense archaeological and artistic past of Iraq, to show America that Iraq wasn't just this desert wasteland over a big puddle of oil. Few people realized that until the National Museum was looted after American troops seized Baghdad. Then came—the utter hypocrisy!—tear-stained, hand-wringing articles by those big blowhards at the *New York Times:* "Oh, the Bush administration are such awful vandals!" Well, where the hell were all of you last year? Why didn't *you* show the architecture and artifacts of ancient Mesopotamia or Islamic Baghdad under the caliphate? The American people were led to believe that Baghdad was just a bunch of Bedouin tents huddled in the middle of the desert. As I said the last time I spoke with Salon, I also blame the Democratic senators—

KL: A "bunch of weasels," you called them at the time—

CP: Yes, and that word "weasel" went out from that interview and caught fire. *The New York Post* used it by that weekend, and from there it was seized by the right wing, as in the bestselling "Deck of Weasels" playing cards. It's a great example of the power of Salon: We put "weasel" back into the American vocabulary! . . .

We have catastrophically compromised our internal system of defense against terrorism because of this adventure overseas. Our National Guard and reservists are over there—our first responders for emergencies in terrorist attacks here. The failure in upgrading domestic defense was horrendously clear during the Northeastern blackout in August, when 20 million people lost power. It was shocking to see that nearly two years after 9/11, there was still no emergency evacuation plan in New York to get people across the Hudson River to New Jersey. I monitored the TV for six hours from Philadelphia as over 20,000 people, including old people and pregnant women, were stranded in the baking heat on those wharves like sitting ducks. There were only a few tiny boats ferrying them across the river. Two years, and still no emergency plan to call in the military or National Guard? And there's been no systematic effort to deal with the No. 1 threat to national security—the container ships unloading at our ports. . . .

As Salon readers know, I am not anti-military. On the contrary, I believe in just wars and would have been proud to serve in the military. But this Iraq adventure was a grotesque misuse of American power unleashed on a Third World nation. What pleasure can we take from a victory where our high-tech arms were blasting poorly armed foot soldiers to oblivion? Most of the Iraqi army weren't necessarily Saddam fanatics—they were working-class people just trying to make a living. U.S. officials don't even bother trying to count Iraqi casualties—including civilians—and the American media lets them get away with it. Only American deaths matter; Iraqis are non-persons.

Paglia, "Vera Wang's Fumble," *Philadelphia* magazine, December 2003. Criticizes Wang's "anemic" and "antiseptic" design for the Philadelphia Eagles cheerleaders' uniforms. "Since when do Philly girls lack pizzazz and va-va-voom?" Rather than "chasing after effete Manhattan chic," Eagles owners Jeffrey and Christine Lurie should have hired Donatella Versace instead.

Paglia, column, in conversation with Ingrid Sischy about child stars, *Interview* magazine, February 2004.

Paglia, "What Makes a Woman Truly Sexy?: The Costume Institute's latest exhibition, *Dangerous Liaisons,* reveals those fashions of the 18th century that demonstrate the provocative power of clothes," *Harper's Bazaar,* March 2004.

Patricia Leigh Brown, "Go Fish (Or, Deconstruct This)," *The New York Times*, March 21, 2004. "Theory Trading Cards," created by a British professor. Playing cards with photos of "21 darlings of literary postmodernism." Contacted by the *Times*, Paglia "called the description of her theories on the back of her card 'careless libel.' 'I'm happy to be with Simone de Beauvoir, whose *Second Sex* is one of the biggest and best books written by women. She was disrespected by Foucault, who ripped off Erving Goffman, an inspirational figure for me.'"

Paglia, column, in conversation with Ingrid Sischy about "rock-star style," *Interview* magazine, annual music issue, August 2004. *IS:* "What about women rock stars of that era, like Janis Joplin?" *CP:* "Janis Joplin was an oddity, a Texas blues singer fronting a San Francisco acid-rock band. Her style was eclectic and bizarre, a kind of slatternly, New Orleans hooker look with Moroccan fabrics and backless harem slippers. It was almost Jean Harlowesque—a ripe, womanly thing that was out of sync with contemporary fashion. . . ." *IS:* "Deborah Harry?" *CP:* "A brilliant singer! What crystal clarity and perfect emotional pitch. In the '70s, Blondie turned rock retro. . . . There's a direct line from Harry to Belinda Carlisle of the Go-Go's, who also jumped back to the '50s. . . . Fashion-wise, Belinda Carlisle as a spunky, bratty blonde was the crucial transition between Debbie Harry and Madonna in the '80s."

Paglia, "Mud and Sweat and Joy and Tears: Playing back the sounds of 1969," *Interview* magazine, October 2004. "Rock music split down the middle in 1969." Surveys the major musical events of 1969: the Woodstock Music Festival, the Beatles' last performance, Led Zeppelin's first album, Bob Dylan's *Nashville Skyline*, the Allman Brothers' debut album, David Bowie's "Space Oddity."

Paglia, review of *Zappa*, a biography of musician and composer Frank Zappa by Barry Miles, *The New York Times Book Review*, November 14, 2004.

Sheelah Kolhatkar, "Notes on Camp Sontag," *The New York Observer*, January 5, 2005. "'Mary McCarthy once told Susan [Sontag], "I hear you're the new *me*,'" said Morris Dickstein. . . . 'It's absurd to think there had to be only one woman intellectual, but it's clear that Camille Paglia had that same *All About Eve* feeling toward Susan Sontag that Susan Sontag had toward Mary McCarthy.'" [The *All About Eve* analogy originated with Paglia's essay, "Sontag, Bloody Sontag," in *Vamps & Tramps*. About Sontag's disastrous 1973 visit to Bennington College, Paglia wrote: "It was *All About Eve*, and Sontag was Margo Channing stalked by the new girl."]

Franklin Foer, "Susan Superstar: How Susan Sontag became seduced by her own persona," *New York* magazine, January 14, 2005. "It was telling that Sontag felt such chilliness toward Paglia. Over the last two decades of her life, Sontag became an eloquent critic of the culture's turn away from 'seriousness,' its relinquishment of *Partisan Review* high-mindedness for Paglia-like frivolity. She began to worry that her writings may have played an unwitting role in this change."

Editor-in-Chief Kerry Lauerman, "Warrior for the Word," interview with Paglia after release of *Break, Blow, Burn*, Salon.com, April 7, 2005. Paglia: "Another thing I object to, and the media seems to really ignore, is how many books by prominent academics have been supported by graduate assistants and research assistants, often paid for by the university itself. They're the ones doing all the book-running, checking quotes, accumulating examples, assembling the footnotes and bibliography. As a scholar, I can see it in people's work from major universities. I can tell who are the professors who actually did the reading and gathered the quotes, as opposed to people who are so busy running this or that and exercising academic power that they have to have examples and evidence supplied to them. And what gets me is when a reviewer says in awe: 'This is a very erudite person—there are so many pages of footnotes!' I want to laugh! Well, pages and pages of footnotes in the back of a general-interest humanities book usually indicate weakness. You don't need all that if your scholarship is solid. And the idea that the trendy professors of the elite schools have actually *read* all those books is usually false. Not only haven't they read them, they haven't even gone to the library to get them. I have no research or clerical assistance whatever. I teach at a small college where I must do every single thing myself. But that is what, I believe, sympathetic readers are sensing: quality control."

Paglia, Culture Klatsch column, in conversation with Ingrid Sischy, "Camille Paglia on the Great Academic Meltdown of 2005," *Interview* magazine, May 2005. Paglia: "Universities are always talking about diversity, by which they mean more women, more blacks, more Hispanics—but they never mean intellectual diversity. And so, unfortunately, it's been left to conservatives (like the former radical, David Horowitz) to address that issue and to demand that in courses on politics or gender, both sides be explored. It is our responsibility as teachers to articulate the other side—there should never be a party line in a classroom. Too few teachers these days try to ensure that the classroom is a neutral arena of discourse. In fact, many professors claim that it's their obligation to change the world. They'll say things like, 'Yes, I'm trying to change minds,' or 'The purpose of the university is to effect change in society.' Humanities professors all over the country have been saying that openly for at least 25 years. Well, I don't agree with that at all. A professor is there to help students use the mind in a detached, objective way to analyze society and culture. The moment you attempt to *convert*, you've sold out and become a missionary or ideologue."

"Stan Knows Best," *American Dad,* Fox Broadcasting Company animated TV series, Season 1, Episode 3, aired May 8, 2005. Stan's daughter Hayley is brusquely told by her dictatorial Women's Studies professor at Groff Community College that she cannot attend school without paying her full tuition bill. Hayley takes a job as a waitress serving beer at a strip club. "At least I'm not being exploited like these poor strippers," she says to the woman bartender. "Exploited?," the gravel-voiced bartender retorts. "These girls are being empowered." "Yeah, right," Hayley replies. "Think about it," the bartender goes on: "All they do is show their breasts, and men hand over hundreds of their hard-earned dollars. Who's really being exploited here?" A bespectacled guy slouching over a beer at the other end of the bar pipes up, "Plus, to quote Camille Paglia, these ladies are sexual conquerors controlling the channel between nature and culture. [*shouts across room*] Take it off, bitch!" Hayley [*meditatively*]: "Camille Paglia, huh . . . ?" When Stan unexpectedly turns up for lunch at the strip club, Hayley, sporting a cowgirl outfit in her new persona of "Dusty," waltzes onstage whirling a lasso and ripping her halter top off to the cheers of the crowd.

Cathy Horyn, "The Sweet Smell of Celebrity: Star perfumes are giving a jolt to a business that has known some dismal years," *The New York Times*, June 30, 2005. Color cartoons by Matt Collins of various fantasy perfumes. The "PAGLIA" perfume atomizer is a black, formidably spiked, high-heeled dominatrix boot standing next to its heavily zipped and buckled case, labeled "SCRATCH SNIFF SNEER" (parodying Paglia's new book title, *Break, Blow, Burn*, a line from a John Donne poem).

"Passions," *Philadelphia* magazine, July 2005. On-site photos of the hobbies of high-profile Philadelphians. Paglia says her hobby is the Hollywood film, *The Philadelphia Story* (1940), which she has watched "hundreds of times": "And I still find it mesmerizing. It's such a magical version of gracious living, in an ideal harmony of art and nature." Here Paglia is impersonating Elizabeth Imbrie, the tart-tongued photographer who accompanies Macaulay Connor on a secret mission for *Spy* magazine to the Main Line mansion of Tracy Lord, which was modeled on the Merion house behind Paglia. Full-page photo of Paglia in combat-like paparazzo mode wielding a small camera (duplicating Imbrie's classic Argus C3 rangefinder) on the manicured Lower Merion lawn.

Paglia, "The Thinking Woman's Women: Radio 4's 'Greatest Philosophers' poll yielded an all-male Top 20. But is philosophy really a female-free zone? On the contrary, insists Camille Paglia," *The Independent* (U.K.), July 14, 2005. "Philosophy has shrunk in reputation and stature—it's an academic exercise. . . . The thinker of modern times should be partly abstract and partly practical. . . . Today's lack of major female philosophers is not due to lack of talent but to the collapse of philosophy. Philosophy as traditionally practiced may be a dead genre."

Emily Cox and Henry Rathvon, "Acrostic," *The New York Times Magazine,* July 24, 2005. Paglia and the title of her study of Alfred Hitchcock's *The Birds* are an acrostic, whose filled pattern is a quote from her book: "After shooting had finished, most birds were released. However, fifty crows refused to leave the studio lot and perched near Hitchcock's bungalow. They soiled his car until the tree they were roosting in was cut down."

Paglia, interviewer, "Joni Mitchell: Interview," *Interview* magazine, August 2005. Paglia talks with Mitchell after celebrating her lyric for "Woodstock" in the final chapter in *Break, Blow, Burn,* a study of poetry starting with Shakespeare.

Paglia, "Guardsmen's Deaths Strike at the Heart of America: Their units doubtless had a powerful sense of mission. But it is difficult for me to understand what they died for," *The Independent* (U.K.), August 27, 2005. Paglia condemns "misuse and abuse" of the National Guard by Secretary of Defense Donald Rumsfeld after seven Pennsylvania National Guardsmen are killed in four days in Iraq. Sidebar: Photo of Madonna wearing a sling after breaking her hand, collarbone, and three ribs after falling from a horse at her British country estate. Paglia is quoted from elsewhere criticizing Madonna for her "disrespectful use of horses as props and fashion statements," as on the August cover of *Vogue.*

Paglia, review, *The First Poets: Lives of the Ancient Greek Poets* by Michael Schmidt, *The New York Times Book Review,* August 28, 2005.

Paglia, "Hurricane Katrina Has Demolished This Administration's Mask of Confidence," *The Independent* (U.K.), September 3, 2005.

"Hurricane Katrina is simply the latest chapter in the epic of American nature. It is a subject that Europeans rarely show understanding of in their often dismissive comments on U.S. culture. . . . American history is crammed with tales of fortitude in the face of hostile geography and punishing weather, from the struggle of the *Mayflower* Puritans to survive their first New England winter to the desperate march of pioneers in the 1849 California gold rush through the baking desert of Death Valley."

Amy S. Rosenberg, "The Cosmo Girl at 40," *The Philadelphia Inquirer,* September 7, 2005. "When Cosmo Took the Plunge: Helen Gurley Brown shook things up when she put her sexy imprint on *Cosmopolitan,* now marking 40 years of the Cosmo Girl and her cleavage." Paglia [rejecting early feminist attacks on Brown's magazine]: "It was new, it was radical. So much has become Cosmopolitanized, it's hard to recover how original it was. . . . The Cosmo Girl was an embodiment of personal freedom. . . . It's an Amazonian beauty. They look armored. They're like galleons in full sail—Elizabethan. They dominate men. They have great savoir faire—a sense of poise. They're seductive. There's an active energy that they always projected. Nothing masochistic, nothing vulnerable about them."

Paglia, "Dancing as Fast as She Can: Madonna cannibalizes herself in a misguided attempt to appeal to today's youth," Salon.com, December 2, 2005. Paglia registers disappointment with Madonna's new album, *Confessions on a Dance Floor,* whose evocation of 1970s disco music (revived by Madonna at her debut in the '80s) is flat and uninspired. Includes "Camille Paglia's Disco Playlist," 116 of her most highly recommended songs from soul and funk to disco (1960s–1980s).

Paglia, "The Rise and Fall of T.O.: Terrell Owens enjoyed mythical status in America's toughest sports town." On the controversial Philadelphia Eagles wide receiver. Salon.com, December 14, 2005. Paglia also wrote a cover story on Owens for *Philadelphia* magazine, February 2005.

Roundtable, "Feminist Writers Pay Tribute to Betty Friedan" (after her death), *The Guardian* (U.K.), February 7, 2006. Paglia: "Simone de Beauvoir kept the feminist flame alive after women won the right to vote. Betty Friedan was a pragmatic facilitator who re-created the political organization of the suffrage movement. But Friedan did not, as has been repeatedly claimed, inspire an entire generation of women to ambition and achievement. Those forces were well launched before she published her first book in 1963. Friedan did not create Germaine Greer, nor did she create me. Women in the wake of the sexual revolution rebelled flamboyantly in the 1960s. The women's movement was one strand that emerged from that decade; it was never the whole story. And with her defiant personal history and epic overview of art and politics, Greer remains for me far more central a figure than Friedan."

Paglia, "Academic, Heal Thyself," *The New York Times,* March 6, 2006. Starts: "What went wrong at Harvard?" Postmortem following the resignation of Harvard president Lawrence H. Summers after charges of sexism. Paglia criticizes Summers' "strategic blunders" as well as the "ideological groupthink" and "insularity and excesses" of Harvard faculty, and she condemns the "climate of persecution and extortion around gender issues" on American campuses. "Corruption and cronyism became systemic" in the past three decades of post-structuralism and postmodernism.

Paglia, "Journey to Art," *Gay America Guide,* Winter/Spring 2006. "Five major works of art in the United States that every gay man and woman should have on their radar." Paglia's choices: Bronzino, *Portrait of a Young Man;* Dante Gabriel Rossetti, *Lady Lilith;* Rosa Bonheur, *The Horse Fair;* Jamie Wyeth, *Draft Age;* Andy Warhol, *Kitchen* (film).

Lois E. Beckett, "Paglia Pans Education at the Ivy League," *The Harvard Crimson,* April 12, 2006. "Offending feminists and conservatives alike, Paglia has defined her own political territory. . . . But lambasting higher education—especially at Harvard—seems to have a special place in her heart." Paglia asserts "a very rapid decline in the quality of the humanities" taught in the Ivy League. She says that when she meets recent graduates, "I am shocked at how little they know and what little cultural sense they have."

Robin Abcarian, "Face Up to the Perky: Katie Couric can't escape the adjective. Some say it's descriptive. Others call it sexist," *The Los Angeles Times,* April 15, 2006. "Katie Couric, who is leaving NBC to join CBS, is becoming the first sole female anchor of a nightly network newscast in September." Paglia argues that "gravitas" is real and that many women have possessed it: Simone de Beauvoir, Lillian Hellman, Ayn Rand, Toni Morrison, and Dianne Feinstein. Paglia: "Women, if they ever expect to ascend to the presidency and be commander in chief, had better learn what 'gravitas' is and stop blowing it off as some sort of backlash word." Paglia says Couric is indeed both perky and "girly." About Couric, who interviewed her during a 1994 book tour, Paglia says, "I found her pleasant but weightless, depthless. Backstage in the green room, she said to me with a look of wonderment in her eyes, 'But Camille, why do you say all those controversial things when you know you will be criticized?' I was dumbfounded."

Paglia, "Mercurial Girl," *Rolling Stone* 1,000th Commemorative Issue, *Rolling Stone* magazine, May 18–June 1, 2006. Paglia was asked to comment on Steven Meisel's "Flesh and Fantasy" portfolio of Madonna, published in *Rolling Stone* in 1991. Paglia calls it "a tribute to Brassai": "In the lacquered hard glamour of Meisel's cover image, we see Madonna shedding her early identification with the tender comedic vulnerability of Marilyn Monroe and Judy Holliday. She has become a sophisticated, world-weary Marlene Dietrich, a cynical dominatrix of Prussian discipline."

Tom Chiarella, "The Problem with Boys," *Esquire,* July 2006. Paglia: "The masculine impulse is limits testing, even self-destructive. We don't want to extinguish it. In the age of terrorism, who will defend us? Young jihadists sure aren't tempering their masculinity. Americans are in unilateral gender disarmament."

Paglia, "Marie Antoinette Ascendant," *The Chronicle Review, The Chronicle of Higher Education,* September 22, 2006. Review of new books, a Hollywood movie, and a PBS documentary on Marie Antoinette. "The Marie Antoinette story, with its premonitions of doom amid a giddy fatalism, seems to signal a pervasive guilt about near-intractable social inequities." Reprinted in *The San Francisco Chronicle,* October 8, 2006.

Mark Adnum, interview, "Cruising with Camille," *Bright Lights Film Journal,* outrate.net, November 1, 2006. *MA:* Oliver Stone once said that every gay man thinks they're a film critic, and Quentin Crisp said that he went to the movies "incessantly and reverently." Yet, as far as I know there's no particularly deep relationship between cinema and lesbian culture. How would you account for this?

CP: I noticed this odd phenomenon while I was still in college. I had a community of response to film with gay men but virtually zero with lesbians. It's partly why my dating life was such a frustrating blank! My theory is that gay men, unlike lesbians, have an innate, hyper-acute visual sense. It's related to what I have speculated to be the genesis of much (but not all) male homosexuality: an artistic gene that ends up isolating sensitive young boys and interfering at a crucial moment with the harsh dynamics of schoolyard male bonding.

I loved *Cruising*—while everyone else was furiously condemning it. It had an underground decadence that wasn't that different from *The Story of O* or other European high porn of the 1960s. I bought the *Cruising* soundtrack, which was really radical for its time, and played it for years. . . . The gay opposition to *Cruising* prefigured the dismayingly Stalinist gay and feminist picketing of *Basic Instinct*—in which Sharon Stone created one of the most indelible, charismatic dominatrixes of all time. It's why I was so pleased to be invited to do the audio commentary for the DVD of *Basic Instinct* (which I recorded in a Philadelphia studio famed for its old soul and disco hits)." [The recording session for the 1996 DVD was in the historic Sigma Sound Studios, where David Bowie had recorded several tracks with producer Luther Vandross for *Young Americans.*]

"Camille Paglia Says Madonna Gave Britney the 'Kiss of Death,'" *US* magazine, December 8, 2006. Paglia: "A great promise was contained in the moment when Madonna kissed Britney [Spears] at the MTV Awards. She in a sense was saying, 'I'm passing the torch to you.' It was a fabulous moment. Britney looked toned, in control of her career, and it was up to her to take the next step. Literally from that kiss, from that moment onward, Britney has spiraled out of control. It's like Madonna gave her the kiss of death! Britney is throwing it away!"

Roundtable tributes to Betty Friedan (after her death), *Entertainment Weekly,* year-end special, December 29, 2006–January 5, 2007. Paglia: "Betty Friedan wasn't afraid to be called 'abrasive.' She pursued her feminist principles with a flamboyant pugnacity that has become all too rare in these yuppified times. She hated girliness and bourgeois decorum and never lost her earthy ethnicity."

Paglia, "What I See in the Mirror" (recurring feature), *The Guardian Weekend Supplement,* January 6, 2007. "When I look in the mirror, I'm glad to see anything at all. Shrinkage is one of the more outrageous aspects of aging. . . . Unlike Susan Sontag and Germaine Greer—tall, majestic, and commanding every eye—I've always been small and nondescript. . . . 'Dimples are death,' a gay fellow confided darkly to me in college. Alas, his dire prophecy has proved all too true. . . . Fortunately, my earliest fond memories are of bossy, hyperkinetic old Italian widows with sun-crinkled faces. Hence it's probably no coincidence that my lifetime idol is Keith Richards, that piratical pioneer of the weathered look."

Paglia, column, in conversation with Ingrid Sischy about Paglia's "worship" of Elizabeth Taylor during the Doris Day–Debbie Reynolds era. In cover story package on Taylor, *Interview* magazine, February 2007.

Paglia, "Wonder Women: Camille Paglia on Dames Who Rise to the Top," *The Globe and Mail,* March 24, 2007. "Why can't a woman . . .

As more and more strong women rise to the top of the political world, Camille Paglia ponders the paradigms of power and gender." Reprinted in *The San Francisco Chronicle* as "Women Warriors: From Hedda to Hillary—the long struggle for power, success," April 8, 2007.

Paglia, Salon.com column, April 11, 2007. Response to reader question about global warming. "As a native of upstate New York, whose dramatic landscape was carved by the receding North American glacier 10,000 years ago, I have been contemplating the principle of climate change since I was a child. Niagara Falls, as well as the even bigger dry escarpment of Clark Reservation near Syracuse, is a memento left by the glacier. So is nearby Green Lakes State Park, with its mysteriously deep glacial pools. When I was ten, I lived with my family at the foot of a drumlin—a long, undulating hill of moraine formed by eddies of the ancient glacier melt.

"Geology and meteorology are fields that have always interested me and that I might well have entered, had I not been more attracted to art and culture. (My geology professor in college, in fact, asked me to consider geology as a career.) To conflate vast time-frames with volatile daily change is a sublime exercise, bordering on the metaphysical.

"However, I am a skeptic about what is currently called global warming. I have been highly suspicious for years about the political agenda that has slowly accrued around this issue. As a lapsed Catholic, I detest dogma in any area. . . . From my perspective, virtually all of the major claims about global warming and its causes still remain to be proved.

"Climate change, keyed to solar cycles, is built into earth's system. Cooling and warming will go on forever. Slowly rising sea levels will at some point doubtless flood Lower Manhattan and seaside houses everywhere from Cape Cod to Florida—as happened to Native American encampments on those very shores. Human habitation is always fragile and provisional. People will migrate for the hills, as they have always done.

"Who is impious enough to believe that earth's contours are permanent? Our eyes are simply too slow to see the shift of tectonic plates that has raised the Himalayas and is dangling Los Angeles over an unstable fault. I began *Sexual Personae* (parodying the New Testament), 'In the beginning was nature.' And nature will survive us all. Man is too weak to permanently affect nature, which includes infinitely more than this tiny globe. . . . Environmentalism is a noble cause. It is damaged by propaganda and half-truths."

Response to reader question about the publishing by Susan Sontag's former lover Annie Leibovitz of "the photos and details of her final days": "Last fall, I was astonished at the inert lack of response by cultural commentators to Annie Leibovitz's gross publication of her photos of Sontag's corpse, as well as of the bloated Sontag hospitalized before her death. When *Newsweek* posted the weird corpse photo online (to accompany its October 2, 2006, cover story on Leibovitz), I could find very little intelligent reaction on the blogosphere—which is one reason I decided it was time to return to Salon.

"For Leibovitz to use those photos to sell a new book seemed callously exploitative to me—though I have been one of Sontag's most outspoken critics. The major media, presumably cowed by Leibovitz, raised no questions about longstanding reports of a bitter ending to her relationship with Sontag years before. Were no red flags raised for editors or journalists at Leibovitz's sudden candor and exhibitionism when Sontag was safely dead?

"Nor did anyone seem to blink at Leibovitz boasting about buying Sontag an apartment in Paris and helping maintain Sontag's lifestyle in her private Manhattan penthouse with a gigantic wraparound terrace (pictured in the book; Leibovitz lived elsewhere). . . . What does it say about so prominent a leftist intellectual that she was being effectively supported by *Vanity Fair* magazine (Leibovitz's employer)?— whose orientation is toward an entertainment and celebrity culture that the public Sontag ostentatiously opposed. . . .

"And as long as I am lodging complaints, what about the excessive number of friends and acquaintances who were allowed to write Sontag's major obituaries two years ago? Their personal anecdotes were naïvely vain enough to unintentionally reveal what a party animal she was. Parties were Sontag's element: it was there that she played the philosopher queen bee, dazzling with her Delphic pronouncements and curtly giving the cold shoulder to the unworthy. And it was there that she embedded herself with the powers that be in the publishing and literary world, which closed ranks around her. (In contrast, I avoid parties wherever possible and have even declined my publisher's offer of book parties.)

Over time, Sontag's reputation will stand or fall not on her compulsive socializing and networking (which should raise doubts about her putative seriousness) but on her writing. Others will make those judgments. I myself feel that Sontag was a serial name-dropper who made gestures at subjects rather than saying something new, true, or memorable about them. Except for a few essays, when she was a witness to the surging avant-garde scene in downtown New York, Sontag rarely delivered what she advertised."

"Go Hillary: Camille Paglia on the remarkable reinvention of Mrs. Clinton" (cover line), *Harper's Bazaar* (U.K.), May 2007. Paglia describes how she was "a huge fan of Hillary" at the start: "I thought she embodied the feisty, outspoken spirit of my generation of postwar American women. However, I became swiftly disillusioned when she mishandled her first assignment: healthcare reform." A huge opportunity for bipartisan consensus was lost because of Hillary's "arrogance and obsession with secrecy." Paglia says that she was the first to compare Hillary to Eva Perón ("the analogy became standard after that") and that she considered Hillary's behavior during the Lewinsky scandal to be "reprehensible." However, "my views moderated when *The Times* [U.K.] asked me to review Hillary's memoir, *Living History*, in 2003. I was pleasantly surprised at the case made in it for Hillary's lifetime of political commitment."

Paglia, review, *Teenage: The Creation of Youth Culture* by Jon Savage, *The New York Times Book Review*, May 6, 2007. Reprinted in the *International Herald Tribune*.

Margaret Wente, interview, "Camille Paglia: Hillary can't win—and shouldn't. The kids are all right, but academia is not," *The Globe and Mail*, September 15, 2007. Paglia responds to Wente's description of Hillary having done "pretty well on her own" as a U.S. senator from

New York: "She was able to succeed as a carpetbagger in New York State because she's the very image of the corporate-legal meritocracy of Manhattan. I cannot stand the snobbery and elitism of this lawyer-heavy superclass. Hillary and her friends are symptomatic of that class. She can glide through those corridors extremely well. But one feels that she has no real pleasures. There's something about Hillary that's anhedonic—the inability to take pleasure in the moment. Everything for her is this beady-eyed scheming for the future, combined with this mass of resentments for the past, the people who have done them wrong."

Paglia, "Gender Studies and Male Sexuality," *The Chronicle Review, The Chronicle of Higher Education,* September 21, 2007. Inside headline: "Rigid Scholarship on Male Sexuality." Pull quote: "When any field becomes a closed circle, the result is groupthink and cant." Generally negative review of three books from university presses: *Images of Bliss: Ejaculation, Masculinity, Meaning* by Murat Aydemir; *Impotence: A Cultural History* by Angus McLaren; *Sperm Counts: Overcome by Man's Most Precious Fluid* by Lisa Jean Moore. "All three of these books, in different ways, share the same dourly judgmental gender-studies doctrine. . . . The stultifying clichés of gender studies must end."

Roundtable, "Can Politicians Solve Climate Change?," Democracy Special, *The Observer* (U.K.), September 30, 2007. Paglia: "Whether we are presently experiencing genuine climate change, or whether the global weather system, powered by the sun, is simply undergoing a transient fluctuation of the convection patterns of average temperatures, remains ambiguous. Politicians hawking hysterical global-warming dogma do a disservice to science."

Kerry Reid, "Hell in a Handbag takes 'Birds' on Wild Flight," *Chicago Tribune,* October 12, 2007. Theater review of the remount of a 2001 show originally staged by Sweetback Productions: an "astute and hilarious deconstruction of Hitchcock's 1963 ornithological nightmare" by David Cerda and Pauline Pang. The script was inspired by Paglia's 1998 book on Alfred Hitchcock's *The Birds* for the British Film Institute. Paglia is a character in the play, "the on-set acting coach/therapist" for Tippi Hedren. The fictive Paglia also "pursues an affair with doomed schoolteacher Annie Hayworth," played by "a brilliant Cerda" in drag.

Liz Smith, Celebrity News, *The Baltimore Sun,* December 19, 2007. " 'I revere Norman Mailer as a unique modern voice. Shrewd, sly, and oddly cherubic, he was like a garrulous blogger, tirelessly processing the stream of contemporary events through his brilliantly scintillating intellect.' So writes Camille Paglia in the year-end issue of *Rolling Stone*" [after Mailer's death].

Paglia, Salon.com column, on the presidential primaries, January 9, 2008. "Hillary's feckless, loutish brothers (who are kept at arm's length by her operation) took the brunt of Hugh Rodham's abuse in their genteel but claustrophobic home. Hillary is the barracuda who fought for dominance at their expense. Flashes of that ruthless old family drama have come out repeatedly in this campaign, as when Hillary could barely conceal her sneers at her fellow debaters onstage—the wimpy, cringing brothers at the dinner table.

"Hillary's willingness to tolerate Bill's compulsive philandering is a function of her general contempt for men. She distrusts them and feels morally superior to them. Following the pattern of her long-suffering mother, she thinks it is her mission to endure every insult and personal degradation for a higher cause—which, unlike her self-sacrificing mother, she identifies with near-messianic personal ambition. . . . Hillary's disdain for masculinity fits right into the classic feminazi package, which is why Hillary acts on Gloria Steinem like catnip. . . . The Clintons live to campaign. It's what holds them together and gives them a glowing sense of meaning and value."

Gary Kramer, "Horror Comedy 'Teeth' Glistens," *The San Francisco Bay Times,* January 24, 2008. Interview with writer/director Mitchell Lichtenstein, whose new film was inspired by the myth of the vagina dentata: "I learned about it years ago in college [Bennington] from Camille Paglia, who referenced it in late-nineteenth-century literature.

It was fruitful territory. The myth is pervasive in ancient cultures and religions. It deals with fears men had about women. It had not been addressed much in pop culture, and I thought it would be informative and fun." [Paglia rewrote the passage in Lichtenstein's script where the heroine intently surfs the Web to inform herself about the vagina dentata. However, in a piquant surprise, the Writers Guild overruled Lichtenstein's granting Paglia a writing credit in the final cut because she is not a Guild member. So he simply thanked her in the closing credits.]

Paglia, Culture Klatsch column, "Why the Melting-Pot Ideal Must Not Melt," in conversation with Ingrid Sischy about immigrants and immigration, *Interview* magazine, February 2008.

Paglia, "Why Women Shouldn't Vote for Hillary," *The Sunday Telegraph* (U.K.), April 20, 2008. "Is Hillary Clinton the savior of feminism? Or its albatross, dragging feminism backward under a weary weight of old-guard victimology and male-bashing? . . . Any woman with the temerity to endorse Barack Obama (as I do) is condemned as a 'traitor' to her sex. . . . Hillary has always been a policy wonk, a functionary attuned to bureaucratic process, but she has never shown executive ability, which makes her quest for the presidency problematic. . . . Well into her second term as a U.S. senator, Hillary lacks a single example of major legislative achievement."

Paglia, Salon.com column, May 14, 2008. "Most of the media fell hook, line, and sinker for the 'Iron my shirt!' stunt at a Hillary campaign event in January in New Hampshire, where two scruffy male hecklers were clearly in collusion with her staff. (The signs—including one suspiciously permitted on the stage itself—were carefully positioned and lit, and Hillary had a pat prepared line to draw camera attention to them.) Those dorky guys, at least one with a link to a radio station, are far too young to have the slightest knowledge of an era when women ironed men's shirts—or when shirts needed ironing at all! Businessmen's shirts go to the cleaners nowadays, and everyone else's gear is just tossed into the dryer. That hoax was designed to reawaken the atavistic resentments of older women voters—and it worked."

Kate Ward, interviewer, "In Defense of the Working Girl," in cover story package on *Sex and the City* (at release of the first *Sex and the City* movie), *Entertainment Weekly*, May 23, 2008. Paglia: "*Sex and the City* is extremely important in entertainment history because of the way it foregrounded the pro-sex feminist movement of the 1990s that I was part of. The show is the most visible result of that generational shift away from the anti-pornography crusade that had dominated feminism in the 1970s and '80s. It was a tremendous explosion, proclaiming that the young modern woman was no longer afraid of sex and was an independent agent who actively embraced it. On the one hand, *Sex and the City* is a love poem to New York and to the glitter of Manhattan. But on the other hand, there's a chilliness to it because it starkly shows how young, unmarried women are at the mercy of men who have more wealth and power. . . . Over time, the show really turned into an accurate anthropological chronicle of the bittersweet dilemma faced by the modern career woman. For every big career gain she makes, there's a trade-off in her personal life."

Paglia, "Hillary Clinton's Candidacy Has Done Feminism No Favors," *The Telegraph* (U.K.), May 24, 2008. "Hillary has tried to have it both ways: to batten on her husband's nostalgic popularity while simultaneously claiming to be a victim of sexism. Well, which is it? Are men convenient sugar daddies or condescending oppressors?"

Paglia, Salon.com column, June 11, 2008. "And here's another whopping female advantage: Hillary could jet around the country with an elaborate, color-keyed wardrobe and a professional hair and makeup crew, who plastered and insta-lifted her with dewy salon uber-ointments and cutting-edge technology before every appearance. No male candidate has ever had that theatrical privilege. (John Edwards, in contrast, was heaped with scorn for his simple yet pricey haircut.) When the mega-prep for some reason failed—as on a frigid morning in Iowa—the resultant photo of Hillary in realistically wrinkled 60-year-old mode caused repercussions around the world. Golda Meir, with her robustly lived-in face and matriarchal jowls, would have given ever-primping Hollywood Hillary a derisive Bronx cheer."

Paglia describes receiving a backstage gift of DVDs from the staff of Brazilian superstar Daniela Mercury after an illustrated lecture on "Varieties of the Erotic in 20th Century Art" in the Frontiers of Thought series at the Teatro Castro Alves in Salvador da Bahia, Brazil. "Watching Daniela Mercury in action, I realized just how bored and disillusioned I have become by American popular entertainment over the past fifteen years, when Madonna went corporate and lost her grip on the Zeitgeist. All that passionate, improvisational, open-air vitality has been going on in Brazil while American music fans have been trapped like doped steers in the commercial stockyard of overpriced, over-packaged arena concerts, where performers trot out canned patter in between the computerized special-effects lighting. Low-budget 'alternative' musicians are just as programmatic, with their rote political bromides or their dated affectations of urban irony."

Paglia, preface to *Camp Nest (Place Space),* book series produced by American designer Todd Oldham (2008). "Located near a small pond in the Hudson River valley between the Catskill and Berkshire mountains, Joseph Holtzman's Camp Nest is a singular fusion of several antecedents in American architectural history. . . . The British town-and-country shuttle of the rich and famous was mimicked by U.S. tycoons in the Gilded Age. . . . As a country retreat, Camp Nest rejects the pomp and circumstance of America's landed gentry and opts instead for a more casual, vernacular idiom. It aligns itself with Adirondack Mountain cabins, with their rustic local materials and humble display of natural wood."

Paglia, Salon.com column, August 13, 2008. "On the pop front, Madonna's life has been passing before our eyes like a decadent German expressionist film. . . . Sex for sternly workaholic Madonna has become a brittle concept rather than a sensual reality. . . . What happened to Madonna? I have had a series of revelations about this since my trip to Brazil in May. . . . Thinking about Daniela Mercury [dubbed 'Brazil's Madonna'], I suddenly realized that Madonna is a displaced person, a refugee. She has lost her roots—Motown, the city of Detroit (called the Motor City because of its auto industry), outside of which she grew up. Detroit had been a major capital of black music in her youth, but its vitality ebbed, partly because of the economic recession that devastated so many Midwestern industrial cities. Madonna would be instrumental in giving artistic legitimacy to disco music, once an underground style of black and gay clubs. As a dancer, she zeroed in on the propulsive, percussive African rhythms at disco's heart.

"Second, the immigrant Italian-American culture from which Madonna emerged also disintegrated over time. I too am a product of it, and I am heartsick that, because of social assimilation, very little is left (except for the vulgar libels of *The Sopranos*). . . . Daniela Mercury, in contrast, has never left her roots [in her native city of Salvador da Bahia.] . . . Bahia is the most Africanized region in Brazil. Up to 80 percent of its inhabitants have been estimated to have some African lineage." Discusses "religious syncretism" and the survival of Yoruba cults in modern Candomblé in Bahia. Annotated list of video links illustrating Daniela's artistic superiority to current work by Madonna.

Paglia, "Why Philly Matters: Ribbons in the Skyline. Springsteen famously sang about the streets of Philadelphia, but our most stunning achievement lies a bit higher. Touring the city's breathtaking, sadly unheralded architecture, Camille Paglia offers a simple piece of advice: Look up, people," *Philadelphia* magazine, December 2, 2008.

Roundtable, "Women on the Verge: The real meaning of heels," cover story, *The Sunday Times Magazine* (U.K.), December 13, 2008. Among the contributors: Germaine Greer, Vivienne Westwood, Antonia Fraser. Paglia: "In our time of amplified bosoms, liposuction, and Botox, pretty feet are the one thing that can't be faked. Male-to-female transsexuals can get it all chopped off, but they're often still stuck with those big, bony feet. Today's ultra-high heels are unforgivingly candid about legs too—showing off great ones and cruelly exposing thick ankles and knock knees. Height does indeed equal power in a man's world—which is how shrimpy Napoleon's name ended up on a complex."

"Pleasure Is My Business," *Criminal Minds,* CBS crime-drama series, Season 4, Episode 16, aired February 25, 2009. Directed by Gwyneth Horder-Payton. A high-priced call girl is killing top corporate executives in Dallas. FBI agent Aaron Hotchner (Thomas Gibson) in opening voiceover: "The prostitute is not, as feminists claim, the victim of men but rather their conqueror, an outlaw who controls the sexual channel between nature and culture—Camille Paglia."

Paglia, Salon.com column, June 9, 2009. "Barack Obama was elected to do exactly what he did last week at Cairo University—to open a dialogue with the Muslim world. Or at least that was why I, for one, voted for him, contributed to his campaign, and continue to support him. . . . The Cairo speech is well-organized, ticking off central thorny issues region by region. But there is an unsettling slackness and even sentimentality in its view of history. . . . It is also puzzling how a major statement about religion could be so detached from religion."

Paglia calls Judge Sonia Sotomayor's reference to herself as "a wise Latina" (whose Supreme Court deliberations would trump those of "a white male") "a vestige of the bad old days of male-bashing feminism when even the doughty Ann Richards was saying [in her keynote address] to the 1988 Democratic National Convention: 'Ginger Rogers did everything that Fred Astaire did. She just did it backwards and in high heels.' What flatulent canards mainstream feminism used to traffic in! Fred Astaire, idolized even by Mikhail Baryshnikov, was one of the most brilliant and peerless dancers and choreographers of the twentieth century. The agile but limited Ginger Rogers, a spunky, smart-mouthed comedienne, is only a footnote. Get real, girls! This is the kind of mushy balderdash I doggedly had to plow through for five years in trying to find a good feminist poem for my collection, *Break, Blow, Burn.* I never found one. Rule of art: cant kills creativity!"

Cathal Kelly, "Contrarian Queen: The gospel according to Paglia," *The Toronto Star,* June 13, 2009. Paglia interviewed as the third and final speaker in a lecture series on the Ten Commandments at Toronto's Royal Ontario Museum, marking an exhibit on the Dead Sea Scrolls. Christopher Hitchens was the first speaker two weeks earlier. Paglia: "Hitchens is a cynic, and he knows nothing about religion. It's one thing to attack it from the basis of knowledge. I thought that book [Hitchens' *God Is Not Great*] was awful. Awful book! That could have been a great book. He's lazy! He just wants to sit around and have dinner parties and drink in Washington. The book is like, *chatted*. . . . Unlike Christopher Hitchens, I take books seriously."

Paglia, Salon.com column, August 12, 2009. "Obama's aggressive endorsement of a healthcare plan that does not even exist yet, except in five competing, fluctuating drafts, makes Washington seem like Cloud Cuckoo Land. . . . You can keep your doctor; you can keep your insurance, if you're happy with it, Obama keeps assuring us in soothing, lullaby tones. Oh, really? And what if my doctor is not the one appointed by the new government medical boards for ruling on my access to tests and specialists? And what if my insurance company goes belly-up because of undercutting by its government-bankrolled competitor? Face it: virtually all nationalized health systems, neither nourished nor updated by profit-driven private investment, eventually lead to rationing. I just don't get it. Why this insane rush to pass a bill, any bill, in three weeks? . . . Somehow liberals have drifted into a strange servility toward big government, which they revere as a god-like foster father-mother who can dispense all bounty and magically heal all ills."

Paglia, Salon.com column, September 8, 2009. "Why has the Democratic party become so arrogantly detached from ordinary Americans? Though they claim to speak for the poor and dispossessed, Democrats have increasingly become the party of an upper-middle-class professional elite, top-heavy with journalists, academics, and lawyers (one reason for the hypocritical absence of tort reform in the healthcare bills). . . . Affluent middle-class Democrats now seem to be complacently servile toward authority and automatically believe everything party leaders tell them. Why? Is it because the new professional class is a glossy product of generically institutionalized learning? Independent thought and logical analysis of argument are no longer taught. Elite education in the U.S. has become a frenetic assembly line of competitive college application to schools where ideological brainwashing is so pandemic that it's invisible. The top schools, from the Ivy League on down, promote 'critical thinking,' which sounds good but is in fact just a style of rote regurgitation of hackneyed approved terms ('racism, sexism, homophobia') when confronted with any social issue. The Democratic brain has been marinating so long in those clichés that it's positively pickled.

"Throughout this fractious summer, I was dismayed not just at the self-defeating silence of Democrats at the gaping holes or evasions in the healthcare bills but also at the fogginess or insipidity of articles and op-eds about the controversy emanating from liberal mainstream media and Web sources.... There was a glaring inability in most Democratic commentary to think ahead and forecast what would or could be the actual snarled consequences—in terms of delays, denial of services, errors, miscommunications, and gross invasions of privacy—of a massive single-payer overhaul of the healthcare system in a nation as large and populous as ours. It was as if Democrats live in a utopian dream world, divorced from the daily demands and realities of organization and management....

"Having said all that about the failures of my own party, I am not about to let Republicans off the hook. What a backbiting mess the GOP is! It lacks even one credible voice of traditional moral values on the national stage and is addicted to sonorous pieties of pharisaical emptiness. Republican politicians sermonize about the sanctity of marriage while racking up divorces and sexual escapades by the truckload. They assail government overreach and yet support interference in women's control of their own bodies. Advanced whack-a-mole is clearly needed for that yammering smarty-pants, Newt Gingrich, who is always so very, very pleased with himself but has yet to produce a single enduring thought."

Margaret Wente, interview, "It's a Landscape of Death in the Humanities," *The Globe and Mail,* May 1, 2010. Paglia (scheduled to talk about education at the Open House Festival in Toronto): "The long view of history is absolutely crucial. There are long patterns of history. Civilizations rose and fell, and guess what! It's not a fiction. I believe in chronology, and I believe it's our obligation to teach it. . . . The problem today is that professors feel they are far too sophisticated and important to do something as mundane as teach a foundation course. So what the heck are parents paying all that money for?"

Sarah Kaufman, "Books That Inspired Art, from Sculpture to Rap," *The Washington Post,* August 15, 2010. Septime Webre, Artistic Director of the Washington Ballet, "created a ballet called 'Fluctuating Hemlines' after reading Camille Paglia's provocative dissection of what drives Western culture, *Sexual Personae.* 'It was a very incendiary, outrageous book,' says Webre. 'The central thesis is that we are essentially raw, animalistic beings. . . . I was starting to feel we all had an underground life, inaccessible to anyone else. That seemed like an interesting notion for a dance.' . . . 'I'm interested in theatricality,' Webre says. 'I come from this big Cuban family where there was lots of drama, so heightened drama is a natural state.' "

Roundtable (23 contributors), "Defining Idea of the Next Decade," *The Chronicle Review, The Chronicle of Higher Education,* September 3, 2010. Paglia: "Revalorizing the Trades."

Paglia, "Lady Gaga and the Death of Sex: An erotic breaker of taboos or an asexual copycat? Camille Paglia, America's foremost cultural critic, demolishes an icon," cover story, *The Sunday Times Magazine* (U.K.), September 12, 2010. "Lady Gaga is the first major star of the digital age. . . . Since her rise, Gaga has remained almost continually on tour. Hence she is a moving target who has escaped serious scrutiny. . . . How could a figure so calculated and artificial, so clinical and strangely antiseptic, so stripped of genuine eroticism have become the icon of her generation?" Paglia on the contributors' page: "For two years her publicity juggernaut has rolled over supine journalists on both sides of the Atlantic. Why was there so little protest and even less analysis? Has cultural criticism gone moribund?"

"Op-Ed at 40: Four Decades of Argument and Illustration," *The New York Times,* September 25, 2010. Paglia's "Madonna—Finally a Real Feminist" (December 14, 1990) is republished as one of the most significant op-eds in *The New York Times* since it invented that editorial format 40 years earlier. A video interview with Paglia (taped in Philadelphia) is also posted in the online package: "For Op-Ed's 40th Anniversary, author and professor Camille Paglia recounts the story behind her 1990 op-ed about feminism, Madonna, and the music video 'Justify My Love.'" [It was this hugely controversial op-ed, commissioned by *The New York Times,* that catapulted Paglia from obscurity to infamy, after the publication of her first book, *Sexual Personae,* earlier that year. In discussion with a skeptical editorial board, editor David Shipley boldly supported the article's pioneering use of slang, which broke traditional protocols at the august *New York Times.*]

Paglia, "So Bold, Bad, and Beautiful: Elizabeth Taylor was brazenly sexual in an era of ponytails and bobby socks. She thrilled Camille Paglia, the feminist and culture critic, who says we will not see her like again" (photo of fetchingly half-dressed Taylor on the set of *Giant* taking up entire front page), cover story, News Review, *The Sunday Times* (U.K.), March 27, 2011. Reprint of Paglia's tribute to Taylor in Salon .com after her death that week.

Paglia, "A Cry of Lost Womanhood," *The Sunday Times* (U.K.), June 12, 2011. Photo of Slutwalk marchers the prior day in London. Paglia: "Prostitutes, strippers, pornographers—these are my Babylonian ideals. . . . The swift global spread of Slutwalk strikingly demonstrates the energy and aspirations of young feminists. But its confused message is a symptom of the sexual chaos and anomie of the Western bourgeoisie. Don't call yourself a slut unless you are prepared to live and defend yourself like one. My creed is street-smart feminism, alert, wary, and militant—the harsh survival code of streetwalkers and drag queens. Sex is a force of nature, not just a social construct. Monsters stalk its midnight realm."

Paglia, review, *The Doors: A Lifetime of Listening to Five Mean Years* by Greil Marcus, *The New York Times Book Review,* December 4, 2011.

Paglia, "The True Voice of America—Adele from Tottenham," News Review, *The Sunday Times* (U.K.), February 19, 2012. "The singer swept all before her at the Grammys. You Brits have found us a genuine new superstar, says the cultural critic Camille Paglia."

"With her armload of six trophies, Adele was the golden girl of the Grammys last weekend, matching Beyoncé's record for the most awards received by a female artist in one night. Adele's performance of 'Rolling in the Deep,' which won Grammys for record of the year and song of the year, triggered one of the biggest, loudest standing ovations in the history of award shows. . . . Partly energizing the audience's response to Adele's performance was its subliminal recognition that 'Rolling in the Deep' (co-written and produced by Paul Epworth) belongs to the magnificent tradition of African-American music that produced Whitney Houston.

"From its opening raw guitar strum to its soaring, thunderous climax, 'Rolling in the Deep' recapitulates the entire history of black music. We hear the percussive accents of early rural Southern blues, with its hand-clapping and foot-stomping, along with a defiant touch of Native American war drums. Next is Adele's incarnation as a voluptuous belter in the 'big mama' style of rowdy roadhouse blues, typified by Bessie Smith. As an agonized torch song, 'Rolling in the Deep' also evokes the subsequent phase in musical style, the urban jazz sophistication of Billie Holiday and Lena Horne.

"Black gospel music, originating in 19th-century negro spirituals, is wonderfully captured in 'Rolling in the Deep,' with its commenting background voices, the 'call and response' format that has been traced from field songs under slavery all the way back to West African communal ritual. . . . At the Grammys, Adele was a revelation, bringing back to America one of our authentic native genres: the spiritual power and purity of the unadorned human voice. It wasn't just the live audience who leapt to their feet and shouted in ecstasy: it was music-loving television viewers from coast to coast."

Paglia, "Mad About the Girl: Henpecked misogynist or fearless vision-ary who bottled the very essence of womanhood? As two new films put Alfred Hitchcock in the spotlight, Paglia reappraises the direc-tor's obsession with blondes," *The Sunday Times Magazine* (U.K.), July 15, 2012. Cover line: "Camille Paglia on Hitchcock's Obsession with Blondes."

Matthew Reisz, interview, "Voluble Radical Gives Old and New Puri-tans a Tongue-Lashing," *Times Higher Education* (U.K.), August 30, 2012. "Camille Paglia talks to Matthew Reisz about the U.S. academy's prejudices and what the secular and the religious fail to understand about art." Paglia rejects "the male gaze" in feminist film theory.

Carol Kino, interview, "Always Ready with a Barb: Camille Paglia scowls at the Metropolitan Museum," *The New York Times,* September 28, 2012. Paglia calls the Met's current Egyptian wing "underwhelming": "Talk about wasted space!" As a child, she had been electrified by the Met's Egyptian galleries, which have "lost their drama." She blames it on "the blockbuster mentality" and curators "underestimating the appetite of the public for detail."

Roundtable, "007 Deconstructed," *The Washington Post,* October 2, 2012. Paglia, "The Women": "The James Bond films were the van-guard of the sexual revolution. . . . But Bond's cavalier womanizing, as well as the overt sexuality of the Bond girls, rubbed second-wave feminism the wrong way. One reason I got drummed out of the women's movement from the start was my embrace of the vampy, Amazonian Bond girls and of the spunky TV characters they inspired on *Charlie's Angels,* a show denounced by feminists as degrading to women. But in the 1990s, both the Bond girls and *Charlie's Angels* returned in triumph during the Madonna-inspired pro-sex feminist insurgency that swept the puritanical old guard into the dustbin of history."

Paglia, "Gender Roles: Motherhood gets a raw deal from feminists," *The Globe and Mail,* October 6, 2012. Working mothers: the controversy over the quick maternity leave of Marissa Mayer, CEO of Yahoo. Paglia calls for "massive adjustment of our tyrannically rigid system of higher education": "Universities must adapt to women students who choose to have children early." Married students in the classroom "would revolutionize" the current academic discourse of gender studies, which is "arrogantly divorced from practical reality."

Paglia, "How Capitalism Can Save Art," *The Wall Street Journal,* October 6–7, 2012. "Camille Paglia on why a new generation has chosen iPhones and other glittering gadgets as its canvas." Starts: "Does art have a future?"

"Powell's Q&A: Camille Paglia," PowellsBooks.Blog, October 11, 2012.

What's the strangest or most interesting job you've ever had?

Night-shift ward secretary of the emergency room at St. Joseph's Hospital in downtown Syracuse, New York. This was a summer job when I was in college. I wore a uniform and sat at a little table inside the emergency room, right next to all the action. When an ambulance brought in a patient—often with bullet wounds on the night shift—the medical staff would rapidly evaluate his or her condition and shout out to me which specialist I should contact. I had a list of doctors on call for that night and immediately dialed the answering service. Of course it was highly stressful when people arrived dead or dying and there was a great outcry from their families in the hallway. But most of the time it was quiet, and I used the pre-dawn hours to read through the shelf of medical textbooks.

Why do you write?

Ever since childhood, I have always felt that the number and intensity of my observations exceed my ability to express them in conversation. People cannot be burdened with a constant flood of commentary on life and the universe! My Joan Rivers fast-talking can only go so far before audience fatigue sets in. So I write! Readers can turn me on and off at will. But I'm always there on the shelf—like a jack-in-the-box, ready to rumble.

If you could have been someone else, who would that be and why?

David Hemmings as the ultra-cool Mod London photographer based on David Bailey in Michelangelo Antonioni's 1966 film, *Blow-Up*. So deft yet so robust. Such oscillation between brooding thought and explosive action. Professional mastery. Detachment, wandering, discovery, obsession. And what's not to like about playing cat-and-mouse games with Jane Birkin, Veruschka, and Vanessa Redgrave?

Paglia, "George Lucas' Force," *The Chronicle Review, The Chronicle of Higher Education,* October 19, 2012. Essay adapted from last chapter of *Glittering Images.*

Paglia, "Beauty: The pursuit of beauty leads in unexpected directions," *Smithsonian Magazine,* November 2012.

Brian Kellow, "Coda: Listeners of Note: Camille Paglia," *Opera News,* November 2012. Paglia talks about her favorite operas: *Madame Butterfly* strongly influenced her Emily Dickinson chapter in *Sexual Personae.* Of Wagner: "My anthem as a writer (I've loved swords since childhood) is the Nothung motif—Siegfried calling his sword, and the hammering sound of the forging. To this day, my hair stands on end when I hear it. That is so *me.*" On opera radio broadcasts: "But I hate this intrusive business of talking to the stars in between acts. It kills the magic! Never, ever should outsiders speak to a performer in the middle of the dream. It's so reductive! It's vandalism—dragging these virtuoso performers back to mundane reality."

Paglia, "Camille Paglia: Taylor Swift, Katy Perry and Hollywood Are Ruining Women," *The Hollywood Reporter,* December 6, 2012, commissioned for the annual Women in Entertainment issue: "The influential female academic, writing for *THR,* calls out their 'insipid, bleached-out personas.'" "When *Forbes* released its annual list of Hollywood's highest-paid women in October, it was no surprise that Oprah Winfrey passed everyone else by a mile. . . . It's staggering that 22-year-old Taylor Swift earned $57 million and Katy Perry $45 million.

How is it possible that such monumental fortunes could be accumulated by performers whose songs have barely escaped the hackneyed teenybopper genre? But more importantly, what do the rise and triumph of Swift and Perry tell us about the current image of women in entertainment? Despite the passage of time since second-wave feminism erupted in the late 1960s, we've somehow been thrown back to the demure girly-girl days of the white-bread 1950s. It feels positively nightmarish to survivors like me of that rigidly conformist and man-pleasing era, when girls had to be simple, peppy, cheerful, and modest. Doris Day, Debbie Reynolds, and Sandra Dee formed the national template—that trinity of blonde oppressors!

"As if flashed forward by some terrifying time machine, there's Taylor Swift, America's latest sweetheart, beaming beatifically in all her winsome 1950s glory from the cover of *Parade* magazine in the Thanksgiving weekend newspapers. In TV interviews, Swift affects a 'golly, gee whiz' persona of cultivated blandness and self-deprecation, which is completely at odds with her shrewd glam dress sense. Indeed, without her mannequin posturing at industry events, it's doubtful that Swift could have attained her high profile.

"Beyond that, Swift has a monotonous vocal style, pitched in a characterless keening soprano and tarted up with snarky spin that is evidently taken for hip by vast multitudes of impressionable young women worldwide. Her themes are mainly complaints about boyfriends, faceless louts who blur in her mind as well as ours. Swift's meandering, snippy songs make 16-year-old Lesley Gore's 1963 hit 'It's My Party (And I'll Cry if Want to)' seem like a towering masterpiece of social commentary, psychological drama, and shapeless concision.

"Although now 28, Katy Perry is still stuck in wide-eyed teen-queen mode. Especially after the train wreck of her brief marriage to epicene roué Russell Brand, her dazzling smiles are starting to look as artificial as those of the aging, hard-bitten Joan Crawford. Perry's prolific hit songs, saturating mainstream radio, hammer and yammer mercilessly. She's like a manic cyborg cheerleader, obliviously whooping it up while her team gets pounded into the mud.

"Most striking about Perry, however, is the yawning chasm between her fresh, flawless 1950s girliness, bedecked in cartoonish floral colors, and the overt raunch of her lyrics, with their dissipated party scenes. Perry's enormous commercial success actually reflects the tensions and anxieties that are afflicting her base audience—nice white girls from comfortable bourgeois homes. The sexual revolution launched by my baby-boom generation has been a mixed blessing for those who came after us. Katy Perry's schizophrenia—good-girl mask over trash and flash—is a symptom of what has gone wrong. . . . Whatever sex represents to this generation of affluent white girls, it doesn't mean rebellion or leaving the protective umbrella of hovering parents. . . .

"The insipid, bleached-out personas of Taylor Swift and Katy Perry cannot be blamed on some eternal law of 'bubblegum' music. Connie Francis, with her powerhouse blend of country music and operatic Italian belting, was between 19 and 21 when she made her mammoth hits like "Lipstick on Your Collar" and "Stupid Cupid." Movie ingénues once had far more sophistication and complexity than they do today: Leslie Caron was 20 at her debut in *An American in Paris;* Elizabeth Taylor was 19 in *A Place in the Sun;* Kim Novak was 22 in *Picnic;* Natalie Wood was 17 in *Rebel Without a Cause.*

"Paradoxically, a key problem with the current youth cult, which is devouring both entertainment and fashion, is that aging women have become progressively invisible. If girls are helplessly stalled at the ingénue phase, it's partly because women in their 40s and 50s are, via Botox, fillers and cosmetic surgery, still trying to look like they're 20. Few roles are being written these days for character actresses— parts once regularly taken by Marie Dressler, Marjorie Main, Thelma Ritter, or Maureen Stapleton. . . . Middle-class white girls will never escape the cookie-cutter tyranny of their airless ghettos until the entertainment industry looks into its soul and starts giving them powerful models of mature womanliness."

Paglia, "Return to the Valley of the Dolls: Peppy, demure, and insipid," *The Sunday Times Magazine* (U.K.), January 13, 2013. Expanded version of article on Taylor Swift and Katy Perry in *The Hollywood Reporter,* December 6, 2012. Asked for a blurb for the Contributors' Page,

Paglia said: "Worshipping European art films in college in the 1960s, I dreamed the revolutionary new woman would be modeled on Jeanne Moreau, Catherine Deneuve, and Julie Christie. How wrong I was!"

Paglia, "The Princess and the Showgirl: Why Rihanna is the new Diana," cover story, *The Sunday Times Magazine* (U.K.), February 17, 2013. Below the masthead on the *Sunday Times* newspaper front page: "Camille Paglia on the startling similarities between the singer and the late princess." Starts: "Rihanna is in love with the camera, and the camera is in love with her. Not since Diana rocketed from a shy kindergarten aide to a lean, mean fashion machine has there been such a ravishingly seductive flirtation with the world press. Like Diana, Rihanna has worryingly drifted into using photo ops to send messages of allure, defiance, or revenge in a turbulent relationship with an errant partner." Paglia wrote another cover story appreciatively surveying Rihanna's career for *D*, the weekend style magazine of the Italian newspaper, *La Repubblica*, November 23, 2013.

Roundtable, "The Revolution is 50: Read what some women think of the iconic *The Feminine Mystique* book," *Elle* magazine, March 2013. Commissioned for the golden jubilee re-release of Betty Friedan's book. Paglia calls *The Feminine Mystique* "one of the most influential books ever written by a woman" but says Friedan's sample was "heavily skewed toward affluent housewives in suburban New York." The book is "a catalog of misery" that resembles "a horror film" with women called "walking corpses." Friedan was "ungenerous to men, who are portrayed as infantile and exploitative." The book is "hostile to popular culture and contemporary art": Friedan attacks the Beats, abstract expressionism, Tennessee Williams, and Fellini's *La Dolce Vita*. Homosexuality is portrayed as "a murky smog," a blight of "shallow unreality and immaturity." Despite Friedan's major status in feminist history, "she did not, as is commonly claimed, liberate my baby-boom generation, which was already in a ferment of rebellion against social constraints" after John F. Kennedy's presidency as well as the late 1950s civil rights movement.

Paglia, "Let's Dance: How David Bowie kick-started a sexual revolution," cover story, *The Sunday Times Magazine* (U.K.), March 10, 2013. Marking the opening of a retrospective show of Bowie's costumes at the Victoria & Albert Museum in London. Adapted from Paglia's essay on Bowie in the V&A catalog.

Emily Nussbaum, "Difficult Women: How *Sex and the City* lost its good name," *The New Yorker,* July 29, 2013. "When Carrie sleeps with a dreamy French architect and he leaves a thousand dollars by her bed, she consults her friends. 'Money is power. Sex is power,' Samantha argues. 'Therefore, getting money for sex is simply an exchange of power.' 'Don't listen to the dime-store Camille Paglia,' Miranda shoots back.' " ["The Power of Female Sex," *Sex and the City,* Season 1, Episode 5. Directed by Susan Seidelman and aired on HBO, July 5, 1998.]

Katie Glass, "The Naked Truth: Was porn's first superstar vamp or victim? Amanda Seyfried brings Linda Lovelace's story to life," cover story, *The Sunday Times Magazine* (U.K.), August 11, 2013. Paglia: "*Deep Throat* was an epochal moment in the history of modern sexuality. It was an exciting period, when young, middle-class women raised during the stiflingly respectable 1950s were boldly forging the new frontier. Enjoying porn films alongside men was a radical gesture in the sexual revolution. I thought it was terrific."

Tracy Clark-Flory, interview with Paglia, "It remains baffling how anyone would think that Hillary Clinton is our party's best chance," Salon.com, August 21, 2013. *TC-F:* "Any hopes, fears or predictions for the presidential elections in 2016?" *CP:* "As a registered Democrat, I am praying for a credible presidential candidate to emerge from the younger tier of politicians in their late 40s. A governor with executive experience would be ideal. It's time to put my baby-boom generation out to pasture! We've had our day and managed to muck up a hell of a lot. It remains baffling how anyone would think that Hillary Clinton (born the same year as me) is our party's best chance. She has more sooty baggage than a 90-car freight train. And what exactly has she ever accomplished—beyond bullishly covering for her philandering husband? She's certainly busy, busy and ever on the move—with the tunnel-vision workaholism of someone trying to blot out uncomfortable private thoughts.

"I for one think it was a very big deal that our ambassador was murdered in Benghazi. In saying 'I take responsibility' for it as secretary of state, Hillary should have resigned immediately. The weak response by the Obama administration to that tragedy has given a huge opening to Republicans in the next presidential election. The impression has been amply given that Benghazi was treated as a public relations matter to massage rather than as the major and outrageous attack on the U.S. that it was. Throughout history, ambassadors have always been symbolic incarnations of the sovereignty of their nations and the dignity of their leaders. It's even a key motif in *King Lear*. . . ."

TC-F: "You're such a beloved and divisive figure, I had to solicit questions from folks on Twitter. Here's a funny one: 'Why do you come down so hard on skinny white girls? Your views on sexuality leave so much room for individuality, so why is it so bad if I am attracted to Meg Ryan or Gwyneth Paltrow?'"

CP: "When have I ever criticized anyone's fetish? I am a libertarian. Go right ahead—set up plastic figurines of 1950s-era moppets to bow down to in the privacy of your boudoir. No one will scold! Then whip down to the kitchen to heat up those foil-wrapped TV dinners. I still gaze back fondly at Swanson's fried-chicken entrée. The twinkly green peas! The moist apple fritter! Meg Ryan—the spitting image of all those perky counselors at my Girl Scout camp in the Adirondacks. Gwyneth Paltrow—a simpering sorority queen with field-hockey-stick legs. I will leave you to your retro pursuits while I dash off to moon over multiracial Brazilian divas."

Paglia, "Miley, Go Back to School: Cyrus' derivative stunt reveals an artistically bankrupt music culture," *Time* magazine, August 27, 2013. Paglia denounces Miley Cyrus' lewdly tongue-wagging and crotch-tickling performance at the MTV Video Music Awards. "The real scandal" was how artistically "atrocious" it was, "clumsy, flat-footed and cringingly unsexy": "How could American pop have gotten this bad?"

"The Cyrus fiasco" demonstrates "the still heavy influence of Madonna," whose videos of the 1980s were "suffused with a daring European art film eroticism": "Madonna's provocations were smolderingly sexy because she had a good Catholic girl's keen sense of transgression. Subversion requires limits to violate."

Bari Weiss, interview, "The Weekend Interview with Camille Paglia: A feminist defense of masculine virtues," *The Wall Street Journal*, December 28–29, 2013.

Tricia Barr, interview, "The Art of *Star Wars*," *Star Wars Insider* magazine, Issue 147, released January 2014. Paglia discusses the chapter on *Star Wars* closing her art book, *Glittering Images*. Pull quote: "*Revenge of the Sith* will remain a classic beloved by worldwide audiences long after most of today's over-praised leading novelists, poets, and painters are forgotten."

Paglia, "Philosopher King: The art of Eminem," cover story, *The Sunday Times Magazine* (U.K.), February 16, 2014: "Portrait of the Artist." Starts: "Lady Gaga never saw it coming." The upstaging of Gaga's heavily promoted but poorly selling album *Artpop* by Eminem's eighth album, *The Marshall Mathers LP2*. "Eminem, now 41, did few interviews and personal appearances for this formidable double album. As with Adele sweeping the Grammys two years ago, his instant commercial triumph demonstrates the readiness of a discerning world public to respond to power and passion of voice, rather than to manipulative gimmicks or exhibitionistic stunts. . . .

"Eminem's rap saga is its own House of Atreus. As in the Greek myth cycle, with its cannibalism, treachery, sexual delusion, and blood sacrifice, he seems to be battling an inherited curse. Like Orestes, who killed his mother, Clytemnestra, for murdering his father, Agamemnon, Eminem is beset by vengeful furies, whose punishing voices penetrate his brain and pour out in his convulsive rapping. . . . If Eminem has a weakness, it is his dependence on spontaneous allusions to a currently thin pop culture of celebutante gossip, video games, sci-fi, and action-adventure films. He does see its mediocrity: 'So what's left?' he asks about his rivals. . . .

"While Gaga panders to fans, inviting their symbiotic attachment to her as 'Mother Monster,' Eminem takes the courageous route of the true artist: he dares the audience to hate him. He breaks every shibboleth, every rule of decorum. He raves with the defiant, repellent spirit of Baudelaire and Rimbaud, the *poète maudit,* cursed and exiled. 'I want to dig my way to Hell!' thunders the majestic chorus of 'Wicked Ways,' the final song on the new album. 'Imagination's dangerous,' he says elsewhere here. Gaga, with her constant costume tat, fatigues the eye. Eminem, in his simple hoodie, looks like an ascetic monk, fed on apparitions and devoted to art."

Interview, "Camille Paglia Pays Tribute to Joan Rivers: From 'scorching candor' to populist appeal," *The Hollywood Reporter,* September 5, 2014 (the day after Rivers' death). "Joan had a huge influence on me for over four decades. She was one of my primary models as a public figure. Not since Dorothy Parker had an American woman been so shockingly fearless in her aggressive speech and gleeful violation of taboos. . . . I was a guest on her TV show in the early 1990s and on her radio show in the late 1990s. . . . She held herself to the highest standard. There was never anything slack or careless about her. On the contrary, she focused the laser beam of her energy and attention on every detail—to give the audience maximum value."

Paglia, "Tina's Turning Point," Roundtable on the pivotal year 1984, *Billboard,* November 1, 2014. Contributors included Annie Lennox and Jon Bon Jovi. Paglia lauds Tina Turner's brilliant comeback album, *Private Dancer,* released May 29, 1984. "Showing off her lion's mane wig, runner's legs and dominatrix high heels on the album cover, the 44-year-old Turner stunned the world with her ferocious, mature sexuality. Released at the puritanical height of the feminist anti-pornography crusade, the album daringly invoked prostitution in its title. But 'What's Love Got to Do with It' makes a feminist statement, as Turner embraces a radical freedom of sexual choice. The five-times-platinum album projects her as a hybrid superwoman, her Amazonian militance melting into bluesy yearning. She is both hard and soft, raw and smooth, a truly modern woman for all seasons."

Paglia, "Vanished Aviator Remains a Magnet for Hype," letter to the editor, *The Philadelphia Inquirer,* November 1, 2014. Criticizes the *Inquirer* for having fallen victim to "the tabloid- and TV-driven hype doggedly generated by Ric Gillespie about the fate of Amelia Earhart ('A key piece found in Earhart puzzle?' October 31). A cursory fact check would have revealed the widespread debunking of Gillespie's absurd, self-aggrandizing claims over the past 25 years. The typhoon-swept tidal bays and atolls of the North and South Pacific are littered with debris and wrecks from a century of commercial shipping, as well as World War Two."

Paglia, "Do Cover Up, Madonna—You're Lady Bracknell Now," *The Sunday Times* (U.K.), December 7, 2014. On Madonna's nipple-baring photo shoot by Mert Alas and Marcus Piggott for the December issue of *Interview* magazine. "The muddy, slack-jawed cover image makes Madonna look as paralytically congealed and mummified as a Celtic bog body. What is shocking in these ugly photographs is not their tiny nudity but their mediocrity and monotony."

Linda Stein, "Feminism and *The Philadelphia Story:* High society topic of Cabrini talk," *Main Line Suburban News,* April 5, 2015. Reports on Paglia's illustrated lecture, "Three Modern Women: Katharine Hepburn, Hope Montgomery Scott, and Tracy Lord," co-sponsored by the Radnor Historical Society and the Radnor Memorial Library at Cabrini University in Radnor, PA. In this public lecture, Paglia was the first to argue that the role of Tracy Lord's prankish sister Dinah was based on Hope Scott's tomboyish younger sister, Charlotte Ives, and that both Philip Barry's play and Donald Ogden Stewart's screenplay contain numerous in-jokes about the family swimming pool and the devotion to dance and music of Hope's other sister, Mary Binney, as well as the latter's rumored alliance with conductor Leopold Stokowski. Paglia also found that the renowned London-based artist Philip de László, who painted Charlotte Ives' portrait, noted in his diary that he saw her and Hope "riding like man-fine wild girls" at Ardrossan, the family estate. Both Hope and Charlotte Ives were champion equestrians throughout their lives. Paglia has acquired (via eBay) old newsroom photos of Charlotte Ives jumping fences in competition and considers her lost story crucial to full understanding of *The Philadelphia Story*.

Paglia, "My Fair Lady: As a blockbuster exhibition celebrating Audrey Hepburn prepares to open, Camille Paglia explores the enduring allure of the icon of screen and style," *The Sunday Times Magazine* (U.K.), June 7, 2015. Commissioned to mark the launch of an exhibition of photographs of Audrey Hepburn at the National Portrait Gallery in London. Paglia says that, like Leslie Caron, Hepburn "represented a new type of postwar woman—a pert, buoyant, charmingly mischievous boy/girl with wispy cropped hair." She "started a raffish line that ran from Jean Seberg to Edie Sedgwick, Twiggy, and the waif-like Mia Farrow. It was a transition to the cheeky, coltish, and more defiant free spirits of the 1960s, such as Julie Christie and Ali MacGraw."

Editor-in-Chief David Daley, The Salon Interview with Camille Paglia, Part One, Salon.com, July 28, 2015. Paglia: "Right from the start, when the Bill Cosby scandal surfaced, I knew it was not going to bode well for Hillary's campaign, because young women today have a much lower threshold for tolerance of these matters. The horrible truth is that the feminist establishment in the U.S., led by Gloria Steinem, did in fact apply a double standard to Bill Clinton's behavior because he was a Democrat. The Democratic president and administration supported abortion rights, and therefore it didn't matter what his personal behavior was.

"But we're living in a different time right now, and young women have absolutely no memory of Bill Clinton. It's like ancient history for them; there's no reservoir of accumulated good will. And the actual facts of the matter are that Bill Clinton was a serial abuser of working-class women—he had exploited that power differential even in Arkansas. And then in the case of Monica Lewinsky—I mean, the failure on

the part of Gloria Steinem and company to protect her was an absolute disgrace in feminist history! What bigger power differential could
there be than between the president of the United States and this poor
innocent girl? Not only an intern but clearly a girl who had a kind of
pleading, open look to her—somebody who was looking for a father
figure.

"I was enraged! My publicly stated opinion at the time was that
I don't care what public figures do in their private life. It's a very
sophisticated style among the French, and generally in Europe, where
the heads of state tend to have mistresses on the side. So what? That
doesn't bother me at all! But the point is, they are sophisticated affairs
that the European politicians have, while the Clinton episode was a
disgrace. . . .

"In most of these cases, like the Bill Clinton and Bill Cosby stories, there's been a complete neglect of psychology. We're in a period
right now where nobody asks any questions about psychology. No one
has any feeling for human motivation. No one talks about sexuality
in terms of emotional needs and symbolism and the legacy of childhood. Sexuality has been politicized—'Don't ask any questions!' 'No
discussion!' 'Gay is exactly equivalent to straight!' And thus in this
period of psychological blindness or inertness, our art has become
dull. There's nothing interesting being written—in fiction or plays or
movies. Everything is boring because of our failure to ask psychological questions.

"So I say there is a big parallel between Bill Cosby and Bill
Clinton—aside from their initials! Young feminists need to understand that this abusive behavior by powerful men signifies their sense
that female power is much bigger than they are! These two people,
Clinton and Cosby, are emotionally infantile—they're engaged in a
war with female power. It has something to do with their early sense
of being smothered by female power—and this pathetic, abusive, and
criminal behavior is the result of their sense of inadequacy.

"Now, in order to understand that, people would have to read my
first book, *Sexual Personae*—which of course is far too complex for
the ordinary feminist or academic mind! It's too complex because
it requires a sense of the ambivalence of human life. Everything is

not black and white, for heaven's sake! We are formed by all kinds of strange or vague memories from childhood. That kind of understanding is needed to see that Cosby was involved in a symbiotic, push-pull thing with his wife, where he went out and did these awful things to assert his own independence. But for that, he required the women to be inert. He needed them to be dead! Cosby is actually a necrophiliac—a style that was popular in the late-Victorian period in the nineteenth century.

"It's hard to believe now, but you had men digging up corpses from graveyards, stealing the bodies, hiding them under their beds, and then having sex with them. So that's exactly what's happening here: to give a woman a drug, to make her inert, to make her dead is the man saying that I need her to be dead for me to function. She's too powerful for me as a living woman. And this is what is also going on in those barbaric fraternity orgies, where women are sexually assaulted while lying unconscious. And women don't understand this! They have no idea why any men would find it arousing to have sex with a young woman who's passed out at a fraternity house. But it's necrophilia—this fear and envy of a woman's power.

"And it's the same thing with Bill Clinton: to find the answer, you have to look at his relationship to his flamboyant mother. He felt smothered by her in some way. But let's be clear—I'm not trying to blame the mother! What I'm saying is that male sexuality is extremely complicated, and the formation of male identity is very tentative and sensitive—but feminist rhetoric doesn't allow for it. This is why women are having so much trouble dealing with men in the feminist era. They don't understand men, and they demonize men. They accord to men far more power than men actually have in sex. Women control the sexual world in ways that most feminists simply don't understand.

"My explanation is that second-wave feminism dispensed with motherhood. The ideal woman was the career woman—and I do support that. To me, the mission of feminism is to remove all barriers to women's advancement in the social and political realm—to give women equal opportunities with men. However, what I kept saying in *Sexual Personae* is that equality in the workplace is not going to solve the problems between men and women which are occurring in the private, emotional realm, where every man is subordinate to women, because he emerged as a tiny helpless thing from a woman's body. Professional women today don't want to think about this or deal with it.

"The erasure of motherhood from feminist rhetoric has led us to this current politicization of sex talk, which doesn't allow women to recognize their immense power vis-à-vis men. When motherhood was more at the center of culture, you had mothers who understood the fragility of boys and the boy's need for nurturance and for confidence to overcome his weaknesses. The old-style country women—the Italian matriarchs and Jewish mothers—they all understood the fragility of men. The mothers ruled their own world and didn't take men that seriously. They understood how to nurture men and encourage them to be strong—whereas current feminism simply doesn't perceive the power of women vis-à-vis men. But when you talk like this with most men, it really resonates with them, and they say 'Yes, yes! That's it!'

"Currently, feminists lack sympathy and compassion for men and for the difficulties that men face in the formation of their identities. I'm not talking in terms of the men's rights movement, which got infected by p.c. The heterosexual professional woman, emerging with her shiny Ivy League degree, wants to communicate with her husband exactly the way she communicates with her friends—as in *Sex and the City*. That show really caught the animated way that women actually talk with each other. But that's not a style that straight men can do! Gay men can do it, sure—but not straight men! Guess what—women are different than men! When will feminism wake up to this basic reality? Women relate differently to each other than they do to men. And straight men do not have the same communication skills or values as women—their brains are different!

"Wherever I go to speak, whether it's Brazil or Italy or Norway, I find that upper-middle-class professional women are very unhappy. This is a global problem! And it's coming from the fact that women are expecting men to provide them with the same kind of emotional and conversational support and intimacy that they get from their women friends. And when they don't get it, they're full of resentment and bitterness. It's tragic!

"Women are blaming men for a genuine problem that I say is systemic. It has to do with the transition from the old, agrarian culture to this urban professional culture, where women don't have that big support network that they had in the countryside. All four of my grandparents and my mother were born in Italy. In the small country towns they came from, the extended family was the rule, and the women were a force unto themselves. Women had a chatty group solidarity as they did chores all day and took care of children and the elderly. Men and women never had that much to do with each other over history! There was the world of men and the world of women. Now we're working side by side in offices at the same job.

"Women want to leave at the end of the day and have a happy marriage at home, but then they put all this pressure on men because they expect them to be exactly like their female friends. If they feel restlessness or misery or malaise, they automatically blame it on men. Men are not doing enough; men aren't sharing enough. But it's not the fault of men that we have this crazy and rather neurotic system where women are now functioning like men in the workplace, with all its material rewards. A huge problem here is that in America, we have identified ourselves totally with our work lives. In most parts of Southern Europe, on the other hand, work is secondary to your real life. It's often said that Americans live to work, as opposed to working to live."

Editor-in-Chief David Daley, The Salon Interview with Camille Paglia, Part Two, Salon.com, July 29, 2015. Daley asks about Donald Trump (six months before the presidential primaries). Paglia: "Well, my view of Trump began in the negative. When he was still relatively unknown nationally, he jackhammered a magnificent Art Deco sculpture over the main doorway of the Bonwit Teller department store on 5th Avenue. It was 1980, and he was demolishing the store to build Trump Tower. The Metropolitan Museum of Art had offered to take the sculpture, but Trump got impatient and just had it destroyed. I still remember that vividly, and I'm never going to forget it! I regard Donald Trump as an art vandal, equivalent to ISIS destroying ancient

Assyrian sculptures. As a public figure, however, Trump is something of a carnival barker. . . . He has no political skills of any kind. He's simply an American citizen who is creating his own bully pulpit. He speaks in the great populist way, in the slangy vernacular. He takes hits like a comedian. . . . Like claiming John McCain isn't a war hero, because his kind of war hero doesn't get captured—that's hilarious! That's like something crass that Lenny Bruce might have said! It's so startling and entertaining."

Scott M. MacDonald, *Binghamton Babylon: Voices from the Cinema Department 1967–77* (2015). Paglia interviewed about the enormous impact on her of the Harpur Film Society during her college years (1964–68) at Harpur College.

Michael Harvey, "Interview: Talking leadership with Camille Paglia," *Leadership and the Humanities* 3, no. 2, September 2015.

Roundtable, "The Female Gaze: 100 overlooked films directed by women," cover story, *Sight & Sound* (U.K.), October 2015. Paglia nominates Donna Deitch's *Desert Hearts* (1986): "Although it has become a cult classic due to its explicit lesbian sex, *Desert Hearts* is a wonderfully well-made film with a host of appealing attributes. Steeped in moody, classic country-and-western music, it conveys romantic longing and confusion with bittersweet intensity. The casting is superb, starting with Helen Shaver as a primly proper New York professor and Patricia Charbonneau as a charismatic Reno cowgirl, but also extending to a riveting supporting cast, who do humorous, sharply observed vignettes across the spectrum of social class. Crisply edited subplots are effortlessly woven throughout. The gritty, monotonous sense of place is accentuated by Shaver's endearing disorientation in wide-open Nevada. The film has a beguilingly hypnotic atmosphere, like Shakespeare's magical green world, where things change shape and identities are transformed. As we contemplate the aching degrees and varieties of love, we must laugh at the eternal muddle of human aspiration and absurdity. With neither cynicism nor sentimentality,

Desert Hearts charmingly asserts the centrality of emotion, as well as its prankish surprises."

Paglia, "Camille Paglia Takes on Taylor Swift, Hollywood's #GirlSquad Culture," *The Hollywood Reporter,* December 10, 2015. "Can group selfies advance women's goals?" Commissioned for *THR*'s annual Women in Entertainment issue. Paglia: "Do girl squads signal the blossoming of an idealistic new feminism, where empowering solidarity will replace mean-girl competitiveness? Hollywood has always shrewdly known that cat-fighting makes great box office. In classic films such as *The Women, All About Eve, The Group,* and *Valley of the Dolls,* all-star female casts romped in claws-out bitchfests. That flamboyant, fur-flying formula remains vital today in Bravo TV's boffo *Real Housewives* series, with its avid global following.

"A warmer model of female friendship was embodied in Aaron Spelling's blockbuster *Charlie's Angels* TV show, which was denounced by feminists as a 'tits-and-ass' parade but was in fact an effervescent action-adventure showing smart, bold women working side by side in fruitful collaboration. A similar dynamic of affectionate intimacy animated HBO's *Sex and the City,* whose four feisty, mutually supportive professional women prefigured today's fun-loving but rawly ambitious girl squads. . . .

"Young women performers are now at the mercy of a swarming, intrusive paparazzi culture, intensified by the hypersexualization of our flesh-baring fashions. The girl squad phenomenon has certainly been magnified by how isolated and exposed young women feel in negotiating the piranha shoals of the industry. . . . Given the professional stakes, girl squads must not slide into a cozy, cliquish retreat from romantic fiascoes or communication problems with men, whom feminist rhetoric too often rashly stereotypes as oafish pigs. If many women feel lonely or overwhelmed these days, it's not due to male malice. Women have lost the natural solidarity and companionship they enjoyed for thousands of years in the preindustrial agrarian world, where multiple generations chatted through the day as they shared chores, cooking, and child care.

"In our wide-open modern era of independent careers, girl squads can help women advance if they avoid presenting a silly, regressive public image—as in the tittering, tongues-out mugging of Swift's bear-hugging posse. Swift herself should retire that obnoxious Nazi Barbie routine of wheeling out friends and celebrities as performance props, an exhibitionistic overkill that Lara Marie Schoenhals brilliantly parodied in her scathing viral video 'Please Welcome to the Stage'. . . .

"Women need to study the immensely productive dynamic of male bonding in history. With their results-oriented teamwork, men largely have escaped the sexual jealousy, emotionalism, and spiteful turf wars that sometimes dog women. If women in Hollywood seek a broad audience, they must aim higher and transcend a narrow gender factionalism that thrives on grievance. Girl squads are only an early learning stage of female development. For women to leave a lasting mark on culture, they need to cut down on the socializing and focus like a laser on their own creative gifts."

Todd Leopold, "Camille Paglia Rips Taylor Swift for 'Nazi Barbie Routine,' Frenzy Follows," CNN.com, December 11, 2015. Paglia's passing reference to Taylor Swift the prior day in *The Hollywood Reporter* sets off an international furor. "Taylor Swift an 'obnoxious Nazi Barbie,' writes Camille Paglia," headlined *The Guardian,* as did *The Daily Mail,* which assured its readers that "Taylor Swift has no affiliation with the Nazi party." *The Sydney Morning Herald* and *The Times of Israel* reported that the chairman of the Australian B'nai B'rith Anti-Defamation Commission, invoking the Holocaust, called Paglia's comments "obscene and insensitive" and demanded that she apologize. Paglia, bemused at this wave of global literalism, of course rejected all policing of satiric metaphors.

Editor-in-Chief David Daley, interview, "'A Bold, Knowing, Charismatic Creature Neither Male nor Female': Camille Paglia remembers a hero, David Bowie. Bowie named Paglia's *Sexual Personae* one of his favorite books. But he helped inspire her to write it." Salon.com, January 12, 2016 (two days after Bowie's death).

Paglia, "Hillary's Blame-Men-First Feminism May Prove Costly in 2016," Salon.com, January 27, 2016. "During her two presidential campaigns, Hillary Clinton has consistently drawn greater support from women than men. Is this gender lag due to retrograde misogyny, or does Hillary project an uneasiness or ambivalence about men that complicates her appeal to a broader electorate?" This piece was commissioned by the op-ed department of *The New York Times* but rejected within hours of its submission. It was published by Salon.com the following morning and immediately became the lead item on the Drudge Report—a good example of how the Web has facilitated free speech and thwarted the gatekeepers of the once omnipotent media establishment.

Paglia, "Sexism Has Nothing to Do with It," Salon.com column, February 11, 2016. "With Bernie Sanders' thrilling, runaway victory over Hillary Clinton in the New Hampshire primary, the old-guard feminist establishment in the U.S. has been dealt a crushing blow."

Paglia, Salon.com column, February 25, 2016. "Democrats face a stark choice this year. A vote for the scandal-plagued Hillary is a resounding ratification of business as usual—the corrupt marriage of big money and machine politics. . . . What you also get with Hillary is a confused hawkish interventionism that has already dangerously destabilized North Africa and the Mideast. This is someone who declared her candidacy on April 12, 2015, via an email and slick video and then dragged her feet on making a formal statement of her presidential policies and goals until her pollsters had slapped together a crib list of what would push the right buttons. This isn't leadership; it's pandering.

"Thanks to several years of the Democratic Party establishment strong-arming younger candidates off the field for Hillary, the only agent for fundamental change remains Bernie Sanders, an honest and vanity-free man who has been faithful to his core progressive principles for his entire career. It is absolutely phenomenal that Sanders has made such progress nationally against his near-total blackout over the past year by the major media, including *The New York Times*. . . . A vote for Bernie Sanders is a vote against the machine, the obscenely money-mad and soulless juggernaut that the Democratic Party has become. . . .

"The Sanders theme that is closest to my heart is his call for free public universities. . . . The public education that I received at Harpur College during the 1960s (I appear to have been its first second-generation graduate) was superb, not simply for its excellent faculty and cultural programs but for its dynamic student body with a large constituency of passionately progressive Jews (like Bernie Sanders) from metropolitan New York City. . . . The cost to my parents for my four years of college was amazingly minimal.

"It is an intolerable scandal that college costs, even at private universities, have been permitted to skyrocket in the U.S., burdening a generation of young adults with enormous debts for what in many cases are worthless degrees. The role played by the colleges themselves in luring applicants to take crippling unsecured loans has never received focused scrutiny. Perhaps a series of punitive, class-action lawsuits might wake the education industry up. Until the colleges themselves pay a penalty for their part in this institutionalized extortion, things are unlikely to change."

Paglia, Salon.com column, April 21, 2016. Responding to a question about Leonard Cohen from Prof. Lance Strate of Fordham University: "There can be no doubt about Cohen's manifest intellect, emotional depth, and productivity. The problem for me is first, the labored, lugubrious monotony of his sepulchral singing style (I feel like I'm trapped with Morticia in a Charles Addams cartoon) and second, the painful over-calculation of his lyrics, which seem designed for the page rather than for performance. There's no room for intuition, inspiration, ecstasy, surprise—every promising detail seems buried in rationalist preconception and plodding delivery.

"Leonard Cohen belongs to the Susan Sontag generation of existentialist Big Think—the drearier the better. Sontag's zany brainstorm for cheering up the shell-shocked citizens of war-torn Sarajevo was to stage *Waiting for Godot* among the ruins. Cohen's version of hip feels like a paralyzing, suffocating stasis. Would a few spoonfuls of syncopation kill him? He clings to words and doesn't trust music.

His verbal overkill parallels the convoluted preciosity of French post-structuralism (he was born in Quebec).

" 'Suzanne,' of course, became a late-1960s counterculture classic, but it was because of Judy Collins' gorgeous, luminous delivery, freed from Cohen's heavy hand. . . . My favorite Cohen song is 'First We Take Manhattan'—I adore anything apocalyptic—but the best thing in it is the rippling Euro-disco beat, borrowed from the school of Giorgio Moroder, my idol."

Emily Hill, " 'The Woman Is a Disaster!' Camille Paglia on Hillary Clinton: A wide-ranging interview with the iconoclastic professor," *The Spectator* (U.K.), October 29, 2016. [Paglia was in London for a talk on free speech with Claire Fox at the Battle of Ideas at the Barbican Centre, two weeks before the U.S. presidential election.] "Paglia says she has absolutely no idea how the election will go: 'But people want change and they're sick of the establishment. . . . If Trump wins it will be an amazing moment of change because it would destroy the power structure of the Republican party, the power structure of the Democratic party, and destroy the power of the media.' "

Matthew Campbell, interview, " 'Sociopath' Hillary Scared Off Better Rivals," *The Sunday Times* (U.K.), November 12, 2016. Paglia: "Any Democratic candidate other than Hillary Clinton would have beaten Donald Trump. Any other Democrat would have won this election because so many people voted for Trump just to stop the utterly sociopathic Hillary from gaining office. The problem is that no other candidate was allowed to run. It was undemocratic. And it was going on for years before the actual primary process as the Clintons crushed any possibility of a primary challenge to Hillary. All the best candidates in my party, the younger senators and mayors and governors in their early forties and fifties, did not dare to run. The party would not permit them to run."

Peter Lloyd and Erica Tempesta, " 'It's Truly Tragic to See Her Maudlin Displays of Self-Pity': Feminist Camille Paglia hits back at Madonna's claims [at the *Billboard* Women in Music Awards] that she was rebuffed by her female peers at the start of her career," *The Daily Mail*, December 13, 2016. Paglia: "I was Madonna's first major defender, when she was still considered a pop tart and a sham puppet created by shadowy male producers. . . . It is absolutely ridiculous for Madonna to now claim that she longed to ally with other women at the start of her career but was rebuffed from doing so. The media, in the U.S. and abroad, constantly asked Madonna about me or tried to bring us together, and she always refused. . . . The real issue is that while Madonna's world tours have remained highly successful, her artistic development has been stalled for 20 years. . . . Madonna has become a prisoner of her own wealth and fame."

Paglia, "How to Age Disgracefully in Hollywood: The social critic and academic blames 1960s disruptions of gender roles (and not the entertainment industry) for Madonna's and J.Lo's difficulty in letting go of their youth as she chastises them to 'stop cannibalizing the young,'" *The Hollywood Reporter*, January 13, 2017. "In December, at the Billboard Women in Music Awards in New York City, Madonna was given the trophy for Woman of the Year. In a rambling, tearful acceptance speech that ran more than 16 minutes, she claimed to be a victim of 'blatant misogyny, sexism, constant bullying, and relentless abuse.' It was a startling appropriation of stereotypical feminist rhetoric by a superstar whose major achievement in cultural history was to overthrow the puritanical old guard of second-wave feminism and to liberate the long-silenced pro-sex, pro-beauty wing of feminism, which (thanks to her) swept to victory in the 1990s. . . .

"I was singled out by name as having accused her of 'objectifying' herself sexually (prudish feminist jargon that I have always rejected), when in fact I was Madonna's first major defender, celebrating her revival of pagan eroticism and prophesying in a highly controversial 1990 *New York Times* op-ed that she was 'the future of feminism.' But I want to focus here on the charge of ageism that Madonna, now 58, leveled against the entertainment industry and that received heavy, sympathetic coverage in the mainstream media. . . .

"If aging stars want to be taken seriously, they must find or recover a mature persona. Stop cannibalizing the young! Scrambling to stay relevant, Madonna is addicted to pointless provocations like her juvenile Instagrams or her trashy outfit with strapped-up bare buttocks and duct-taped nipples at the Metropolitan Museum of Art Gala in May. She has forgotten the legacy of her great precursor, Marlene Dietrich, who retained her class and style to the end of her public life.

"In her Billboard Awards speech, Madonna oddly cited David Bowie as her 'real muse.' But Bowie did not cling to his revolutionary, gender-bending Ziggy Stardust in the way that Madonna doggedly regresses to the sassy street urchin of her 1980s debut. Bowie retired Ziggy after a single sensational year and evolved into other personae, such as the suave, enigmatic Thin White Duke. Neither Dietrich nor Bowie would have begun an event as Madonna did after Anderson Cooper handed her the Billboard trophy: 'We already had sex with a banana' and (about her microphone) 'I always feel better with something hard between my legs.'

"Two years ago, Jennifer Lopez (then 45) made a similar misstep with her crudely repetitious, faux-porn "Booty" video with Iggy Azalea. At ABC's recent *New Year's Rockin' Eve* show, Mariah Carey bungled more than her singing: in her needlessly risqué nude bodysuit, she looked like a splitting sack of over-ripe cantaloupes. All women performers should study the magnificent precedent of Lena Horne, a fiercely outspoken civil rights activist who maintained total dignity and gorgeous elegance over her 60-plus-year singing career. Today, graceful aging by veteran stars is wonderfully modeled by Jane Fonda, Sharon Stone, and Tippi Hedren, as well as the British actresses Judi Dench, Helen Mirren, and Charlotte Rampling. Lucy Liu, at 48, displays luminous self-possession and impeccable taste. . . .

"Women in or out of Hollywood who dress like girls and erase all signs of aging are disempowering themselves and aggressing into territory that belongs to the young. They are surrendering their right of self-definition to others. Men are not the enemy: they, too, are subject to nature's iron laws. For the sake of its own art, Hollywood needs less sex war, not more." [Apropos Madonna's strange confusion or senior moment at the Billboard Women in Music Awards, where she surreally conflated Paglia with the latter's longtime *bête noire* Gloria

Steinem, Paglia was philosophical: Madonna's grasp of history has always been shaky at best.]

Molly Fischer, "Camille Paglia: What the '90s provocateur understands about the Trump era," *New York* magazine, March 7, 2017. Asked about Donald Trump two weeks after Inauguration Day, Paglia (who voted for Jill Stein) says, "He is supported by half the country, hello! And also, this ethically indefensible excuse that all Trump voters are racist, sexist, misogynistic, and all that—American democracy cannot proceed like this, with this reviling half the country." Paglia praises the "solidarity" of the Women's March but says she was "horrified" by the pink pussy hats, which she calls "a major embarrassment to contemporary feminism": "I want dignity and authority for women. My code is Amazonism. I want weapons."

Mitchell Sunderland, interview, "Camille Paglia Discusses Her War on 'Elitist Garbage' and Contemporary Feminism," broadly.vice.com, March 14, 2017. Sunderland asks how young people can preserve free speech. Paglia replies: "Stand up, speak out, and refuse to be silenced! But identify the real source of oppression, which is embedded in the increasingly byzantine structure of higher education. Push back against the nanny-state college administrators who subject you to authoritarian surveillance and undemocratic thought control! . . . The rapid, uncontrolled spread of overpaid administrators on college campuses over the past 30 years has marginalized the faculty, downgraded education, and converted students into marketing tools. Administrators are locked in a mercenary commercial relationship with tuition-paying parents and in a coercive symbiosis with intrusive regulators of the federal government. Young people have been far too passive about the degree to which their lives are being controlled by commissars of social engineering who pay lip service to liberalism but who are at root Stalinist autocrats who despise and suppress individualism. There is no excuse whatever for the grotesque rise in tuition costs, which has bankrupted families and imposed crippling debt on students trying to start their lives. When will young people wake up to the connection between rampant student debt and the administrator-sanctioned suppression of free speech on campus? Follow the money—the yellow brick road leads to the new administrator master class."

Paglia, "A 'Fractious' Feminist Decries the Ruthless Thought Police Stifling Free Speech on Campus," *Time* magazine, April 3, 2017. Cover: "Is Truth Dead?" Excerpt from *Free Women, Free Men*.

Jonathan V. Last, interview, "Camille Paglia: On Trump, Democrats, transgenderism, and Islamist terror," *The Weekly Standard*, June 15, 2017. Paglia: "My position continues to be that Hillary, with her supercilious, Marie Antoinette–style entitlement, was a disastrously wrong candidate for 2016 and that she secured the nomination only through overt chicanery by the Democratic National Committee, assisted by a corrupt national media who imposed a virtual blackout for over a year on potential primary rivals. Bernie Sanders had the populist passion, economic message, government record, and personal warmth to counter Trump. It was Sanders, for example, who addressed the crisis of crippling student debt, an issue that other candidates (including Hillary) then took up. Despite his history of embarrassing gaffes, the affable, plain-spoken Joe Biden, in my view, could also have defeated Trump, but he was blocked from running at literally the last moment by President Barack Obama, for reasons that the major media refused to explore. . . .

"There seems to be a huge conceptual gap between Trump and his most implacable critics on the Left. Many highly educated, upper-middle-class Democrats regard themselves as exemplars of 'compassion' (which they have elevated into a supreme political principle) and yet they routinely assail Trump voters as ignorant, callous hatemongers. These elite Democrats occupy an amorphous meta-realm of subjective emotion, theoretical abstractions, and refined language. But Trump is by trade a builder who deals in the tangible, obdurate, objective world of physical materials, geometry, and construction projects, where communication often reverts to the brusque, coarse, high-impact level of pre-modern working-class life, whose daily locus was the barnyard. It's no accident that bourgeois Victorians of the industrial era tried to purge 'barnyard language' out of English."

"Rihanna Feels the Love," cover story, *Elle* magazine, October 2017. Tributes from (among others) Venus Williams, Tyra Banks, Eminem, Wyclef Jean, Laverne Cox, Olivia Wilde, Pharrell Williams. Paglia: "Rihanna is today's most fascinating performer, a mysterious amalgam of amiable warmth with glittering charisma. With her keen creative eye for line and color, she has become a fashion icon like Audrey Hepburn. Yet she is a tempestuous wild child and international adventuress like Ava Gardner. Most importantly, as an artist in this over-mechanized age, she bravely draws on deep wells of pure emotion, endearing her to millions of fans worldwide."

Interview, "Camille Paglia on Hugh Hefner's Legacy, Trump's Masculinity, and Feminism's Sex Phobia," *The Hollywood Reporter,* October 2, 2017 (after Hefner's death). *THR:* "What would you say was *Playboy's* cultural impact?" *CP:* "Hugh Hefner absolutely revolutionized the persona of the American male. In the post–World War Two era, men's magazines were about hunting and fishing or the military, or they were like *Esquire,* erotic magazines with a kind of European flair. Hefner reimagined the American male as a connoisseur in the continental manner, a man who enjoyed all the fine pleasures of life, including sex. Hefner brilliantly put sex into a continuum of appreciative response to jazz, to art, to ideas, to fine food. This was something brand-new. Enjoying fine cuisine had always been considered unmanly in America. Hefner updated and revitalized the image of the British gentleman, a man of leisure who is deft at conversation—in which American men have never distinguished themselves—and the art of seduction, which was a sport refined by the French. Hefner's new vision of American masculinity was part of his desperate revision of his own Puritan heritage. On his father's side, he descended directly from William Bradford, who came over on the *Mayflower* and was governor of Plymouth Colony, the major settlement of New England Puritans. . . ."

THR: "What do you think about the fact that Trump's childhood hero and model of sophisticated American masculinity was Hefner?" *CP:* "Before the election, I kept pointing out that the mainstream media based in Manhattan, particularly *The New York Times*, was hopelessly off in the way it was simplistically viewing Trump as a classic troglodyte misogynist. I certainly saw in Trump the entire *Playboy* aesthetic, including the glitzy world of casinos and beauty pageants. It's a long passé world of confident male privilege that preceded the birth of second-wave feminism. There is no doubt that Trump strongly identified with it as he was growing up. It seems to be truly his worldview. But it is categorically not a world of unwilling women. Nor is it driven by masculine abuse. It's a world of show girls, of flamboyant femaleness, a certain kind of strutting style that has its own intoxicating sexual allure—which most young people attending elite colleges today have no contact with whatever. . . ."

THR: "Is there anything of lasting value in Hugh Hefner's legacy?"

CP: "We can see that what has completely vanished is what Hefner espoused and represented—the art of seduction, where a man, behaving in a courtly, polite, and respectful manner, pursues a woman and gives her the time and the grace and the space to make a decision of consent or not. Hefner's passing makes one remember an era when a man would ask a woman out on a real date—inviting her to his apartment for some great music on a cutting-edge stereo system (*Playboy* was always talking about the best new electronics!)—and treating her to fine cocktails and a wonderful, relaxing time. Sex would emerge out of conversation and flirtation as a pleasurable mutual experience.

"So now when we look back at Hefner, we see a moment when there was a fleeting vision of a sophisticated sexuality that was integrated with all of our other aesthetic and sensory responses. Instead, what we have today, after *Playboy* declined and finally disappeared off the cultural map, is the coarse, juvenile anarchy of college binge-drinking, fraternity keg parties where undeveloped adolescent boys clumsily lunge toward naïve girls who are barely dressed in tiny miniskirts and don't know what the hell they want from life. What possible romance or intrigue or sexual mystique could survive such a vulgar and debased environment as today's residential campus social life?

"Women's sexual responses are notoriously slower than men's. Truly sophisticated seducers knew that women have to be courted and that women love an ambiance, setting a stage. Today, alas, too many young women feel that they have to provide quick sex or they'll lose social status. If a guy can't get sex from them, he'll get it from someone else. There's a general bleak atmosphere of grudging compliance."

Paglia, "A 'Strange Joke': The pro-sex feminist on the meaning behind the 'childlike' Playboy Bunny costume," sidebar to "Hef's Hollywood," *The Hollywood Reporter,* October 4, 2017. "When it came to that infamous Playboy Bunny costume, the one that Gloria Steinem wore undercover at the Playboy Club for a *Show* magazine exposé in 1963, second-wave feminists were irate. They felt that it reduced women to animals. Yes, it's animal imagery, but a bunny is charmingly harmless. Hugh Hefner's iconic creation could certainly be criticized as infantilizing to women, but it's the *type* of animal here that is key to his unique sensibility.

" 'Multiplying like bunnies,' we say: Hefner was making a strange joke about the procreative process. It seems like a defense formation— Hefner turning his Puritan guilt into humor. It suggests that, despite his bland smile, he may always have suffered from a deep anxiety about sex. There was nothing dark or threatening in Hefner's opulent sexual universe. It was a childlike vision, sanitizing all the conflicts and turbulence of the sex impulse. Everybody knows that Hefner's sexual type was the girl next door: the corn-fed, bubbly American girl who stays at the borderline of womanhood but never crosses it. She was like an ingénue in a postwar musical comedy like *Oklahoma!*— uncomplex as a personality but always warm and genuine.

"Hefner's bunnies were a major departure from historical female mythology, where women were often portrayed as animals of prey— tigresses and leopards. Hefner was good-natured but abashed, diffident and shy. So he re-created women's image in a palatable and manageable form. I don't see anything misogynist in that. Woman as cozy, cuddly bunny is a perfectly legitimate modality of eroticism. I think feminism goes wildly wrong when it portrays men as oppressors. What I see is Hefner's frank acknowledgment of his fear of women's enormous power."

Tim Hains, "Camille Paglia vs. Identity Politics: Return to Authentic 1960s Vision Where Consciousness Transcends Divisions of Gender, Race, Ethnicity," RealClearPolitics.com, October 5, 2017. "An Earth-shaking meeting of the minds takes place between Dr. Jordan Peterson and feminist icon Camille Paglia. Peterson interviews Paglia, only to find that they agree on just about everything. They riff on their concerns about modern feminism, the myth of the Patriarchy, and the future of Western civilization." The one hour and 43 minute dialogue ("Modern Times: Camille Paglia and Jordan B. Peterson") was videotaped by a Toronto film crew at the University of the Arts on September 21, 2017, and posted on YouTube on October 2. Paglia was astounded and delighted to learn that Jordan Peterson and she had both been deeply influenced by Jungian analyst Erich Neumann, above all his major work, *The Origins and History of Consciousness.* (See Chapter 56 in *Provocations,* "Erich Neumann: Theorist of the Great Mother.")

Sarah Lyall and Dave Itzkoff, "Charlie Rose, Louis C.K., Kevin Spacey: Rebuked. Now what do we do with their work?," *The New York Times,* November 24, 2017. "Some people, like the feminist scholar Camille Paglia, argue that art—no matter who created it—should be beyond the scope of punishment. 'The artist as a person should certainly be subject to rebuke, censure, or penalty for unacceptable actions in the social realm,' Ms. Paglia said via email. 'But art, even when it addresses political issues, occupies an abstract realm beyond society.'"

Ed Pilkington, "How the Drudge Report Ushered in the Age of Trump: Twenty years ago, Matt Drudge's reports on the Lewinsky affair nearly brought down Bill Clinton," *The Guardian,* January 24, 2018. Numbers Paglia as among Matt Drudge's "devoted fans": "She was one of the first established voices to break ranks and endorse the site at a time when it was still being almost universally derided. 'I saw in Matt Drudge the triumph of the populist tabloids,' says Paglia. 'It's amazing how no one, in all these decades, has been able to imitate, displace, or supplant Drudge—because he is a true American original.'

Paglia is right: it is amazing that the Drudge Report continues to enjoy the influence it does."

Executive Editor Mish Barber-Way, interview, "Camille Paglia, Agent Provocateur: Going deep with America's most electric mind," *Penthouse*, January/February 2018. Reprinted: the fox-in-a-henhouse color photo of a very happy Paglia ringed by strippers at Stringfellow's Pure Platinum club in Manhattan in the October 1994 issue of *Penthouse*. *CP:* Demanding equal rights for women is crucial, but mischaracterizing men as oppressors and brutalizers throughout history is such a distortion! Of course, there have been brutes, but it's a minority of men who have behaved in a dishonorable way. Overwhelmingly, when you look at world history, it's men courageously giving their lives and their energy—sacrificing themselves for women and children! . . .

MBW: My husband is a metal fabricator and a craftsman. He was raised in a working-class family from Arkansas and since meeting him, I have developed a different appreciation for this kind of work that I once took for granted. I think that's why your writing has resonated with me. Why do you think culture has become so blind to these essential male contributions? *CP:* I've been calling for decades for vocational training to be reinstituted. I want a restoration and revalorization of the trades. For all of my career, I've been teaching in art schools, so a lot of my students work with their hands. . . . In rural Italian culture, it's assumed that you show true character by your willingness to do physical work. However, now we're in a period where manufacturing has fled overseas. Over the past 50 years, we've moved into a service-sector economy, which has been a disaster for working-class men who used to be able to walk into a factory off the street and earn a very good living working with their hands. Look, in Italian culture we pay attention to infrastructure. That's just the way I was raised. Workmanship is important. . . . The Romans developed concrete. In my family—oh my God—they could talk about concrete forever! The right way to pour it, the wrong way to pour it. My whole life I would hear the men in my family evaluating craftsmanship. My mother sewed—all the women did. Among my earliest memories is women fingering my sleeve or lapel and complimenting my mother on the stitching! . . .

MBW: You see us going down in the same rubble Rome did? *CP:* Rome became impossible to sustain. The lesson of history is that all bureaucracies eventually expand to the point where they collapse of their own weight. All bureaucracies become inefficient, convoluted, and self-involved, whether you're talking about ancient Rome or Soviet Russia. The whole Russian experiment began as a revolution in 1917 to liberate the people, and all of a sudden it became state-run farms and collectives—a horrendously inefficient mode of operation. The only way to run it was an authoritarian surveillance state. That's the lesson in all this. The bigger and wealthier a culture gets, the more you get an expensive, overgrown bureaucracy. We can see it now in Washington and on college campuses. This is a decadent phenomenon—a parallel to ancient Rome. . . .

MBW: Finally, because it's *Penthouse,* what value does pornography bring to sex and art? *CP:* My position has always been that pornography shows us the truth about sexuality, which connects us to the animal realm of primitive urges. Sexual desire and sexual fantasy are perpetually churning on the subliminal and unconscious levels, surfacing in our dream life. . . . Pornography is vital to freedom of the imagination. It's only in pornography that we can discern the shifting, shadowy structure of contemporary taboos. We call something "hot" when there is a subtle or not so subtle violation of taboo beneath the surface. Hence I view pornography as both art and anthropology—an alluring cultural projection that also reveals the hidden compulsions and conflicts of sexual relations in every era.

ACKNOWLEDGMENTS

My most fervent gratitude and appreciation go to my longtime editor, LuAnn Walther, who acquired the paperback rights for my first book, *Sexual Personae*, shortly after its publication by Yale University Press and presciently before the media storm began. As commander-in-chief of six of my subsequent books, she has been absolutely central to my public career. The debt I owe to her support, patience, understanding, and professional expertise is incalculable.

Catherine Tung was the tireless coordinator of the vast project of *Provocations*, with its multiple sources and formats crossing three decades. Her contributions to the editorial organization of this book (culled from a mountain of material) were truly heroic, as were her meticulous precision and persistence, particularly during the byzantine permissions process. Altie Karper, Cat Courtade, and Rita Madrigal were the formidable triumvirate of production: I am deeply grateful for their acute attention to detail as well as their supremely high standards of quality control. Josefine Taylor Kals, my publicist at Pantheon Books, has been a master strategist and keen cultural consultant. Many thanks again to Michael Lionstar for his discerning author photos. Janet Hansen's stylish, dynamic jacket design (based on a Lionstar photo and inspired by Andy Warhol) eloquently expresses my world-view and method in a way that I never thought possible. The Warhol Foundation was most gracious in giving its blessing to this splendid cover.

My profound thanks are owed to the bold and innovative editors who commissioned many of the pieces in this book, often at a time when my work was being attacked or censored elsewhere. Foremost among them are Herbert Golder and Nicholas Poburko, the erudite editor-in-chief and managing editor of *Arion* at Boston University. Nick was very generous in expediting the urgent digitization of my early *Arion* articles for production of this book. I was fortunate indeed to have been invited to participate in David Talbot's cosmopolitan vision for Salon.com, for which I wrote as a co-founding contributor from its first issue in 1995. I am also very grateful to the other Salon editors who were so hospitable to me and my work: Kerry Lauerman, Gary Kamiya, and David Daley. Some day, when the pioneering visual design of early Salon is systematically documented, the brilliant satiric spirit of artist Zach Trenholm (represented in this book) will be fully recognized and celebrated.

Jeff Yarbrough was very courageous in offering me a column at *The Advocate* during a highly contentious period in gay activism. It was a huge pleasure to work for several years with Ingrid Sischy and Brad Goldfarb, the editor-in-chief and managing editor of *Interview* magazine. Sarah Baxter has kindly offered many exciting (and mischief-making) opportunities at *The Sunday Times* in London. Jeanie Pyun's open door at *The Hollywood Reporter* has been like a dream come true for this lifelong movie fan.

Thanks to Jamie Malanowski for commissioning my "agony aunt" column in *Spy* magazine in 1993—the snappish ancestor of my later Salon column. I am grateful to editor Dian Hanson for commissioning my tribute to Tom of Finland for Taschen's collected works. Lance Strate of Fordham University was instrumental in providing a forum for two major pieces in this book, "The North American Intellectual Tradition" and "Dispatches from the New Frontier: Writing for the Internet." Anne Savarese, executive editor for literature at Princeton University Press, was extremely kind in supplying emergency assistance for digitization of my article on Western love poetry in *The New Princeton Encyclopedia of Poetry and Poetics*.

My literary agent, Lynn Nesbit, remains a steadfast source of wise and sympathetic counsel in any crisis. Finally, hearty thanks are due to my friends, allies, and family members (in alphabetical order) who have been so loyal and supportive over the decades: Gunter Axt, Glenn Belverio, Robert Caserio, Lisa Chedekel, Kent Christensen, Jack DeWitt, Matt Drudge, Kristoffer Jacobson, Ann Jamison, Mitchell Kunkes, Kristen Lippincott, Alison Maddex, Lucien Maddex, Lenora Paglia, Christina Hoff Sommers, and Francesca Stanfill.

No research assistants were used for this or any other of my books, articles, or lectures. Whatever errors may appear are entirely my own.

INDEX

PREVIOUS PUBLICATION INFORMATION

"The Grandeur of Old Hollywood" originally appeared in *The Hollywood Reporter* as "Camille Paglia on Oscar Glamour Then and Now: 'The Mythic Grandeur of Old Hollywood Is Gone'" on February 23, 2017.

"Art of Song Lyric" originally appeared in Salon (www.Salon.com) on March 31, 2016. An online version remains in the Salon archives. Reprinted with permission.

"On Rihanna" originally appeared in *V* magazine as part of an interview with Alex Kazemi on March 27, 2017.

"The Death of Prince" originally appeared in Salon (www.Salon.com) in response to a reader question on May 5, 2016. An online version remains in the Salon archives. Reprinted with permission.

"Theater of Gender: David Bowie at the Climax of the Sexual Revolution" originally published as a chapter in *David Bowie Is,* ed. Victoria Broackes and Geoffrey Marsh (V&A Publishing, 2013). Copyright © 2013 by The Board of Trustees of the Victoria and Albert Museum.

"Punk Rock" originally appeared in Salon (www.Salon.com) in response to a reader question on January 20, 1999.

"Living with Music: A Playlist" originally appeared in *The New York Times Book Review* on July 16, 2008.

"Oscar Style" was originally an interactive live event hosted on AOL.com/ABC Cyberplex on March 26, 1996.

"A Love Letter to Joan Rivers" originally appeared in *The Hollywood Reporter* on June 12, 2013.

"Rock Around the Clock" originally appeared in *Forbes ASAP* magazine on November 30, 1998.

"*The Guardian* Questionnaire," interview by Rosanna Greenstreet, originally appeared in *The Guardian* magazine in January 2008.

"The Death of Gianni Versace" originally appeared in Salon (www.Salon.com) on July 22, 1997.

"The Italian Way of Death" originally appeared in Salon (www.Salon.com) on April 18, 1996, and was subsequently published in *The Italian American Reader,* ed. Bill Tonelli (Harper, 2003).

"Women and Magic in Alfred Hitchcock" originally appeared as a chapter in *39 Steps to the Genius of Hitchcock,* ed. James Bell (British Film Institute, 2012).

"The Waning of European Art Film" originally appeared as "Art Movies: R.I.P." in Salon (www.Salon.com) on August 8, 2007. An online version remains in the Salon archives. Reprinted with permission.

"The Decline of Film Criticism" originally appeared in Salon (www.Salon .com) on December 9, 1997.

"Movie Music" was originally a segment on BBC Radio 3 titled "Essay: The Sound of Cinema," broadcast October 2, 2013.

"Homer on Film: A Voyage through *The Odyssey, Ulysses, Helen of Troy,* and *Contempt*" originally appeared in *Arion,* Fall 1997.

"Sex Quest in Tom of Finland" originally published as a chapter in *Tom of Finland XXL,* ed. Dian Hanson, copyright © 2009 by TASCHEN GmbH, Hohenzollernring 53, D-50672, Köln, www.taschen.com.

"Women and Law" originally published as a preface to Gunter Axt's *Historias de Vida: Mulheres do Direito, Mulheres no Ministerio Publico* (Florianapolis, Brazil, 2015).

"On Jewish-American Feminists" originally appeared in slightly different form as part of an interview with Adam Kirsch in *Tablet* (tabletmag.com) on March 9, 2017. Reprinted with permission.

"Portrayals of Middle Eastern Women in Western Culture" originally published as a foreword to Birgitte C. Huitfeldt's *Usensurert: Midtøstens kvinner/ Ti møter* (Oslo, Norway, May 2017).

"On Ayn Rand" originally appeared in Salon (www.Salon.com) on October 28, 1998.

"The Death of Helen Gurley Brown" originally appeared in *The Sunday Times* (London) on August 19, 2012.

"Legends of Diana" originally appeared in *The Sunday Times* (London) on August 29, 2004.

"Deconstructing the Demise of Martha Stewart" originally appeared in *Interview* magazine in June 2004. Courtesy of BMP Media Holdings, LLC.

"Feminism and Transgenderism" originally appeared in *The Weekly Standard* (www.weeklystandard.com) on June 15, 2017.

"Movies, Art, and Sex War" originally appeared in *The Hollywood Reporter* as "Camille Paglia on Movies, #MeToo and Modern Sexuality: 'Endless, Bitter Rancor Lies Ahead' " on February 27, 2018.

"The Unbridled Lust for Blurbs" originally appeared in *Publishers Weekly* on June 3, 1996, copyright © Publishers Weekly PWXYZ LLC. Reprinted by permission.

"Teaching Shakespeare to Actors" originally published as a chapter in *Living with Shakespeare,* ed. Susannah Carson (Vintage, 2013).

"Scholars Talk Writing: Camille Paglia" originally appeared in *The Chronicle of Higher Education* on November 9, 2015.

"Shakespeare's *Antony and Cleopatra*" originally published as program notes for production starring Helen Mirren at the National Theatre, London, October 1998.

"Tennessee Williams and *A Streetcar Named Desire*" originally appeared as "Tennessee Williams" in *A New Literary History of America,* edited by Greil Marcus and Werner Sollors, Cambridge, Mass.: The Belknap Press of Harvard University Press. Copyright © 2009 by the President and Fellows of Harvard College.

"Dance of the Senses: Natural Vision and Psychotic Mysticism in Theodore Roethke" was originally the keynote lecture of a conference celebrating the centenary of Roethke's birth, University of Michigan, Ann Arbor, 2008, and was subsequently published in *Michigan Quarterly Review,* Winter 2009.

"Final Cut: The Selection Process for *Break, Blow, Burn*" originally appeared in *Arion,* Fall 2008.

"Western Love Poetry" was originally an article in *The New Princeton Encyclopedia of Poetry and Poetics,* ed. Alex Preminger and T.V.F. Brogan. Copyright © 1993 by Princeton University Press. Reprinted with permission.

" 'Stay, Illusion': Ambiguity in Shakespeare's *Hamlet*" was originally a lecture in a series on ambiguity in Western culture, Intellectual Heritage Program, Temple University, October 18, 2003, and was subsequently published in *Ambiguity in the Western Mind,* ed. Craig J. N. de Paulo et al. (Lang, 2005).

"*Columbia Journal* Interview: Writing" originally appeared in *Columbia Journal,* Issue 39 (2004), pp. 79–88.

"The Death of Norman Mailer" originally appeared in Salon (www.Salon .com) on November 13, 2007. The Hochswender letter and commentary appeared in Salon on April 8, 2008.

"Dispatches from the New Frontier: Writing for the Internet" originally published as a chapter in *Communication and Cyberspace: Social Interaction in an Electronic Environment,* ed. Lance Strate et al. (Hampton Press, 2003). Reprinted by permission of Hampton Press.

"On Andy Warhol" originally appeared as part of an interview with Priscilla Frank in *Huffington* magazine on November 7, 2012.

"Millennium Masterworks: The *Mona Lisa*" originally appeared in *The Sunday Times* (London) on April 18, 1999.

"Picasso's *Girl Before a Mirror*" originally appeared in *ARTnews,* Volume 95, No. 1, January 1996. Reprinted courtesy of Art Media Holdings.

"More Mush from the NEA" originally appeared in *The Wall Street Journal* on October 24, 1997.

"Dance: The Most Fragile of the Arts" originally appeared in *Dance* magazine, July 2005. Reprinted by permission.

"Controversy at the Brooklyn Museum" originally appeared in Salon (www .Salon.com) on October 6, 1999.

"The Magic of Images: Word and Picture in a Media Age" was originally a lecture at the "Living Literacies" conference, York University, Ontario, November 15, 2002, and was subsequently published in expanded form in *Arion*, Winter 2004.

"Free Speech and the Modern Campus" was originally a lecture for Pennoni Honors College Free Speech Forum, Drexel University, on April 21, 2016.

"On Canons" originally appeared as part of an interview with Gunter Axt in *CULT* magazine (Brazil) on August 15, 2014.

"The Right Kind of Multiculturalism" originally appeared in *The Wall Street Journal* on September 30, 1999.

"Cant and Fad in Classics" originally appeared in *The Washington Post Book World* on March 29, 1998.

"Intolerance and Diversity in Three Cities: Ancient Babylon, Renaissance Venice, and Nineteenth-Century Philadelphia" was originally a lecture for the Ethics, Religion, and Society Program at Xavier University, Cincinnati, April 5, 2013, and was subsequently published in *Justice Through Diversity?*, ed. Michael J. Sweeney (Rowman & Littlefield, 2016).

"On Genius" originally appeared in Salon (www.Salon.com) on February 3, 1999.

"The Mighty River of Classics: Tradition and Innovation in Modern Education" was originally a lecture at Santa Clara University, May 5, 2001, and was subsequently published in *Arion*, Fall 2001.

"The North American Intellectual Tradition" was originally the Second Marshall McLuhan Lecture, Fordham University, February 17, 2000. Excerpted in *The Globe and Mail* and subsequently published in *Explorations in Media Ecology* 1, no. 1 (2002).

"Erich Neumann: Theorist of the Great Mother" was originally a lecture for the Otto and Ilse and Mainzer Lecture Series, sponsored by Deutsches Haus, New York University, November 10, 2005, and was subsequently published in *Arion*, Winter 2006.

"Slippery Scholarship" originally appeared in *The Washington Post Book World* on July 17, 1994.

"Making the Grade: The Gay Studies Ghetto" originally appeared in *The Advocate* on September 5, 1995.

"Gay Ideology in Public Schools" originally appeared in *The Wall Street Journal* as "It Wasn't Romeo and Julian" on February 22, 1999.

"The Death of Claude Lévi-Strauss" originally appeared in Salon (www.Salon .com) on November 10, 2005.

"The Columbine High School Massacre" originally appeared in Salon (www .Salon.com) on April 28, 1999.

"Vocational Education and Revalorization of the Trades" originally appeared in Salon (www.Salon.com) on March 21, 2001.

"No to the Invasion of Iraq" originally appeared in Salon (www.Salon.com) on February 7, 2003.

"Language and the Left" originally appeared in *The Advocate* on March 7, 1995.

"Camp Insensitivity" originally appeared in *The Wall Street Journal* on July 30, 1998.

"Bill Clinton: The Hormonal President" originally appeared in *The Advocate* on June 25, 1996.

"Sarah Palin: Country Woman" originally appeared in Salon (www.Salon .com) on September 10, 2008.

"Donald Trump: Viking Dragon" originally appeared in Salon (www.Salon .com) on May 19, 2016.

"Jesus and the Bible" originally appeared in Salon (www.Salon.com) on January 14, 2009.

"That Old-Time Religion" originally appeared in *The Advocate* on December 26, 1995.

"Cults and Cosmic Consciousness: Religious Vision in the American 1960s" was originally a lecture for the Institute for the Advanced Study of Religion,

Yale University, on March 26, 2002, and was subsequently published in *Arion*, Winter 2003.

"Religion and the Arts in America" was originally the Cornerstone Arts Lecture, Colorado College, broadcast by C-SPAN, American Perspectives series, 2007, and was subsequently published in *Arion*, Spring–Summer 2007.

"Resolved: Religion Belongs in the Curriculum" was originally an opening statement supporting the resolution, Yale Political Union, Yale University, on April 11, 2017.

"St. Teresa of Avila" was originally broadcast on BBC Radio 4 on December 31, 1999.

"Powell's Q&A: Camille Paglia" first published on October 11, 2012. http://www.powells.com/post/guests/powells-qa-camille-paglia.

PERMISSIONS ACKNOWLEDGMENTS

Grateful acknowledgment is made to the following for permission to reprint previously published material:

Alfred A. Knopf, a division of Penguin Random House LLC: "Occupational Hazards" from *Field of Light and Shadow: Selected and New Poems* by David Young, copyright © 2010 by David Young. Reprinted by permission of Alfred A. Knopf, an imprint of Knopf Doubleday Publishing Group, a division of Penguin Random House LLC. All rights reserved.

Alfred Music: Excerpt of "Pirate Jenny" from "The Threepenny Opera," English words by Marc Blitzstein, original German words by Bert Brecht, and music by Kurt Weill. Copyright © 1928, copyright renewed by Universal Edition. Copyright © 1955, copyright renewed by Weill-Brecht-Harms Co., Inc. Renewal rights assigned to the Kurt Weill Foundation for Music, Bert Brecht, and The Estate of Marc Blitzstein. All rights administered by WB Music Corp. All rights reserved. Reprinted by permission of Alfred Music.

Counterpoint Press: "Strategic Air Command" from *Axe Handles* by Gary Snyder, copyright © 1983 by Gary Snyder. Reprinted by permission of Counterpoint Press.

Downtown Music Publishing LLC, on behalf of Chandos Music Company (ASCAP): Lyrics to "Silver Dagger" written and composed by Joan Baez. Copyright © Chandos Music Company (ASCAP). All rights reserved. Reprinted by permission of Downtown Music Publishing LLC, on behalf of Chandos Music Company (ASCAP).

ILLUSTRATION CREDITS

ABOUT THE AUTHOR

Camille Paglia is the University Professor of Humanities and Media Studies at the University of the Arts in Philadelphia. She is the author of *Free Women, Free Men*; *Glittering Images*; *Break, Blow, Burn*; *The Birds*; *Vamps & Tramps*; *Sex, Art, and American Culture*; and *Sexual Personae*.

A NOTE ON THE TYPE

This book was set in Scala, a typeface designed by the Dutch designer Martin Majoor (b. 1960) in 1988 and released by the Font-Font foundry in 1990. While designed as a fully modern family of fonts containing both a serif and a sans serif alphabet, Scala retains many refinements normally associated with traditional fonts.

Composed by North Market Street Graphics,
Lancaster, Pennsylvania

Printed and bound by Berryville Graphics,
Berryville, Virginia

Designed by Betty Lew